The Pearl and the Hut

Soul Wisdom for Growing up and Living Between Divorced Parents

Yiana Belkalopolos

FriesenPress

One Printers Way
Altona, MB R0G 0B0
Canada

www.friesenpress.com

Copyright © 2021 by Janice Amy Belcher (Yiana Belkalopolos)
First Edition — 2021

All rights reserved.

Practices in this book are used worldwide and can help people challenged with some mental health issues. Since mental health systems, practices, supports and laws differ between countries, provinces, and states, the author takes no responsibility for a formal therapeutic relationship with any reader without a legal contract negotiated directly and confidentially between the reader and the author. Having therapeutic support from a counselor, social worker, licensed psychology professional, anthroposophical psychotherapist, anthroposophical doctor, or curative eurythmist is recommended for readers who are children or adult children of divorce. Workshops, on-line courses, or discussion groups offered by the author may not constitute contracted counseling.

Due to changing cultural conditions in Canada, the author chose to write and do artistic pursuits for almost 30 years under her paternal family's original Greek name, Belkalopolos. That name was changed to an Anglican name by Canadian authorities when her grandfather immigrated to Canada in order to be accepted in society. With 30 years of legal documents in the Anglican name, the author has kept that name, Janice Amy Belcher, for ease in legal purposes and to honor her Anglo family side. Copyright and all legal matters for this book reside under the responsibility of Janice Amy Belcher.

No part of this publication may be reproduced in any form, or by any means, electronic or mechanical, including photocopying, recording, or any information browsing, storage, or retrieval system, without permission in writing from FriesenPress.

ISBN
978-1-5255-7935-6 (Hardcover)
978-1-5255-7936-3 (Paperback)
978-1-5255-7937-0 (eBook)

1. FAMILY & RELATIONSHIPS, DIVORCE & SEPARATION

Distributed to the trade by The Ingram Book Company

Divorce can have a devastating effect on children. It raises questions of meaning, social chaos, and fear of change. The author uses deep knowledge and understanding of the spiritual development of the human being in this caring exposition.

Glenn Charles
Business Systems Analyst
London, UK

Traditionally, the family has been the cornerstone of communities and civilization itself. Divorce used to be rarely encountered. A reality of the modern age is the increase in the numbers of broken families. While legislators and the courts make laws for the financial and physical protection of children, what has been missing is practical advice from those who experienced growing up in the middle of the often, on-going disruption of parent separation.

Stephanie Georgieff
Cultural Researcher
Albania

Belkalopolos sets out to heal residual divides in the "Pearl" children of divorce, applying the anthroposophical wisdom behind Waldorf education, biodynamic farming, anthroposophical medicine, curative eurythmy, and Goethean art and color theory. This resource book is filled with integrated healing practices and techniques; using fairytale, biographies, visualizations, verses, myths, practical exercises in childcare, anthroposophical movement, meditations, and vocal toning. It brings natural spiritual understandings to the pain of divided hearts.

Adriana Koulias
Author, Anthroposophical Researcher
Sydney, Australia

Here is a lifetime of research into the soul experiences of the child and adult child of divorce. The author brings the unique background of having befriended many rich spiritual traditions, along with her depth of understanding as a professional in the realm of psychotherapy. This is a path of healing, of reaping a harvest of painful experiences and transforming them for the good. The human soul is renewable, indeed.

Elizabeth Roosevelt
Waldorf Teacher
Maine, US

TABLE OF CONTENTS

Preface
What to Find Here, and Who This Book Is For 1

Introduction
Growing Soul Gardens on the Rocks 7

Chapter One
The Pearl and the Hut:
A Fairy Tale for Adult Children of Divorce 17

Chapter Two
Coming Out of Darkness 37

Chapter Three
What Do Waldorf Philosophy and Anthroposophy Do? ... 77

Chapter Four
Modern Psychology and Anthroposophical Perspectives . 185

Chapter Five
Spiritual Bypassing Gives Way to Warm,
Life-Supporting Illumination 229

Chapter Six
Anthroposophical Human Development 275

Chapter Seven
Adolescence and Bridging the Abyss: Ages 14–21 321

PREFACE

What to Find Here, and Who This Book Is For

The topic of divorce, and children of divorce, is a massive and profoundly complex social phenomenon in the Western world. It is one that is re-shaping our societies. The issues for many children, over several decades, have shown to present many psychological dangers. The research is staggering on the side of negative outcomes, especially the lower the economic standing of the families involved. The impact of divorce on children is an emotionally charged subject. On the more challenging side of the spectrum of broken families, it is one that is testing society's coping capacities as a result of homelessness, poverty, and drug addictions. Many grown children of divorce, myriad professionals, and civic society workers believe it is one in urgent need of addressing.

This book is the first significant introduction to address the topic of child-of-divorce soul-psyche issues through *anthroposophy*.[1] *Anthropo* (the human being) plus *sophy* (wisdom) is the science and philosophy behind Waldorf schools, biodynamic farming, anthroposophical medicine and homeopathy, the eurythmy movement, progressive forms of economics and civil society awareness, and a vast body of artistic and cultural understandings and works. As a pioneer piece, *The Pearl and the Hut* offers some foundational thoughts, insights into, and practices relevant to anthroposophy.

As a resource, this book is the first in two volumes designed to help readers to understand the vast, lifelong developmental soul-psychological issues that can be associated with the child-of-divorce phenomenon. It is based on the child pedagogy and adult soul-spiritual philosophies of Rudolf Steiner, the forward-seeing twentieth-century Austrian scientist, Goethean editor, sculptor, architect, biodynamic farming developer, medical-holistic health researcher, holistic health intuitive, and community socio-economics innovator.

The experiences of many people who grew up with the phenomenon of divorced parents, and split homes and lives, now inform this reference book to help others. *The Pearl and the Hut* shows how child-of-divorce issues are not simply the "medical model" of mental health and social issues that they have often been presented as in the past, but whole health, practical, rational, and valuable human concerns that work deeply into soul patterns, social innovations, and new human challenges regarding spiritual development.

The Pearl and the Hut reference books are seed works. Much will follow and blossom as adult children of divorce come together, with gathered strengths and common experiences, to develop greater understanding and loving resiliency from a soul and spirit perspective.

Having lived the scenario of the child of divorce and adult child of divorce, while researching diverse angles, I see that today the task of anthroposophy is to help those most profoundly and even dangerously affected.

Rudolf Steiner was the founder of anthroposophy. His psychological insights integrate both logical reasoning and insights into human consciousness development. Knowing how the soul develops, therapeutically, works to bring self-awareness to people of the soul-psyche workings happening at the different ages and stages of life. This lets a child eventually arrive, in rightful timing, at a healthy ego that can become a selfless instrument for working in the world. A child is supported to move forward in soul and spiritual growth at child-level stages, rather than engaging in adult-level psychological issues that come out of adult conflicts and unaddressed traumas.

As I often tell divorced parents, children are not developed enough in their wholeness capacities for coping in adult situations or society, in real self-dominion, until they have certain personal physical, imaginal, conceptual, inspirational, and resilient-will capacities developed by about age twenty-one. That includes readiness stages in the soul-psyche and having been through the late adolescent neuron-growth and pruning stages that lead to full executive-mind, prefrontal-cortex brain health. This is the part of the brain that helps adults keep neurologically balanced and able to plan, think through difficult experiences and problems, and seek appropriate, collaborative help, without overloading the fear and reaction centers of the brain.

Until then, children are truly still like chicks in the nest or cubs in the den. Imagine the adult birds or bears pulling their offspring out of the protected space before they're ready and casting them into adult creature activity with no protection. Imagine the adults fighting over them and pulling them about between one nest and another nest or one cave to another cave, then hauling them back regularly into the energy of a stand-off or brawl with the other parent creature. Children and parents are not animals, but this scenario highlights the great unnaturalness that many parents of divorce expect their children to endure before they have grown into adults themselves.

The ability to embrace life and a wealth of spiritual freedom as an adult is the difference in psychological health that anthroposophy provides. The practices of anthroposophy support self-authority and self-responsibility, even when one struggles with serious, psychologically damaging circumstances. This comes out of knowing healthy, adult, soul-development stages, as well as those of the child. This book is about pointing out why divorce can be so harmful to the child soul. I hope to clarify why anthroposophy can be one of the most important ways to assist soul development for children of divorce is the only solution that the family has been able to work out.

By necessity, the focus of *The Pearl and the Hut* series (an illustrated fairy-tale book is also in the works) is on the children and the adult children of divorce. For practical reasons, these reference books cannot offer an investigation around the parents' issues or needs regarding divorce. Those topics have been covered extensively in modern social studies, psychology books, and other self-help manuals. Although most adult children of divorce can attest that they have heard much about the parents' struggles, complaints, and issues in the divorce, encompassing every angle and participant in the issue here would expand these initial books beyond the mandate of a first-case set of works of their kind on the children themselves. My hope is, however, that what is brought here will assist both parents who were themselves children of divorce and parents who are guiding their own children of divorce.

Until now, nothing has been written about divorce in light of anthroposophy. It is a perspective brought through the children's inner-soul point of view. Hopefully, this work will inspire divorced parents to engage the insights of anthroposophy toward meaningful relationships with their children through more wholesome family dynamics. It is also my hope that teachers, doctors, and therapists will find it enlightening for understanding, in more practical depth, how to help these children in their development.

Foremost, *The Pearl and the Hut* volumes are about keeping the children of divorce masters of their own lives when they become adults. Anthroposophy's astute soul observations and practical methods, as indicated in the spiritual research of Rudolf Steiner on child development and adult biography, have proven to be profoundly insightful and vital for our modern times.

A Starting Place

There are mind-bending levels of complexity in the families of divorce today, resulting from one or more parents divorcing more than once, or parents breaking up with other, post-divorce partners. Psychotherapeutic healing approaches for children of divorce have required diverse interventions and creative solutions. Though it would be ideal to offer a vast array of individual interventions for specific family scenarios, I could not practically do so in a first book. I do, however, refer to some foundational and general practices and indications for children and adults of different ages and stages. These can be springboards for applying anthroposophical work to various family configurations.

What I offer here comes from years of soul connecting with others who were experiencing the issues. Volume One speaks to the whole body, mind, and soul complexes of children of divorce, from birth to the end of the child-development stages at age twenty-one. It includes four biographical stories, including the broad-ranging story of Sarah, a pioneer in the West as an early child of divorce during a time when almost nothing was known about soul-psyche issues related to growing up in split families.

Volume Two tells the stories of adult development according to Rudolf Steiner's soul-spiritual development indications for adults. Through the biographies of Melissa, Forest, Leiko, Jocelyn, Saverio, and my own midlife developmental experience, the reader can gain insight into some long-forgotten rites of passage brought lawfully into modern times. That soul-spirit lawfulness, and how we can work with it today to support holistic, well-balanced health, and a more stabilized psyche, is discussed throughout both volumes.

Insights in both volumes also come from my work with children and adult children of divorce in education, arts, psychotherapy, spiritual communities, cooperative garden-farming, and various business ventures, as well as in health-food collectives. I have also touched on aspects of child family trauma issues through work in community initiatives in India, the US, and Mexico, as well as through Waldorf teaching in Canada and anthroposophical study in Europe.

In the later chapters of Volume II, I share Western, evidence-based psychosocial theories and interventions as a registered clinical counselor in Canada, to be considered along with anthroposophical practices.

A Resource

In both volumes of *The Pearl and the Hut*, I have striven to point readers to where they can go to research more and to get help with this work. The knowledge can, initially, be complex, and so it is important that responsive adults can take up the ideas and have resources to continue developing their own research for their families, students, or therapeutic clients.

Adults can hold the space for the children of divorce with compassionate and informed wisdom. They can find inspiring and realistic approaches to educating and healing these regularly strained human beings. A main task for the adults around these children—the therapists, doctors, teachers, parents, and artists—is to support the children to find their own most whole and sustainable ways to keep soul-strong in the middle of conflicted family issues and societal conflicts as well.

Ultimately, the hope is that self-aware and whole, adult children of divorce will be able to work together to bring about some of the healthiest soul support and understandings around this world-changing phenomenon.

Those Who Helped and Inspired this Work

In rooting these first books on the children and adult children of divorce, I found it imperative to share the biographies of people of various ages who have experienced both parental divorce and anthroposophical education, spiritual work, or healing. Anthroposophy as it lives in practical application is a big canopy, and many people worldwide are already part of this organically expanding network.

Some people in the references and stories were introduced to anthroposophy through Waldorf education in early childhood, grade school, or high school—in one country or another. Others came to it seeking a healthy soul education on their own. Still more came for different matters and found themselves working to understand soul-spiritual insights to overcome the pain and harm arising from the modern-day divorce phenomenon.

I extend the most heartfelt gratitude to those grown children of divorce for their courage to share and bring understanding. My experience of gratitude is like glistening spirit, fed like a spring from the soul through the heart, and offered in reverence. It is also an inspirational loop. According to anthroposophy, inspiration arises out of imagination, intuition, higher thinking, and the active working into good deeds with others. Children and adult children of divorce inspired this book as we entered each other's lives, full of the striving for life that could revive an imagination of love.

We helped each other to affirm our intuitions about the possibilities of greater inner peace. We also sparked positive problem-solving to keep us healthy and whole enough to engage our own work and a communion with goodness in life. I am grateful to many other young and grown children of divorce for keeping my compassionate strength alive and keeping my will strong to get this book into form for others.

The imagination that I had to write *The Pearl and the Hut* series in 2011 was given a boost in moral value one day in a visit with Virginia Sease at the Goetheanum in Dornach, Switzerland. Dr. Sease, now retired, was the spokesperson for the English-speaking members of the Anthroposophical Society in the world. Later conversations with a psychotherapeutic mentor in Sacramento, California, the late Dr. William Bento, an anthroposophist and licensed psychotherapist who helped to create the Association for Anthroposophical Psychology,[2] solidified my commitment to provide a transpersonal psychology informed by anthroposophy to care for children and grown children of divorce. Dr. Bento was a child of divorce and a respected therapist in the US.

Former anthroposophical publisher, Claude Julien, gave his selfless assistance to the early process of developing the books, and Faith Moore brought valuable editorial input as well as perspective from the viewpoint of a concerned parent of adolescent and grown children of divorce. Artist and content editor, Chris Manvell, whose grandparents on both sides were divorced, has brought an insightful, English-Turkish heart and soul nature to this book series through the lens of having formed his own, very loving and connected family with insights out of anthroposophy and Waldorf child development theories. An added thank you goes to Gotthard Killian for content input and networking for the books.

Other kind and good souls to thank for participating in the process of preparing this book are Adriana Koulias, Kristina Kaine, Suzanne Downe, Carolyn Jourdan, Frank Chester, Kim Graae Munch, Cynthia Hoven, Gabrielle Armenier, Mary Brian, Beatrix Hachtel, Jaimen McMillan, Ruta Hallam, Danny Fortier, Dennis Klocek, Katherine Carpenter Perlas, Chantel Kingsbury, Alara Miles, Stephanie Georgieff, Andrew Linnell, Macarena Kalj, and Nesta Carsten. There are others who cannot be named for confidentiality purposes, but who will read this book and know that their voices are here, too. Thank you, for the sake of many.

Finally, I would like to thank my father, Kenneth Belcher, for sticking through the tremendously difficult work of maturing through this pioneering process with his own children. May my mother, in the spiritual world, always know my love for her. She gave her all, out of what she could know at the time, to be the full-hands-on single parent to my brother and me at the very beginning of the wave of family divorces in the West. I truly sense that she would have been grateful that I took on this extensive investigation on behalf of children of divorce.

Endnotes

1 F. Edmunds, An Introduction to Anthroposophy: Rudolf Steiner's World View, (Forest Row, UK: Rudolf Steiner Press, 2005), retrieved June 18, 2020, https://www.amazon.com/Introduction-Anthroposophy-Rudolf-Steiners-World/dp/1855841630

2 J. Dyson, R. R. Nelson, D. Tressemar, K. Derreumaux et al., "Who We Are," (Boulder, CO: Association for Anthroposophic Psychology, 2020), retrieved June 18, 2020, https://anthroposophicpsychology.org/Who-we-are

The Pearl and the Hut:
Soul Wisdom for Growing Up and Living Between Divorced Parents

INTRODUCTION

Growing Soul Gardens on the Rocks

Childhood physiological, mental, or emotional pain leads in adulthood to spiritual-scientific research. In trying to understand the suffering, a person comes to know oneself. Knowing brings compassion to the heart, determination on the soul path, and connection to spirit.

Anthroposophical practices keep a person attuned to lawfully evolving spiritual developments. One becomes capable of more sustainable psychological stability as the tides of life turn. Great spiritual insights, mature love, and inner peace become possible even if parent conflict doesn't end.

It is only with the heart that one can see rightly.
What is essential is invisible to the eye.[1]
- Antoine de Saint-Exupéry

One grim city night, twenty-five years ago, I was steered to the hospital with a stabbing chest pain that was taking my breath away. I was a young, long-term substitute teacher in the public-school system in Toronto, Canada. I had been in an extended and grueling stretch of testing and essay-marking, while preparing students for end-of-term exams. I was also implementing newly government-enforced, standardized-testing regimens.

Someone in the apartment building across the street from where I lived had jumped to his death from the balcony a month before and a yellow police line haunted my dreams with rattling frequency. My relatively new skills in meditation, although helpful on my one day off a week, didn't seem to be resolving my day-to-day life stresses or my family problems. A search for meaningful counsel from religious leaders in my region offered no solace for what I later understood was my long-term, locked-up shock and inner grief.

Earlier in the night of the ambulance run to the hospital, I awoke from sleep and couldn't breathe for what seemed in the moment like several minutes. My heart was tight, as if I was being stabbed. I was thirty-one and newly into a teaching career in a high school that was fully immersing itself in computer technology. It also had a program to prepare students for a life in the space program. I called my father, who lived only a few blocks away. He immediately said that the heart pains were nothing and I shouldn't worry about it – and nothing more. In a packed, noisy hospital room, the doctors found no physical reason for the attack that I was certain I had experienced. I felt ashamed.

I wasn't known for histrionics or falseness and, as I returned home that night, I grappled with what was happening. I had recently experienced my first, conscious anxiety attacks that woke me out of sleep, imagining that I was falling from the balcony of my apartment. The day after the hospital check-in, one of the country's most public young comedians, John Belushi, was reported dead of a heart attack. I called a friend on the west coast in complete distress about life. She encouraged me to come to the ocean and the mountains. Within a month, I began one of many complex and profound life transformations. Away from the noise, concrete, and hustle of the city, I immediately realized what I was struggling with.

Our family divorce at age seven had never felt resolved for me. I felt broken and weakened, and though I had kept up a brave face for years, I now was finding it hard to cope with all the other difficult challenges that modern life was presenting to everyone in general. Living in a complex, multicultural life setting, with increasing noise, escalating electromagnetic influences all around, denuded and denatured food in the markets to which my limited budget had access, and competing to just stay in the job market, with no family to turn to when my emotions overwhelmed my reason, I was regularly getting sick and returning to an empty apartment with a pharmaceutical drug in hand but no one's loving understanding or comfort. I received regular messages from people around me that love really didn't matter much anyway.

I knew then that divorce was not just about two adults severing their ties to each other, but that it could sever children from important growth and resilience forces that normally become ensouled in whole families. No one in the society that I lived in seemed to be consciously addressing this for the young people in the emerging divorce wave.

I had never been asked for my feelings, thoughts, or intuitions about family divorce. I had no counseling around my intense heartache and trauma. It seemed that I had deeply, and unconsciously, absorbed the feelings of betrayal, separation, and the quietly bitter infighting of my parents. As a seven-year-old child, the destruction of respectful relationship modelling left me at times with unmanageable fears, insecurities, and beliefs. In adulthood, the missing experiences of loving family life were constricting my sense of life. Like so many children of divorce, I had been left alone in unmanageable trauma.

Our mother's death from cancer some years earlier and our father's behavior around it revived in me intensely difficult feelings about how my parents treated each other. I had for so long been without a safe elder to help me understand the complex pain. My family was a cultural mix of British Anglo-Saxon and Greek, and I had unconsciously risen to an old-world Greek practice of stoicism. However, it became clear that the old ways weren't enough to help me. The stress was coming out in my body, even if it had not come out strongly enough yet to land a serious diagnosis.

Soon after, I left the city to get free and breathe, freshly, a sense of my own life. I remember, vividly, a meeting on my apartment balcony with my father just before my departure. It was a dramatic scene of individuation, much later than most adolescent rebellion, since my innate sense of responsibility toward my sick, single-parent mother had kept me from many social activities that adolescents in the West normally engaged in during their teens. I told my father that his behaviors around the divorce, and what I saw as his subsequent sexually inappropriate behavior in my presence with other women, were so painful to me that I could not remain in the same city with him. I was finally setting some personal values and boundaries.

We had been estranged since I was seven years old. That was when he and my mother sat my brother and me on their bed one afternoon to tell us that my father wasn't going to live with us anymore. Although they did not tell us this then, my father had engaged in a sexual affair and my mother had told him to leave. The shock for my brother and me that our father would not live with us anymore was immediate. We were in tears, but no one held us, told us how to cope, or arranged for us to kiss our father goodbye. Our parents were in too much pain and anger with each other to reach us, or to even realize the profound nature of our own pain in this breaking apart. We were sent downstairs and nothing more was addressed about our feelings or needs during this trauma and throughout all the subsequent changes. The pain within all of us seemed to just get locked away, unaddressed, in a festering and unhealthy stasis.

I didn't see my father leave the house. My parents' marriage was on the rocks and we were left on denuded and barren soil from it. When the legal divorce came through three years later, I was told not to cry, and the sense of loss and repression was almost more than I could endure. I couldn't finish my favorite projects at school. Even harder, no court heard our feelings or asked us who we wanted to be with or how we saw the situation. No adult took us aside to comfort us. People said we were young and that we'd just get over it.

Takotsubo Cardiomyopathy: Broken Heart Syndrome

Physiological research, started thirty years ago in Japan and supported more internationally today, points to a condition of the heart associated with heartache, called Takotsubo Cardiomyopathy (TC).[2] It presents as one part of the heart, often the left side, ballooning out, but is not due to any known heart disease. A person can feel tightness of breath and chest pain without having any recognized heart disease. It is now believed that people have suffered this for a long time.

Because TC doesn't show up in regular echocardiograms (ECGs) or most other standard tests, it has not often been recognized. TC is medically related to a negative heart-enzyme state, but it is not treated well with heart drugs. Researchers use the adjective "stunned" to describe the effect on the myocardium of the heart. This *stunned-heart* feeling was very real for me even until my late thirties, so much so that I could have moments, even in public, where I felt stopped in my 'heart tracks', almost blinded by emotion, and unable to think. I felt arrested by heartache, although I was perfectly healthy and strong.

In Japan, the first tests of TC showed that intense emotional stress, especially among women, can cause a heart reaction that can physically mimic heart congestion or myocardial infarction of the anterior heart wall. Though the number of people believed to experience this in a full-blown way are few, the more hidden and earlier somatic realities may be much more common.

For years I had inexplicable heart-wall pain that some doctors associated with menstruation. Yet, the pain was not consistent with menses. A team of doctors at Wellesley Hospital in Toronto determined that I had an unusual heart murmur that would need to be checked regularly. I had heart tests every year for thirty years, always with the strange result and no answers or remedy.

Somatic Illness

The mainstream definition of somatic illness[3] comes from the Greek word *soma*, meaning body. Somatic symptoms are early, sensed symptoms experienced in the body—physical sensations, movements, or experiences. Some examples may include pain, nausea, dizziness, and fainting. Somatization is a normal human experience, but sometimes these body symptoms cause problems in everyday life that inhibit our ability to function well. However, the deepened consciousness work of anthroposophy and anthroposophical medicine perceives soma somewhat differently.

(This book cannot cover the vast understandings of anthroposophical medicine practiced by certified medical doctors, but many elements of their work are mentioned here through pedagogical and other anthroposophical understandings. A helpful book from Adam Blanning, MD, is *Understanding Deeper Developmental Needs: Holistic Approaches for Challenging Behaviors in Children.*[4])

Somatic illness manifests as small or subtle states of illness that do not show up in modern medical tests, but which are noticeable to the person experiencing them and which can become chronic if not attended to. Somatic illnesses can be the early warning signals that a person's etheric life forces are being eaten into, through a decompensating effect, or distorted away from human truth in our times. Inwardly, people may be noticing illness pending, or in the case of TC, potential early heart disease before it becomes fully perceptible in a physical illness.

Although beta-blocker medications and even acetylsalicylic acid (ASA), or Aspirin, are sometimes prescribed for TC, along with exercise, the most effective treatment has shown to be the act of supporting the emotionally distressed person one-to-one. What is most unusual about this condition is that the person can experience a literally depressed, or lethargic, energy-depletion in one of their heart ventricles, putting other stress on the heart walls.

In my case, heart testing confirmed the diagnosis of an uncertain, potential, innocent myocardial prolapse that would need to be watched every year at medical check-ups, but which never, over time, revealed anything significant despite my ongoing experiences of this heart strain and pain.

I was only in my mid-twenties, fit and healthy, with an almost enviably disciplined dancer's diet for most of my childhood and adult life. Yet for years, I researched to try to understand why I had a deeply felt, inner sense that my heart and hormones were under too much overwhelming pressure. It was frightening enough that researchers were beginning to suggest that serious heart and brain health issues were arising from intense electromagnetic influences in cities from communications technology being installed for cell phone reception and other effects. I had what I felt as heart strain for much of my adult life and I still notice it if I allow external life to override my inner knowing or harm my sense of heart strength and love for myself or humanity.

What we all missed then, until I was well into my early thirties, was that the heartache that I was continually experiencing was connected to my very rational and practical inability to grow beyond the ongoing emotional triggers related to my parental divorce. I simply had no solid ground to stand on for safety, inner security, and ways to get my practical needs met while taking the necessary time out for conscious healing. Being emotionally locked up, I also couldn't find or create very well the common ground that I needed to build wholesome and resilient relationships with others.

Many years along, and after a richly meaningful time working as a teacher in a new organic life on the west coast of Canada, I moved to the Rocky Mountains with my new husband. A parent of one of my classroom children had suggested, prior to our move, that I had the right nature to become a teacher in the local Waldorf school in our new community.

I joined that Waldorf school as a classroom assistant for two years and then took Waldorf teacher training. This is when much came home for me. Through anthroposophical herbal remedies, homeopathy, rhythmical massage, biodynamic farming, flowing intergenerational eurythmy movement, community visual arts, poetry, singing, clay work, sculpting, international spiritual community, and Rudolf Steiner's detailed lectures and meditation work, I realized that I had found a path to more wholly heal the wounds of being a child of divorce.

I learned that the inward questioning I had been doing about my pain and suffering was leading me to a wholeness that I could not find in any other system of healing or awareness. It was also affirming many experiences of self-knowing and spiritual insights that had never made sense before, but that now made perfect, rational, imaginative, and even inspirational sense. I had found a personal grail of life meaning and a practical capacity in life that I did not consciously know I had been seeking. In addition, it was a grail of understanding that would help me to navigate the world of egos and the higher life of selflessness in ways that I had no capacity for before. Later, I even came to understand that this knowledge was also seeking me in a form of karmic destiny.

Consciousness Soul

Rudolf Steiner has spoken of the *Consciousness Soul* period of human consciousness development. He indicated that humanity is in the Consciousness Soul stage of spiritual development today. It is sometimes spoken of in New Age circles as the Age of Aquarius, although that is a misnomer, since we are, by true cosmology, living in the Age of Pisces.

Steiner investigated more deeply, and in a more comprehensive way than many other spiritual teachers or psychology researchers prior, on how we can apply ourselves during this challenging, mind-and-body-altering time in human history. He showed ways for all people to remain deeply human, progressive, less stressed-out about tension and body strains, and more connected in relationship through the generations. Steiner indicated ways for managing our individual states of being without false and unfree associations and comparisons.

In my early Waldorf work, I could see that it was not lost to the very humanistic teachers with anthroposophical backgrounds, anthroposophical lecturers, musicians, architects, engineers, physicists, and artists that I met and worked with, that treating heart and soul issues is an important process of development for all of humanity in our point in time in human history.

The painful and alienating soul-psyche disconnections that *Pearls* (a term I apply to children of divorce, explained in Chapter One) often experience, become clearly understood through anthroposophy. This is part of a profound process in the actual conscious and physiological changes happening in all human beings on a large scale on the planet today.

Pearls, in their emotional pain, have often had important elements of their lives regularly suppressed through emotional-regulation psychiatry or psychology interventions, or overly expressed through the opinions of their non-objective parents or reactive siblings and friends, and not through their own self-informed voices. They are often given pharmaceutical balms, through synthetic medications, to be peaceful about their struggles. They can also be pressured to believe that diet alone, extreme exercise, or even intellectual and spiritual bypassing activities are the cures for their soul ailments.

Soul issues, however, are not fully physical or outer-world matters. They have an inner, occult (meaning "hidden") nature connected to the journey of human consciousness. Pearls have been affected not only by the intense and psychologically disruptive family issues, but with the overall general growing pains associated with the larger collective shift in human consciousness. Humanity is developing new soul organs of perception toward self-relating, inter-relating with others, and relating to the world-cosmic reality. Their issues are as systemic as they are social and internal.

Pearl Child pain can be truly debilitating at times when healing help is not present. The stresses of ongoing triggers, neglect, stigma, or other forms of unconscious issues for the children of divorce today cannot be treated briefly, or purely with pharmacology. That is, not if Pearl Persons are to gain a sustainable sense of their own conscious humanness, warm-hearted relationship with others, or direction around how to meet a vastly reorienting future.

Today, individual human soul-psyche development foundations must prepare people to withstand a myriad of changes, including environmental crises and adaptations, population pressures, increasing cultural integrations bringing new human connections but also confusions and clashes, and sustainable natural resource transformations and conflicts.

It has become evident, after decades of research and efforts on this subject, that the very practical soul issues of children of divorce today need to be treated consciously and in healthy relationships of conscious, understanding people prepared to offer mutual support.

Anthroposophy, more than any philosophy that I have discovered along a very astute path to knowledge of this issue, shows, in minute details at times, how to grasp a sense of personal rhythm and wholeness in the changes that humanity is in now. Anthroposophy also indicates in specific ways, with complete freedom to investigate for oneself, how a person can navigate the sometimes intensely rocky terrain of this new world while maintaining personal connection to beauty, intuition, peaceful engagement, practical capacities in the world, spiritual courage, and societal skillfulness.

The Pearl and the Hut books are cultivated out of a love for a group of heart-aching souls who often live out a substantial segment of their lives caught in parent conflict. These volumes bear knowledge supported throughout a worldwide community available to Pearls in person as well as online. I feel hopeful that many children of divorce will have the chance to overcome desperate feelings, disturbing somatic sensations, and real, physiological illnesses, including the psychic illness of mental health pain. I hope that some of the hardest issues will be healed and archived to history.

Yiana Belkalopolos
Spring, 2021
Vancouver Island, Canada

Endnotes

1 A. Saint-Exupéry, K. Woods, The Little Prince (New York, NY: Harcourt, Brace & World, 1943).

2 Y. J. Akashi, D. S. Goldstein, G. Barbaro, and T. U., "Takotsubo Cardiomyopathy: A New Form of Acute, Reversible Heart Failure," CirculationAhA 118:2754-2762, retrieved June 18, 2020, https://doi.org/10.1161/CIRCULATIONAHA.108.767012Circulation. 2008;118:2754–2762

3 K. Glise et al., "Prevalence and course of somatic symptoms in patients with stress-related exhaustion: does sex or age matter?" BMC Psychiatry 14, no. 118 (2014), https://doi.org/10.1186/1471-244X-14-118

4 A. Blanning, Understanding Deeper Developmental Needs: Holistic Approaches for Challenging Behaviors in Children (Great Barrington, MA: Lindisfarne Books, 2017).

CHAPTER ONE

The Pearl and the Hut:
A Fairy Tale for Adult Children of Divorce

This is a fairy tale about a prince and princess whose parents, the king and queen, disagree on how to run the kingdom. Troubles heighten and the royal adults launch into a war with each other. The children are whisked away from the palace and taken to live with an elder couple in an old wooden hut, deep in a forest far from home.

Hidden from the war for years, the children come to know the wisdom of nature, as well as practices to keep their souls strong and resilient for the future. Becoming skilled in their heads, hearts, and hands, they become capable of overcoming intense emotional fears, doubts, and a lack of self-trust. They are prepared for self-acceptance, and to meet the earthen world of tensions and challenges with love. Despite their parents' divided worlds, they can move forward with a new sense of enlivened, inner harmony.

Just as our body has to have nutritive substances circulating through the organism,
the soul needs fairy tale substance flowing through its spiritual veins.[1]
Rudolf Steiner

In times of great difficulty or loneliness in our adult lives, often images or thoughts of childhood stories come to mind. We might know the stories from puppet shows we saw as children, or from the times in childhood when a family member read fairy tales to us before sleep. We might remember the prince or princess in a castle, a cavalier figure on a horse charging through a forest glade to save the villagers, or a strange but infinitely kind old man or woman in a welcoming cottage.

Keeping watch over a dwelling place was often a seemingly magical owl, raven, or eagle. Sunlight cast from another side of the world glowed upon a quiet moon, stirring the unconscious, as well as a sense of safety, in the otherwise pitch-black nights. The elder, with work-gnarled hands, long white hair, and a heart as warm as the worn and glowing embers in a fire, seemed to know things about the world that no one else knew.

In good stories, there was always a child, a simple village character, or powerful seeker who went about a task or adventure through which he or she would have to endure the challenges of tricksters, villains, or untimely loss. Important events in the stories usually coincided with special numbers, such as three essential items to find or adventures to complete, seven creatures to encounter, or twelve special people who ritualize a heightened event. These numbers reflect certain aspects of our soul development and sustenance that are described more in the following chapters of this book.

> *The starting point of all true tales lies in time immemorial,*
> *in the time when those who had not yet attained intellectual powers possessed*
> *a more or less remarkable clairvoyance, the remains of the primeval clairvoyance.*
> *People who had preserved this lived in a condition between sleeping and waking*
> *where they actually experienced the spiritual world in many different forms.*
> *This was not like one of our dreams today, which have for most people*
> *(but not for everyone) a somewhat chaotic nature.*
> *In those ancient times, people with the old clairvoyance had such regular experiences*
> *that everyone's were the same or very similar.*
> *Rudolf Steiner* [ii]

Rudolf Steiner had much to say about the importance of stories for the soul. For that reason, the first rough-hewn fairy tale known for children and adult children of divorce, "The Pearl and the Hut," begins this book. To begin and end are sayings that Rudolf Steiner indicated to be said to set the appropriate mood for a fairy tale telling.

Adult children of divorce are encouraged to take the story in while being gentle with themselves, considering how they might write the fairy tales of their own lives.

Yiana Belkalopolos

The Pearl and the Hut: A Fairy Tale

Once upon a time it happened ... Where indeed was it? Where indeed was it not?

A king and a queen lived in a land of great rolling hills of every shade and hue of green and blue. Gentle farmlands shimmered in the warming sunlight, strengthening from the darkness of winter. Many feisty lambs and calves arrived in the spring to keep the husbandry folk busy.

The young prince and princess of the land loved to go by the misty royal pond in the mornings. They would wait to watch the shepherds open the regal, carved-wood gates to the meadows. They gloried to watch the ducks, long-necked geese, and swans being caressed by streaming morning sunlight, the skies above layering the lightest green, yellow, vermilion, and brilliant gold through dissipating clouds.

Carefully wood-sculpted into the well-protected gates were roving chains of purple amethyst, green tourmaline, and orange citrine. Among them, inlaid in fine gold, were twelve glowing pearls. Legend told that the pearls had arrived at the kingdom many centuries before, from honorable merchants of the land of Sumer. That was the land of another king whose name was Gilgamesh. The children knew the story of the pearls held great wisdom and that one day they might know of their magic.

In the crisp, refreshing air, the children would bound along with the lambs and calves toward the dewy grasses that were the animals' daytime meal. The prince and princess knew that in a few hours, the moist air would fill with rain to wash the forests and to feed the rivers and lakes. The adventure of running about with the geese, sheep, and especially the goats—who sprinted gleefully and bucked up their legs—would send the children into reams of laughter. Often, their royal morning knickers and jumpers ended splattered and stained from sliding on the slippery grasses or from an encounter with a mud puddle. Even for a prince and princess, children would be children, and that was good.

One day, a great argument broke out between the king and queen. The king expected the soldiers and knights of the kingdom to gather together for months of jousts and competitions to prepare them for the future threat of war. The queen, weary of wars, wanted the strongest men of the land to dig more gardens, build better stables for the animals, and create the finest crafts in the land through their metal forges and woodworking. The king and queen railed day and night, calling in their individual advisers. Neither seemed willing to give up the fight, and their fiery tongues began to hurl insults at each other that frightened the children terribly.

—∞—

One morning, before the children rose to greet the meadow animals, they were hastily collected out of bed and whisked away on magnificent horses by a knight of the kingdom and a lady-in-waiting. In the morning dark, the children did not know where they were going, and they were afraid. Deeply through a forest glade they rode, bathed in shadows.

At full sunlight, the horses galloped up to a simple earthy hut. Dismounting, the riders met an elder woman with a warm but practical voice. Inside the hut, tending to the woman's needs, was a coppersmith. He walked with a yew wood cane that was carved at the top in the form of a plush, mythical bear.

One of the man's feet had no toes, the result of a bear mauling when he was a young man. The cane had become a symbol to this kind man of his rise from fear after the attack, and his mastery of the forest through knowledge of its nature and its creatures. He had learned a hard lesson once in the presence of a great creature of God's nature, and he now used the hardest wood of the forest to rest his elbow as he kept about his daily tasks. He worked metal into trinkets and household items. Every month he would slowly pull them in a cart to a village several days' journey away.

The children knew nothing of this old couple, nor of the people in villages far away. They were scared and cried to be taken home. But the knight and the lady turned and charged away upon their horses into the shadows, promising before they left that the palace would be there for the children again one day.

The old woman of the forest, sorting baskets of colorful wool through gnarly fingers, told the children that war had broken out at the palace, something the children would not understand. They must not succumb to fear, but rather wait it out and learn the rules of creative patience. They would learn to live with the hut people, and to know their ways of survival and the secrets of the forest.

That night, the bewildered and grief-stricken royal children cried themselves to sleep under a new moon. Unknown to them, nocturnal owls quietly announced wisdom to come. Twice the old woman checked in on the children in their beds. She left knitted blankets of the softest red wool that she had warmed by the fire for each of them. On a small nightstand by each child, she left a mug of hot goat's milk sweetened with honey and lavender. She did this every night for a month, retrieving sometimes empty cups, sometimes full ones.

—∞—

The morning after the children arrived at the forest hut, following a breakfast of warm goat's milk, oats, and salmonberries, the prince and princess looked around the forest for geese and other water birds. There were none. The only sound of feathered creatures in the forest now were the echoing calls of black ravens and the little-known trill of the occasional eagle with his mate high above the forest glades.

The forest seemed shadowy most of the time compared to the open valleys where the children had lived before. Yet, in special moments and places near a small garden and pond, it gleamed in sunlight and veils of radiance. It seemed at once both calming and eerie.

Seven wizened goats spent their days on the roof of the old woman's hut, coming down a wooden plank to the forest floor when they cared to. They provided milk and cheese to eat.

In time, the children learned to work the chores of the house and the small forest garden that surrounded it. They cultivated semi-wild roots, leafy plants, and colorful mushrooms.

Slowly, as they grew, they built bigger gardens in the dappled sunlit glades by a small and pulsating nearby waterfall. They came to know of the snails, the worms, the sultry foxes, and where to find the rabbits' dens and the badger setts, dug from sandbanks and surrounded by the rich and fertile loam. Often, they would be delighted to discover a brilliant red or green salamander beneath an old and decomposing log. Often there was not much to do except play by the streams, adventure in the woods, and make up songs. They built small drums and lyres by honing forest wood with iron files and blades. They strung the instruments with deerskins and strings of animal sinews.

The children grew and learned to flint a fire and warm the goat milk with chamomile and sage to drink before turning in to their beds of dried vines, leaves, and animal fur. When the old woman was ill or when the coppersmith's wounded foot bothered him too much with pain to get up and around in the darkness, the princess tended the night stove to keep herself and her forest family warm.

When the princess turned twelve, she began to slip out into the night to gaze at the stars. She grew to wonder at the moon and the many star pictures that seemed to tell a story in the darkness. A longing arose in her heart, and she developed a deep fondness for her quiet time in the evening solitude.

The prince learned to scout the forest on his own. When he was barely fourteen, he discovered a cobbled path in the opposite direction from which he and his sister had arrived at the forest hut. Excitement overcame him, and he followed it for three days to the nearest village. When he returned, wide-eyed, filthy, but very lively and out of breath, he expected to be scolded for disappearing. Instead, the coppersmith introduced the maturing prince to the coppersmith work.

He showed the now-lanky boy the rocky hills where the copper was mined and introduced him to foresters in the village who knew the lands and all that they had to offer. The prince was soon apprenticed to a woodsman who taught the young man how to manage the forest and to tend its needs so that it would last a very long time. He also learned the skills of a carpenter.

The forester told the boy both great and harrowing stories. Some were of mountain creatures big and small across a distant ocean. Others were of girls with mocha-cream skin who strummed light, lilting harps and beat elk-skin drums for vigorous village dancers. He told of lands where men worked all night and slept all day. The prince learned of perilous passages of people wandering from land to land.

In time, the elder man carefully relayed stories of dreaded battles that turned beautiful homesteads into some of the darkest places on earth. With great expression, he created heartfelt imaginations of great men and women who rallied side-by-side to save people in floods, earthquakes, hurricanes, and from bandits.

It was hard for the prince to hear of the horrors and human bitterness in the forester's descriptions. He could barely believe that this could exist. His heart was on fire to become one of the saviors of the stricken people. Yet, he also came to appreciate the lively forest home that had become a refreshing sanctuary to their tender feelings and their still-youthful need to explore, experiment, and wonder.

The forest caregivers did their best to soothe the children's fears when they remembered the words of the knight and the lady of the palace who had carried them away from their home. "War has broken out," they had warned, firmly. "You must remain here in safety until we know who is left standing at the palace."

The old coppersmith, no stranger to war in his youth, would play a peaceful wooden flute at night to calm the children before bed. The woman would hold each child close and murmur a verse for courage. She warmed stones in the fire and set them in skin bags full of wild chamomile, hops, and comfrey to put at the feet of the children's beds. Sometimes the children would warm some cheese or milk to eat before hearing a bedtime story from one or the other of the hut parents. They drizzled it with bees' honey that they had collected out of wooden hives they had made and hung from the trees. On cold nights, some fat from a rabbit carcass, or from a fish caught in the stream that ran down from the mountain lake, was warmed in the milk.

—∞—

Most evenings, the adolescent prince sat up with his sister and told her all that he had seen and learned in the far town. The princess, in turn, shared songs and poems that came to her in the night as she watched the lights in the night sky. She shared her dreams of great past ancestors who seemed to call advice into her ears first thing in the mornings.

She recalled premonitions of kind and unusual people who would come into their lives in the future. One such was an old man with a silver-white beard. Sometimes her brother wasn't certain if her visions were true or if she made them up to make him feel better.

Each sibling felt the fascination of each other's daily stories. Each also felt the pain of not having their real parents present with whom to share their lives. They wanted their parents to know what they were discovering about life. They wondered how their parents had become lost to them. They wished to know if their parents were alive, or if they had succumbed to evil.

The court knight and lady had told them they would return to the palace one day. Though the children had badgered and pleaded with the hut couple many times to tell them what the tragedy of a palace war could possibly mean to their family, nothing came to bring resolution to their hearts.

There were times when the young adolescents cried in the night, sleeping little. Other times, they were filled with the desire to find a place for themselves where they could make something better of the outside world. They longed for the mysterious places that they had heard about from the forest couple. They wondered at the elder woman and the copper man. How had they come to live where they did and why did they want to help hide and protect children who were so different from them?

The warm glow of the night fire seemed to warm their hearts when they thought of the tending that they had received from the strangers. They were too young and unclear about their past to understand the kind of love this meant. Love was a confusing feeling for them. They knew that they loved the creatures of the forest, and they cherished the stories they heard from the forest couple about people long gone or in foreign places. They also loved the rare occasions when visitors from the distant village came to stay for a night or three.

—∞—

One early summer evening, at eighteen-and-a-half years old, the young prince dared to venture through the forest in the direction the children had always been told to avoid. He followed along the path that the castle knight and lady had galloped along on steaming horses, years earlier. At the break of evening, he foggily recalled the morning of semi-darkness ten years earlier that had changed the royal children's lives forever.

When he arrived at the forest edge and a clearing by a babbling brook, the prince heard immediate warnings from his longtime raven companion in the trees above. He was surprised to notice the bird silhouetted before a glowing and moody, orange-ember moon. Through the dusk and shadowy stands of fir, oak, and maple, he was certain that he spotted the distant spire of an old stone abbey at the far end of the palace grounds. The raven echoed an ethereal, "Cloak, cloak, cloak." Soon, he was swooping down and snatching the hat off the young man's head, screaming like a ratty crow.

The prince lashed out at his friend to get back his hat. His heart was hard that day and he would have no interference from his lightweight, airy friend when he knew that he was at the edge of some dark but intriguing disaster from the past. He looked for the spire again but tumbling clouds had overtaken the moon. Within minutes, the forest was awash in rain. The prince ran back to his hut family. That night, he told his sister that he had discovered the way back to the palace. She shuddered to know what that must mean for them now.

After three nights' sleep and three days' work, when the chores were done, the youths wrapped up their afternoon snack of cheese, fiddleheads, and acorns, and stuffed it into small, goatskin bags. They placed some stones and sticks together at the entrance to the hut, creating a sign for the old woman and the coppersmith, pointing in the direction that they were heading.

The siblings, full of feelings of gratitude as well as loss, left the hut before their foster parents returned from a three-day journey to market. Their love for the couple could not override their youthful need to venture into the wholeness of their full lives again. The old woman had not journeyed to town before with the coppersmith, but this time she had insisted. The royal youths had been relieved, feeling concerned that if they had been obliged to tell their caretakers where they were going, they would have been stopped. Little did they know that the caretaker couple had gleaned for some time that the younger ones would have to leave them soon enough.

The Pearl and the Hut

Just before they left, the youths bundled a handful of eagles' down, four red berries, and a birchbark note into a deer-skin bag they had made, and left it for the elder couple. The note read: "Four heads, four hearts, and many hands. Thank you."

—∞—

The children had not seen their real mother or father for two-thirds of their lives. Knowing of both the exciting world, and also of some of the painful realities that lay beyond their safe boundaries, did not frighten them to stay away. They felt the full pulse of life that only very young adults can feel, enlivened by the passion to find their parents, and to know the truth of how they might carry on. That same day, an eagle from afar followed them silently, high in the treetops. His gaze was stern, but no disruptive dives or hat tricks came from him.

Halfway to the entrance of the forest, the prince forgot a landmark from his earlier adventure. Soon he and his sister were lost. Dusk set upon the already shadowy forest. Brother and sister, who were normally kind to each other, began to curse and blame each other for becoming distracted on the trail. Soon, the princess burst into unrelenting tears alike those she cried on her first night in the strange forest.

For a moment, the youths' fears were great, but not so great as the pain of never knowing their parents again and of learning how a family could fall apart in hate and destruction. While they had lived with the strange but loving man and warm-hearted woman, they had regularly struggled in their souls about what to do or what to think about their own family.

Their forest family had told them not to worry, but that had not been as easy as it sounded. Now they did not know where they were at all. In their excitement, they had forgotten to set landmarks along the trail, and they did not know how to return to the hut. They looked around for a safe space for the night but found nothing to allay their increasing anxiety.

The siblings fought and yelled, and their anguished calls reached a height wild enough to silence a night owl that was attempting to call solace into the otherwise sleepy forest night. Then, without warning, a small elfin man stepped onto the path. He brandished a walking staff with a glorious and rhythmical stroke; up and down, back and forth, and crossing his chest like a blissful and passionate music conductor. He carried a lantern in his other hand. His chin bore a long, white beard.

—∞—

The man's elegant staff was embedded with a glowing pearl, encased in gold. He was an aging shepherd who no longer tended the flocks, but wandered the meadows and forests daily, eating plants and roots, fried grasshoppers, and dry, salted worms. He drank freely from the refreshing, fern-arbored stream leading to the palace. When he spoke, his voice was warm and lyrical.

"Please do not fear, young bloods," he bade them. "I was once a shepherd at the palace." He spoke quietly, polishing the pearl of his staff with his right thumb. The children gazed upon the familiar-looking pearl with amazement. "I recognize you from when you were children at the palace," he said. The youth hesitated, searching the man's eyes, which were partially buried by long, silvery-white curls. Something told them that they could trust this man.

He bade them join him by the hearth in his cottage and they were surprised by the regal, silk-woven carpet on the floor. In its corners were bundles of tiny crystals. Something comforted them to also see round stones there, with white stripes running about their edges. The stones reminded them of the palace stream that emptied far beyond into the ocean. For a moment, they struggled between this good memory and old memories of loss and grief.

The princess recalled the likeness of the stones, similar as they were to those she had dreamed of not so long ago. As the elfin man spoke, the princess felt that she knew what he was going to say. "These are called grandmother stones. They hold the ancient, ongoing wisdom of the seasons. They also hold the circle of love of the ancestors, the angels, and the greater spirits who are with us at all times," he said.

Almost without a breath or beat, the princess spoke. "Yes," she said. "I recognize them. They were in my dream." She spoke with a sense of awe. "A kind woman was holding them and said that we must not fear. She said to remember to feel fullness in our hearts and stay away from hatred."

"Ah," said the elfin man. "Your dream life has stayed alive and wise in the mornings. That is good."

The princess was surprised for a moment by the man's knowing comment and by her own, newfound boldness. She hadn't realized how the forest and her woodland life had strengthened her courage, and yet she knew she also sensed foreboding shadows around her. In an instant she felt both heartened and humbled.

Comforted and filled with a sense of trust with the little man, she blurted out: "How will we find home now? Why is it so hard to be fully in our hearts?" She paused, fighting back tears. The old man's eyes softened. The prince spoke up forcefully.

"There has been little help for us to know who we are from the past, or what we must do outside of the forest." Without hesitation he launched on. "We are in search of our parents to find what has happened to them, and why we have been forsaken!"

The elfin man gazed upon the children, his eyes sparkling like the crackling embers in the stove. "If I may guess, you feel a sense of betrayal and some deep loneliness. I hear tender sadness in you," he said, as a tremor caught his voice for a moment. "I am not unfamiliar with such feelings," he revealed, as if about to tell a tragic tale, then he stopped. "It can be wrenchingly painful to be away from your loved ones and not know if they have been lost to you for good."

The youths considered the man with wonder. The prince murmured, "Who did you …?" but then quickly thought not to ask more since it might not be right and the elder was concentrating.

"Feelings can come like lightning strikes in a storm of activity," said the tiny man, "Or like a rainbow of beauteous color when we are full of joy and contentment, glancing into a shimmering waterfall." He said this with a look in his deep hazel eyes that seemed far away and hidden at the same time. He stirred the fire with his staff. The youths thought that the old man must be speaking in riddles.

"Come," he said, leading them to the back step of his cottage. He looked out onto the forest floor that was covered in newly fallen leaves of vermilion, crimson, and gold. A heady fragrance of musty toadstool spores hung in the air. A small bubbly, tumbling spring coursed downhill through several round rock pools embedded in a sloping, moss-covered path.

"Love and courage flow through whirlpools of feelings. The churning inside you purifies your heart when you take time to think through your feelings and those of people who have harmed you."

"Nonsense," said the prince. "I always churn when that foolish raven makes my adventures so frustrating. I never feel better, though I know he's just a ratty bird."

The elfin man raised his eyebrows. "Such a bird has given the tiniest amount of grief compared to what the world will show you!" He laughed. Then he stopped and thought more deeply about his mocking.

"Yes, I understand. His hijinks only add to your grief, after years of your parents being absent, in their own worlds, and not close to offer you heart-warmth. That is why his antics lead you to churn too much and to feel so sensitively."

"When we learn to tame our feelings into forms," he kept at it, "we can put those forms into goodness and help ourselves along the way. We purify our anger and tears by forming good ideas, with trustworthy people in our hearts and minds. Then we put our will and imaginations into action. Some good planning, and practice, are also important."

The youths weren't quite sure what to think. The man was creating forms in piles of forest leaves with his staff, circling and running the carven stick through them as if they were water. The princess looked stern for a moment. "How will this help us to meet our parents again? They abandoned us." She began to tear up and her eyes scanned the dark sky for something to hook her hopes to. Still young, it could not occur to her yet that she grieved both her lost parents and leaving the forest couple and home for the unknown.

The elfin man took her hand kindly, but firmly, and wrapped her fingers around the golden-pearl staff. He showed her how to stamp a five-pointed star on the dirt before her with the end of the staff. He did this while speaking a verse:

"We are starlight come to earth.
Five points of light hold a hearth.
Wise heads keep feet and hands alive.
Courage draws love, like bees to a hive."

He repeated the verse two more times, each time more slowly. The princess' tears, and fears, waned momentarily.

—∞—

"What do you imagine of your parents?" the man asked.

"They didn't really want us," the prince let out quietly.

"I doubt that is true in their real hearts," the man said as he turned and had the prince hold the staff, "but I can see how you might feel confused about their love." He put his warm hands over the hands of both children. "Some people have an immature or false heart that hardens over their real one," said the elder man as he led the prince to stamp the star for himself.

"Your parents' choice to war with each other to find their true hearts broke your hearts." He reached into his pocket and pulled out a second pearl encased in a golden ring. He gestured to the princess to open her hand, and he placed the ring in her palm and warmly closed her fingers around it.

"Now that the war has ended, they have to face honestly what their war has done," he said.

"Do parents do that?" the prince asked.

"Yes, some do," the man assured them.

"There are more pearls where these came from," he continued. "Your parents will help you to find them. Just don't expect the pearls to be like these."

The prince and princess weren't sure what he was saying. "Do you know that our parents are alive and well?" asked the prince.

"I do not know if your parents are alive or well," said the old man. "But I know that they are both standing."

"If that is true," the princess whispered very slowly, "and if our parents' hearts are so hard or hurt that they won't or can't help us, then what?" Her gaze seemed to drift away.

"Then appreciate if they try, and find the better help you need through others and your angels," the old shepherd assured them, "by being the best healers you can possibly be of your own hearts. Tell people what happened and what you seek. Carry the goodness of your helpers in your heart all along the way. And don't let anyone say that you are wrong for claiming the love and wisdom of the pearls. Just don't gather the goodness for yourselves only."

—∞—

"This is the form of a chalice, one that, using my imagination, I hope to have fire-blown into golden, rainbow-colored glass, iridescent like dragon-fly wings, before I die," he said. The old man mixed some leaves in with forest clay. He sculpted the earthen mixture with his hands, creating a vessel.

"You see, with hope and an imagination, you start slowly, and you build your heart vessel—possibly many times before it becomes something that serves your needs and those of others."

"Do you mean," the princess asked, "that we build a story that we want about our lives and our parents?"

The prince nodded because he feared what others would think about the real story of his family and the war they had created.

"You can make up a different story about yourself, because you are free to do so," said the elfin man, his staff pointing them into the cottage as a cool breeze arose. "That will only help you so far, though. Better to build a life story about what makes your heart open and full, with others, when life feels good, but also when you and others suffer most. Drink that goodness in every day and you'll have a golden life with loving people."

"Remember, too, you always have a special being with you." He layered sheepskins and woolen stoles on wooden cots across from the hearth fire, then pointed the youths to make their beds in them. "Just like the eagle who watched over you tonight in the darkening forest, an angelic being that we cannot see is with each one of us. Each speaks to us in the night with our ancestors and from a great love surrounding us, even in the stars and sunlight."

The royals felt awkward with this kind of talk and yet comforted. The man's deep voice seemed to resonate through the whole forest and the night sky at once. The old man continued as the youths settled into bed.

"What I tell you is eternal wisdom," the old man said. "Take it with you in your quiet times, like the glowing pearls. Make sure to have quiet times."

The prince could hardly keep his eyes open. Yet, worry worked upon him and he struggled to sleep.

—∞—

The elfin man looked at the royals with kind and patient eyes. "Not everything can be known or done at once, my dear friends. One feeling at a time. Fear—what do you want to make out of it?"

"I want to make a friend," the prince said quietly.

"Good," said the man. "Now, place into your grateful remembering all the friendly things that others have done for you. Who has been a friend?"

We have not had many friends, the princess thought. "We have been alone for a long time in the forest."

"Who cared for you?" asked the man.

"The old man and woman," the prince replied.

"They are your eternal friends," said the man. "They cared, they helped you, taught you, and watched out for you to get the food, shelter, and clothing that you needed. They gave you steady tending and took care of you when you were sick. You will carry kindness from them all the rest of your days. Friends give you kindness. Revere them in prayer and thankfulness."

"The knight and lady took us to safety too," the princess added.

"Wonderful," cried the man. "More friends! People who helped to protect you when you were most vulnerable. Anyone else?"

"The shepherds who let us into the fields every morning when we were young," laughed the princess, sleepily, remembering the joy she felt very young while watching the shepherds herd geese out of their way and into the royal pond.

I was one of those shepherds, though you don't recognize me, the elfin man thought, his eyes moist, and his heart soft.

"Notice the people who come to you with what you need when you open your own hearts. Ask what ails the other person. Listen to their wisdom and be ready to act out of pure goodness in right moments. Have curious questions."

The two youths had by now fallen asleep by the fire. The old shepherd watched their slumber, conversing with their angels, and singing ever-so-quietly to the ancestors.

—∞—

In the morning, the shepherd was gone, and at the door of the hut were four notes on dried layers of birchbark. A small sack of grandmother stones sat beside them. On the first note was a tree map leading to the entrance of the forest. Near the bottom were drawn six ethereal wolves. The princess read the note below to her brother.

"Six shiny-coated female wolves will appear to you when you get to the clearing at the entrance to the forest. They will seem friendly, but each will try to eat you for dinner if you give in to fear. You must not, though you may feel very frightened. Don't pretend, just don't let fear win. Stand straight. Breathe. Pause."

"Take charge with each," demanded the second note. "Show them that you are strong in heart and courage, and that you lead your own pack. If you trust yourself and forgive yourself when you make mistakes, they will settle beside you and protect you. You won't even know that they are there. Sing your own heart songs with them and listen if they need to howl at the night. They will respect you."

"If you do this for twelve nights," the note continued, "and if you keep a fire within these stones with dried ferns and bristles to smoke the food that the wolves bring to you, they will eventually leave, and you will be ready for the last trial. It will seem like an eternity."

The prince picked up the third note of instructions and read. "Don't hold your breath and don't over-blow yourselves either. Recall and retell to the night stars every good story that you have ever heard from your parents and caregivers, and every good moment in the forest. Remember yourself and others with a full and open heart."

The prince wondered if he could endure all of this, but the elder's note went on. "You can take a stone for every hard or fearful thought that arises in you and, after you feel the painful feelings, toss the rock carefully into the stream, asking the stream to ease your pain and suffering for now. Pay attention to what the stream tells you. Then look at the fire and ask the warm light to enter your heart. Watch the smoke from the fire rise and ask yourself where it is going."

The mysterious man's vision concluded on the fourth and most clear piece of bark. "If you persist in this way for twelve days, a pearly white male wolf, with a tuft of gold on his forehead, will appear - called into your circle of loving courage. He has no teeth anymore. All the wolves, as they leave, will honor him by walking around him once, for he is very old. Yet, he has done well by his pack. He will lead you to the palace."

"The wolves bring earthly lessons of respect and self-respect that every person must learn before they can truly live. In the twelve nights in the forest with the wolves, you will learn from inside of you the most important things to take with you when you meet your parents again. Pay attention to the goodness in your own heart."

"Lastly," the youths read, "never forget to review your day, every night, backward."

—∞—

For a moment, the brother and sister looked at each other with bewilderment, doubt, and fear. Then they started to walk. They still felt alone. Could they trust the shepherd and the forest creatures to lead them out of darkness so that they might see the ongoing sunshine again?

They reviewed where they had been and what they must do. Their caregivers had been kind throughout their childhood forest days, but their differences had challenged the prince and princess also. The knight and the lady had left them years ago with a riddle they said the young ones would not understand then. Would they understand war now? Would others understand their unique upbringing? Would they be accepted? Would anyone love and care?

The prince and princess read the notes again and then each tucked equal sections of the birchbark into their layers of deer-hide clothing. The princess recalled the elfin man's staff and thought of the glowing pearls on the meadow gates of their early palace life. She wondered where the elfin man had gone. She knew that she must let that question go unanswered, since she and her brother had no more room for grief right now. They had hope and imagination to move on to.

The princess turned to her brother. "We've had each other to trust and we have shared many painful feelings. We can do many things, and we live with a family of stars, the sun, the moon, crystals, plants, and the animals, too. We have had the love of important and caring human beings when we needed them. Let us not fight, but rather, let us agree to always be friends."

Her brother looked upward for a moment in such a deep feeling way that the two almost teared up again. "I'll be here beside you, so long as I can be true to you as your brother," said the prince. "I can't promise that I won't feel angry at times, or afraid," he owned, "and I don't know if I will meet these dragons in my belly in the best way every time. I want to imagine something good." Then he flung a stone into the forest creek.

"The forest parents told us that we come from noble bearings," the princess said, picking up two sticks and pretending to shoot an arrow into the treetops. "We can watch out for each other when we face the darkness. We've learned what to do to survive in the darkness. Let's see what we can do in the light!"

—∞—

I now come to the end of this fairy tale. I can say that I once saw this, and if what happened in the spiritual world did not perish, if it is not dead, it must still be alive today

Therapeutic Stories Transform Outer-Life Trauma

The tale of "The Pearl and the Hut" is my version of a soulfully lawful story of childhood divorce. The events in the story are metaphoric, meaning heightened for emphasis, but not necessarily meant to be taken literally.

For instance, we may not take children directly away from their parents when their parents start their divorce battles. In some violent cases, however, this is the first approach to keeping the children safe. Most Western societies have worked out somewhat sophisticated systems to address protecting children—even fostering them in other families and homes—when parents and their other family members show themselves to be incapable of keeping young children safe in the middle of parent conflicts.

This fairy tale is also metaphoric. It suggests the important need for some children of divorce to be supported in having retreat times away from their parents, be it to the "hut" space that I outline later in this book, or away from parent's homes through the help of trustworthy relatives, social workers, or community members. In esoteric terms, the hut itself is a further metaphor for later life development, symbolizing a cultivated and inward meditation-space that we become conscious of slowly and develop through adulthood. Awareness and practices that strengthen meditative consciousness lead to healthy spiritual development and a freer sense of openness in the heart and life forces.

"The Pearl and the Hut" fairy tale has many of the elements of imaginative storytelling that can bring healing and help to open intuitive and creative thinking. The fairy tale suggests many creative uses in puppetry and drama work. For Pearl Adults, and potentially even their parents, it can also be an inner life contemplation. For healers and caregivers of children, it can stir important thoughts that I have worked to address later in this book about appropriate, anthroposophical childcare and development principles for children of divorce.

The fairy tale scene where the children are whisked away on the eve of parent wars is presented as a firmly-stated boundary against bringing adult harms upon children. It suggests not allowing children to be directly exposed to spousal abuse and caught in the middle of soul-destroying power struggles. It is meant to duly emphasize that growing children should not be exposed to heavy adult conflicts, or made into divorce pawns, if we want them to become healthy and sustainably capable adults able to bring effective work and goodness into their own lives and the civic arena. The biographies in this book explain this from the point of view of the grown children themselves.

Do the fairytale story and the book volumes overall suggest that societies should legislate more effectively in favor of child-of-divorce protections? Possibly. For the adult children of divorce, it helps to clarify that what happened in their family life, while they were still not capable of mature, human understanding and self-agency, was not, according to soul lawfulness, their responsibility. Their capacities to cope through their natural human will-forces, their feeling life, and their higher thinking were not developed enough to help them through parent conflict well, and those capacities were not meant to be developed to adult levels while they were still children and youths.

Only adult level soul development can deal effectively with adult level conflicts. Soul-spiritually, it is also not a child's karma to address adult issues while in childhood development. It is the author's belief that children have a right to protections from parent divorce conflicts until the children reach full adult capacities at age twenty-one.

Harms brought when children are incapable of coping with them are soul-crippling and often psychologically dangerous to life itself. Greatly limiting the exposure of children to toxic relationships, be they blatant or insidious, and prior to age twenty-one, is the responsibility of parents, extended family members, benevolent and responsible community members, or accountable, formally acknowledged societal leaders.

It is an anthroposophical view that having children sitting alone in therapy rooms talking about their deeply challenged feelings in adult ways with psychology professionals is also not the most appropriate or effective approach to supporting child development through parent conflict. It is the author's view that far more of this kind of work needs to be expected and even legislated for parents and not the children. The children and youths need processes that meet developmental ages and stages that are not the same as those of adults.

The elders in the naturally life-giving forest glen in "The Pearl and the Hut," who take the children in and teach them skills for living in nature and connecting back with primeval soul wisdom, reflect the life-giving practices embedded in anthroposophical child-development pedagogy and healing practices that can help children of divorce. The ideal is to bring the awe and wonder of the imaginative layers of nature, in their outward forms and inward essences, into the children's lives in a safe space. This provides a sanctuary for the children's souls while they wander the emotional wilderness between parent homes and highly divergent or conflicted parent belief-systems.

The best-case scenario is to encourage parents to be willing and able to examine and practice anthroposophical approaches to child-raising. However, even just one parent doing so can be helpful and soul-saving. When both parents bring soul-destructive negativity to a child, then truly developed adults in society, who have achieved the ability to realize greater selflessness, are called upon for benevolent assistance. Sometimes that means bringing help in very practical and even material ways.

Anthroposophy works out of the lawfulness of the soul's wisdom, as explained throughout this book. A child-of-divorce fairy tale is brought here to remind us that stories, even the stories of the children of divorce themselves, need to keep connections to true, soul-spirit lawfulness. We reach for transformational stories in life because they stir us back to a sense of wholeness, courage, and capability in the face of adversity. Fairy tales and storytelling bring us in touch with our inherent and even primeval life forces of wise nature. They cultivate levels of soul lawfulness that lend a meaningful and positive culture to the children and youths that can offer wholesome resourcing for them in the face of future life challenges and conflicts.

Adult children of divorce, and caregivers of young children of divorce, can use this "Pearl and the Hut" fairy tale as a starting point to create and tell the stories that relate to difficult times in their own lives. The task is to heighten the positive strengths and transformations in the story, while not shying away from presenting the harder trials as well as the most soulfully lawful resolutions to them. For instance, a Pearl Youth can recall a time when it felt as if wolves were all around and she didn't feel able to hold courage in her heart. What happened? Who helped her get back her strength and stride? What surprised her? Gave her hope? How did she respectfully acknowledge the person or people who helped her?

Dark moments in the story always need to be paired with transformational moments of goodness and light. This is not for bypassing hard realities, but for balancing them. Balance and equanimity are big challenges for many Pearl Children to trust, since they have felt little sense of home and family life as being just, fair and balanced. A creative storytelling tool uses the diversity of experience living in the storyteller's soul in order to bring unbalanced elements into a transformation from darkness to balancing, strengthening, and freeing light.

Much begins to change in the body, mind, and soul by doing this. It is important to consider what is being touched in our natural human wishes, wonders, and surprises through what is revealed through good storytelling. If we are clear in our highest heartfelt intentions, the healing comes out of our imaginations, inspirations, and intuitions. Anthroposophical speech practices offer just the right awe-inspiring sound, breath, and life-giving etheric nature to a well-told tale for young people. These stories can also be tenderly designed, in a strengthening way, for elders who lived the life of the adult child of divorce.

Healing happens at all ages, and thus, reading fairy tales, myths, and inspirational tales, or seeing them acted out on stage or through live drama, or even performing them, can be very helpful at different points along the life spectrum. Children in Waldorf schools experience many fairy tales, myths, and stories throughout all of the grades, and often they act out the stories through verses, poetry, and songs in classroom plays and school performances.

Adult children of divorce can affirm their soul's truth by picking up a fairy tale picture-book—like Grimm's fairy tales, which don't shy from the dark side of human behavior—or by creating one for themselves that integrates lawful elements of good soul stories when they feel the need for a renewal of their higher life forces. (More on this lawfulness is explained in later chapters.) The workings of good stories stir our hearts awake and light a certain clarity in our eternal souls.

An important adult fairy tale that Rudolf Steiner brought to early anthroposophical students, about bridging divides and entering into the heartfulness of our times, is Johann Wolfgang von Goethe's "The Green Snake and the Beautiful Lily."[2] It can be complicated to understand upon first reading and is best experienced first through seeing it acted out in a play or drawn in pastel chalk pictures.

Endnotes

1 R. Steiner, The Poetry and Meaning of Fairy Tales (Spring Valley, NY: Mercury Press, 1989), retrieved May 6, 2020, http://wn.rsarchive.org/Lectures/PoeTales/PoeTal_index.html

2 J.W. von Goethe, The Green Snake and the Beautiful Lily (Forest Row, UK: Rudolf Steiner Press, 2006), retrieved June 17, 2020, https://www.amazon.ca/Green-Snake-Beautiful-Lily/dp/0880105704

CHAPTER TWO

Coming Out of Darkness

Modern Western statistics create perceptions of children of divorce. The lived experience of the grown children brings the human soul to hard facts. Opposite, angled, and diverse views naturally arise. Mythology heightens historical understanding of how developing consciousness stirs deeply human conflicts and struggles in our times. Escapist tendencies and tensions can ensue in the development toward love. Managing the cosmos of the nervous system becomes crucial.

Love is higher than opinion.
If people love one another, the most varied opinions can be reconciled.[1]
Rudolf Steiner

Child-of-Divorce Statistics

According to statistical research in the United States, 35 to 50 percent of marriages ended in divorce in 2014.[2] Higher rates have been recorded in the European Union.[3] Much of what the Western world holds in greater awareness, sixty years following an unprecedented wave of family divorce beginning in the 1960s, is that childhood trauma from family divorce is real. It can have ongoing and highly detrimental effects on the lives of children through their growing years and in their adult life. This is so even if the breakup happens after completion of the childhood developmental years.[4]

Extensive research and theories that we have come to depend on regarding these issues, which emerged from Western psychological and sociological colleges over several recent decades, have not necessarily had substantial follow-up studies. Follow-up would have shown whether the interventions put into place to therapeutically assist the children and adult children of divorce had the effect of helping them to resolve divorce-trauma distress and gain individual self-dominion.

Practices have been created and implemented in therapeutic counseling offices to meet the stress of these children in a patchwork array of interventions since the 1970s. Often, children with emotional grief, fear, anxiety, hopelessness, or anger have been diagnosed with psychological illnesses and given medications to ease their emotions but not their souls. As the generational waves of children of divorce have grown up, they have had more than a little to say about what divorce and the healing theories have meant for them.

Despite forty or more years of Western therapeutic treatments for the heavy emotional issues of children of divorce, an exceedingly large number of people affected by family breakup or multiple breakups experience ongoing distress about it on periodically pathological or significantly dysfunctional levels. Divorce and child-of-divorce issues are still a strong topic in psychology research in the West, with an upsurge of studies, to 1,980 studies, in the United States alone in August 2009.[5]

During the height of the Western economic recession fallout in 2008, a search on the internet revealed 125 million mentions of divorce and 45 million searches of children of divorce. Today the numbers are harder to cite as adult children of divorce pull out from online sharing because of new awareness of the emotional manipulation and dangers of the internet and social media.[6] Others have blatantly acted out their conflict conditioning in spaces such as Facebook and Twitter.

Many grown children of divorce have come to hear challenging stories from others like them. Some have been able to share their pain, wisdom, and efforts to bring understanding and healing to one of the most controversial and complex social issues of the last half of a century. Many others have gone down self-harming routes or have histories of lengthy psychotherapy. Some of their parents have also.

Taboos, Stigmas, and Natural Complexity

Some of the mood and personality disorders considered by conservative Western psychology standards to be associated with child-of-divorce issues are known to be the ones that many professionals (clinical therapists, as well as marriage and family therapists) most prefer not to take on because of the heavy emotional charge. Litigators in family court have found it a duty to speak up in courts, books, and sociology studies to say that the truly tangled emotional load of divorce on children is one of the hardest experiences with which a child must cope.[7] One thing is definitively clear—the soul experience of these children is highly complicated.

One by-product of the divorce revolution has been to diminish the value of marriage in the eyes of children in hopes that the idea would gel that relationships are no longer meant to be sustainably whole or harmonious. A belief that often adapting and changing relational family structures is appropriate for our times and for most adult personal-growth needs, has set in across much of the Western social landscape.

Philosophically, myriad questions arise considering such a phenomenon. Is this a true state of humanity and relationships for modernity - the revolving door of marriage and procreative partnerships, leaving children ricocheting between parents' and partners' issues like balls in olden pinball games? Are family members' lives fodder for marriage Minecraft[8] fantasy, and reconstructive social-surgery, whenever the former construction isn't in style anymore? Parallels could also be brought with The Sims.[9] Can children truly fit easily into parent divorces like app accessories into new technological products?

In a holistic, life-forces-based life of growth and sustainable existence, one that is respectful of other human beings sharing the planet, the research does not show divorce or revolving-door parent relationships to be a strong wellness path to psychological health or long-term functional success for grown children. Or at least, not as it has been largely carried out in the last several decades. The harmful and soul-distorting experiences of children when they are caught in the emotional burdens of their parents' conflicts show a remarkably disconnected picture between divorced-parent perceptions and those of grown children of divorce. Many Pearls are far more honoring of relationship stability today than their parents are.

Who Becomes Free?

Many parents often feel much freer after a divorce. However, the intense emotional burden that millions of children of divorce actively struggle with, post-divorce, is often far less of an experience of freedom for them.

Today, we have an unprecedented experience in the Western world where parents and elders are living a far better life than their children. Lacking well-crafted soul guidelines, and often without support or models to show children of divorce how to live a truly developed and moral soul life upon emerging through parent conflict or even violent hatred, the children suffer while some parents, who did not grow up in divorces, seem to flourish post-divorce.[10]

Masses of young adults who were children of divorce have a different view of relationship and marriage today than their once-divorced or multiple-times-divorced parents. Many want intimacy as a main feature of life, and they work on attachment responsibility and sustainability in their relationships much more than their parents did early in their relationships. Too many reflect on their parents' divorce as a deadening or hindering factor in their lives, rather than an enlivening and supporting freedom factor.

At the same time, many parents who divorced are convinced that their decision at the time was right, for better or for worse, as far as the children were concerned. This discrepancy has, for many children of divorce, young or adult, created a confusing and even emotionally devastating wedge in interfamily and intergenerational relationships. We see it writ large today as part of the fabric of a Western society that is clearly having a civic meltdown in societal shared values.

As Chris Manvell, one of the editors of this book has pointed out, some people, like himself, wished their parents would have broken up. That is because of the fighting that his parents did when they thought that the children were asleep, and the ongoing silent battle underlying their marriage that pitted Chris against his brother. Chris felt significant pain in his heart about this most of his adult life.

My work as a registered clinical counselor has shown that family conflict can bring significant harm to many children and adults who did not experience parental divorce. My focus here, however, must be on the very specific issues and needs of those who lose family connections and significant supports as a result of parent divorce, including the fallout from often contentious and alienating court battles and ongoing volleys back at ex-spouses that divorced parents engage in overtly or covertly to prove winner and loser after the breakup.

As I've shared with many people over the years, this work around the children of divorce, and the research represented in *The Pearl and the Hut*, has come not to say that divorce should never happen. Rather, the intention is to place the issue where it belongs by taking adult-level conflict off the children, who can't handle it in their growing systems, and show ways to make divorce a more healthy and developmentally whole process so that the worst-case scenarios don't plague Pearls in their adulthood.

It is crucial that Pearls—like anyone else who is challenged with serious healing and developmental issues from family struggles and societal, systemic problems—can realize a sense of soul-spirit freedom, the ability to love, the courage to realize meaning, purpose, and value in their lives, and the resilience and strengthened confidence to form appropriately nurturing relationships with themselves, with others, and with their children or children of other community members.

Trust and trustworthiness are precious virtues for many people today in the social realm. Pearls as young as nine are known to be in therapist offices working with strangers on trust issues and often with no parent present. Yet, they often have no guarantee that either parent is working as consciously or diligently on their own relational trust and trustworthiness problems.

After years of this expectation, many grown children of divorce have come to realize that they, in some ways, have been doing the trust and trustworthy work far more than some of the significant adults in their lives. They are not always prepared any more to take on such work as their sole responsibility. This is leading to further family and societal conflict.

Children of divorce holistically experience energetic deficits, unfairness, stigmatization, and even social scapegoating when one or both parents step away from the hard work of family trust-building and mutual responsibility in the personal relationships that challenge them. This is still so despite the six or seven decades of greater awareness of divorce culture. Divorced parents, whose own parents were not divorced, still often expect trust from their children in a way their children cannot necessarily safely offer. They have not had the family social material or the opportunities to live in a committed sense of trust with their primary caregivers. Some rarely see a soulful trustworthiness in their parents' actions with new spouses or partners.

For those who do get to experience trustworthiness, when one or both parents remarry or re-partner into stable and growth-oriented relationships, the stability and earnest soul effort in the family make a great difference to the children throughout life.[11] If one parent manages good relationships and the other does not function nearly as well in life, it can still be tumultuous for the child, who often feels an underlying love and compassion for both natural parents.

The child can become alienated from one parent or the other, with joy on one side confusingly mixed with a sense of deep unfairness, disgust, betrayal, or hopelessness on the other. As a promising, clear, or better-realized life may appear on the outside for the one parent (with a new partner and family, for instance) the child in the middle suffers more. He is young, developing, and challenged with highly complex feelings, with only emotional tools but no understandings geared to a child's ages and stages, and few age-appropriate practices, to move through the pain. Too often, in psychotherapy, his emotions are treated but his soul feels sick, oppressed, or it experiences a strange sense of imposed dysphoria.

Bringing Imagination to Practical Love and Light

In highlighting the strengths and challenges of the child-of-divorce path, and how anthroposophical healing and practices can assist the children, youth, and adults toward growth and stability, I'll regularly use the terms "Pearl Child," "Pearl Children," "Pearl Youth," "Pearl Adults," "Pearl Parents," and sometimes "Pearls." One reason for this is that the term "child of divorce" has come to represent something depleting for certain children and adults. For others, the word divorce alone is trauma-triggering.

I also use the Pearl term to simplify some complexity. Since many readers will understand the confusion and negativity that can arise in sorting the details of the child and grown child-of-divorce issues, I've chosen to use a psychological intervention called reframing to bring simpler and more meaningful terms for children of divorce. This is also to increase respectful positivity and valuing for the children and adults who are the focus of love and concern in this book.

> *For the pearl is born from the sickness of the oyster, from the destruction inside the pearl-oyster. As the beauty of the pearl is born out of disease and suffering, so are knowledge, noble human nature and purified human feeling born out of suffering and pain.*[12]
> *Rudolf Steiner*

The pearl imagery of olden times represented stamina, resilience, patience, and great value. Actual pearls are cultivated in the wild as irritating earth particles enter an oyster shell. The oyster surrounds the sand particle with healing saliva to calm the irritation. In time, the healing creates a strong, yet not exceedingly hardened, sphere of lustrous, shiny beauty and wonder. It can keep its luster out of its birthed environment for decades and even centuries if cared for well.

Since the souls and hearts of Pearls can be pained and irritated by the ingrained conflicts of their divorced parents, the pearl identifier seemed apt to me, with the gracious strength and tender wonder that it also represents about the hearts and souls of these persons.

> For the purposes of this book, *Pearls* means the children of divorce and the grown child of divorce in general. *Pearl Children* are aged from birth to eleven. *Pearl Youth* are adolescent children from age twelve to age twenty-one. *Pearl Adults* are age twenty-two or over. *Pearl Parents* are adults who grew up as children of divorce and are now parents themselves.

Staying Positive

An important note needs to be added as we reframe the Pearls' experiences in ways that can make life more helpful. The positive psychology[13] approach of modern psychotherapeutic intervention in the West, which has been strongly promoted as healthy psychological therapy, is helpful if used consciously and not allowed to represent some process to bypass real and practical issues or times of very real grief and mourning.

Positive psychology earnestly seeks a brighter way of seeing a negative situation and hopefully buoy a person up in spirits to keep them moving forward. However, when used as popular psychology by people who are not conscious of the extensive and complex issues of divorced children, it can leave Pearls and their parents in a kind of blind and unrooted faith about their resilience and their future well-being.

If not worked well, positive psychology can urge Pearls to mentally scatter or dissociate, to take off pressure from undue pain or confusing responsibilities. This can prevent them from identifying important feelings and needs, hindering them from working through family relationships, and causing them to disregard real, practical needs and considerations. Pearls have often been told to just look at the bright side of things and have been disregarded for the very real and mature help they need to permeate the distinct and often practical issues causing their darkness. They can become avoidant of circumstances that can feel negative and tense. With the help of trustworthy, ongoing connections with empathic others, they can be encouraged again into an active life that can be beneficial to everyone.

While we know that not all Pearl Children experienced family divorce in the most harmful ways, and that some have done reasonably well with healthy, conscious, blended-family situations, others have seen blended-family life in some of its darker and more dangerous ways—with abusive stepfamily members or secondary family breakups. Complexity is a standard for most Pearls. It can feel like too much sometimes. Overwhelm and numbness are common experiences.

Weary, confused, and suffering questions can arise for the grown child of divorce: What would happen if there was no chance to dump unhappy, uninspired, or undeveloped feelings onto a spouse or family member anymore? What would it be like if we couldn't discard a person in our life because they didn't suit our changing tastes or if they didn't always see things the way that the other person wants? Should people simply have the right to toss out or disregard a spouse, regardless of what the harm is to the child's inner environment? Is this part of truthful soul development in human striving or is it a consequence of a consumerist, disposable society mentality toward other human beings?

In a spiritual age of freedom, a moral person can be very challenged to know where freedom ends and abuse sets in. What must happen in life for the children of divorce to believe that relationships can be life-sustaining and not destructive or soul-distorting, even if parents decide to go separate ways?

Finally, are the children of divorce, who long for sustainable relationships deserving to be ridiculed, or scoffed at as overly idealistic, as has happened for many Pearls? Harmfully, such characterizations often come from people who have not lived the experiences of family divorce themselves but who have observed it from a kind of outside, laboratory view, or from a stigmatizing social distance. Sometimes it comes from authoritative social leaders who have not actually managed particularly healthy relationships themselves.

The Deeper Questions

As couples' divorce becomes a more common reality in countries around the world, such as in Brazil,[14] China,[15] and Egypt,[16] the issues of a new culture of children worldwide become significant not only for the children and their families, but for the world society. What is this new world culture? Are the children of divorce wrong, lost, unhealthy, born of "sin", even "mistakes" as some have tried to elude over the years? Are the issues that Pearls face to be simply dumbed-down, smoothed over, or thrown into a general-melting-pot mindset of "needy people's issues"?

Are the trends toward modernized and distilled spiritual practices of Buddhist mindfulness, yoga bliss and unity, or eco-tribal, intentional-living community enough to realistically stabilize, de-stigmatize, and support the soul and the necessary ego wholeness of the Pearls today?

It is helpful to keep in mind that Pearl Children often regularly negotiate conflict between divorced parents who don't live simple or peaceful lives and who don't understand the Pearls' strong needs for extra sanctuary, rest, and peace. These children grow up to meet a world where other people around them may have stronger inner resources to cope with the intense world outside because others didn't have the kind of serious, damaging, and too often, irreparable battle to live out between their parents when they were growing up. Can Pearl Children truly live into a healthy, soulful existence and social life like anyone else—in soul lawfulness? (This kind of lawfulness will be explained throughout this book.)

If being a child of divorce is something to stay transcendently positive about, despite the real and practical challenges that it brings about in the structure of daily life and in socio-economic realities, then serious, follow-up social studies would show positive psychology as a successful intervention for the stabilizing systemic and basic socio-economic survival issues that so many Pearls end up facing. Such studies haven't manifested. Those who do "better" in life seem to do so most effectively because of inherited higher income levels leading to more access to societal comforts and general therapeutic healing.

The many children who become impoverished by divorce don't have as much positive energy to share among the societal figures who may or may not help them to get educated, find decent homes, manage well-paid work, and access ongoing psychotherapy support. The lack of real family support often leaves a psycho-emotional gap that can set the Pearl up for a string of crises in life, or the inevitable fall from grace or even chronic health issues. They can end up spending much of their free time from work just trying to heal because their experience with the outside world is regularly raw. Their foundations are regularly vulnerable compared to others from holistically healthy, stable families. Many fall through the cracks.

Rudolf Steiner, the founder of anthroposophy[17] and Waldorf[18] education, was clear that the cultivation of positivity is an important value and practice. However, his point was to cultivate that which rests morally well in the heart and soul, and in ethical relationships to economics, rights, and spiritual freedoms as they align with cosmic and human truths. There must be ethical considerations for Pearl experiences and needs, along with a truly moral consideration of the unrealistic expectations by others that Pearls just simply be positive that life will get better, more manageable, or outright harmonious and successful without significant systemic interventions and practical help.

Fantastical notions of the effects of blind Pearl positivity can push a Pearl's consciousness into a kind of "high" or false escape. It can also represent a simplistic distraction from real needs and the problems that require complex thinking about very negative home-life circumstances. In addition, it requires steady patience while reworking complex feelings, relationships, and living arrangements, representing the kind of energy that some people despise. Today one might say that, in spiritual terms, the issues of Pearls today are karma-sized.

That means that responsibilities remain with parents when a child is harmed by their adult conflicts. Much repair may be needed to clear the record and prevent the domino effect of later cross-generational abuse. Neuroscience today shows that there is a level of intense striving for positive "highs" that can push a person's nervous system above the recommended "window of tolerance"[19] for neurological harmony and well-being.[i]

The nervous system is vulnerable to chemical cortisol spilling as the nervous system tries to put out neurological inflammation fires after a significant stress, often leading to small depressive crashes later. Chronic or traumatic situations can lead to a major depressive state that is long-lasting and often accompanied by general exhaustion.

The Neurology of Overcoming Relationship Strain or Abuse

It is helpful to bring an encapsulated point to this early part of the discussion of the stressful effects of complicated Pearl Child experiences. This regards the complex neurological stresses, which will be discussed later in the book.

When the neurological memory banks of our brains are formed in the developmental years, with heavily loaded stress memories and stress-chemical overloading in the brain during times of unmet needs, together with recurring emotional triggers, the whole human organism suffers. Imagine a fresh garden bulb that seeks to renew its flowering blossom every year but is subjected to regular, unnatural, and unpredictable climactic storms and low-level soil nourishment when it is just working its way to uprightness and strength to meet the sun. Most gardeners or farmers would predict that such a plant won't flourish, will be knocked down to the point of permanently wilted, or it may not sprout at all after a few harsh seasons. The Pearl in adulthood, and even younger, planted in poor soil, can regularly struggle to calm the brainstem from inflaming out of fear reactions and the harsh, negative energy of others. The Pearl's life forces struggle from the exertion, then wilt and die.

What both children and adults need in the regularly stress-bound times that we live in, even during normal life tensions and hurts, is to be experiencing a sustaining balance of warm, resourcing, and naturally-balanced dopamine washing, along with loving caregiver attention and appropriate reparation experiences that can be trusted. Blocking the child's expressions of pain and need can cause the child to ruminate to try to self-calm, thinking over and over the hurt, if not immediately, then at some future point, and continuing the cycle of neurological

---

i   The window of tolerance is our neurological home base of health and well-being, where we are not spiking high from stress responses, and where we are not in a depressed state from the tiredness and biologically sick feeling following a toxic spilling of neurological chemicals after a stress event.

cortisol flooding. The neglected child is not just left alone to find some distraction but is rather suffering real neurological stress that is being increased by the neglect.

Soul-Psyche Splitting

To expect a child to override real needs with seemingly positive distractions that don't connect with his authenticity can cause him to split from his own soul-knowing in a kind of spiritual mindlessness or blind faith. It asks the child to go unconscious and "spiritual" in moments that really require astute and mature, adult-attending, soul-connecting and problem-solving. Growing healthy humans needs a holistic consciousness. The child with a mindlessly positive adult coaching him is in a bind otherwise.

Parents may feel free by diminishing or ignoring the child's harsh truths and needs, but the child is left bound up in feelings, and nervous-system experiences that are too intense and even destructive to manage alone. In adulthood, the Pearl can experience serious frustration at not achieving what is a felt sense, conscious capacity in life because early childhood neurological strains related to divorce stressors prevent sustainable adult functioning.

When the heart and mind can't move reasonably and consciously into workable social solutions, the soul struggles to find an opening to life-giving, practical survival applications without some level of mounting or even extreme tension. This happens unless a person can trust a bigger and existential life perspective for himself and others. It takes significant maturity to know how to appropriately balance patience with anxiety about life, about the future, and about death.

Many adults themselves find this self-management to be a major life challenge. For adult human beings in natural growth and development, it takes time and life experience to come to this higher soul-psyche skillfulness. For children, it is unfair and even abusive to expect this of them even before their bodies and brains have fully developed. Though a child may try to please his conflicted parents and numb or swallow the emotional affect for a while, such locking-in of early tensions can express outwardly in adulthood in mental, emotional, or physiological illness, sometimes chronically, or leading to a devastating end.

Positively Distorted Relationships for Pearls

All human beings cultivate relationships to steady and foster their path of growth, to help assuage anxieties, to build loving connections, and to help give them some sense of security and rest. This allows for space and safety to think and contemplate more deeply into life experiences and matters to which the external life can give no answers.

Many people start developing these supportive relationships beginning with their family. They may not stay within the family fold in adulthood, and it is a positive sign of individuation if they don't. Yet, they have learned skills for respectfully relating with others in ways that keep them able to live somewhat freely and capably into life. Pearls have often not had good early experiences of this relationship-building, family scaffolding.

Their less integrated relationship lessons and experiences can leave them with big gaps that they must fill with strangers or societal professionals and authority figures. These are usually people with little emotional investment in the child's lifelong welfare, and Pearls are often painfully aware of that lack of long-term resourcing and soulful acceptance of everything that they are about in relationships.

These are crucial and practical facts and issues to consider when Pearls need someone trustworthy to watch their backs when they need sanctuary and important life lessons that don't just serve to damage, once again, their ability to live capably in life.

A very real despair can set in for some Pearls because they didn't know how to cultivate nurturing or protective relationships well in their childhood, youth, or early adulthood, and so they cannot build on any firm relationship ground in adulthood. Missed experiences influence how Pearls receive resourcing support to bridge experiences of anxiety that arise naturally for everyone in life.

In cultures that don't have room for those who struggle with less strong resilience mechanisms because of humanly challenging and sometimes resource-weakening experiences in their family past, a numbness, frozenness, and even various forms of spiritual-socio-economic dysfunction can be the only go-to for Pearls. They can lose faith in themselves, or in other human beings at times, for the lack of compassion and moral or practical assistance and acceptance.

Morally integral feelings and actions are often very important for Pearls, who are largely sensitive to neglect, abuse, heartache, or social alienation from others. They also often naturally offer help to others with these needs because their pain cultivates a natural compassionate kindness with others who suffer. They can often be more helpful and kind to others than they are to themselves, or than others have been to them.

Ironically, if older Pearls bypass in various ways, using ineffective survival solutions to address their emotional and spiritual neglect, or for the sake of keeping themselves above despair, they can be ridiculed and ignored by others as airy, spacey, ungrounded, or unfocused. They are often then diagnosed by psychologists with dissociation. Or they are left out of positions of responsibility and leadership for being too idealistic or seemingly unrealistic.

Alternately, the opposite can happen; they are recognized for spiritual truthfulness and social sensitivity, and given a kind of dreamy social status, while their practical and material needs are ignored, elevated to sacrificial avatar status, or simply taken over by others. This disconnects Pearls from steering their own material and practical matters well, and that can be damaging with the loss of guardians, friends, colleagues, or family members to death or other circumstances. Pearls need to be independent and self-capable like their social peers. They often have all the right capacities, and hard-earned skills, but the wrong supports and personal relationship strengths.

Inner Resources

Pearl Children can not necessarily count on their inner resources the way that other children can do more easily. Children from whole families have parents who found ways as adults to maintain connection, respect, and integrity in their human relationships that provided an emotional base, even in hard times. Good families provide a network of good and helpful people to surround the child. This puts much less pressure on the child to become independent too early, and it eases physiological fear centers near the stem of the brain.

When children do not have adults holding appropriate calm and responsibility to allow children's nervous systems to grow un-assailed by issues that are too sophisticated for their age and stage, they often either recede into themselves in a kind of locked-up emotional way, or they act out as a cry for appropriate attending.

It is not always easy for a child to experience all the right amount of patience from people in society. Pearls are often left among strangers who don't perceive them as warmly or sustainably as they do their own family members, and who give their time or energy to the Pearl based on a cool, paid, time-bound work schedule. The lack of earnest warmth and empathy adds damage to the Pearl soul.

Pain, Suffering, and the Phenomenon of Human Consciousness Development

Perhaps the most poignant question of all for Pearls is this: Does the tide of pain associated with this movement of children represent a new world phenomenon and part of the growing pains of a deeper and wider human Consciousness Soul shift, rather than just some highly complex, sometimes pathologized, social matter? Pearl Adults often realize relationships with a new spiritual awareness, greater self-responsibility, and a deeply earthed, flexible, and alive heart.

This is often cultivated on the compassion that arises from their early suffering. It can also come from having sent themselves into mature psychic places and emotional experiences early—seeking to realize a more expansive and tolerant level of love and compassion with others than what their parents were able to achieve.

These heightened experiences and relationships with others are often, however, unsustainable. That does not mean that some of that refined higher spiritual work is not relevant. However, according to Rudolf Steiner, a kind of higher, mystical spiritual work is not the lawfully whole or right picture for our times. How much of this striving and achievement in more refined spiritual relationship for a young person is healthy and whole, and how much is a dissociated, hyper-idealized attempt to overcome pain and neglected missing pieces?

Is some of this expansive, high compassion in young Pearls just a prescription for endless nervous-system disruption or other diseases later in their adulthood? Is this the spiritually lawful way of the future for fifty percent of young people in the Western world today? Are Pearls simply all bound for neurologically disruptive lives in our times, pacifying themselves endlessly with mood-altering substances, or medicating themselves on antidepressants,[20] benzodiazepine calmers[21] or opioids?[22] It seems to be much of the trend of expectation toward many Pearls today.

Striving for a Connection that Parents Couldn't Get

Pearl Adults tend to be soulful, forgiving, and emotionally open with each of their parents when they leave home, even when their parents created a great deal of conflict in their life. They don't necessarily want to hang out with their parents, but they also don't fully condemn them. Many, many Pearls tend to love their parents unconditionally, and want to spend time with both parents, despite regular emotional turmoil.

Love is a complicated matter, yet some therapists might be forgiven to believe that this love of both conflicted parents is based on a kind of trauma response, akin to when a dependent person responds in love to an abuser simply to survive. For adults, trauma can bring about a much-needed spiritual maturation. For children, however, it can bind them into servitude to a parent's life organization and soul journey, however healthy or unhealthy it is, rather than to their own.

The trauma response triggers an inner, higher-mind escape to override chronic fear. However, sticking around in the soul-churning of the Pearl-and-his-parents dynamics, with skill, can have other values and gifts that sometimes go unseen, but are necessary for the Pearl's soul development. Yet, the effort to hold oneself in peace in the middle of parent conflict that seeks no resolution, can invest soul skills of some Pearls that are much higher than their own parents' skills. This has the potential of creating another level of alienation from one or both parents if the parents have become locked in egoism due to incessant conflict.

Are these shifting, relationship breakup times suggesting that all human beings should now simply grieve and let go of a belief in familial love all-together, to live fully out of some form of high-spirited, mature, and detached *agape*[23] love—and even before a child has the more earthly, incarnate, and everyday *philia*,[24] or family love?

Agape is a universalized and societally interdependent love without family attachments, meant to be realized by individuals after childhood development has fully matured at age twenty-one. Rudolf Steiner had much to say to affirm the possibility that our attachment to our hereditary family is lessening by the age of seven for a higher spiritual reason. However, he considered children to be ready for higher love only after healthy childhood development has occurred—with a healthy child-development period fostered until age twenty-one. Earnest, humanistic, and trustworthy parenting for children is as necessary today as it has always been.

Left with heart-and-soul-threadbare parenting, are Pearl Children then destined to a high spiritual life, with gaping holes in their childhood soul development, due to reaching desperately for some sense of peaceful meaning in life that wasn't available with their parents? Are they to live in an artificially enforced, falsely joyful, spiritual maturity that even their parents haven't really realized in relationships? Or will the great suffering of soul lead these children to a fuller brotherhood/sisterhood spiritual compassion and inter-dependency not yet realized in many other people in this human time—despite the initial, neurological strain and pain that being pushed to get there so early in life may bring?

Steiner's anthroposophy provides extensive insights into a spiritual rising that people are indeed part of in our human evolution today. Yet, Steiner was clear about how and when spiritual life must be brought for children to protect their wholesome development while living into spirit-rising lives. This is to help human beings cope as naturally as possible with physiological and neurological disruptions along a rocky path to human and earthly changes.

A Rightful Maturation Process

Anthroposophy suggests that higher consciousness shifts happen in humanity naturally and within a spiritual lawfulness and timing, something explained at points throughout this book. Essentially, cosmic patterns and timings that are understood through geometry, mathematics, and physics, show how our solar system is designed, and how those designs affect all living matter on the earth, including the more highly developed sentient beings—animals and humans.

It also offers practices to protect how human children need to be "held" as real, non-mature beings who are in full development processes for twenty-one years before they are ready to flourish and fend in the world for themselves. Human children are exceptionally different from the offspring of animals, some of which mature in only a few months or a short number of years.

No living being can meet the world well if it is forced to grapple with mature tensions before it has reached maturity to do so. That is why, for instance, in "The Pearl and the Hut" fairy tale, the children are removed from the heavy adult war of their parents. This action is a metaphor for keeping children as children, and not exposed to a kind of adultification before they are ready for adult issues.

Steiner gave many clues to deciphering what is spiritually lawfully true for our times and for human development ages and stages. He presented them practically, consciously, and soul-spiritually within the picture of an advancing human society that would desperately need to develop an increasingly human and compassionate social and spiritual consciousness. That is, if humanity wished to avoid devastating conflicts, harmful distractions, completely unsustainable paths of materialism, and the potential, highly disorienting technological onslaughts that he said would need to be appropriately managed but could not be avoided.

Steiner was clear that some of the coming technological advances represent other important stages in human consciousness development. However, he warned that people today, and in the future, can very easily take untrue life approaches and technological paths directly toward the destruction of the earth. (More on this is addressed in the coming chapters of this book.)

A great deal of insight and practical application work has come out of anthroposophy in the more than a century since Rudolf Steiner's time—from researchers in anthroposophical communities worldwide, and from teachers in Waldorf early-childhood care, elementary schools, high schools, and communities integrating biodynamic farming and natural product development with arts development programs and human rights activities.

Outlines of this work can be accessed through other written articles and books from venues such as Anthroposophic Press, also known as Steiner Books, in Great Barrington, MA, USA,[25] Mercury Press, The Threefold Educational Foundation and School, Chestnut Ridge, NY,[26] Waldorf Books, Des Moines, IA[27] Rudolf Steiner Press, Forest Row, East Sussex, UK,[28] Floris Books, Edinburgh, Scotland, UK,[29] Rudolf Steiner Archive online,[30] and Dale Brunsvold's online audio site.[31]

Spending time involving oneself in anthroposophical communities and in activities happening in Waldorf schools and anthroposophical healing centers in over a hundred different countries is also a great help. These can be searched through contacting the head office of the Anthroposophical Society at the Goetheanum in Switzerland,[32] or their official representations in various countries. There is also an online Facebook resource called the " Anthroposophical Directory of Michael Impulses Today,"[33] run by Danica Folksier.

Getting on the Path. Practices to "Know Thyself"

In my Pearl life, after years of cultivating and pruning modern Western psychotherapeutic techniques for emotional stability and personal awareness, and following deep study and practices in world spiritual traditions for deeper soul-spirit understanding such as Christianity, the Jewish Kabbalah, Eight-Limb Yoga, paganism, Buddhism, and shamanic health-and-wellbeing rituals (while working with natural health food and wild-crafting), a friend handed me a Waldorf education book titled *Education Towards Freedom*[34] by Rudolf Steiner.

Two Steiner books later, and after a year in Waldorf teacher training, something remarkable sparked from the reaches of my past. I later understood that this had opened a significant level of karmic awareness in me both about myself and about my family. This later opened my much broader understanding of the thoughts, feelings, and karma underlying much that was going on in society at large.

The profound wisdom shared by this tender, thoughtful, and extraordinarily productive man, as well as the practices that he indicated for the future, seemed to fill in vast empty questions in my life around why I experienced life as so painful and why human relationships, even though so far along in human consciousness development, could often turn hateful.

While too often other practices and philosophies had taught me to seek high ground, Dr. Steiner's insights showed me how to stay in the middle ground of the heart and the soul work without thinking that I could somehow run away from human problems. Anthroposophy also helped me not to want to just give up on life when I was constantly pushed out of societal comforts and accepted, traditional social systems.

Anthroposophy essentially woke me to my truest core connection to our soul-spirit times. The human capacities that I had felt for so long that I had been born to work into the world, aligned inwardly in ways that I could not achieve in the past. I was able to bring aspects of myself to the world that were buried in self-doubt, insecurity, and my habit of giving my personal authority and goodness over to others who stood in a constant state of superior judgment over me. I stopped letting other people make me small, wrong, and insignificant.

Some answers that I had come up with myself had been deeply affirmed by Steiner's work and by thousands of others worldwide who had done their own inspired, humanistic research. Profound experiences that I had lived through had never been addressed by any wise elder, leaving me feeling as if no one would ever understand. Yet, in one short book, *How to Know Higher Worlds*,[35] Rudolf Steiner spoke to my inner experiences and understandings so completely that I felt I knew him.

I realized soon that this feeling for Steiner's work came to me because of how he characterized and expressed the human, soul-spirit condition of our times so thoroughly, clearly, and prophetically. Yet, like the finest of modern spiritual initiates, he never claimed power over anyone, and spoke to the freedom of the soul as the only true higher order and supremacy in the human world. That is a supreme nature of the human being that requires strong responsibilities toward others and that can turn to darkness and destruction easily if not self-monitored vigilantly. It is also free for all to take up.

Steiner was also clear, in the most spiritual and scientific terms, that this higher order in a human being comes not from who we are or what we have, but from what we do in goodness for and with others. After a lifetime of living out the inner memory of the two people in my life who battled for supremacy over each other, this higher truth spoke directly to what I already knew inside of me.

In the meantime, many people tried to tell me that the knowing that I felt with my whole being was wrong. Steiner's insights validated and encouraged the experience of self-knowing that helped me to gain greater personal dominion over my own actions, feelings, and ways of relating with others. This knowledge strengthened me to navigate ego activity and distorted egoism better in myself and in others.

I also learned to stand more firmly in my own values and light in the face of lies, half-truths, and dark manipulations all around. I gradually developed my own appropriate path for work, social engagement, and healing. It also strengthened my ability to serve the community and others more maturely, individually, and in a more wholesome light. I could trust myself in my imperfections by truly knowing myself in cosmic-earthly spirit light, and I could work to understand and trust others in theirs.

Self-Trust

With trust being one of the hardest virtues for children of divorce to recover after their parents' marriage breakup, anthroposophy helps individuals to learn to trust themselves and their purpose in life. For me, it has become a dynamic practice from which I can live soul-freely while regularly reviewing my own humanness and spiritual inter-connectivity with others.

In much of my early life, my struggling parents had given too little attending to the real needs of my brother and me as Pearl Children. They knew nothing of the effects that a bitter divorce could bring upon undeveloped children. I took that personally to mean that I was not lovable and would have to be perfect to mean anything to anyone, or to have any reason to live. My brother took it differently, but in an equally self-denying and negative way against himself.

I refused ever to hurt anyone or use people intentionally because I felt so hurt and rejected myself. Though such intentions were good, most other people were not living by such rules. I pushed myself into some intense loneliness because I went too far and inadvertently set myself up to be responsible for everyone else's feelings and responses to me. I couldn't be a real human being, only an archetype that certain people would shuffle about a playing board according to their own beliefs, needs, and meanings. I was highly vulnerable to other people's abuses.

These are some typical reactions for children of divorce who experience mental, emotional, or even physical abuse or neglect. I had to learn that relationships are my responsibility, but not my sole responsibility. The other person in a relationship picture carries at least half of the soul-load when two people engage, unless each person has contracted otherwise with adult, free choice, out of some conscious or unconscious soul contract. Children do not have any higher responsibility with adults until they are fully developed at age twenty-one.

Children in dysfunctional family relationships don't have the soul power and autonomy to hold the adults to account. They can't have true and full responsibility until they become adults. Even then, they can't have individual freedom if the parent is inappropriately holding something over the Pearl Adult, which often occurs in divorced families. Parents often end up highly entangled in their adult Pearl Children's lives, in a very unfree way. That soulfully changes the responsibility equation, and can disrupt the relationship's spiritual lawfulness, with regard to the freedom of the child and the parent after the child reaches maturity. Such dynamics are highly problematic today.

According to Steiner's soul-spiritual insights, parents today are responsible for their growing children until adulthood—each parent—whether each chooses to take up his or her responsibilities or not. I speak of spiritual law here and not of Roman law. Essentially, we do not get to disregard our responsibilities in childcare, leaving them to someone else or to simply others in the village or community to take up fully. This irresponsibility will land on someone negatively and unfairly.

If that does happen, something will likely happen to cause the irresponsible or incapable parent to need to pay back the responsibility sometime down the road. These are the laws of karma. Children are not responsible for the karma they bring from a past life. They are responsible for it only when they become adults who are fully developed enough to understand it and do something restorative about it.

In my case, the more I learned of anthroposophy, the more responsibility I could take for myself despite gaping holes in my upbringing and despite parental entanglement on one side and almost complete parental disregard on the other. I learned to discern more easily how to accept or rehabilitate my choices and how to hold myself in the face of choices that coworkers, friends, and family members made. This was partly because I felt the support of spiritually mature community members who reasonably understood the workings of human soul journeys, of ego and egoism, and of the practical life in the stream of conscious, human development today.

Practiced students of anthroposophy can show extensively how human perspectives may seem in opposition to one another, and yet how an individual's place or stance in the cosmic-earthly picture can still be valid. This is so, even though persons may be at different stages of soul development in different areas of a truly human life. The soul works in ways that are not standardized and that are not necessarily formal. That is why, for so long, people have spoken of the mysterious workings of divine grace. Today, and into the future, more of those "mysteries," according to Rudolf Steiner, will be openly known to all.

Understanding oppositional perspectives and how to see them in ways that a person can meet them with an honorable and appropriate level of higher soul respect, artistic working, and practical application, greatly alleviates irrational fears and anxieties. This can be a huge step for children of divorce who can become lodged in tight caesura-like[36] personal boundaries of intolerance, having a metaphoric double-line drawn on the relationship ground with others, blocking out any real human understanding on both sides of the parent conflict and pausing any real development for themselves with others out of fear and pain.

The healthy caesura, which could represent simply a poetic pause in a person when he or she encounters a conflicted person and attempts to understand that person's pain, becomes an inward block in many Pearls, being stronger or weaker, depending on the level of antagonism they have already experienced between their conflicted and divorced parents. It is also something not well understood by other adults from whole families who were able to be in the presence of parent conflict at home and not feel destroyed by it because it didn't lead to family breakup, lingering resentments, or attempts at ego-and-soul destruction between family members.

Mythology Makes Meaning in Strife

The higher metaphor of the pearl, from the title of this book, *The Pearl and the Hut*, is drawn from one of the many stories of the Babylonian king, Gilgamesh. This story originated in the middle-eastern region of Mesopotamia, in Sumer.

Gilgamesh was a great but increasingly tyrannical king living in the fertile belt at the head of the Euphrates and Tigris rivers, five thousand years ago. He was a bullish man who was considered part god. He built walls to keep out what he considered to be the heathen people living beyond the border walls of the city. He was a man of great responsibility whose ambition, but also impatience, made him obsessed with the search for the pearly knowledge of eternal youth.

The southern coastal region of his ancient kingdom was acclaimed for the youthful divers who would winnow deep into the ocean waters of the Persian Gulf to gather oysters, ripe with pearls. These they would sell at market or to the town jewelers. The swimmers had to be in ultimate fitness to do their work. Thus, it became known that the pearls of wisdom and eternal youth lay at the bottom of the Gulf.

One day, Gilgamesh, who by then would not be shown up by any other man, decided to gather up a great pearl of wisdom for himself. Without a thought, he dove into the rough waters and grasped a pearl from a shell at the sea bottom. Once he ascended to the beach, he was so exhausted that he fell asleep by a tree. There, a giant snake stole the pearl out of his hand.

The Gilgamesh story is today an allegorical one, representing spiritual truths through human adventures. The allegory of the pearl, for Gilgamesh, reveals the great king's misguided and disintegrating, patriarchal, tribalistic consciousness. His story emerged in the time of the evolution of human consciousness when most human beings had only the minutest of soul seeds regarding an individualized, wholesome ego to distinguish themselves as their own persons.

These were pre-Egyptian times, and Gilgamesh was trying to realize a new level of himself as a human being, but without the tools and the appropriately ensouled life to do so. Thus, he could not experience the eternal sense of youthful soul renewal that higher soul-spirit development brings. Developing people, even today, can have insights into a future consciousness, without realizing that there are many steps (and even many lifetimes needed) to achieving that consciousness in full.

For Gilgamesh to evolve in his time, he did not know at first that he would have to meet and embrace the "other," the man who was his opposite and who he initially despised. In his case, in the undeveloped consciousness of his times, he would have to harmonize his opposite through a potentially deadly battle. Only through time could he grow and realize a more eternal aspect of himself, coming to understand the real pearl of eternal soul youth that was presented to him in a friendship with his foe. In the far distant future, this integration of the opposite would have the potential to bring him eternal love.

Gilgamesh, in his time, was a man who was destined to begin a new stage in a long story of the struggle for the healthy incarnation of an individual, human ego. His barely rooted, newly forming ego-essence, like a nine-year-old's today but in a grown man, brought potentially destructive forces, and Gilgamesh was losing his grasp of truth to guide his people, represented symbolically in his loss of the grasp on the pearl. He was fortunate to soon meet his match and his teacher in the form of a forest hermit, Eabani.

Eabani was a man still so innately connected to cosmically attuned nature that he could little be distinguished, on the outside at least, from the forest and animals with which he spent his days and nights. He was purified, by cosmic nature, of the inoculating seeds of egoism that most human beings would sprout in the future, prior to the arrival of the Christ. (A later being close in nature to Eabani was St. John the Baptist, of the Christian Bible.) Eabani still held primordial spirit-knowing, and thus the seeds of an emerging, healthy ego capable of a more transcendent humanity.

Humanity was about to initiate, a short three millennia after Gilgamesh's time, and through Christ Jesus, a new world of individual egos and well as new, individual responsibilities toward others. Following the Christ appearance, human beings would begin to be capable of developing truthful, humane capacities regarding earthly love, through a never-before-known process. Yet, this process was still far away from Gilgamesh's time, although there are always initiates being prepared ahead of the rest of humanity to prepare other leaders to help humanity along. Eabani was one of those initiates, and Gilgamesh would become a devoted disciple.

This ancient, pre-Christian story has it that Gilgamesh became jealous of the forest man when a musical mistress of the court became intimate with Eabani. The two men came to a great fight, high upon the walls of the despotic king's palace. Just as the king was about to lose his life by falling from a wall ridge, the wise forest man grabbed the king's hand and pulled him back up to safety. The decadent king and the rectifying forest man faced each other in the ultimate confrontation of opposites. That moment sealed a friendship between them, and it is one that people say still exists in the spiritual world today.

Gilgamesh's unmanaged small self, lacking the new ego of the future Christ being, could not be well-evolved in his time under the strain of his societal responsibilities. This led to his desperation to grasp, without appropriate discipline, for that which inwardly leads a human being to eternal, youthful spirit. He didn't know how to bridge the two in the way that spiritual truth would later lead. Humanity still had a Chaldean-Egyptian cultural-spiritual period of sun gods and master builders to evolve through.

This ancient story, however, is the story of many of the parents who divorce and who hope to grasp a new youthfulness and freedom through the relationship breakup. They sense an evolution, but without appropriate soul processes, and a strong, truthful ego to hold respect for opposite human perspectives, they can't get out from under the post-divorce negativity. Without a whole and healthy ego, they can't see how they push that negativity onto the children in order to try to free themselves up from responsibilities.

They know they will have a greater sense of freedom one day, although they do not have the awareness and skills to know how to work well through many aspects of the modern, complex life and still hold soul-spirit reverence for the "other" in their life with whom they share a child and who represents their opposition. Too many have battled on the palace walls, but they haven't brought in the purifying, eternal soul-spirit responsibility to find the way to higher friendship with their former spouse or partner. Thus, they have even less sense of how to steward the healthy heart-soul issues of their children, who are even less the same as them because their children represent a different generation with a different collective-soul purpose than their parents.

This naturally encompasses the story of many children of divorce. In some ways the children themselves become the Eabani character in their parents' divorce or divorces, locked in the despotic battle of opposites, unconsciously hoping to awaken and enlighten the paternal and maternal forces of old in their parents and bring them to loving understanding of the other, or at least a respectful and peaceful resolve and cooperation.

Conflicted parents relying almost exclusively on divorce to solve relationship disputes today will only meet the real needs of their children by becoming more of their own, inner-powered, compassionate, and deeply human beings, leaving personality and egoism aside, and harmonizing with the Christ forces of love toward the other parent who gave them such challenges to grow "up." Only by truly tuning up with the lawfulness of the loving and benevolent cosmic-earthly, higher marriage described in Chapter Three in *The Pearl and the Hut, Volume II*, can conflicted parents become, or remain, young in heart enough to deeply understand their children's hearts, souls, and struggles.

Children are always closer to spiritual lawfulness than parents, who have been on the earth longer and subjected to its distracting forces and responsibility worries more intensely. Only when children have been seriously abused do they tend lose their clearer connection to spirit lawfulness.

Some parents know, from an evolving intuition, that they are striving for something eternally higher and true, but they have not developed the higher power capacities to realize it soulfully. Parents are grasping for pearls, their youth, and their children, but their real understanding of eternal, spiritual youthfulness can get buried in personal conflict and court battles. The capacity of love in their children gets stunted or stolen away by the snakes of avarice, jealousy, and hate that are cast as shadows about them when parents carry out conflictual divorces and the residual bitterness and resentments that often accompany them.

It is as if the Pearl Children experience Gilgamesh's story now in a kind of regressive and reverse order of human development; regressed because humanity, two millennia past the coming of Christ, needs to advance more beyond old, despotic battles; and in reverse order because children are forced to learn the lessons of the despot and the wise forest man before they are ready and sometimes long before their more life-experienced parents have learned the lessons themselves.

Humanity today has had the chance to develop much further than in Gilgamesh's time, and yet the striving to realize a healthy ego, including engaging the new, sustainable will forces and practices required to do so, has become greatly distorted in world society through outer distractions. It's as if Gilgamesh got too busy playing golf when he lost the pearl to struggle with Eabani on the rooftop and to meet his opposite in an appropriate way for the sake of bringing new insight and great leadership to the people. And the modern Eabani is too busy retreating with ganja and sexual pleasure to bother bringing the higher insights to the town gates to save humanity from its evils. For many Pearl Children and their families, this is just leading to heavy addictions, alienation, drug deaths, and suicides. (More on these distortions is addressed later in this book.)

While Gilgamesh's distortions were the result of his time, when the ego was only forming in a delicate process, today, when humanity has moved much further along in ego development, Pearl Children can have their healthy ego process thrown backward if they are not met well in their family and earthly societal circumstances. Anthroposophy recognizes the dark outer and inner forces of life that would try to pull humanity's development backward.

Parents need to become conscious of these forces in themselves and rein them in through soul disciplines to keep their own development going forward as well as that of their children. The greatest challenges today and into the future are the distractions that grandiose materialism wields against the soul and the sustainability of the earth itself, and the manipulations and confusions of truth that people will use to rationalize not doing the true soul-spirit work.

The Hardening and Tightening of Society and Relationships

For children of divorce, the sense of being drawn backward in the inward soul development can raise a kind of inner-soul panic that leads to any number of human distress issues. Their perceived "acting out" battles, or their avoidance and stringent self-control to the point of self-hatred, as well as the tumultuous insecurity and anxiety that Pearls can experience around decision-making at too early ages, can lead Pearls too often into feelings of despair and to a wish to die and be done with life—in a distorted belief that all will be fine in their soul after such a death. The flip side to this is the constant battling that a Pearl can get into with elders to resist being dragged into old consciousness behaviors. Suicidal ideation, blame of others, and life-death fantasies become mass, critical phenomena working to wake people up to something bigger and more eternal in the soul and spirit of the world.

These phenomena work outwardly as a cry to change the picture of a hardened, materialistic, and conflicted human social life on earth to one of self-responsible, conscious, and peace-honoring cooperation along with creative inner growth. It is a cry for change from the tight, authoritarian, power-dominance of a tradition-obsessed kingly character like Gilgamesh, toward the freer wisdom of the newly compassionate and earth-honoring heart that brought someone like Eabani together with the king in an unbreakable, spirit-brother friendship.

"Sibling Society" Revisited

Despite the diminishing experiences that Pearl Children often have in childhood while tied up in their parents' fights, they know that many of them have been raised and "saved" by their brothers, sisters, and friends. Being raised by those who don't bear the immediate conflict responsibility has exposed many Pearls to selfless and compassionate people and thus to the wisdom of some of the most important values in human life for the future.

However, for some siblings, the behaviors of the parents become acted out between themselves, whether or not they wanted to be caught in the same behaviors. Like the fairy-tale princess and prince, without someone to help them to advance their development, such as the elfin forest man, they can only bring to relationships what they have been shown in early life. Those siblings who often find ways to transcend with each other can also, detrimentally because of youthfulness, speed up spiritual consciousness processes inappropriately for their age and stage of development, or even for our particular consciousness times.

Relating together, or even blissing out together in one way or another, may be good for quite some time, until some greater life issue triggers old conditioning or simply unaddressed practical issues that bring a sense of a fall. The depressive nature of ongoing falls can make each trip over oneself harder to pull out of mentally, emotionally, or practically the next time.

Many of the children and young adults who turned to their peers as parents have been criticized for living within a sibling society,[37] with no authority figures to keep them in check. For school-aged children, there can only be partial truth to this since the life of school children is surrounded by authority figures much of the day, unless the children are being home-schooled. However, as applied to home life, these problems coming from a lack of appropriate, modern, parental authority, can hold some truth.

Still, for Pearl Adults, this further negativity against their rational efforts to create a sibling society for support for themselves surfaces fears of the authoritarian church fathers of the past, who believed that individuals could not find their way in Christ alone, through the true Christ suffering path—in the way that the Gospels and Christ's life spoke to humanity. The new Christ way gleans truth and higher consciousness through shared wisdom, but also through individual suffering that comes through the trials and errors that naturally arise in the practice of leading higher lives of self-dominion, self-responsibility, and compassionate action toward others. It is a path of freedom rather than the path of old authoritarianism. It cannot be without some pain. The ultimate gift is the increasing courage to meet death with equanimity of mind, bringing peace to the soul, and a reverent love for the higher lessons of the earthen journey.

Eabani, in the past, represented the higher Christ-seed of brotherly love and compassion, and a self-responsibility that moved beyond just individual, personal circumstances. Love strives for a roundtable brotherhood-sisterhood, rather than a purely hierarchical, elder-age-powered authoritarianism represented in Gilgamesh. Many spiritual teachers of our modern times, including Rudolf Steiner, have foretold that much of humanity will eventually develop to this point of compassion and brotherhood-sisterhood, but not all. More and more people will take individual responsibility to care for each other and help each other to develop beyond only family bonds and their old, heavily attached and entangled dysfunctions. We see the growth of this in many pockets of world societies today.

Pearls who strive to create a whole-hearted sense of loving friendship out of the rubble of family divorce conflicts are often "saving" their parents' heart growth by showing them love, despite the often-hateful energy one or each parent continues to hold against someone so deeply connected to that Pearl. Some parents mature later in life, find friendship with ex-spouses, and recognize how their Pearl Children made them better persons. Others don't.

Parenting the Parents

When divorced parents don't grow in soul-spirit maturity through the breakup and after, this often shows up differently in children's or youths' maladaptively immature and often dangerously rebellious behaviors. Pearls often struggle with balance and transitions as they strive to stay in their soul truths and in their own ages and stages.

A common demand on developing children by parents is to somehow help their own parents toward more stability after the divorce, or in the face of the conflicts with the ex-spouse. Unresolved, this can spread to protecting one or other parent from conflicts with other people in general. The child is now expected to be a buffer for the parent to the outside world, even though that child is not a maturely developed being yet.

This social behavior expectation put onto the children by the adults is not a child's responsibility and needs to be handed back to the parents or supportive adults to work out, leaving the child, youth, or very young adult to matters that are right for their development level. Truly, well-functioning adult thinking does not set in for a developing child until age twenty-one. Prior to that, the child or youth can seem to mimic adult behavior, but that can be a hindrance on their inner forces in a way that comes out only later in chronic issues or maladaptation.

To cope with the stress and pressures of needing to deal with the family divide better than their parents, many children of divorce go "high." This can pressure the very finest and delicate levels of the prefrontal cortex brain[38] before the appropriate mid-brain is developed, leading to nervous strain and other body stresses and ailments. This brain region is believed to come maturely into formation only when a person is well into their twenties. Neuroscientists are discovering that the highest development of the prefrontal cortex brain seems to happen when middle-aged or older adults become interested and capable of sustaining investigations in different states of consciousness,[39] associated in anthroposophy with the loosening of the etheric forces from the astral sheath. Done at the right age and stage, this work is not an unnatural strain or dangerous to normal age-and-stage life functioning.

For children and adolescents with developing nervous systems, this striving for dopamine[40] highs (the effect of a brain chemical that washes the nervous system under stress, bringing a feel-good sense), to bring themselves into socially transcendent coping skills beyond their rightful development stage, has been termed in psychological theory, "spiritual bypassing".[41]

New research has confirmed that children who become addicted to highs—be it through drugs, dangerous thrills, excessive sports, or even social media—are unconsciously flooding their neurology with dopamine to feel high and stave off low feelings or to bring down anxiety.[42]

Considering the levels of prescribed medication[43] that many Pearls experience for symptoms ranging from anxiety, to attention deficit and hyperactivity, this theory of neurological and spiritual bypassing may have real relevance. We do know that much nervous-system stress is showing up in Pearl Children.[44]

Cultivating the Hut

The hut in the fairy tale of "The Pearl and the Hut" is, in anthroposophical esoteric wisdom, a metaphoric place inside of us. We go there to reflect on a middle way toward solving our peace, stability, and comfort issues. It is the place of prayer, meditation, mindfulness, and contemplation that, when fostered and developed, keeps us more centered and less subjected to the up-and-down, back-and-forth swooning in our emotions and keeps our thoughts stable and earthed. (This is something that Rudolf Steiner called the fluctuations of "sympathy and antipathy.")[45] The hut is also a space where we can listen to our higher self and get to know our own inner nature better.

The hut represents the inner spiritual refuge and the foundational place to safely practice more sophisticated levels of self-calming and to build higher consciousness thoughts and practices. It is a contained inner experience. It is sometimes associated in Eastern philosophies, with the home of the third eye.[46] It is also linked with the health and strengthening of the biological pineal gland.[47]

Figure 1.1: The Pineal Gland and the Egyptian Third Eye (Eye of Horus)

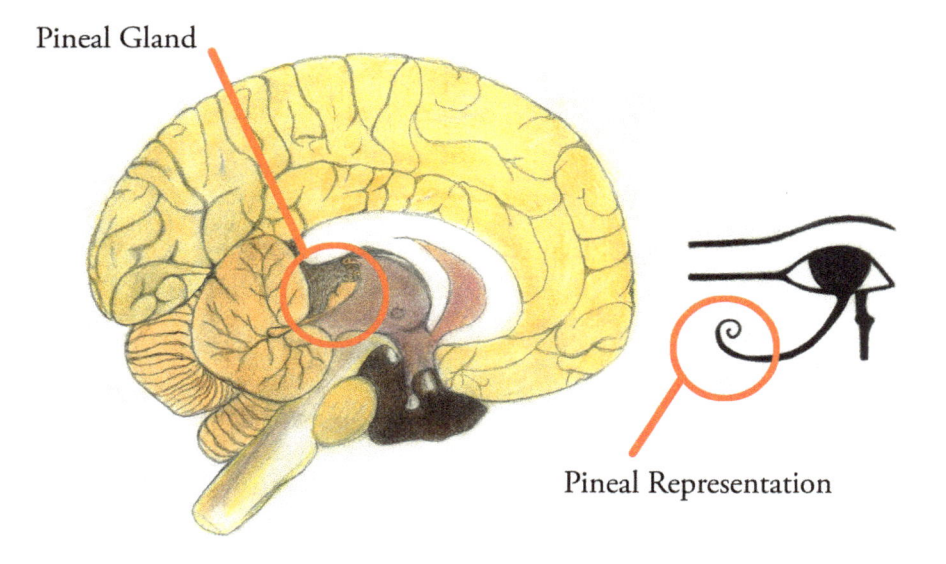

Esoteric understandings indicate the pineal gland in the brain as the place of higher knowing that is associated with sense-free thinking, intuition, imagination, inspiration, and even modern clairvoyance. The pineal gland is set back from the region between a human being's two eyes. It is believed that the ancient Egyptians had consciousness of this gland, sometimes called the third eye, and that it signifies the hidden meaning behind the Eyptian Eye of Horus.

This pineal gland holds tremendous forces for the social and spiritual health of a mature human being, as well as physical, hormonal health. This profound energy center of the mind, located slightly above the place between the eyes and esoterically known as the hut, has a physical location in the body but resonates with no finite earthly place. It is like a human point of reception for higher, inner insight that goes beyond time and place. Many well-practiced meditators know the power of this cosmic-earthly integration point in the body. An adult

Pearl, with some community support, and practice, can learn to connect with that space and ensoul it with etheric life in a way that heals the body, heart and negative thinking. It offers a sense of luminous resonance with a higher force without taking a person high. It is ultimately connected to an outer and inner function of the wider, *agape* heart.

In today's world, cultivating the adult hut can mean having a place to go for fostering a personal inner passion and potential for life that is not smothered or held back by non-empathic others or bound to old ritualistic practices of controlling the breath or excessive body worship. It is a place to strengthen a sense of both trust and vulnerability that builds resilience and readiness for action in the daily efforts of life and when the necessity or grace arises to help others.

The adult hut space is where we work on nourishing ensouled substance through self-development and soul practices as a buffer in the moments of our hardened projections of likes and dislikes onto others, or when faced by them coming from others toward ourselves. Staying present in the hut helps us to develop the inner, poignant capacities of love in ourselves that we long and need to share with others. However, it can become hardened when we put our focus to too much electronic media and outer material attachment to things. It is fostered when we share loving reverence with others.

The inner hut is a truly free place on earth, sustained only through conscious, spiritual practices that are appropriate at the right ages and stages of adulthood. It is a place to feel a sense of incarnate, warm wholeness that is not dependent on sensual stimulus. It is where no thoughts, judgments, or beliefs work to dislodge us from our tender, compassionate heart-truth. Harmonized thoughts, natural, rhythmic breathing, and stillness support the opening of the third eye, or adult-level hut.

It is where we can go to buffer overwhelming outer input, to be close with ourselves, to take a break, and to focus a feeling for kindness. It is also where we go to find our higher self or *I-being*, without lifting ourselves up and out of grounded connection with earthly life and others, something that often happens in times of fear or the sadness of loss. The hut gives us a place inside wherein we can cultivate a reverence and respect for those we might normally push away or feel divided from, by contemplating how their souls may be striving or how their hearts are hurting.

Here, in the hut, often in the warm light of morning, or beneath the early evening stars, we also find the room to cultivate interest and self-respect for our connection to the natural world and the elements that sustain our physical health. It is our portal to knowing insights beyond what only our physical senses can tell us.

When we can be truly still, with attention on that hut place and focused on a single object in a warmly lit space that is calm, we in time come to foster the cosmic strength to silently perceive esoteric phenomenon. (More on this kind of practice is discussed in further chapters in this book and in *The Pearl and the Hut, Volume II*). Musicians and singers, for instance, in time, often learn to hear the music of the celestial planets while in this meditative, or calmly attuned place—even while making music. We become sensitively aware of sound and energy that moves our hearts to more expansiveness and our souls to greater lightness.

Initially, the hut can be the place we settle inwardly into, to pause in a busy day, breathe better, and to think of nothing for a moment. Metaphorically, it is the space of spiritually ripe potential between the two fishes in the Christian sign of spirit, the Vesica Pisces.[48] In Zen Buddhism, it is the "no-mind."[49] In yoga, it is "yoga sutra" occurring along with "karma yoga," the practice of regularly stilling negative thoughts of desires and attachment in the mind while participating in the livelihood of the community.[50]

In the life of the anthroposophical practitioner, this place of the hut is where the *etheric body*, or our higher sense of spirit life, meets the etheric world,[51] or the world of human heart life. This resonant consciousness comes about with self-disciplines. In the hut place, one is not quite "out" of oneself so much that one loses consciousness of one's lower-self needs, and also not quite "in" so much that one loses consciousness of others and the material and spiritual worlds.[52]

Morals and Ethics

The moral of "The Pearl and the Hut" fairy tale is two-fold and a unity at the same time. In general, it reveals what we grasp for unconsciously in life without more considered and expansive thought, and often in the face of unacknowledged or unowned fear. Misguided, authoritarian fear in this story is personified by the king and the queen of the seven-pearled, gated kingdom in the fairy tale. They are each grasping for a competitive win over the other in their argument, rather than a win-win solution that might have saved their kingdom from war and kept them fostering healthy, unafraid, independent children.

In the tale, seven gated pearls, coming out of antiquity and belonging to the regal parents who gave into tyranny, ended up lost in the battle. Only two remained, which were revealed later to the forest youths by the elfin elder. One became the spiritually valued pearl encased in the wooden walking stick of the elder shepherd of the palace and given to the maturing prince. It was used for years for meditative inspiration in the elder, guiding him to keep awake and be in the right place at the right time. The other was a soul-touching pearl designed in a golden ring to highlight the circle of human diversity found among the good forest people. It was placed in the hand of the princess at the height of her adolescent maturity.

Without the hut couple to teach the children how to cope meaningfully in the world, the royal children might have had to scavenge for love on their own, tasked unethically to care for themselves alone, and much too early. Overcoming the debt of war had become the higher soul task of the good people of the forest and village, to raise the young royals to have a chance to be more deeply human than their parents could muster in their circumstances. This is to become the process of many human beings in time—to be raised by a compassionate community of soul beings prepared to make sacrifices toward others for the good of all. However, those who parent will be responsible members of those communities.

Being set onto an unsteady and insecure path through parent antipathy and aggression, children or youth can be deeply challenged to accept that they have a welcome place in a healthy, earth-life incarnation. Anthroposophy works to acknowledge these painful challenges showing up in people today, for one reason or another, and to help to secure more healthy life patterns for our times, and right into the soul. Rudolf Steiner's indications for child-raising highlight the imperative, appropriate care of children by bringing the right soul-development practices at the right time, and from conscientious people. It is all meant to keep souls free to be responsible in an increasingly karmically clear way, for themselves and toward others. Much of this book speaks in various ways to the practices for doing that.

In "The Pearl and the Hut" fairy tale, as in life today, an egoism-based kingdom could not offer children what they needed, but a tiny hut in the darkened woods could because of the selfless love of two committed people who knew that children need loving guidance, wise care, and experiences of wholesome, sense-world interactions. The hardened world of bitterness, divisiveness, and even violence, that was being cultivated in the battle between the king and queen had to be set well away from the children.

We know today that grasping for grandiose power over another, in usually an unrecognized and undeveloped egoic need, leads mostly to crisis—be it in a family, in a community, or in a nation. In the West today, such activity is leading to greater and more severe mental health crises that is ultimately the fallout of a lack of higher love in societies. Just as when Gilgamesh could not hold onto the Gulf pearl or win supremacy in the battle with Eabani, today human wholeness can only grow well out of an acknowledgment of the "god" in each other and the mutual need of a friendly, higher brotherhood-sisterhood.

In the case of "The Pearl and the Hut" fairy tale, wisdom comes in the loving care of the cottage couple, and in the figure of the hermit shepherd with the one-pearled, glowing staff. Each has little to gain in the outer world, but all have much to give from the inner place of deep human valuing.

Like Eabani, the forest hermit of ancient times, each has the naturally cultivated compassion to give both a practical and spiritual hand to those who are lost or flailing in the face of egoic life challenges. In this case, they help and protect the war-threatened children—a metaphor for those who help the Pearl Children caught between warring or substantially conflicted parents.

In the fairy tale, one might think that the lost ones were the prince and princess. As the biographies in Chapters Five to Seven show, Pearl Children today are not "lost," as some have labeled; they usually know, on some level—often very rationally—where and how they stand. Some may be disempowered to change certain familial and societal constructs that don't meet their needs. Certain opportunities may have been restructured for them, and different ones have opened, but they are often put in situations that traditional societal structures are often inadequate to help meet or accommodate. Many Pearl souls sense an eternal nature within them that guides them when all else in society fails. Lost is often a characterization that adults project onto challenged children when they themselves are at a loss to understand what to do to help.

The venerable and humble keepers of the child-appropriate hut are people who self-reflect, who pass on practical help and wisdom as freely as possible without neglecting their own responsibilities for personal well-being, and who see their lives as a selfless reflection of a higher purpose. Historically, in our modern era, people who searched intently for answers to life inwardly in the soul, in order to dedicate their lives toward work to transform society for the good, have only been known quietly in the world.

Others, because of karmic necessity, have been more fully in the outer world arena to do the same. Some of those great world figures in time were the Knights Templar, Joan of Arc, the great Renaissance painters and sculptors, and more recently, Mahatma Gandhi, Martin Luther King, and the modern-day young student from Pakistan, shot by the Taliban while advocating for education for women, Malala Yousafzai.[53]

In the adult hut, a person has the quiet and presence to ask oneself what might need changing inside that would help one become more human toward another person in more peaceful and constructive interactions and relationships. It also gives a safe space to think of another person's perspective. (Marshall Rosenberg presented a popular modern practice for this out of his "nonviolent communication"[54] theories and studies.)

Anthroposophy for older adults can go further with this work with its deep understandings of karma and how it works in a world moving through evolutionary changes of consciousness.

Child Hut Space for Sanctuary and Child-Level Soul Practices

Time that a Pearl Child can spend in a safe space at each parent's home, following parental divorce and a co-parenting agreement, can be important for a child over five years old, a Pearl Youth, or a very young adult Pearl who may not feel ready to leave home. That is a space that represents an inner, esoteric hut for creative expression and a seed of contemplation—one that should not be brought conscious at all for young children, and only brought somewhat conscious for youth when in later adolescence. Before that, it is more of a calm, "me" place to play, work, rest, or just be creatively quiet.

This hut is a downtime space in each parent's home and is a place to relieve their sensitized, holistic systems that may have experienced images, sounds, and felt-sense impressions of conflict that were hard and unnerving, sometimes for long periods. Children can be taught simple, amygdala-calming meditations, self-massages, body poses, or short eurythmy movements to restore calm. They can also use foot rollers, gently scented creams, or warm, salted foot baths in this hut to feel warmed and relaxed. The space should allow for some messiness without becoming concerningly unhygienic, such as with food or wet towels left to mold. Parents make a kindness contract with the children to come into the space regularly to check the hut for health needs.

The hut is a place to have an outlet for feelings to play out safely with sounding instruments that provide gentling or rhythmical sound, and artistic tools that encourage creating. There should be freedom of movement in the space without opportunities to experience harm in a hardened environment. A child could have a creature to care for in the hut that a parent checks in on to be sure of proper upkeep. There can be a wooden project to rasp, sand, and sculpt away at to relieve some absorbed parent angst or annoyance and allow the child to disregard, for a time, rigid parent behaviors or beliefs.

Holding space for the child's hut space takes great patience and trust on behalf of parents, but Pearl Children need to see a lot of trust from their parents when they feel that the family trust has been broken. They want to know that their parents will trust their own humanness, since they've seen a loved one diminished and cast out for his or her very human problems. The child can not necessarily discern a parent's harmful behavior, and thus cannot understand why one parent may have left, or been asked to leave, the family scenario. The child, unprotected, will simply resonate with the harsh divisiveness between the people that the child has the greatest felt sense with from a genetic and/or karmic connection. The time to break an intergenerational harm pattern is when the child is still in child development.

There can be an unconscious child rebellion for a while after a parent relationship breakup that is a test of how much of a human being that child can be in the family now. As a young adolescent, the youth can be testing how far to go before getting kicked out or disowned from a sense of being loved—the way the child saw the parent relationship go.

For a young child, a child whose behavior gets too intense in the hut needs to be companioned outside of the hut in the other areas of the home or outside in the park, forest, or other amenable place, until any heavy acting out is resolved. The parent rehearses and offers practices for the child to find a more resonant experience again in his hut space when he wants to retreat in there again.

The parent checks in on the child regularly, with permission, unless the parent senses that something is wrong that the child clearly can't handle, then the parent must intervene in the hut without permission. The parent expresses empathy and curiosity for what the child might want to share from the hut, and shares imaginations of what the parent might need to express in a personal hut if his or her parents weren't together in marriage anymore.

A parent can share this in the form of a story the parent writes, using child images and language, but not by using commercialized characters the child might recognize. Checking with Waldorf teachers and bookstore staff about appropriate story figures for certain ages and stages is helpful. The parent always affirms that the child has the right to meaningful time in the hut to calm, feel, play, create, sleep if necessary, cuddle with a pet, listen to music, eat a healthy snack, think about the other parent and even make little cards, pictures or gifts for him or her, or just read quietly.

There should be no wi-fi, computers, televisions, or cell phones anywhere close to the home hut. Restrictions should be minimal other than for safety reasons for children from ages five to sixteen, such as no matches or lighters, only a protective water source as opposed to a pool, no sharp cutting tools, and no toxic plants or cleaning products. For young children there should also not be synthetic fabrics that can be unexpectedly suffocating (cottons, wools, silks, and some kinds of hemp, bamboo, sheepskin, or other natural fabrics are best in the hut).

Older children need fewer and fewer restrictions, depending on age and proven understanding and responsibility around the dangers, for instance, of lamps that can start a fire if fabric is put on them or if a lamp breaks and falls over. Youths can still be encouraged to use hut space as time without computers or phones, but adolescents may need a great deal of convincing to encourage them to invite a friend or two to hang out in the hut rather than spend all kinds of time on a cell phone or in a computer interface. I encourage each parent to work hard at that convincing. Your child will be grateful later that you put the hard work into them.

The child builds a "practice," with creative tools, to put into imaginations and pictures. This child forms the feelings that are hard to wrestle with at times through drawing, knitting, wood-whittling, soapstone carving using safe files, through wax sculpting, or through craft activities.

The hut time is not a substitute for close, meaningful time with each parent, who attends to the child's *seven life processes* (detailed in Chapter Three), and who offers imaginative and loving stories, poems, images, and tales from nature, as well as biographies of inspiring people and stories of hardship overcome in relationships. It is imperative that the child's true nature not get lost in parent relationship distractions and new lifestyle challenges with new partners.

The child must be shown how to build up courage, resilience, a sense of heart resonance, and the ability to be known for who he or she truly is in the middle of difficult family times. He or she must be allowed to ask the difficult questions, even if the parents don't feel that they have full answers about how good relationships survive or struggle through challenges. Children need to hear that their parents are working on finding out those answers for themselves. They should not be hearing a parent outright blaming the other.

In being supported by a caregiver to create a warm and welcoming hut space, a Pearl Child can work through some issues alone, but with parents giving loving attendance to the needs of the hut space itself as a reflection of the child's individual soul nature. Simplistically, in esoteric terms, the hut represents the space for taking a breather, noticing natural breathing rhythms, creating space within our body and heart, and letting the human organs return to organic, wholesome, rhythmical life through quiet and/or lively playfulness designed by the child.

With a parent's help, a child can build a structure at home into which he or she designs a creative, exploratory place with access to materials, foods, instruments, and sensual, textured furnishings that invite a child to deepen into himself or herself without distraction. It should not be a bedroom. For Pearls, it is helpful for a child to have such a space in each parent's home, as long as each parent understands the nature of the space and does not allow it to become purely an escape place wherein the child does not have to engage with others at home much at all and which a parent need not offer any attending to.

It should not just be a closed-door room, though space in the home may require that it be a special room where the parent doesn't enter much except with permission. A parent ought to be able to hear some sounds and sense some activities happening in the hut with a child aged between five years old and fourteen. If the hut is simply another room in the house, try to architect it in a special way with the child's imaginative input. For an older child, it could be an outside cabin or tiny home with a connecting hallway to the main house that is heated and has healthy, ambient lighting.

Hut time is a place for a child to go to practice soulful, self-regulating skills through reciting verses, singing songs, doing body-practices such as tapping rhythms on energy points on the body, or reinforcing code behaviors used to signal stress to each parent in transitions from one parent's home to the other's.

It is also a place where a child can draw out the stories of discomforting experiences with stepparents or stepsiblings and, with trust and no judgment, be able to show them to their parents or other caregivers who give real, empathic presence to the potential feelings underlying the images. Again, this puts an expectation on the parents to be mature about what they experience from their child of divorce, and to get help outside of the child's realm to learn to identify what the child might be feeling and experiencing and work on practices and solutions to cope with what the child is feeding back to them. A parent should not force a child to outright accept a stepparent with no empathic practices and skills in the relationship for negotiating tensions and challenging feelings between child-level experience and the stepparent's adult-level experience. Once again, it is the parent's responsibility to make good bridges, not the child's.

In the Greek language, the breath is the *psyche*. When children are given protective space and time to manage the breath well, unconsciously, they can maintain a healthy, modern psychology. When a parent engages his or her own soul inwardly, warming it compassionately toward the child's heart by helping the child to create an inner hearth, or heart hut, then the traumatized Pearl can retrieve important soul integration, finding the secure sense of self and personal higher nature and the natural, unforced connection with spirit and higher healing.

As the child grows, the hut will change in form and nature to become something deeply internalized, bringing resourcing self-support throughout adulthood. In spiritual practice later in life, it represents the nourished, etheric third-eye space of meditation, and the subtle, self-accepting spaces in a gentled heart that enlivens with spiritual light. (More on the gentled heart can be found in *The Pearl and the Hut, Volume II*, Chapter Four.)

Leaving the Darkness with a Different Lamp

In "The Pearl and the Hut" fairy tale, the old woman, the coppersmith, and the forest itself, all seem somewhat mundane to the children when they reach their adolescence and as they are naturally tempted to seek greater inspiration and excitement in life. Yet they find that in their adventure to go further afield and to claim some of what the larger life offers, there is a need to look back and to review what was valuable to learn, to take a truly mindful moment of reverence toward those who loved them (or to even create a ceremony of gratitude for those who cared for them, and think over what was held ethically and responsibly for them in their growing years), and to remind themselves of practices they learned for coping with difficult feelings and experiences.

In their futures, to manage feelings of fear, anger, and despair well enough to live through whatever life will bring to them, the life-valuing Pearl Adults will need to visit the meaning of the pearl and the hut often. This is because the world outside could bring frequent, triggering reminders of their painful past, throwing their ego into potential egoism, and causing emotional pain to lock up again in memory. With healthy capacities ensouled in them through anthroposophical practices, the chances for them to dissociate or distort into fantasy rather than into healthy, spiritually lawful illusion leading to intuition, imagination, and inspiration, can be greatly lessened.

The inner dragon that Pearl Children will need to bring to bay with resilient efforts over time is the dark shadow that emerges when circumstances begin to distort or overwhelm their ability to experience heartwarming meaning in life. They need to know how to fill their inner holes with warmth, joy, light, and good actions in a way that is regenerative and substantial. Knowing what the dragon is and how it can be overcome is the work of parents to come to understand before their children take it on themselves. Parents can do this through the resiliency mentorship of anthroposophical workers in all fields.

When Pearls can become well-practiced with anthroposophical interventions and soul-strengthening practices through to their early adulthood, they will reach a point of more capable independence in the mastery of their own dragons. That will not mean that they will never be vulnerable again or need to ask for help. Yet, they will have achieved much greater freedom to direct both the fulfillment of their own needs and lives, as well as their own healing and the ability to offer selfless help to others. They can reach self-fulfillment, a crucial step toward a still-distant future of full self-realization.

This is a central goal in the developing impulses and initiatives of anthroposophy in the world. Rudolf Steiner foresaw the needs for many people to become more capable consciously of building, managing, maintaining, and protecting their inner life forces in ways that would foster healthy relationships with others in greater freedom and wholeness. This need was to prepare humanity for even greater changes that Steiner spoke of in detail regarding human development in the future.[55]

Parental Neglect Resulting in Decompensation

In Chapter Six, the discussion of psychological decompensation[56] addresses a problem seemingly endemic to Pearls. It comes out of parental neglect. When a child does not get the inner benchmarks of healthy development met, at important ages and stages of growth, the soul knows it is not going to manage well those problems that it will need to meet with deep humanness in adulthood.

Two things can happen: a) the child's soul registers lack, and b) there can be a sense of an inner fall into distressing discomfort, displayed outwardly as undeveloped behaviors, regressive behaviors, or excessive dependencies. In psychological language, this is called decompensation. Educators often see this when parents don't uphold healthy disciplines and practices at home and the child regresses rather than affirming their learning and moving forward, when the right capacities are developed at a certain age. It is similar in the soul.

Grown children are often deeply affected by this backward effect on their life forces, to the point where they become depressed or even despairing, experiencing a sense of deep failure and wallowing in an abyss of unhealthy patterns due to sheer energetic exhaustion and lack of specifically important soul development. They are not able, mostly, to be conscious of what they are doing or feeling.

This also happens for children who get entangled in inappropriate, adult-level emotional relationships with one or both parents after the divorce, or with the parents' new partners or spouses. That is when healthy boundaries are obscured between parent and child, and demands are exacted upon children that are not right for their age and stage.

As described earlier in this chapter, there can be a physiological-neurological association in these energetic fallbacks and strains. When a child's attempts to get compensated again are not heard, understood, or met, this contributes to many acting out behaviors at home or elsewhere in the child's community. Some children take the decompensation quietly inward, stoking a dangerous self-hate.

Ultimately, when the pearl and the hut are truly understood, and practices are second nature, love unfolds in Pearls because they can recognize how and when they are heading for a fall, and what decompensation that fall represents, and how to fulfill a crucial need. They can see how their behavior is systemically tied to that of others, and thus not take everything upon themselves in self-blaming ways.

In this way, family members can keep entangled and deadening emotional lines clearer as adults. They can begin to see what reparations are needed by whom, toward whom, in order to deactivate the ongoing negativity cycles. That is because when grounded, whole, warm-hearted hut moments are cultivated in the middle of busy family life, a higher grace can come to the innate knowing of the child.

Injustices in families are real, and as the Pearl Child grows, inner knowing can begin to form a process by which the young adult can address the parents from a place of discerning what is fair and just behavior between family members. Some people call this a process of karmic discernment. This can only happen with the healthy, ego-I development needed by all people today. That will be described more in the following chapters.

Endnotes

1 R. Steiner, "At the Gates of Spiritual Science, Lecture II: Post-Atlantean Cultural Epochs" (lecture, Stuttgart, August 1906), retrieved June 16, 2020 from: https://wn.rsarchive.org.lectures/GA095/English/RSPAP1986/19060091p01.html

2 National Marriage and Divorce Rate Trends (US), Center for Disease Control and Prevention, retrieved April 4, 2017, https://www.cdc.gov/nchs/nvss/marriage_divorce_tables.htm (page discontinued).

3 D. Seijo et al., "Estimating the Epidemiology and Quantifying the Damages of Parental Separation in Children and Adolescents," Frontiers in Psychology 7 (2016), https://doi.org/10.3389/fpsyg.2016.01611

4 P. Amato, "Research on Divorce: Continuing Trends and New Developments," Journal of Marriage and Family 72, no. 3 (2010): 650-666.

5 Amato, "Research on Divorce."

6 D. Boyd, (2015). "Untangling Research and Practice: What Facebook's 'Emotional Contagion' Study Teaches Us, Research Ethics 12, no. 1 (2015): 4-13, https://doi.org/10.1177/1747016115583379

7 H. Brownstone, Tug of War: A Judge's Verdict on Separation, Custody Battles, and the Bitter Realities of Family Court (Toronto, ON: ECW Press, 2009).

8 Minecraft (video game) (Sweden: Mojang, 2009), retrieved May 7, 2020, http://www.imdb.com/title/tt2011970/companycredits

9 Prima Games, The Sims: House Party (Rocklin, CA: Prima Communications, 2001), retrieved June 16, 2020, from https://dl.acm.org/doi/book/10.5555/516843

10 W. M. Williams-Owens, "The Behavioral Effects Divorce Can Have on Children," CUNY Academic Works, retrieved May 27, 2020 from: https://academicworks.cuny.edu/gc_etds/2314

11 R. Steiner, "Supersensible Knowledge, Lecture III: The Origin of Suffering" (lecture, Berlin, November 8, 1906), retrieved May 27, 2020 from: https://wn.rsarchive.org/Lectures/GA055/English/AP1987/19061108p02.html

12 C. Peterson, A Primer in Positive Psychology (New York, NY: Oxford University Press, 2006).

13 R. A. Nunes-Costa et al., "Psychosocial Adjustment and Physical Health in Children of Divorce," Journal do Pediatria 85, no. 5 (2009).

14 Q. Xu et al., "Is the 'Seven-Year Itch' Real? A Study on the Changing Divorce Pattern in Chinese Marriages," The Journal of Chinese Sociology 163, no. 17 (2016). https://doi.org/10.1186/s40711-016-0038-x

15 A.-M. Al-Youm, "Egypt's divorce rate up the highest in ? years: CAPMAS," Egypt Independent (September 8, 2016), retrieved May 7, 2020, http://www.egyptindependent.com/news/egypt-s-divorce-rate-its-highest-two-decades-capmas

16 R. Steiner, Anthroposophy: An Introduction (London, UK: Rudolf Steiner Press, 1931), retrieved May 7, 2020, https://wn.rsarchive.org/Lectures/GA234/English/RSP1931/AntInt_index.html

17 J. Petrash, Understanding Waldorf Education (Lewisville, NC: Gryphon House Inc., 2002).

18 F. M. Corrigan et al., "Autonomic Dysregulation and the Window of Tolerance Model of the Effects of Complex Emotional Trauma," Journal of Psychopharmacology 25, no. 1 (2010): 17-25, https://doi.org/10.1177/0269881109354930

19 "Depression: How Effective Are Antidepressants?" National Center for Biotechnology Information, retrieved May 27, 2020, https://www.ncbi.nlm.nih.gov/books/NBK361016/

J. McCormack and C., Korowynk, (2018). "Effectiveness of antidepressants," BMJ 360, no. 8146 (2018): k1073, https://doi.org/10.1136/bmj.k1073

20 C. E. Griffin, et al., "Benzodiazepine Pharmacology and Central Nervous System–Mediated Effects," The Ochsner Journal 13, no. (Summer 2013): 14–223, https://www.ncbi.nlm.nih.gov/pmc/articles/PMC3684331/

J. Brett and B. Murnion, "Management of Benzodiazepine Misuse and Dependence, Australian Prescriber 38, no. 5 (2015): 152–155, https://doi.org/10.18773/austprescr.2015.055

21 L. Manchikanti, S. Helm nd, B Fellows, et al. "Opioid epidemic in the United States", Pain Physician. 15(3 Suppl) (2012):ES9-38, https://europepmc.org/article/med/22786464#impact.

22 S. Tasselli, "Love and Organization Studies: Moving beyond the Perspective of Avoidance," Organization Studies (2018), https://doi.org/10.1177/0170840617747924

23 V.L. Provencal, "The Family in Aristotle", Animus 6. Retrieved June 17, 2020 from: https://d1wqtxts1xzle7.cloudfront.net/30641608/provencal6.pdf?1361694747=&response-content-disposition=inline%3B+filename%3DThe_Family_In_Aristotle_1_In_memoriam_J..pdf&Expires=1592434696&Signature=fTmHlVRMBhA4B2qPGNADI-B3~-OK3DokUuj2CIgnr7kqloLrQkeKRfsj6b878vO4KyIv0XwSVh95rBS8yruGYXE~92UFyeyTpWloP2gckoNiq3IdZXeV-J5xFytHNqBCtBmfPWiJdziHcAHXzhN9eMOaOJXRVh9Knz2fH~TxbU-g9qa2gz~edE3nskXup7cVhGIkEHQecVWB6TgCqLajK40BwANB-q6T9cK9bZnCpZ2neBZsKrLrR8n4sYsjjOVQPNQtSqPMUXFzeJuu99qEtEaI-QOZbRDCabXlXhBIycbwi-wsn0N6JazCdahLy-pQ3OZwWECQ4IfJqIj1vGByKg__&Key-Pair-Id=APKAJLOHF5GGSLRBV4ZA

J. Wellman, "What is Philia Love in the Bible?", Patheos Christian Crier. (2015). Retrieved June 17, 2020 from: https://www.patheos.com/blogs/christiancrier/2015/05/20/what-is-ph

24 Anthroposophical Press, "SteinerBooks," (Great Barrington, MA, Anthroposophic Press, Inc., 2020) retrieved May 7, 2020, https://steiner.presswarehouse.com/Books/Features.aspx

25 The Threefold Educational Foundation and School, Threefold, (Chestnut Ridge, NY: The Threefold Educational Foundation and School 2020), retrieved June 16, 2020 from: threefold.org

26 The BEarth Institute, "Waldorf Books," (Des Moines, Iowa: The BEarth Institute, 2020), retrieved May 7, 2020, https://earthschooling.info/thebearthinstitute/product-category/waldorf-books/

27 Rudolf Steiner Press, "About Us," (Forest Row, UK: Rudolf Steiner Press, 2020), retrieved May 7, 2020, https://www.rudolfsteinerpress.com/about.php

28 Floris Books, "Floris Books," (Edinburgh, Scotland: Floris Books, 2020), retrieved May 7, 2020, https://www.florisbooks.co.uk/index.php

29 J. Stewart, ed., The Rudolf Steiner Archive & e.Lib, retrieved May 7, 2020, https://www.rsarchive.org/

30 D. Brunsvold, ed., Rudolf Steiner Audio, retrieved May 7, 2020, http://rudolfsteineraudio.com/

31 Goetheanum School of Spiritual Science, retrieved May 27, 2020, https://www.goetheanum.org/en/

32 D. Wolksier, admin., Anthroposophical Directory of Michaél Impulses Today (Facebook page), retrieved May 7, 2020, https://www.facebook.com/groups/919713598104973/

33 R. Steiner, Education Towards Freedom: Rudolf Steiner Education, A Survey of the Work of Waldorf Schools Throughout the World, 3rd edition (Edinburgh, Scotland: Floris Books, 2008).

34 R. Steiner, C. Bamford, ed., and S. Sieler, ed., How to Know Higher Worlds: A Modern Path of Initiation (Hudson, NY: Anthroposophic Press, 1994).

35 "Caesura," Literary Devices: Definition and Examples of Literary Terms, retrieved May 27, 2020, https://literarydevices.net/caesura/

36 R. Bly, The Sibling Society: An Impassioned Call for the Rediscovery of Adulthood (Menlo Park, CA: Addison-Wesley Publishing Company, 1996).

37 S. V. Siddiqui et al., "Neuropsychology of prefrontal cortex," Indian Journal of Psychiatry 50, no. 3 (2008): 202–208, https://doi.org/10.4103/0019-5545.43634

38 R. Carter, The Human Brain Book: An Illustrated Guide to its Structure, Function, and Disorders (London, UK: Dorling Kindersley Limited, 2009).

39 C. G. DeYoung, "The neuromodulator of exploration: A unifying theory of the role of dopamine in personality," Frontiers in Human Neuroscience, (2013), https://doi.org/10.3389/fnhum.2013.00762

40 C. S. Cashwell et al., "The Only Way Out is Through: The Peril of Spiritual Bypass," Counseling and Values 51 (2007): 139-148.

41 N. Kardaras, "It's 'Digital Heroin': How Screens Turn Kids into Psychotic Junkies," New York Post, retrieved May 7, 2020, http://nypost.com/2016/08/27/its-digital-heroin-how-screens-turn-kids-into-psychotic-junkies/

42 M. Olfson et al., "National Trends in the Office-Based Treatment of Children, Adolescents, and Adults with Antipsychotics," Archives of General Psychiatry 69, no. 12 (2012): 1247-56, http://dx.doi.org/10.1001/archgenpsychiatry.2012.647

43 S. E. Gilman et al., "Family Disruption in Childhood and Risk of Adult Depression," American Journal of Psychiatry 160, no. 5: 939-46, https://doi.org/10.1176/appi.ajp.160.5.939

44 R. Steiner, "Study of Man: Lecture II" (lecture, Stuttgart, 1919), retrieved May 7, 2020, http://wn.rsarchive.org/Lectures/GA293/English/RSP1966/19190822a01.html

45 "Pinecone History and Symbolism," Third Eye Pinecones, retrieved May 7, 2020, https://thirdeyepinecones.com/history-symbolism

46 S. Stephanie, M.D. Erlich, M. L. J. Apuzzo, "The pineal gland: anatomy, physiology, and clinical significance," Journal of Neurosurgery 63, no 3 (1985), https://doi.org/10.3171/jns.1985.63.3.0321
F. Lopez-Munoz, F. Marin, C. Alamo, "The historical background of the pineal gland: From a spiritual valve to the seat of the soul," Revista de Neurologia 50(1) (2009): 50-57, https://europepmc.org/article/med/20073024

47 A. C. Sparavigna, M. M. Baldi, "A Mathematical Study of a Symbol: The Vesica Piscis of Sacred Geometry," PHILICA No. 560 (March 17, 2016), https://ssrn.com/abstract=2748242

48 G. Pagnoni, et al., "Thinking about Not-Thinking: Neural Correlates of Conceptual Processing during Zen Meditation," PLOS ONE 3, no. 9 (2008): e3083, https://doi.org/10.1371/journal.pone.0003083

49 Baba Hari Dass, "The Yoga Sutras of Patanjali: A Study Guide for Book I Samadhi Pada", Sri Ram Publishing, Edition 1, (1999): ISBN-13 : 978-0918100207

50 R. Steiner, "III: Concerning Man's Etheric Body and the Elemental World," The Threshold of the Spiritual World, retrieved May 27, 2020, https://wn.rsarchive.org/Books/GA017/English/GPP1922/GA017_c03.html

51 Steiner et al., How to Know Higher Worlds.

52 "Malala Yousafzai: Biographical," The Nobel Foundation, retrieved May 27, 2020, https://www.nobelprize.org/nobel_prizes/peace/laureates/2014/yousafzai-bio.html

53 M. B. Rosenberg, Nonviolent Communication: A Language of Life (Encinita, CA: Puddledancer Press, 2003).

54 R. Steiner, "Preparing for the Sixth Epoch" (lecture, Dusseldorf, June 15, 1915), retrieved May 27, 2020, http://wn.rsarchive.org/Lectures/19150615p01.html

55 "Decompensation Definition | Psychology Glossary," AlleyDog.com, retrieved May 27, 2020, https://www.alleydog.com/glossary/definition.php?term=Decompensation

56 "Decompensation Definition | Psychology Glossary," AlleyDog.com, retrieved May 7, 2020, https://www.alleydog.com/glossary/definition.php?term=Decompensation

CHAPTER THREE

What Do Waldorf Philosophy and Anthroposophy Do?

Foundational insights into the history of the development of human consciousness in terms of anthroposophical insights. A holistic, anthroposophical, whole-view-down-to-the-parts look at some main aspects of child-of-divorce trauma and anthroposophical insights that address it.

Anthroposophy does not want to impart knowledge. It seeks to awaken life.[1]
Rudolf Steiner

Anthroposophy means the wisdom of the human being. At its foundation is the reverence for the human soul life, connected with nature, and deeply woven with the freeing forces of the spiritual cosmos.

The philosophy of anthroposophy was developed by the scientist and spiritual researcher, Rudolf Steiner, at the beginning of the twentieth century in Austria. Steiner eventually moved his work to Germany, then created an artistic, intentional-living community in Switzerland, with a biodynamic farm, skilled craftspeople, and a soulful political structure. In the shadow of the First and Second World Wars in Europe, Steiner lectured throughout Europe on an anthroposophical, life-giving approach to the struggles of the times.

Steiner developed anthroposophical insights and practices to foster a human being's innate and cultivated capacities to be authentically intuitive, imaginative, and inspired—in relationship with the earth, other human beings, and the spiritual world. This included a person's relationship to the earth's resources; to other people through mindful, artistic, and reverential practices; to oneself; and to the reality of birth, life, death, and life beyond death. Even the life that comes back into an earthly nature upon rebirth was given meaningful consideration.

Human nature and activity, through the anthroposophical lens, is permeated and influenced by natural cycles within an earthly organic and cosmic-spiritual patterning of existence. Anthroposophical work helps an individual to sustain a practical and structured life that is informed by free creative thinking. It is brought to consciousness through timely cosmic-earthly understandings and awareness. Anthroposophy seeks to reveal, remedy, and revive the relevant soul-spiritual understandings that were being blocked by a one-sided, overly materialistic, science-based world perspective that came to dominate much of the Western life view in the centuries of Western economic industrialization.

Anthroposophy is also the philosophy behind Waldorf schools and their child-development pedagogy. It is based on the foundational understanding that a child goes through a longer maturation process than any other sentient being on earth. Rudolf Steiner saw that the human maturation process recapitulates in the soul, through seven-year stages, the history of human consciousness since the fall of Atlantis.[2]

Anthropo (human) + *sophy* (wisdom) looks at the development in the soul life of humans, from early childhood, as a gradual awakening of capacities developed in the human being through approximately the last 12,000 years of history. The inner-soul record of human evolution, Rudolf Steiner taught, is revisited, sifted, sorted, and updated to present times through an unconscious process in a child's growing years until age twenty-one.[3] What happens after maturation is up to the free capacities of the adult human being, with an innate responsibility to spiritual lawfulness guiding adult soul development. Aspects of this lawfulness are taught during the high school years, but many adults only become wholly conscious of them after age thirty-three. (More on this lawfulness will be explained throughout this book.)

Although a thorough explanation of anthroposophical human development and its association with Waldorf education for children is not possible here, a short description follows of the association between child development today and human evolutionary development over millennia.

The Seven Post-Atlantean Epochs and Child Development

As Rudolf Steiner perceived, early life for children, who are birthed out of a profound and still somewhat mysterious process, is about the soul and body getting familiar with earthly life again. The very young child is becoming incarnate and coordinated while remaining in a kind of non-discerning, fairy-tale consciousness of innocence and wonder.

This is how humanity was itself in its earliest stages of development, following the time of the great world flood about 12,000 years ago, an event noted by ancients the world over. Steiner's anthroposophical, spiritual-scientific research shows that following the great world flood that ended the Atlantean era,[4] humanity entered a new era of consciousness development.

In historic time, and long prior to the great flood, a necessity had arisen for human beings to experience a falling out from the pure but unconscious attunement to the spiritualized, natural world. Described in the Christian Old Testament, this was the event of the banishment of Adam and Eve from the garden of Eden.[5] This "fall" was a planned, consciousness event out of the spiritual world that would foster the descent of man into cooperation with all that was given in the earthen world, through the gaining of knowledge and experience.

Later, following the flooding of Atlantis, the Indian cultural epoch[6] began and ran from approximately the eighth millennium BC until the sixth millennium BC. Human beings who survived the Atlantean flood became completely engaged in physical needs while still living by a sense of oneness of consciousness with the divine world. They were also guided by great spiritual teachers, the rishis. These were clear spiritual initiates who had not lost spirit memory out of the cosmic-earthly forces alive at the beginning of human time. Human beings didn't think much in the early Indian epoch. The outer, physical earth was still covered in mists. Human beings and animals existed together in a kind of hazy consciousness. Life was body-and-senses oriented, and people had a strong heart-longing for wisdom from the spiritual world.[7]

A sense of human affinity with the gods still existed then, gods that acted and looked somewhat like human beings. However, a slow human separation from such forces was soon to begin. No longer would man simply reap earthen fruits without any struggle or without planning what was available on earth. Rather, men and women would need to work the land and create items from nature to keep themselves alive and evolving. They would also develop social orders and the arts.

In the very earliest period of this epoch, life on earth resembled something of the original, misty garden present on the planet for millions of years. It was through the necessity of learning to become more earthen and incarnate that human beings were more spiritually invested into the natural world to fend for themselves, reaping understanding and honing deeper physical senses. Life would no longer be about simply hunting and gathering in a blissful state slightly more conscious than animals. It would require struggling with the elements to secure longevity.

Following the Indian epoch came a 2500-year Persian epoch[8] when human beings articulated and charted the patterns in earthly cosmic life, heralding early astronomy, simple calculus, and greater human organizational trends. As humanity struggled along, together as group-minded souls, many small and large catastrophes challenged human tribes, causing society leaders to order and organize the people harshly for survival purposes. A period of great, and sometimes minutely detailed, discipline began through the Persian epoch.

The next Caldean-Egyptian epoch,[9] of the same length, went further to delineate ritual and traditions, particularly those regarding life after death, and recorded sophisticated practices for health and well-being, as well as recording astrological patterns in the cosmos. Leaders were considered half-human and half-gods of the sun.

Following that progression that ended around the beginning of the first millennia BC, a new process of individual, intellectual thinking characterized the Greco-Roman epoch.[10] In the middle of this epoch came a momentous human event with the birth of Jesus of Nazareth, who would be baptized as the Christ. This would be a preparation for individuals in our modern times to begin to eventually realize the highest and subtlest levels of human and worldly consciousness, as well as a state of firm self-dominion while still on the earth.

In 1914, the present Anglo-Germanic epoch[11] began, heralding a period within which humanity would find the ability to evolve to expansive human and earthly consciousness, including through advancing, human-friendly technologies. Full individuation and capacity to manage certain levels of humane technological mechanizations are characteristics of this epoch, again 2500 years in length, and through the painful challenges of that process, a deepening sense of human empathy and compassion. Human beings will become deeply conscious of the processes of their bodies, minds, and souls, as well as the differences between soul cultures around the world. Karmic awareness, and how negative karma can be resolved between people, will be revealed more in individual human souls.

In the future, Rudolf Steiner spoke of a Russian epoch[12] and a time when humanity will be ready to experience a much fuller state of individual, spiritual consciousness. The detailed characteristics of this epoch are yet to be revealed to humanity, though such details can be known early by high spiritual initiates – prior to these details being understood by greater humanity. All human beings will be able to know them if they seek them, and if human spiritual striving remains on track and doesn't devolve too dangerously.

Since human consciousness development is not without perils and could be blocked along the way by non-benevolent forces, human beings will need to strive diligently in the future for spiritual development in the process to future ascension. Rudolf Steiner spoke of a future, potentially catastrophic, human event that will foster humanity into appropriate spiritual humility to overcome the hardening forces of the earth and human conflict, causing them to reach for the greatest human capacities of inner love, peace, and refined consciousness. This is mentioned in more detail later in this book.

Finally, an American epoch, [13] about 4,500 years into the future, will prepare souls for full ascension back into spiritual worlds in the future. The end of the last post-Atlantean epoch will be in about 7,000 years.

Healing from the sufferings of survival, conflict, and earth disintegration over time will leave human beings wizened and with expanded hearts. They will then be prepared, through individual effort but in conscious community with each other, for the courage necessary to imagine life beyond earthly human existence, coming at the end of the post-Atlantean epochs. Much, according to Steiner, will transpire in human physiology and in the soul in the coming millennia to prepare us for this eventuality.

Human Consciousness Epochs are Recapitulated in Child-Development Years

The epochs of human consciousness that have happened prior to our modern consciousness epoch are set in soul memory, according to Rudolf Steiner. These memories recapitulate somewhat in the soul, bringing to a human being a sense of continuity of existence, and an inner harmony with all that has represented what it means to be a human being in our times. This inner memory will help us to understand personal past actions, errors, and olden seeds of karmic character that need to be developed more wholly, and psychically helpfully, in the future.

These mostly unconscious moments of recapitulation of the past begin during childhood. Since we are in an epoch time of bringing much more consciousness of our human story to light, Waldorf pedagogy brings stories and activities to school-aged children that fit with the recapitulations that naturally happen in the child soul.

The early childhood years, and kindergarten, tend to reflect the first post-Atlantean epoch of the earlier Indian culture. It is an altruistic time for children, when they play freely while mimicking highly idealized adults in tasks of cooking, cleaning, gardening, and the socialization around eating together. Small children, when protected and nourished in healthy environments, have an early East-Indian, altruistic nature of openness, trust, and a sense of the cosmically guided delight of earthly discovery. Children deeply, sensually, work away at their play.

In grades one and two, at ages seven and eight, children tend more toward an inner sense of the Persian epoch, wanting to learn how to order things, such as in learning to count. They can be fascinated with the stars and their patterns. They like learning rhythmic form drawing, and simple geometric properties associated with lines and curves. They are getting more familiar with learning disciplines and social ones.

The fall of humanity, before the post-Atlantean era, is recapitulated in the child soul around the age of nine when a child has a period of unconscious awakening that life has hardship and struggle. By the time a nine-year-old child enters grade three, he is beginning to feel himself more deeply separate from his early childhood unconsciousness and is becoming aware, as mirrored through the grade three curricula, of how people have farmed, built houses, used their hands to make practical items, and generally worked in the world.[14] The children now become aware of the reality of earthly suffering. Children at nine years old can have a moody and rebellious time with this awakening.

Grade four is a special time when children begin to integrate forces that they will need to meet the struggles of human life, through a fortitude of will. The soul recapitulation of the Egypto-Chaldean epoch, and its qualities of life after death consciousness, are rebutted somewhat through mythical studies of the mighty and resourceful Nordic gods. Now, children start the human journey of wrestling in the soul with the existential dark-side aspects of life, striving to instill a more iron-willed, heroic nature for the sustained tasks of a lifetime.

By grade five, or age ten, the child is entering into another, fuller recapitulation of the earlier epochs, leading up to the Greco-Roman epoch of history. Starting with direct lessons on the history of India, they unconsciously relive the innocence, resistance of evil, peacefulness, and devotion that was taught to the masses back in that epoch, through the spiritual wisdom of the Vedas of the seven great Indian rishis.[i]

In the middle of grade five, or age ten, modern children revisit the soul affinity with the Persian cultural epoch—from the sixth millennium BC to the third millennium BC. They often study the story of Gilgamesh, work more with mathematics, and begin to learn more sophisticated patterns in eurythmy movement work [15] and Spacial Dynamics®,[16] as explained in other chapters of this book.

Also, in the middle stages of age ten, children relate in the soul to the Chaldean-Egyptian cultural epoch—from the third millennium BC to the first millennium BC. These were times when, in history, people were becoming even more earthbound and deeply fixed in the sense world. Egyptian death tombs, for instance, were filled with material artifacts for the deceased to take on the journey beyond the threshold of death. Great pyramids were built with tomb temples within for the burial of their half-human gods. Human beings were becoming aware of a human/godly nature that they would, in the next epoch, take inside of themselves fully.

The ancient Babylonian, Assyrian, Chaldean, and Egyptian influences underlying the ten-year-old child soul recapitulation is noted in school, or learning in general, when children

---

i   The Vedas were scripture written by the sacred initiate rishis that taught man to seek truth above everything. The human being had no separate identity from the gods. All that was material in life was known as an illusion. The Vedas also taught lessons on healing, astrology, and mathematics. Rules for how different people should live their lives were established in the Vedas and seen as making it easier for the common man to establish a discipline for the sake of a happy life.

begin to exhibit higher cognitive interests. Their innate interest with the science of the stars and simple geometry stirs, sometimes along with exuberant reading abilities. They long for more complexly structured social activities requiring almost ritualistically ordered, cooperative skills, such as with physical and mental games, including riddles. Math learning includes measurement. Children live into greater imaginations and stronger memories.

Leaders of this ancient era began to organize the masses through sun-god rituals, to realize the great material development that led to finely detailed architecture and artistic expression in household crafts, such as mosaic tiles, rug making, and pottery. Merchant trade of every conceivable and naturally resourced item moved up and down the river Nile. Form drawing, and accounting skills became firmer and more reliable in memory for schoolchildren at this time.

People began to depict themselves, in temple wall art, for instance, as more integrated with natural phenomena and connected to each other in orderly procession with higher beings, gods, and sacred animals. Collective, religious life was based on understandings of an absolute, authoritarian, patriarchal sun god.

These sun-god leaders, called pharaohs, and riveting goddess-queens, such as the goddess Isis, were now depicted as beings who were separate but still permeated by nature; drawn as part-human beings and part animal-like, cosmic creatures that humans revered in ritual. Cave drawings, and later tablet and papyrus recordings, showed slaves and workers who were upright and disciplined in collective rituals and in higher, mentally oriented, stately work.

The Hebrew culture also featured strongly in this period of soul development, bringing a distinct purification of body and soul. Great spiritual leaders in the Chaldean-Egyptian epoch reminded the people of the higher significances of the "magic" of life and the cosmos. This was the incubation period in the spiritual world for the later Magi kings.[17][ii]

Toward the end of the Chaldean-Egyptian epoch, a pure, orderly, and balanced sense of grace and beauty had begun to stir in some of the peoples of the region of the Mediterranean crescent, areas known today as Turkey, Jerusalem, Bethlehem, Lebanon, Cyprus, Northern Egypt, and Italy. This heralded the next human consciousness stage, the Greco-Roman epoch—from the first millennium BC to the middle of the second millennium AD.

The child at the end of age ten seeks a new inner balance and is ready for those images and activities that inwardly remind the soul of the Greco-Roman epoch. This is when they are gaining a greater sense of symmetry in their bodies, human values, and imaginations.

A greater capacity emerged in individuals in this historical stage, rather than solely in the designated sun-god leaders of the past. A consciousness of full, three-dimensional symmetry and human balance blossomed, manifesting in sculpture, classical pillared temples, and in the emergence of theatrical dramas of tragedy and comedy. Individual human beings slowly began

---

ii   These wise men were known in Christian teachings for their role in sacred astronomy. Their later holy pilgrimage to Bethlehem, during the Greco-Roman epoch, insured the highest honoring of the infant Jesus Christ at his birth. Human beings were soon to witness not just a sun god, but the very human son of God himself.

to intuitively, imaginatively, and inspirationally know that they themselves were now vessels of the gods and that godliness was not simply outside of themselves but part of their own nature.

In this period of the Greco-Roman cultural epoch, mythologies and legends depicted human beings in struggles with the gods, wrestling for authority and divine recognition in the eyes of each other. Life-striving was not just in the sight of gods who lived far beyond them or who were far greater in their abilities than those of humans.

Now, striving was seen to bring a sense of the godly directly into the human being. However, this god-mindedness still lacked a fully developed human ego-I nature, leading human beings into decadence and disease because they did not have the healthy ego capacity yet for self-responsibility. That would come in the mid-stage of the Greco-Roman epoch with the coming of Christ.

Christ was about to show people, whose egos were willing to listen, how to do this new humanness. Human beings were about to begin a process toward freedom, wherein they could freely choose to listen to spiritual truth or not, to the benefit or detriment of their souls. They would also be able to take up their own healing and raise themselves up from the individual fall as well, if they chose to truly learn what would be necessary in the new human spirit times.

Human grace in bodily stance, movement, feeling, thought, and in a more brotherly and sisterly gesture toward each other, began to form in the sculpted images of the ancient Greek statues of the Pantheon gods and in an emerging awareness of moral laws between individuals. Great teachers of human-earthly cosmic lawfulness emerged, such as Plato[18], Aristotle[19], Socrates[20], and Pythagoras[21].

The Greco-Roman epoch is recapitulated in Waldorf schools in grade five. Bothmer Gymnastics[22] and Spacial Dynamics® move children's physical education toward complex and rhythmical ball games, toward balance activities, symmetrical stick games, graceful javelin, and discus-throwing skills. Children prepare for Greek Olympics competitions and celebrations with students from other Waldorf schools. Later in adolescence, this Greek and Roman awareness is reconstituted around the fifteenth to sixteenth year.

In the ancient Greek cultural epoch, balance, uprightness, and the hints of a developing self-responsibility were reflected in the great epic stories of heroes such as Odysseus. Warrior protagonists moved beyond outward battles, where they hoped to retrieve beauty, grace, and honor from the foe, only to find that the outward battle wasn't enough to soothe the soul. Odysseus' attempt to rescue Helen from the romantic capture by Paris is an example of an ultimately empty battle from which the great warrior would retreat to come to some higher understanding of himself in society in general.

Human beings were about to learn a new way. The pre-Christian, inner retreat that Odysseus underwent upon his return to his home-life after battle, via a seven-year stay on an island with the nymph, Circe, is an early example of a process that Christian human beings now undergo regularly to examine their inner conscience after a struggle or outright battle with other people.

This time of change for the old warrior archetype in all human beings was about to begin the long, upward, and entirely human climb out of self-created misery toward a new, inner, heart-soul tendency of will. According to Rudolf Steiner, in a few short millennia from now, this capacity will ripen and fully and reveal itself for humanity through the Christ consciousness. This insight is in harmony with revelations from many great spirit traditions worldwide.

Jesus Christ brought, in the middle of the Greco-Roman epoch, the astounding capacity for this inner transformation toward compassionate self-responsibility in all people. With him came a worldwide, human impulse that would guarantee that no human beings on earth would ever remain as they had been if they wished spiritual salvation in the future of the earth life. The heart-spirit forces in all people will be able to grow, open, and purify inwardly in ways never known prior to the Christ-consciousness era. The only catch was that individuals would have to trust this new capacity within themselves and take it up, with humility toward others.

For Odysseus, who's battle and transformation occurred just over a century before the coming of Christ, reformation from warrior to peacekeeper meant that the spiritual warrior within him could take more orderly dominion over his life in relationship with his family and society. After the coming of Christ, all human beings would eventually go further than that, making reparations for harms and raising each and all upward.

By about the middle of the Greco-Roman cultural epoch, the seeds were fully ripe in some human beings to receive the teaching of the Christ consciousness. These people were the apostles of Christ, who would then go to selflessly plant the seeds of future spiritual awareness for the rest of humanity. To spread the word in every way and in every learning discipline, humanity moved into a highly intellectual era. It lasted until 1413 AD.

This Christ-led change is reflected today in children who, even if they or their family members do not identify as Christian, emerge at age twenty-one into full adulthood with an intact ego capable of loving self-discipline in actions toward others, despite mistakes they make as they navigate the world on their own. A whole and healthy ego provides the capacities for a mature human being to think alone, and to own an individual stance in the world, with grace, personal healing, and self-responsibility.

Children from ages eleven and up begin to experience the influences of the Roman part of the Greco-Roman epoch, learning how to make sophisticated projects using human thinking and practical skills. They learn the qualities of the earthly elements and how they are made into helpful items for humanity. Geography helps children to understand how the manifestations of earth elements—such as metals, crystals, rocks, water, gases, and plants—are found, how they are composed, and how different elements work together, such as fire and wood creating charcoal that they can use for drawing.

Children at age twelve go deeper into what an individual human being is all about, studying, for instance, simple biology, and drawing the human face in right proportions. They learn about personal health hygiene. Mathematics and sciences strive to show the child what the lawfulness of these arts means to their human needs, such as with simple accounting practices and with food preparation chemistry. Children might learn ratio in relationship to the gear differentials on their bicycle.

Pre-adolescents come right up to the modern, Anglo-Germanic epoch at age thirteen, in grade eight. Now, they begin to learn about some modern technologies, such as electricity, hydro, and computer components, and how they have worked to support and better human freedom and individual striving. They learn the biographies of people who stood up for human freedoms and rights, such as Martin Luther King and Gandhi.

Young adolescents practice compassionate action by doing service in the kindergarten or grade one classroom. They might learn about composting in the school's biodynamic farm and how to steward farm animals ethically. Often, in this year, children are given individual projects. They take charge of their learning significantly with this project, to fully research, design, and carry out—through their own thoughts, creative impulses, and practical examinations of the topic—the planning needs, costs, social implications, or the needs and qualities of the physical materials used to complete the project.

High School

Adolescents, from age fourteen and up, recapitulate once again the earlier epochs, through deeper and more sophisticated insights into the human and physical world that they have touched on earlier in their imaginative, age seven to fourteen years. They use more scientific, conceptual learning to investigate understandings and practices that will become an important kit for their future adult lives.

Youths continue all of their earlier studies, such as languages, mathematics, sciences, physical education, art, music, biology, chemistry, and geographic studies. These are all designed to bring to youths ways of greater human understanding about themselves in nature, as connected with the cosmos, as well as understanding of others interacting in the universal and more objective worldly society. Youths learn about their changing, sexually maturing bodies, responsibilities about being skilled practitioners of life who also live to create new innovations and important social dynamics to support a healthy future society. Youths are supported to know what it means to be creating anew in the world and attempting to make moral/ethical decisions through reading biographies and staging heart-provoking plays.

Youths in the later adolescent years, around grade eleven, come to wonder if some life activities have become distorted from cosmic-earthly human lawfulness and they work to learn to discern truth from false thinking, such as on the internet and in scientific discovery. They learn that people can present polar-opposite thinking, as well as a roundtable of truths that make up the whole truth. Eurythmy movement activities might reflect the astrological wheel as a representation of twelve planetary forces influencing the earth, the solar system that we live in, and our human energies. They learn to look to history to see what errors in thought back in time may be stirring similar or more problematic thoughts and actions in society today.

Rudolf Steiner spoke of errors in leadership thinking in the historical, Roman Epoch times that went counter to the true Christ teachings of individual freedom of thought, consciousness, and responsibility. These errors can override clear human thinking today. This will be discussed later in this book regarding the 869 AD Roman Catholic ecumenical council.

However, for this discussion, it is important to note that adolescents struggle very much in the social realm today, partly as a result of world social and spiritual order distortions. Older adolescents unconsciously struggle with the legacy of the spiritually incorrect view that permeated from the Roman epoch into the present Anglo-Saxon and Germanic cultural epoch.[23] Adolescent psychological health needs some monitoring today for signs of psychological splitting, while not hindering adolescent urges to freedom that are entirely appropriate for their ages and stages.

The current, fifth post-Atlantean, Anglo-Germanic epoch, running from 1413 AD to 3574 AD, is a period projected to take us into higher spiritual attunement in the coming millennia. Firstly, however, we will struggle with distorting, controlling, and heavily materialistic forces that would seek to draw us downward and chain us indefinitely to a heavy, entangled, and unfree existence. This, in the face of unheard-of-before technological advances that are meant to aid humanity, but also some that could have very harmful effects.

The incarnation of Christ was one of the most significant, turning-point events of the post-Atlantean epochs, and of all time. This epoch, unconsciously working upon the adolescent and on all adult souls today, reflects another important turning of human time. As Rudolf Steiner and many other great spiritual researchers have indicated, the human heart is going to become a greater power in life, as well as a kind of human radar for truth. We are in training now to realize our greatest, humanitarian deeds.

In the light of our current epoch, older adolescents, with healthy developmental holding, start to realize a healthy ego that is capable of tuning into the highest good for society. However, those teens also learn today that they may not get to manifest this strength of soul into society without significant resistance from certain elements in the large and complex world. They learn that in order to keep a firm resolve to the good in life, they will need to have practices to tackle their own inner dragons that stir out of fear, frustration, and epic social anxieties. They are learning to engage the issues of our times without sabotaging their own natural higher needs for soul-spirit development.

In later chapters, the phenomenon of artificial intelligence technology is introduced in association with Rudolf Steiner's insights on certain earthly forces advancing in the world that will resist human soul-spirit development. A new era is being prepared for humanity that is so unfamiliar that most people are not yet aware of how to meet it. Meanwhile, dark, life-resisting elements in the world will attempts to allow human, earthbound fears and egoism to override higher human truths. Anthroposophy strives very hard to prepare adolescents to meet this well as adults and to not lose healthy soul-psyche connection. One hundred years ago, Rudolf Steiner predicted that we would face very challenging times now and in the future. He also indicated many things that will help us. The following chapters explain this more, regarding Pearl Children and Adults.

The Anglo-Germanic epoch signifies a time when uprightness includes a human being's ability to school oneself on broad new economic/technologic, social, and cultural topics. Artistic and creative innovations have the potential to raise humanity to long-forgotten heights of action and creativity. At the same time, the modern era offers the free will for human beings to believe in lies and errors, rather than soulfully and spiritually identifying with eternal and universal human truths, and without reconciling harms or stewarding the earth together respectfully. Steiner was clear to indicate that some people will choose not to advance consciously into the future. They will choose to hold life back untruthfully. We will have to summon all the courage and trust in our heart and soul natures to resist that drag backward.

Anthroposophical Psychology

Counselors in psychotherapeutic work that is informed by anthroposophy hold the awareness that the human soul is working out of spiritually lawful rhythms and cosmic patterns. As human beings, we are not enlivened by purely, earthly-materialistic reality, though we do live by earthly cycles and patterns; for example, day-night, spring-summer-autumn-winter, and birth-transformation-death.

The many natural, earthly cosmic patterns that inform our lives open our awareness of ourselves. Yet much of this lawful patterning is not always in our consciousness during busy school or work lives. Other levels of these phenomena are not sense-perceptible. Some profound experiences occur, for instance, while we sleep. Counselors practicing anthroposophical psychotherapy recognize the role of sleep-waking rhythms in the increasing developments of modern, human, soul-psyche growth. To cultivate forces that assist the soul in the nighttime, often a therapeutic client is asked to take a question into sleep for three days, and to listen inwardly for answers in the mornings.

Anthroposophical doctors and therapists working with people on psychotherapeutic issues avoid firm diagnoses in the way that some modern clinical psychologists or psychiatrists tend. Rather, therapists refer to soul sketches based on extensive criteria, within which the person seeking healing will flesh out the hues, tones, and deeper colors of a problem's history. Anthroposophical therapists consider the timings of problems in the course of the client's life, in relationship to cyclic patterns, and work with remedies and practices in relationship with adult, soul-development patterns.

Some features of anthroposophy's psychological health indicators live in the following themes: a) the fourfold human being, b) the seven life processes, c) the twelves senses, d) stages of human development, and e) the life constitutions of the human being.

Other anthroposophical understandings discussed in the coming chapters are a) moral-cosmic laws, b) the lemniscate as a caregiving technique, and c) personal biography.

Yiana Belkalopolos

The Fourfold Human Being

In human development, Rudolf Steiner saw that very specific capacities of soul emerge in the human being between birth and age twenty-one. These capacities gestate inwardly, like auric or energetic sheaths, that stay nestled within each other until it is time for each to open more fully and successively.[24]

The first sheath brings the energy and light to form the child's developing physical forces, those unfolding from pre-birth to age seven. Briefly, this is the force from which the child lives into a new body fully—developing bones, mature teeth, inner organs, nerves, and brain structures, as well as establishing natural breathing processes and metabolic rhythms. A child uses the freed cosmic potential of this first sheath to explore the earthly senses, playing into how the body receives the impulses of the earth and lives fully into them.

The very young child naturally leaves more complex thinking, planning, cultivating, and physical survival needs to the responsibility of the parents and caregivers, since the natural soul sheaths that would help develop those capacities within are not yet open or evolved. This child can be harmfully pressured to try to develop higher capacities early, by mimicking others or through inappropriate, imposed levels of hard discipline, stress, or traumatization.

The child's biological organisms will likely, as Steiner indicated, take the strain right into the formation of the inner organs, limiting a child's future adult capacities through disease or bodily dysfunctions. This causes physiological and mental health problems from the reduction of life forces. The results can bring more serious health issues around age forty and beyond.

Steiner spoke of how those early and unnatural stresses and strains can affect one's ability to engage life fully later in adulthood.[25] Looking at how natural systems work, it is not natural, for instance, for a tree to be in a trunk stage if it is still not formed in the root stage. People do not expect an apple tree to have branches and leaves before it has roots and a trunk.

A human being, also, cannot be expected to be in the second sheath stage of the etheric body development, from ages seven to fourteen, if the physical body has not evolved sufficiently from birth to age seven to hold the tasks of the later stages. [iii]

The physical-sheath in-forming that happens for a child comes, for instance, through playing in natural settings and with natural toys, eating natural foods at good times, wearing and touching natural fibers, having warm, close-body connections with safe family members, and having consistent, life-rhythm habits such as healthy bedtimes.

The second human sheath to open, from ages seven to fourteen, is the etheric, or life-force sheath. In this period, the child becomes, without self-consciousness, supported in the vitality

---

iii   This does not mean that a child will not live into the second of the fourfold stages—the development of etheric life forces—if that child has been born with a physical exceptionality such as a limb missing or needing childhood heart surgery. The way that parents and society support the nurturance of the life forces of the child is what most matters in such a situation.

and great imaginations behind a truthful life. A child learns about the world, for example, through well-crafted fairy tales, such as Grimm's fairy tales,[26] that keep them imaginatively connected to nature, people who work with nature, number rhythms, noble beings, and opposing beings such as trickster animals or naughty thieves. Many different tales are orally shared by an adult, tuning the child to the heart-warm, lyrical, epic, or dramatic voice of the storyteller.

At home, school, and in the neighborhood, the child increasingly warms into interests and friendships with other children through exposure to a musical environment where the child is free to move together with others. Rhythmical habits based on natural day-night progressions allow the spirit and soul to experience incarnate belonging on the earth while not losing the subtler connection to higher worlds. The body begins to coordinate in a more disciplined way through rhythmical exercises with the other children, doing movement games with bean bags, copper rods, balls, and through much outdoor play that includes group games and special, dynamic activities mentioned more fully in later chapters.

The third sheath is that of the astral sheath or the feeling-body. This period, between ages fourteen and twenty-one, brings a fascinating, and sometimes disturbing, reality to the child. Life is felt more intensely than it was before, and a child knows on unconscious levels that they must do something active and practical with these feelings. The challenge of this time is that the child, moving into adolescence, continues to have experiences with craftwork, garden-farming, art, and other practical skills that tune the soul to the work of the earth. Keeping imagination alive and protecting the sense of wonder for the world and its more conceptual workings is important as the brain and hormones design a whole new layer of body-mind functioning in the youth.

Without this astral, feeling period, the growing child will not get an accurate picture or plan of how to cope independently with the intensity of life, thwarting the development of the next developmental sheath, that of the ego. The healthy ego emerges once the brain's pre-frontal cortex is fully developed. This part of the brain is designed for complex planning and organizational skills and completes its higher development in a way that gives the emerging adult executive-thinking capacity.

Such capacities allow an adult to think and act upon many possibilities, practices, and needs in life at once. It hones the very human ability for a person to contain one's desires, think in terms of long-term goals rather than just impulsive and short-term interests, allows the youth to distinguish wants from needs, and helps a person to resist harmful reactions and impulses. Higher, conceptual thinking that develops in the child throughout adolescence balances the strong, astral, feeling capacities.

Without higher, executive-mind functioning, the feeling-desire astral pole in the human soul would overrule logical thinking. The new adult would be far too driven by almost animalistic tendencies toward sense-world fulfillment, sexual activity with no responsibility, and procreation with no boundaries, limitations, or rational practices to take care of oneself or others. A person would have no way to see oneself in perspective in relationship with others, with society's needs, or with the finite and vulnerable resources of the earth. This youth can become an overly egoic adult bringing many personal issues upon oneself, as well as complex challenges upon society.

As the final ego sheath comes into mature formation, the youth wrestles with the feelings and thoughts of a higher destiny, learning new patience while navigating through the astral, feeling-life unfolding. Only in time can this youth design the inner softening for a life plan, according to that soul's own, natural, knowing. The youth is becoming the artist, author, and designer of their own approach to an individual destiny.

A new capacity opens for the youth to assimilate expanding experiences of life, beyond the purely physical senses, that live into the youth's relationship with the surroundings and with others. Some of the youth's earlier-developed life forces are being channeled into some personal, karmically destined patterns for her future. That happens while some inner experiences that were steeped in childhood distill into unconscious memory.

This is also happening while physiological changes are bringing new formations such as with a new menstrual cycle or testicular growth, as well as little "deaths" within neural pathway development.[27] Today, this inner and physiological re-ordering may bring gender disturbances and adaptations. It is best to allow the full ego to emerge at age twenty-one before undergoing any gender reconstruction if one feels a real sense for it. Decisions then will be aligned with a fuller and more capable ego. Gender dysphoria heralds a future state for human beings that Steiner foretold—one where all human beings will become more androgynous.

Adolescents at this point are letting go of some of their lower sense-life interests, and they are inwardly becoming guided toward higher, managerial, and organizational capacities. Developments in the mid-sections of the brain are being completed now, and growth forces are working more substantially, and in a more sophisticated way, on the prefrontal cortex in the forehead region of the brain. What the adults around do to support or thwart this can have a significant impact on the young person's life in adulthood.

In this time, parents often experience seeing their teenage children seem to lose interest in certain foods that they always loved before, or they notice the adolescent forgetting to take the dog for a walk. They see a youth take almost no interest in the forest hikes that they absolutely lived for on weekends with the family in the past. Instead, the youth is now holed up with complicated hobbies on their own, putting together strange inventions or quirky creations. Or, another youth begins to network more complexly with friends on the basketball team or on social media. That youth may now be imagining experiences very far from home.

Teens often move into a world of their own at home now. They are individuating. They are registering intensely, internally, and mostly unconsciously, what kind of organizational refinements are going to be necessary to realize full, individual needs and potentials as an adult. That includes coming to manage higher insights revealing themselves through dreams. Adolescents test themselves socially and skillfully, with awkward and even risky experiences, resounding with this new astral-feeling life that is accompanied by refreshing, new, sexual forces. These may be subtle, or strongly pushing a youth into motion for relationships of one kind or another.

The inner experience of the adolescent is as if a master builder inside is constructing a destiny-planned, inner cathedral, heightened beyond early processes of physical-sheath wonders, etheric-sheath enlivening, and astral-sheath likes and dislikes. Youths develop a true, individual, soul-spirit-connected, ego-I sheath. Metaphorically speaking, after about age twelve, the inner, higher systems of the head, and the frontal brain architecture, start to decide if this cathedral is going to have a domed roof, minarets, steeples, or some sort of fusion, Asian/American, A-frame feature with solar panels and pagoda-like wings coming off of all four corners! All of this takes place internally, within a lawfulness set clearly for the uniqueness of this individual.

The self-testing that adolescents engage in, and their testing behaviors toward others, comes as an innate process for youth inner frameworks to receive feedback about how their higher-mind natures can work in an integrated way with the other parts of themselves. The brain begins to form codes for how the youth will interact with outer circumstances, including the immediate socio-economic ones influencing the youth. There is a process whereby some neurological functions get pared away in the teen—from a younger-stage neurology. It is important to acknowledge regularly with an adolescent the nature of some of these inner changes. Also, affirming that higher, human characteristics of the human mind coding are far more supple and soul-spirit sophisticated than computer coding, even if a computer robot can intellectualize certain types of practical information better than a human.

This adolescent era brings a process of learning what parts of oneself are being pared away or restricted, and what that will gather as a full, unique, and flexible expression of that soul well into the future.

As a healthy ego-function arises, the adolescent becomes more capable of sorting through life with new conceptual models. Youths are refining capacities for integrating experiences with others without becoming overwhelmed. This begins a lifelong process, and it happens in tandem with the integration of more mature physical secretions newly forming in a maturing, adult body. This pulsing physicality is there to remind youths of their earthen nature, and to remind them of the constant task of self-care in life while bringing all of their other interests to bear on the world.

The fourth, ego-I sheath[28] is the marker for a mature human being who can speak of themself as an individual with authentic feelings and needs, with empathic awareness of others, and with a sense of responsibility for themself and their actions. This is also the emerging new adult's conduit to the spiritual lawfulness informing the rest of life activity. Without a healthy "I" awareness, and a sense of responsibility, the young adult at age twenty-one is unable to act in true freedom and can become objectified by the lower egoic will of others in myriad ways.

Young adults with patchy I-forces, a symptom coming out of the poor development of the other sheaths, are often without a personal voice, and without the ability to claim rights, to draw to themselves and foster appropriate resources for ongoing survival and soul growth, or to realize higher insights into actions. They are at risk of being hindered in their higher capacities and relationship connections because of their inability to discern for themselves truth and goodness in others. They can struggle to know how to extricate themselves from others' lower behaviors toward them. They may, as well, be hindered from their evolving, mature, self-compassion. That can hinder their sense of empathic and etheric responsibility toward others regarding the innate and complex challenges of human existence.

Confusion: The Sign of the Times

Rudolf Steiner knew that humanity would meet the coming modern era with still-undeveloped, human ego-I natures. Human beings would struggle with confusion, fear, hubris, over-the-top emotional highs and lows, and distorted desires to control the actions of others or even to try to turn back time. He also saw the dangers of how undeveloped ego-I beings would easily allow others to take over their rights and freedoms and subject them to abuses, bringing despair. The process of coming into full, healthy egos, those that are capable of transcending egoism and selfish action through a fully formed I, is a necessary process for our times that he called the Consciousness Soul era. This process, Steiner made clear, will last for about nineteen more centuries to come.[29]

As Steiner indicated, full I-achievement will not happen for every person at the same time. He also saw that it would be impossible for humanity to go backward without massive strife, or without people realizing, ultimately, that regression is not the answer to the Consciousness Soul evolutionary period. Creative, compassionate, and innovative thought, brought with the mood of artistry and creativity, would be the route toward modern socio-economic and cultural-spiritual health in this epoch.

Steiner lectured in the shadow of the First and Second World Wars in Europe. Back then, he took the great responsibility to show the people of Europe a different and more spiritually truthful and humane route to solving life's problems in these increasingly complex times. He saw the massive, materialistic-scientific disaster that human beings were headed for in Germany and Russia. He predicted how human beings could turn hateful if their souls and spirits were not nurtured appropriately for the Consciousness Soul evolution.

Rudolf Steiner's soul capacities were developed in such a way that he could articulate indications for others, within six thousand lectures, thirty books, and in hundreds of undocumented private conversations with people. The processes that he indicated would help people to be able to monitor and strengthen their own soul and I-forces while developing economic, social, and cultural-artistic-spiritual wholeness with others. Some of those indications involved working with the seven life processes.

The Seven Life and the Seven Learning Processes

Two, interconnected, seven-fold processes are observed and worked with in anthroposophical psychotherapeutic counseling with children and adults. They hold important considerations for parents, caregivers, teachers, and healers raising Pearls or helping them to heal. The Seven Life Processes and the Seven Learning Processes help to structure a reliable set of observations and reflections that give Pearl Children and Pearl Adults practical, inspiring and creative support for working through difficult transition issues and challenges in different stages of development. They bring wholesome, soul-spirit connected imaginations and individualized, authentic insights that help Pearls to stay balanced and self-connected through the dynamics of a family divide, particularly while transitioning between parent homes and their parents' two different personal life "cultures".

The Seven Life Processes are: Breathing, Warming, Nourishing, Secreting-Absorbing, Maintaining, Growing, and Reproducing.

The Seven Learning Processes are: Observing, Relating, Digesting, Individualizing, Practicing, Growing a New Faculty, and Creating Something New.

The Seven Life Processes and the Seven Learning Processes happen naturally in developing children when a child has warm, reliable and predictable, soul-spirit-connected and attentive caregiving. These processes get easily distorted by adult conflicts and adult societal pressures that are an increasing challenge upon children in the confusions of the modern and changing consciousness times. The processes represent how human beings, in their bodies and their inner, unconscious minds integrate what they experience and interact with through the natural elements and rhythms of the earth, the seasons, connections to creatures, family members, other human beings, and life itself. Working mindfully with these processes provides insight into how to transform mundane, stuck, or negative thoughts, feelings, and unhealthy physical life patterns, including disrupted sleep patterns, into more supportive and appropriate etheric life practices. This is done through authentic, expanded, and life-giving imaginations for children and adults.

The processes foster age-appropriate, heart-centered and also spiritually heightened interactions with others when necessary, using the deeply important sleep-life cycles. These cycles bear great significance since we spend much of an earthly lifetime sleeping at night. The processing practices also help us to find the essence of what matters most to our hearts in a situation, helping us to retain an alive and inspired sense of self while managing to bring our hearts to the experiences of others non-judgmentally, yet in a connectedly discerning way.

The *Seven Life Processes* begin before and even shortly before conception. The *Seven Learning Processes* begin to develop after birth. Each are involved in the maintenance of the wholesomely, heart-connected human being throughout life. Here, I describe these interconnected, seven-fold processes in a general way for the perceptions of adult caregivers first since children ought not to be expected to lead themselves through these understandings.

Starting with the discussions on child development that begin in Chapter Six of this book, and that continue in the adult development chapters of *The Pearl and the Hut, Volume II*, I offer prompts regarding how to observe the sevenfold Life and Learning Processes in Pearl Children and Pearl Adults at different ages and stages. This is to support Pearl's needs for stability, wholeness and a creative, inspiring life. As a child matures into later adolescence, the processes that the parents have continued to hold for the child can be made more conscious, offering the youth an age-appropriately disciplined, personal self-dominion that is a natural pathway to a wholesome life and innovative thinking in adult maturity.

Since practicing these seven-fold indications involves some direct guidance (that will be offered in future on-line work from this book through the www.anthropearl.com website), here I offer them in a holistic, combined approach for a simplified and early understanding of these seven-fold processes. In anthroposophy, it is important to take an overview of a subject at first and work into a deeper understanding of it over time, with periods of time where the ideas are put to rest to gestate.

Seven Life Processes	Seven Learning Processes
Breathing	Observing
Warming	Relating
Nourishing	Digesting
Secreting-Absorbing	Individualizing
Maintaining	Practicing
Growing	Growing a New Faculty
Reproducing	Creating Something New

1.) *Breathing/Observing*

In life and learning in general, we thrive by observing various earthen and cosmic phenomena and breathing into active experiences with the elements of the world and in human social interactions. When we deeply observe life around us, even as small children, we are affected in our breathing. When we focus and engage our will in something, we tend to narrow our breath. When we finish, we change our posture or seating, move around, and literally take an out-breath or a "breather". Alternately, even if we're taking an out-breath with no specific focus or will-engagement, and something occurs that is harsh to our sense of beauty, life sustenance, or natural order, we often become stifled in our breathing.

Anthroposophical practices, brought differently for children and adults, help people to stay present and engaged in natural, rhythmical breathing and to manage ways to bring breathing back into harmony if it becomes distorted. This happens without using old yogic practices of breath control or other forms of intentionally controlling one's breathing. One initial and simple example that works for both children and adults is through artistic activities in observing and drawing plants in nature.

By applying oneself in a focused way to an in-breathing activity of observing and sketching a plant that has a personal attraction for the individual, and then stepping back and observing one's work with a wider, out-breathing gesture, the soul-breathing comes into balance. This allows for a broader sense of etheric life and light to inform one's narrowed thoughts, feelings, and imaginations and literally en-lightening our psyches while not ungrounding them. Entering into focused, in-breathing activity creates a breathing contraction, while stepping back and away with a wider focus acts as a breathing expansion. Our breathing follows our attention. It contracts and expands in natural and soul-engaged way unless our attention becomes too fixated out of some traumatic or unnatural reason.

2.) *Warming/Relating*

The human soul is a warm, malleable, and relatable inner force that draws people and even creatures (who have a somewhat different soul configuration) together in heart-stirring ways. The earth, by contrast, though a living being that is variously warmed by the sun and that is essential for human life and living inspiration, is still a colder, harder entity than a human being. Often, the thinking around its resources can cause heart-hardening as well as division between people and also inside of themselves. Our attachments around earthen matters and resources often cause battles between people or between our feelings toward the earth.

We often variously love but also hate or deeply dislike the earth for it's hard and hardening challenges. Often, we're not even aware of our antipathy toward the earth and we unconsciously build up hardened resentments and project our rejection of its hardness onto other people. We blame others for an unconscious sense of inner hardening and particularly if that hardening results over time in physical manifestations such as any number of kinds of illness, strained muscles, various bone or ligament degradations, fractures or simply body stiffness.

When we live into the *warming/relating* steps of the seven-fold Life and Learning processes, we bring our sensing and our feelings to what we observe in nature or in various practical tasks, or to a person that we engage with. We observe ourselves in the ways that help us to stay warm-hearted to the experiences of life or others while avoiding becoming entangled with simply mundane perspectives or endlessly perpetuated, negative storylines.

The younger we are, the more we carry our story about with us if we've experienced early traumas, especially if we aren't listened to by empathic adults or if our emotional needs are not respected in our youth. If what we sense into of our growing inner knowing about what will enhance our etheric life forces (even if that sensing is mostly unconscious in youth) becomes disregarded or degraded by significant others, we shut out important imaginations for how to manage stuck and mundane life issues.

This kind of neglect can lead a person to becoming an adult who lives out of a self-absorbed, dark or irresponsible personality rather than out of something more deeply soul-authentic, warmly human and lovingly selfless. That stuck person can become a drain on others who sense their superficial disconnect from self and who want little connection. A neglected Pearl can become and adult who becomes entangled in relationships of "love" based purely on money or other material things and not for any inner and more sustainable and enlivening, as well as freeing, qualities. They can also draw to them people who use intimidation and control to keep overly sensitive and insecure Pearls in unhealthy and unfree relationships.

This is different for children than for adults. More sensual, material attachments and more blinded absorptions in personal interests are natural and healthy for developing, young children and this represents the state of childhood physical and emotional growth. Expecting inappropriate levels of expansive and objective thinking from young children can be damaging to their natural development. This is where parents with good seven-fold processes practices and understandings can hold the space for Pearl Children caught in self-sabotaging conflicts by being in their own, adult, expansive, seven-fold development and creativity and staying conscious of the distinct differences between adulthood and childhood.

As human beings in the *Consciousness Soul* epoch, we are now challenged to make extra-conscious efforts, out of our own will forces, to warm ourselves inwardly in the heart and soul and outwardly in relationships of loving goodness with others consistently. This is an extra challenge at times when souls, lacking maturity, strive to be regularly "cool" about life and relationships while actually fearing intimacy and the honesty and integrity necessary to sustain close relationships. What we may have come to believe about human beings as being more naturally warm and lovingly connected in relationships before this epoch is more likely an effect of television and cinema movies, that put modern ideas of love into historic settings, than actual truths of the human condition in the past.

Developing loving relationships today requires the full commitment and consciousness of the individual who is willing to do the self-development and practices to warm themselves into sustainable and regularly changing, inter-relating. This is hard to do when true human egos are not yet fully developed and much reactivity bolsters false, personal egoism. Yet this is an important moniker for our cold, technological times; the clear struggle for human beings to maintain relatable warmth of heart and soul while being pressed to become conscious in higher imaginations and deeply human thinking about everything that happens in and around us. (Later, in Volume II, I describe this multidimensional consciousness more and how Pearl Adults can work with it psychologically.)

An exercise for *warming/relating* that a person can do while alone is to observe a plant or animal, draw it, stand back from it to see if from a wider, out-breathing perspective, and then sense into what is relatable about it to them. By bringing feelings to it while not attaching too much thinking about it out of the past, present, or future, a person suspends or pauses judgment while opening space to discern something more meaningful about what has been observed. The observer senses, feels, then steps back to be simply and quietly present to it. The person opens up to notice what imagination or inspiration might come about from a wider-focused experiencing. The person returns to observe the initial sketch with any imaginations, intuitions, or inspirations from the process.

3.) *Nourishing/Digesting*

In our daily lives, we take in many nutrients, impressions, images, and counter-images. Some of these are positive and life-sustaining, and others are not. Nothing enters the human body or awareness without a process or a sequence of inner events that either reject, or digest in a nourishing way, these impressions, integrating them in a certain order or series of orders. Our inner soul digests and absorbs impressions coming from outside of us also though we are often unaware of this happening. We can absorb impressions that sit well in the soul, digesting wholesomely, or those that do not and cause us a sense of being ill-at-ease or distressed. We may digest food, but we may also digest something that someone says to us. How well we do this digesting and then assimilate understanding and higher consciousness into our being, is reflected in our body-heart-mind, soul, and spiritual health.

To digest in the way of seven-fold processes anthroposophical working, we step back from what has been observed, taken in, or experienced in a focused way, and enter into a more expansive perception of how we are experiencing this "digesting" within us. We consider in an open, out-breathing way if we are bringing only earthen-attached awareness to the subject or experience, or bringing a more expansive, imaginative, or higher consciousness to it as well. Are we able to absorb a sense of opposites, including the opposite views of other people, or are we simply bringing a limited, and perhaps too ego-centric focus to how our experience sits in our inner nature and our heart? Children digest best through play and being witnessed and guided committedly, responsibly, and non-judgmentally by adults who are able to process consciously for themselves.

4.) *Secreting-Absorbing/Individualizing*

In the same way that we digest and assimilate experience in the body and the soul, what we consequently do with it contributes to what we are secreting and absorbing through our whole being as evolving individuals. We may secrete and then absorb into ourselves that which is positive and life-giving. Conversely, we can assimilate that which creates a toxic inner environment and works to separate us from ourselves or causes us to lose ourselves in others. This is particularly so in the trials of alcoholism, drugs, or sexual obsessions and abuses.

We may, through our mental, emotional or thinking nature, secrete and absorb those life and learning nutrients and essences that bring clarity to our I-sense. With that, we increase our ability to connect more clearly with our own heart and with higher, loving capacities for human connection with others. Learning to discern the quality and differences in what and how we absorb, and what that means to our healthy individuation that allows us to act selflessly and in compassion with others, is key to soul-psyche wholeness today.

For both children and adults, the practice becomes one of observing an issue or experience as a more objective "it", relating "to it", finding something of ourselves "in it" by seeking the nourishing essence that can resonate in our heart, and then holding this essential thought up to a nourishing imagination (for children especially) or to our sense of a higher "I" nature (for adults). This includes holding it up to an imagination and sense of spiritual beings that are not necessarily directly perceptible to our senses. This can be aided along for adults with anthroposophical knowledge of sacred geometry, the cosmic nature of music, understandings of the elementals behind growing plants or whole gardens or forests, and the experiences innate in Eurythmy movement.

The adult I-sense can look beyond purely selfish intent without disregarding healthy, individualized ego needs that nourish body, mind and soul. In this way we strengthen the soul-spiritual container of our being into a vessel that has capacity to see, hear, and engage with phenomena or other persons, out of increasing levels of soul-spiritual brotherliness and sisterliness. For children, this is done through loving adult authorities bringing age-appropriate imaginations, inspiring stories, seasonal celebrations, a child-appropriate focus on angelic beings, and the stories of saints and greatly inspiring people through time.

5.) *Maintaining/Practicing*

Since in our times we must bring our will to consciously ensoul goodness, community with others, and warm understanding of the human condition for people close to home and also worldwide, knowing how and when to make firm commitments is a precious need of the soul today. Forcing ourselves to do something because culture or old tradition said so for eons is not helpful, as it creates a hardness that brings about resistance. We are simply not in olden circumstances anymore.

Practicing something over time with a rhythm, however, is a positive, ensouling technique. Steiner indicated that today, it is healthy to take up to seven attempts or practices for a process to sink into the soul as a warm and life-enhancing and supportive, etheric impression and memory. The more rhythmic a practice is, the deeper into the soul it impresses and the more memorable it becomes. It is positive if the rhythm remains earth-rhythm-oriented and not bound for some level of mechanistic or technologically oriented hyper-speed. It must not consistently lift oneself up and out of oneself, yet still attune to cosmic consciousness. Such sped-up practices, as in some Eastern traditions for raising the human vibration to an unearthly, spiritual vibration, are considered by anthroposophy to be out of step with the Consciousness Soul times. Sped-up practices can elevate one's consciousness away from the love of the earthen challenges of being human, causing a person to become increasingly resistant toward other human beings or the earth itself.

The intention in some olden Eastern and even Middle Eastern practices is not to be soulfully in complete acceptance of the challenges and tensions of an earthly life, but rather to long for escaping that life. In Anthroposophy, good seven-fold processes "practicing" means going back to what one was *breathing/observing* in the presence of, and *warming/relating* to it, *nourishing/digesting* about it, and *secreting-absorbing/individualizing* around it by holding it up to the higher I —and repeating the process with an added piece that comes to one's consciousness directly after a night's sleep. By adding in another insight that comes imaginatively, intuitively, or out of an inspiration through the night, the situation, thing, experience, or person being observed and processed around may be offered something different to move them forward that is still authentic and relatable to their true circumstances. No bypass or disconnected fantasy is cultivated. Newly ensouled steps in the evolution of that thing, experience, or person can grow naturally and with ensouled, etheric life forces. One sees how everything truly human grows well over time if tended to well and patiently.

Once again, a person observes with focused attention first and then with a wider, open attention, letting go of ingrained or repetitive thoughts from the past or out of some sense of a projected future. Rather, a person seeks a new insight that relates to the former but that is an advancement of it, even if it is a very small move toward something new. In time, with more practice, something distinctly new reveals itself from this *Practicing* ensoulment. The rhythmical pace of the practicing creates a mindful vessel or chalice that provides grounding for the new or the futuristic.

6.) Developing/Growing a New Faculty

When we have practiced something to the point where it is laid down in a healthy and enlivening etheric memory, meaning one that has malleability while still holding sustainable rhythm and form for our sense of practical sustenance in life and a personal sense of balance and stability/equanimity, we have consciously and inwardly earthed that practice. Now, we have a foundation to work with to develop a whole new capacity for awareness in cultural, spiritual, artistic, social or practical/economic matters. This is the beginning of what becomes a mature, adult, alchemical process.[30] (A deeper discussion on the alchemical wheel is in Volume II.)

Here, we think of an upward loop, taking early observation and then allowing our sensing, and our thoughtful discerning of the essence of that which is observed, up an ascending and then descending loop. We move our thoughts to a higher purpose and then bring back out of inspiration that which is a helpful integration for understanding and soul-enlivening that which was observed.

When we have established the earlier seven-fold processes and have practiced them, we become capable of engaging new and expanded knowledge. We bring our feeling nature to our subjective impressions, experiences, and inspirations, and then move along the alchemical loop toward a sense-free essence, and a higher-I perception of it. We allow this process to "steep" through the night and then stay open in the morning to whatever related, sideways, or even opposite impressions come about it, including ideas that may seem to come out of left or right field.

By example, Nicanor Perlas, a Philippine anthroposophist who won the alternative Nobel Prize for environmental right livelihood, and who has worked with thousands of people as a social systems change advocate, and who ran for the presidency of the country while researching with business leaders, technology industry experts, astrophysicists, biodynamic farmers, and teachers, has spoken of the capacity to think of important, inspirational and life-applicable ideas that move six degrees in separation from how we normally think.

It is known to some dedicated researchers that when we do that, we find someone or some idea that aligns well with our own idea or inquiry, but that brings new insight from missing places in our normal consciousness that can reveal new solutions that align even more truthfully in the soul and psyche. We may reveal to ourselves something entirely opposite to what we have believed until now, yet we see a more expansive truthfulness in that opposite thought or idea. The edginess of anxiety or frustration can be relieved by working with these opposites and becoming more whole in our thinking and in our soul. In time, and with integrated earnestly, oppositions can rest in the soul well and even our sleep can in time become more restful and renewing.

These can represent areas of our beliefs and attachments that we don't like to explore but that are often brought to our attention anyway. Sometimes, they are thoughts that we have made firm arguments against within ourselves and have shut off all discussion about. If we allow ourselves to move further right or left in a circle of degrees away from our traditional or safe thinking, we can learn something important from our blind spots. We can create important and even spiritually lawful, new innovations that can serve ourselves and others.

As we play with these thoughts without having to commit to them right away, we begin to form a kind of thought hologram around the practices that we have already affirmed in our lives and the feelings that we have about them. We create a healing wheel of new perceptions around old and stuck patterns. This thought hologram can be inclusive of opposites and sideways impressions. Or, as with the cosmology of the medicine wheel of North American First Nations peoples, we contemplate north, south, east, west, up, down, inward, and outward directions, representing many sides or aspects to earthly life, and how we and others relate to them. We move from seeing unknown situations as problems toward opening possibilities for new, evolutionary, timely, and humanly renewing ideas and solutions. In the process, we actually become more deeply human.

Figure 3.1: Example of a North American First Nations Medicine Wheel

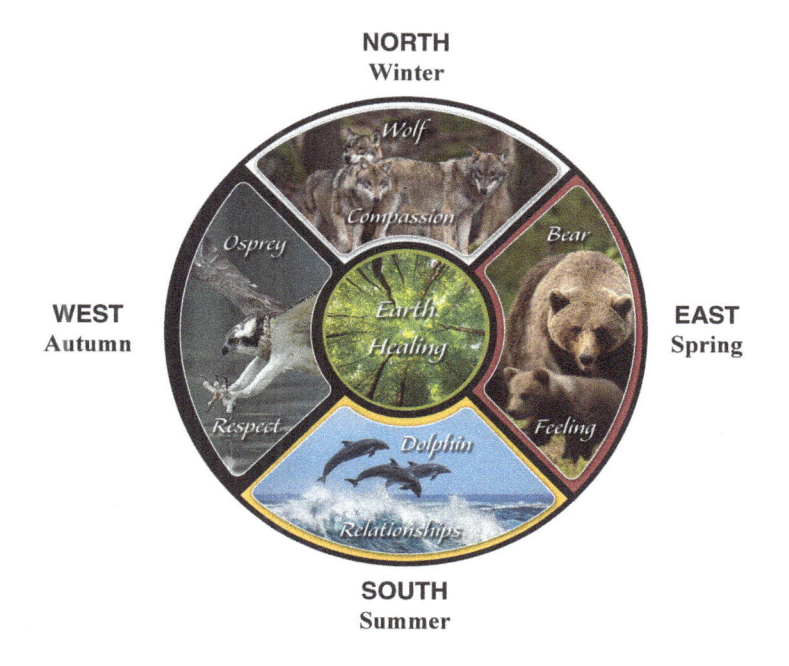

The Medicine Wheel is a sacred symbol denoting seven teachings regarding: the unity of all people in the circle of life, the directions of the earth, the seasons, the elements of earth, water, air, and fire, animal and plant wisdom, the heavenly bodies of sun, earth, moon and stars, and the life stages of birth/childhood, youth/adolescence, adulthood/parenthood, and elderhood/death.

What we find is that, by working the wheel of thoughts and feelings, we are indirectly including other souls into inner dialogue with us that we may have given no consideration to before. Our new faculty is one of objective truth now, and not just our own, subjective desire or opinion. We have held our truth while expanding it to touch others' truths. This alchemical process—where a person moves an earthed practice into feeling, and then into diverse and even oppositional thoughts, patiently within oneself—is a soul process for developing new inner faculties of perception, intuition, imagination, and inspiration.

This is where the I-sense inside of us begins to master our experience for us. Working the wheel while taking the impressions with us into sleep at night, soon brings about an "ah-hah" moment about that practice that can lead us into unique, inspired, and loving actions.

7.) Reproducing/Creating Something New

Out of the inspirations that reveal themselves while developing these new life-process faculties of awareness and higher perception, come new creations, directly out of the individual's own soul intelligence and impetus. Nothing is more freeing, comforting, and affirming for the inner life of the soul than to be able to move a well-considered experience into something with greater objective truth, for a higher or fuller connection with others out of our own, honest connection to a practice and to a set of deepened impressions. If a person struggles excessively to bring about this new inspiration, then a review of the other life processes can reveal some of the obstacles to their clarity and vision. Working another life process more firmly can bring a greater strength to the soul for this *creating something new* stage of the seven life processes.[30] If one remains stuck, further practices in this book can help bring greater light for inner resilience.

Examples of Counseling with the Seven Life and Seven Learning Processes

1. Breathing/Observing Example

When a Pearl Child is in a new co-parenting family situation following family divorce, a counselor, parent, or caregiver carefully notes, when applying the first life process of observing and breathing, whether the child knows sufficiently the habits, routines, or plans of the parent's home life that the child is transitioning into that day, weekend, week, or month. The child may need more time to observe what the new situation is looking and feeling like at each parent's home, and what the others in the house are doing. The child needs to not feel pressured to join in; to act happily and positively, or to just relax and be "part of the furniture" like everyone else. The child many feel somewhat vigilant for a while, and may seem stiff or unnatural to the others in the home. This stiffness needs attending to in soulful ways.

The child's breathing may consciously or unconsciously begin to change or constrict. This may happen before arriving, while wondering (and worrying) about the home transition on the way between homes, or while still at the first parent's home. This can depend on previous experiences or how much the life picture at the one parent's home seems to contradict or conflict in some way with the life-picture with the other parent. Just this experience alone is enough to begin to demonstrate the extra energy and alchemical work happening within the child of divorce in a co-parenting situation, particularly if there is still animosity between parents.

A counselor, parent, or caregiver needs to acknowledge the extra work and feelings impressed upon the child and help the child to practice calming and strengthening activities to manage anticipatory anxiety and restore the child's etheric forces. This may include giving an older child practices to do in the car, on the subway, or for the train ride on the way to the other parent's house. The child may need calming Bach flower essence remedies, money to purchase a warm, natural tea/soup/health-food hot-chocolate to sip out of a cup on the train, earplugs to keep subway noise from over-straining the nerves, an extra-warm hat, scarf, or hoodie, a pair of drumsticks to tap out a rhythm on the thighs while sitting waiting at a bus stop, or a mbira instrument in a knapsack that the youth can pluck quietly in the corner of the cafeteria after lunch at school, gently encouraging calm digestion before classes start again.

Extra shy or introverted children can be given small bodily codes and signals to practice in the car on the way to the other parent's house. These signals will have been practiced with each parent to show each of them quickly what the child is feeling when first arriving at one or the other's home where there are stepbrothers or stepsisters. Using this stress-signaling system needs to be taken seriously by the receiving parents but not as something to be taken personally or against the other parent.

The child can decide if he or she wants stress signals known to stepsiblings or not, in the early stages when parents are moving in with a new partner or spouse, and when Pearl Children are being brought together with stepchildren in a new blended family. The signal can provide a contract and an impetus for the parent to slow the moment down a bit and allow the child to be seen and heard for what ails him or her in that moment.

2. *Warming/Relating Example*

A child may feel an inner-soul coldness in the new setting, having left one parent behind in life for a while, or when returning to this same parent having adjusted to the other parent for at time. The child may need specific practices from a counselor or caregiver to bring a sense of inner-soul warming to steady inwardly enough to connect better in relationship with each parent and others in the families in each home. The child can do this by carrying pieces of warming clothing, having warm transition drinks in the car on the way to the other parents' house.

The child might need to request some family pet time alone with the dog, cat, gerbil, or cockatoo upon arriving at one home or another. Gently rubbing the heart area (heart chakra) or cupping a natural fibre scarf, or a wool hat, around the nose and mouth, breathing warm air into it to warm it then holding it to the chest area of the heart, are practices to use in a pinch when a child feels fear or a sense of disconnect.

Warming ointments such as Uriel's Copper or Aurum[31] creams can be helpful to rub on the chest and/or kidney area upon arriving. Keeping the kidneys extra warm at times can be important, along with extra nourishment that supports kidney strength. Though the liver likes to be clean and that can lead some people into fasting, Rudolf Steiner warned that fasting won't be so helpful to the human being today and could serve to excarnate them too much. Eating nourishing, organic whole foods and diverse vegetables and fruits, potentially with some cleansing herbs, can keep the liver warmly functioning. (For adults, avoiding alcohol as much as possible is important for liver and kidney functioning.)

3. *Nourishing/Digesting Example*

The third life process is one worth highlighting. The unknown is hard for young children, and especially when the unknowns are based on the changing and potentially non-accepting moods of divorced parents regarding behaviors and feelings that the child has picked up from the other parent's home and life. Digesting and assimilating experiences of adjustment between homes, parents, and lifestyles can be less-than-fluid or "clean" for a Pearl. Some experiences in each home situation may, in fact, feel entirely indigestible to the soul, but the parent expectation is that the child will find some way to assimilate it anyway. This is a red flag for emotional and behavior issues at some point.

A child can be helped with creative-expressive activity, using nature props and costumes in a counseling session to naturally play out frustrations and expel/transform unacceptable and indigestible issues. Counselors can help the child to rework the play with images and verses that bring goodness, courage and light to permeate the less digestible elements and manage the darker impressions. Examples can be passages from the Waldorf school play performed every autumn about the Archangel Michael.[32] He tames the dark dragon and helps people to apply the energy of strife to work and skill. The counselor always watches for signs of reportable child abuse. A parent should take severe signs of non-assimilation as important red flags regarding mental or emotional lack of safety in their child.

Even if the child knows certain routines in each home, changeovers can fluster the feeling and sensing nature of the child, and many questions may be repeated until the child gets strong affirmations of acceptance. This is a process of warming into the emotional and procedural lay of the land with that parent that day or week. The child may need to find a sense of how to relate to what is happening with others or to what is being expected in this particular week. Expectations for small children should be as consistent day-to-day, week-to-week as possible for deeply rooting a long-term psychological memory of stability, which will be increasingly important during Pearl adulthood stresses.

So much happens in a Pearl Child's day or week, depending on the age and stage of the child. Extra time or attention may also be necessary to warm up to how that child can remain inwardly authentic in relationship with the others in the parent's home. This may require an expression of feelings and what seems unfair. Having warm hut time is important for centering.

Thirdly, the child may feel confused about what feelings are actually arising. Parents can attend to the child with a simple feeling language, using the feeling words of fear, sadness, anger, worry, love, and joy. It is most appropriate anthroposophically for an adult to bring a story to the child about a fairy-tale character who felt the same way as the child, or a similar animal story. Older children are helped by hearing the biographical story of another person who struggled with similar feelings and circumstances.

If the child is not attended to with patience and helped to sort personal impressions and allowed to express in some authentic way, while being expected to adjust, the child may well swallow, insinuate, or expel tensions in self-sabotaging ways rather than getting the support to manage the tensions and find a sense of balance and groundedness in the situation. Practical balancing/grounding activities are best for young children, such as walking across logs in the forest, rolling on grassy hills, making food with their hands such as with baking, playing skipping games, massaging pets, helping turn soil and plant seeds and vegetables in the garden, or helping to hammer and construct a new fence in the backyard. There are many practical grounding activities that help the child feel in body, connected to the soles of the feet, and warmed in the blood. At home or in the classroom, balance boards can be available for a child who is off-kilter at times.

Ultimately, adjustments will need to be made by the adults to help a child digest and assimilate the family dynamics better, rather than putting the work and strain on the child. This process might take substantial work and time to hone if there is a real disconnect between parents, new partners, stepsiblings, or lifestyles.

In the early stages of sharing a parent with the parent's new partner or spouse, the Pearl may struggle very hard to have a safe felt sense with that parent who is now energetically different from what the child was accustomed to previously. Once the child has had a warming time (to observe, breathe, ask questions, digest, process, feel out needs, identify and express authentic self to the others that day, and negotiate and practice a sense of place with others until they feel comfortable and unconditionally accepted), that child can more easily avoid the buildup of a sense of rejection and abandonment.

Unless this transitioning is negotiated well, based on concepts of fairness that may or may not have developed well when the child was with parents who were in regular conflict, a deep, inward feeling of ethical or moral betrayal can set in, and the child has no real way to know how to access and get a grasp on that negative felt sense before it becomes acted out or suppressed in harmful ways.

When Parents Don't Digest or Assimilate the Divorce Well

Healthy human beings have a way to feel into other human beings and their feelings and energetic states. Neuroscience has identified this very real ability based on mirror neurons in the body that read neuron activity in another person.[33] Despite society's attempts to resolve divorces legally in or out of courts, often divorces are not resolved in the hearts and minds of the parents for years to come, and sometimes they never get harmonized. Children of divorce can usually feel if one or the other parent is still holding onto bitterness about the divorce.

Children also absorb and assimilate negative impressions of their situation from outsiders. Clearly, in my phenomenological research, many children of divorce minutely noted what their parents and other adults carry in their spoken tones about each parent in the divorce. It is very hard for a growing child to digest and assimilate something so directly or insidiously negative in their lives that the adults have not found their own way through, and which keeps coming toward the child through subtle sense impressions that are very alive for children. Human beings as children have a great need to feel sanctuary and trust with their parents, and a sense that a circle of the important people in their life are valued and loved by others in the circle.

4. Secreting-Absorbing/Individualizing Example

Finding a way to personal discernment is hard for many Pearl Children. Depending on how much they have been involved in their parents' divorce conflicts, they can absorb negative feelings and tension that are not their own to sort and resolve. Since what we take inwardly during our physical, etheric, and astral development becomes the fodder for our individuation toward a fully functioning ego, having child forces entangled with demeaning parent issues can mask the youth's own developing soul work. This can go unnoticed in some children until much later in their young adult years.

This is often noticeable when Pearls are out on their own as adults and unable to make decisions for themselves, or when they are overly vulnerable to the constructive input of others because of a lack of early parent presence and protection that leaves their sense of self-esteem crumbly. Counselors support children of divorce to sort their own interests, feelings, wonders, and strengths, and they can help to spot the signs of neglect, abuse, and emotional abandonment.

In North America, some of these abuses evoke serious legal issues requiring court-ordered child removal from one parent or another, and reparations. Today, particularly in First Nations communities, every effort is being newly made to avoid such outcomes. Counselors can help the children to recognize what kinds of behaviors and messages around their parents are life-giving and those that are life-reducing, or that get stuck as negative blocks to the individual child's developing "I" realizations.

If a child hears the message, "What you feel doesn't matter," elders and counselors help the child to know that what they feel in their heart does matter, but that the parent is struggling to know how to accept that and work with it. Then the counselor helps the child to work with it in creative and practical ways. The child's imagination is supported since, often, parents caught in spousal conflict can't imagine well into what a child is fully about as a soul until that child is an adult, and sometimes not until the child is a more capable adult than them in relationships.

A small child can be supported through balanced fairy tales and moral animal fables to discern positive and negative traits of human behavior. They need to learn affirming songs and rhymes for themselves. Elementary-age children can use imagination and creative-expressive therapy to reinforce what is age-appropriate and positive for them to focus on. Counselors can guide creative work to move through negative programming, using dark and light color play, or discerning through music what is a natural and healthy tone of voice to be hearing at home about the other parent and what is too hardened or hurtful.

A child can be given some simple rhythmical verses or mantras to speak and internalize to soften the situation for themself if they hear one parent demeaning the other. The child can also find some healthy ways to care for friendships and to help other family members to know their feelings and needs.

Tandem counseling, with each parent at different sessions, aside from the child's safe time with a counselor alone, can sometimes be effective, but more often, different counselors work with each family member. With permission, counselors can confer together. Parents can also work through artistic or skilled-craft work, such as creating a clay sculpture of their former spouse, to find the right balance of thoughts and feelings, and to work out their own strategies, or mindful ways of defusing negative statements at home about that other parent.

As the former partners work to strengthen their own physical, etheric, astral, and I balances,[iv] they can more easily pull back their projections on the other parent. Each can notice more clearly when they bring inappropriate issues into their child's process. Parents can also be supported with verses, mantras, meditations, and visualizations for looking at their challenges and moving away from defensiveness, and for discovering what oppresses or overstimulates their will forces, and how to manage that.

Middle-school children need support to have practical, hands-on hobbies and skills to cultivate positive interests, with extra attention to help them move through frustrations in the otherwise joyful work. This could mean creating anything from sewn jungle-animal dog jackets, to building "rad" squirrel-and-bird condos, to reconstituting old shoes with First Nations glass-bead fringe, designing outdoor garden-stone carpets, collecting broken-teacup pieces for carport-wall mosaics in concrete … well, the creative list is endless. If a pre-adolescent feels a creative block for ideas, they can ask any hobbyist, craft person, artist, or engineering/construction person for some imaginative help. (It's better in person than just pulling some instruction off the internet.) Better yet, ask a safe, responsible adult artist friend to arrange a forest picnic with the child to imagine creations with them.

Hobbies can be anything with some imagination, repetition, crafted qualities, and time for reflection. This can steady thirteen-year-old children significantly when they need to take in some hut time during difficult moments with stepparents or siblings. Hut time can entail gently puttering around with a creative hobby project while having no pressure or expectation of anything put onto the Pearl. Middle-school children can learn songs and balancing verses to recite to themselves during hut time to stay centered in their own age-appropriate tasks and issues. Parents should not try to know or express along with their child with these particular songs and verses unless invited or given permission by the child. (Chapter Five begins several chapters devoted to the age-appropriate needs of each developmental stage.)

Pre-adolescents and young adolescents can benefit from short, overnight, or weekend stays at the homes of extended family members who can stay neutral about the divorce for the sake of the children, or offer a truly non-judgmental open ear. These youth ought to have the chance for sleepovers with their friends' families who are safely known to one or both parents. Retreats, such as school camping trips with a counselor present and couple-escorts who have strong relationships, can help create safety for the youths and pattern for them what can happen in good relating. They can also offer campfire discussions, through stories, about

---

iv I use the term "former partners" and not "ex-husband/wife" because of the literally cutting and hardening nature of the prefix and how negatively the ex-spouse terms have affected many Pearls.

when people were given burdens that were not theirs to carry and how they got free of them without harming others or themselves.

The Burden Boundary Game

This can be made into a game for six or more children between ages ten to thirteen. It uses three, individual camp-gear backpacks. The counselor serves as referee purely for safety and to mediate any arguments over the rules. Here is how the game works:

1. In the group of children, two people are chosen to be 'it'. They have the three gear-packs available to them. The packs are filled with some rocks as well as items of necessity for camping, and also a balance of things children don't like but parents might want them to have. The children work together to decide what to put into the burden packs.
2. Children choose sticks to decide which two players (the ones who chose the two biggest sticks) will be the "loaders." The loaders stand with the pile of three backpacks, and as soon as one of the loaders picks up a pack, the "players" run.
3. One loader tries to catch a player to be the "mule." A player can only be caught and unfairly loaded if they do not create an authentic boundary for themself.

   3.i One authentic boundary symbol (ABS) for a player is to put a square of sticks around themself with only one side open. That means that the player is guarded but open to seeing if there is anything in the camp packs that might be appropriate to carry. The loaders must let this player look inside the pack and take out what they are able and willing to carry. The child will know because it is true to their own feelings, needs, or abilities.

   3.ii (The other players can come close to see the choice and even encourage this player if the player is asking for help in decision-making, but they are not protected once the mule has taken up the appropriate burden-pack from the loaders. As soon as the burdened one has taken the burdens, the loaders go back to their starting place with what burdens have been left. They then start running after players again with a fresh pack. They can put the burdens left over from the first pack into the second pack.)

   3.iii Another ABS is to stand by a water source like a stream. This means that the player is boundaried but willing to listen to the loader's feelings and needs, discerning what seems right to help the loader out with. The player reserves the right to say no if the loader doesn't offer an earnest and considerate argument. Players must stand by a water source at least once in the game.

   3.iv A third ABS is to stand on a higher spot or hill, making the player appear taller than the loader. If there is no hill, the player can stand on a tree stump, a raised pile of dirt/leaves sticks, or on anything else he or she can think of that raises the body up at least 10 inches/25 centimeters. A player can go to a hill if she has been caught and loaded by the chaser two times already.

3.v The loaders must stop chasing if the mule has climbed twice as high as them, such as on a tree, or on monkey bars, or onto a ladder placed in the playing area at the start of the game. This is a special move in the game only. The player can climb twice as high if the loader has disregarded the rule-contract in any way. This represents divine guidance. If a loader sees a mule up twice as high the loader must drop the gear, go to the player, sit, and just be present to the mule to hear what rule has been broken. The player must come down to the loader's sitting level to explain what rule has been broken. If they can't agree that the rule has been broken, the counselor comes to clarify or mediate.

4. The game ends when all three packs have been loaded onto mules, or when 20 minutes run out. Integrated social discussions can follow. Loaders can ask what it was like for the player to be able to decide what burdens to carry. They can ask what it was like for the player to listen to what the loader argued were good reasons for the player to carry certain burdens. Players who never got caught can ask what it was like for mules to get burdened. Mules can ask what it was like for loaders to try to negotiate with them about what they should carry. They can also ask how players felt who did not get caught but who watched others being loaded with the gear. Each child can later write a story about burdens and boundaries.

Older adolescents may want to work with music or social media to find expressions for sharing their love and appreciation for their parents while giving them the message that some life lessons are just not for school kids, or that some dark, over-stimulating or fanciful thoughts are too much of a burden for the youth's reality.

Video-work and other artistic media can be used by older adolescents to give parents a pause and to require of them some thought in their actions. Parents often need to be reminded not to suffocate adolescent ideals, and to keep in mind the importance of finding reasons for tolerance and kindness for all beings. Children are a deep spiritual practice for parents and other adults.

5. Maintaining/Practicing Example

Practicing something for the sake of the soul is different than practicing for something of temporary or superficial importance in a lifetime. In our times in the West, if a person was only allowed to hit nails with a hammer to build one kind of product for forty years, with no creative input or variation to the work—simply earning a subsistence wage and returning someplace to eat and sleep and start all over again the next day—that person would most likely achieve a deadened appreciation for life and for others. They would have nothing enlivening and heartfully inspiring to share with others in relationship, and would have no real sense of higher freedom. They might turn to abusive behavior toward others in the time away from work, out of a distorted reaction to the deadness within himself.

With few inspirational thoughts, creative impressions, honest joy experiences with coworkers, friends, or family, or with no exceptional rhythms to this mundane existence, that person will likely achieve only a very dull or even fatalistic perspective on life and human beings in general. It is likely, also, that they would suffer from many illnesses, including mental illness. This is one reason, for instance, that in the middle of the industrial revolution in Europe, workers' unions struck up to help laborers bring better work hour rhythms and wages to their lives. Those workers needed to have a more meaningful life with their wives, children, and other family members. This is also why, in many places in the industrialized world, health benefits became of great importance. Human beings had to begin to increase their knowledge and awareness of their own soul needs to survive in spirit and keep working.

A materialistic practice in life is cultivated by having self-obsessive, repetitive thoughts and desires about money, land and home ownership, earthen or functional "things," or about consuming excessive food and drink. These lower needs don't foster anything beyond base, materialistic desires. Imaginations and intuitions about the origins and possibilities of those material things as they relate to shared human resources and life—with understanding, coming out of selfless perspectives and out of questions of the long-term implications of industry on human systems, or through inspirations about how to create material items in life that truly foster well-being in society as a whole—moves a materialistic focus to a higher level of good for all involved.

Without a cultivation of feeling and thinking to go along with mechanized willful practices regarding resource things, at age-appropriate levels, the I cannot take hold of the practice and move it into higher purpose. When this can't happen, the breath/psyche suffers innumerable distresses that either get addressed with natural doctors, therapists, or other soul helpers, or get suppressed until some major crime, personal self-destruction, or personal, economic fallout happens, affecting others.

Let's imagine a Pearl Child who grew up with heavy poverty issues living with one parent while the other parent was, for the most part, absent from that child's life. Later in the Pearl Child's adult life, the absent parent is struck with terminal cancer and feels remorse for neglect or absence and decides to leave a substantial inheritance for the impoverished child. The grown Pearl had always wanted to be a farmer, knowing what it was like to go hungry. The Pearl jumps on an opportunity to invest with a farming friend and go into the agriculture business. The farmers cultivate a bio-distorted and heavily chemically sprayed series of crops to make some hefty harvests, despite the damage to the environment.

The two spend the winter months playing the commodities markets online to get the biggest buck for their labors, to get more equipment to plant bigger crops, and to make more money on the stock market for less labor. The business practice is great for a while, and they think night and day about pouring profits into more land and more crops, and into retirement savings.

They de-stress through long drinking bouts at the pub, two or three days a week. The Pearl Adult at first feels a sense of security not experienced before and lives more in charge of life than previously. The work buddies don't share much in common other than work and drinking, but their bank accounts are full, and they sometimes talk about the properties on tropical islands they'd like to own when they retire.

They know that markets can drop at any time, so they work with complete focus and the most high-yield farming practices known, for years. Neither of them has much luck with forming relationships because they don't communicate well, they have consistent work angst, and their long work hours don't leave room for personal development or children.

The Pearl Adult gets older, gets more reclusive and misses a day or two on the farm more frequently, due to kidney issues and a general lack of energy. The Pearl has formed no personal, intimate relationships, being afraid of what the parents went through, and simply lacking relationship role modeling. Secretly, the Pearl hopes to be wealthy enough to retire early and meet someone who likes the house and financial freedom, the adult toys and the hunting quad collection. All sense of etheric life has been materialized into possessions and predatorial amusements.

The Pearl has come to satisfy sexual desires through pornography, the occasional one-night stand, or a prostitute. A mean streak comes out toward others who dote on their children or who are on welfare. "A proud, working citizen deserves to feel angry about that" is now the adopted social motto. The Pearl never looks inward to examine moods and angry projections, the annihilation of the value of others, or the heavy cycle of materialism. The Pearl secretly hates most other people.

The Pearl does not contribute to the well-being of all, since the focus is on personal, material gain, and is simplistic, non-creative, and non-charitable. Any threat to the secure holdings of wealth and land accumulation and the fantasy relationship in the future is defended with clannish, belligerent, and aggressive behavior toward others.

The Pearl supports war proponents politically, especially if war would benefit stocks or keep secure sales happening. The Pearl would never join the armed forces and secretly both envies and despises the attention that armed forces people get. Suggestions by anyone for creating a more whole life pass right by. Constant bitterness against an absent parent keeps the Pearl from ever imagining what that parent might have gone through in life.

Although their business practice is in full swing and mature, the Pearl has cultivated nothing new, creatively innovative, socially just, or philanthropic in the economic, social, or artistic/spiritual life. The Pearl only values a base life, resisting every idea about taxed earnings being used to help others and never thinking to support immigrants or refugees from political wars that helped protect the farm business.

The Pearl ignores or tyrannizes others for wanting an education on how to better sustain farm cultivation environmentally and how to tackle earth-warming effects in the region. When a community crisis happens, the Pearl simply doesn't help, believing that all crises are someone else's issue and the result of something they did wrong anyway. Blame is a regular psychological feature.

This story is clearly one that shows the dangers for Pearls who are given support only in the material realm but not in the soul-spirit or even heart realm, which was essential food for growth as a child.

Too often, purely materialistic reparation in a neglectful family relationship exacerbates emotional shutdown behaviors. Unmet anxiety, grief, loneliness, and trauma can lead to a walled-up intolerance of anything that stirs the heart. It deadens imagination and restricts the empathic capacity for caring for others' challenges and suffering.

The stockpiling farmer here, in the elder years, may still withhold all capital from any kind of humanitarian cause, or even practical venture for the benefit of future generations. Without real, human connection that represents anything but money, the Pearl may draw endless attention to a long retirement and self-congratulatory, self-glorifying behaviors without a thought to whether that serves the greater humanity.

Loyalties of other family members may be tested for how much abuse the members are willing to take to connect with this Pearl. Having inherited money from a neglectful, divorced parent has done little for the "missing pieces"[34] of an unfulfilled soul that is clearly as thin as a wheat sheaf.

In counseling, practicing soul exercises is the foundation for fostering inner strength and courage to meet the challenges of a non-materialistically focused life—without negating the need to engage with economic activities that sustain a life. Anthroposophical biodynamic farmers, for instance, know that it would be easy to get bogged down in practical work and thus, thin in their soul connections with others.

Instead, they work daily with practices to keep a view to the elemental spirits, higher worlds, and the work of others. They relate their world to a world of equally important social or creative, artistic, and spiritual activity. They help the economics-focused soul groups stay connected to others who may not share the same soul path or callings, but who share humanness and a sense of responsibility to the evolving human culture, planet, and spiritual lawfulness. They work with the earth's materials, but they don't attach their identities or souls completely to them. They keep compassionate awareness toward others' suffering and struggles.

For a Pearl Adult, this means developing greater practices and skills around hearing and communicating and sharing clear interests and needs with others. It entails having ways to relate to others who are not just like them, sharing resources, and being morally and ethically responsible with the earth's resources. It might also require extra-comprehensive self-care practices around nutrition, hygiene, sleep schedules, and sensory over-stimulation—to increase one's own awareness of self-care and caring for and about others.

It also often incorporates and reinforces hut time routines and rhythms for coping, in meaningful ways, with relating to people who from time to time oppose them. Soul practices birth unique and creative ways of making meaning every day for a life that is not just about things, but about discovering the innate value in earthen life and the other aspects of human activity and higher humanness.

6. Developing/Growing A New Faculty Example

One of the essential routes today to soul freedom for a Pearl is the ability to embrace as fully as possible what is available in the workings of our lives as divine tools, brought through our I-being, out of both our soul history and our intuitions about the future. We do this while resisting judgments floated by others—in their estimation of their life values—that the Pearl person is inadequate or deviant from some perceived norm decided by a society that may or may not have soul-spirit lawfulness to it.

Somehow, we use our creative higher thinking to move beyond other people's personal and unloving opinions. We come to be able to do something that we never thought that we could do before. It does not, in this stage of the life processes, need to be something exceptional, or something no other human being has done before. It often represents an area of ourselves that the tensions or missing pieces of our family experiences may have inhibited us from even imagining that we could do.

An example might be of a Pearl who, for fifteen years, has been told that she is so orderly and fine in her mental perception that she is an exceptional accountant now despite the regular health struggles she has had to maintain her work. She has worked in her field since her mid-twenties and has enjoyed some level of financial security. However, her relationships have, to her, seemed disastrous, and she never seems to meet the right people for what she considers to be a healthy love life, or even social circle.

For her entire adult life so far, she has been almost mesmerized by the complex work of architecture and the messier work of building construction and renovation. Her house is full of magazines on the subject and, through her accounting firm, she has been invited to ribbon-cutting ceremonies for some inspiring civic building openings where she got to meet some of the people involved in the raising of the building.

She has always felt some level of being in the right place at those gatherings and has often felt depressed afterward when she returned home. She may feel that building construction work is well beyond anything that anyone supported her to do in life, despite her deep, albeit hidden interest in it. Construction work may go against everything that people in her upbringing had to say about her acceptability, since they saw her as they wanted her to be—the orderly thinking, simple, but effective money organizer. She knew that family members didn't see her for her true self, and only valued her as the humble and reserved banking mind that fit the strongest-willed parent.

She wrestles with this image imposed unconsciously onto her since childhood, knowing full well that no one in the family divorce melee ever listened to what really mattered to her. Yet her depression after each construction company event leaves her in such distress that she continually gets chronic illnesses, despite her strong attention to her health. Every now and then, she lies and misses a week of work because she is locked up and numb about the disconnected life she is living. She feels she'll fail if she ever tries to realize her real goals and interests.

The Pearl hesitates about personal rights and values, since they bear some similarity to her mother's, and she knows her father frequently told her how her mother was a failure at such things. She becomes worried when she finds that her mood with others is getting touchy and resentful. She thinks that something is wrong with her and is now attending therapy with a psychologist to see how she can be a more patient and compassionate person toward others and thus, maybe have an intimate relationship with someone once, before she dies.

Although the therapy work represents the woman's development of a new soul capacity, it may have never occurred to this frustrated woman that her soul may be calling for her to broaden her practical horizons and inner capacities for important soul reasons. She may, in fact, be telling herself, unconsciously, that her soul needs to develop some new practical skills, creative imaginations, and renewed belief system capacities. Something in construction work is clearly enlivening for her inner, higher being. Something missing or abandoned in her is wanting to reform and reconstruct now.

Talking in a therapy office about mindful meditation and what would make her more compassionate is not really leading her through the life processes in the way that creative, investigation of her soul passages can. What she discovers with some anthroposophical *biography*[35] work, experience with soul geometry, creative clay sculpting work with Platonic forms, and rhythmical practices with verses enlivening thoughts of a dodecahedron-based architecture, is that her organizational mind is more suited to a broadened, multitasking, socially organic, and foundational way of working. She clearly realizes that her will forces need to collaborate with creative, structural-minded souls who have a conscious, organic nature that wants to manifest buildings and homes that inspire environmental resourcefulness and loving interaction between people.

Continuing with an imaginative example, this woman begins to see that she may feel truer to herself in work that allows her to be developing a not-for-profit center for innovation in joint public-private housing architecture. She organizes this in her spare time, through her connections with some of the architects and construction people that she has met. With a sense of her solid connection to soulful, selfless, but thought-provoking, philanthropic work with others, and with empathy for those who lack understanding of her journey and who project negativity about her new initiative, she reaches out to gather a small group of similar-minded friends.

They meet to share ideas and skills, giving room to their visions about a better life for those with issues of low income or homelessness. In the process, she is visiting building sites with architectural interest that fill her soul and spirit with higher longing and wonder. Moments of deja-vu cause her to wonder if she has been in the presence of great architecture that she can't seem to place in memory this lifetime. Her soul feels stimulated in a way she never previously imagined.

Within three years, the woman organizes a first presentation for a group construction project with the input of city council. A new woman seems to have emerged who has a warm and inspiring group of friends, is offering creative input that she never imagined she could reveal out of herself before, and who feels more alive as well as content in her life. Not only has she developed new faculties of cooperation, creative construction, inward seeking, and civic organization, without relinquishing the most important aspects of herself that carried her through life before, she has prepared herself to move forward in the next level of the seven life processes and create something original and new. She never allows failure storylines about her abilities to negate her self-beliefs again.

7. Reproducing/Creating Something New Example

When an individual has a level of awareness and self-understanding of the seven-fold life and learning processes of breathing/observing, warming/relating, nourishing/digesting, secreting-absorbing/individualizing, maintaining/practicing, and developing/growing a new faculty, and often when that person has a sense of those processes in others, that person experiences what it means to move naturally into a realm of higher-mind and higher-world connecting. This does not mean being high as in disconnected from others, escapist, or in consciousness distortion through consuming mood-altering or cognitively distorting substances.

When a person has a creative grasp of the *seven-fold processes*, the craving for substances to reach a higher level of awareness and creative elevation dissipates. This represents a profound state for a human being today and although it may not necessarily be sustainable regularly, in one person, it is the sign of the future of humanity as seen through anthroposophy.[36] It is something worth celebrating by letting the imaginative, intuitive, and inspirational impulses come into manifestation.

The Twelve Senses: Whole Health from Infancy

A century and a half ago, Rudolf Steiner noticed that people have more than the five outer senses of seeing, hearing, smelling, tasting, and touching. Steiner indicated twelve senses in the human being.[37] He also recognized that some senses are foundational, and others are more developed or refined as a child grows into adulthood. These senses are associated with the many complex features of the incarnating or earthing soul.

Table 3.1 below shows the twelve senses in basic relationships with each other and the relationships with the twelve cosmic constellations of our earth's solar system. It helps to read the twelve senses table from the bottom upward, since the senses are worked and developed from the beginning stages of touch in infancy and up through the middle senses into the adolescent stages toward the fully knit ego-sense. The senses come to full flourish between the twenty-first and twenty-fourth years.

Table 3.1: The Twelve Senses

Spirit Senses:

Ego	Initiating out of individual effort	Aries
Concept/Otherw	Purifying earthly desire to make room for another	Taurus
Word/Speech	Speaking the insights of spirit	Gemini
Hearing	Engaging compassionate association with all phenomenon	Cancer

Soul Senses:

Warmth/Temperature	Raying heart forces outward and inward	Leo
Taste	Discerning substance, assimilating spirit	Pisces
Smell	Distinguishing hygiene in heath, thought and action	Aquarius

Physical Senses:

Balance	Adjusting for equanimity	Libra
Self-Movement	Intuiting higher beings of will	Sagittarius
Life	Transformation of soul and substance	Scorpia
Touch	Earth sensing	Capricorn

Rudolf Steiner perceived that human beings had twelve innate senses, rather than the commonly known five. Each sense is associated with gross or subtle organs of perception that are stimulated by cosmic forces embedded in the earth's solar zodiac of stars and planets.

Ego	Aries	Taste	Pisces
Concept	Taurus	Smell	Aquarius
Speech	Gemini	Balance	Libra
Hearing	Cancer	Self-movement	Sagittarius
Warmth	Leo	Life	Scorpio
Vision	Virgo	Touch	Capricorn

The senses harmonize through opposition. Oppositions in the twelve senses do not mean that one side discounts the other, but rather that each opposite informs and challenges the other to come to a healthy and balanced center for clear thought, feeling, and action.

They work in this way:

Touch	opposes	Ego
Life	opposes	Concept
Self-Movement	opposes	Speech
Balance	opposes	Hearing
Smell	opposes	Warmth
Taste	opposes	Vision

The twelve senses are developed to their utmost in anthroposophical education, health, and creative activity. This can be done in early life in varied ways. The following is a short checklist of how a connection to each sense might be expressed through early life for incarnation, and in later life for balance and healing.

Touch: Baths, massage, hugging, holding, body contact play, dance, feeling the textures of natural/unnatural earthen resources; gardening, farming; sculpting, crafting; caretaking animals, caretaking of babies, the sick, and the elderly. Sexual touch and noticing unsafe touch, bonding touch, communicating touch. Culturally differentiated touch.

Life: Nutritious food, clean fluids, fresh air, healthy environments; positivity; herbal and homeopathic remedies, knowledge of minerals, gardening and farming, time with nature; rooting oneself, opening to new people, places, or adventures. Sense of potential. Sense of purpose. Sense of belonging. Sense of self-valuing and being valued. Sense of grace. Sense of love.

Movement: Sense of flexibility in the body, body coordination, awareness of the movements of the elements of earth, water, air, fire, ether; sense of expressing that which can be seen or not seen. Rhythm. Sense of difference between self-directed and natural movement verses technology-assisted movement. Sense of transformation. Sense of body in reactive or responsive patterns with others.

Balance: Sense of opposites, poise, sure-footedness, symmetry, polarities, finding a center or finding the capacity to bridge divides. Finding stillness, controlling urges, alkaline/acid diet tailoring; sense of sympathy toward something or someone as well as antipathy away from something or someone. Sense of harmonizing prudence versus excess.

Smell: Noticing attraction or aversion to scents and aromas. Sense of sickness or purity. Sense of familiar or foreign, moist or dry, clear or obstructed. Sense of truth.

Taste: Sweet, salty, pungent, sour, or astringent. Simple or sophisticated. Discernable taste or indistinguishable. Cravings. Sense of known tastes or risky tastes, palatable or disgusting tastes. Sense of life-supporting or toxic. Sense of grace.

Vision: Light, dark, bright, dull, clear, hazy. Sense of something appearing solid or ethereal. Colorful, subtle, brilliant. Real, surreal, abstract, naturalist, dreamlike. Sense of beautiful or appalling; sense of perspective or distortion. Sense of focus, periphery, angularity; sense of attractive or repulsive. Sense of depth, texture, veneer, or substance.

Warmth/Temperature: Since cultivating inner warmth is such an important soul issue for our times, this sixth sense merits a little more discussion and description. An easy way to sense if we might be losing touch with inner warmth in the modern era is to pay attention to how often we use words about something or some action or event, such as saying that it is "cool," "interesting," or "blowing me away!" Intellectual work is cooling in the nerves and so must be continually balanced with heartwarming and active, humanistic experience.

Adolescents love to do things to send a vibe or chill up their spines for excitement. This can easily carry into adulthood. Rarely, when we don't have awareness, do we realize how much of a cold effect this is having on our inner organs. We usually don't notice until we've had so many out-of-body experiences accompanied by illness, that we realize that we are constantly chilling ourselves into stress, sickness, and energetic distortion.

It is easier to gauge what the weather temperature is doing outside than it is to gauge whether we have enough inner warmth to offer kindness, loving attention, or sustained will-force activity for important work, relationships, or humanitarian projects. We often don't realize when we've given our energetic warmth to something that is not going to give any warmth back to us. Over a lifetime, the practices for keeping warmth energy close within us, while having enough to share with others, require some deep insight and even planning.

People who help others to die, such as hospice volunteers or palliative nurses, know that to die well, with consciousness and a loving heart, in the end, requires energy. When we ignore the forces of warmth inside of ourselves on a regular basis in life, we can find that closer we are to the end of life, or even in middle age, we don't have the energy to keep a warm nature with the people that we love. This is painful for all involved. Knowing the importance of cultivating warmth inwardly, consciously, and sustainably is a very big advantage for the soul in these modern times.

Hearing: Sense of connection; sense of communion; sense of music, tone, voice, pitch, activity, nature's creatures. Discerning natural or man-made sound; stimulation or calming. Sense of rhythm, cacophony, distress, harmony, listening. Opening or filtering; distant, close, high, low. Sense of electric or acoustic; octaves, soft, loud. Allegro, andante. Earthly or angelic.

Word/Speech: Sense of openness, stiltedness, protection, defensiveness, pride, humility, vitality, steadiness, lyricism, epic, drama. Critical, non-judgmental, competitive, domineering. Sense of strength, weakness, vulnerability, commitment. Pressured, impatient, capable, irreverent, or devotional. Haughtiness, reluctance, undependable, uncertain, illogical, emotive, overwhelmed. Heavy, light, whimsical; engaged, illusive. Enunciating or mumbling. Quality of tone.

Concept/Other: Sense of trustworthiness, moral, ethical; logical, intuitive, imaginative, inspirational. Honorable, adaptable, open, honest; slyness, manipulation, egoism. Sense of danger, safety, respectfulness, communicativeness, silence, cooperativeness. Sense of selflessness or selfishness. Committed or flirtatious. Sustainability or recklessness. Generosity or stinginess. Goodness or deceit.

Ego: Continuity, authenticity, compassion, discipline, frankness. Self-reflective, intuitive, imaginative, inspirational. Creative, procuring, innovative, respectful, honoring, positive. Reverent. Gracious. Whole. Contemplative, thoughtful. Philanthropic. Charitable. Merciful. Initiator. Responsible and reparative. Healing. Practical.

Note on autistic children: It is known that many autistic children experience the sense impressions very intensely. Adults who tend to autistic children know that they must temper their expectations of how a child will respond and react to sense-based activities. One friend has shared that his adult autistic friend, who has managed significant capacity in his life and is a father himself now of an autistic boy, must always wear sunglasses to buffer the intensity of light.

Early Childhood: Warmth/Touch, Life, Movement, Balance

To help children to begin to feel comfortable and at home with their new life after birth, and to help them to begin early to have a felt sense of belonging here, connected to the profound gifts and sensual responsibilities of the earth, newborn babies in anthroposophical care are kept close to the fold of nature and natural experiences.[38] They are, for instance, clothed and nursed in soft, naturally-spun and dyed cloths, such as wool, cotton, and silk. Mothers are encouraged to maintain quality organic or biodynamic diets.

Babies are protected from too much adult or even older-child activity for the first forty days of life, while they gently become familiar with the new and intense sensations of the outer world. Infants need significant time to adapt to light, smells, tastes, and sounds from which they were significantly buffered in the womb.

Although the Anglo-Germanic impulse is still to keep children separate from mom in a crib during sleep, other cultures, even if anthroposophic in their practices, have kept the traditions of having a family bed for the child to be close to the parents' body warmth and touch. In the very challenging trauma times of the twenty-first century, worldwide, many parents are allowing this practice to continue for children even past the ages of four or five.

Modern trauma research shows that the vagus nerve system of the body, which runs through the lower, threat-response areas of the brain and moves down the arms, both shoulders, and connects with the heart and stomach, is calmed through safe warmth and touch. Research also suggests that the memories of human warmth and closeness that the brain registers and stores in childhood help a child to cope with stress and trauma as an adult.

Too much stimulation around an infant too early while nursing, or while in everyday activity with older children and adults, can be harsh on a baby's development and nervous system, and too hard on the healthy malleability of the child's body tissues and developing organs. It is a practice for families with newborns to reflect upon this delicacy, as if pondering the awe and wonder of a refreshing, almost opaque, early-spring morning. They need to remember that an infant's first three years are a mirror of the mood of spring.

Even with the strength of wisdom that many adult parents have today, they sometimes forget that their own "survival suit," physical-sense body took time to adjust to when they were an infant. As adults, they've had many years in their bodies to adapt and create buffers to the challenges of the earthly elements and human-made sense impressions. Even if they are young parents, it has still already taken many tests in their lives to become resistant to some of the heaviness and harshness of earthly existence. A baby is only just beginning to feel it all, and he or she can only slowly come to deal with the major adjustments of earth life.

Tracking an infant's breathing is a healthy practice for parents to notice a baby's stressors. It is important that an infant's new exposure to the earth be paced, rhythmical, and protected in as mindful, measured ways as possible if the child is to find soul safety to incarnate deeply enough to develop in a wholesome way to sustain a full life.

Rudolf Steiner steadily petitioned teachers, farmers, and social leaders to remind parents and caregivers that children are not animals that are born into direct exposure to harsh elements, adapting to a pure survival instinct. Human beings are not very comparable to wildcats, wolves, or fawns. The bone structures in our skulls, thorax, and limbs show that we are beings born with a much more upright nature in time, with rounded skull, no snout, no fur, no hardened and protective incisor teeth, claws, or hooves, and with stomachs that take time to integrate mother's milk and other foods. We hold brains with neurological networks resembling the highly complex cosmos, and an integrated, design-purpose clearly different from four-legged creatures.

Even a giraffe, with a clearly upright, long neck and an exceptionally large heart, is still biologically designed to hold a brain system that is geared toward seeking and scavenging rather than thinking and having choices around long-term survival. In beasts, much of their skeletal design is arranged around impulses based on sense-stimulation, predation, and instinct, but not necessarily balance, reasoning and choice in the face of perceived threat.

A human being is not created with a forward-reaching skull and the elongated snout of an animal who follows mostly his nose and experiences a perpetual lust for food and sexual pheromones. The human being is upright, with retracted eating and smelling apparati, with an upward-raised skull resting centered, and freely moving, on an upright torso containing very free limbs. Mature human beings are physiologically designed for free thinking, as well as for a kind of free will in love and relationships that has human, karmic responsibility regarding spiritually lawful action and the necessity of repair and reconciliation if harms are brought upon others. Human beings can choose association in any number of ways with people similar to their cultural and genetic norm, or with people who are seemingly very different from them. This is not true with animals.

If young children are treated like animals, they can mimic animalistic behavior, but they will in time sense that they are not being true to the very body and brain for which they were designed. Something in their soul is bound at some point to reject some aspect of the animalistic life that they have been cultivated toward.

Heavily abused children, however, may go the other direction, becoming as animalistic and dangerous to others as their abusers, having had violence so fully and monstrously ingrained in them. Children who are able to resist being raised purely according to animalistic beliefs have a strong soul-spirit sense in their innate knowing that they have a purpose beyond that which the animals were made for. That does not deny the important purpose of animals in the world, but it begins to clarify the distinct consciousness differences between them and human beings.

An animal can know the earth, but a human being can at the same time know the ocean, the earth, the sky, and the dark and starlit cosmos beyond the very planet itself. The human being has the mature option in time to venture in any of the earthen realms out of free choice. Creatures do not have that free choice.

If treated like full, upright human beings, children will grow into the great earthly and cosmic potentials that are distinctly the birth rite of human beings, and literally mirrored in their physiology and in capacities that they hold that reach beyond the merely physical and sensual.

Attachment and Trauma

Sadly, too many parents still today do not register in their higher thinking and perception that an infant, toddler, or young child can experience significant harm to their developing physiology, mental orientation, or emotional life, from being caught in the turmoil of conflicted parental aggression. When responsible individuals become blind or inured to the consequences of the buildup of traumas and abuses toward infants, third-party intervention is necessary to find appropriate care for these highly vulnerable souls. Classically, for some Pearl infants, this has meant years of healing interventions from extended family members, social workers, and foster parents. Some Pearls, including First Nations children who experience parent abuse or neglect, are safely given over to the care of their grandparents, who can be an important source of unconditional love.

Emotional Trauma

As noted earlier, subtle traumas that can occur in even the seemingly more civilized parent divorces can have serious long-term effects on the life of the child since the child experiences somatic sensations in a divorce, bringing a kind of cold storm upon the spring-child's organs, brain plasticity, and unconscious emotional memory.[39] Despite healing and moving forward in development, stressful triggers can plague the child into adulthood, bringing chronic diseases.[40] The greater and more violent or terrifying the parental conflict is that the infant is exposed to before and even after a divorce, the more of a crisis the child can be holding within the body and neurology. As Bernd Ruf indicates in his book, *Educating Traumatized Children*, trauma is an impingement on the child's natural, holistic growth forces, and it has inevitable and direct consequences on the psyche.[41]

Undue infant and toddler stress and trauma affect the threefold organic systems: a) the rhythmic system, or blood circulation and lung respiration; b) the metabolic/limb system, which allows the child to digest, grow, and assimilate life experiences; and c) the nerve-sense system, which registers higher thinking and psychic well-being.

Healthy, Abnormal, or Dangerous Psychological Splitting?

In a stable early childhood, an infant will begin to trust the safety and felt bodily warmth of the parents as well as the open-hearted sense of the outer-life surroundings. As a toddler and preschooler, this child will feel free to explore surroundings without anxious fear. The child senses the harmony, resilience, and tuned, relational sensitivity coming out of the parents' relationship connection and skills. This comforting and stabilizing resonance in the body is known in neurological work as the mirror neuron effect.[42]

In an atmosphere of sustained distrust between parents, psychotherapeutic attachment theory[43] has recognized that a young child easily picks up on the instability and uncertainty of the parental relationship. A toddler may fear moving about freely, may cry in despair rather than seek the parent for comfort when his parent leaves a room, or may become frozen in fear in the presence of a stranger when a parent leaves the room for a short period. A child whose needs have been ignored or neglected may seem, in a room with one or both parents, uninterested in the parents and unable to respond to them much.

These behaviors can have long-term and even chronic potentials and consequences for the child of divorce when conflictual parents decide that they can no longer live with each other. Some people have imagined that once the parents no longer live together, the child will now relax and become trusting again. Long-term research and observation do not necessarily bear such conclusions.[44]

An unattended and emotionally unprotected child can lodge tension in body-mind "bank accounts" and that poor investment may surface later in poor social behavior, illness, or self-destruction. A child may contract their inner as well as outer forces, causing blockages in metabolism, respiration, and even blood flow. A screaming child who is unattended to in stress shows the pent-up blood in the face and often overall stiff body tension. This pent-up experience, unaddressed with real loving and stable attention, can seed ingrained physical illness later.

An infant—being a human, holistic, living being connected in every way to lower and higher nature—registers levels of safe/unsafe, confusing/comforting, overloading/manageable, terrifying/joyful, healthy/poisonous, good/harmful, and loving/hateful within their biology in ways that are disguised on the outside. This is especially so if the child has learned to block her crying or other emotional expression out of fear, shock, or neglect.

When a child gets regular, loving, warm, and gentle responses to frights, that child responds in the heart and soul like the ebullient and sparkling earthen nature does itself when nurtured with refreshing water, sunlight, and nutritious soil. Everything grows and glows. That is what some call having a healthy aura. It is also an outer mirror showing if the child is absorbing life-giving impressions or harmful ones.

Though the soul itself is eternal and moves in purity from lifetime to lifetime, the samskaras,[45] or harmful impressions that it picks up during earthen life, can resonate throughout a life. Unhealed, some say these samskaras register even into the next lifetime.

The Traumatized Infant

For a traumatized baby, warmth and rhythm are crucial to inviting the soul to feel welcome again for healing and incarnating into the body. Close, warm attending by a heart-centered adult, steady bedtimes, consistent feeding times according to a baby's nature, the sounds of the gentlest of pentatonic lyre music, or soft, and mid-toned bells are helpful for the atmosphere of the healing, living, or sleeping room.

Gentle hums and tender, lyric sounds are also good for a baby to hear any time when the mood of the home or relational circumstances become discordant and heavy from adult tensions. Soft and light-colored silks to touch, and sheepskins, or natural woolen afghans to grab onto, offer healthy textures for a baby to touch and to be wrapped in when tensions in the home have been excessive.

Deeper healing can come through the gentlest of rhythmical massage with rarified skin oils such as Weleda Comforting Baby Oil[46] in a warm bath or massaged gently on the baby's skin, especially around the kidneys, liver, and the back of the neck. Warm lavender oil poured on a washcloth, or some purified Lavender Moor Mud Cream[47] massaged on a baby's feet can also be helpful for a child in the first three years, who has experienced the harshness of a family relationship breakdown. Massage has the benefit of calming the developing vagus nerve, the lightning rod nerve organ in the body that responds instantly to stress and tension.[48]

Some babies may even require adapted forms of cranial-sacral therapy after experiencing parental fights or violence. With a confident caregiver, the child will know that they can be safe again and surrounded by goodness.

Insecurity in the adults around a traumatized child, when the child needs to heal and feel confident and incarnate again, can be further destabilizing or excarnating. The baby's soul, in essence, lifts 'high' or to the very edge of the body. Some say that the infant soul, in extreme stress, will lift right out of her body, not wanting to come back in.

For the caregivers, holding the consciousness and feeling inwardly of the sense of the warm blood and waters of the mother's womb is helpful for infant-healing purposes. It is a mood held more in balance, in the later toddler stages, so as not to overly promote a watery welcome to life as the baby becomes older and is working to become more firmly incarnate. Depending on when the child experiences the trauma, the womb mood and a fresh spring mood may be necessary for some sustained periods.

The very young child will strive to pick up a normal stage of development as the child begins to feel safe, flowing, and confident again. As a toddler, the child ought not to be pushed to articulate feelings on any adult level. Understanding what a child may feel requires the empathic understanding of the caregiver, expressed through the caregiver's own healing sounds and affirmative words, his or her warm and sensitive felt-sense nods, gentle humming, or references to soft healing creatures such as rabbits, purring cats, or snuggly, protective dogs. (Such healing creatures will vary from culture to culture).

Fairy tales presented with pastel-colored, silken, or brushed-cotton puppets literally resonate for the toddler in a way that the child is *touched* by the sensual gentleness while receiving appropriate, child-level, emotional stimulation.

Soft environments to play, such as a mossy forest floor by a sunlit glade or pond, grassy and treed spaces by a garden, or on a soft wool, crawl-friendly carpet, are ideal for the infant to explore and move, processing stress through connections with a natural environment. The caregiver needs to work to notice the child's breathing and moods, phenomenologically witnessing how the child is adapting and overcoming fears.

An older toddler must be encouraged, but not pushed, to gain confidence with the earthier and harder textures, and inherent bumps and bruises of life, in right timing. A child between ages three and seven will need to begin to experience some levels of self-comforting around knee scrapes, small injuries, and play wounds with appropriate, but not necessarily trauma-attuned healing responses from the caregiver. Otherwise, the child can increasingly come to associate nature's natural bruises in life as requiring a trauma-attuned response. This takes sensitive discernment on the part of the caregiver with a child who was earlier traumatized but has had some healing. Triggers do weaken earlier healing at times, but the child also needs to be encouraged in the healed resilience.

Young children will gradually need opportunities to meet tensions, but the wrong tensions at the wrong age and stage can bring physiological and neurological strain. When a young child is exposed to larger society outside of the family home, many observances are necessary for protecting the developing inner forces and the nervous system from too much, or too hardened, stimulation. Warm hats and clothes are important for both infants and toddlers. In warm or hot-climate environments, a cool cotton or silk hood is helpful.

An infant who has become overheated neurologically, for instance after screaming from being caught in the middle of a parent conflict, may need to have the kidneys warmed with an herbal oil, but the head cooled with a geranium-water wipe and a light cotton head covering. Rocking the child rhythmically in one's arms or lap, or holding the child while walking in a slow and rhythmical way, are also important interventions mimicking the womb experience again.

Warm, non-ultraviolet light is soothing and important to bring the infant's system back into balance. It is okay and good for a baby in the first three years to see safe candlelight frequently, or a well-tended bonfire occasionally in the early evenings. Candlelight ought to be ideally from the naturalness of beeswax candles, for the burning beeswax itself is purifying for the air and brings a calming, fully natural scent to the room.

Natural colors in the baby's environment are also important, and keeping the hues integrated, and in the warm spectrum of reds, pinks, oranges, peaches, yellows, and golds, is helpful.

A warmly lit room painted in anthroposophical lazure[49] layering and coloring is ideal. The aromas of chamomile tea being steeped, or raw milk being warmed with vanilla bean essence are also soothing. Warmed, natural apple cider can bring a calming aroma to the child's environment, as well as the natural smells of home cooking, and the scents of natural wood and herbal soaps.

Natural, Gentle, Sensual Stimulation at Natural Prices

Some of these environmental adjustments can represent costly purchases, depending on many family factors. However, beeswax candles, for instance, can be made at home. Some thrift stores save bags of collected beeswax. A parent can put out a call on social media to community members to save up old beeswax for when they can and arrange a day to pick it up every few months or once a year.

Setting up even a balcony herb garden of lavender, geranium, and chamomile can be an inexpensive way to have the herbs on hand to steep in some kitchen olive oil. One can sew each of these herbs into clean, second-hand cottons to put by the baby in the carrier or by the bed while sleeping. Silks can often be recycled from lightly used, thrift-store blouses, pajamas, or skirts.

There are many recipes online now for making home-prepared herbal or felted soaps. For lazured rooms, renowned anthroposophical lazure artist Charles Andrade has created reasonably priced lazure painting kits sold online to allow families and individuals to lazure their own home and work-space walls.

If the child is in a place where there is little access to nature or plants, fill the house with non-toxic plants and let the baby see seeds sprouting and other things growing. If you live in a home in an urban center, or in an apartment with no outside gardens that allow play time in the soil, greening your home is becoming more creative today than ever. There is a seeming endless array of ecologically sustainable pots for indoor planting, as well as wall hangings with earthen pockets for growing plants on a wall or on indoor patio pillars with a light source. Give the child regular experiences to smell and feel organic, high-enzyme, well-composted-mulched-aerated soils.

Yiana Belkalopolos

Staying Close, Keeping Resonant

For a very traumatized child, it is good for the caregiver to keep the child in close touch proximity for significant periods of the day. Holding the child more regularly can be helpful for a time. Babies can sleep in a baby sling on the caregiver's back or belly while the caregiver does regular household tasks such as cooking, cleaning, washing, making crafts, or even playing a gentle musical instrument, writing by hand, or gardening.

This will be temporary but important for the child to experience consistent touch, the warm-heartedness of the caregiver on a moment-to-moment basis, and frequent, soft moments of "right eye to right eye" contact, where the caregiver holds the child in his or her left arm and gazes to the child's right eye.

Try to keep up regular activity as much as possible but be prepared for outbursts or other expressions as the child unwinds what he or she may have been holding inside while unsafe. Gently affirm for them that you hear them and that you understand.

Affirm the child's pain and, in time, that child will feel free to let it go. If the child's need to be noticed and attended to is neglected while processing trauma, the child will build up a greater need for attention that could easily become some level of compulsive or addictive, compensatory behavior down the road. Any child can internalize a level of low self-respect that gets missed by sensitive adults, with the child moving into too much aggressive mimicry of the close adults, for acceptance and survival. This aggression needs transformation through consistent healing and loving patterning by the parents.

This does not mean that the caregiver must get into hovering parent behavior. An affirming humming sound or short affirmations that you are there and aware of the child's potential feelings is helpful while the child explores on their own. Even a few strums on the guitar or a small lyre or harp, or the calming sounds of a wooden flute, are enough to show that you are gentling the space for a child, and noticing them regularly, and that can be enough. Avoid ignoring neediness in the early stages of trauma processing.

Nursing Mothers

If a mother is nursing, it is good to remember that stress chemicals easily affect a mother's milk as they are released into the blood from neurological triggers. Self-care is important for a mother who is caring for an infant or child who has been significantly traumatized.

Creating an anthroposophical environment and atmosphere can be soul-calming for mothers and caregivers as well as the children. Many Waldorf mothers find themselves significantly changing the atmosphere at home. Taking a mindful few moments to soak in the warm colors of a lazured room, while lighting a candle and watching the light dance for a few moments before breastfeeding, can bring just the necessary calming mood to the mother and the baby, as well.

A nursing mother can also chip a piece of natural, herbal-scented soap into a specially colored, second-hand store bowl, filled with boiling water, allowing the aromas to fill the room both inexpensively and easily. Putting a small towel beside the aroma bowl, on a table by the nursing chair or bed, can let a mother dip her free hand from time to time in the cooling, scented water and wipe her brow, the back of her neck, or her upper chest. This can bring calming and an awareness of the soulfulness of connecting with the baby and with nature at the same time. Olive-oil based, herbal-scented soaps are good for this and easy on the skin.

A baby's digestion may or may not react immediately to early tensions between parents, but it could develop something chronic as the child grows and continues to be exposed to parent divorce tensions. Also, any kind of constant fight, flight, or freeze response that the baby might have to harsh sounds or danger signs in the parents can cause a restriction in digestion or elimination. This is a natural, neurological reaction stemming from the earliest-developed aspects of the baby's protective signal center in the brain, the amygdala. Rudolf Steiner referred to the malformation that can happen in the development of the organs, such as the liver, when child's etheric forces are pressed upon by levels of emotional hardness from adults.

Sometimes it is the father or another male caregiver who must take up the care and feeding of an infant after a parental conflict or divorce. It is important to not become gender identified when it comes to feeding or caring for traumatized children. There is no male or female way to care for a child in this case. What is needed is simply a loving, attentive, naturally calming process, with lots of patient, warm-hearted breathing, as well as sensitive effort around making the feeding environment calm and sensually natural and appealing.

Rudolf Steiner clearly indicated to anthroposophical medical doctors, and to teachers, that what happens in the first three to seven years of life can affect the capable development of the child's inner body organs and thus the regulatory life systems. This includes the nervous system. In a world of over-stimulation at every turn, and particularly for families with a great deal of tension, the old notion that a baby must be stimulated early and often, to think and engage with the outside world and other children, is not a set rule or recommended now in many cases.[50] Allowing the child to take on what he or she signals readiness for is much more the norm in anthroposophy and Waldorf-based early-childhood parenting.

This means that parents or caregivers are mindful and attending to the wholeness of the metaphorical garden around the child. This is necessary for the child to be ready to take the next growth steps in tune with the child's own inner-soul forces. That tending also requires that the parents tend to their own inner work and relationship wholeness. Encouraging parents who get caught in conflict to do anthroposophical biography work offers a wholesome process for parents to work on their own inner healing issues.[51]

This is often not possible in conflictual relationships or divorces. Even if one parent, however, tends to the inner soul-processing work well and with conscious skill, this can have a strong effect on the child. It is naïve, though, to think that this is all that will be necessary for the child. These issues are not simple, but once one is started on the conscious path to healing child trauma, other insights will reveal themselves, and a collective sharing of insights brings the wisdom and collective heart of the community to light for the sake of the child.

Yiana Belkalopolos

The Two-Year-Old Ego Flare

One big toddler development period occurs, in clearly attuned rhythm with the child's own soul forces, around the ages of two to three. That is often when the parents experience the child speaking for individual desires and rejecting the mother's and father's directives. "No" becomes a big word for the child of two to three as the child asserts a level of deep innate knowing that cannot be expressed in any other whole or capable way yet.

While the child is resisting parental control, to assert the tiniest new levels of independence, the parents still need to be deeply present to the child and the the close, warm, and attentive tending of the "soil" around the child's explorations. Parents still need to assert the natural and nurturing elements of safety, predictability, and truly felt-sense heart love. This requires huge patience, and a sense of non-derogatory humor, but it is worth it later.

Parents and other caregivers should not associate this early toddler rebellion with anything having to do with the marriage breakup, with the other parent's "bad parenting," or any other deficiency in one or other of the parents. Two-year-old rebellion is normal, and it is important to not project any more tension onto it than it already creates, especially for new parents on their first time around.

There are many resources today for parents and caregivers on the anthroposophical development of wholeness for very young children, including Karl Koenig's *The First Three Years*[52] and *Simplicity Parenting*[53] by Kim Payne. They are among dozens of other resources available in anthroposophical bookstores, and online, giving helpful Waldorf approaches to overseeing a child's development in all aspects.[v]

The outcomes for people who have had their childhoods held well with anthroposophical approaches, as witnessed phenomenologically and empirically[54], show the strong ability of these children to grow into steady-on-their-feet adults who can face the myriad outer-world challenges of our times with a healthy sense of personal freedom and extensive skills for scientific and creative work, social cooperation, and practical collaboration. Unfortunately, there has been no research data on the strengths and gifts of Pearls who grow up in anthroposophical environments. Yet, anthroposophists who have worked with them know that Pearls can have effective practical skills, intuitive, imaginative, and inspirational thinking leading to creativity and innovation, and a sense for the necessary and healthy rhythms in daily life. Their human potentials fall within a healthy spectrum of capable people.

An increasing number of Pearl Adults hold valuable memories of having dedicated caregivers in their childhoods, having experienced inspirational, heartwarming will-engaged activities in creative, inter-collaborative, commons-like communities and intentional living communities in North America, northern Europe, and in the United States. (Some of the progressive

---

v   Personal care specifically for parents in divorce cannot be further elucidated in the space of this book, but many resources are available now in mainstream, book-sourcing centers.

work of young anthroposophical students today will be explained in the section on threefold social order[55] and the story of Forest in Chapter Seven.)

Waldorf graduates often have natural, holistic, diversity-honoring, balanced, socio-economic-cultural-spiritual perspectives on life. They carry capacities for pure thinking and higher-mind approaches to problem-solving without getting disconnected from humane intentions or from nature. Increasingly, Pearl adolescents and young adults find a place in such company and in anthroposophical communities.

Marriage and Moral/Cosmic Law

Earthly and cosmic laws were known and understood in ancient mystery schools the world over through the post-Atlantean era. Middle Ages Europeans were aware of such honorable laws residing in the spiritual wisdom of the Templar Knights. Great masters wove these truths within the inspiring imaginations of the artistic and masterful craftwork and masonry of the European Renaissance period. The paintings and drawings of Leonardo da Vinci and Raphael, the sculptures and frescoes of Michelangelo, and the grand cosmic structures of Chartres Cathedral in France[56] reflect the mystery-school wisdom.

These outer laws are reflected practically and artistically in the mathematics and geometry that affect our everyday lives, though we are often not conscious of them. In the past, these laws were understood as being connected to both inner and outer, soul and spirit needs. They informed the moral righteousness of our human working in society and life. Anthroposophy is one of the great wisdom paths helping humanity to restore its connection to the soul-spiritual truths as they have adjusted in our time, accordingly, through lawful, evolving advances.

These natural, soul-spirit orders lie within the features of the Golden Mean[57], the series of set and reproducing ratios that are present in the fundamental structures of plants, animals, and the human body. People have known the dependable nature of these cosmic-earthly laws that permeate all life on earth. When human life is attuned to the rhythms and patterns informing this lawfulness, life feels right and whole.

When life goes awry or even chaotic for a period, coming back into rhythm and structure can help guide Pearls back into soul harmony. They sleep better and experience less anxiety, despite evolutionary and even revolutionary change around them. Since many cosmic laws around in our solar system are undeniable and consistent, despite some perilous human activity on the earthly plane, a very distraught person can find one level of stability and comfort by knowing that every aspect of their human beingness is reflected in the laws of the universe. They are star matter, and they are entirely a part of all that happens on this earth. This is the place where they are meant to be, and they are welcome to be the very human being that they are.

Individuals can do practices to remind them of their lawful connection to the earth and the heavens. By doing so, they reaffirm an inner, lawful soul hologram of consistent, holistic truth about who they are and how they fit the world and the times.

A clear demonstration of the Golden Mean lawfulness is in the spiraling shape of seeds in a sunflower or the spiral of a nautilus shell. Varied lawful patterns permeate chemical structures and the planetary orbits of our solar system, as well as musical theory. They show up in everything living on the earth as structures underlying all that holds form. They move in higher and finer eternal integrity in the living world just as the cosmos mirrors it to us.

Figure 3.2: The Golden Mean in nature

A well-understood cosmic-earthly lawfulness exists in nature. The Golden Mean is an expanding number sequence made manifest and visible in spiral formations in plants, animals, the human being, and in cosmic phenomena.

Figure 3.3: Fibonacci sequence – numerical

The Fibonacci Sequence

1,1,2,3,5,8,13,21,34,55,89,144,233,377…

1+1=2	13+21=34
1+2=3	21+34=55
2+3=5	34+55=89
3+5=8	55+89=144
5+8=13	89+144=233
8+13=21	144+233=377

In the fibonnaci number sequence, each number in the sequence is the sum of the two numbers that precede it. Thus, each starting number in the next addition sentence is the second factor number of the first addition sentence that is added to the sum number in the first addition sentence. 1+1=2 is followed by the last two numbers becoming the new factor numbers in the next addition sentence: 1+2=3. These last two numbers, and 3 become the addition factors in the next addition sentence:,2+3=5, 3+5=8, 5+8=13 etc.

The Fibonacci sequence is a number series observed in living nature that moves natural growth in earthly things from a simple and base development through a sequential, measurable, expanding, and often spiraling progression.

Figure 3.4: Cosmic Fibonacci with verse

Cosmic nebulae can appear in a similar spiral to the Fibonnaci spiral in the earthly plant. Here is a verse for children or adults to show the wonder of the Fibonacci spiral mirrored in the stars that can lift our sense of spiritual wonder in the dark night or in dark emotional moments.

Within wondrous cosmic light on high,
lives the self-same patterned life,
that in our human nature grows,
inspiring hearts in darkest woes.

Figure 3.5: The Fibonacci sequence on a grid with verse

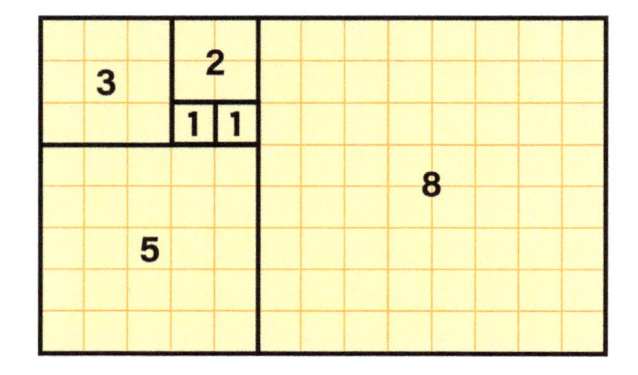

A geometric drawing grid shows the pure Fibonnaci pattern in number only – as if on tiles on the ground floor of a building. The motion of the numbers moving around the tiles is the same motion of cosmic formative forces in nature.

Fibonacci curls my fate,
1+1, 3, 5, 8.
Moving right, up, left, down, 'round,
grows life forces, stars to ground.

Figure 3.6: Classic Fibonacci in a rectangle with verse

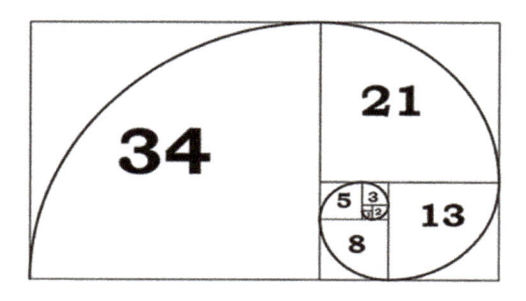

Here is the floor version without the tiles, drawn in reverse, showing the verstility of the sequence when made into a line pattern. Versatility in life offers a sense of the freedom of the cosmic life forces. The accompanying verse suggests directing one's gaze along the line as if unfurling out of the center of the spiral and also gazing along back into the tight center of the spiral for a balance of attention and inner, etheric motion.

Fibonacci starts my whirl,
letting free forces unfurl.
Yet, to keep my balance true,
lawful in-out spirals rule.

Figure 3.7: Fibonacci conch shell with verse

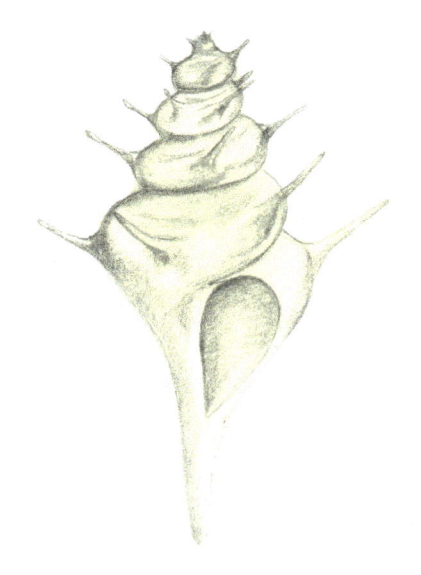

Even within the formative forces of the ocean, the Fibonacci unfurls from a simple, tight equation to an expansive form that stays in an elegant lawfulness. The verse speaks to the wondrous sense of an artistic harmony and aesthetic in the sequence as it sculpts natural earthen forms within the rhythms of the ocean's tides.

Lively ocean waters pool,
to sculpt sea creatures' homes to rule.
A shell to house a beauteous life,
flows in rhythms with the tide.

Figure 3.8: Fibonacci plant with verse

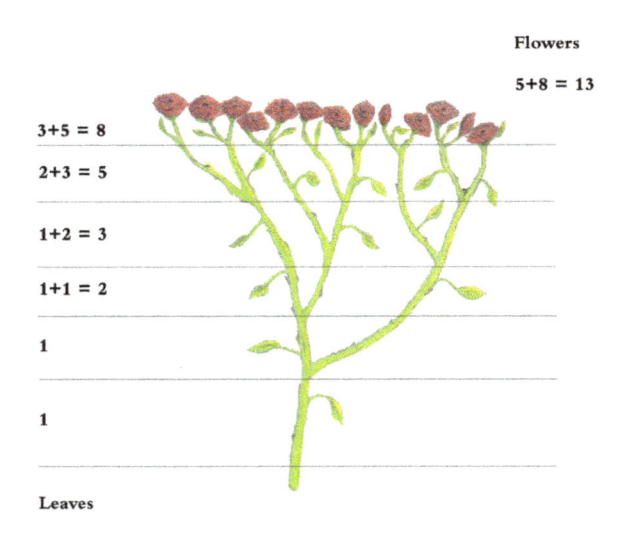

Flowers
5+8 = 13

3+5 = 8
2+3 = 5
1+2 = 3
1+1 = 2
1
1

Leaves

A plant stems and blossoms in Fibonacci rhythms.

Though a seed roots life below,
beyond the seedling we can know;
branches, leaves, and budding blossoms,
fill the spring with ordered offerings.

Figure 3.9: The Fibonacci nature of the embryo with verse

The Pearl and the Hut

Artist's renditions of a stylized tree and of an embryo in nubile life-growth forces. The Fibonacci similarities are visible in the unfolding growth of the embryo and that of the tree branches that also resemble the nerves of the brain. The sequence that is perfect in higher thinking manifests imperfectly in nature, but with identifiable similarity.

Cosmic unfolding begins human life,
from mysteries contained in minutest space.
How comes this body from a simple seed?
What force has brought about this great deed?

Cosmic-earthly laws manifest in nature in degrees of perfection. There is nothing stagnant in earthen life, since everything in life has fixed, mutable, and cardinal patterns, with cycles and repetitions of life and death. That means that their growth seems at times to stay still, become flexible or changing, and then move actively forward at certain points. They do so even if only on a minute, molecular level not noticeable to the unaided eye or to the other outer senses.

Active periods turn into more slowed and seeming still periods again, and flexible periods have different rates of flexibility. Growth sequences in earthly and human developments present what feel like peaceful or harmonic states, move through variations and deviations into gross or subtle dissonances that feel disturbing and stressful, and then onto homeostatic harmonies again.

In this way, although the Golden Mean archetypically and mathematically has certain set ratios; as, for instance, related to the human body and the lengths and segmentations of the limbs of the human body, these ratios are reflected with small imperfections or variations when present in a real, and whole, human body. Dissonances in growth show up in disease or formations outside of the lawful archetype, such as when a person is born with a missing or poorly formed body limb. Human beings recognize a problem with the lawfulness of a malformed limb in a newborn baby and usually work diligently to help that child to have a fully functioning body, perhaps by creating a prosthetic limb.

This is how we all know a sense of order, but also, accept that earthen life does not always fit an absolute and perfect, non-adapting form, despite that fact that all things living have some set, and recognizable, form. For instance, we know that some parts of the human archetypal body have disappeared in time, or have remained but lost much of their use, such as the tonsils and appendix. Though the lawfulness of form is still there in the human body with these organs, the lawful usefulness no longer serves human beings. Many people have these organs removed without consequence.

These lawful determinants, of which Rudolf Steiner and the mystery-school teachers of old have reminded us, come not out of earthy life alone, but from ongoing planetary and star effects influencing all earthly and human development. Out of the spiritual cosmos they offer higher intelligence, and onto the earth, they offer direction, structure, love, and moral-ethical insights.

One example of a lawfully attuned variation in geometry, being examined for its relationship to the heart and the sequence of earthly building blocks called the Platonic Solids,[58] is in Frank Chester's heart geometry[59] in the last chapter of Volume II. Since certain geometry is lawfully connected to human development, geometry can literally give a soul-spirit reflection of what is changing and developing in the literal, physical hearts of human beings.

(In Volume II, we'll see how Rudolf Steiner has indicated that a lawful developmental change, starting to happen in the human heart today, on subtle body levels, is preparing the way for significant lawful change in the physical heart in the future. It will change humans as we evolve well into the sixth post-Atlantean epoch. The formative life forces affecting the emergence of this heart change are capable of becoming powerfully consistent in human beings who connect with them through sacred practices in the present and in the future of humanity.[60] This will fulfill what great initiates through time have prophesied and sought to describe in poetry, prayer, parables, and songs.)

Old Roman Marital Laws

In the West, there are old Roman social laws that persist today in fixed ways due to humanity's attachment to holding on to unfree traditions around blood-lineage and material ownership. According to anthroposophical wisdom, much in these laws now have no soul-spiritual bearing on our present times. These old laws are naturally receding and slowly being replaced by a new, conscious experience of soul relationships and community.

The transition has been awkward and severely distressing for individuals and society. It has come, partly, out of the freeing impulse of Christ consciousness that is rejecting certain untruthful human laws that were imposed in the Roman cultural epoch. Many who resist have brought heavy stigmatization to families that change, a reaction coming out of an ancient, "illegitimate" social-status mindset regarding children who were not living in legally recognized marriages between their parents.

Roman marriage was not originally organized for the sake of love, but rather to produce children to continue the race and to help with family farms and businesses. Marriage was an economic contract. Children born into a legal marriage would be considered legitimate heirs to their father's property. Legal marriage bestowed citizenship on a couple and their children. If you were born outside of a legally recognized marriage between citizens, then you were inferior in the eyes of the law. You had few rights and an uncertain economic future.

Your lack of access to responsible activity in the "polis" or city center meant that you had far less chance of personal development, advancement, or freedom. You became a lowly servant or slave to economic masters. Religion strove to keep the lowly people within acceptable behavior in the eyes of the business leaders.

This was a distorted twist on the truths of Christ's teachings, brought during the changeover from the Greek human consciousness development epoch to the Roman one. Despite the new spiritual laws that Christ pointed to as cosmically correct changes for the new epoch and beyond, Roman leaders maintained the olden patrilineal culture that had been dominant prior to the coming of Christ.

Following on ancient cosmic-spiritual developments foretold in Jewish, Egyptian, Persian, and East-Indian sacred texts, Christ had changed those rules for all beings. Yet, even lineages of Roman clergy who accepted Christ's teachings reverted to old beliefs eight centuries after Christ's death. They were not prepared for the spiritual freedoms of individuals, and even less prepared to move from economic domination and control to recognizing the rights and economic capacities of all.

Originally, in the era of the dominant Roman Empire, women had no say in who they married. Parents chose the groom for the young woman. Girls were normally married at age fourteen, although some were betrothed as young as seven years old.[61] Women were expected to remain under the *manus* or control of their fathers when they married, except in the case of marriage to a priest of Jupiter. In this case, the wife came under the control of the priest under certain religious rites. In this way, the woman was also made a citizen.

Slaves could establish a relationship known as a contubernium,[62] which allowed for children to be born to slaves. Such an arrangement needed the permission of the slave owner and the couple remained non-citizens. If a woman had no legal status to become a wife due to being of a lower class, she could be a concubine with no legal protection but with recognition by society that she was a permanent feature in her partner's life. A widower might free a slave and take her as a concubine. Slaves who had been legally freed became citizens, but they could only marry if they had their patron's permission.

Many such patriarchal marriage laws, based on material ownership, still exist in various places in the world, such as in many Middle Eastern, Eastern European, and Asian countries, although this is now changing. Changes to the status of women in marriage relationships in the Western "advanced" countries only came into effect in the last century, and only on a grand scale in the last five or six decades. This has not come easily or without great social conflict.

In most countries, there are people who still seek to set back the free status of women in marriages and other forms of relationship. They would attempt to return to an old lawfulness that does not reflect the new lawful variations being brought by the advancing human and spiritual consciousness of our era, as initiated by the Christ. Thus, they don't mirror the nature of spiritual truth and freedoms. They are unlawful, and human beings recognize this on some levels, although many don't know yet how to express this deeply in their consciousness and move forward into the new ways. That is because human focus has not yet found the right soul-spirit-materialism balance for our times and that the Christ heralded. Has modern divorce been the only way for some to break the heavy, old and material blood bonds?

A modern question arises regarding whether the divorce phenomenon of recent times reflects a true variation to lawful relationships that was needed for advancing freedom. Was there another method of freeing relationships being called into form in our times, yet left uninvestigated by some for the sake of sensual and material desire and convenience, rather than spiritual, social truth?

Clearly, a great many children of divorce feel deep soul offense from the way that family breakups have happened and disregarded their developmental needs. This may well suggest that something did not fit the emerging, newly lawful pattern in familial relationships.

Men and women in the West enter marriage relationships more freely now and with the choice to dissolve a relationship when it no longer suits the circumstances of what they see as a freely evolving society and personal life. Yet, the economic status and rights issues have been much slower and harder to reconcile and bring into spiritual wholeness. The child neglect and abandonment issues remain some of the most dysfunctional symptoms of a humanity looking to free itself of the old paradigms.

As lawfulness cycles come back around, this revisiting of the balances of freedom and form in relationships, especially where the raising of children is involved, is one of the main dissonant points today in the changes of marriage and family status and the raising of Pearl Children. The question of responsible parenting in divorce matters is very much up in our spiritual, economic, and litigious times.

Since not enough generations of Pearls have had time to bring their say into the fold of this issue in our times, it may be that we have not reached the full lawful variation regarding new parent relations, relationship breakups, and the moral issues of child-raising in the middle of such a widely divisive divorce phenomenon. When significant generations of growing children become thrown into dangerous suffering due to new social contracts in which they have no say, society cannot simply take one view over the other and claim that the emotional outbursts and adjustment problems are with the children and not with the adults and the social contract itself.

The laws of Platonic Solids and evolution can bring a much more complete, and truthful, picture of what it really takes to innovate a new variation of soul-spiritual lawfulness. There is nothing simple, easy, or quick about it. In some ways, Pearl Adults as children have been thrown into the dark side of quick and easy relationship dissolutions. Others took the painful issues upon themselves. A few have been able to hold a more conscious, open-heartedness with former spouses in their own divorces, sensing that the divorce issues need much more visitation and clearer thinking on the part of parents first, for the sake of healthy, whole children.

True Christian consciousness laws, based on the true, maturing freedoms of all individuals to receive the power of divinity and life-direction into themselves (through the masculine-feminine integrated Christ sun-being), became distorted by the Roman church fathers during the Ecumenical Council of Constantinople in 869 AD. This is when congregants other than clergy were informed that they were only composed of body and soul, and that spirit could only be accessed through the patriarchal church priests, not by the congregants of the church or individuals themselves. This was a regression of Christ's teachings, back to old testament ways.

When male priests decided that human beings could not be trusted to take up spiritual life freely for themselves, despite the truth of the teachings of the Christ himself, human society experienced a grave setback. This edict also preserved a psychological distortion for women who continued to be dominated by men who, through olden biblical beliefs, assumed a sense of greater righteousness over women, despite the true teachings of Christ. The Ecumenical Council allowed the church males to presume that women could never reach their own spiritual truth by themselves, thus preserving a dependency and perceived deficiency in women rather than an increasing equality worthy of a higher, spiritual, male-female harmony. These were old economic, enslaving standards that divorced the clergy and mass congregations of worshippers from Christ's true teachings.

Real freedoms, although outlined in the Gospels, became curtailed by these new Roman religious beliefs in the ninth century. By example, a female figure as important as Mary Magdalene was painted for centuries as a lowly whore rather than as the legitimate free woman that she was, steeped in the deepest understandings of spiritual laws. (Recently, the Roman Catholic Pope, Francis, has rescinded some of the shadow status that the church bestowed on Mary Magdalene, recognizing her as the forgiven and legitimate apostle and the beloved disciple of Christ that she was.)[63]

The modern battle of the sexes in the last six decades, which has been partially responsible for the strained relations in marriages and divorces, came about as a rebellion against the heavy-handed issuances of the priesthood in Roman times.

Some children of divorce, whose parents have managed the breakup amicably, have created a more harmonic, grounded, and forgiving experience in the family divorce. Pearls whose divorced parents truly overcame bitterness and animosity toward their former spouses tend to feel calmer and are more comfortable with their incarnation. They feel at ease and in their rightful place on the earth. Their parents have approached the breakdown in marriage with fairness, conscious co-parenting, and with mature empathy for themselves and their former spouse. They have also tended more closely to the emotional upheavals and *etheric* "needs-management" of their children. Some carry a real sense of soul friendship with their former spouse.

This is in great contrast to the lives of many others whose parents dealt with breakups (or continue to deal with breakups) by ignoring feelings and needs, blaming each other for the marriage breakup, or disregarding the real, internal challenges for the children. Few, in this case, have begun to look at the bigger heart picture.

Going Higher in Human Behavior in the Midst of Strife

Human beings are higher beings with greater capacities than animals and plants. Humans have the potential to advance, out of their own free will, in spiritual truth and thus in the variations of lawfulness, even down to genetic changes. Human thoughts, however, if not elevated in higher lawfulness, can hold back a healthy level of evolution through attempts to stagnate the true etheric life forces in others that are naturally available through committed spiritual consciousness. This is an awareness that is free to be taken up individually by human beings.

It is easy in these massive, human-transitioning times, for people to become confused about the evolution of cosmic-spiritual laws and what they mean for human beings. The complexity of the changes taxes a person's sense of how these modern-world transformations will affect their humanness here and now, and their survival for a full lifetime, or for the health of the soul for millennia to come.

In the human, soul-descending past, as people strove to deepen their connection with earthly matter and organic cycles, they lost touch with direct impulses from the spiritual world. People followed orders of patriarchal family law and religious leaders. These laws were designed to bring certain disciplines into group activities while humanity was in a descent into a heavier, earthly integration. People were going to be taught earth-orientation laws to keep sharing the earth's resources in specific and orderly ways depending on the resource and technology circumstances of the times in different regions of the world.

This is the history of the Christian Old Testament. These laws were of the bloodlines of tribes and religions, with the elevation of initiated priests, and the secret preservation of the highest holy teachings above the everyday consciousness of most working-world people. People would only be exposed to higher-world knowledge through lower rituals performed by priests and priestesses at holy sites, sacred healing centers, and temples. The highest understandings were studied and protected by initiates and developing initiates, who put full focus on priestly practices and preparations for ritual and sacred celebrations to be performed at lawful times for the masses. The great initiates knew that in time the sacred wisdom would come out to all. Prophets foretold some of this to the everyday people.

The New, Christ-Taught Approach to Lawfulness

Two millennia ago, at the time of the lowest descent of spiritual mankind on the hardened earth, the deed of Christ brought the new word of the whole and highest, unified godhead. At the epitome of humanity's education about earthly matter and earthen life, and also at the greatest state of human decadence about it all, the son of God came to reveal how every human being was to begin to loosen from the old laws and from a materialistic belief about life.

Human beings would be preparing from then on to return to the spiritual world, away from the earth, for good. That process would take several millennia, but souls were going to need to learn how to bring what they had learned about being human on earth with them. They would have to purify their understandings of the value of a human life first. This was symbolized by Mary Magdalene washing the feet of Christ and anointing him before his crucifixion.

The new understandings of how to interpret one's life in the light of a soul-ascent process, rather than a descent one, came through Christ. The lessons and practices of life now had to be about how to lighten and enliven inwardly what one had learned in the heart and soul as a reflection of human-cosmic good.

Through the teachings first delineated in the recollections of Christ's apostles in the Christian Gospels, Christ's life and parables brought indications as to how people who cared for the highest life could bring the most important essences of the earth learnings with them as they began the ascent to the light and spirit of the cosmic heavens, and to the life away from earth that would come in time. This vessel of human wisdom that will distill and etherize all human experience and bring it as an inner chalice into the heavens, is the human heart.

Lawfulness now was going to be directed not through old earthen laws, but increasingly through the cosmic order and the karma purifying ways that each person would find to make the trip back home to God. Individuals would be given the direct help from divine grace to refine, cleanse, and etherize the life that they had led on earth. The Christ guidance would help them distill toward the heart center all essence of that experience, essentially transforming into "light luggage" their human experiences for the journey beyond the earth in a few more millennia. The heart is increasingly becoming the final vessel of humanity's human treasury.

According to the Christ, and later explained in more specific ways by the higher servants that he initiated, the heart is about to transform—even physiologically. It will hold the human offerings of our most important earthly experience—those of love—and then alchemize them into a new kind of essence that will be held in the soul when we pass the earthen-body threshold. This happens on certain levels every lifetime now when we die, but it will reach a full and final rapture well ahead into the future.

How we go forward in lawfulness now and in the future is going to be different for every human being, with some similarities. That is because different life experiences, with unique karmic issues, will be cleansed and resolved in individual ways out of each person's increasing understandings of what has happened in his or her soul throughout past earthly lifetimes. The veils to our spiritual existence that fell over human consciousness at the time of the *fall* into matter and earthly learning, will increasingly fall away. We will see in this dissolution of the old what needs to be attuned through love and self-discipline, and repaired among others, in order that we may move on when the stars of heavenly ascension make their final call to us.

Cleansing through the Eight-Fold Path

The Christ consciousness, which is present and available to anyone in the world who seeks to attune to that heart and light consciousness, even if they do not consider themselves "Christ"-inspired beings, is flooding humanity with ever profound forces now in the Consciousness Soul era. That means that we are not in need of others to follow, but rather that we can each help direct each other to the conscious lawfulness of ascension, wherever we are on the earth.

The earthen sacred sites and centers will be less and less necessary, as we fill our own practices and hearts with understanding, moment to moment. We will still need to take care of earthly human needs, including homesteads of increasingly communal nature, but in a way that does not drag individuals down into an old, overly earthen heaviness. We are refining slowly away from the earthen consciousness while keeping as naturally and healthily awake for the transformations that will continue for a few more millennia to come. Both helpful and unhelpful technologies will accompany our journey through the Anglo-Germanic epoch and beyond, making the soul-spirit process a highly vigilant one. We are in the process of discovering which of these technologies will truly free us and which will bind us too heavily to the earth.

It can seem mentally challenging to perceive what is a cosmically natural and evolving change in oneself and how it relates to inner and outer personal activity. That is because we have moved recently from Intellectual Soul consciousness into Consciousness Soul awareness. We will not understand everything now through mental attachments. We will, however, understand much more through heartfelt intuition, imagination, and divine inspiration that can come through paying close attention to practices that keep us inwardly cleansed and bathed in human compassion rather than selfish egoism.

For growing children, the indicators of wholeness and attunement come through the natural harmony of their fourfold physical, etheric, astral, and I-being development. For adults, we have manifold ways to keep our thinking and feeling spiritually tuned and resonant today. Some are indicated through the chapters of this book. In societal working, anthroposophy has also offered understanding through the threefold social order[64] and the perceptions of Steiner's world economy.[65] These are discussed further in Chapter Seven.

Discerning truth in the Consciousness Soul times means being able to look at ourselves objectively while not losing touch with our subjective intuitions and needs for taking up individual karmic issues, purifying them and doing the restitution work. We don't give ourselves away to simply personal opinion, nor fully into the details of other people's points of view without thought and contemplation. If we become too subjective and can't see objectively into ourselves in life with others, then we are likely to get caught in imposing personal opinions on others rather than true perceptions about what other souls around us in these times are truly destined to do. We can lose our spiritual truth in the morass of emotions, desires, accumulated grievances, false protections, and projections.

To prune and stabilize these consciousness swings, Rudolf Steiner proposed practices to cultivate conscious equanimity in times of challenge as well as in times of ease and well-being. These practices emerge out of a next-stage evolution of olden Buddhist practices as the anthroposophical Eight-Fold Path.[66]

The Eight-Fold Path

Saturday: Right Thinking	(Richtige Meinung oder Anschauung)
Sunday: Right Resolves	(Richtiges Urteilen oder Denken)
Monday: Right Speaking	(Richtiges Wort)
Tuesday: Right Action	(Richtige Handlungsweise)
Wednesday: Right Way of Life	(Richtiger Standort oder richtiger Lebensberuf)
Thursday: Right Endeavor	(Richtige Gewohnheit, richtiges Streben)
Friday: Right Remembrance	(Richtiges Gedächtnis oder richtige Achtsamkeit)
Plus: Right Meditation	(Richtige Beschaulichkeit oder Versenkung)

Eight-Fold Path Exercises

Saturday — Right Thinking

Admit only significant ideas and thoughts. Learn gradually to separate the important from the unimportant, the real from the unreal, the eternal from the ephemeral, the true from the false. Listen to what people say with inner quietness, refraining from approving or disapproving judgment and from criticism. In this way, one arrives at the habit of forming opinions that are not influenced by sympathy or antipathy.

Sunday — Right Resolves

Cultivate steadfastness. Make resolutions only after full consideration of even the most insignificant points. Avoid thoughtless acts and meaningless ones. For every act, have sufficient reasons. Do no needless thing. When convinced of the rightness of a resolve, abide by it unfalteringly.

Monday — Right Speaking

In speech with others, say only what has sense and meaning. Make your conversation thoughtful. Do not be afraid to be silent often. Try not to use too many or too few words. Never talk for the sake of talking, or merely to pass the time.

Tuesday — Right Action

Make your actions as far as possible harmonious with your surroundings. Weigh all actions carefully so that the eternal may speak through them, so that they may be good for the whole and for the lasting welfare of others.

Wednesday — Right Way of Life

In the management of life, seek to live in conformity with both nature and spirit. Be neither over-hasty nor idle. Look upon life as an opportunity for work and development, and to live accordingly.

Thursday — Right Endeavor

Do not attempt what is beyond your powers, but also omit nothing for which they seem adequate. Set before yourself ideals that coincide with the highest ideals of a human being; for example, the aim of practicing such exercises as these is to be able better to help and advise one's fellow human beings, if not immediately, then later in life. One can also say that this exercise consists of making all these exercises into a habit of life.

Friday — Right Remembrance

Strive to learn as much as possible from life. All experiences have something to teach. When opportunity offers, one should handle a situation more wisely than previously. Experience is a rich treasure, and one should consult it before doing anything. Watch the actions of others and compare them with the ideal—but lovingly, not critically. One can learn much from observing others, including children. Aim to remember all that one has learned in this way.

To Accompany Each of the Above — Right Meditation

Each day, at the same time, if possible, turn inward and take stock, test one's way of life, run over one's store of knowledge, ponder one's duties, consider the aim and true purposes of life, reflect on one's own imperfections and mistakes. In short, distinguish what is significant and of lasting value, and renew one's resolve to take up worthwhile tasks.

Marriage Today

Cultivating greater consciousness and cleaner responses to relationship problems and crises is the mark of successful partnerships today, and successful relationship dissolutions as well. This is necessary in intimate relationships and especially those in which the foundations of children's whole future lives are being cultivated.

Marriage, or partnerships within which couples are raising children, are still earthen crucibles of change. Because of natural earthly stresses, the immature human soul tendency is to want marriage relationships to be perfect, purified, and easy sanctuaries of love, offering relative comfort, convenience, but also regular, hidden self-indulgences. We shut out any conscious understanding about what those indulgences represent and why we consider them something to be hidden and repressed, rather than working them into healthy understanding with soul practices. In this way, we repress the chance to deepen inner forces of soul that can offer more inner stability as well as flexibility, including more freedom from anxiety and sleeplessness.

We essentially pretend away a dark double side of ourselves by walling it up inwardly, in order to carry on a life of money-making and the externalization of a perfect, good-life fantasy that can only bring ease through greater and greater accumulation of things or the fiats that represent things. When the excess wealth is not there to keep up the perfection fantasy, or it disappears, there is little or no goodness between people, since meager soul substance has been cultivated. Despair and/or hatred arises out of soul-depravity.

This creates a hardened, tired, rejecting soul that doesn't find an appropriate energetic outlet on earth, which can literally lash out at others and even reject the whole world with death fantasies. Whole aspects of our naturally inner, supple nature get iron-shut, and we become like prisoners in our self-created reality, continually rattling up against ourselves but blaming others for our discomfort.

We shut out a side of ourselves that could become a compassionate force of good toward others. Since we're denying natural aspects of human nature, we project exclusion and hate upon others when the dark inner dragon arises. Or, we indulge it with irreverent rejection of others who we expect to judge us for even having a dark side of ourselves at all. We set up a constant battle, with ourselves or with others. Marriage or close relationships become battlefields or military bunkers.

Raising sacred, incarnate human beings who maintain soul connection with themselves and others for upwards of seventy or more years of life is much like running a kind of sustainable, organic garden-farm rather than a military organization. It is a garden requiring habitual attending, exertion, and full engagement with the beauty of life, but also acceptance of the need sometimes of digging into human understanding from cosmic-earthly awareness and working the muckier soil issues into lawfulness again. Compassion for the human soul-struggle is paramount to the success of a lawful human sustainability on the earth that allows individuals the inner foundations to cultivate a soul capable of enlightening appropriately into an ascendant state in the distant future.

With faith in the regularly life-giving aspects of reconstituting our earthen, inner foundations with spirit-light awareness, we gain respect for the cyclical processes of inner and outer growth. We notice our responses to the natural elements of earth/water/fire/air, recognize the human need for sustained warmth to nourish a living heart, observe, weed, and prune unhelpful negative thoughts and energetic distractions, celebrate the blossoming and flowering gifts of original and heart-connected ideas, harvest the fruits of those ideas in order to feed the hearts and souls of others, and allow natural downtime for reseeding, composting, and an enlivened, human-lifted re-sprouting of goodness in relationships.

We tend the laws of the earth as they apply to the less noticeable laws of the cosmos in order to create a truly soul-protective lawfulness unbound by blood but entirely related to a sustainable brotherhood-sisterhood.

Out of our old consciousness, we simply expect that someone in our direct family will be by our side through anything, out of a base belief in genetic blood bonds that need no work, no growth, and are just a forced attachment. When the soul naturally strives for a true soul-spirit freedom, one that does not require running away anywhere but rather a coming closer to oneself as a human being, it cannot remain in this blood-bound, undeveloped, and backward-seeking circumstance. Relationships break up, children are left in the fallout of battles and rejections, society gets more anxious, and the outer elements stir up a fury. The ages-old spiritual dictum that what happens within is reflected without is writ large into earthly dramas.

Wise caregivers, capable and responsible in soul-spiritual and earthly ways, are required to step in to help until parents and relationships can be restored to some level of capability for the Pearl Children in the middle to have a chance to become whole again.

When hard antipathies arise between parents of children, and divorce is the solution, the "family farm" kinds of soul needs of children don't just go away. The child who seems at first just a small being is going to be a grown soul-spirit force on the earth in future with the power for good or the power for great evil.

Shared, two-household parenting has become the norm over several decades for divorced couples. Yet, it hasn't necessarily served the broken inner issue of Pearls, which they often associated with a broken heart. Co-parenting doesn't guarantee that the inner-soul work is working better now on either side of the relationship divide, especially if one or the other parent is incapable of forgiveness toward the other.

Even co-parenting arrangements have shown to be challenging for children, as reported in large numbers of research studies[67] and by grown children themselves. Too often, the stresses for the children have revolved around trust destruction in the child, or the failure of the parents to repair the bond the child needed to overcome divorce insecurity. Pearls simply carry the unresolved trauma into the new households with their single parents, stepsiblings, other family members, or stepparents.

Society is not evolved enough in Christ consciousness to have established many soul-wholesome, universally conscious, intentional-living communities outside of blood-family contracts—to ensure the truly good development of a Pearl Child who is lacking two soul-spirit committed parents. Many Western-world families are experimenting with intentional-living communities for this purpose today. Foster homes today, in the Western world are the segue homes, but too many children in foster care systems have had nightmarish experiences of lack of safety and care.

Karmic lawfulness protects children and puts child-raising responsibility onto the parents, whether one or another parent takes up their responsibility or not. When one or the other parent doesn't take responsibility for their own children, new caregiving relationships must be formed. Society too often bears the brunt of irresponsibility in child-raising. However, society itself often means government-funded mental health or fostering programs that are often too adult for child-development needs, or too political and economically conflicted. They don't necessarily help heal the inner bonding conflicts for the children or help children develop a rooted sense of warm, loving, and authentically positive resilience and wholeness. This makes it exceptionally hard to help a foster child feel fully welcome on this earth as part of a larger family of humanity.

Some divorced parents, or split, non-married parents, are trying out new forms of semi-familial homesteads for raising children. They've revived a concept of the olden tribal village, wherein groups of people related and unrelated to the children raise each other's children communally. Life in some such communities becomes like a melting-pot of married and single parents, overriding boundaries and suppressing individual freedom for the sake of a kind of group-mind. Other similar communities are more on the way to clearer, ego-conscious relating with healthy gradients of boundary-setting based on individual soul needs and negotiated collective societal and spiritual needs.

Those communities do the inner-soul work practices, of various descriptions, to manage the necessary suppleness of individual souls and also of the collective soul of the community. The best of such communities can handle the coming and going of certain spirit-seeding individuals who help keep the soul work from getting too tribal, ingrained, or closeminded and thus uncreative or no longer capable of innovating necessary, new impulses. Anyone coming into higher spiritual truths and understandings can become those spirit-seeding travelers between communities if they have instilled the inner-soul understandings and practices as well. This is necessary to keep even innovative thoughts from sending communities into destructive devolution rather than evolution.

Positive outcomes for Pearl Children, regardless of the living arrangements worked out between split parents, are still predicated upon whether the parents can be forgiving, respectful, and significantly harmonious between each other; in other words, situations where the children are in emotionally safe environments where the adult, soul-based, conflict-resolution and higher love work is being done by the parents and not left to the children.

In such arrangements, although the parents may be applying more appropriate soul-spiritual insights to their own relating work, many still try to bring adult-level spiritual expectations to the children's development. This is where anthroposophical insights can help bring the soul harmony into greater balance for the families, regarding how the children themselves need to be in soul-spirit development at appropriate ages and stages. Chapter Four explains more on this.

Plato, Adaptation, Innovation and Collaboration

How do we discern if a phenomenological change in society, such as masses of family divorces in the space of six decades, is soul-spiritually lawful? Investigating mathematical phenomenon helped me on this. It gave me much more information on keeping grounded and whole internally, helping me stay more incarnate and not jumping out of myself, in an old unconscious strategy from childhood, when faced with family and societal conflict and change triggers.

With geometric awareness, I could create some lawful, earthly holding for myself that was not coming from any soul-denying family member or societal members. I needed to consciously bring geometric Solids into my toolkit of self-understanding to stay emotionally, mentally, and physically even-keeled and more incarnate—to withstand the extreme social divisions massively permeating society after the 2008 economic restructuring crisis. These were exacerbated by the feeling-manipulating influences that worldwide social media suddenly brought onto world society.

Now I could understand the lawfulness of our evolving bodies and the soul holograms morphing in the middle of cosmic-spiritual changes. Without this understanding, I was regressing into running myself ragged and overly nerve-stressed, denying the forces greater than myself all around, and trying to keep in perfect self-control in socially chaotic and distorting times.

Math and geometry offer insights into pure, archetypal forms that inform earthbound beings. They bring the *spirit* into soul working, providing insight into how cosmic structures are held together in the earth and in the human body, as well as what kind of adaptive patterns human beings face and evolve through in the light of these influences. Without geometry and measurement, in architecture, for instance, we could spend endless amounts of time, and waste significant resources, building or renovating a home, business, or civic structure, being bogged down in purely individual perspectives or *planes*, losing sight of our purpose halfway through, and losing coworkers who reject the chaos and move onto other projects.

It is known in geometry that an infinite number of planes can be drawn on the many arcs of a sphere. The key word here is "infinite." Creative ideas are infinite and necessary, but so are structures that give form and an appropriate moral sense for inner stability.

A sphere may seem set in shape, and yet its uses are multidimensional. In our times, having the consciousness of these truths can be enlightening and hopeful, but it can also be confusing and, for some, even threatening.[68]
Rudolf Steiner

Without forms considered for their lawfulness, as well as creative imaginations, no clarity could inform a successful innovation. We would develop little capable executive functioning in the higher cortex of our brains. We could not manage efficiently complex tasks involving many people and many needs at one time. We would get lost in pure, personal opinions rather than spiritually insightful, and intuitive feelings combined with heartfelt approaches to rational thought.

Figure 3.10: Planes projected from a sphere

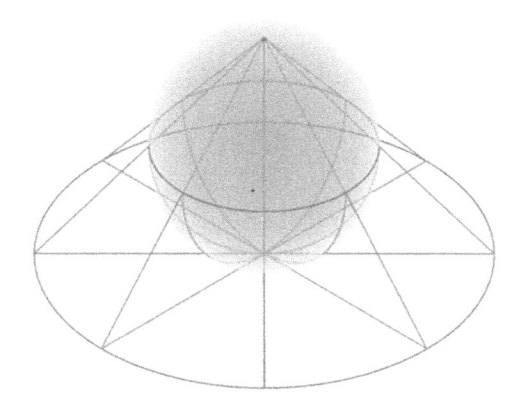

When human beings think of earthly matters only as the naked eye perceives them, and without imagination that extends beyond, we miss the potentials for greater understanding about our needs and our capacities as creators of helpful human inventions. We can also miss the lines of thinking that can lead us to greater cosmic-earthly understandings, and thus 'spiritual matters'. This figure shows lines and planes extended beyond a sphere, just as human beings can imagine and use lines of knowledge to know creative existence beyond the sphere of the earth.

If we know that a sphere is a geometric shape that appears to be set and certain, but we also know that an infinite number of lines or planes can be drawn on its surface, we know that in its practical application, humanity can find any number of creative solutions to problems that arise as we adapt to life's movements and changes. We just have to figure out what design we want to work with that will still have a lawful progression from one state to the others, keeping a harmony to it and thus maintaining necessary social stability for society and for the growth of new generations of young souls.

When we understand that geometry moves from star movements, to lines on a page, to solid earthen forms such as pyramids, squares, hexagons, icosahedrons, and dodecahedrons, we gain clarity of soul. These earthen Solids, emerging out of lawful geometric designs in spheres and cycling cosmic patters, provide the lawful standards to gauge human development. They help us to clarify the incarnate or disincarnate human problems that arise when people only engage simplistic, personal-senses-based thinking and feeling when life presents challenges.

Life on earth has some solid forms and structures to it. It also has imaginative, intuitive creativity that arrives freely in our consciousness in what seems like formless states. We take this information up and create form or not, depending on our destiny and cultivated will forces. This gives us the freedom to assert ourselves into activity on the earth that is individual and creative.

When we know how to tap into lawful forms together with flexible thinking, while choosing how to heal and strengthen our individual inner-soul needs, we become freer to meet what collective society needs for clear thinking and free, untangled association. A natural, enlightening consciousness raises our spirits, and our hearts feel opened and calm. Activity together starts to move with ease, grace and less heavy thinking. We sleep better and have less fear and anxiety.

These are signs of the spirit-imbuing processes that the incarnation of Christ brought for all individuals. That is, the capacity of consciousness to bring these healing and helpful insights to ourselves without becoming bogged down in sense-life-based opinion about how what we do is the absolute right thing for everyone.

When, as a result of destructive, developmental experiences in our childhood years, our life just drifts along in boundless emotion or desires, with no good habit-forming, or disordered discipline, and without ability to bring creative and lawful soul effort to the problems, we live in a state of lowly, bound-up heavy-heartedness. We become vulnerable to using external fantasy creations to make us believe we're okay despite the niggling knowing that something's not right inside.

We can be set into disharmony with higher truth, then seek the highs through harmful substances or activities, trying to reach falsely for higher spirit knowing in the attempt to raise our spirits. However, poor choices entangle our thinking further. In the ensuing chaos and roller-coaster feelings come the hidden costs of reinforcing a false stability, bringing hopelessness, or preserving graceless, rigid, absolute thinking that hardens a person into angry divisiveness once again. The cycle becomes a vicious one.

The issue becomes how to manage the knowledge of such a vast subject as a sphere with endless planes of existence, when we know that there are also five set and related, lawful Platonic Solids creating form on the earth, with more possibly to be revealed in time. Add this query to the higher spiritual truths of humanism, technological assistance for humanity, and future human ascendance, and what might begin to seem clear also gets very complicated. However, the Christ forces are going to help us get more comfortable with complexity.

Figure 3.11: Platonic Solids drawn through circle geometry

The circle is the starting point for conceptual, geometric drawings of all Platonic Solids. The Solids begin to take form in perception when the circle is made into a sphere. Waldorf students create Platonic Solids out of balls of clay after drawing them in geometric form.

Figure 3.12: Dodecahedron and the sphere of the earth

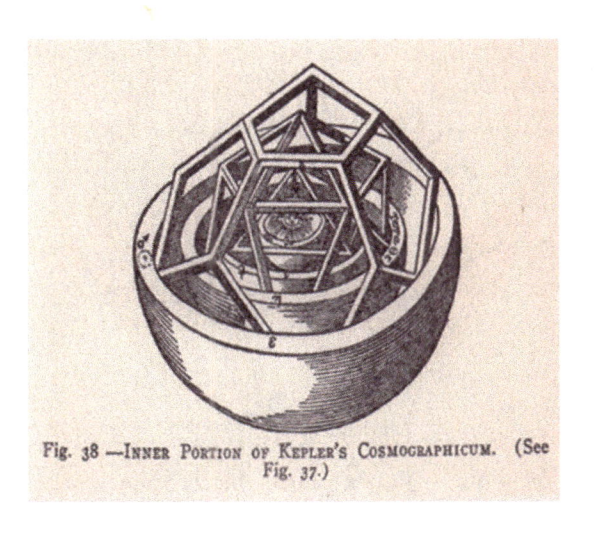

Some philosopher and artist attempts to describe the inner geometry of the earth.

Rudolf Steiner affirmed the mature spiritual truth that human beings are going to have to embrace a comfort zone again with complexity. With self-knowing, personal responsibility, and self-authority we may need some new kind of expansive heart force to cope well with it all. More in-depth discussion on the heart and soul work with Platonic Solids is discussed in Volume II.

The Platonic-Aristotelean Crucible of Conscious Relationship

The soul needs of our times marry earth-based, karmic knowledge and self-knowledge with spiritual lawfulness. These cosmic-earthly patterns help us clearly notice personal karmic reactions to life developments, and how we move forward, bringing more inner harmony, or regress backward, bringing blame, soul strife, and a decadence that tries to refute a true, higher lawfulness.

When individuals can't find inner harmony between what they think, feel, experience, and want, they need to spend some time with practices that attune them to the evolving structures of our times, and away from sense-world fixations as the only answers to all earthly problems. Fantasy thinking abstracts one entirely away from the laws of earthly cosmic humanity and severs a person from clearly seeing how those laws evolve. Dark, egoic forces on the earth thrive on distracting human beings from inner truth through greater and greater forms of fantasy cultivation. These forces tend to prey on younger people who have not yet developed mature soul-spirit practices and deeper capacities.

Physical laws, social laws, and spiritual/cultural/artistic laws evolve. Spiritual initiates have a sense of calm *knowing* when something evolves on the earth that symbolizes real progress and innovation for the sake of all. They see also that which is a controlled manipulation of forces and resources for selfish interests and know how to stand in the presence of such manipulations without being taken in. They know what is from the past and what is for now, and they do not allow emotions and desires to distract or confuse them either way. They can maintain a peaceful equanimity about what is occurring in the world.

When painful or horrific soul-searching questions arise, untamed dark forces work to distract people from bothering to work on personal development. Individuals can backslide in consciousness to old traditions and conventions that do not serve consciousness times. Vulnerable Pearls, and well as many other people, avoid practicing reflection, noticing personal breathing, examining our inability to be patient, sensing into others, and finding the courage to create new, non-familial relationships for growth, change, and soul-spirit attunement inside and out.

Some of us use only outer practical work, to ground ourselves in external reality. Yet, denying the work needed to transform our inner-soul understandings to stay human, humble, and cooperative with healthy human progress at work, at home and/or in the child-raising worlds of nurseries, doctors' offices, and schools, often leads to some kind of a soul crisis. We are caught in the breezes and storms of the natural environment while forgetting the actual, consistent, and creative nature of soul-spirit lawfulness and light that permeates all human existence.

It can at first be a disorienting awareness for some modern people to realize that they have come to understand many things about the laws of physics (even if it is as simple as the laws of energy and chemistry that allow a person to bake cakes over and over again consistently) while forgetting higher lawfulness in their own inner life. They may feel comfortable in the scientific constructs of the natural world or even political rules regarding rights or national sovereignty, and they can accept evidence-based science regarding personal health, commerce, and even architectural and engineering protocols that keep high-rise buildings and bridges standing, but they have forgotten the lawfulness of the cosmos permeating and informing everything living in this earthly world, including their own hearts and souls.

This has not always been the case. In fact, it is a consequence of a forgetfulness that set in with the increasingly hardening effects of a deepening, materialized mentality that has gripped Western societies since the European Renaissance. With the Industrial Revolution then came a belief in materialistic science and earth-based physics that began to cloud higher thought, coupled with industrial inventions to drive mass production and profits for growing companies and increasing populations.

This heavy emphasis on product that escalated in the 1980s, particularly in the United States, that accelerated resource extraction, production, profit-making, and the advertising of endless "things" that people should believe they needed, empowered advertisers to work to foster in "consumers" (rather than real human beings) addictive materialistic drives to survive, even though most human beings had survived and even thrived with much less for millennia. Marketers began to distort thinking toward a belief that only what is completely sense-perceptible is real and valuable to human beings. Mass numbers of human beings forgot that something mysterious happens before birth and continues after we die. Yet, at the same time, people with near-death experiences have explained in detail why they changed their own completely materialistic lives, often drastically, after the awakening from what they were deeply convinced was an experience of crossing the threshold of death and perceiving the cosmic world again.

Without something more than a purely materialistic belief, humans would never determine how to get a spaceship to the moon and back based on a certain level of sense-free, higher thinking. An obsessive materialistic belief would suggest that the space lab technicians would have needed to touch, smell, taste, and directly hear the moon before they could step onto it.

Mathematics and geometries come closer to the higher truths than pure materialism, but not merely the kind that only calculate that which can be touched or made and counted as earthly product. Man did not fly to the moon based on materialistic math alone. Today, physics has moved toward quantum physics, astrophysics, and closer proofs that spiritual truths, coming out of imaginations, intuitions, and inspirations, and written down and spoken of by human beings over millennia could be entirely true.

Sometimes, when we can get more deeply honest with ourselves, we realize that we seem to have stepped away from our authentic selves, leaping too far forward from what our human hearts tell us is true, or conversely, holding too tightly to a way of being that is not serving our sense of humane life. We have been perhaps riding on someone else's coattails or shoulders to get ahead in life while our feet are not really on the ground and we're rarely thinking of anything higher or of anyone else.

Or we've ignored the repressive effects of our fantastical, or even megalomaniacal and desirous material ambitions upon others' sustainable well-being. Our once truly human relationships with our children have become corrupted, and now some of those children are threatening suicide, lost in addictions, or bullying and even killing people. We may need to take more than a few deep breaths and reflect on our beliefs and perceptions.

Too often, in marriage breakup, unlawfulness presents itself as scapegoating one person or one group of people into being the lightning rod for most of the wild electricity flying in a discontented, non-evolving, or too quickly evolving personal life. Someone else becomes the appointed martyr, failed hero, or some other projected-upon character or stereotype for our distorted, unmet expectations, or unowned responsibilities. We fly off in great fantasies of freedom that are more about temporary sexual or nerve-stimulating titillation, or self-aggrandizement, than any whole and meaningful human encounter or endeavor for cosmic goodness in the world or the recognition and reparation of suffering in others all around. We blame and game the systems of society without really working to truly transform them into clearer lawfulness.

When our actions and our soul's knowing are far apart, then we feel a great deal of distress that can come out in physical, etheric, astral, or I-being illness or mental illness. Adjusting through soulful checking in and adjusting stages, our ability to cooperate with the universe and become more conscious in our relationships or work, builds resilience within, and stamina for hard outer tasks throughout life, including our end-of-life dying. With reverent thanks to the deed of Christ, we can now do the inner investigations and screenings of our soul lives and our spiritually lawful attunements more successfully for ourselves.

No overseeing and absolving priest, teacher, guru, or politician can do it for us or take away our self-dominion to be our own person. No one person or group gets to direct our healing or our awareness solely for us. We can offer each other help and insight, in unentangled, brotherly-sisterly love, but the willful higher and holy, or more whole, work and practices we must do ourselves. This truly requires Christ-natured courage.

Healthy, conscious working, with full focus and absorption, is when an enlivening and enlightening new offshoot of inspirational lawfulness comes into effect in our lives, seemingly at times from nowhere. The magical sense that we get is rational, but from a higher cosmic, divine rationalism. This keeps relationships resonating in social and relational renewal, evolving contracts with each other as transforming, Christ-conscious beings.[69] More of this is explained in the coming chapters.

Heart and soul contracts can be full of life for parents who are going through difficult life transitions and general life fears and confusions. That is, so long as we keep a level of respectful, human sensitivity with others. This does not guarantee a tension-free life. Life has tensions, even when the whole of an individual life appears to be functioning well in society, and even well spiritually. That is because we are still earthbound. When tension gets too heavy, we need to move to a kind of Platonic Solids consciousness, alchemically, to see what we can move around in our foundational, material, inner awareness, to stir creative life there again too. (Alchemy and Platonic Solids, as applied to psychological awareness, will be explained more in the coming chapters.)

It is our absolute blocks, or our complete resistance to cosmic-earthly form, structure, or creative innovation, that cause soul harm and social damage, because rigid old stances or "walls" wreak havoc on spiritual truths within humanity. Conflict and duality are not the rightful energy of our times. Only intra-human movement, when people exist within a closed system, such as the earth's boundaries, will cleanse our karma now. We are asked to rub up against each other, but in less hardened ways, as if like flows of water tumbling through a purifying flow-form water fountain—sometimes intensely, other times more gently.

Figure 3.13: Anthroposophical water purifying flow form

The anthroposophically conceived flow-form aerates and purifies water in an energetic, rhythmic vortex created between specially designed basins. The basin surfaces are mathematically designed with path curves involving a polarity between point-like and plane-like processes. This reflects an energy field that has both earthly and cosmic resonances.

We either flow with each other together in rhythm, bringing the refreshing aeration of ideas to help sustain etheric needs, in freedom, or become entrapped in dark surveillances that will bind human thinking to deadening technologies and bring rote, punitive consequences from authoritarian leaders acting out of regressive, underworld-like, and animalistic, cruelty.

Change For the Sake of Change or Power?

If it was so that any change, or complete change, based purely on personal opinions and ambitions that people sometimes call "personal dreams," is healthy for human, holistic nature, we would not have any repetitive cycles of seasons, or chemical constituents that maintain a consistent number of positive and negative ions in the body, or any number of human beings that continue to be born with recognizable hands, fingers, toes, limbs, skulls, and other features that clearly indicate that this is a human being and not a pimpernel. (This is not a derisive comment to disregard those people born with physiological exceptionalities and challenges, just a statement highlighting the consistent state of natural human developmental nature.)

Human evolutionary changes happen slowly and experience recurring and advancing cycles. There are elements within the process of human struggle and suffering. There is no truth to disconnected, unilateral, hyper-projectile change in human, earthly life that will bring perfect ease. Soul immaturity or denial make some believe that. Rhythms are a soul-spirit truth despite what some materialistic scientists, war arms dealers, and technology moguls would like us to believe about the nature of human systems.

Though certain forms of technology are going to be truly evolutionary for humanity, and although human beings will go through significant physical changes in time, the acts of violently pressing humans forward on time-lines directed by the pursuit of selfish personal profits or soulless beliefs not for our times. Nothing whole evolves in selfish timing, though some living entities evolve a little faster than others.

Everything has a soul-spirit process of emergence, and those timings, even cosmically, are cyclical rather than purely straightforward. A straight-line, masculine light-beam approach to life carries with it, naturally, a round, cycling, earthing feminine approach. It is the nature of human, upright balance and earthly cosmic impulses. Striving beyond such processes of lawfulness brings lawfully opposing responses.

Human changes are indeed occurring, and it is important to bear in mind that human beings, en masse, will struggle over time with losing the use of certain body parts or aspects of body functions. In the past, we lost the usefulness of the third eyelid, tailbone, and wisdom teeth.[70] As humanity progresses further toward ascension, people will begin to lose the function of more body parts. That is one reason that the practicalities of human robotics and other technologies are coming into fruition now. However, many forms of this technology will be profit-fantasy-selfishness driven only. That is going to tax humanity to stay even more connected to human heart consciousness and moral-ethical-cosmic lawfulness.

Rudolf Steiner suggested that in time, several millennia from now, we will lose our sexual connection to reproduction.[71] We may have seen the start of this phenomenon with shortened menses in women and impotence issues in men in the last few decades in the West. As we evolve into new human stages, leaving known processes of reproduction behind as some level of new birthing evolution emerges, the reality that we still birth through sexual activity will remain until that massive shift. Until then, responsibility remains between parents and society to raise children with whole and soulfully conscious practices.

Phenomenological Observation

Phenomenological observation of events, and changes, is a form of watching and noting what is happening around us and in us, to see if something is in personal development, change, and innovation, or if something seems to be in collective change. It is another way to know how to track if an eventuality in life is morphing for the greater good of humanity and in connection to lawfulness developments.

This is important for our consciousness times, since everything that occurs in us and to us today is affecting the collective consciousness that younger generations take in unconsciously. Generations from the ages of about thirty-six and older hold the consciousness for the young to fully develop into maturity and then get their feet wet in the world for a decade or so. The collective tracking of elders can't take the form of a tribalistic, generational oppressiveness, despite elders still holding some responsibilities for the youngers. Elders must hold cosmic understandings through their conscious, spiritually striving deaths.

Phenomenological tracking looks to see what kinds of cycles have been happening in humanity over time, and where the next adaptations fit in the cosmic-human future picture—including information coming through younger generations through the cosmic cycles they represent—even though the youngers won't have consciousness of themselves yet. This helps us to understand when events in our personal consciousness meet the new innovations being brought slowly into consciousness through younger generations.

We still have a human soul need for the understanding of history and to hear other people's biographies, elder and younger, and their intuitions about the future. We need to commune well with each other. Consulting others who commit to seeking clear perception is helpful, if we don't give over our responsibility to them or forgo our own need to work on our conscious development, including generational development. As the light of the Consciousness Soul progresses, human souls will feel the threat of oppression quicker when one person is given too much power to guide them. Yet, we must not stop asking questions of each other or learning from the collective wisdom of soul-spirit transformation.

The recent leap from real-time, verbal communication with each other to cyber-talk has clearly created another soul investigation and phenomenological tracking challenge for humanity. We can only track humanness if we have real access to other human beings in real time. Rudolf Steiner clearly foresaw that humanity would integrate more with machinery and technology as our bodies evolve and lose functions, while our hearts and souls increase in expansive, spirit-mind functions. However, tracking through the internet has shown how easily untruth and evil slips in.

Different Streams, Different Points of View

One of the finest features of olden Anglo-Saxon mythology, within the story of King Arthur and his knights, is the idea that wise people consult many voices at the table on significant matters. (King Arthur's twelve knights are important allegorically for the notion of the higher initiate speaking at his round table of advisers.) To see the social life truthfully, one must be able to see several perspectives on one subject, freely given, and united in the cause of goodness for all. Here again is the higher sense of the cosmic circle—the circle of higher striving.

Reflecting on an action from many points of view can bring a much more whole storyline of intuitions from the past, present, and future that didn't create a break in conscious development, but rather provided a well-knit transition from one collective societal understanding and stage of development to another.

This twelve-points-of-view awareness has been true through time, with the peoples of the Indian, Persian, and Egyptian epochs consulting the zodiac of twelve cosmic influences. The Hebrew peoples knew that the spiritual and cultural life of their people had the history and experiences of twelve tribes to take into consideration.

In anthroposophical study and practice, people come to the work from many different soul streams, including a Celtic stream, an Asian stream, and a Germanic stream.[72] Some are more Platonist and thought-minded; some are more Aristotelean, meaning practical and feeling-oriented; and others are a mix of both. Hearing from many points of view can raise more questions than it answers at times. However, living balanced in the question is an important indication of anthroposophical work. (A very clear elder spirit woman once said that consulting from different angles means also consulting different angels.)

In the recent past, in Western society, we would see this balance and consultation with many sources displayed in the news media, in public forums, and in post-secondary educational settings. Human experience was imagined, discussed, reworked in the minds and souls of many people, and opened to wide reflection and scrutiny. Living was not a process of impulse and pure physical reactionism.

If life today is all in our hands now, as Rudolf Steiner has affirmed out of spiritual-scientific research and Christ-consciousness understandings, and if any choice we make to live is okay so long as we prepare to face the consequences of harms we bring to others and make repairs, how do we know if we are truly prepared to face what we've done that may have reduced the life of another? What helps us to decide what's morally and ethically right for ourselves and society? How do we distinctly tune individual conscience to cosmic-earthly, soul-spirit lawfulness? How do we trust that this will all turn out okay?

This questioning may have been the prime reason that church fathers of Constantinople came to believe that they alone could be the free-hold spiritual beings and everyone else would have to follow their spiritual guidance. Prior to Christ's incarnation, everyday people did not much question the priests. This allowed the priests to keep an established order. How could society survive without human-created orders, and only spiritual orders to guide them?

This questioning highlights fearful and anxious perceptions that stick in our beliefs about how we should act soul-spiritually now and how we should behave when our comforts or our set ways and desires are held up in the mirror of change. Instead of being incarnate, flexible, questioning, and cooperative, we become hardened and try to reconstitute ourselves in recognizable ways from the past. It temporarily gives a sense of rootedness, bringing a low-consciousness sense of solidity and protection. Some people even try to become as heavy as the earth, metal, and rocks—through as much land ownership that they can acquire, through the stockpiling of capital machinery, holding the biggest herd of cattle, the largest gold mine, or the biggest military complex in the world.

This is all a level of olden, materialistic fantasy covering over anxiety and uncertainty about change. It is also egoic. It happens partly because we don't track what's really happening in us and in the record of being truly evolving, spiritually responsible humans on the earth. We overlook or wall up the scary parts of life rather than facing them full-on with truth and working through observance of life around us. We identify where we need help or how we can help others that is true to the times.

Instead, as a result of the regressive actions of spirit leaders in 869 AD, people in the Western world don't take responsibility between each other out of individual freedom, a process that brings the most to learn individually. We hide within the masses and try not to be awake. We even try often to hide from the truth that human beings naturally die in time.

When we can't find a soulful understanding for our feelings and needs in real and flexible relationship with others, we lose touch with our fluid capacities of love. We stop one of the most important qualities of our ascendance development—the ability to be malleable, flexible, and sculptural (*plastisch*[73] in German), as well as inwardly moveable beings. Without that human quality, we resist others that we need for our future development. We make ourselves exceedingly sensitive and vulnerable.

Due to fear, we forget to observe the seven life processes within ourselves and in our deepest heart places, and we doubt the power of speaking a heartfelt truth while we observe what is occurring in the transformations of everything around us. We tend to associate human life with the kind of perception that we have for trees. We just want to stand there and hold firm, praying that everything will work out for us but not rattle our simple earthly understandings.

Sometimes, we can recognize that things must change in the earth life, because we see some advantage about that for ourselves, such as when we clear land to build a new house or to set up a better community water system. Yet, too often we are not willing to accept or forgive a person when that person is changing inwardly, and freedom sets them out of alignment in some way from their higher truth, or from ours. We give no room for them to chart inwardly, with some time, what is happening in their soul consciousness and find their way to a new soul wholeness through an innovation crisis and its associated healing journey. If the changes don't seem to have any immediate or quick benefit for us, we are quick to disown them or others, to our soul-spirit detriment.

The Internet

The internet makes this quick condemnation and toss-off of others intensely easy to do today—with knee-jerk responding and impulsive reactions on every topic under the sun. Too often, individuals give no real thought to situations that arise on internet social media, or fair consideration to what has occurred in the past, what is present, and what gleanings they have been getting about the future.

The social soul art for individuals today is finding the right balance of self-awareness and selflessness. This is to keep new aspects of oneself growing while staying incarnate enough to register inwardly, for enough time, what changes are personally soulful, truthful, and benefiting heartfelt connection with others. Unregulated fear and anger direct our attention to changes that are based on immediate, selfish, or grasping-hoarding fantasies or self-delusions.

On the internet, masses of people were initially manipulated into such behaviors by the psychological design features within certain social media forums that play both on human emotion and advertising power features. The forums were implemented to be addictive and hook participants who could then be surveyed for marketing purposes, without knowing consent, and then subjected to steady, on-line advertising. Some people have gained awareness of the manipulations inherent in social media platforms and have freed themselves of addictive and anti-social behaviors. Governments have begun attempts to regulate the platforms to force the platform leaders to censor out violent and hateful content that has been supported by the psychological programming in the forums themselves.

In the short span of one human life, it is not always apparent that changes may be part of a much longer-term and higher order for humanity. This is especially so for people who believe that humans live one life only, as opposed to those who for millennia have understood that human souls reincarnate. Anthroposophy acknowledges reincarnation, and that there are features of being human that are spiritually distinct as a result of our ability to be aware of other incarnations.[74]

For a human being to have relationships only with animals, exclusively with plants, or merely with minerals would seem absurd to the healthy human consciousness, and for good reason. The human being, although connected to the innate wisdom of those other beings and elements on earth, is more complex, capable, and profound than all other living beings. This is so when the human inner life and its capacities toward intuition, imagination, and inspiration come into effect to open a person to knowledge of higher worlds. According to Rudolf Steiner, this full understanding will come to its highest human standard in a not too distant future.[75]

The Lemniscate as Counseling and Caregiving Technique for Pearls

Earthly cosmic lawfulness helps a growing child to feel stability and safety. It is not appropriate to bring adult understanding of such things to young children by talking about such higher matters. Conscious caregivers hold the higher awareness for the children until the growing children have developed various inner capacities to be able to address this awareness safely and consciously for themselves as adults. For now, they don't need to know what these laws are all about. However, moral dilemmas, and many aspects of sacred lawfulness can be introduced at a child level, imaginatively, such as through fairy tales, myths, and biographies.

Caregivers also work to help keep children tuned to natural rhythms of life, such as keeping good bedtimes, eating within natural times that allow for good digestion and important sleep.

As well, they support the children in celebrating the turning seasons as reflections of changing light and the lively presence of elemental beings and angelic forces. Waldorf school celebrations include acknowledging the yearly meteor showers, lantern walks in nature as the season turns darker earlier, and a spiral nature circle with candles to honor the important form of the spiral as well as any number of light ceremonies in the world that include Christian Advent.

These practices inwardly instill for children strengthening soul-spiritual forces in appropriately child-friendly and incarnating ways for a sustained life. In caring for the young, it is also important to promote in appropriate ways a rhythmic habit life for strong life-will forces.

The understandings of these inner rhythms may go unconscious in older children for a time until about their early thirties. It is important to keep in mind that Christ-imbued, cosmic-spiritual lawfulness today does not set rigid constructs, but rather healthy, archetypal outlines. In our transitioning times, both routine and flexibility are crucial in raising heartfelt children. Observing how children respond to flexed habits tells a caregiver whether the child needs a more simple and dependable form for now, or if they have resilience for an adapted form or habit. For most children up to adolescence, these adaptations ought not to be too frequent or adult-oriented.

For stressed or traumatized Pearl Children, as well as Pearl Adults who need healing, one lawful construct that therapists can keep in mind when attempting to understand what the young soul is needing, is the lemniscate.[76] The lemniscate chart here, in Figure 3.2, is a tool for counselors and caregivers (including doctors, teachers, parents, or other guardians), to assess what can inwardly be happening in the Pearl Child's seven life processes as the child is moving back and forth between the homes and lives of each parent within custody arrangements.

Charted here onto a lemniscate diagram, or as some have called it, the *infinity line*, is the classic path of the Pearl Children's back-and-forth travels between their parents' lives. This back-and-forth experience, often daily, weekly, or biweekly, depends on the distance between parent homes and other custody considerations. It is helpful for a counselor to observe the seven life processes at each stage when the child is arriving at, or leaving, one parent's world for the other.

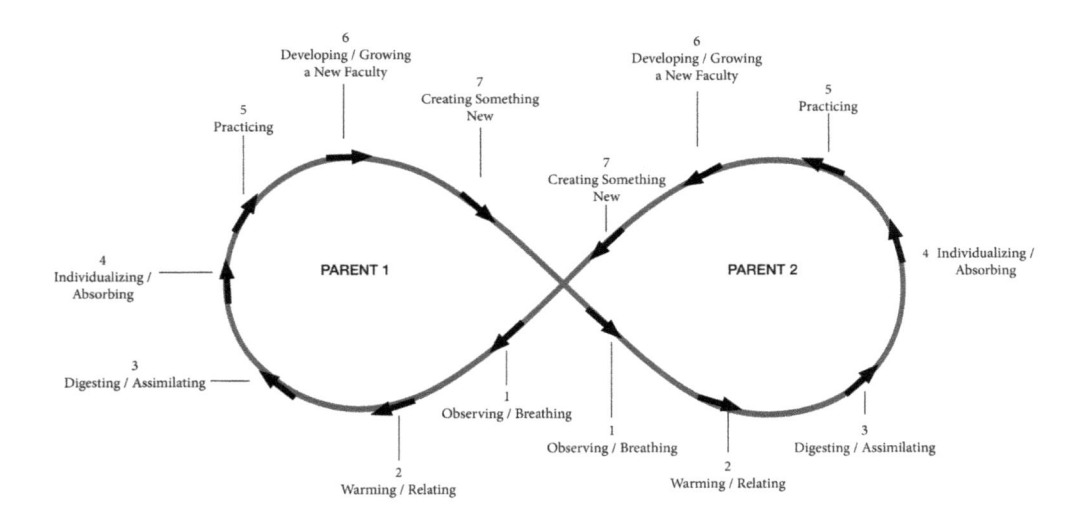

Figure 3.2: Seven Life and Learning Processes Lemniscate Chart

```
                    6                               6
         Developing / Growing              Developing / Growing
            a New Faculty      7              a New Faculty         5
     5                   Creating Something                     Practicing
  Practicing                    New
                                        7
                                Creating Something
                                       New
   4                                                                  4
Individualizing /        PARENT 1           PARENT 2           Individualizing /
   Absorbing                                                       Absorbing

   3
Digesting / Assimilating                                              3
                             1                               Digesting / Assimilating
                      Observing / Breathing
                                        1
                                Observing / Breathing
                     2                              2
                Warming / Relating              Warming / Relating
```

Track the processes of a child moving between parents or parent homes. As the child moves from one parent to the other, he or she unconsciously adjusts through the seven life processes, adapting to each parent's soul nature and practical circumstances. The child moves through processes of 1. Observing/Breathing, . Warming/Relating, 3. Digesting/Assimilating, 4. Individualizing/Absorbing, 5. Practicing, 6. Developing/Growing a New Faculty, and 7. Creating Something New.

Therapeutic Method: The child arriving at the other parent's home in a conflictual parent situation, however subtle the conflict, begins the unconscious check-in process of the seven life processes. To keep the child's natural soul processes healthy, the young child cannot be expected to weather this alone. With the help of an older family member, caregiver, anthroposophical doctor, counselor, remedial educator, or teacher, the child can adjust.

Caregivers track the processes unconsciously through the child's comments, actions, creative expressions, and emotional outbursts when moving between parent's homes. They watch the child's strategies for relating, finding belonging, protecting autonomy, and giving and receiving love with others in the house.

If the child is struggling, the adults offer insights, practices, interest, curiosity, and empathic understanding. Parents can journal what they observe to help the child to gain self-awareness later in life of the processes that were needed to engage and stay well and whole in the family dynamics. A record of it can be very helpful to a Pearl in case one or both parents die early. Pearls often struggle to create an accurate picture of their growing up process when they are adults.

Having helpful practices to do in the stages of transition, to strengthen the seven life processes and clear parent-conflict impositions on the children, can mitigate development damage and keep the child engaged in healthy rhythms even if one or the other parent is not holding up routines and the child's habit life well. This helps to keep a Pearl Child's habits and life processes from being regularly eclipsed by the parent's unresolved adult issues. Older children, from about the age of sixteen onward, can begin to track their own passages between parent homes and lives through writing stories, songs, poetry, and/or prayers.

> **Note:** Questions that a caregiver, teacher, or counselor can ask themselves regarding the Pearl Children and the seven life processes are outlined at the beginning of each chapter on child and adult development (Chapters Five, Six, Seven, and in Volume II).

The child in *Seven Life and Learning Processes* therapeutic work—be it at home, school, in a spiritual community, or in a creative-expressive arts environment—has time to process and adjust to what has been happening with the other family members. Age-appropriate awareness of this is especially important at each age of the growing child. Never accelerate the child's perspective on family issues beyond the appropriate age-and-stage needs of the child. A ten-year-old, for instance, should not be aware of parent sexual issues.

A therapist can offer outside support by checking in about any changes in rules or routines in each home that evolved or changed abruptly, leaving the child with no inner tools for adjustment. In the best-case scenario, an outside supportive caregiver is welcomed to observe each of the home-and-family routine activities for a short time. That caregiver can help parents to notice adjustment needs and work with the parent to bring about sensitive and creative solutions.

A parent, caregiver, or therapist can notice if a child is holding the breath in any way. Older children will need some coaching to know what a deep breath, shallow breath, and a held breath look and feel like. These are not practices designed to have the child control breath, but to help gauge what the breath is doing.

This is especially so in the initial stages of a divorce, family split, and change or adaptation around the child's residence. For a small child, a patient adult observes and notes the child's reactions and offer stories, practices, and creative opportunities for real connection and empathy. This helps the child to not become stuck or distorted in any of the seven life processes.

In the times when a child cannot have outside therapeutic support, a parent who is working consciously with the seven life processes can help track this for the child. The parent, upon releasing his or her child to the other parent for the scheduled stay-over can make a phone call to the child before bed that night to do a gentle processing review in child-appropriate language, using codes that the child has been prepared for.

The child can signal if they are feeling "tight breathing," "easy breathing," or "fear breathing." The parent can ask what the child saw when they got to the other parent's home and what was new, cold, hardened, or scary, or what made them feel warm and flowing. As well, the child can share what they did that felt safe and good with the other family members.

> **Note:** These suggestions are for building practices for the child to strengthen the *Seven Life and Learning Processes*. It is not a way for a parent to spy against the other or log a critical check-in on what is happening at the other parent's house or in that family's relationships. Any betrayal like this will cause more harm than good.
> * This does not mean disregarding any signals from a child who may be experiencing legitimate mental, emotional, or physical abuse from the other parent. All caregivers should familiarize themselves with understandings, societal guidelines, and laws around child abuse detection and reporting.
> This phone call assessment technique is only recommended for the youngest children if there is not a parent in the other home who can do empathic observing and assessing for the child. It is highly recommended that adults, on each side of the transition, schedule for time to do this seven life processes check-in, having been coached by a therapist or anthroposophical counselor, a doctor, curative eurythmist, or teacher.

The next three observations for the *Seven Life and Learning Processes* will be about how the child is making meaning (digesting/assimilation) out of what is happening at the parents' homes. A child needs an opportunity to examine stressful events and be able to safely process out what is happening in one home or another.

A Pearl Child may need a check-in on eating habits and whether the child can eat what is needed (not necessarily wanted) when that child needs to, and if the child's stomach feels calm through the digestion process. Gauging healthy habits, as well as feelings, is important, since a child asking for sweets suddenly in one parent's home may mean that the child's nervous system is overstimulated, or that the child feels unconscious sadness or fear that isn't being attended to well with warmth and patience. The parent may need to spend deeper understanding time and do some anxiety-relief practices together with the child to bring a sense of greater resilience.

A child entering a new co-parenting arrangement between two homes might have a legitimate ailment brought on by a virus or bacteria that needs to be treated, or by a new allergy to something in the new parent home.

When children feel safe, they naturally set into rhythm with natural, relaxed play coming out of their own imaginations and interests. This could be expressed through drawing, doing crafts, building forts in the backyard, creating soundscapes on a musical instrument, making food in the kitchen, taking care of the family pets or farm animals, hammering away on a wood construction project, or talking to an older stepsister on the phone.

Homework will get done reasonably and contentedly with parent attention and help when needed if Pearl Children feel that they are valued members of the family in all of their struggles and joys. Feeling free to experience healthy touch with either parent in either home is important. If a parent doesn't feel sure what healthy touch is with a child at different ages, that parent should consult a childcare specialist or counselor.

This unthreatened state will allow the child to manage much more life force than the child can manage in a state of alienated tension around parent feelings and grievances. Pearl Children who feel loved, valued, and safe also own responsibility for any harms against siblings or stepsiblings. Pearl Children can hear what the other children need without panicky jealousy or insecurity.

With holism working its natural way in the child now, the delights of innovative and creative new discoveries can emerge, even in small ways, and bring much joy, inspiration, hope, and confidence to the child and the family. The Pearl can feel free to share what is coming up in his or her heart, imagination, intuition, and inspiration. This will not necessarily come out consciously, but through thoughts, actions, projects, jokes, experiments, and refreshingly unusual moments of child brilliance.

When it is time for the child to return to the other parent's home, there is some emotional danger in the crossover if the child is not able to freely share what has recently been happening with the other family members. Since this can be a challenge for the receiving parent to listen to and honor, it is important to begin the *Seven Life and Learning Processes* check-in again as the child enters the other parent's life and home again.

Parents to do their own *Seven Life and Learning Processes* check-ins also, though not outwardly to the child. Keeping conscious needs-awareness happening in the transitions is crucial to safe passage for the child, to avoid blocking his or her capacities, or throwing the child off-balance after the child may have worked hard inwardly to get attuned at the other home.

> <u>Important note</u>: Always watch for signs of overtiredness, which can come out as moodiness, and resist criticism about it. The child has a lot of work to do to reconcile the parent/homestead/sibling issues, and the constant transitions, even when the child has been going back and forth for some time already.

Parent Expectations of Pearl Child Harmony

When parents are sharing custody of a Pearl Child, while maintaining conflictual beliefs, expectations, and actions regarding the other parent and that parent's influence on the child, there is no lawful way for the Pearl Child to maintain a regularly peaceful and harmonious life inwardly. This can be shown by the lawfulness of the lemniscate itself.

Figure 3.14 shows the parents' hopes and desires that the child will somehow manage a steady and even successful life, and in good relations with them, despite their ongoing conflicts and distance from each other's lives and views.

In the overly idealized vision of co-parenting and its possibilities for the children, too often parents believe that the child can create a life wherein the grown Pearl feels a sense of togetherness, wholeness, and full, individual capacity in the world, despite parent conflict.

This expectation is often in the thoughts of divorced parents despite the child's exposure to parents who remain judgmental and conflictual with each other. They expect the child to adapt some level of personal balance in between them on their own, and naturally.

Figure 3.13: Parent expectations of a whole, harmonious child between them, despite repeated parent conflict

Figure 3.14i: Ideal Co-parenting Scenario

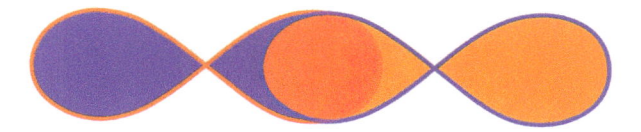

Former spouses, each represented in a complimentary color, and with the child as the center of focus (in red), work diligently and respectfully together to hold the child in empathy, love, and healthy developmental practices. They maintain separate households close to each other.

Figure 3.14ii: Conflict and Distortion

An alienated parent begins to pull further away from the former spouse and child. The child's heart and soul forces become insecure and lessened/decompensated.

Figure 3.14iii: Spousal Standoffs

Spouses cut off all civil communication between each other and prohibit the child from sharing much or anything about life with the other parent. What lives in the child as a part of each of them is shut out. The child's true soul life doesn't exist for them.

Figure 3.14iv: Child's Heart Alienation

One parent excludes himself or herself from the child's life completely, either from choice or as a result of one form of legal action or another. Some aspect of that child's heart forces is left alone and in limbo, consciously or unconsciously holding soul memory of the lost parent. In the soul memory, this can be the case even if the parents' partnership broke up when the child was only an infant or early toddler.

The self-harmonizing expectations that parents and extended family members regularly put onto growing Pearl Children are not backed up in any empirical studies as bearing any reality on what a child is able to do in such circumstances. What parents hope for or fantasize about does not necessarily equate with the true, soul-spirit lawfulness regarding the developmental needs of an at-risk child. Too often, parents try to resolve the child's stresses with adult talk about how the parent is coping with the tensions with the other parent. This behavior risks establishing adult maturity in the child that the child can't really handle and may resent later, knowing on some level that part of that child's important childhood was taken away.

Figure 3.15: Early consequences for a child "shared" between conflictual parents

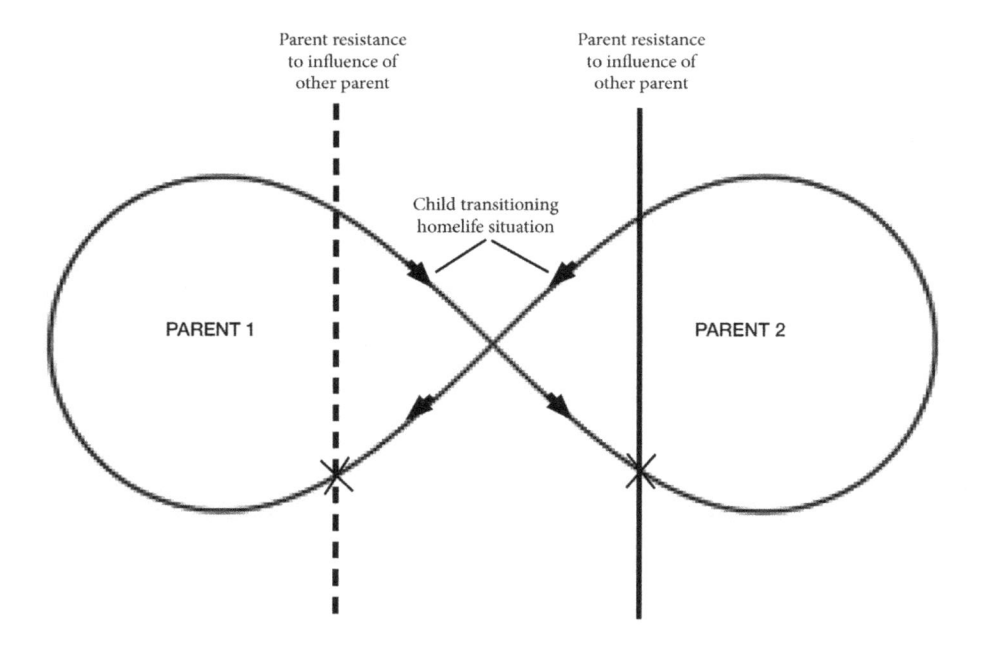

When each parent holds resentments toward the other parent, hidden or otherwise, the child's inner-soul development cannot rightfully fit into the expected triple lemniscate of parent expectation. Parental tensions and overt or subtle conflicts, representing blockages to higher love and respect, create breaking points for the child's development. The child's soul begins to be distorted or shut out.

Without a parent-supported ability to create peaceful refuge between them, and with the child being made to act out adult, loving, peace-keeping practices that don't actually get patterned in the parent's lives, a child can unconsciously chart an individual path too early. The child ducks out on trusting the parents, knowing unconsciously that she is being expected to be in unlawful expectation and hypocrisy. The child must move away from each parent in some way, although the child is not developmentally ready to do so. Such forced independence exacerbates insecure, disorganized, ambivalent, or other subtler forms of unstable attachment with the parents. On the other scale, a child may "swallow the wrongful expectations, taking harms inwardly in a way that raises eating disorders or deep-seated resentments later."

Figure 3.16: Triple lemniscate of a Pearl's reactions to parent conflict, according to rational lawfulness

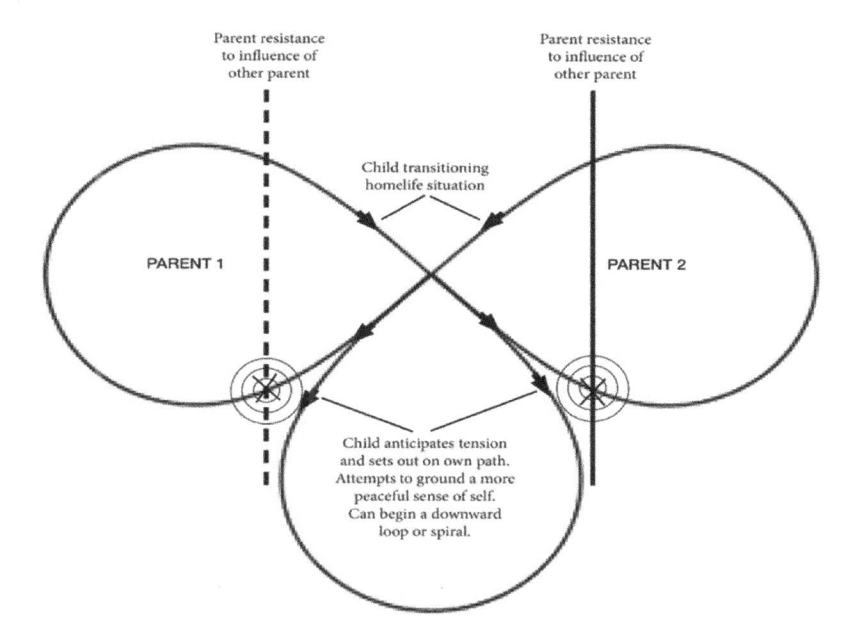

The child, unprepared in the physical, etheric, astral, or ego-I developments, naturally and lawfully seeks the flow to health. Since the child is not yet appropriately prepared for individuation at this level, he or she is at risk of falling through the cracks or into a sub-nature depression and despair. Parents, especially of teenagers, often don't notice the early signs of this fall.

Figure 3.17: The spiritual bypass or depressive fall of the child

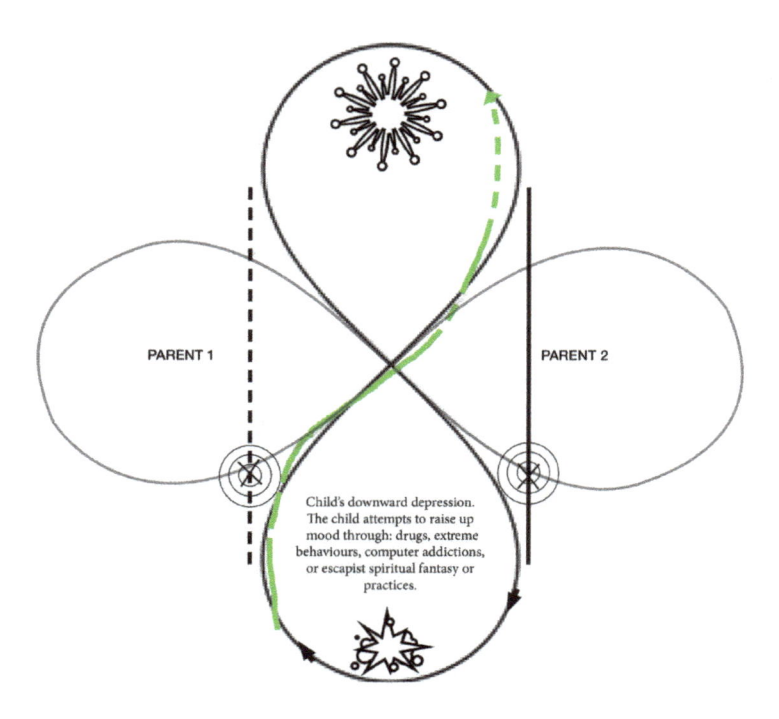

[Diagram: vertical lemniscate with PARENT 1 and PARENT 2 loops on either side. Text in lower loop reads: "Child's downward depression. The child attempts to raise up mood through: drugs, extreme behaviours, computer addictions, or escapist spiritual fantasy or practices."]

Faced with regular conflicts with the home parent about the other parent, (conflicts represented in lemniscate drawings by reverberating circles with crosses inside), the child does one of two things:
- Reaches for an escape, some kind of a high (area of the exploding star in the top loop of the vertical lemniscate). This is an attempt to overcome the heaviness and dark feelings and to try to achieve a sense that everything will somehow be okay.
- Falls low in an emotional crash or harmful/sabotaging behavior (represented by the distorted star in the bottom loop of the vertical lemniscate.) The child can lose the will forces for activities that otherwise motivate joy or interests. The child is at risk of depression in this state. The child may attempt to rise out of the low state with the use of drugs, extreme behaviors, computer addictions, or other escape-oriented practices.

The child's unconscious reactions are not necessarily observable or predictable. A parent may have no sense of whether the child is jumping out in a high in some way or beginning to sink into an unhealthy low. The child seeks escape (spiritual comfort for pain and suffering) in unconsciously desperate and ineffective ways. This is because the undeveloped child is unrealistically being expected to bridge points of conflict that the parents themselves could not.

A polar reaction often occurs, where the child or youth makes chronic efforts to find a high to pull out and away from energetically decompensating conflict. A child is painfully, though unconsciously, aware of the lack of appropriate holding. The child's neurological place of "calm and capable" is likely set off into cortisol-chemical flooding in the brain. The child is forced to "raise the spirits" in an immature spiritual way, but chemical flooding will lead to an eventual shutdown, illness, addiction, obsession, or compulsions.

The child becomes addicted to a cycle of trauma-reactive events in the brain. A neurological, hippocampus brain cycling can lead to neurological burnout later and the need for ongoing anti-depressant medications. Or, the Pearl may need to drop out from outer life to retreat someplace exceptionally calm and protected to try to build up brain resources again. That is, if these youths or young adults don't go directly to using illegal opioid drugs or other dangerous substances to bring calm.

Figure 3.18: Child sacrificed on the cross

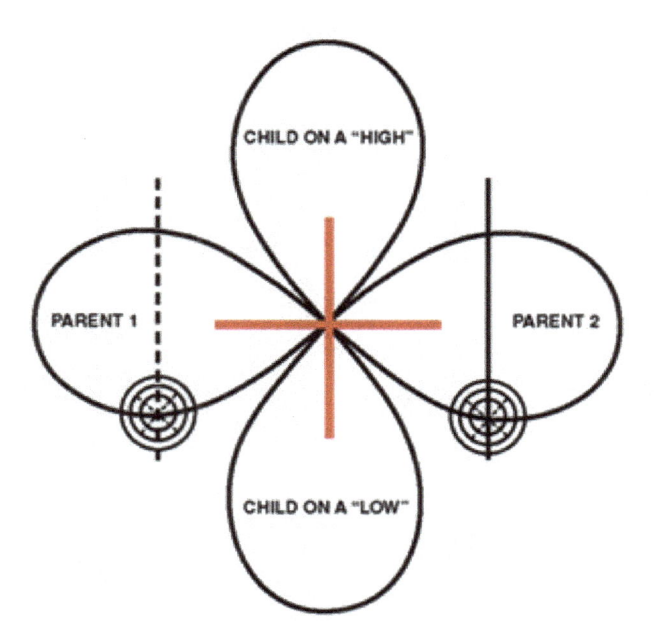

The child is being falsely expected to develop and overcome in a way that has not been proven in soul lawfulness. The child cannot be expected to hold adult-level peace practices in the middle of the conflicted parents. To stay in soul lawfulness, the child must break out and reach for someone or something higher to help bring child lawfulness into proper harmony.

This is seen mathematically. The only triple lemniscate that can be achieved mathematically is apparent in this lemniscate looping downward or upward—not through the center. This sends the child into the need for very complex spiritual capacities and practices long before he or she is ready for that. The exacerbated and exhausting efforts for soul survival can cause inner systems damage in the child—digestive, metabolic, and nerve-sense distresses are typical.

Figure 3.19: Lemniscate cross showing soul complexity expected of a Pearl caught in parent conflict

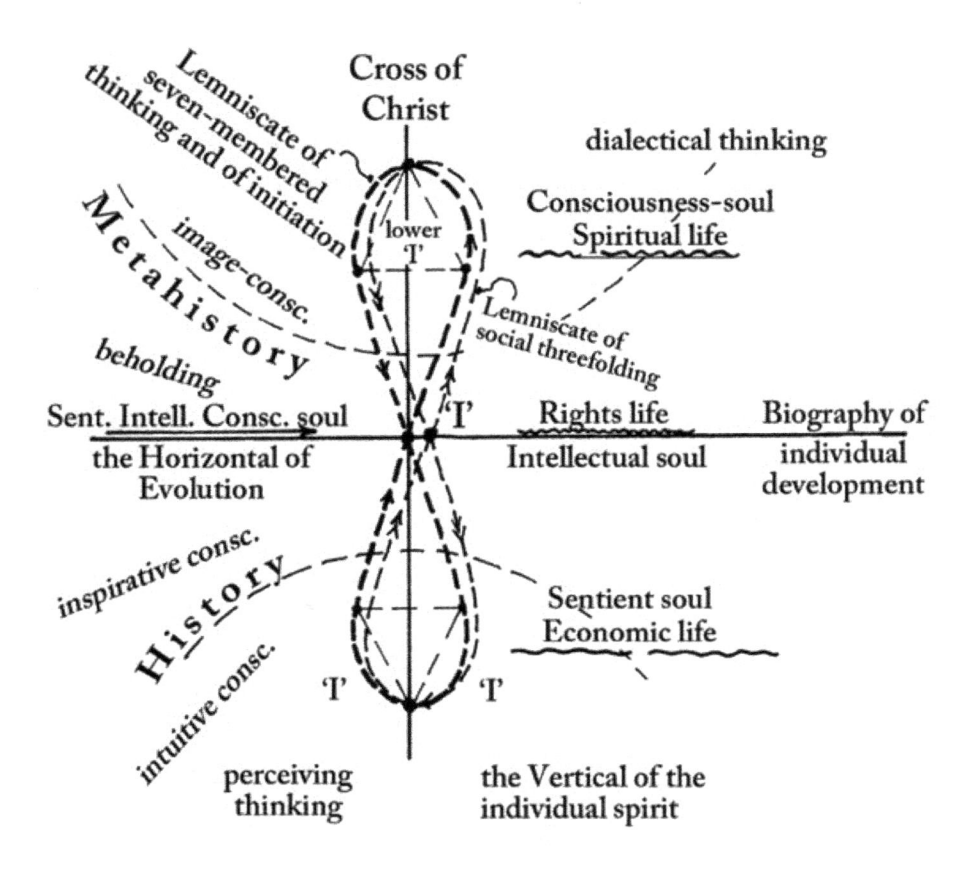

Lemniscate of seven-membered thinking and of initiation
image-consc.
Cross of Christ
lower 'I'
dialectical thinking
Consciousness-soul
Spiritual life
Metahistory
beholding
Lemniscate of social threefolding
'I'
Sent. Intell. Consc. soul
Rights life
Biography of individual development
the Horizontal of Evolution
Intellectual soul
inspirative consc.
History
intuitive consc.
Sentient soul
Economic life
'I'   'I'
perceiving thinking
the Vertical of the individual spirit

The sophisticated lemniscate cross that children in conflicted divorces can experience in the soul, despite being too young to cope with the high levels of complex spiritual truth being now demanded of them to keep their souls-psyches in wholeness and harmony. (Image courtesy of Kim Graae Munch.)

Figure 3.20: Artist's lemniscate rendition reflecting many parents' unrooted and often superficial expectations of child success despite a conflicted, divorced family life.

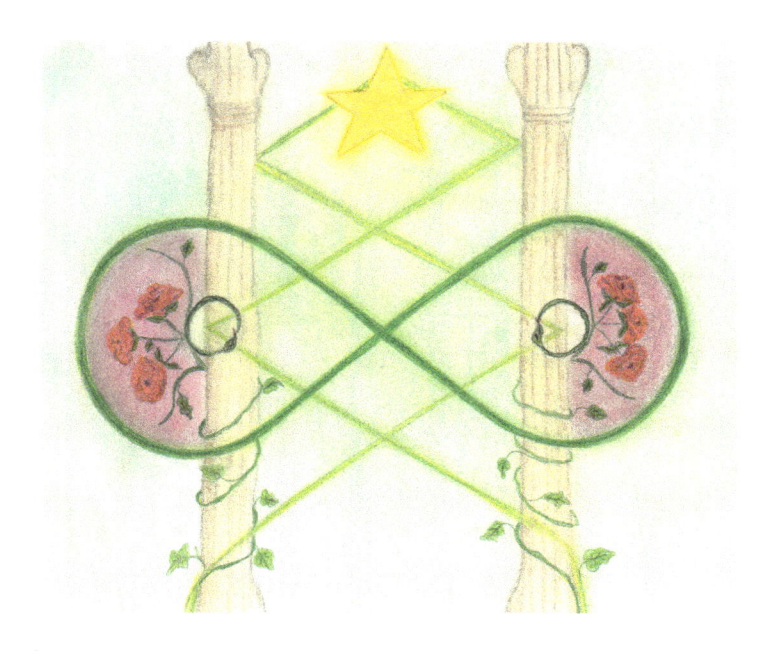

Each loop, with a rose inside of an ouroboros (sacred snake biting its tail), represents a parent, divided well apart from the other, who wants to believe that their way of life is best. The edgy, woven pattern in the middle, leading to a lopsided star, represents the thin-souled child caught in high but unsubstantiated expectations.

This rendition is a fantastical image and metaphor for the Pearl Child that can be created artistically but not through mathematical lawfulness. Although lovely and pleasing to the eye, it shows both a clearly unrooted, and spiritually blown-open, rendition of the individuated child in the middle of the more rounded parents.

With fantastical beliefs put upon the Pearl Child, a kind of untethered transcendence is expected of the child who is trying to get two feet on the ground, self-capable, and whole enough to manage a soulfully attuned life on his or her own for several decades to come. Abstract art does not represent the real spiritual laws of humanness. For a true soul, being expected to act in false, abstract ways, that can feel like being a decorative accessory is clearly unsustainable for a human life.

When a Pearl can have no lawful respite, and no escape from parent impositions, and if that child does not want to fall into abuses that lead to highs and lows, the child risks being relegated to a life of décor in the middle of the parent's main egoic events. If the passive child attempts to express the real pain, suffering, and soul indignation, he or she may be ignored, hushed, medicated, or expected to be more psychologically sophisticated than the parent, at stages in life when their biology and neurology are not even fully developed. Many Pearl Adults attest to the feeling of being made insignificant, but also hyper-responsible, in the light of their parents' conflict. In essence, they were made to feel unreal.

Figure 3.21: Life-giving, human DNA double-helix loop compares with triple lemniscate

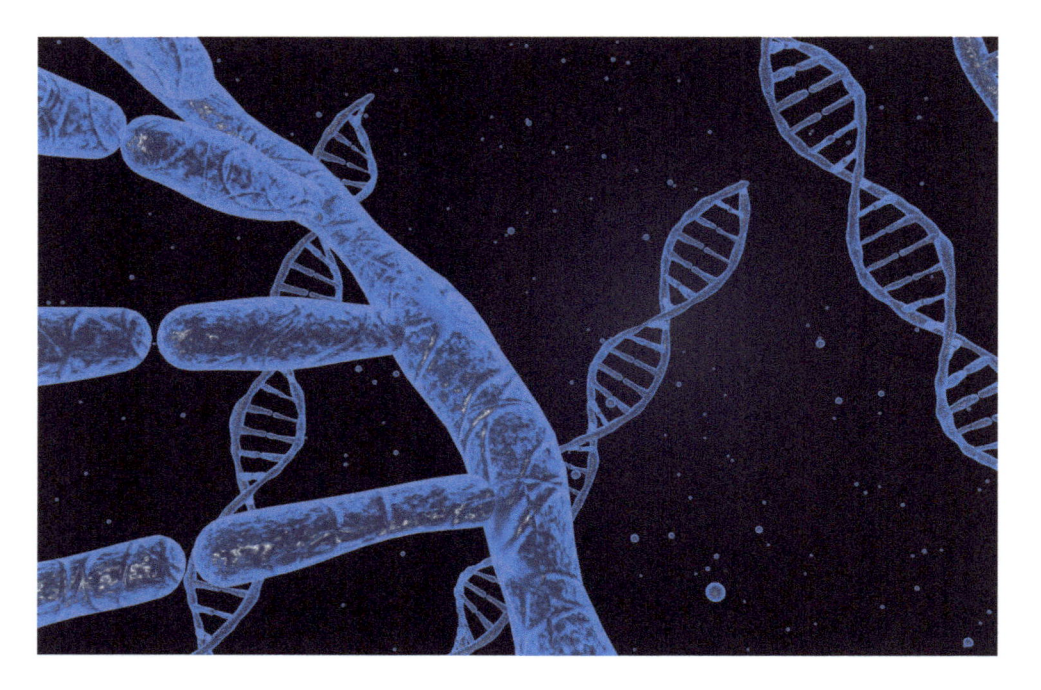

Human DNA, appearing as a series of open-ended lemniscates, is created out of biological lawfulness, organically, with an astute and even mysterious process coming out of the integration of masculine and feminine markers. They seek harmonious, healthy functioning for the system in every way possible. DNA does not naturally set out to create a conflict between two opposing systems.

How is it that human DNA can create a lawful triple lemniscate, although geometric math and algebra cannot create such with the noted conflict points that represent parent conflict above? This is despite the human-earthly-cosmic awareness that all organic life in the natural world follows a lawfulness that can be traced, tracked, and even at times, predicted through mathematical rationale?

Harmony in a biological entity entails various aspects of that entity cooperating for the sake of the wholeness, effectiveness, and reasonable stability of that system. Likewise, harmony for a child caught in a parental divorce requires that all entities in that system cooperate for the stability and well-being of that child and for the broader implications of that child's long-term life and the family system.

Where does the Pearl Youth or Pearl Adult soul turn if this is not the case—the one who wants to go forward, and not fall into old, heavy matter again, but stay on the earth well until the time is right to ascend from it forever?

Walking and Living as Angels

If human beings were able to live in pure, archetypal lawfulness, entirely in tune with their masculine and feminine natures, as in their DNA, would they be able to develop a life free of events of disharmony and unlawfulness?

Living in a purified, archetypal lawfulness on earth would be like walking as an angel. No earthly hardship or phenomenon would have any significant effect on us. No astral emotion would be stirred. No earthly diminishing of etheric life-forces survival would really affect anyone. Our struggle with the hardened earth would be taken care of by robots or other technologies while we continue to need to walk the earth.

We would be as highly enlightened beings on the earth—entirely transcendent of earthly effects. We would seem to live in a kind of untouchable radiant beauty, not fully engaging the earth and somewhat ethereal, seeming closer to the sky than earth's other living beings. We would, however, have a great deal of work to do helping other human beings to become ascendant also

If this sounds like the story of human, spiritual ascendance, it is. The problem with that story is that it is millennia away. What do we do until then? What soul work are we here for? What kind of angel should we be, here and now? Will everyone on earth work to become the archetypal angelic beings that the great spirit teachers and initiates have foretold?

According to Rudolf Steiner's esoteric science, the angelic forces moving humanity today come out of St. Michael's archangelic guidance. St. Michael, slaying metaphoric dragons and real evils with his mighty sword, is the spirit of our times. He builds iron forces in us as we head into the wintery, dark times of the year and the heavier earthly challenges, encouraging us to keep mindful attention on our own dark double natures, transforming them and putting them to use for the good.

The dark double represents those aspects of ourselves that work to deny our humanness, and the humanness of others. They harbor non-virtuous qualities in us and seek to keep us heavily attached to the earth. To bring the sword of truth to our human development, we must tame, and even slay, our inner and hateful demons to walk rightly on the earth today. To do this, we need to take the time to look inward at ourselves and see where we are being unloving, selfish, excessive, arrogant, greedy, slothful, vengeful, and harboring a host of other unsavory qualities that make us less than human and bound to snaky attachments that are not for our times. What happens if we take up this sword in earnest? We become loving beings.

However, there are dark angelic beings hovering about the earth as well, like snakes, seeking to keep us low and in turmoil and horrendous suffering. The challenge is to clearly discern if we are following Michael, our personal angels, or these other beings.

What does this mean for Pearl Children whose parents can't find a way to be humanly respectful with each other, even if they decided to be far apart? How do these children get Michaelic protection from soul regression or destruction? Are these children angelic beings planted among hardened beings to transform them? Can they do this while they are only young?

Pearl Children need protection from parent hardenedness. When parents don't overcome this, should the children still be in the homes with them? Some children, exposed to parent violence or neglect due to parent drug use, get taken away into foster homes. What's the difference between fostering and regular parenting?

Foster parenting is a sacred societal trust. Good foster parents are not going to benefit from any familial attachment from a child. They are parenting out of a strong measure of unconditional selflessness, to help a child to grow in wholeness and manage a sustained life, hopefully among people they can trust to also have a measure of selflessness. Conflictual divorced parents too often can't find that selfless nature in their child-raising, and that leads to attachment conflicts with their ex-spouse, and to child alienations and estrangements. Foster parents work like angels with the kind of angelic nature that walks the difficult, real-life heart stuff.

The Hut as Sanctuary, Temple, and Honored Space

Rudolf Steiner has indicated that a process is taking place now, very slowly and bringing transforming life forces right down into our DNA. We are growing a new, lawfully attuned space in our hearts that can lovingly withstand intense conflicts or polarizing thoughts, feelings, and activities between others. What will this inner nursery of heart growth be like for children, youth, and young adults going through great heart pains?

On an adult level, cultivating inner hut space is about maintaining our own sacred practices toward ascended cosmic nature. We prepare ourselves now for a future, finer presence, and seek as angels to grow our hearts and do good in the presence of others. For Pearl Children that space may need to be externalized in a material and practical way as a start—taking the form of a protected heart hut in the home that is purely a physical play space for that child. It is held as a sanctuary by the parents. The hut needs to have an element of incarnate and precious warmth. Parents help Pearl Children keep the hut sacred by encouraging them to be loving with it, helping to care for the items that the Pearls have put there, or that an older sibling, cousin, or friend has chosen carefully to put into it with permission from the hut owner.

The hut at home needs to be more special than just a play or activity room. It might be a room constructed within a room with some handcrafted wood from the trees around the property. It might be a tiny yurt in the recreation room, a terra-cotta, rammed-earth hive in the enclosed porch, or a firmly created sultan's tent with a fine carpet and silks (found perhaps at a thrift store or second-hand auction) hanging across the ceiling in the loft. It could be a small, self-sewn or designed tent in a corner of the living room. The hut should have a window with a curtain, and good air circulation.

The space should be ripe with a few nourishing items that the child likes to eat, such as sweet figs, strawberry leather the child made, or a warm, almond-milk-and nutmeg drink in a special, low-spill-potential, clay bottle with a cork or a Thermos cup. The choices of food items in the hut need to be mindfully considered by the child but monitored by parents to avoid over-indulgence or overstimulating foods.

The hut needs a musical instrument, like a lyre, wooden flute, tambourine, drum, or mbira. It needs easily accessible art or craft supplies such as pastel sticks and paper, with a soft clean up cloth. Some soapstone and files can provide a focusing activity for a child, lowering anxiety. Inspiring, colorful crystals can reflect the seasons and lift the mood in the hut when a Pearl is sad. A particularly meaningful image, such as a painting or wall hanging can be changed from time to time. Story-character dolls, finger puppets, and stuffed animals are also helpful.

The hut may be very simple and quiet, or it might invite the child's singing or poetry reciting, filling the space with sounds to override loneliness. A child can select a prayer or reverent verse that is spoken only in the hut. Sand-tray[77] creatures, figures, nature-table beings made of felt, dress-up clothing, and play props are all items that a child can create within the hut.

The purpose of this room or space is not to promote indulgence, but to offer a traumatized boy or girl a resourceful place of natural sanctuary in each of the homes that the child shares with parents (and other family members) and not in the place where the child is always sleeping. It is a therapeutic space. It is to ensoul self-solace, with both patterned as well as unstructured practices for the child to engage when complex emotional processing needs can't be attended to by a parent or other caregiver right away. It is not a place to replace important emotional experiences with the parent and extended family members. It is a place the parent pays attention to, nonetheless, when noticing the child retreating there.

Soulfully, the hut space is a place where the child can go to have early experiences of self-calming and self-loving. This ritualized sacred space can have essential oil scents if the child approves, can be made up with warm lighting, beeswax for play (not candles), and things to access for self-expression. It is best developed slowly and changed when necessary.

The child who is taking hut time gets check-ins from the parent or stepparent, and can create boundary rules around it with others in the family. Codes can be established with other children in the house regarding when the Pearl is ready or willing to share something in or about the hut. Other children are taught to be deeply respectful of the Pearl's need for that space. They can be encouraged to create their own huts, if they need to.

If parents in each home have been consistent with helping a Pearl with the seven life processes check-ins during crossover transitions, the need for hut time may be minimal. It is important if the transition times are not going as well as they could, to not underestimate the need for a hut space that is warm, welcoming, clearly made up with loving artifacts of soul goodness in the likeness of the child's open interests, and clearly bounded as that child's space only. A parent can "mail" love notes to the child's hut at times, and playfully leave a delivery of some item that the Pearl can use in the hut. Parents can also offer a favorite drink or food when it seems appropriate.

The practice wherein parents help with divorce transitions is a necessary event to minimize what is a stressful back-and-forth life for young children. The practice may be needed right up through late adolescence. It helps to rebuild an inner sense of security that was disrupted in the soul in the parental breakup. It can help to keep the child's nervous system balanced and in the healthy neurological "window of tolerance."[78]

The Counselor and the Lemniscate

Since there are going to continue to be parents who fight for partial custody for their children but who do not want to do any psychosocial processing with their children when they have them in their lives for periods of time, and even if the other parent is open and willing to do so, the option of having a well-trained counselor to help with the divorce transition processing becomes an important one. History and practice have shown that one parent cannot take on everything for a child after a divorce.

A counselor, teacher, counseling-skilled family member, or even a therapeutically informed friend can use the *Seven Life and Learning Processes* lemniscate to help process a child's inner experience of the parent home-life transitions. The more consistent the helper, the better in the first year, and the best case is that the same person be able to help at times throughout at least grade school. This is not necessarily possible for many people, but if possible, it is best. All must suspend judgment.

The counselor can give practices for the child to use in the hut and elsewhere, and help design the hut, quietly holding space sometimes to just listen and acknowledge if the child needs to share about the parents. (That person must follow confidentiality protocols for someone past the age of legal minority, and abuse and self-danger protocols for a child of any age). The helper needs to have good rapport so the child can safely share anything that is distressing to the soul. The counselor might see some consistent and differentiated needs patterns that the parents simply have a hard time seeing due to their own biases. The likelihood of bias is very strong in conflicted divorces.

The Keepers of the Fairy Tales of Darkness and Light

In Waldorf education and healing, children are brought the whole picture of an idea, story, or experience before having it broken down into smaller parts for more specific understanding. This describes the humanistic perspective of anthroposophical education and healing where all of life's activities are interpreted from their holistic, human connections.

Waldorf education also strives to prepare grown children to recognize, address, and come to some acceptance of the many conflicting and countering forces present in real, human endeavor. This is addressed, in child-appropriate ways, for instance, through Grimm's dark and light fairy tales, which are told regularly in Waldorf lower schools, homes, and in community puppet plays. The tales themselves weave many elements of natural and cosmic influences within the moral stories of good human behavior coming to be challenged by others' trickery and the various characters' struggles to uphold the moral goodness and light.

Children hear of characters taking the rocky and yet magical trails to a better sense of personal judgment and to their places in the bigger picture of life. Tension happens in fairy tales, and yet children feel the truthfulness of the struggles depicted in the tales and are not overwhelmed by them. Rather, they are helped to know that they can overcome adversity and tension through the many healing and creatively practical skills that Waldorf education brings through the child's development years. Soul adventures in the fairytales offer inner rehearsals for the life of the young child.

Still, a child who has been through divorce conflict or trauma with their parents can get extra-triggered or numbed with fairy tales, so it is something for educators and therapists to watch for and prepare to offer further processing around. This needs to be done in child-appropriate ways, such as some watercolor painting over lunchtime, or having the child create a clay sculpture at a desk while hearing the story. The Pearl can do this also with some hut time during free play periods. I encourage teachers to create a hut in the classroom.

A counselor, teacher, or caregiver at home can reinforce for the Pearl Child the positive points or images in a fairy tale. Kingdoms in fairy tales often portray the bigger world with its intrigues and hard-felt consequences, but also with its joys. Give more time to the joys with a Pearl in distress, and what aspects of that joy the child can access internally, right there and then. The caregiver may need to review for the Pearl, in living, imaginative pictures, the story elements that showed how a character overcame a darkness.

Elders in a story are often the moral keepers of the land. These seemingly magical people arrive to point people out of darkness and despair and bring the protagonist in the story back onto the path of light and goodness. A caregiver can share with a child how to identify a kind, safe, and helpful elder—and how to make a graceful request of one.

A therapist or parent can ask a child when they have had magical moments when a special person showed up unexpectedly and did something for them. If the child has truly no recollection of such a scenario, the adult can help arrange an experience for the child with compassionate elders in the community. Good elders in the Pearl's community may need to advocate for Pearls, in general, bringing awareness of Pearl issues, and petitioning for helpers and people who will just offer a graceful kindness to Pearls when they see them or if they get a request from one.

Gems, creatures, and magical numbers in fairy tales remind the child of the truly creative and sometimes stunning beauty and mystical power of the original forces in earthly life. Tricksters in the fairy tales, who are often frustrating to characters in the stories, also bring out our sense of humor. If a child can find no humor in the tricksters, do a short role-play about a trickster to see what does arise for the child. The adult in the room can work alchemically (processes described more later) to turn the experience around to appropriate humor for the child that is not in any way put-down humor. Pearls too regularly hear put-downs of one loved one by another. They can be super-sensitive to it and can get emotionally triggered by it.

As with the comforting stories of the old coppersmith, the forest woman, and the elfin man in the fairy tale of "The Pearl and the Hut," a soul-psyche-informed teacher, caregiver, or counselor can, through therapeutic storytelling, offer a bridge between healthy stories and the conflicts of the child's own relationship world. In "The Pearl and the Hut" story, although the children couldn't really know or understand this, they were kept safe and hidden from the serious soul destruction going on in the kingdom between parents caught in hateful competition. This is a similar need to when parents of Pearls are in heated court battles for child custody. Children need to be kept far away from their parents' courtroom scenarios. This is a special time to receive creative, artistic, imaginative support.

In "The Pearl and the Hut" story, the children do not know the whole truth of their parents' conflicts, and Pearls, in general, ought not to know at such young ages and even well into adolescence. Instead, in the fairy tale, they are given the chance to have their natural, development needs met by the coppersmith and the forest woman, at the right ages and stages. We don't hear what the resolution of the parents' battle was, but we know the children are whole and steeped in loving examples to carry them back into the world of their once-warring parents. Their growing organs and nervous systems have been protected in the quiet forest with the mature, soul-respecting, and selfless elders.

The metaphoric story of "The Pearl and the Hut" is not shared to suggest that all Pearl Children be completely removed from their parents in stages of divorces. It does, however, suggest a clear, zero-tolerance policy regarding exposing children to traumatizing parent divorce violence, bitter reprisals, constant negativity, and destructive thinking. Children need safe, loving, and predictable experiences to enter the harsher outer world when they are grown and examples of people with a loving vigor for life. "The Pearl and the Hut" fairy tale reinforces that.

Chiron's Wound

The children in "The Pearl and the Hut" tale are increasingly aware inside of themselves of a Chironic[79] wound in the soul, usually raising feelings of deep loss, grief, and betrayal, by the time they are older adolescents. That is, a deep psychic pain that many people experience about something from their childhood that makes them suffer but also grow in ways that they may not have thought they wanted to.

Some Chiron wounds take much of our lives to understand and resolve to some level of peace or acceptance. That striving is evident in the fairy tale through the children's continual questing for knowledge about what happened to their parents. It is something from childhood that despite other positive aspects of the child's life, the grown child can't let go of. The soul needs to transform the Chiron wound with deep meaning in order to bring it into higher good this lifetime and without pretense or false spiritual bypassing.

The Modern Elder Earth Magician

Counselors act as feeling attendants and self-care coaches today. They are often the elder, earth magician. They witness, recognize, and parse out the sources of pain and distress in children and parents. If they really have their hearts and souls in it, they inspire loving confidence and offer practices for clients to create deeper and fuller relationships with themselves. Counselors also help Pearls to practice trusting adults again.

A main goal for anthroposophical counselors is to be available as consistently as possible for children in undue stress, and to encourage the fostering of strengths and the safe sharing of vulnerabilities. When their work really touches the core, human needs of a Pearl Child, then the child's soul sheaths and processes can evolve safely and in full of capacity.

Children whose life situations require outside counseling because nothing else is available to them need new kinds of counselors, like the forest couple and the earthen, elfin man. These counselors require courage and wisdom to walk the darkened woods with them. To do so, they need a higher view to know, without question, that the lustrous glowing pearls forming around the grating sands of the children's family dissolution, and the incumbent heart pain that the incessant, burning irritation is causing, are part of a much bigger divine plan. Counselors of Pearls must enter in with the children's hearts with the highest reverence, and with a Christ-natured, Michaelic love, that will protect and foster the newly expanding heart forces as reverently as they protect their own.

The following chapters offer some training ground for the caregivers in that honorable, Pearl Children knighthood.

Endnotes

1 R. Steiner, "Lecture 2: Laughing and Weeping," Metamorphoses of the Soul: Paths of Experience, Vol. 2 (1910), retrieved May 31, 2020, https://wn.rsarchive.org/Lectures/GA059/English/RSP1983/MetSo2_index.html

2 R. Steiner, Karmic Relationships: Esoteric Studies, Vol. VII (1924), retrieved May 31, 2020, http://wn.rsarchive.org/Lectures/GA239/English/RSP1973/Karm07_index.html

3 R. Steiner, (1909). "An Outline of Esoteric Science, Chapter IV: The Evolution of the Cosmos and Man,", retrieved May 31, 2020, http://wn.rsarchive.org/Books/GA013/English/AP1972/GA013_index.html

4 R. Steiner, Cosmic Memory: Prehistory of Earth and Man (1904), retrieved May 31, 2020, https://wn.rsarchive.org/Books/GA011/English/RSPI1959/GA011_index.html

5 M. Ruef, The Nine-Year Change and Child Development Between the Ages of Seven and Twelve (Chatham, NY: Waldorf Publications, 2015).

6 S. Prokofieff, Steiner and the Founding of the New Mysteries, (Forest Row, UK: Temple Lodge Publishing, 2000), retrieved June 18, 2020, https://www.amazon.ca/Rudolf-Steiner-Founding-New-Mysteries/dp/0904693619/ref=sr_1_1?dchild=1&keywords=9780904693614&linkCode=qs&qid=1592514608&s=books&sr=1-1

7 R. Steiner, An Outline of Esoteric Science, (Toronto, ON :Hushion House Publishing, 1997), retrieved June 18, 2020, https://www.amazon.ca/Outline-Esoteric-Science-Rudolf-Steiner/dp/0880104090/ref=pd_lpo_14_img_1/147-9279141-5637559?_encoding=UTF8&pd_rd_i=0880104090&pd_rd_r=1381fbea-5695-47ba-83d2-48d5c6625012&pd_rd_w=knkM9&pd_rd_wg=h10C1&pf_rd_p=256a14b6-93bc-4bcd-9f68-aea60d2878b9&pf_rd_r=N4GMC2424ETG8V8YX8ER&psc=1&refRID=N4GMC2424ETG8V8YX8ER

8 R. Steiner, An Outline of Esoteric Science.

9 R. Steiner, An Outline of Esoteric Science.

10 R. Steiner, An Outline of Esoteric Science.

11 R. Steiner, An Outline of Esoteric Science.

12 R. Steiner, An Outline of Esoteric Science.

13 R. Steiner, An Outline of Esoteric Science

14 M. Ruef, The Nine-Year Change and Child Development Between the Ages of Seven and Twelve (Chatham, NY: Waldorf Publications, 2015).

15 M. Baker, "Movement Education: The Origins of Bothmer Gymnastics," Waldorf Resources (July 2014), retrieved May 31, 2020, http://www.waldorf-resources.org/articles/display/archive/2014/07/28/article/movement-education-the-origins-of-bothmer-gymnastics/c19f05f1ec6fa0291b8600b16487dfc9/

16 Spatial Dynamics Institute, "Spatial Dynamics," (2015) (Blogspot). Retrieved April 25, 2017 from: https://www.spacialdynamics.com/definition-of-spacial-dynamics/

17 R. Steiner, "From the Contents of the Esoteric Lessons, VI, On The Three Magi," extract from a lecture, (Berlin, Germany, 1904), Rudolf Steiner Archives, retrieved June 18, 2020, https://wn.rsarchive.org/Lectures/Dates/19041230p01.html

18 R. Steiner, "Christianity as Mystical Fact," (Berlin, Germany, 1902), Rudolf Steiner Archive, retrieved June 18, 2020, https://wn.rsarchive.org/Books/GA008/English/RPC1961/GA008_index.html

19 R. Steiner, "Philosophy and Anthroposophy: An article by Rudolf Steiner," (London, UK: The Anthroposophical Publishing Company, 1929), retrieved June 18, 2020, https://wn.rsarchive.org/Articles/GA035/PhlAnt_index.html

20 R. Steiner, "Christianity as Mystical Fact," (Berlin, Germany, 1902), Rudolf Steiner Archive, retrieved June 18, 2020, https://wn.rsarchive.org/Books/GA008/English/RPC1961/GA008_index.html

21 C. Dunn, "Pythagoras the Master: Philolaus, Presocratic Follower," (Berwick-upon-Tweed: Lindisfarne Books, 2018), retrieved June 18, 2020, https://wn.rsarchive.org/Articles/GA035/PhlAnt_index.html

22 M. Baker, "Movement Education: The Origins of Bothmer Gymnastics," Waldorf Resources (July 2014), retrieved May 31, 2020, http://www.waldorf-resources.org/articles/display/archive/2014/07/28/article/movement-education-the-origins-of-bothmer-gymnastics/c19f05f1ec6fa0291b8600b16487dfc9/

23 R. Steiner, An Outline of Esoteric Science, (Toronto, ON: Hushion House Publishing, 1997).

T. Boardman, "The 'Abolition' of the Spirit: The Enigma of Canon XI – The Year 869 & Its Significance in the Destiny of Europe,"threefold Society (July 13, 2012), retrieved June 17, 2020, http://threeman.org/?p=1092

R. Steiner, The Knights Templar: The Mystery of the Warrior Monks, (East Essex. UK: Rudolf Steiner Press, 2014).

24 R. Steiner, "Cosmic Memory: The Fourfold Man of Earth," (1904), Rudolf Steiner Archive, retrieved June 18, 2020, https://wn.rsarchive.org/Books/GA011/English/RSPI1959/GA011_c18.html

25 Steiner, R. (1920). Spiritual Science and Medicine: Lecture XVI," (Dornach, Switzerland, 1920), retrieved April 27, 2017, http://wn.rsarchive.org/Lectures/GA312/English/RSP1948/SpiSci_index.html

26 R. Steiner, "The Poetry and Meaning of Fairy Tales," (Berlin, Germany, 1908), Rudolf Steiner Archive, retrieved June 18, 2020, https://wn.rsarchive.org/Lectures/PoeTales/19081226p01.html

C. Natale, "Fairytales in Waldorf Education", The Wonder of Childhood (February 26, 2011), retrieved June 17, 2020, https://thewonderofchildhood.com/2011/02/fairy-tales-with-christine-natale/

27 D. J. Siegel, "Pruning, Myelination, and the Remodeling Adolescent Brain: The Brain Rewires During Adolescence to Increase Integration and Efficiency," Psychology Today (February 4, 2014), retrieved May 31, 2020, https://www.psychologytoday.com/blog/inspire-rewire/201402/pruning-myelination-and-the-remodeling-adolescent-brain

S. Blakemore, "Adolescent brain development," (Barbican, London: Welcome Trust, 2014), retrieved June 18, 2020, https://thinkneuroscience.wordpress.com/2014/01/22/adolescent-brain-development/ JANUARY 22, 2014

28 Camphill School Aberdeen, "Understanding and Applying the Fourfold Approach to the Human Being," (Aberdeen, UK: Camphill School Aberdeen, 2015), retrieved June 18, 2020, http://www.camphillresearch.com/content-stuff/uploads/2015/08/Bruell-Understanding-the-Fourfold-Human-Being.pdf

S. Prokofieff, "The Riddle of the Human "I", (Forest Row, UK: Temple Lodge Publishing, 2017), retrieved June 18, 2020, https://www.amazon.ca/Riddle-Human-i-Anthroposophical-Study/dp/190699997X

29 R. Steiner, An Outline of Esoteric Science, (Toronto, ON: Hushion House Publishing, 1997).

30 W. Bento et al., The Counselor . . . as if Soul and Spirit Matter: Inspirations from Anthroposophy (Great Barrington, MA: Steiner Books, 2015).

31 Uriel Pharmacy. "Aurum Lavendar Rose Body Oil," (East Troy, WI: Uriel Pharmacy, 2018), retrieved August 30, 2018 from: https://www.urielpharmacy.com/aurum-lavender-rose-body-oil

32 R. Steiner, "The Mission of the Archangel, Michael," (Dornach, Switzerland, 1919), Rudolf Steiner Archive, retrieved June 2, 2020, http://wn.rsarchive.org/Lectures/MissMich/19191123p01.html

33 L.Winerman, "The mind's mirror: A new type of neuron-called a mirror neuron-could help explain how we learn through mimicry and why we empathize with others," American Psychological Association: Monitor on Psychology, 36, 9, (2005), 48. Retrieved June 18, 2020, https://www.apa.org/monitor/oct05/mirror

34 G. Klein, "Missing Pieces: The Skill of Noticing Events that Didn't Happen," (Psychology Today , 2016), retrieved May 31, 2020, https://www.psychologytoday.com/blog/seeing-what-others-dont/201607/missing-pieces

35 R. Steiner, "Practical Training in Thought, Lecture, 1909" (Carlsruhe, Germany: Rudolf Steiner Archive), retrieved June 18, 2020, https://wn.rsarchive.org/GA/GA0108/19090118p02.html

36 A. Soesman, Our Twelve Senses, (Stroud, UK: Hawthorn Press, 1999), retrieved June 18, 2020, https://www.amazon.ca/Our-Twelve-Senses-Albert-Soesman/dp/1869890752

37 E. Olofsson, "Children of Divorce: Long-Term Psychological Effects and Neurological Consequences: Bachelor Degree Project in Cognitive Neuroscience," (Skovde, Sweden: University of Skovde, 2019), retrieved June 19, 2020, https://www.diva-portal.org/smash/get/diva2:1349746/FULLTEXT01.pdf V.K. Schaana, A. Schulza, H. Schachingerb, C. Vogelea, "Parental divorce is associated with an increased risk to develop mental disorders in women," Journal of Affective Disorders, 257, 1(2019), 91-99, retrieved June 18, 2020, https://www.sciencedirect.com/science/article/pii/S0165032718330957

38 Canadian Mental Health Associaton, "The Relationship between Mental Health, Mental Illness and Chronic Physical Conditions," (Toronto, ON: Canadian Mental Health Association, 2008), retrieved June 18, 2020, s://ontario.cmha.ca /documents/the-relationship -between-mental-health-mental-illness-and-chronic-physical -conditions/#:~: /#:~:text=People%20with%20serious%20mental%2

39 B. Ruf, Educating Traumatized Children, Waldorf Education in Crisis Intervention. (Herndon, VA: Lindisfarne Books, 2013).

40 L.Winerman, "The mind's mirror: A new type of neuron-called a mirror neuron-could help explain how we learn through mimicry and why we empathize with others," American Psychological Association: Monitor on Psychology, 36, 9, (2005), 48. Retrieved June 18, 2020, https://www.apa.org/monitor/oct05/mirror

41 R.C. Fraley, "A Brief Overview of Adult Attachment Theory and Research," (Champaign, Il: University of Illinois), retrieved April 27, 2017, https://internal.psychology.illinois.edu/~rcfraley/attachment.htm

42 R. E. Emery, Marriage, Divorce, and Children's Adjustment, (Thousand Oaks, CA: Sage Publications, 1999), http://dx.doi.org/10.4135/9781452220574

43 Wikipedia: The Free Encyclopedia, "Samskara (Indian Philosophy)," (Wikipedia, 2020), https://en.wikipedia.org/wiki/Samskara_(Indian_philosophy)

44 Weleda, "Comforting Baby Oil – Calendula", (Weleda, 2020), retrieved June 17, 2020, https://www.weleda.com/product/c/comforting-baby-oil

45 Dr Haushka, "Moor Lavender Calming Body Oil," (St. Jean-sur-Richelieu, QC: Dr. Haushka, 2020), retrieved June 18, 2020, https://www.drhauschka.ca/body-care/body-oils-lotions-powders/moor-lavender-calming-body-oil/

46 D. G. Alexander, "Freeing the Heart: The Importance of the Vagus Nerves/Cranial Nerve X," Massage Today 13, no. 7 (2013), retrieved May 31, 2020, https://www.massagetoday.com/articles/14777/Freeing-the-Heart-The-Importance-of-the-Vagus-NervesCranial-Nerve-X

47 C. Andrade, "What is Lazure Painting?" (YouTube video, November 17, 2014), retrieved May 31, 2020, https://www.youtube.com/watch?v=afdvh9nMRP4

48 G. Burkhard, Biographical Work: The Anthroposophical Basis, (Edinburgh, Scotland: Floris Books, 2007), retrieved June 18, 2020, https://www.amazon.ca/Biographical-Work-Anthroposophical-Gudrun-Burkhard/dp/0863155987
G. O'Neil, The Human Life: Understanding Your Biography, (Chestnut Ridge, NY: Mercury Press, 2012).

49 K. Konig, The first three years of the child: Walking, Speaking, Thinking, (Edinburgh. Scotland: Floris Books, 2004), retrieved June 18, 2020, https://www.amazon.ca/First-Three-Years-Child-Speaking/dp/0863154522

50 K. J. Payne, L. M. Ross, Simplicity Parenting: Using the Extraordinary Power of Less to Raise Calmer, Happier, and More Secure Kids (audiobook) (Old Saybrook, CT: Tantor Media, 2012), retrieved June 18, 2020, https://www.amazon.ca/Simplicity-Parenting-Extraordinary-Calmer-Happier/dp/B072HXWLTR

51 G.W. Mohi, "Positive outcomes of divorce: A multi-method study on the effects of parental divorce on children," University of Central Florida Undergraduate Research Journal, 7(2), 2015, retrieved from https://www.urj.ucf.edu/docs/mohi.pdf. . Retrieved from from https://www.urj.ucf.edu/docs/mohi.pdf

52 N. Dodwell, "Financial Crisis, Threefold Social Order and Rudolf Steiner's Organic System of Money," Insitut für soziale Dreigliederung (July 2012), retrieved May 31, 2020, http://www.threefolding.org/essays/2012-07-004.html

53 B. Harris, S. Zucker, "Part 3: Cathedral of Notre Dame de Chartres, c.1145 and 1194-c.1220" (YouTube video), Smarthistory (2011), retrieved May 31, 2020, https://www.youtube.com/watch?v=vAtQB9wLkUA

54 Homeschoolmath.net, "Fibonacci Numbers and the Golden Section," (Homeschoolmath.net, 2020), retrieved June 18, 2020, https://www.homeschoolmath.net/teaching/fibonacci_golden_section.php

55 R. Steiner, "Man As A Picture of The Living Spirit" (London, UK, 1923), Rudolf Steiner Archive, retrieved June 1, 2020, http://wn.rsarchive.org/Lectures/19230902p01.html
J. Blackwood, Mathematics Around Us (Edinburgh, Scotland: Floris Books, 2006).
P. Calter, "The Platonic Solids," Dartmouth University (1998), retrieved June 1, 2020, https://www.math.dartmouth.edu/~matc/math5.geometry/unit6/unit6.html

56 S.T. Miller, A New Sacred Geometry: The Art and Science of Frank Chester, (Portland, OR: Spirit Alchemy Design, 2013), retrieved June 18, 2020, https://www.amazon.com/New-Sacred-Geometry-Science-Chester/dp/0988749203/ref=sr_1_1?crid=3LRE17S0AUISF&keywords=a+new+sacred+geometry

+the+art+and+science+of+frank+chester&qid=1559366093&s=gateway&sprefix=A+New+Sacred+Geometry+%2Caps%2C195&sr=8-1

57 Haertl, R. (tr.), "The formation of a new etheric heart organ in the light of the present Michaelic mystery culture as Rudolf Steiner required for our age in his lectures,"(2000), retrieved June 4, 2016 from: http://www.rsarchive.org/RelArtic/GoldM/etheric_heart.html

M. Glöckler, "Understanding the Etheric Organization in the Human Being: New Insights Through Anthroposophical Research," Research Institute for Waldorf Education Research Bulletin 3, no. 2 (June 1998), retrieved May 31, 2020, http://www.waldorflibrary.org/journals/22-research-bulletin/483-june-1998-volume-03-2-understanding-the-etheric-organization-in-the-human-being-new-insights-through-anthroposophical-research

58 J. E. Grubbs, Women and the Law in the Roman Empire: A Sourcebook on Marriage, Divorce, and Widowhood (New York, NY: Routledge, 2002).

59 A. J. French, "The Christian Mysteries and Modern Consciousness" (electronic thesis, The University of Arizona, 2017), retrieved June 2, 2020, http://hdl.handle.net/10150/579325

R. Steiner, Christianity as Mystical Fact and The Mysteries of Antiquity (West Nyack, NY: Rudolf Steiner Publications, Inc., 1961).

60 J. E. Grubbs, Women and the Law in the Roman Empire: A Sourcebook on Marriage, Divorce, and Widowhood (New York, NY: Routledge, 2002)./

61 D. Montagna, "Mary Magdalene, 'Apostle to the Apostles,' Given Equal Dignity in Feast," Aleteia (June 10, 2016), retrieved June 1, 2020, https://aleteia.org/2016/06/10/mary-magdalene-apostle-to-the-apostles-given-equal-dignity-in-feast/

62 N. Dodwell, "Financial Crisis, Threefold Social Order and Rudolf Steiner's Organic System of Money," Insitut für soziale Dreigliederung (July 2012), retrieved May 31, 2020, http://www.threefolding.org/essays/2012-07-004.html

63 R. Steiner, "World Economy: The Formation of a Science of World-Economics," (Dornach, Switzerland, 1922), Rudolf Steiner Archive, retrieved June 18, 2020, https://wn.rsarchive.org/Lectures/GA340/English/RSP1972/WldEco_index.html

64 S. Prokofieff, Rudolf Steiner and the Founding of the New Mysteries, (London, UK: Temple Lodge Publishing, 1986).

65 C. K. Buckley, Co-Parenting after Divorce: Opportunities and challenges," (The Family Institute at Northwestern University, Evanston, IL: Clinical Science Insights, 2013), retrieved June 18, 2020, https://www.family-institute.org/sites/default/files/pdfs/csi_buckley_co-parenting_after_divorce.pdf

66 B. Matherne, "The Christian Mystery, GA# 97, by Rudolf Steiner: 29 Lectures on Christianity, 1906-1908" (Book Review), A Reader's Journal, vol. 2 (2003), retrieved May 31, 2020, http://www.doyletics.com/arj/christia.shtml

67 R. Steiner, "Man As A Picture of The Living Spirit," (London, UK, 1923), Rudolf Steiner Archive, retrieved June 1, 2020, http://wn.rsarchive.org/Lectures/19230902p01.html

68 R. Steiner, "World Economy: The Formation of a Science of World-Economics," (Dornach, Switzerland, 1922), Rudolf Steiner Archive, retrieved June 18, 2020, https://wn.rsarchive.org/Lectures/GA340/English/RSP1972/WldEco_index.html

69 S. Prokofieff, Rudolf Steiner and the Founding of the New Mysteries, (London, UK: Temple Lodge Publishing, 1986).

70 C. K. Buckley, Co-Parenting after Divorce: Opportunities and challenges," (The Family Institute at Northwestern University, Evanston, IL: Clinical Science Insights, 2013), retrieved June 18, 2020, https://www.family-institute.org/sites/default/files/pdfs/csi_buckley_co-parenting_after_divorce.pdf

71 B. Matherne, "The Christian Mystery, GA# 97, by Rudolf Steiner: 29 Lectures on Christianity, 1906-1908" (Book Review), A Reader's Journal, vol. 2 (2003), retrieved May 31, 2020, http://www.doyletics.com/arj/christia.shtml

72 R. Steiner, "Man As A Picture of The Living Spirit," (London, UK, 1923), Rudolf Steiner Archive, retrieved June 1, 2020, http://wn.rsarchive.org/Lectures/19230902p01.html

73 H. Scoville, "4 Vestigial Structures Found in Humans," (New York, NY:ThoughtCo., 2019), retrieved June 18, 2020, https://www.thoughtco.com/vestigial-structures-in-humans-1224772
M. Glöckler, "Understanding the Etheric Organization in the Human Being: New Insights Through Anthroposophical Research," Research Institute for Waldorf Education Research Bulletin 3, no. 2 (June 1998), retrieved May 31, 2020, http://www.waldorflibrary.org/journals/22-research-bulletin/483-june-1998-volume-03-2-understanding-the-etheric-organization-in-the-human-being-new-insights-through-anthroposophical-research

74 R. Steiner, "Fall of the Spirits of Darkness: Lecture 5 – Changes in Humanity's Spiritual Make-up," (Dornach, Switzerland, 1917), Rudolf Steiner Archive, retrieved May 31, 2020, https://wn.rsarchive.org/Lectures/GA177/English/RSP1993/19171007p01.html

75 R. Steiner, "Preparing for the Sixth Epoc,"(Dusseldorf, Germany, 19150, Rudolf Steiner Archive, retrieved June 18, 2020, https://wn.rsarchive.org/GA/GA0159/19150615p01.html
R. Steiner, "Faith, Love, and Hope: II, Towards the Sixth Epoch," (Nurnberg, Germany, 1911), retrieved June 1, 2020, http://wn.rsarchive.org/Lectures/GA130/English/GB1964/19111203p01.html#sthash.Iv7olM8R.dpuf

76 R. Steiner, "Lecture 11," The Mission of Folk-Souls: In Connection with Germanic Scandinavian Mythology, (Christiana, Oslo, 1910). Retrieved June 18, 2020, https://wn.rsarchive.org/Lectures/GA121/English/APC1929/MF1929_index.html

77 R. Steiner, The Education of the Child: And Early Lectures on Education (Forest Row, UK: Rudolf Steiner Press, 1996). Retrieved June 17, 2020, https://www.amazon.ca/Education-Child-Rudolf-Steiner/dp/0880104147

78 R. Steiner, "Reincarnation and Karma: Their Significance in Modern Culture," (Stuttgart, Germany, 1912), Rudolf Steiner Archive, retrieved June 18, 2020, https://wn.rsarchive.org/Lectures/GA135/English/SBC1977/ReKarm_index.html

79 R. Steiner, "The Reappearance of Christ in the Etheric: I," (Stockholm, Sweden, 1910), Rudolf Steiner Archive, retrieved April 27, 2017 from: http://wn.rsarchive.org/Lectures/ReapChrist/ReaChr_ index.html

CHAPTER FOUR

Modern Psychology and Anthroposophical Perspectives

A short recapitulation of modern Western diagnostic views of children and adult children of divorce. Includes research on neuro-scientific thought regarding their mental health issues. An introduction to Rudolf Steiner's approaches to soul discernment and development. A description of the earthly life constitutions of the child.

It may be said that all sorts of people who feel drawn to psychoanalysis today are earnestly searching for the spiritual foundations of existence, for the inner realities or the greater meaning of the life of being a human being.[1]
Rudolf Steiner

Mood and personality disorders associated with child-of-divorce issues, with respect to conservative Western psychology standards, are known to be the ones that many marriage and family therapists prefer not to take on. This is due to the strong emotional expressions and the practical life habits and skills that need to be developed or redeveloped in the children.

Pearl therapy carries the additional issue of cost, for children in families of low income or who have no insurance coverage, or whose coverage only allows for brief periods of therapy. Pearls with minimal healthy family or social supports tend to need long-term counseling.

Some skilled therapists have helped Pearls of varying ages, to some effect, with interventions from emotionally-focused therapy[2] and dialectical behavioral therapy."[3] Having the skills and appropriate supervision to handle the emotional transference and projections is necessary for counselors who help with Pearls, at any age and stage, to endure the breaks in trust that can happen. (Other Western therapies used to help Pearls are discussed in Volume II.)

One of the most skillful helpers that I experienced before discovering anthroposophy was the rare, silent, yoga initiate, Baba Hari Dass. Dass ran an orphan home in India, as well as intentional-living consciousness centers in the US and Canada. He had the wisdom to know that certain childhood trauma and oppressions can take decades or a lifetime to overcome or manage. He rarely pushed anyone's true healing path but rather worked patiently with people to instill basic rhythms, routines, and soul-spirit development practices without judgment, while helping community members get past psychological obstacles. Rudolf Steiner's work is deeply similar, but from a Western perspective.

Although Hari Dass' eight-limb Ashtanga Yoga met some souls who only approach a soul-spiritual life through yoga, his centers were open to all. He offered teaching and advice to any earnest person who came seeking safe mind-body healing and spiritual practices. Similar in some ways to Rudolf Steiner, he understood the differences between Eastern and Western spiritual life and healing, encouraging many Westerners to take a more individual approach to self-enlightenment. He and his community members offered seekers numerous nutritional, earth-practical, arts-integrated, and somatic healing approaches to care for their health and soul-spiritual faculties without becoming overly detached or attached about the sense-world life.

Dass was entirely practical in daily life matters and the running of ecologically sustainable, intentional communities, two of which had full, organic fruit and vegetable gardens. He also encouraged individual artistic, intellectual, and personal consciousness work. He saw the role of much of the technology of our times as a support to human development.

Dass, like Rudolf Steiner, was clear that physical yoga itself was not going to sustain a spiritual life in the future. People would need to take up individual soul paths more, and school their own spiritual awareness. He encouraged insights from many spiritual streams.

He fostered equanimity among individuals, creating long-term, and temporary accommodations for many people struggling with early family issues, including many Pearl Children and Adults. Dass helped to bring some early understandings for people about the future spiritual levels of self-realization that many more people would achieve in the far future. These higher states are the same as those that Rudolf Steiner spoke of in his anthroposophical work—the states of manas, buddhi, and atman.[4]

Like Steiner and modern transpersonal psychotherapists, Hari Dass did not focus on mental and emotional pain as diseases or stuck pathologies. He saw mental-emotional health issues as moral/spiritual troubles of the soul, requiring personally refined practices and disciplines, and community support that honors differences and healing. Finding what works best for the virtuous individual, through self-awareness, and through understanding others' approaches to heart-soul reasoning and resonance, provided the key to his very committed, sustainable, and wholesome living communities. They have been some of the most sustainable and successful intentional communities in the world.

Several anthroposophical communities worldwide are seeding similar communities, some with diverse groups of people at all different ages and stages of life, and of ego and spiritual development. Many of those communities include Waldorf schools.

Both Dass and Steiner knew that healing practices and experiences are ensouled through extended periods. Issues can take much longer to heal than what North American insurance companies can help with through funding brief therapy[5] psychotherapeutic counseling for Pearls and others. Often, the realistic amount of time and resources needed to bring about healing for traumatized Pearls—who are often rebuilding healthy egos from very debilitated states—are not accessible to them. Parent financial strains after divorce often prevent Pearls from affording private counseling. Child-of-divorce trauma and neglect issues often go unaddressed, except if they come out in greater societal struggles later.

Exhaustion

The general load of growth and self-healing responsibilities that Pearl Adults can be carrying on their shoulders can lead to debilitating exhaustion. It often leads to physical ailments resulting from being unsupported, worn-down, and overstretched. Many of the children have had to mother or father themselves the best they could for a long time and often in survival-personality[6] circumstances.

Most Pearl Children, when they take up counseling, will transfer feelings and attachments they have for their parents onto the counselor. They can paradoxically both desperately seek, and zealously reject, role models. The therapist becomes the focus for a range of potentially frustrating reactions around receiving and rejecting help.

Studies reveal that socio-economic-cultural support systems around Pearls, upon the divorce of their parents, often become unstable or dissolve substantially.[7] Non-profit organizations such as churches and service organizations that traditionally helped oppressed people or those suffering intensely without socio-economic support, can be places today that stigmatize children of divorce. Others strive to help, but with limited resources, staff, and capable volunteers.

In adolescence and young adulthood, many Pearls find themselves energetically and emotionally threadbare from seeking and trying to hold within themselves some workable sense of positive self-image and sustenance. The double-whammy of ongoing negativity from family members and societal stigma about a divorce, or unmarried parent breakup that was not of their choice, can create another negative—the youth's ability to experience a sense of justice.

This occurs while the outer-world demands that the adult Pearls meet "normal" educational, economic, and societal work and social standards. Those standards do not necessarily negotiate any room for the awkward needs and extra burdens of the Pearl Child or Pearl Adult. In my teaching experience, young Pearls often arrived in my classroom in the morning exhausted and limited in their ability to engage in the activities that the other children were deeply involved in. Others, with single parents, began the school day in a slight bewilderment from bridging between parent homes. Teachers often have little or no support to meet the extraordinary circumstances of the Pearls.

This lack of significant understanding in society about real Pearl issues often contributes to the inner alienation of the Pearl Children, triggering behavior issues because the children can't feel safe to cope with what they face. If they are pushed to be just like the other children from whole families, they often suffer some energetic consequence that can lead to other problems later. This is not due to a lack of potential or skills capacities, but rather because of being overburdened and ill-supported at home. Children in whole families don't carry these kinds of loads. Often, the burdens that parents thought they'd avoided by divorcing the spouse got transferred as other burdens onto the children.

Pearl Adults are often spending their own financial resources, and even taking time away from work, to get the counseling help that they need to maintain emotional balance and to get relationship mirroring and self-reflection. These financial burdens can affect their long-term ability to care for their overall survival needs.

The Burden of the DSM Diagnostic Approach

The American Psychiatric Association's *Diagnostic and Statistical Manual of Mental Disorders* (DSM), fifth edition, applies some of the bleakest pathologies in psychology to the children of divorce. These are labeled as "Narcissism," "Borderline Personality Disorder," "Antisocial Personality Disorder," "Manic Depressive Disorder," and various designations related to addictive personality issues.[8]

The DSM is a controversial but consistently used manual, referred to by psychiatrists, psychologists, and some clinical psychotherapists, when sorting and categorizing a person's psychological (soul-psyche) symptoms. Categories and diagnostics are used to get counseling funding, to apply standardized therapeutic practices and interventions, and to prescribe medications.

Daily or periodic conditions that doctors and mental health professionals in the West test for and treat in children of divorce range from anxiety, depression, trauma, "separation anxiety," "selective mutism," "reactive attachment disorder of infancy and childhood," and "attention-deficit/hyperactivity disorder."[9]

Early-childhood divorce-trauma issues, through the lens of modern psychology, are seen to have the potential to blossom into imbalanced reactions against authority figures such as "conduct disorders," "alcohol and substance related disorders," and as mood, sleep, eating, and even "gender identity disorders."[10] Some children are treated for suicidal ideation.[11]

Youths can be vulnerable to acting out their pain and grief in conflicted and confusing behaviors called "externalization."[12] This can happen toward even those people most willing and desiring to share the youth's life or be there for them in their troubles. The opposite pole to this is "internalizing"[13] behaviors, meaning that youths act out their pain and grief inwardly on themselves in self-hating or self-sabotaging ways.[14] Some teens and adults can even get into situations where they are physically harming themselves by cutting, bruising, hitting, or using other methods to injure themselves.[15]

Mental health expert Steven Levenkron speaks of the self-injurer as someone who has found that physical pain can be a cure for emotional pain.[16] Most people experience moments and degrees of these various psychological states, and even minor psychic splits, at different times in modern life. Many people, however, who have family trauma from parental divorce, including those whose parents' marriages break up when they are in their early adulthood, can experience more severe levels or episodes of these states. This can lead to dysfunctional or socially alienating experiences and pathologies. What is more serious is if substance or pharmaceutical abuse turns into an addiction. Chronic drug use for Pearls is increasingly dangerous and even fatal today due to fentanyl lacing[17] of easily accessible opioids promoted on the street as pain relief and a calming escape.

Neuroscience and Stress on the Psyche

Neuroscientists today are investigating how brief periods of poor brain health, or mental illness, can become chronic or pathological states in the same way that heart stresses can become full-blown, chronic heart disease.[18] Some of the findings suggest that physiological illness issues originate in the organ of the brain where over-stimulation leads the brain to become flooded with brain chemicals and hormones that attempt to bring calm to the strain. The amygdala-hypothalamus axis[19] is the immediate fright, fight, and flight danger-recognition center of the brain.

It can flood with chemical responses when stimulated during states of fear, panic, or grief. This can happen as well when we inwardly or outwardly review in our minds our fear-filled or traumatic past experiences. Without proper calming techniques and other interventions for moving the mind to focus on positive thoughts and stop the wave of brain chemicals, we can trigger chronic states of flooding that deplete or burn out our hormonal and chemically balanced nerve centers.[20]

The hippocampus is another area of the brain that can go into overrun, straining chemicals and hormones into chronic flooding.[21] The serotonin-firing system between neuron cells is also a well-known site in the brain that becomes drained and loses its fertility and capacity to function well. In this way, our thinking and imaginative abilities become deadened or calcified. We feel a depressed sense of connection to life, and that usually stirs the heart's emotional centers. Overly emoting as a child or adult is a strong red flag that a person needs help to bring the soul-psyche back into homeostasis, a state that is frequently offset by parent divorce tensions and conflicts.[22] Labeling these stress signals as mere attention-seeking is simply cruel.

Research has suggested that neurological illnesses happen due to the soft tissues of the brain becoming nutrient-depleted, tissues wearing out, and chemical energy centers misfiring or failing to fire at all. Neuroscientists who study the higher prefrontal cortex and its associations with mind-consciousness might agree more with Rudolf Steiner's holistic view of illness in the body organs.

Rudolf Steiner saw that when something goes against the grain of higher, soul-spirit necessities in the human being, illnesses arise that affect the body-mind-soul complex right down into the physiology of the body and nervous system.[23] The holistic human system, being asked to compensate in unnatural ways, can experience wounds and constrictions on developing organs, which often show up negatively in somatic symptoms on the way to becoming full-blown physiological or neurological illnesses.

Some researchers suggest that certain strains or brain illnesses cause lesions in the brain.[24] These are energy gaps between normally resilient neuron passages, which cut back the brain's capacity to facilitate the many malleable and efficient messages signaling about in the organism for healthy functioning. Although neurological researchers, and even Rudolf Steiner in his time, have suggested that the body's organs, including the brain, hold healing plasticity and can become more whole, they still require a process, time, and insightful practices to support healing and change.[25]

Ethically, Pearl Children who require healing work to overcome exposure to violent parenting are not likely to be put back into a violent parent environment. Yet, Pearl Children who work on their emotional issues often return to living with parents who continue to subtly abuse them emotionally or mentally through a lack of the parent's own psychological work and growth. Thus, the wounds that are trying to heal are strained again through re-triggered stress signals.

Mental Override and Memory Bypassing

Bigger questions now arise as to whether there is a higher reasoning in this wounding. Neuroscience suggests that the brain can heal and grow in capacity by overriding neural passages and forming new ones, if a person can leave old or rigidified thought patterns alone and let new networks form. This may represent a kind of physiological bypassing and raises the question: Does the soul ask us also to move on and not bother to use those parts of the brain anymore that may have been harmed in significant stresses with others?

Is this what the Christ meant when he said to turn the other cheek (Matt 5:39 NIV) when someone's actions deeply harm us? Is this about forgiveness? Is it the child's place to forgive and forget something that seriously affected that child's ability to function in life? Can the forgiveness only happen when the negativity is fully stopped for good? Is it like the story of Christ seeing the woman being stoned in the hating crowd and telling those with the stones to stop the barrage, clean up their own sins, and stop judging?

What if newly healed places in the brain are re-exposed to the same ingrained messaging of old—stimulating the brain to access depleted or only recently restored neuron energy to try to stream out calming chemicals once again—to offset toxic cortisol spilling? What if too many areas of the brain's functions get worn-down and dysfunctional because the growing Pearl Child, or Pearl Adult, is rarely safe from repeated, negative, parent imprinting? At what point does the negativity become recognized as a full-out assault on the Pearl's neural functioning?

Is medicating the Pearl Child or Pearl Adult with anti-depressant drugs then simply allowing the assault to continue with no consequences for the ones bringing the assault in the first place? Why is society's response so often reparative with the child rather than preventive with the parents, not expecting ongoing psychoeducation for divorced parents, and accountability and consequences if nothing is done to change the constant negativity barrage between former spouses? How can children be educated to seek help beyond the family if they are regularly being exposed to negative, divorced-parent mental abuse?

Without parent cooperation, Pearls are led to develop new, mindful practices in the expanding consciousness of our times. They may need to leave some areas of our thoughts dormant or dissociated for a while or even long-term—to heal lesions or burnout areas. Does that do anything to their genetics or other functioning?

Some details are known in neurological science about what gets lost when old dendrite nerve formations in the brain are left dormant or bypassed for other, newly created passageways. It is known through magnetic resonance imaging (MRI) research on dementia that brain networks that are not used over time can die away, affecting mental cognition.[26]

Do we necessarily have to lose the connections between neural pathways and other parts of our holistic biological system, such as our heart or other organs, to get past traumatizing triggers from past events? Was bypassing the only way for me to overcome my own experience of Takotsubo Cardiomyopathy (TC)?[27]

If we learn to shut off the spinning chemical soups in the brain's hypothalamus and hippocampus, with retreats, natural supplements, meditations, and practices supported by wholeness-seeking communities, are we just avoiding or trying to bypass human truths? Do we make ourselves "wimps" who can't cope with any hard problems in the world? Shutting out thoughts to not have to medicate, be in pain, or address the work to change the negativity around them, because a parent won't take the harms up seriously and responsibly, is surely a drain on the etheric life forces of a Pearl. So too is continually jumping around in consciousness. The exhaustion factor for many Pearls raised in conflicted families disproves that we make strong, resilient adults from exposing children to regular adversity.

People with brain injuries from car accidents, strokes, or other physically damaging incidents can lose their access to sensory activities such as sight, speech, body coordination, and even most of their movement. To regain function, much hard work must be done—with serious assistance and emotional/moral support. Brain injury patients have been known to recover some old circuitry with exercises and practices that stimulate and build newly connected nerve cells in the harmed areas of the brain. This can't occur, however, if the brain-injured person is continually exposed to experiences that re-injure the brain.

I bypassed family relationships for several years, having the latest psychological practices, ancient meditation knowledge, and a spiritual community close by. I consciously worked with healers over decades. And I enjoyed greater peace and the most important love relationship of my life. I may have healed nerve issues as a result, although I felt that I was pacifying them more than addressing sustainable repair. Later in adulthood, when a family tragedy happened with a loved one, the old strains and neurological pains came back. I had skills to overcome them to a point, yet I needed significant help to overcome draining dissociation.

I learned that nothing would change if I didn't directly address the root causes, or karma, of the problems. This time, to stay functional in life, my restoration meant going into the problem and weeding out the systemic harms, finding understanding and also the strength to hold accountability around them, even if some of the harms came out of my own choices around conflicts. I would also examine my early rights as a child to mental safety, stability, and child-appropriate nurturance.

I would need to become a very firm guardian of my lost childhood in order to restore and rebuild some sustainable capacities. I would stand up for myself or my healthy soul-spirit connection would die. I could feel the edge of despair that I had felt as a child, but this time, righteous Archangel Michael inside knew that I had been taking up my own dragon for decades. Grace was now going to propel me past any fear of rejection by my remaining parent. I was prepared to put my physical life on the line to be free of the mental oppression.

The mind, being an earthen reflection of the cosmos and a receptor for higher perception and impulses from higher worlds, can move our heart courage into clear attunement with our spiritual times in order to clean up past karma and negotiate reparations. That happens when the wholeness of the higher mind's functions are developed enough with committed practices. Either healthy child development supported that into adulthood, or "missing pieces" therapeutic work helped to restore higher insight.

In my case, the years with my deeply understanding and healing husband had brought much restoration. When he died, I was vulnerable again to the old, negative harming playing out in my family of origin. I would succumb to more neurologically harmful negativity or step up to root out anything in myself that allowed the negative messages to stick when I knew they were not deserved. I would call on the higher light of the Consciousness Soul, and Christ inspiration, to help me do what no one else could help me do, despite my years with therapists and coaches.

In anthroposophy, this is called taking up a "Michaelic impulse,"[28] and relates to the character-strengthening inspirations summoned up through the study of karma, and the transformative practices of soul-informed creative work in community. When we take up the gifts of anthroposophical insight in a Michaelic way, investigating our sympathies for certain people and actions, and our antipathies toward others, we find our own answers to healing karmic wounds. We find our own moral rule that fits the ethics of the soul-spirit times and sometimes that means righteous anger.

No one walks what another person walks, and thus no one else can know the individual healing path but the one walking it. However, the highest spiritual forces, guiding us through our sleep, keep our insights attuned to right action in our time, including right action regarding systemic world phenomena. These are the new laws of Christ, the lord of karma. If we seek, we shall truly find the grace that heals us, even if the method doesn't seem to fit olden patterns. Thus, my healing led me to complete this book through impulses that had been speaking for some time out of my sleep.

Moon Nodes

One of the helpful insights that helps us tune up to soul-spirit truth in our own biographies is work with the moon nodes that we can understand through our astrological birth chart. (More is addressed about astrological work later in this chapter.)

This book was completed at the end of my third moon node event, at age fifty-six. Work with lunar moon nodes[29] helps us identify individual gifts that our soul has come into the world with this lifetime, and which seem to speak out in some way every eighteen years or so, starting at age eighteen and a half.

Lunar nodes are points where the sun and moon's orbital paths around the earth intersect. There is a north moon node and a south moon node, and they are found in opposite astrological signs. We come into life to learn something opposite to what we learned in another lifetime. Spiritually, the south node marks karmic work that we completed in the past life. At around eighteen and a half, the moon revisits the cosmic place where it was when we were born and stimulates something in our sense of life destiny. It pushes us forward into life to learn something that is not something that we feel we already know well. At this age, it can still be something very vague in our consciousness.

The north node marks what work we're guided to accomplish this lifetime to find a balance to that which we did before. It suggests an element of soul destiny. At the lunar return stages in our life, we can review our life and observe how our whole being responds to inner insights and outer reflections from others about something that we feel very strongly that we must know, repair, or do. At the first lunar node alignment at eighteen and a half, we often ignore the impulses and information coming our way about our destiny, since we are often quite happy to live out of what we already know.

By not being in our adult Consciousness Soul development stage at eighteen (something discussed later in this volume), it can be hard to discern what is being spoken to us out of the spiritual world at that point. The next nodal return, however, at age thirty-six to thirty-seven, happens when we're more ready to look at ourselves and consciously notice what messages just keep coming up for us about a life issue. The messages may come up in our dreams or when we wake. Or, they may come blatantly at us from others if we've been really off soul-spiritual track.

With some review help from family or special friends who were in our lives when we were age eighteen and a half, we may start to glean what task is destined to send us burrowing through our Chironic wound, bringing conscious light, love, and wisdom to transform it to the good and to help others. If we fail to grasp and try to work with this destined piece of our biography, and can't find a deeper way into self-knowing, depending on our earlier childhood mental health, we can develop psychological splits.[30]

Psychological Splitting

For the general, human population—meaning not just specifically Pearls but not excluding them—people can function with moments of psychological inner-splitting for insignificant periods of time in their lives. This splitting comes from cognitive dissonance between what the soul needs to be following, and what that individual may have taken up by force, or through their incapacity to make a different choice. The destiny to heal a Chironic wound usually brings our life work and journey into alignment with our authentic self. Our soul is strengthened in significant ways when we take the healing up.

Psychological splitting is often stabilized or held from being entirely self-destructive for a short time with unconscious help from outside carriers or holders like siblings, friends, a healthy parent, role models, inspiring coaches, or even a significant partner who seems to understand many of the Pearl's important issues and needs. However, without taking up the split oneself, the Pearl can easily be dissipating energy, or smothering inner forces that are wanting to move into great energy for other things in later years.

After a while, staying stuck can literally throw the adult in two or more directions simultaneously, causing varying levels of inner havoc. Certain schizoid kinds of behaviors can start this way with an episode that can feel profoundly frightening or painful to the Pearl.

A sadly common example is when a child is sexually abused by an adult in the immediate family, or someone very close, like a relative or priest, and is told by the abuser that they will be greatly harmed if they tell someone. That child, with a truly safe and stabilizing adult at home or in their life who is unaware of the abuse, or with other siblings who are not being abused, may manage to continue life for a short or long time with unrecognized signs of distress or behaviors that are strange but accepted. (This is complicated because sometimes the child is tricked into believing that what they are experiencing from the abuser is pleasurable and okay for the child.)

Yet, with that safe other person holding loving tending with the child, the signs of disconnect can begin to show in the child's distrustful or slightly bizarre behaviors. An attuned adult may notice and ask what is wrong. In real safety, that child can inwardly break free and share what has happened, bringing significant protection, healing, and readjustment. Many do not make this early breakthrough, however, and the issue doesn't come up until much later in life. It is the kind of issue that can peek through more at the second lunar node around age thirty-seven, or later, around age fifty-six.

People can superficially relieve the worst aspects of childhood wound stress until an ingrained stress dysfunction catches up in more serious personality or mood disorders. At that point, certain wounding issues come to look more like post-traumatic stress disorder, severe nervous-system breakdown, or so much self-regulation deterioration that the Pearl begins projecting aggression toward others.

Some very psychologically distressed Pearls can convince themselves that adaptations they have superficially made since childhood, or on simplified advice of family, friends, or medicating doctors, are sustainably healthy ones. There can be positive movement forward for some time. Struggling people can form friendships and relationships with people who relate to their pathology for any number of reasons and who accept them and share coping strategies. The distressed Pearls feel loved and helped, and they can develop other positive aspects of themselves. This can also have a strong and positive effect on neurology and the body, not to mention the heart and soul.

However, often the result of brief or superficial therapies and healing help, is that healing is only maintained until something much more extreme triggers the ingrained issue to come to the surface, or when support people are no longer around or alive to help the Pearl. Today, many people the world over experience mental health strains and triggers through endless, external, shocking events happening in the weather, in society, or by being exposed to criminal events shown in the media. It is harder to block the psyche from such potentially triggering events.

Re-triggered, traumatized persons and their loved ones are often faced with illness, overwhelm, or ethical dilemmas around how to manage and cope with increasing mental strains. Do they trust doctors to just increase medication doses, or add other meds? Can they bring their early wounds to a new caregiver or intimate relationship to try to find understanding and support? Can they trust themselves to take a more thorough look at an underlying psychological distress issue, and put some energy into understanding it with the chance to release more life forces and lighten their hearts?

Betty Broderick

An example of unaddressed triggers in divorce comes in the tragic story of a divorced woman and parent, Betty Broderick of San Diego. Broderick went into serious, narcissistic and psychopathic psychological splitting after her divorce from her husband. Rather than seeking or receiving appropriate soul help to manage her emotional burden, she sought emotional backup from friends and even a new partner.

However, due to her lack of deeper soul-spirit investigation about how her thoughts, feelings, and actions might affect her children, and bringing the will to change and find a space of higher love for her newly shared parenting with her former husband, Broderick clearly triggered in the worst way after the remarriage of her ex-husband. She murdered him and his new wife in 1989. This has become a classic training case for lawyers and psychologists, alike.[31] The harmful effects of this horror on the divorced couple's children were substantial.

The outer implications of soul-psyche splits may also surface as serious physical illnesses, such as from somatic and visceral pains related to depression and known to lead to heart disease for some people.[32] Many children and adults are given medications as quick or inexpensive solutions to help them to function. Medications such as selective serotonin reuptake inhibitors (SSRIs) or antidepressants,[33] work to re-stimulate the burned-out stress hormone mechanisms of the brain.

Currently, the levels of prescription of antidepressants in the United States are at an all-time high. A *Journal of the American Medical Association* report in 2015 shows the percentage of people on these medications doubling in two years to thirteen per cent of the population, not including hospitalized, imprisoned, and institutionalized people. Some medical workers believe that statistic to be very low compared to what they experience in practice.

Anthroposophical Health: A Renewable Soul Environment

Anthroposophy is a major healing philosophy with extensive, substantial soul foundations. One of its prime considerations is the awareness of the human being as having a fourfold nature, with a physical body, etheric body, astral body, and an individual ego. It also sees the fourfold bodies revealing themselves in stages throughout childhood, while the child's whole living organism is experiencing and refining seven life processes and the management of the twelve senses mentioned in Chapter Three. Three more indicators bring psychological orientation for an anthroposophical healer or caregiver. These indications gauge what a person's soul nature might be working with at any time. These are the temperaments,[34] the twelve cosmic archetypes of the zodiac,[35] and the life constitutions.[36]

Temperaments

As far back as ancient times, and still observed up to the great human cultural Renaissance of William Shakespeare's time, people showed characteristic tendencies and traits that tended to form a basis for their behaviors and their responses to life. These traits, identified in olden Mesopotamia and Egypt, and recorded in the Greek times of Hippocrates the Healer as humors,[37] were seen to have associations with different bodily organs. Their health or imbalance could stimulate beliefs, values, and thoughts upon which people based their life priorities and choices. Rudolf Steiner called these temperaments.

The four temperamental natures of the human being are: a) phlegmatic, b) melancholic, c) choleric, and d) sanguine. These reveal themselves as singular human features, as well as oppositions and blends within the individual. They tend to indicate not only individual characteristics, but varying characteristics within a person's lifespan.

Generally, to be phlegmatic is to have a thick, heavy, un-chiseled nature that is characteristic of a baby in swaddling, longing for the comfort and nurturance of the mother and of all that represents the sensual goods of the milk and juices of life. It is the temperament of the brain organ, known for its soft, watery, curd-like consistency. It signifies a potentially cool and ebullient character, prone to the sicknesses of dampness, excess, and lack of physical activity.

The phlegmatics, associated with the moon, can be generously spirited, but usually with lots of moody ties and binds around giving and receiving, a reflection of the mysterious changing phases of the moon. The phlegmatic is comfortable with ownership and access to many emotionally tied relationships and resources. They may be big boned and have weight concerns.

The melancholic can often be a less incarnate soul who focuses more on purification of earthly matter and blood. Melancholics feel the pain of life's changes personally and are challenged to realistically let go of old structures and to accept loss. The melancholic is often a supersensible and spiritual being; cool, detached, and dry as opposed to mucoid, yet with deep empathy for others. Melancholics can feel overwhelmed by emotion, which can be perceived in a lack of boundaries about what are their own feelings to feel and manage and what are feeling-associations best left to others to be tested in their own heart fortitude and empathy.

Many melancholic-natured people tend toward spiritual and creative life and work to ease their sense of earthen loneliness through compassionate service to others. They tend to need a loving and creative outlet for their pain and compassion. They may become avoidant in relationships or clingy, giving ground and taking ground rather coolly, always wishing for deeper connection, depending partly on what kinds of matters and losses their melancholy is focused on.

Choleric people, strong in the features of fiery will, can have great will forces and wells of energy that require outlets for creative action lest their bodily forces and strong feelings become pent-up and frustrated. The gall bladder is a strong influence in the choleric, who can be attention-seeking and off-putting, like a hot desert wind. Meaningful activity into which cholerics can pour both focus and passion can help to remedy this.

Choleric children often need to learn to keep their hands to themselves unless they get an agreement from the other child or children to be hands-on and physical. Otherwise, they can be too much full-on force for the others around them, who are left feeling mentally, emotionally, or even physically invaded, or metaphorically burned. Choleric people can become great performers, actors, leaders, laborers, farmers, adventurers, and athletes. Without discipline in the face of unexpected hardship or opposition, they can become aggressive and even violent.

Finally, sanguine temperament people are light-hearted and full of thoughts, wishes, dreams, creative notions, games, and experiments. They are literally striving for the higher heart organ, and they can be friendly and chatty, as thoughts stream quickly in them. They are often very fast to catch onto a concept or a way to embrace and make mental connections for a new device or idea. Ruled by expansive Jupiter, they may entirely miss feelings in others or practical concerns while they whirl together fantasies or enjoyable illusions of parties and activities for people they know to get together for experiments and adventures.

They are often the life of the party and warmly sensual, which can sour when they overlook the life in others being presented in different, demure, or quieter ways. Sanguine people can offer a great deal of refreshing insight in artistry, science, mathematics, social planning, and even entrepreneurial inspirations. They can be less strong in carrying ideas through into function, in understanding the hard workers, and in bringing about project completion. While most people throughout life represent more than one temperamental type, and different life stages are associated with different temperaments, the eternal nature of these human soul characteristics are as common today as they were in the classical Renaissance when Shakespeare considered: "Every humor hath his adjunct pleasure/ Wherein it finds a joy above the rest."[38]

More Modern Traits?

Recent theories in Western psychotherapeutic diagnostics have turned toward Myers-Briggs's testing[39] for distinguishing the personality traits of extroversion and introversion, and the natures of sensing, intuiting, feeling, thinking, judging, and perceiving.

Transpersonal psychological theory adds the Enneagram's nine personality characteristics as a rubric for determining personality characteristics in individuals.[40] They are: a) the reformer, b) helper, c) achiever, d) individualist, e) investigator, f) loyalist, g) enthusiast, h) challenger, and i) peacemaker. Though it is not possible to extend this discussion here, it is important to consider that there can be differences between external personality expressions and a more karmic, and often unconscious, soul nature.

The Twelve Cosmic Archetypes of the Zodiac

Centuries ago, prior to the mechanistic, human-reductionist, industrialization period in the eighteenth and nineteenth centuries, human beings felt and saw themselves as interconnected with aspects of nature and life that are not directly seen by the eyes. Human beings knew that supersensible forces affected all of life on earth. The moon, the sun, the sun aura reflected in the northern lights, the meteors, the stars, and the planets in an earth-connected solar system, have all affected human life as far back as human outer technology and inner-soul memory have been able to reveal. People not only sensed this in themselves and the world directly around them, but they also saw that people of other cultures, far distant, new these connections.

A zodiac of archetypal influences has been known in many cultures and represented in distinct symbols for millennia. From thousand-year-old script paintings in the burial chambers of the ancient goddess Nut in the Egyptian Dendera Temple, to a carved-dolerite Saura Hindu zodiac wheel from thirteenth-century Andhra Pradesh, to the mosaic-inlaid zodiac floor in the church of the Dormition in Jerusalem, human beings have been creatively depicting and recording the influences of the stars and planets upon their lives.

The following are the Western archetypal, zodiacal influences still referenced today and informing some of the aspects of anthroposophical understandings of the human being. Some mundane or practical traits, and also negative opposite, or dark double aspects of each archetype are offered here, in simplified form, in what is sometimes called the mundane expression of those forces. They are presented here to begin to show how people can work to see opposite natures and egoic behaviors shadowing positive behaviors in themselves, as well as balancing them to find the higher heart space in between positive and negative forces.

Table 4.1: Zodiacal archetypes

The following table shows the twelve zodiacal archetypes of western astrology with the positive expression of each sign, the negative or dark-double expression, and the spirit forces attributed by Rudolf Steiner.

Name and type	Double	Spirit forces
Aries, Ram or Initiator	Egoist	Christ
Taurus, Bull or the Founder	Acquirer	Holy Spirit
Gemini, Twins or Collaborators	Scatterer	Seraphim
Cancer, Crab or the Feeler	Avoider	Cherubim
Leo, Lion or Courageous Heart	Amusement Seeker	Thrones
Virgo, Virgin or Health Purifier	Critic	Kyriotetes
Libra, Scales or Justice Seeker	Irresolute One	Dynamis
Scorpio, Scorpion or Power Processor	Power-seeker	Exusiai
Sagittarius, Archer or Higher Seeker	Gambler	Archai
Capricorn, Goatfish or Overseer	Tyrant	Archangels

Aquarius, Water-bearer or Humanitarian	Unbounded One	Angels
Pisces, Fishes or Cosmic Guides	Fear-based One	Humans

Table 4.2: Rudolf Steiner's images and characteristics for the zodiacal archetypes

The following are Rudolf Steiner's indications for how each zodiacal influence facilitates spiritual impulses. For instance, Aries perceives the immediate impulse, while Taurus acts on it directly, Gemini considers the vast capacities for the impulse on the earth, and Cancer nourishes the impulse into a wholesome initiative. When the impulse has ripened through all of the human archetypes, Pisces ritualizes the meaning in it and reflects it back in reverence to the spiritual world.

Aries	The event
Taurus	The action itself
Gemini	Capacity for action
Cancer	Initiative
Leo	Burning enthusiasm
Virgo	Soberness
Libra	Weighing process in thought
Scorpio	Thinking
Sagittarius	Resolve
Capricorn	Connect thought to the world
Aquarius	Man striving after balance
Pisces	The event becomes destiny

Figure 4.1: Rudolf Steiner's zodiacal drawings

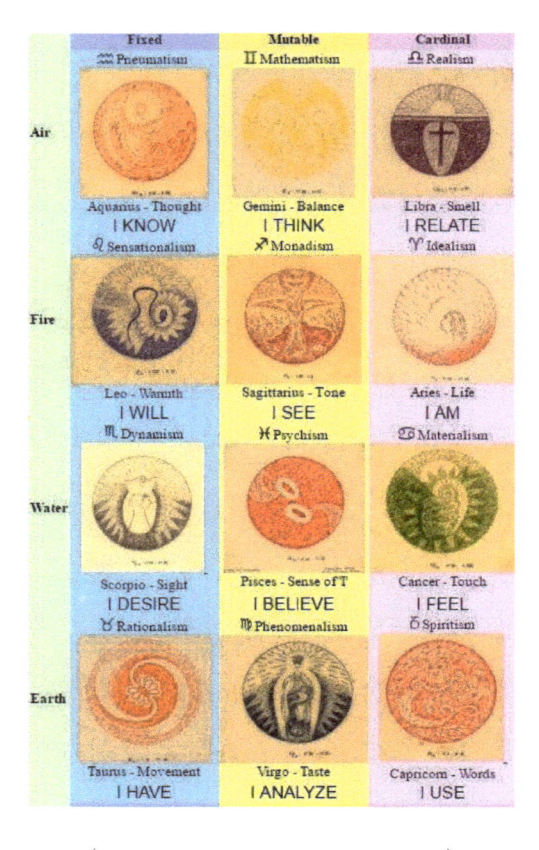

(Image courtesy of Kim Graae Munch)

Steiner's new representations of the zodiacal archetypes, offering updated, and even futuristic, etheric visions for each.

Zodiacal archetypes are helpful to perceive spiritual essences in the capacities of individual human beings. These essences have stages or trimesters of maturity. The sun highlights each zodiacal sign as it passes by for approximately thirty days. The therapist can encourage a client to consider each sign as having ten days of early development, ten of questioning and budding new insights, and the last ten days of deeper assurance of the impulse for that sign in that year.

A therapist working with zodiacal influences takes in the whole trajectory of the thirty-day transit of an archetypal energy in a person's birth chart, and sees how these forces are aspected by the sun's radiance and the effects of other planets and stars. He reflects on the inward and outward experiences of those archetypal forces and intuits insights regarding future transits. He encourages this knowledge and exploration in the client.

Pisces Example in Counseling

An example of the zodiacal sign trimesters in counseling is shown here, while working with a client during the Sun's entry into Pisces—the Fishes or Cosmic Guide. In the first trimester, with the Sun in Pisces for ten days, there are vague spiritual, creative, and compassionate impressions arising. The client wants to allay a sense of impending fear or insecurity—a typical Pisces trait, or on the opposite scale, discern and revere something benevolent in the impression.

In the middle of the Pisces transit—the next ten days—the therapist finds that the client is having an ah-hah moment when something strikes the client about that distinct month, year, or season. The client may feel impressions that seem to be wandering about in the client's feeling life but which can't be pinpointed. Something is occurring in the world that sparks a mystically or compassionately creative, Piscean imagination. Or, the client may have headed off into a fantasy interest or may be wanting to retreat into alcohol or drugs.

The therapist may encourage the client to volunteer at a food bank that month, or start an art project to save the whales, or invest more marketing research into a new herbal drink product. Together, they consider what building fears the client might be having about executing a creative or compassionate impulse into action.

In the third trimester, an urgency can build to complete the task and follow through on the epiphany of that transit as it applies to the client's actions. The client needs feelings support to not back out on the impulse to put an inspiring thought into something that will touch the feelings of others. The overwhelming fear may cause the sensitive Piscean just to leave the thought in limbo and retreat. The therapist and client discuss courage and do exercises to stimulate some will-fire for the Pisces client to initiate, fulfill, and bring sustaining energy or closure to the task. This is one way that the zodiacal archetype trimesters can work in counseling.

Anthroposophy is an esoteric path to knowledge, meaning a path that directs one to look at underlying or more subtle activities in the natural and spiritual worlds that affect our soul working on the earth. An exoteric path would be one that looked only at external events as perceived purely through the immediate senses or sense memory. It is an esoteric protocol to not examine a child's birth chart until after age seven with the change of teeth, since the child's real soul life is rightly still enfolded within the protective and hereditary forces of the parents, and rather strongly in the first three years.

Interpreting a child's birth chart too early is cautioned against, since it would be easy for the adults around the child to begin to innocently impose astrological ideas or understandings onto the young child before that child had begun to naturally show how the expression of some of the natal chart forces are really wanting to come through directly from the child's soul. It is best to have awareness of zodiacal archetypes, but to allow the young child slowly to begin to reveal an authentic soul nature before looking into the natal chart to see what kinds of important karmic challenges might present themselves in the child's life and through childhood.

Later, especially after age eighteen, consulting the chart can be helpful to look at a Pearl's birth planets and transits to see how the child is working through a transiting planetary influence on a cosmic influence in the chart, at what trimester stage it is occurring, and what maturity level of the archetype the child seems to exhibit or struggle with.

Since a person's sun sign forces progress as a person ages, becoming tempered and influenced by the next sun sign, and even by up to three consecutive sun signs, it is advisable to have an experienced natal chart reader for Pearls to see the complexities that can inform a person's soul life through one lifetime. The most trustworthy readers only suggest the potentials of a chart, but never give absolutes about how a person's cosmic influences may unfold. An honorable reader will also offer, on a spectrum, the immature or more negative potentials for the planets in a constellation sign through to the more mature and positive potentials. That would include offering ways to see, and work with, the progressions from negative to positive.

A qualified transpersonal counselor, or an anthroposophical psychotherapist working with a very afflicted adolescent, can look closely at certain inspirations in the natal chart and offer suggestions in practical ways for the Pearl Youth to see that some things that affect them may have little to do with the parents or family but more the timing of bigger life cycles and events. The counselor can show how planets move through the signs in the seasons, for instance, changing the way we feel life inwardly in early autumn and late autumn, as well as the different stages of each season. This can help the Pearl know that certain difficult stages do pass and change, both seasonally, and through the longer seasons of our lives.

The transpersonal therapist can know this by having experienced, with strong, conscious tracking, the very nature of cosmic transits. The therapist's life experience can speak with affirmation coming out of real authority from observing the influences directly over time.

Another influence for a Pearl is that the young person's parents may be living out of an opposite zodiacal consciousness, and one that is not so easily relatable this lifetime. None of this is shared directly with most very young adolescents—it is simply to inform the counselor, parent, or caregiver of what the forces behind a child-parent conflict can be when no other interventions are working well to bring understanding through an objective, archetypal, traits-based story. Zodiacal, archetypal-transit awareness allows the counselor to bring something mythologically interesting and (cosmically) relevant to the youth through zodiac-sign qualities in modern biographies and related stories. For instance, the story of a fallen warrior may feel very relatable to an Aries or Scorpio youth client.

The Pearl Youth whose parents never listened to each other or collaborated to plan family trips, is told a story and shown some archetypal nature that might be relatable about his parents' natures. Set in a noble context, a story can show what might have been a cause of a relationship issue that never got resolved, but which could have had a good resolution with a lesson to learn.

A Pearl with opposing Sagittarius-Gemini parents, for instance, can consider the conflicts through an objective, traits-based story, where the Pearl works to identify the traits of the protagonist on a scale - from least helpful traits in this instance to most helpful ones. An adventure story is best, (Sagittarius) perhaps this one about an impulsive but earnest young man who didn't want to think out the details of a ski trip in the backwoods of a mountainous valley with a close friend. He'd known that area from childhood and thought it was not a hard trail to figure out, even in the snow.

The friend had wanted the adventurer's help to plan a ski trip, and to figure out the orientation details of the backwoods ski-trail. The adventurer, however, was more interested in spending time that weekend at an indoor wall-climbing course. The adventurer told the friend it was okay to go it alone because he would be able to figure out the trail along the way since the friend had grown up there also.

Shortly after, the friend (Gemini), who was always astute at working on some detailed computer game, became lost on the backwoods ski trip. The adventurer begged the search and rescue responders to allow the adventurer to search with them, but they said no. The adventurer did not know the details of search protocol and it would be too risky for them. The searchers couldn't find the friend as a snowstorm set in. Three days passed with no sign of the friend.

The adventurer spent three days and three nights with a recurring dream of a monster wandering behind a mountain. Each day, the adventurer awoke with a throat dry and hoarse, as if calling all night for the friend. The adventurer could hardly talk to anyone, despite longing to share the feelings of grief that the friend might have been lost on the mountain for good. The adventurer's heart was breaking.

When the searchers did find the friend, frostbite had permeated three fingers, and the tips of his fingers had to be amputated. Waiting at the hospital through the surgery, the adventurer wondered if the friend would ever be able to forgive him.

A Pearl could examine in this story what might have happened for the adventurer if the friend never forgave, or if the adventurer treated the forgiving friend nonchalantly again and stopped hearing from the friend for a long time. They might struggle in the heart about what better behaviors might have caused the two friends to help each other more and maintain a meaningful friendship of goodwill, rather than a broken one filled with heart pain. They could talk about blind spots in understanding the relationship needs of others who are very opposite to each other (Sagittarius-Gemini opposition shown in this story).

Archetypal, zodiac-based stories can bring greater meaning to a Pearl's investigations of relationship struggles and pain by removing personal details about a person for a period and looking at objective traits.

Capricorn Counseling Example

In an example for a Pearl during a Capricorn transit who's not sure how to feel about the discipline measures of his stepfather (Capricorn), a different archetypal story can be shared. This one is of a man who has no significant Aries initiator energy and a youth who has three planets in Aries. It is the Greek myth of Prometheus.

In a distilled summary of the Prometheus myth, Prometheus, a reformed Titan, in an impulsive passion (Aries impulsivity), steals fire from his father Zeus (Capricorn authority) to give to all of the people of the land to make their lives better (Pisces compassion) while receiving youthful glory. The pre-Christian Zeus, seeing that the world was not quite ready for humanity to take up fire for themselves and step toward independence, has Prometheus chained to a rock where an eagle continually eats at his liver (the irritating discomfort of facing the sometimes-harsh consequences of good actions done in wrong timing).

The Prometheus tale is best told with time available, and with rich imagery, rhythm, build, climax, resolution, and denouement, to sit well with the adolescent soul. For the sake of space in this book, I have offered the stark Prometheus summary only to tweak the reader's interest for an example of a myth to possibly consider researching further for a Pearl in such a situation.

Through the story of Prometheus, a youth can learn how his own impulsive, youthful energy and actions might have a righteous purpose, but can feel irritating and uncomfortable to an older, Capricorn-natured man who knows, from wisdom, that righteous actions still need to be done in right timing.

The therapist gauges an appropriate level of empathy, while bringing the story in a way that the youth feels able to be heard for some suffering being inevitably felt by having a stepparent who is relating out of significant differences from him about discipline, and often bumps up with him on it, unlike with his own father, who rarely disciplines him.

When a Pearl Youth can see that a consequence brought by his Capricorn-natured stepfather might have been enacted because of an archetypal and cosmically lawful truth about human souls, a truth that is even written into the mythologies of the past, but that must still adapt to the present, he can buffer and strengthen his trust.

He can also see if and where his own father may be out of soul truthfulness by not offering discipline very much at all. He can talk to the therapist about whether it would be right to try to be the father archetype with his own father to show him discipline, teaching his own father what he needs. Or he might want to discuss feelings of confusion about whose way is better, the discipline love of his stepfather or the rarely disciplining love nature of his birth father.

Rather than set up a competition, the therapist can clarify why it is not the Pearl's job to be his father's father, but that an interest in archetypal discipline is good. They can look at how he can take more of that up himself for his own needs and who might be best to offer him some support about personal disciplines, since it is often hard to set oneself a new task or habit and stick to it well without rigidity, or the opposite, giving up. They can discuss which parts of discipline, and flexible discipline such as working in space and time in the day to be free thinking and creative, are most appropriate to his needs and his age and stage of life.

The Pearl is reminded that old mythologies are not meant to be translated into direct and exact action today. No one today, even if he feels angry, is right to chain someone to a rock and knowingly leave them to be attacked by dangerous creatures to teach him a lesson. If the youth himself reveals, through the telling of the myth, that he has been subjected by his stepfather to seriously harmful abuse disguised as life lessons, then the therapist has a responsibility to follow abuse-reporting protocols with the youth.

A Pearl may cope easier with disciplinary action from his stepfather or societal authorities, if he knows that good discipline is normal with "good enough" fathers in whole families, or those who are in the youth's home and life regularly.

"Weekend" parents in divorce have been known to struggle with appropriate discipline with their children because they are disconnected from those children during much of their weekly life. Even if they bring an appropriate consequence, a Pearl can resent the absence of the parent the rest of the week and resist the consequence anyway. Weekend parents often try to make the time they have with the child seem like fun. This can lead to other problems when the child associates that parent only with the light parts of parenting, and the parent gets used to light parenting also.

Capricorn/Cancer Opposition Example in Counseling

Another example of zodiac archetype counseling might happen when a young Pearl Adult has been having a rough time with parents when strong Cancer influences are in opposition to her Capricorn sun sign for several weeks. That might happen with Mars transiting through Cancer.

The young Pearl Adult may have been working in the world at a job and at college studies and tasks. She is testing her daily life structures and routines on her own now in the world and applying them outwardly with great discipline. She has been feeling the expectation from society that she should begin to get into full societal career ambition (Capricorn).

Yet, a Mars in Cancer transit speaks to possibly having to fight for some inward healing or relaxation time, impulsively searching for a new home and comfort zone, having sexual urges related to having children, spending active time in rural environments, or learning to manage calm and stillness in the middle of a developing social life to balance work-life stress.

The Pearl may not have been considering marriage or committed relationship yet or ever, or she may have recently felt that she'd like to spend more significant and intimate time with a boyfriend she knows from school, but she doesn't know how to open into the conversation about raising children.

Her sense of fatherly discipline (Capricorn) says to her that her boyfriend should just know that now is the time to have such conversations. She really loves him and feels that he would be a good father and a healing influence in her life, but she feels intensely irked with him for not stepping up and introducing the conversation responsibly himself (Mars in Cancer).

A Mars in Cancer transit is a good time for this conversation about anger moments in relationships involving raising children. Yet, if the Pearl has unconsciously resisted this conversation before, due to Pearl insecurities about being able to have a family (conflicted Cancer energy), the Pearl may feel unbearable awkwardness now, coming out as strong irritation at the boyfriend.

She may be experiencing pressure from a family member (Capricorn opposite Mars in Cancer) to push the child-raising topic now. She could find herself projecting anxiety issues around the divorce of her parents in authoritarian ways (Capricorn) with her boyfriend, who is perplexed because he feels her annoyance with him but doesn't know what it's about, since Capricorns like his girlfriend often struggle to discuss feelings.

Or, the Pearl may have been meeting the pressures, structures, and demands of work well for a year or so (Capricorn), but now feels that she has to make some kind of self-care adjustment, and maybe she's not in the right job. She may want to go on an ocean cruise (Mars in Cancer), irking older family members who might consider that irresponsible so early in her work life and while she's still taking some college courses.

For six to eight weeks, the young Pearl Adult may get into heavy battles with a family member about the trip, only to discover than when the transit has passed by, she doesn't feel so compelled to go, or she drops the ambition for self-care but not the hurt feelings about being so opposed by others. She, and possibly the others are now holding grudges, and nothing significant has been settled (Cancer stillness). She's not interested in addressing family stress now because her ambition (Capricorn) has picked up again and she's thinking of working extra hours to be financially ready to have a vacation when she wants in the future without having to consult family members at all.

Post transit, the young woman is secretly holding onto anger (Mars) against the family, disgusted with, and alienated by, both parents for not understanding anything in her life. Cancer transits for young adult Pearls can be loaded with moody trauma triggers and resentments.

In counseling, the young adult can benefit from an exploration of what the continuum is for the Cancer mother-healer archetype, from most undeveloped to most developed and how its characteristics can manifest in relationships in general, in individual practices of health and well-being, and in the outer collective of work life, the community, the nation, or the world. She also looks at Mars influences to see how impulsive, and even selfish thinking can make her expect things from others that they aren't thinking about at all.

This is a deeply conscious intervention and it can help people to stay conscious of many progressions in life that bring short-term stressors, which may seem to come powerfully out of the blue for a short period of time. Through role-plays, social boundary strategies, drawing home-and-family maps, or by looking at how to bring her vacation sense of spaciousness and retreat into her daily life more, she can help herself to initiate some practices to get her Cancer-natured needs better met. With the initial need satisfied, she may be ready to work through relationship issues to manage triggers and reactiveness.

Life Constitutions

Rudolf Steiner saw that children incarnate into life with a greater or lesser affinity for earthen existence. These affinities affect how the child enters the first years of life through the nerve-sense system, metabolic system, and respiratory-circulatory systems. Rudolf Steiner identified, in the early twentieth century, six challenges and gifts that children tended to incarnate with and how to work with those children therapeutically as well as educationally. These came to be known in anthroposophy as the "Six Constitutional Types in School-Age Children."[41]

A therapist can apply the wisdom of these types to what is learned about the Pearl from recounting early school-age years and observing in the present healthy or dysfunctional adaptations and adjustments. Since human constitutions and their remediation can sometimes involve medical remedies, it is important to have the collaboration of anthroposophical doctors, nurses, Camphill caregivers, and even anthroposophical homeopathy practitioners.

Healing centers connected with Camphill communities for mentally disabled people, biodynamic farms, curative eurythmy, anthroposophical senior's residencies, medical centers, and anthroposophical arts institutes, with their balanced routines and rhythms, can have the right conscious capacities to help children of divorce to balance their shaky constitutional natures.

Many of these centers—such as the Threefold Educational Center in Chestnut Ridge, New York, the Rudolf Steiner Health Center in Ann Arbor, Michigan, Kultuurcentrum Järna in Ytterjärna, Sweden, the Ascura center and Hesperus House in Richmond Hill, Canada, and the Goetheanum in Dornach, Switzerland—have anthroposophical doctors, teachers, and therapists on-site or nearby to help facilitate this warming into a balanced and graceful connection with life.

The Six Constitutional Types in School-Age Children

A curative eurythmy[42] movement therapist can also observe constitutional adaptations during growth and development that may or may not be serving a child. Among many of the developmental observations for children that eurythmists, doctors, teachers, and therapists apply are the indications that Rudolf Steiner gave regarding the forces in a child as they present in the physical body, and particularly in the head. The following are some of his insights into the physiology of the head in relationship with the body and emerging soul expressions.

The Large-Headed Child

Large-headed children (and not implying children with encephalitis, a condition of water on the brain) tend not to want to embrace the sensual workings of all of life and prefer to move about in something of a dream world, lost in thinking. Rudolf Steiner associated the skull with an enclosed cosmos. With modern neuroscience, it is even easier to see it as such with the profound workings of firing and connecting neurons within the head resembling, in pictures, many fine, starlit nebulae. Steiner did not need today's neuroscience to see that the head is its own universe, with the brain resting in fluid, somewhat afloat and adjusting its balance atop of the body.

The human head and the organ of the brain allow us to think, imagine, and envisage well beyond what we might experience with just physical movement and our senses. We may see stars in the galaxies, but will never touch, smell, taste, or hear them. We can, however, imagine great thoughts about planets and stars, and even design a rocket that will travel to one. We can feel subtle body connections to their movements, sometimes through the help of acoustic music, or other times just in silence. Pure thinking has brought mathematics, science, and technology to a point that some human beings who develop the understandings have direct, supersensible experiences of other cosmic bodies in space.

More people can tell a story or two of dreams, imaginations, and the like, as well as sensations, beliefs, or direct knowing of experiences coming toward them from vast distances that they know on some level affect them. They may be hundreds of miles from a loved one but just know that something is terribly painful and challenging for them, only to find out that there was a restricting Saturn or Pluto alignment that day. Or the opposite, something deeply positive just happened like a birth and they feel as if they really experienced the moon's affect that morning. If no false theories, stigmas, or judgments were tossed about, it is likely that many people would trust their intuitions and have a story or two to tell about such cosmic experiences. They are often shared between people following a loved one's death.

Anthroposophy does not bother with the denials. It is well understood that the head carries consciousness far differently than just that which the limbs, muscles, and the torso are doing as parts of an integrated *survival suit* with earthly senses. The concern for the large-headed child is that he tends not to be conscious in his head region and so does not clearly grasp things as they are. He can't quite differentiate about material things in nature, and he may not focus well. He is neither oriented well to the cosmos and spiritual concerns, nor is he well oriented to the earth.

This child can be a dreamy, jovial, and rich soul, but with no strong tethers one way or the other. It is as if many of his life forces are still arranged in his head as he unconsciously decides if he's coming in to do earthly deeds or not. The soul's astral and ego forces are only tentatively attached to the nervous system of the body. This can feel very disconcerting on some level for the child and rightly so for the soul.

These undecided children, Rudolf Steiner suggested, can benefit from very hot or very cold body wipes or water drips on their face and upper body in the morning, to gently wake the soul after the body awakens. The child is requiring a bit of a bite to life, as with icy water wipes, to shake awake the soul forces and make them aware of the body and the differentiation of the earth realm from the thought realm. This daily practice, he suggests, could take a year or more to impress the soul with the reality of its new earthly existence.

The Hippocratic oath of the healer is paramount here: "Do No Harm."[43] Literally shaking a child to wake him out of daydreaming is not only an unhealthy practice because of the damage that it can do to the child's body and nervous system, it is a form of child abuse and illegal in many Western jurisdictions. This is not the suggestion that anthroposophy makes. It is known that the soul invests knowledge, willfulness, and awareness through practice, rhythm, and time. The winter nature of the cold-water therapy for the child is one that is brought as a slight, awakening chill. The process is not to keep the child in that cold state throughout the day and night. It is a wake-up procedure only, for the soul, in the morning.

Pearl Child

A Pearl Child, prior to the parents' divorce, may or may not have had a good constitutional balance between nerve-sense activity, metabolism, and breathing. A large-headed child today in the often chaotic and nerve-wracking world circumstances of environmental disasters, climate change, war, human displacement and divorced family disruption may become too shocked out of sleep daily, depending on the parents' or caregivers' composure in today's realities. This child may need a very different approach to keep the soul engaged with the day and not resorting to regressing back into their loose-headed connection out of fear and escapism.

The important point is that this kind of child tends to live in the head but not in connection to much that is distinct or related to earthy nature. In a traumatized child's case, oil massages surrounded by gentle, acoustic music, and even hot stone body treatments, may work very well to introduce this sensitive soul warmly into the body and its earthiness again. Then, a lively run through the woods or park with a family therapy dog, watched by mother or father, before heading to school, might be the right wake-up.

Divorce trauma can cause the constitution to become distorted, especially if the child was previously disposed to a tentative incarnation such as that with a large-headed child. A child after divorce can be like the dreamy, loosely incarnate, large-headed child; in this case, frightened about bringing the body into engagement with the earth and the sense life. Such a child may also be feeling inwardly ungrounded and unsafe, unable to reach up into a spiritual mood, either, to self-soothe and make life more bearable or welcoming.

Another issue for this child is that they may have become leery about who to trust in life to offer welcoming stimulation and consistent remediation. This child may need more long-term and frequent healings such as hot, lavender-mud massage around his neck, back, and kidneys. This is best done in a warm room with healing, peach-toned colors. A woodstove, fireplace, or beeswax candle burning nearby is good. The massage can go from calm to lively to calm again.

In this case, the child needs to feel the heart warmth foremost, to become encouraged back into the cool, earthly life. In a hot-climate region, this healing might be adapted with cool, tangy lemongrass, lavender, and geranium-leaf baths followed by warm, sesame-oil reflexology on the foot soles and toes. A warm, sesame-oil drip on the forehead can be grounding and calming. The need to keep clear, differentiated, and rational with this child, while bringing joyful imaginations, continues to be a priority. Sense-stimulating warmth or coolness that doesn't contribute to further shock is asked for here. Tuning up with ball-tossing play with mom or dad before school can be just the lively connection the child needs to enter the day safely.

This child's diet may need more salt to encourage metabolism. For some young children, and particularly girls due to their naturally social nature, bringing a friend or relative into the healing with the therapist and/or practitioner can help in time to gain trust and establish comforting and active relationships again. A therapist can attempt to establish with the child a better sense of natural and balanced breathing, often through sculpting, copper-rod exercises, or wet-on-wet, watercolor painting.[44]

The Small-Headed Child

The small-headed child is not so connected to the nerve-sense or thought and spirit organs. They are uncomfortable with metabolic activity, so the child acts in a tense and driven way, as if trying to move along in life without becoming too affected by digestion and metabolism. The small-headed child is often impulsive, and food processing and elimination can be very non-rhythmical and even blocked for a day or two.

Food substances may not be regulated and moving through the body well, which can leave the child run ragged by metabolism. This child can struggle to bring imaginative pictures to mind, to be constructive, and to move artistically in the limbs. The child's astral body is struggling to connect in an integrated way with the metabolic-digestive system.

Rudolf Steiner indicated warm tummy wraps after meals for this child, encouraging quiet time with a safe and comforting parent or caregiver. Some sweet food is helpful, such as honey in chamomile tea or maple syrup in some warm, non-gluten drink such as rice or almond milk. Just enough of the sweetness is needed to provide an invigorating effect on the metabolism while stimulating higher, joyful thoughts.

Stories about the nectar-giving flower spirits and the bees nesting in their honeycombs can be very effective to bringing the child's astral forces in line with digestion and a sense of the earthly home and nature's sentient cooperation.

Any biodynamic farm stories offered during a tummy wrap time can be effective for this when they focus on digestion, such as the cow's four stomachs and its ruminating activity, as well as the warmth and loving nurturance. The storyteller can add some insights about the good caretaking relationship of farmer to the farm animals, vegetables, fruits, and the dedicated farm helpers.

Pearl Child

Pearl Children can have any number of metabolic and digestive concerns today. Eating disorders can be a big problem. Children of divorce often begin a conscious or unconscious search for the love that seemed to be lost when their parents separated. Yet, their perception and understanding of relational love can be distorted, particularly as they absorb what each parent models after the marriage breakup.

There is much to digest and absorb through the blood system, brain, and heart when a family breaks up. Even hormonal and brain chemical systems in the child can become overwhelmed or out of healthy order by the loss and trauma of divorce. If there has been violence in the family breakup or leading to it, then many factors are now involved in healing the Pearl Child's relationships with the three pillars of their human constitution: a) the nerve-senses, b) the metabolism, and c) the breath.

Eating Disorders: Searching Incarnate, Non-Reductionist Love

When a child, adolescent, or young adult begins a search for love outside of themselves, in whatever way, the child can easily become exposed to a modern barrage of supposedly powerful experts telling or showing them what love is, or what to love and what not to love. The constant product advertising promotion and manipulation around male and female desires, even at very young ages, is offensive not only to child senses but to the "common sense" of being human. It has required tremendous courage for anthroposophical and other parents not to be swayed by the reductionist advertising and fantasy images of love, beauty, and materially or emotionally manipulative sexual relationships that many children see all about them today.

Human reductionism is a way of putting focus on parts of a person's body, or on ideas and images of people in their worlds, with only a small part of the person's or peoples' whole value depicted, leading to a minimization of them. A young child driving in a car on the city freeway can be exposed to frequent billboard visuals on the street of womans' behinds or of mens' chests, that are often sexualized or demeaning. A woman on an advertising billboard for a whiskey company is shown for the lowcut blouse prominently, or the slit-cut slacks and spiked heels hanging loosely over the end of a sofa with a half-empty bottle of 'spirits' in her hand, face down, with slightly lifted, tight-slacked buttocks showing and flowing hair, but no face. Or color and lighting effects highlight the rounds of a man's buttocks in extra tight, black, business suit pants, in the forefront of an image with the newest model sports car – again no face, just the sexually sculpted backside of the man and the go-for-it car.

These sexualized images disregard aspects of the human beings' faces or other features. They are often airbrushed to make the models bodies look inhumanly perfected. The message is that the real value is in the fun of drinking hard liquor with the woman and maybe jumping in intimately with her, but not really knowing anything about her. Or it's about the strong backside of the man who would want to valued for his almost animalistic drive for success and excitement rather than for his connectedness to self and others. Body-image manipulations surrounding children in the West today can wreak havoc on young people's thoughts about eating and thus the metabolizing functions of their connected and disconnected bodies. Images that commodify body parts of men and women (female breast cleavage or men's sculpted pectorals) are exhibited all around young children today, further imprinting a sense of human soul-hollowness as a cultural feature in their lives.

Digestive and metabolic activity is one of the most highly manipulated issues of our times, with the emphasis on speedy internet lives, fast food outlets, and unlabeled, genetically modified foods. leaving natural human diets unprotected. Eating while watching television shows or computer engagements brings no consciousness to the meal, or to conversation and sharing with real, human meal companions. It can leave the soul feeling empty even if the body is full.

Mindless eating can encourage poor nutrition since the addictive nature of the media may encourage a general craving nature in the child. Neonicotinoid-sprayed farm fields, dying pollination bees, and food manufacturing advertising targeting children's media with genetically modified, sugar-laden, or chemically dyed food has reached an alarming rate in the last five decades. There is little wonder why souls are coming into the world not wanting to engage their metabolic or digestive systems too deeply.

This life-diminishing behavior in society thrusts upon parents, caregivers, healers, doctors, biodynamic farmers, therapists, and teachers the even greater responsibility to observe what is happening in the digestion of the children of divorce. It is also important that the adults in the children's lives do not scare them away from having deeply incarnate digestive and metabolic systems through promoting to them nutritionally austere dieting schemes. Some children may be naturally developing toward vegetarianism today, and some may not be ready for that. Holistic eating, in this case, must be designed and monitored for a child to be certain that the child is getting full meals with a variety of seeds, nuts, or proteins along with healthy whole-food grains, fruits, and vegetables.

It can be a challenge to help a child with very light adult attachment and an unsafe family support system to eat a very light diet since heavy, more acidic food can give the child a sense of substance, even while it creates other health challenges. Until safe, stable home-like and family-like circumstances can be available to the most vulnerable Pearl Children, the jury is out around encouraging such children to become vegetarian or vegan. For some other Pearls, their compassion may easily express as a complete aversion to eating animal foods—even to the peril of their own health.

Parents walk a tender balance today regarding just how incarnate they can expect their children to be and how each individual child will meet the tense challenges of a transitioning and globally interconnected world while staying earthed and grounded. Organic foods, homeopathy, herbal teas, tinctures, and Bach flower remedies are recommended for digestion and metabolism in transitions when a parent can afford it. Argentum (silver)[45] is a homeopathic remedy suggested for the small-headed or metabolically reticent child. Rudolf Steiner suggested that therapists, healers, and doctors hold the idea of summer with the small-headed or metabolically reluctant child and winter with the large-headed or nerve-sense disconnected child.

This availability of parental or caregiver commitment remains a concern for children of divorce. Many still can experience, in their growing years, the uncommitted nature of relationship and neglectful parenting as one parent disappears, is reluctant to take up responsible co-parenting, or insists that children should be able to just roll with the punches. Here, the anthroposophical notions of sympathy and antipathy become helpful.[46] Managing the middle-torso sphere of the metabolic-digestive-limbic system becomes a more effective and tuned process by looking at what the child feels sympathetic to and what they resist or feels antipathy toward.

Observing and questioning what it is in a child that is drawing him to always want red meat and heavy breads without balancing these foods with fresh vegetable salads, cooked beans, or digestive herbs, can reveal if there are constitutional, environmental-regional, or emotional issues associated with eating. Is there a potential logic to why a child might be blocking up their inner core and fortifying it with food that will digest slowly but also bring a carbohydrate high after experiencing overt or covert, divorced-parent conflict?

Is the child repressing speaking about some bullying at school and thinks about the need to bulk up while also blocking out depression by stuffing the body with sweets? Did the recent flooding in the city leave the child without a home for a few weeks and the child is now using food to hoard internally, trying to solidify the body against being washed away again somehow?

Sympathy means to be open to something, someone, or some idea. With sympathy, we can laugh and be warm-hearted. *Antipathy* means that we feel a need to protect ourselves from something, someone, or some idea. We put up boundaries, meet things head-on, like a bull with no feeling sensitivity, or close ourselves off. The middle road, between sympathy and antipathy, brings the greatest peace and the most balanced breath, digestion, and metabolism.

The Earthy Child

The Earthly Child has what Rudolf Steiner called the "gift of interest at first sight of everything earthly."[47] An earthly existence is second nature to these children, and they embrace it early and easily, filled with excitement and love for all that earthly life brings. They may show signs of tussled ruggedness, always dirty from the day, since they have been in active play with everything that nature and life offer. These children are often impetuous. They love to move, and any work with movement, dance, music, craft, and outdoor play works well with them. Their need is to cultivate awareness of feelings and beauty. They may need to sit back and watch more beautiful and refined movements in others through observing eurythmy or Spacial Dynamics.[48]

These children love to have craft and art activities patterned for them as they are not so likely to come up with spiritual/artistic inspirations out of their own constitutional abilities. They need to see how others have refined them, so they can be inspired to do that for themselves too. The earthy child needs to experience opposites and may struggle to see things other than as they appear now in the material nature. Their process is one of awakening the feeling realm so that they are inspired to go further than just the practical and sensual.

Pearl Child

An earthy child of divorce is the kind of child who can deeply resent the disengagement from a family member and may spend a great deal of time trying to rework the family dynamics. This child may not even seem to feel much disturbance in their emotional life early in the separation. Such a child may, however, struggle significantly around how to make and hold a claim on things, on the child's sense of ground, on sensual interests and desires, and on family treasures and inheritances. Managing the possessions and tasks of the home can get tricky going between two households with different rules and different parent couples who value earthly, material items differently.

This child, once established in new routines at each parent's home or with the single-parent arrangements, may become more forceful about needs and wants. This child could become confrontational at home and even at school in situations where less food, toys, or opportunities to play reveal in the child's awareness a resource deficit. This can be exacerbated if the child's main caregiving parent, or both parents, experience a dive in income or other resources in the divorce.

This is a classic issue for many divorced families. Decompensation in Pearl-life experiences can be especially painful for the earthy child, who is so aware of the abundance of the world and family relationships, and unable to see any higher purpose for what has happened in the split family. It's likely that this child could struggle with envy and jealousy in the middle of stepfamily dynamics.

This is the kind of adolescent who may have an early pregnancy, or even become dangerously promiscuous to get some of the material things the Pearl felt lacking during childhood. This youth could become a thief. These adolescents need to include subtle thinking and long-term planning with their desire fulfillment, and to address feelings of loss and grief as fully as they address sense-fulfillment. Without addressing loss, this child can easily project cynicism and even ruthlessness in later relationships when the need for beauty, ownership, purely practical activity, or sensual-sexual pleasures are not being met as expected.

The strengths of earthy children are that they are often capable of working hard through trying times to achieve goals. Through the arts and crafts, they can become well-refined adults with creative and balanced constitutions. They need inspiring mentors, though, who share their sensual, material interests in appropriate, non-greedy ways.

The Cosmic Child

When a teacher or counselor has come across a child who seems to have fairies in the belly, endless imaginations, and invisible friends who the child will happily share with you through nature stories, toys, animals, paintings, or collections, it is likely that the adult has met up with a Cosmic Child. This child is often flexible or fluid in the thinking and creative nature. The cosmic child may not be very constituted to the metabolism or to the earthly realm and deep, earthy breathing and rhythms. Yet, the child is so truthfully charming and sweet that it is hard not to be completely enchanted.

This child benefits from studies and activities that foster engagement with spiritual or creative interests in nature, geography, historical events, and people. Rudolf Steiner saw how the cosmic child needs to be given activities that allow the child to take the inner time to reflect on the life of feeling and actions. This child, like the earthy child, has a feeling necessity, and is best helped into a balanced constitution through artistic engagement in several variations.

Eurythmy is helpful for this child, with its musical movement and rhythmical verses that ground imagination. This child needs strong feelings for engaging with nature and the earthen world more fully. The child wants to test life bit by bit, with guidance. A good approach to such a child is to be sure to hear the child out about the options coming up out of imagination for how to do practical things a little differently and creatively, and perhaps with a touch of reverent ritual about it.

Drama is one effective way to grab the imagination of these children. They need to work into musical and dramatic performances, rather than simply watching movies or television programs. They can use lots of creative resources at their fingertips to weave the magic that they can so easily see that others don't.

Pearl Child

Cosmic children are not necessarily earthbound children, so their relationship to traumatic loss and change is one to watch carefully and help to ground in love. These children could need compassionate stories of earth fairies, devas, sylphs, and gnomes to bring them back to earth in imaginative and heartfelt ways. They may need to play in warm water with natural colors, flowers, or with East-Indian, patterned, leaf-and-candle boats to push around in the ripples with a caregiver.

Earthen life is not easy for these children and relationships can be emotionally confusing at best, and entangling and frightening at worst. They can be reached a little easier with puppets voicing feelings, by putting funny voices to the family pet's activities, or having plenty of dress-up play and helping to design, build, and decorate a walk-in playhouse with room for a friend or sibling.

Cosmic children can do very well with intellectual thought in adulthood, making great writers, professors, performers, artists, designers, hospitality workers, therapists, scientists, researchers, technology designers, and sociologists. They can also find much fulfillment in spiritual work.

If these children are supported well through a family divorce, they can avoid falling into rationalizing and keep focused, grounded, and open. They need to be helped to identify and experience grief, to rehearse options for expressing relationship love, and to overcome social shyness through practice support, such as role-playing. They also need encouragement to network meaningful relationships with extended family members and other substantial people in their lives.

The cosmic child can have the tendency to put up hard barriers and boundaries when relationships fail or surface intense feelings that can inwardly feel out of control. The nerve-sense nature of the cosmic children can make them super-sensitive in relationships, and they may need a lot of explaining and investigating to understand what has happened between the parents in the breakup.

Deeply empathic therapists and healers are best to work with these children since these children can more easily take to a warm, water-natured person than an earthy, straight-and-narrow, cool-minded one. Such children benefit from nature-art retreats and an ongoing, biodynamic farm work that help them relate their cosmic affinity to how plants grow and how animals relate to the zodiac and the garden preps. In time, they would also benefit from playing a stringed instrument that they get to design and make themselves, such as a lyre.

The Fantasy-Rich Child

A child who is rich in fantasy will have plenty of inspiration and imagination. This child recalls images, sounds, and events well, and likely with a twist or two of added comic relief or chutzpah. This is also the child who can become enchanted, compulsive-obsessive, and even haunted by an idea of which the child has a very hard time letting go. This can easily turn to psychosis, personal disruption, and pain if the child is not able to receive the guidance that is needed to offset the imbalance.

Rudolf Steiner has used the example of a child who is presented with a thought from a teacher or student that he then holds onto and follows in his consciousness to the complete exclusion of everything else continuing in the room. He indicated that this child is usually in a dance with their I-being. This is a sensitive being who is negotiating with awareness of the spiritual on such a level that the I-force struggles to bring life to the other natural and essential functions of the fourfold human being.

The fantasy-rich child is seen to have had spiritual forces freed up from the rest of the human forces too early. These forces, if in healthy growth and rhythm, would have gone more into embodiment early in life, then into practical tasks of imagination, and then into thought and concept, thereby leading to the formation of a whole and rhythmically structured I or ego. This holistic ego would then use its executive functions to manage inspirations and images coming out of higher consciousness and spiritual thoughts.

This child, when given age-appropriate practices and helpful awareness of holistic earthly activities, rhythms, and self-care methods, can ground personal capacities in a self-responsible way to take full financial, political, constructive, relational, and creative hold of adult life. "Work through play" can become this child's motto.

With self-discipline and an ability to relate to the diverse outer experiences of others, including those who find it almost impossible to connect with a spiritual truth in life, this child can become an inspiration. By staying guided from within, affirming others' spiritual journeys, and pointing in any number of ways to the general truth of a spiritual world and cosmos, this child in time can bring healthy capacities for illusion to conscious and creative expression in ways that can help others. The helpful and creative inventor as well as a healer may be the path for such a child.

This child's deepening spiritual-soulful awareness will encourage for others, homeopathically, the freedom to find their own spiritual connection as well. For this child, Rudolf Steiner suggested activities of movement, cursive writing, form drawing, and music to encourage this child to incarnate and warm up to the inner self again. The warmth of the middle realm of good metabolism and digestion will help the child to experience the loving resonance between spirit and human life on earth.

This could come with a biodynamic farm community of conscious-eating foodies who understand the connection between spirit and the earthly elementals. Singing is also affirming for this child, in all scales and moods, beginning and closing with a heartwarming impulse. Philanthropic deeds are a mainstay for this child.

Pearl Child

Rudolf Steiner gave the following description for the fantasy-rich child: "A disturbance or premature opening in the metamorphosis of the growth forces."[49] It is a definition that can also characterize the experience of many children of divorce at various stages of development. A shock to a child's whole-soul system, which is so far-reaching as to rearrange the emotional, structural, rhythmical, financial, and relational foundations of the child's life, can cause the child to be shaken awake too early in the spiritual life. This can happen whether the child has been exposed to a spiritual community or not. It comes out of a deep fear response.

Parents will also sometimes give higher spiritual meanings for the divorce to their children too early, causing a child to strive unconsciously to realize spiritual and cosmic work on a level far beyond the needs of the child's earthly, natural growth. This can be worse with spiritual beliefs that project gods or spiritual beings as being outside or away from the earth or child, rather than also in the earth, in individuals, and between people.

Archetypal, angelic perfection, for instance, can become an unconscious reason inside the child's thinking for them to be extra good in life so that no one he loves will ever leave again. This can happen despite a parent's good intentions to assure the child that the child holds no blame in the divorce.

A fantasy-rich child can be very susceptible to self-recrimination about the loss of love and goodwill in a family. It does not have an adult rationale, but rather, it is a felt-sense dilemma for the child because coming into body out of the cosmos in the first place was hard for this soul. The family breakup has, unconsciously, confirmed for this child that life can be a place of wretched sadness and unprotected heartache.

The newer unconscious dilemma is how to come into the body now when the original, family rhythms, structures, and relationships have changed. This child's sense of child-protection and innocence may not feel recovered enough in its appropriate ages and stages and may not have been strong to begin with, depending on the early nature of the parental marriage.

Sometimes, the only in-spiriting experiences that remain consistent in the fantasy-rich child's life after a sad divorce are the child's daily hopes, prayers and "happy-ending" bedtime stories, the comforting people at their church, temple, or community worship hall, and the fairy-like or angelic bedroom pictures and storybooks intuitively given to the child by family and friends throughout the birth and childhood.

In a different kind of family, there may be nothing in this child's surroundings that is reminiscent of heartfelt spirit between people, only unrealistic computer memes, cartoon-like dolls, and robot-like media figures in child-geared movies. The soul "jumping out of body" problem can be exacerbated here as it unconsciously seeks safety in something resembling the joyful high of nature and natural spirit light.

This child, male or female, as an adolescent or young adult, could fall into the traps of drugs and easy schemes to get to the top of life and miss the earthy challenges of real relationships. If one of the child's parents disappears, is inconsistent, falls ill, or dies in the transition time of the child recovering courage for life, this child can fall into serious mental illness.

Also, if a parent tries to intellectually rationalize the marriage breakup to the child, and without having resolved his or her own heart pain, the child can lose trust in the middle-realm warmth and consistent state of love that helps to foster appropriate, fourfold human development. This child should also not be given too much cognitive behavioral therapy but rather, expressive and arts therapies.

These children may become particularly demanding of love before they can trust it again, causing issue with young child friends, adolescent peers, authority figures, and early adult relationships. Without appropriate, conscious, and empathic help from the adults around, this child can be helped into a warm, earthy incarnation, but could just as easily be encouraged to become more out of body and dependent on others who look to the child as an avatar or precious spirit needing to be taken care of without challenge. The kind of consciousness of the adults around this child is key. The child must be carefully guided when engaging with computer social media so as not to get caught up in trying to save the world at the expense of good sleep times and time in real life.

Enchanted parents can lift this child up as their own spiritual guru, leaving the child more in a phantom body through life rather than incarnate and freely relational. They can encourage the child into all kinds of fantastical exploits that will simply leave the child's heart hollow, despite how exciting it might seem for a while. Stories that celebrate the heart and soul of human beings doing creative work for the less fortunate are good for this child.

This awareness is important for helping the fantasy-rich, spiritual child stay self-contained with a life recognizable through nature, with grounded people in the child's social network, and an ability to stay consistently upright. Rudolf Steiner suggested eurythmy practices of threefold, toe-metatarsal-heel walking, rope-skipping, rhythmical games, and running as helpful activities for this child to bring the ethereal nature into the other elements of earth, water, air, and fire.

In eurythmy dance-movement, this child can do this without losing spiritual connection due to the cosmic rhythms of the movements and the impulses of the higher worlds in the choreographies, verses, choices of music, rod exercises, and colorful gowns. In speech work, consonant work will be most helpful.

Anthroposophy also stresses the need to do practices with this child to help work into rhythms of remembering and forgetting. The Waldorf school curriculum, for instance, works on "main lesson" learning blocks each morning. A different subject, such as mathematics or geography, is studied in an intensive and holistic way for three to four weeks. The subject of study is enlivened with compelling, feeling-enriched stories, colorful drawing, movement, special projects, music, and even sports and spatial dynamics activities.

Once students are immersed in the subject, the topic closes and the new skills and knowledge go to sleep for a time while another subject is introduced. The subjects are reintroduced over cycles of learning, and often it is the same teacher who picks up with the children with the renewed topic at a new age, stage, and grade.

The Fantasy-Poor Child

It is a good practice for healers who work with fantasy-poor children to take some empathic time and imagine what has brought these children to have so little ability to raise thoughts and images in their minds. Since many healers and teachers tend toward the creative-artistic-spiritual realm of interests and abilities in life, sensing into an embodied human experience where many of one's easiest or most natural capacities are not available is a real awakening.

The pressure and struggle to reconnect with a natural capacity is not lost on these children, who can experience emotional pain from not being able to remember things that other children seem to be able to recall so easily. Much stigmatizing and even bullying can happen toward a child of this nature without skilled and conscious parents, teachers, and caregivers to help clear the labyrinth of misunderstanding, particularly in school.

A fantasy-poor child can be earthy and strong in metabolic processes. This can be the farm child who is deeply invested in the life of the minerals, plants, animals, and the earthen interests of the people around. This is the child who knows what is directly appealing to the earthly senses and has had such consistency with that on the farm that the child hasn't needed to range much further to embody and enjoy life. The child may have parents, siblings, or grandparents who do too much for the child, such as with the youngest child in a large family, and the child is not challenged to be creative in thought or to put problem-solving in action.

This child may be from a cultural background, perhaps an Italian or Argentinian folk-soul experience, where people find it natural to have many people busily talking and debating in the house all at once, collectively solving problems. Into this family has come a more silent, less mental, and impassioned type of soul who is tasked with moving from what would be practical, earthy mimicry to more personal capacities this lifetime because of immigration to a more individualist society.

This child is at risk of feeling lost and frustrated if given a sanguine activity to complete alone, or if not given enough time to reach into memory for the stores of thoughts that have sunk into deep unconsciousness.

Rudolf Steiner reminded teachers that children learn in step-by-step processes that reflect the unfolding of the fourfold life forces of the human being. Rushing or overloading the developmental processes—pandemic behaviors in some schools and early-childhood care programs around the world today—has simply shown to be stressful on children and not of any real benefit to learning or growth. The fantasy-poor child will only awake to the higher developments of thought and spiritual truths in time and with practical accompaniment in life.

A therapist may need to spend time in the exploration of senses and the earthy life with this child, while having an atmosphere of repetitive, rhythmical music and offering the child opportunities to be very practical with music, dance, arts, or other higher work. These are the children who will want to do eurythmy stomping exercises repeatedly until they can find connection to the beat of the music. Many of their experiences need to be repetitive.

These children will enjoy cooking in class and punching dough for bread-making in kindergarten. Finding ways to move from basic rhythms to some syncopation at times, or to beating or stomping, moving rhythms with different sounds such as stomping with slippers, stomping with wooden Dutch shoes, and stomping with bells on ankles, can begin to loosen up for these children their own sense of variety of experiences that will naturally wake up some thought and diverse experience.

Beanbag toss, rhythm games with the therapist, with new colors added in time and a slight change in pace or a clap added in between, and then repeated enough for the effort to register without going to sleep in the child, can be effective. At the point where the child seems too comfortable, that is the time to change the task or to introduce a verse or a song. Repeating the whole new sequence, and asking for sensation impressions, can help this child to integrate several lively capacities.

Creating warmth, mindfulness, and acceptance for these children to feel welcome as they are, and safe to reach beyond themselves on their own timing, is important for the fantasy-poor child. From this, later, a memory bank of diverse experiences can begin to build and knit extensive brain capacity. Practical craft experiences support the fantasy-poor child, such as working with clay or wax.

Helping to hammer together and paint colorful set pieces for a play is also a good activity. The child can be purposeful to the actors in the play. This child's ability to remember parts and lines is not as strong as the other children. This child needs to be the chorus member for a few more years.

Trying to shake these children out of themselves could, because of the lack of a personally engaged imagination, put these children into something of an existential crisis. The path of these children is different than the large-headed children. These children will need to be raised up slowly into complex activity.

Pearl Child

The fantasy-poor child who can be left in complete bewilderment when the parents' marriage breaks up and when life is divided between two homes. The child might fall into deep silence. Or, if the child suddenly has stepsiblings at some point, or finds things gone from the home, and routines shifted when one parent moves out, a crisis can manifest in angry reactions and even bullying.

These children are the most likely Pearls to try to keep things as they were, and to try to stand ground without any openness to reason. They may need to be told and shown over again, with great patience, what is changing and how the new routines work. These children may not open about feelings for a very long time regarding loss, betrayal, sadness, or any complex emotions. The child's priority will likely be to resurrect, at any cost, the unconscious comfort lived since infancy.

The fantasy-poor child may become a very anxious child in a life that can't be brought back as it was. In adolescence, this can become problematic if the youth begins to seek avenues to root feelings with alcohol, manipulation, or possibly stealing. This adolescent may secretively bully or scapegoat others to do the thinking and creative work that eludes this youth. The youth may take things inwardly, getting a range of illnesses from refusing to participate in anything other than sitting in front of the television or hiding away in a room listening to music all day on a Saturday or for a whole weekend.

These behaviors can quickly become signs of mental illness setting in and are best met by companioning this child in the stuckness, silence, and pain for a while. Simple activities in counseling together, such as casually whittling a stick, plucking at an African mbira instrument,[50] or fiddle-filing some soapstone, can boost this traumatized child to open feelings without requiring too much upheaval of deep-seated comfort. This teen might also benefit from working with a lazure painter, applying blended colors—soft, warm, and balancing cool tones—on a wall-painting project at home. Such a task can be both calming and creative.

A casual veil painting project with a counselor could also help this child to dab paint in steady, rhythmic, non-taxing thought, giving the child a lot of room to put the paintbrush down and settle into a chair to gaze at the colors. A veil painting, with many gentle strokes of watercolor paint, overlaying each other, revealing their own imaginative picture after a while, can be steadying yet also exciting as the child maps out what the painting is trying to show. Riddles and the occasional joke can help to relax some fear. The client can open to more self-expression and emotional intelligence with a therapist who is very patient.

If the fantasy-poor youth moves into what modern Western clinical diagnostics in psychology call histrionics,[51] or forms of uncontrolled acting out, one can be assured that the youth has been pushed well beyond comfort zone and needs to have home base established again, with some creative renovating perhaps encouraged. This is the type of child who can become a home builder, renovator, or handyman. The key will be to make the child aware of the vast number of other approaches that people take to life and find ways to respect that.

Endnotes

1 R. Steiner, "Anthroposophy and Psychoanalysis" (lecture, Dornach, November 10, 1917), retrieved June 2020, https://wn.rsarchive.org/GA/GA0178/19171110p01.html

2 K. Stavrianopoulos, G. Faller and L. Furrow, "Emotionally Focused Family Therapy: Facilitating Change Within a Family System," Journal of Couple & Relationship Therapy, 13, 1, (2014), retrieved June 18, 2020, https://doi.org/10.1080/15332691.2014.865976

3 L. Dimeff and M.M. Linehan, "Dialectical Behaviour Therapy in a Nutshell," The California Psychologist, 34, (2001), 10-13, retrieved June 18, 2020, https://www.researchgate.net/profile/Marsha_Linehan/publication/239279018_Dialectical_Behavior_Therapy_in_a_Nutshell/links/00463530be15f63c28000000.pdf

4 Theosophical Society of India, "Atman, Buddhi, Manas," (Chennai, India: Theosophy World, 2020), retrieved June 18, 2020, https://www.theosophy.world/encyclopedia/atma-buddhi-manas
Rudolf Steiner, Theosophy: An Introduction To The Supersensible Knowledge Of The World And The Destination Of Man, (Scotts Valley, CA: CreateSpace Independent Publishing Platform, 2008), 50-56, retrieved June 18, 2020, https://www.amazon.ca/Theosophy-Introduction-Supersensible-Knowledge-Destination/dp/1440431744

5 K. Brasher, "Solution-Focused Brief Therapy: Overview and Implications for School Counselors," The Alabama Counseling Association Journal 34, no. (spring 2009), https://eric.ed.gov/?id=EJ875397

6 J. Firman and A. Gila, Psychosynthesis: A Psychology of the Spirit (Albany, NY: State University of New York Press, 2002).

7 T. Fischer, "Parental Divorce and Children's Socio-economic Success: Conditional Effects of Parental Resources Prior to Divorce, and Gender of the Child," Sociology 41, no. 3 (June 1, 2007), https://doi.org/10.1177/0038038507076618

8 Diagnostic and Statistical Manual of Mental Disorders (DSM-5) (Washington, DC: American Psychiatric Association, 2013).

9 DSM-5.

10 DSM-5.

11 M. K. Nock et al., "Suicide and Suicidal Behavior," Epidemiologic Reviews 30, no. 1 (2008): 133–154. http://doi.org/10.1093/epirev/mxn002
C. Van Heeringen, "Understanding the suicidal brain," The British Journal of Psychiatry 183, no. 4 (2003): 82–284, https://doi.org/10.1192/bjp.183.4.282

12 J. Liu, "Childhood Externalizing Behavior: Theory and Implications," Journal of Child and Adolescent Psychiatric Nursing 17, no. 3 (2004): 93–103, https://doi.org/10.1111/j.1744-6171.2004.tb00003.x

13 C. A. Moylan et al., "The Effects of Child Abuse and Exposure to Domestic Violence on Adolescent Internalizing and Externalizing Behavior Problems," Journal of Family Violence 5, no. 1 (2010): 53–63, https://doi.org/10.1007/s10896-009-9269-9

14 G. M. Johnson, "Self-Punitive Habit Syndrome: A Theoretical Model and Cognitive-Behavioral Intervention Strategy," Journal of Cognitive Psychotherapy 1, no. 3 (Fall 1987).

15 K. L. Gratz and J. G. Gunderson, "Preliminary Data on an Acceptance-Based Emotion Regulation Group Intervention for Deliberate Self-Harm Among Women with Borderline Personality Disorder," Behavior Therapy 37, no. 1 (2006): 5–35, https://doi.org/10.1016/j.beth.2005.03.002

M. Smith et al., "Cutting and Self-Harm: How to Feel Better without Hurting Yourself," HelpGuide, last updated October 2019, https://www.helpguide.org/articles/anxiety/cutting-and-self-harm.htm

16 S. Levenkron, Cutting: Understanding and Overcoming Self-mutilation (New York, NY: W. W. Norton, 1998).

17 L. Nelson and R. Schwaner, "Transdermal Fentanyl: Pharmacology and Toxicology," Journal of Medical Toxicology 5, no.4 (2009), https://doi.org/10.1007/BF03178274

18 "People with mental health disorders twice as likely to have heart disease or stroke," Heart and Stroke Foundation of Canada, (2014), retrieved June 2020, https://www.eurekalert.org/pub_releases/2014-10/hasf-pwm102314.php

19 A. Michel, "Burnout and the Brain," Observer (February 2016), retrieved June 2020, https://www.psychologicalscience.org/observer/burnout-and-the-brain#.WQqdZuQktPY

20 K. Kozlowska et al., "Fear and the Defense Cascade: Clinical Implications and Management," Harvard Review of Psychiatry 3, no. 4 (2015): 63–287, https:// https://doi.org/10.1097/HRP.0000000000000065

21 A. Vyas et al., "Chronic Stress Induces Contrasting Patterns of Dendritic Remodeling in Hippocampal and Amygdaloid," The Journal of Neuroscience no. 15 (2002): 6810–6818, https://doi.org/10.1523/JNEUROSCI.22-15-06810.2002

22 C. B. Nemeroff and P. J. Goldschmidt-Clermont, "Heartache and Heartbreak: The Link between Depression and Cardiovascular Disease," Nature Reviews Cardiology 9 (2012): 526–539, https://doi.org/10.1038/nrcardio.2012.91

A. R. Brunoni, "A systematic review and meta-analysis of clinical studies on major depression and BDNF levels: implications for the role of neuroplasticity in depression," International Journal of Neuropsychopharmacology 11, no. 8 (2008): 1169–1180, https://doi.org/10.1017/S1461145708009309

23 R. Steiner, "Paths to Knowledge of Higher Worlds" (lecture, Christiania, November 6, 1921), retrieved June 2020, http://wn.rsarchive.org/Lectures/19211126p01.html

24 M. L. Berthier et al., "Obsessive-Compulsive Disorder Associated with Brain Lesions: Clinical Phenomenology, Cognitive Function, and Anatomical Correlates," Neurology 47, no. (1996): 353–36, https://doi.org/10.1212/WNL.47.2.353

25 V. James, "Art and the Integration of Head, Heart, and Hand," Waldorf Resources (2015), retrieved June 2020, http://www.waldorf-resources.org/articles/display/archive/2015/11/10/article/art-and-the-integration-of-head-heart-and-and/42b2767f5c9e52c6eec409f409382a10/

R. Steiner, "Spiritual Development: Lecture I, The Inner Experience of the Activity of Thinking (lecture, Dornach, April 0, 1923), retrieved June 2020, http://wn.rsarchive.org/Lectures/GA084/English/LZ0290/19230420p01.html

J. Petrash, Understanding Waldorf Education: Teaching from the Inside Out (Beltsville, MD: Gryphon House, Inc., 2002).

26 P. Lam, "What to Know about MRI Scans," Medical News Today, retrieved June 2020, http://www.medicalnewstoday.com/articles/146309.php

27 E. B. Tomich, "Takotsubo (Stress) Cardiomyopathy (Broken Heart Syndrome)," Medscape, updated July 31, 2019, https://emedicine.medscape.com/article/1513631-overview

28 R. Steiner, "The Mission of the Archangel, Michael" (lecture, Dornach, November 3, 1919), retrieved June 2020, http://wn.rsarchive.org/Lectures/MissMich/19191123p01.html

29 S. Donato, "The Effect of Lunar Nodes on Human Biography: Our Hidden Plan," Waldorf Journal Project The Online Waldorf Library Journals, retrieved June 2020, https://www.waldorflibrary.org/journals/24-waldorf-journal-project/933-waldorf-journal-project-2-the-effect-of-lunar-nodes-on-human-biography

30 G. Simon, "Understanding 'Splitting' as a Psychological Term," Counselling Resource (2011), retrieved June 18, 2020, https://counsellingresource.com/features/2008/10/28/splitting-as-psychological-term/

31 A. Wallace, "Till Murder Do Us Part: Dan and Betty Broderick's Divorce Played Out Over Five Vicious Years." Los Angeles Times (June 3, 1990), retrieved June 2020,http://www.latimes.com/la-me-broderick3jun0390-story.html

32 . B. Pless et al, "Chronic Illness, Family Functioning, and Psychological Adjustment: A Model for the Allocation of Preventive Mental Health Services," International Journal of Epidemiology 1, no. 3 (Autumn 1972): 71–277, https://doi.org/10.1093/ije/1.3.271

33 D. J. Nutt et al., "Evidence-Based Guidelines for Treating Depressive Disorders with Antidepressants: A Revision of the 2008 British Association for Psychopharmacology Guidelines," Journal of Psychopharmacology 9, no. 5 (May 2015): 459–525, https://doi.org/10.1177/0269881115581093

34 R. Steiner, "The Four Temperaments" (lecture, Berlin, March 4, 1909), retrieved June 2020, http://wn.rsarchive.org/Lectures/GA057/English/AP1987/ForTem_cover.html

35 W. Sucher, R. van Schilfgaarde, (ed.), D. Turner, (ed.), Cosmic Christianity and the Changing Countenance of Cosmology (Meadow Vista, CA: Astrosophy Research Center, 1993).

36 M. Gloeckler, "Constitutional Types in School-Age Children," AnthroMed Library (1992), trans. L. Maloney, retrieved June 2020, https://www.anthromed.org/library/2019/1/13/constitutional-types-in-school-age-children?rq=Constitutional%20Types%20in%20School-Age%20Children

37 I. Serageldin, "Ancient Alexandria and the Dawn of Medical Science," Global Cardiology Science and Practice 4 (2014). 395–404, https://doi.org/10.5339/gcsp.2013.47

38 "'And There's the Humor of it': Shakespeare and the Four Humors," U.S. National Library of Medicine, retrieved June 2020, https://www.nlm.nih.gov/exhibition/shakespeare/index.html

39 M. Carlyn, "An Assessment of the Myers-Briggs Type Indicator," Journal of Personality Assessment 41, no. 5 (1973): 461-473, Pages 461-473 Published online: 10 Jun 2010 http://dx.doi.org/10.1207/s15327752jpa4105_2

L. Cunningham, "Myers-Briggs: Does it Pay to Know Your Type? The Washington Post (December 14, 2012), retrieved June 2020, https://www.washingtonpost.com/national/on-leadership/myers-briggs-does-it-pay-to-know-your-type/2012/12/14/eaed51ae-3fcc-11e2-bca3-aadc9b7e29c5_story.html

40 "Tour the Nine Types," Enneagram Studies in the Narrative Tradition (2017), retrieved June 2020, https://www.enneagramworldwide.com/tour-the-nine-types/

41 Gloeckler, "Constitutional Types."

42 Gloeckler, "Constitutional Types."

R. Steiner, "Curative Eurythmy: Synopsis of Lectures" (lectures, Dornach, 1921– 1922), retrieved June

2020, http://wn.rsarchive.org/Lectures/GA315/English/RSP1983/CurEur_synopsis.html

T. Poplawski, Eurythmy: Rhythm, Dance, and Soul (Edinburgh, Scotland: Floris Books, 1998).

43 L. Edelstein, The Hippocratic Oath: Text, Translation, and Interpretation (Baltimore, MD: John Hopkins Press, 1943).

44 I. Perera, "Learn How to Paint Wet-on-Wet – Steiner Style," The Mulberry Journal, retrieved June 2020, https://themulberryjournal.com/activities/tutorials/learn-paint-wet-wet-steiner-style

45 R. Treichler, "Metals and Psychotherapy," AnthroMed Library. Retrieved June 2020, http://www.anthromed.org/Article.aspx?artpk=811

46 R. Steiner, "The Study of Man: General Education Course, Lecture II (lecture, August 1919), retrieved June 2020, https://wn.rsarchive.org/Education/GA293/English/RSP1966/19190822a01.html

47 Gloeckler, "Constitutional Types."

48 J. McMillan, "SDI Movie Promo: Space is Alive! Film: 30 Years of Spacial Dynamics (YouTube video, 2015), retrieved June 2020, https://www.indiegogo.com/projects/space-is-alive-film-30-years-of-spacial-dynamics-education--2#/

49 Gloeckler, "Constitutional Types."

50 M. Holdaway, "Is it Kalimba, Karimba, or Mbira?" Kalimba Magic (February 2016), retrieved June 2020, https://www.kalimbamagic.com/blog/item/kalimba-kalimba-or-mbira

51 F. Novais et al., "Historical roots of histrionic personality disorder," Frontiers in Psychology 6 (September 5, 2015): 1463, https://doi.org/10.3389/fpsyg.2015.01463

CHAPTER FIVE

Spiritual Bypassing Gives Way to Warm, Life-Supporting Illumination

How conscious insight and light work for discerning soul-spirit health. The soul differences between light, illumination, illusions, delusions, and fantasy. A pioneering, adult-child-of-divorce biography highlights the need for practices of spiritual-light discernment, aided by the arts, angelic forces, human boundaries, and cognitive-neurological self-awareness.

Don't limit a child to your learning, for he was born in another time.[1]
Rabindranath Tagore

Working with anthroposophy, people recognize that human beings have an innate capacity and desire to affirm meaning in life beyond the simple and superficial. They respect that human beings experience more in life than a mundane, material reality. That means fully acknowledging that things happen in people's lives that go beyond earthbound senses. To be overly attached to the physical senses, to material matters, and to entangled, codependent relationships rather than interdependent ones[2] does not suit people long in these spiritual times. (Attachment between parents and their developing children is a different, unique matter, as discussed more in this book and further in Volume II.)

Many Pearls end up seeking sheer excitement when they sense that their divorced parents' lives are overly focused on money and battles about material possessions. Excitement-seeking can be a child-level attempt to reach higher spiritual truth. A heavily materialistic focus leads to dull or vacant thinking and limited life-forces. It also denies imaginations and inspirations that can lead to a reverent wonder and natural exuberance for life as it is beyond mere material comforts. Efforts to stay balanced in health and mental well-being are regularly thwarted. The growing Pearl Children can't feel comfort alone in their natural interests.

Thinking too much about the past, without soul-spiritual practices for the present, and without relationship skills for a future of human encounter, can be suffocating and even depressing to the heart and soul progress of a Pearl of any age. It comes from not having a true sense of oneself as a whole being, and losing oneself in the quest for outer things or experiences that can't be recaptured as they were. With energies dragging continually backward or outward, a person can't stand fully alive in the moment, and in any truthful state of harmony. Money, personal gratification and self-glorification become obsessions.

In J. R. R. Tolkien's renowned novel *The Lord of the Rings*,[3] Gollum represents a character who becomes crippled and hardened by his obsession with possessing the most valued golden ring of the kingdom. Other living beings grate on him. His intolerance for the wholeness and natural joy in others fuels his desire to destroy anyone and anything on his quest for the shiny ring that he believes will imbue him with eternal power over all things.

The heavy imposition of materialist thinking in relationships suffocates the true in-and-out breathing that people in families need for realistically relating with each other as holy human and spiritually cosmic beings. There is meager soul substance in this kind of materialistic relationship quest and Pearls who have survived a materialistic divorce between their parents know it. They know that the real heart substance in the partnership was driven into the ground or discarded in a used-up, consumerist way.

For heavily materialistic parents, love often becomes a cool and hardline parade in outer achievements, sexiness, and pride that narrowly defines the other according to one's personal and financial interests. Any divergence from that which defines one partner's competitive edge becomes fodder for belittling the other and demanding that one fit in or be cast out.

If a sense of the illumined, higher individual self is not lit in the soul of each partner toward the other—accompanied by flexibility, warmth, and openness to each other's heart and soul-development needs, including whatever creative activity that might call up—emotional shadows and darkness become immovable fixtures in the relationship. A truer, spiritualized relationship does not have to mean indulgence of the other's every emotional whim. It does mean a willingness to understanding the other's perspective, and to consider together what is best for each person's soul development—with compromise.

In reductionist, materialistic relationships, no one grows beyond the baser forms of human, carnal ambitions. These partners miss the kind of love that has no need for the gross or subtle dominance of the other, mood-altering substances, power-seeking stand-offs, emotional manipulation, or self-righteousness.

Natural, luminous love bears consciousness of the other that brings a healthy dance between human harmony, dynamism, undisturbed inner stillness at times, outward cooperation, and higher empathy. It is the kind of love in which children can grow into the light of their true selves and then face the shadowy issues of adulthood gracefully. With children who can see the light of grace in each other, children can become adults who bring a natural light of goodness to others.

Otherwise, life becomes a sticky and shadowy web that is draining to the heart and life forces. The enlightened nature of loving relationship gets mired in heavy, and even hellish controversies that bind people forcefully to each other, or cloak them in surreal role-plays of irreverence and irresponsibility. Played out too much, each soul must grow to overcome the darkness, or the relationship dies in a cold undercurrent of blame that Pearl Children unwittingly pick up on, to their future detriment.

Lawful Illumination

Spiritually lawful illumination, in relationship with others, or in one's personal connection with oneself and with higher nature, entails experiences that reveal the nature of light. After significant time on the earth, if we have not been overcome by too much human darkness, we naturally emit a light-heartedness toward others in reverent, heart-strengthening ways.

When we're young, the warm, outer light is the initial draw of life on earth. We literally open fledgling eyes, having come out of the dark warmth of our mother's womb, into a world lit by sunlight. We are like seeds, loosed from the pod and planted well on the ground and on our feet as we grow as children who seek the light with energetic enthusiasm in order to survive. This enthusiasm is clear when children feel safe to play. Their energies can hardly be matched by overthinking adults.

Following a naturally illumined childhood, by mid-adulthood we can begin to see natural, golden light in much more profound ways. Today, however, young people are having their life focus overly pushed toward cool blue light in cyber-technologies that keep them separate from nature and natural, human interaction. Life forces are suppressed to stay in the contrived computer or iPhone environment, rather than freed toward warm, sunlit experiences of nature and enthusiastic exploration, hands-on creative activity, and heart-warming companionship.

Regularly observing light—naturally filtering through prisms, refracting off geometrically-cut crystals, cone-filtering through raindrops in a rainbow, sparkling in the stars at night, or sculpting tones and hues of color and shadow on daytime landscapes—is a practice for any person to be reminded of how the soul is participating in the wholeness of cosmic illumination while living out an earthly existence.

The mindful activity of beholding with awe and reverence the gifts of sunlight brings important foundations into the soul. It inwardly enlivens important soul-strengthening forces. Putting focus on these truths naturally balances a person's focus on earthen material. For children, the focus is deeply on the earthen aspects of nature and how light interacts with an earth that is at times in darkness. After age thirty-three, conscious human soul focus begins to shift beyond the sense-nature of light to the relational nature of light between human beings.

Cultivating childhood observation-of-light activities represents an early step toward enlivening the individual Consciousness Soul period that starts at age thirty-five. (More on the Consciousness Soul in Volume II.) When young children play with wet-on-wet watercolor painting, they are seeing light essences brought into closer, earthen hues. At Advent time at the beginning of December, walking a nature spiral on a community hall floor or in a courtyard, carrying a lit candle that is placed firmly along the walkway, is a Waldorf school community activity for children that is warming for the child's heart at the time of year when daylight is at its shortest.

In middle school, Waldorf children do optics experiments, such as blacking out all light from a room to see what they feel and sense. Or they spin a Benham Disk,[4] that is part black and part white, on a pencil to see the disk reveal colors and naturally experience the excitement of the unexpected, or unconscious, effects of light. They notice that sunlight gives a more colorful effect than LED lighting.

Other activities, such as observing a red dot on a white paper for a minute, then switching their gaze to a blank white paper to see what reveals itself, serve to stir the soul through the inward impressions of the counter-images of light. This helps to fire inner imaginations, intuitions, and inspirations that a person can come to understand more consciously in the Consciousness Soul stage from ages thirty-five to forty-two.

These activities can lead a person to discover the qualities of light that are not dependent on the physical senses. That stage is called "sense-free thinking,"[5] a natural, high form of spiritual illumination that any human being can achieve with practice, humility, and patience. Good nutritional practices support this more mature seeing.[6] A person comes to understand why good nutrition sometimes keeps the sense-free awareness clearer than the sense-life awareness.

Yiana Belkalopolos

Filmmaker's Sunrise Visualization

The following is an observation of the transformations a soul goes through in life from sense-based awareness to imaginative, artistic practical applications, and then to higher, inner-soul illuminations. Imagine a filmmaker capturing on film or video a sunrise by a beach that is gently populated by any number of people, plants, and stirring creatures. Everything and everyone is bathed in morning light. The observer sees long, stretched shadows of trees and mountains or beach-village houses and shops around which light spills its early welcome. The shadows naturally shorten as the sun climbs higher in the sky. A golden image of the sun ripples and sparkles on the water at the early morning ascendance of the sun. Slowly, the watery reflection dissipates into a whiter, bluer daylight. The ocean or lake beyond the beach turns from a dark, wine hue at earliest light, into a deepened mirror of the light-blue sky at noon.

The filmmaker, a heart-challenged Pearl Adult who has had some therapeutic practice, sets his captured film images to music and lyrics that he has written. They belie how the rising sun shakes away some of the shadows he inwardly feels, as he surfaces from a dark night of soul pain. He sings of his sleepless nights following an unresolved conflict with a loved one. His lyrics wrestle with the heaviness of relationship fallout, and a literally wrenching discontent in his stomach and heart. In darkness, he can't figure out what the matter is; what that earthy substance is that is blocking the higher nature of his love, his cooperative radiance, and his ability to tap higher and even brilliant inspiration for the selfless sake of others.

With no beloved person there to witness his pain—meaning bring the light of attention and love to his hard night—or to notice him rise through a haze of self-regret the next morning, the pain and loneliness force him to seek the light himself. He automatically remembers his day of filming, and the beauteous calm he felt while being present to the golden sunrise. He is bringing his conscious will forward with a resourcing memory of light and warmth to soothe his soul-psyche pain. His consciousness soaks it up, even though he is not in the presence of the sunrise right then. His haze starts to clear, and he starts to think through a solution to his troubles. Eternal light is literally raising his inner consciousness a little higher. In yoga, this is called raising the *tamas*, heavy earthen consciousness, to *rajas* consciousness, the awareness of the kingly, inner heart of light.[7]

At first, the painful feelings are still strong. The filmmaker resists waking on his own and wants to reach for caffeine or a drug to feel better. He tells himself he's tired from thinking through restless nights. He forgets that the darkness won't bring what he needs, that pushing thoughts through the night help nothing, and that he must regularly practice patience until the morning light brings illuminating forces alive in the soul.

Something stirs in him, and for a moment he feels shame to have an early morning impulse to pick up his guitar or violin when he really should be getting breakfast and getting to the office and starting the editing work. He is reminded of the ocean sunrise in his film. On an impulse, his self-talk trails off into a musical refrain on the violin that crests and breathes. He's not sure where the sounds began, or where they ended. Eternal time sets in.

The filmmaker-musician realizes that in his relationships, he needs to walk his talk a little differently today with others because he's been somehow reminded of some empty spaces in his upbringing and soul history that are not what he thought they were yesterday. He holds an open space inside because who he thought he was before doesn't feel so certain, but he also doesn't want to be dark or hard with others. He needs to get sleep at night. He wants the sun. As he works into his day, some people treat him more sensitively, and he's grateful. With others, he responds to criticism a little less sharply.

The next night before sleep, he remembers the morning sunrise that lifted him briefly from his misery. He thinks, for a time, of how human beings have watched sunrises for millennia. He wonders if all people in time saw those same colors in the sky at daybreak. He imagines what people on the other side of the planet were seeing while he was seeing light arriving over the darkness.

He thinks of the whole other world of people who rest in starlight and moonlight when he rises in the morning sunlight from sleep. They are resting while his day is just activating. Now he will rest, and they will gaze on sunrises. For a moment, he feels a pang of anxiety. He recalls that he didn't resolve his conflict with the most important person today.

Yet, sunrises keep intriguing his thoughts. He's afraid. What is the other person going through right now, and how can my striving make it better for her now? In his filmmaker/artist mind, he turns his inward source of light to ray upon the other person for a moment. Instead of thinking negative or worried thoughts, he slows his breath down and imagines shining a warm and gentle, morning sunrise on that person, reminding himself of patience. He finally falls asleep.

One night prior, this soul was in turmoil. Tonight, he's in deep sleep without harming or abusing himself, or anyone else. Nothing is fully resolved, but his soul has imbued a higher, fuller wonder toward the beloved. What he doesn't fully understand is that he has just undergone sacred soul practices in his twenty-four-hour "dawning".

These sacred soul practices are:
1. Feeling emotional, mental, and/or physical suffering that happens naturally on a hardened earth with others.
2. Inwardly acknowledging a wound from childhood.
3. Slowing thoughts.
4. Observing what is present—meditation on nature.
5. Staying present—allowing light in.
6. Allowing and engaging creative activity without expectation.
7. Allowing impressions and feelings to arise without judging—staying equal.
8. Wondering.
9. Acknowledging the wonder in others.
10. Humbling, acknowledging feeling, accepting incompleteness and the need to look at troubles in a different light to develop oneself.
11. Asking what ails the other and turning one's warm, inner heart light toward him or her.
12. Letting sleep, rather than recycling thought, work on the soul issue through the night, regardless of some awkwardness.

Yiana Belkalopolos

Glory

Throughout millennia, people have had a sense of the presence of a refined source of light that stirred their hearts into restfulness for some unconscious reason. It is the source-same and very present, here-and-now mystery of the sun that helps us to move on in the day and find ways to experience peace, warmth, love and goodness with others. The light of the sun is doing this profound and brilliant dance throughout every morning, day, and evening, and into the night beyond our vision, except as reflected in the stars and the moon.

Even primal beings recognized the sacredness of light. Anthropological discoveries elucidate eternal aspects of our humanness through time as we made connections with life in universal, cosmic ways. This confirmation of a higher striving and purpose has been "illustrated" in cave drawings, pyramid cuneiform scripts, architecture, sculptures, artifacts, and through oral and written literature. A recent discovery of Neanderthal caves in France, dating 47,000 years ago, shows that early human beings created experiences of fire rituals. They practiced in deep, stalagmite caverns for no seemingly practical purpose of living.[8]

The belief that we can bring light to resolve our pain isn't new, and the impressions that light leaves with us can't always be described in modern words, although the effort to do so helps to spread the warmth and light around. Often, words that articulate our sense-world experiences don't seem fully adequate. The answer to how to cope with a painful inner struggle just sometimes seem to come to us out of nowhere, and we say things like: "Something just lit up in me!"

Many songs, paintings, poems, and prayers the world over have spoken to a higher light. Sometimes we see someone in full-on, engaged actions of goodwill with others, in such purity of form, thought, and cooperation that we say, "What a bright light she is!" Or we say, "How brilliant!"

We often hear a more mechanistic version of the inspiration of light today when someone says, "It's like a light bulb went off inside of me."

What Lights Us Up?

After some time on the earth, and if we've been reminded of it, we know that the sun will rise every day and it will bring energy and forces to all that we do. The sun may seem weaker in certain seasons, but we unconsciously trust that it will bring more energy in another season. The filmmaker/artist knows that people have safely relied on this dawn of a new light throughout the hardest moments of human time. He or she often shows this in highlight moments of a great film, either directly with a character alone watching light move about, or indirectly with that character waking in the morning from a dark crisis with insight to move the story along. It is innate to believe the light will be there for us tomorrow when we are in healthy rhythms and feel love from others. When this is not the case, we often don't notice the presence of the sun, there with us always, for our hearts and minds have become clouded inwardly with darkness.

Even today, when an over-warming earth exposes us intensely to extreme heat in the full sun, pressing us to enlighten our thinking about how we live together on the planet, the night comes, but we still know that something life-giving has not disappeared. We know that an illumination in human souls is still happening. We see it in others despite our momentary fears and anxieties about our own survival in massive earthly change, including climate change. When we don't give into the dark fears, we can have thoughts of solutions to our overheating.

When one stays open to the awareness that there is a true light of wisdom, and that we have an endless connection to it which daily washes our soul, we see that the shadows cannot hold power over us. We know that a loving, radiant legacy is always steering our hearts back to us, every day, even if it seems dulled by our sensory perception of clouds, rain, or outright storms. Our unbroken connection to divine light is going to back us up in our struggles. It's always coming again.

This is, in a very simple expression, what the Christian Gospels reveal as the glory of Christ (1 John 1:4-14 NIV), since Christ is considered the son of God whose pure and unhindered soul power came out of the forces within the sun, and whose promise is to be present for us until the end of time.

How Natural Brilliance Works on Us in Sleep

Rudolf Steiner spoke of how our ego-I nature and our astral-feeling nature seem to disappear for the night when we truly sleep. Although our physical body and our life forces are still with us as we sleep, the more conscious aspects of ourselves live into a very different state that we are not aware of except through dreams and insights that we glean upon waking in the morning.

This is when we fully surrender our will up to cosmic forces. Every other moment of the day, our will is under our own conscious or unconscious direction. All people worldwide begin to feel deeply physically or mentally disturbed when they do not get enough sleep and have not given themselves up to higher forces for the night.

When we let our attention in the morning move beyond the disappearing night shadows and pay close attention to the increasing light with humble presence, we ensoul a knowing that we are not alone. That is because enlightening awareness is coming to us all the time.

When we acknowledge the light that is ever-present with us, we can access the golden account, or our resourcing spiritual record, that is held for us, even as we sleep. We access our Akashic record,[9] an inwardly knowable chronicle of the soul's journey through time, and that of the world. This is an important reason that a restful sleep is necessary for soul-psyche health.[i]

---

i   On very high levels of spiritual development, mostly not realized yet in people because of lawfulness, a person's greater self can consciously witness, in lucid dreaming, what is being impressed as higher messages into his or her soul nature in sleep.

When we choose to only think of the darkness, our authentic "light"-ness is not absent, but it is hidden by our own inner clouds of pain, fear, doubt, or distrust. That's why often, when people are suffering terribly, they still know that they are not lost or broken. The divine light of grace still hovers, present to their journey and healing. Extraordinary moments of inner-knowing-light can shine through for anyone at any time.

This occurs while dark forces continually work to entice us not to value our inner nature of light. In the very moments of dawning that most people experience that tell them that they are more than what is in front of them in physically, sense-perceptible, or tangible ways, every nature of distraction is presented to bring about forgetfulness of this truth. Dark forces prey upon human weakness.

By looking more expansively, we give ourselves strength for outcomes that go beyond the stuck conflict with another person. We fill up our awareness with real experience of natural light and work to bathe the other person in it for a time. Doing so, our own hearts become awash in divine presence.

Imagining into the film artist's activity of bringing his darkness into light through a creative process, we see a practice that integrates practical, earthen activity with the inner-soul resourcing that comes from striving for goodness. Feeling into the soul journey of another person, as he or she strives for the light, lays within the soul a resourceful spiritual firmament and a humane soul safety net. His pain does not stay locked up with him; it is illumined by his need to connect it to what is human in someone he cares about, and in everyone.

The moment the artist offers his insights of truthful human light to others, he is raying forth goodness. He is in the light with the other, and the greatness of that in the soul registers in more than a sense-perceptible way, regardless of what comes back to him. When he shares with another the light of his heart-honest truth, a higher, divine grace is present (Matt 18:20 NIV).

Heavy Sense Impressions through Media Pull a Soul from the "I" into Starlit Fantasies

As young people grow into full adult lives, they can come to feel a longing or 'dream' to realize a summit of light and brilliance in their own lives, in some enjoyable way, and often with the expectation that expansive return will come to them in the vein of wealth, attention, connection with others, or even adoration. This can happen for a Pearl, particularly when experiencing emotional tensions. A young person who has not been raised to incarnate a wholesome, felt-sense, lawful, and rhythmical soul structure himself, with heart warmth, can become easily influenced by others beyond that which is healthy or lawful.

All people entering adult life are brought to make deals with the lower nature of being human, in order to be earthen and to manage what could potentially be a long life. With those negotiations often come dark sides of the deals, which lead to the ongoing challenge and growth of personal conscience.

Yet, many people lacking a concept of a true ego-I nature can get caught in endless cycles of suffering and pain that they have no clue how to get out of alone. A young person can literally hook a fragile ego to another person's more dominant personality and ride a wave with that person for a while without learning the progressive lessons needed for personal growth and future ascension.

He is not really sharing his own creative heart and soul forces yet, but rather basking in the rays of the other. He is in danger of selling his soul to the other person. In the darkest vein, this can be to a corrupt boss, a drug dealer, some false gurus, certain priests, a heavily marketed celebrity, a casino owner, or a pimp. But it can also be to someone presenting themselves as a kind of respected community caregiver, or someone who will take care of their desires and tell them everything they need to do to get what they want the easiest or most exciting ways. Any young person can be distracted toward these fantastical, promising personalities, not just Pearls.[ii]

If a young soul hooks up with someone with a stronger personality but who is not a truthful guiding light—either through becoming directly linked with that person or through social media, celebrity infatuation, or with a boss who bullies the Pearl for perfect service under unhealthy conditions—in time the light of truth deep within the soul will know that something is unlawful, be it spirit law or social law. This is almost always so, even if the Pearl has become weakened by the experience of the other to the point where the Pearl can't seem to be fully conscious of the problem that is challenging the inner soul wholeness and freedom.

The lack of honest, spirit-freeing intent in the other registers as disturbances in the Pearl's psyche, such as chronic anxiety, depression, jealousy, anger, sleeplessness, or self-hatred. These are always signaling that the young person needs to find a way into more of the true light of individual self or eternal ego-I. The soul calls the unevolved ego out of delusion and into the illumination—or light—of the times through signaling sometimes unbearable psychic pain. One must wake up first in oneself before one can honestly wake in relationship with another person.

The delusion or fantasy often cultivated in modern Western culture—toward hard-core celebration of power, easy riches, and sex, as well as dark and hardened displays of culture in certain forms of music, video games, movies, and sports—press in on young Pearl souls less like the joyous "thunder-and-lightning-very-very-frightening" joy of a skilled musical artist playing back the hardness of his times (reference to Freddy Mercury and his beloved song "Bohemian Rhapsody"),[10] and more like an inescapable and macabre prison. The Pearl soul must find ways to draw on the inner artist to take back true life.

---

ii Occasionally, a surrogate good parent figure is necessary for some very harmed young Pearls, but if those surrogates are honest, they will ultimately guide the Pearls to see their own light as being potent, creative, full of capacity, and resilient. They will work for the young person to become freely acting.

Often, people in a dark night of the soul react to these influences by ingesting harmful substances, or by regularly seeking an equally fantastic reaction or highlight to the dreariness of life. Since they can harm themselves and even die, if they survive, they can push themselves into even more addictive darkness, with no light of awareness as to why they can't stop themselves in this repetition of cycles. Buddhists call this the dharma wheel[11] of self-created suffering.

The capacities for young people to make healthy choices for the soul, and to gain awareness of choices without experiences that constantly set them back or overly pressure them, are limited until age twenty-one, and still quite vulnerable until age thirty-three. It is necessary for responsible, I-natured adults to speak up at times for the light of freedom.

Fantasy, starlit distractions become obsessions as a result of the hyper-gratification programming that gets invested right into some pop-culture events, products, or music/television/movie/sports/virtual-reality entertainment. The goal is maximum profits for pleasure. Young fans spending time, money, and energy on the celebrity market, rather than on being simply inspired to connect with their own inner light and create their own music, film, local event, play, or sport, become easily stuck in the eye of the bull of materialistic interests heavily masked as fun and celebrity.

Pearls can then become bound by feelings of inferiority, imperfection, and an impoverishment of creative expression that ties up their energies for years. This can have a deleterious effect on the future stability of these young people.[12] They become passive and disconnected observers of life, rather than courageously active participants.

Culture-for-Heavy-Profit Smothers the Seven Life Processes

Heavy, attention-seeking, fame-and-celebrity culture promotes stimulation for youth that easily thwarts their chances for engaging their own seven life processes. A young person's attention is regularly distracted, and their ability to stay present to their personal development, needs, and creativity can be regularly thwarted by entertainments. The Pearl needs to: a) breathe naturally and observe; b) relate from the heart to a sense of human warmth; c) clearly digest and assimilate what is being presented; d) absorb something fresh and inspiring from it and relate it, with a clear mind, to one's own individuality and skill life; e) practice what is stimulated in a wholesome way; f) have a sense of soulful, inner interest stirred to build new capacities out of the experience that ultimately helps others; and g) create something new. The egoic forces of others are easily draining the Pearl's potentials.

Some Western world cultural programmers have caught onto this problem for the average person and have created, for instance, singing and performance competition shows where anyone with a committed and practiced interest to develop as a performance artist can come to the show and compete to get free coaching from accomplished, celebrity performers.

The shows still work from the glamour and glitz of television or social media, and the prizes are often about establishing the winners in the celebrity vein, but the sustainable, harder work of becoming a skilled artist is cultivated somewhat by the coaches, and the soul stories of participants are honored. Earnest compassion for the suffering expressed by artist-participants is "high-light-ed" as something important to the heartfelt endearment of the participant. A more earnest connecting between highly skilled performance stars and newcomer artists of every age is valued.

If a Pearl of any age becomes spoon-fed in the cultural life, or pacified by others' artistic experiences, the person's true inner light becomes overwhelmed. The individual's soul experience has been pulverized into submission while a false high has been driving him like a ghost rider on a gilded, charging bull. Rather than being truly raised into lightness by personal will to embody and ensoul the creative-expressive experience and share it with others for goodness, the fan of other people's creative flames set the striver back in a labyrinth of dull-mindedness. It is tricked into a kind of addictive amnesia. The Pearl gives away important aspects of individual soul capacity to another person's developed creativity or mere attention-getting showiness.

This is not to say that no soul gets inspired by another creative person or shares creative discoveries with more skilled people along the way to developing one's own creative capacities. Yet, there is a difference between inspiration that sparks an individual's development, and celebrity distraction backed by substantial promotional wealth aimed at manipulating public demand for an artist's work. Investors and the artist may get mass attention and wealth, but vulnerable young fans can lose themselves and their will to develop their own creative natures.

A similar process happens with cyber-media today. An unfree, trance-like social life is cultivated using the psychological manipulation of repeated social-media messages, songs, memes, images, or effects. Individual wills are not required to engage much to get psychological gratification. Anger is stimulated online for likes and engagement reactions. The cumulative consequences have been to stimulate a kind of guerilla-fighter mind in people worldwide that soon dulls down the original spirit and impulse of social interaction. In the case of certain worldwide social media, it is also interfering with world social harmony, democratic institutions, and even world trade and financial systems.

Professional, Limelight Sports

An example of the fantastical limelight that is promoted to early young children, is through professional sports such as hockey, baseball, basketball, football, and soccer. Years ago, young hockey fans who were disappointed in the outcome of a game rampaged and rioted in the streets of the city of Vancouver when they left rink-side after the game.

This false soul attachment to the starlight of sport celebrities, and then the disappointed, psychological splitting into violent anger and frustrated entitlement when the joy doesn't meet soul expectations, can quickly happen today with sensitive youth and young adults.

Young souls in regimented sports early in life have a little-cultivated sense of their own inner creative and innovative brilliance. Too much attention is directed, early in their lives, to a kind of ritualized, team effort in activities of speedy, adrenaline-spiking, hard-hitting, adult-minded, and profit-supported sports events.

In the West, such sports have been promoted in a Western military-industrialist mindset, by big-money corporations, into supposedly untouchable, sacred traditions. Rarely does a new sport arise in the collective human consciousness out of the creative light of the children or out of new young adults themselves. Only in amateur sport does that happen, as is evidenced in new Olympic sports such as Big Air Snowboarding.[13]

Practices for children's sports can become so regimented and adult-values driven that the children in adulthood have an ingrained tribal focus and expectation entirely invested in competitiveness. Parents believe that they are instilling good business and social skills in their hockey children and driving out emotional weakness in their future family stars.

When young people are not supported to develop their own appropriate, child-level stages of ego-I growth, through age-appropriate role models, then unaddressed emotional needs can get projected onto what their parents or other adults in society have determined are the icons of their own interests. Young people are pushed into a hardened adult reality based on ingrained past traditions.

What lights up the souls of the youth out of their own inspirations through childhood and adolescence can get crushed or never even allowed to reveal itself to the young people. Any inklings of it are described by the adults around them as childish. Often, the only time it is really given free expression is after a serious accident or crisis, and it is only then seen by some as a healing tool rather than an important part of a whole and sustainable life.

A blatant rejection of certain other people is often instilled in the groomed sports child. The competition and big-money enticement of the industry often sets up intense divisions around what is a successful human being and what is not. Anyone who does not toe the line can get a wicked backlash. Witness the heavy fighting that often takes place in televised hockey games, with fans and onlookers inured to the violence.

A militarized sports child can become a rigid adult, unable to respond to life's turns and changes with flexible, open, and empathic responses to other human beings. As adults, they can disregard for far too long the need for self-reflection, wider social responsibility, and change. The professional sports fan easily succumbs to levels of alcohol or drug addiction with a system behind him prepared to help him deny his dependencies.

When a serious lack of functioning is finally recognized, certain psychologists are called in to get the youth back in tune with the programming, but not necessarily in touch with one's own soul's destiny and higher work. He rejects the psychology and turns to celebrate addictions with others until that person, or someone very important to them, completely falls.

Committing to guiding young people toward creating a healthy, illumined life inwardly, through childhood and into young adulthood, while establishing emotional truthfulness and responsive relationships that allow the young person the freedom of creative brilliance, is rare in the Western world today. Yet, it is one of the most urgent soul tasks of our time.

Enlightening the Adults Around Children First

Christian Rosenkreutz was the last descendant of a German Gnostic Christian family in thirteenth-century Germany. The family castle stood in the Thuringian Forest on the border of Hesse. His family was killed in religious persecutions, and Rosenkreutz, at five years old, was secretly carried away by a monk and placed in a monastery. Later, disguised as a Muslim pilgrim, he traveled to Damascus to study maths, cosmology, and religion. He later studied in Egypt, before returning to Germany to found a deep, spiritual order. His calling was freedom and developing processes for others to find light and truths that harmonized all religions.[14]

Figure 5.1: Christian Rosenkreutz

Artist's sketch of the contemplative spiritual leader who's work is the foundation for the Rosicrucian Christian path of initiation.

The need for bringing to caregivers the practices of spiritual illumination, and tapping into the life beyond fantasy, delusion, and pretense, has kept human beings striving for millennia to enliven human understanding. Harmonizing the outer physical life with the light of inspiring biographies, of people who radiated great light of wisdom in challenging times, is an important strengthening activity for the soul-psyche.

Parents need this soul-spiritual nourishment to raise free, capable, attuned children in these times. Children need to know their parents are not inappropriately anchoring them to old-world themes that will not serve the social and cultural circumstances of their own creative generations and the future times, when technology is taking over so many physical functions.

Great historic figures such as Aristotle, Plato, St. Thomas Aquinas, Hildegard de Bingen, Joan of Arc, Michelangelo, Raphael, Leonardo da Vinci, Friedrich Schiller, Johannes von Goethe, Christian Rosenkreutz, and Nicholas Tesla have, through their life stories, kept this soul-spirit life present in the consciousness of humanity. Although the stories of these great beings are beyond the capacity of this book, I encourage parents and caregivers to look them up.

When Human Beings Bring Light to Earthly Substance

Physically integrated architectural examples of illumined activity by human beings, from ancient, medieval, and modern times, are notable around the world for their eternally natured inspiration. Some instances are:

a) Stonehenge,[15] on the Salisbury Plain in England, with its massive stone markers positioned in ancient times to mark seasonal solar events and sunlight ceremonies. Related to the equinoxes and solstices, sunlight pours through spaces between its stone markers, some weighing 50,000 pounds, and alights directly at the top of the Heel Stone outside of the circle at the summer solstice. This sacred place, once believed to be a burial site for political and religious leaders, is visited by close to a million people every year. Many believe that it holds special, spiritual healing powers today.

Figure 5.2: Stonehenge, England

Originally a place of burial worship, the Neolithic Stonehenge monument was built five thousand years ago

b) Xochicalcan Pyramid in Morelos, Mexico,[16] was designed with an upper portal, allowing sunlight to beam into the body of the building in such a way as to provided natural, x-ray light. Mayan ancients used the light to check fractures and disease in the bones of hands and feet.

c) The Pantheon dome portal of light in Rome,18 built by Emperor Hadrian in 126 AD.

Figure 5.3i: Parthenon Dome, Rome

"[Hadrian] sought honorably for a renewal of the Mysteries and even came near to Christ. That is why he even went to Egypt, far beyond Edfu up the Nile. Egypt caused memories to rise up in his soul, but they blinded him with the power of the Sentient Soul's world of images."[17]

Rudolf Steiner

d) Mystical light beaming through the dome windows and other light portals of the Hagia Sophia in Turkey.[18] Built over fifteen hundred years ago, it was long a spiritual home for Greek Orthodox Christianity, then a muslim mosque, a Turkish museum, a Christian place of worship, and now a Muslim mosque again.

Figure 5.3ii: Hagia Sophia, Turkey

"The Hagia Sophia — brilliant, sad and flooded with the amber-coloured light of ultimate mystery — lifted up my soul which had fallen and was frightened. I looked up into the dome that is like the vault of heaven, and I thought: There it stands, made by the hand of man, and in it men are coming close to the triune god on earth."[19]

Dimitri Merezhkovsky (Russian Novelist/Poet)

e) France's Chartres Cathedral,[20] which holds and preserves 176 multicolored, stained glass windows that bring a range of effects of light and color in the way of allegorical Christian stories.

f) Rudolf Steiner's anthroposophical community house of spiritual-scientific research, the Goetheanum,[21] finished first by hundreds of artists, craftspeople, and architects in 1920, and burned down in World War I. It was rebuilt in concrete by 1928.

Figure 5.4: The Goetheanum, Switzerland

"Gazing into cosmic space today, we see the light shining steadfastly and harmoniously from the stars. In reality, however, the Spirits of Wisdom reveal themselves through the light, which in ancient religions was conceived of as the garment of cosmic wisdom. It was at first celebrated as the unity, the primeval wisdom, then as the duality of light and darkness, and finally as the trinity, the illuminated human being, the teacher and mediator, Mithras.

But mankind could be blessed by this cosmic harmony only when a consciousness of it arose from the human heart itself. The external light, the light that is born out there in the universe, must today be born also in the human heart." [22]

Rudolf Steiner

The Other Side of "You're Caught Up in Illusions!"

Creating enlivening, light-illumined public spaces for social, educational, and spiritual well-being, have had the kind of truly life-sustaining features that bring greater freedom to individual minds and to collective efforts celebrating the human spirit. This has been through imagination and creativity in ways that some more hardened thinkers like to call illusions. However, true illusions, rather than fantasies, are activities that bring our attention away from the constant focus on dark, material accumulations and earthly resource claims, and into the illumination of light, heart radiance, and higher thinking.

These honest and natural, Consciousness Soul era activities are the bread of life for our modern times. They lighten our thoughts, hearts, and souls toward empathic awareness and a naturally heightened celebration of human soul lives that are working in spirit together. The language of divine light has come to permeate modern society. The origins of that language, and the deeply healthy, soul-psyche meanings, are now coming back into human awareness by individuals who can take up the light for themselves.

We take the inspirations in these olden structures and imaginatively turn them through the cycles of time to new inspirations to meet the challenges of now. Today, practical solar panels capturing sunlight and warmth to heat and to power homes is an important innovation in the higher thinking about light in times of climate change and the need to upgrade sources of energy for a sustainable human future. Invention is when light becomes inspiration in human thinking toward willfully creating something for the good of all of humanity.

This fosters:
1. the deeper, and also fuller, heart connection between diverse peoples,
2. soul-resonant, supersensible[23] perceptions,
3. natural highs,
4. positivity that is sustainably alive in persons as they work the earth, provide service to others, offer care and help to those who need it, and
5. bring creative cultural light and insight to lawfully inspire souls—out of dullness and fear into conscious and progressive action.

The Traumatized Child in Light and Sleep

When a craft-artist, parent, therapist, teacher, or doctor, creates for a small Pearl Child or elder Pearl Adult a cloud-like, felted, angelic figure with a gold and white flowing gown and downy wings, they are bringing to that figure a human projection of an idea of a spiritual light and presence.

An illusory image it might seem, in the minds of the grandparents of a young girl, as they read a bedtime story and offer a prayer during family visits. Yet, the figure itself helps to draw the Pearl Child's awareness to spiritual forces that help her cope after a car accident that killed her little brother. When she is older, she can learn about the many qualities of clouds, including their higher spiritual and angelic nature.

For now, a strength that no one knew she had arises in her in the wake of the disaster, having, among other things, an angelic image to gaze upon nightly about which she has been told heartfelt stories along with a prayer or a gentle song to sing to it before sleep. Some natural chamomile or lavender essence oil brushed very lightly on the angel wings offers a calming sensory impression that can be appropriate for some children at bedtime.

The angelic or fairy figure is not an optical illusion, a tool to trick the mind, or some false religious or spiritual icon; it is the very heart-and-soul-invested attempt to depict something of a super-earthly nature connected to matter, with earthly textured color brought out of light to welcome the child to the sense world again in the morning.

The soft felt reminds the child's soul of the etheric, lighter nature of sunlight and matter, as opposed to the dark and heavier sense impressions of the crunching metal, breaking glass, and powerful electrical load that hit her being as mother's car took the accident impact. Her soul can take in the right kind of balancing impression to counter that oppressive trauma. The finer substance of angelic presence will help loosen bound-up fear memory. Soft outer impressions can give her dopamine-releasing brain centers a break.

Fantastical Economy versus Practical, Soul-Spirit Economy

As Rudolf Steiner clearly pointed out in his discussions on world economics,[24] many material things, such as the money that we use to buy items, or machine-made cars, have little etheric life or inspired light in them. Money is literally dead metal, paper, or numbers on a computer screen today. Behind money, tangible economic assets, or even computer cryptocurrencies like Bitcoin (essentially value agreements that have nothing tangible behind them that can be perceived with earthly senses), can lie representative, enlightened human thought.

Too often, deadened thoughts live behind the concepts of money and are based on fantasies about storing up and recreating perceived comforts and traditions out of an old heritage, and a patrilineal or matrilineal past. We naturally have basic needs to meet for survival, growth, and development in the soul. Yet, we too often desire so much more. Hoarding money for false tribalist or clannish security against others who are not just like us bears the element of spiritual delusion.

The more we deny our need to relate to others different than ourselves with the currency of light—and thus love, compassion, and soul substance—the more we stock our safety-stability centers with excess, and wall ourselves off with dark indulgences. We organize our humanness the way we do an accounting sheet, and then strive for as much profit and as little loss as possible for ourselves and our family members.

In the West, we only mix our most basic human needs up with others if we absolutely must, and usually only in the work world. Otherwise, other human beings are more like entertainment to us. We relate to them the way we relate to television characters or restaurant chefs. We appreciate others only if they give us pleasure, service our needs, or obey our orders for our own sense of safety and control. Otherwise, we simply observe, judge, or consider them a drain on our time and energy. We care little about their healing needs.

Polarized, divisive attachments to monetary wealth, rather than empathic, enlightened, unifying agreements to share resources in harmonious, humanly resonant ways with each other, represent dead engagement. We feel stifled in our freedom, but the problem is not just the other person, it is in our own, protective, indulgent, and divisive thinking. Nothing truly enlightening is alive in the soul.

Only with growth that reflects lawful cycles of nature, with diverse expressions of resource distribution, industriousness, a commitment to fair trade, and reasonable competition for innovative, creative new ideas that serve sustainability for future generations, can economy function in spiritual lawfulness. Time has shown, regularly, that greed and selfishness do not contribute to societies of true, appropriately progressive, human light and love.

Today, wealth as an exchange of energy created out of human goodwill and brotherhood-sisterhood, in sustained harmony with nature, is a rare commodity. Wealth as we now know it is hooked to money and material holdings. A strict focus on hoarding material possessions creates a hardening in the individual soul in present time and a disregard of others.

Too often today, the negative or deadening shadow of money and resources is projected onto others when great wealth owners expect something spiritually enlivening to come to them from others with much fewer material resources, and with little effort extended on the part of the wealth owner. An equally small return to the wealth owner results, and the wealthy capitalist with a false social perception and artistic understanding derides the creative or innovative capacities of the others, belittling the everyday person. They start engaging the energies of younger and younger people to feed life to their souls.

The diminishment of the other creates an etheric life-force drain on the everyday worker, student, or artist, and reflects on everyone in an underlying social layer of hateful, death-and-destruction-focused cultural messaging.

One will never experience the fullness and expansiveness of light and spiritual life within an earthen, material object, or with a purely materialist mindset, without human heartfulness and reverence engaged lightness. The spirit that is in material things is enlightened by the efforts of the very human being who worked that matter into something useful for humanity. There is no light in it when it is simply collected, hoarded, or violently guarded.

What was in the heart for the betterment of the people who will use the created products, for the people loved, and for one's own increasing knowledge and grace, is what is invested in that object, not simply the money paid to create it for the manufacturer. Too much of this reverence has been lost in the unconsciousness of materialistic human endeavor in the West through mechanization. Even more may well be lost through cyber-tech and robotics.

When someone working out of the economic realm is acting out of a selfless aliveness that has come from focusing on a) meaningful relationships in and beyond family, b) creative efforts to uplift and enlighten the energetic and spiritual life, or c) innovative guardianship of environmental-material resources for the benefit of all, including future generations, an individual can maintain clear perceptions of enlightened human life.

Those burdened by the deadness of material accumulation and hoarding can project a distorted, self-righteousness jealousy or disdain toward the living efforts of others. Conversely, people living in too much of a spiritually enlivened way often don't think that they should understand or participate much in real economic life at all. They are soon uprooted, or delusional about those trying to find the material-life balance with creative and inspirational initiatives.

People in both realms need the light of understanding of how to negotiate social rights so that people's needs are considered from more than singular or tribalistic perspectives. Polarized political rights in society today represent unintegrated, disconnected human perspectives with limited soul qualities. Mentally annihilating people, who mostly see opposite realities to their own thinking as entirely wrong, represent people who've allowed shadowy, egoic fantasies to set in.

A Living, Spiritualized Divorce, or a Dark Fantasy of the Soul Casting Shadows on Others

The Eastern spiritual term *maya*[25] describes the mental and emotional confusions that fantasies create. The maya and delusions of human beings have become the tomes of great works of art, literature, theater, and music.

There are many examples of art expressing the human struggle between fantasy and truth, leading into and through the Consciousness Soul epoch. Johanne Wolfgang von Goethe's *Faust*[26] tells of a bored man who sells his soul to the devil and then struggles with the freedoms he is granted. French sculptor Rodin's famous *Gates of Hell*[27] shows debauched and desire-riddled human figures climbing over each other to free themselves from the hell they have landed in due to climbing ruthlessly over all others in their lives to get ahead.

Wolfgang Amadeus Mozart's *Don Giovanni* (KV. 527)[28] reflects a man who tries to live from charm and sexual effects alone, without consideration of others, and who succeeds until, in the end, the gravestone drags him into the underworld.

Each artist, in his own way, strove to depict, through imagination, human characters in the struggle to engage desires without conscience while slowly awakening out of the maya[29] to see the significance of their actions.

In Pearl-life realities, when parents dwell on unfair issues in the divorce with their children, rather than working them out in a life-giving way within their own adult relationships, in society, and in ex-spouse understandings, they project a fantasy adulthood onto the children. Often, they hope for some mature level of understanding from the child that the parents haven't worked for well enough with the adults around them. This is a form of maya delusion being imposed upon a child that fosters an unhealthy codependency. It darkens the child's soul.

The child is caught in the sticky web of the unresolved parent relationship. This can lead a child to be drawn into fantasy-like expectations of them to override their own development and act like an adult. This acting is a delusion, merely a mimicking, and damaging to the young one, who still needs to be a growing child or youth who is having good relationship skills patterned for them by a significant adult who can offer appropriate bonding for a time.

Repeatedly recalling the wrongs in the divorce to the children, thinking that this will somehow make things better, means offering dead thoughts lost in old fantasy to a growing being who has no personal capacity to respond as one's real, emerging self. The child is asked to be in collusion and even mimicry with one or both parents' darkness, forcing the child, because of the stuck place in between conflicted parent stances, to be empathic and compassionate in a situation where the former spouses are not.

That is a high capacity to expect of a growing child. If the child rejects, out of healthy soul survival, being put in the role of judge, referee, or priest between immature adults, that Pearl can be excused for acting out, rejecting, or wanting to be far away from the family. The child knows that they are living in shadow homes and relationships rather than ones that celebrate warm-hearted goodness and light.

When divorced parents resolve to make the most of reconciliation, and practice to respect each other after a divorce, then a child can live into the spiritualized warmth of their parents' more enlightened approach to being human. The parents: a) agree to not wage intolerance upon each other; b) continue to recognize and take up the hard, higher work of being responsible adults who can let another significant adult in their personal life be in his or her adult growth and struggles, even if they decide that those struggles are too intense to endure in a live-together relationship; and, c) recognize that they must allow their children to stay at their own ages and stages of holistic development without negative judgment.

These are healthy responses to co-parenting, since the Pearl Children have enough work simply growing up to become full-capacity adults who can take on the complex relational work that their individual karma as well as generation direct for them.

No one enlivens thoughts completely alone, all the time, even with divine light present. Karma directs the appropriate people to enliven the work with us, whether we like the challenges or not. Our tasks ask us to be people who understand the passages of the soul. It takes courage, wisdom, and a high level of commitment to be consciously human, supportive, and loving of children as well as the free and unfree adults in our lives at the same time.

Light as Color, Creative Thinking, and Spirit

One hundred years ago, Rudolf Steiner did not specifically address the issues of divorced children in any of his lectures. Divorce was not a prominent social issue in his time. However, he did predict that serious social disorientation would arise as human beings strove for higher and loftier experience, or regressed into lower behaviors, as earthly change and inherent suffering continued. Human beings would struggle with great difficulty to remain in honest, non-fantasy-bound relationships with each other in which they would inevitably see and even experience some of their darker double natures.

Steiner worked to prepare people to withstand being in the presence of other people's enlightening, shadowy natures without being dragged into greater shadow themselves. The needs of young, growing children could easily be neglected or abused without skill in this at this stage of human evolution. Steiner knew that in the Consciousness Soul era of human consciousness development, people would take escape routes before they found ways to stay balanced, centered, and in responsible, personal discipline with the earth's resources and in relationship with others. This discipline would take balanced will and conscious humility.

The new soul disciplines of our times are not going to come down from olden priests and clergy. They will develop out of knowing oneself well, from deep understanding of the human condition in relationship to nature and cosmic cycles and rhythms, and from cultivating love for connection with people by taking responsibility for our harms toward others fully. We ourselves will be responsible for repairs to others to redeem our harms. To experience the luminous grace of being full I-beings, we will need to learn to make amends with others out of our own initiatives.

A prime consideration that Steiner offered for our times, to keep people's thoughts and feelings out of darkness and fear as they become more personally responsible for their lives, was to bring light, arts, and spiritual matters consciously into human awareness and soul-skill. As human beings work toward their physical needs, they will become creative artists and authors of their own soul destiny with others.

People will in time become "universal human beings,"[30] able to soulfully integrate with peoples from the altruistic Eastern world, with people in the practices of freedoms in the European world, and with peoples of the Americas and their unique cosmogony.[31] This will bring human beings into perspective about what it is to be a truly human being, and will diminish the old, unfree harms associated with old folk-soul traditions that seep into modern times.

People will glean for themselves essential human truths. Respecting those points of light in others, which have nothing to do with earthly ownership and that are human beyond nationalistic boundaries, will help human beings to become like tiny suns, spiritually lighting up much of the world in natural rhythms through an inner, etheric light essence containing a sense of refined warmth.

Most of us are not so deeply aware of what the sun is doing with our souls daily, and thus with others, other than bringing light from one nighttime to another. Yet, it is affecting all of us in similar soul ways. Refracting light, for instance, moves the soul differently at five-thirty in the morning, at noon, and at four o'clock in the afternoon. Sun is daily affecting our food, water, air, heat, and life sense. It affects our automatic digestive rhythms. Thus, it also affects our metabolism that can affect our feeling life. The expression of feeling and light can affect us everywhere in nature as it shows up in color.

The Theory of Color,[32] presented by Johannes Wolfgang Goethe in Germany in 1810, revealed how the many soul qualities of light affect every color environment that we find ourselves in. Goethe included the darkness of the night into the picture of how light and color is perceived and deeply understood in human souls. The light slips into our day like an overlay, or a brightening veil, on the darkness in the morning.

Goethe showed that at sunrise, light slips around the contour of the earth, in front of the darkness, revealing first an almost imperceptible violet purple, followed by blue-green and then orange light, and then the yellow-gold that most people associate with a morning sunrise.

During our advancing night, the colorful light slips by again like a receding veil that moves elsewhere on the earth - revealing to us once again the gold, vermillion orange, the faint blue-green, then the almost imperceptible violet. As the sunset veil recedes below the horizon, more of the light of the moon, stars, and planets is within our sense of sight. The sunset offers an end-of-day reminder of the ever present light, life, joy and strength offered by the sun to all of life on the earth. It also reminds our souls that what is perceived as earthly light soon transforms in our perceptible reality to the cosmic light of the moon, stars and planets. The soul-spirit lawfulness of this often leaves a strong sense of balance, settledness or peace in people as they watch the sun go down in the evening. No complete darkness takes human beings over, despite the sometimes shadowy and challenging thoughts in our everyday life. If we think into where the sense-perceptible light and color go at night, we know that it is in the perceptions of others in the other sun-illuminated places in the world as we sleep.

Figure 5.5: Sunset

The sunset is our earthly perception of the last colors of light as light recedes across the horizon threshold. In timely rhythm, it unveils the night sky and the light reflections of the moon, stars, and planets. The sunset also reflects our time leading up to the passing of the threshold of death. By remembering the true source of light, love, and inner warmth, we overcome the abysmal fear of the dying of the temporary body. The body, a complex organ of earthly sense-perception, carries higher organs of soul-spirit perception and memory – in the same way that the moon, stars, and planets carry light in the nighttime when the earthly light seems extinguished to us. Memories do not remain in the physical organ of the brain-body complex upon death, but stay present in the subtle bodies of the transcendant soul as it passes into cosmic spirit light. In this way, the sunset of our life is a last veil of our earthly sensory body, as our subtle, sense-free bodies move into what resonates more fully as moonlight, planetary light, and starlight. Our loved ones who remain on the earth often remember the colors and shadows of our earthly soul veils for a time, and then perceive a sense of our more subtle, heavenly light and presence after.

Color is also deeply imbued in natural crystals, plants, animals, as well as human bodies. Human beings have the capacity to adorn themselves and their environment in any array of primary, secondary, tertiary, and complimentary colors. Today, the color of clothes we choose to wear seems a choice of arbitrary significance or of personal pleasure. However, in the past and even in modern religious or spiritual traditions, color in the vestments of priests or spiritual leaders was recognized as having divine-light significance.

Goethe considered color to have soulful qualities—such as beauty for red, nobility for orange, goodness in yellow, usefulness in green, commonness in blue, and a sense of the unnecessary in violet.[33] Steiner elaborated on the actual colors of light that human beings could see in the different epochs of human development. We have not always seen the same colors and the same hues of light that we see now.[34] Steiner articulated the connection between how our bodies developed throughout the post-Atlantean epochs and our developing ability to see colors.[35]

Color and Consciousness: The Art of Becoming More Human

According to anthroposophical color understandings, as practiced by color healers such as artist Iris Yves, human beings in the early Indian cultural epoch of civilization, about eight thousand years ago, had different and less evolved perceptive capacities. They could not see much in the way of color except magenta-red. This was a time of deep empathy with nature and the gods.

In the following Persian cultural epoch, people could also see vermilion and other hues and tones such as umber, sienna, and the sepias.

In the Egypto-Chaldean cultural epoch, human beings began to perceive the hues of yellows and golds. At that time, the golden sun god came into full worship.

Later, in the Greco-Roman cultural epoch, viridian green, and darker, earthy greens became familiar in human perception, along with the colors that had come into sight in the progression since the Indian epoch. With the emergence of colors that gave more depth to light, human beings also began to see themselves more complexly. They slowly turned their focus from the workings of the gods to the godlike activities of human beings themselves.

Indigo blue and turquoise are the colors of our current Anglo-Germanic cultural epoch. The indigo blue light of our present times has coincided with the effects of humanity becoming much more conscious of its workings inwardly, outwardly, intellectually, and partially with the spiritual cosmos. Blue jeans came into mass circulation in the West in the last century, while the compassionate consciousness of the needs of the worker, and worker rights, arose. These are important themes in the current epoch.

In the future Russian epoch, all human beings will become more clearly aware of violet hues in light as well as all of the other hues—red, vermilion, yellow, green, and blue. Some people can lightly perceive the coming violet aura of light associated with the epoch to come, the Russian cultural epoch. Most people cannot clearly see the violet hue in light yet they might see it, in a meditative state, in the aura of another person. They see violet or purple in paint, or flowers, but not necessarily in direct refraction of light, for instance, through a prism onto a black or white surface. If they sit quietly gazing upon a sunrise and deeply discerning the different colors arising in the surrounding light, most people will not yet see the violet with any sure sense of its color in the sky. In the same way in the past, people did not see blue light.

In the last epoch of the Post-Atlantean cultural era, the American epoch, we will perceive a magenta color present in the full, perceivable light spectrum.[36]

Color in the Classroom

Since childhood development today recapitulates the earlier evolutionary epochs within the child's soul, the colors of those eras are brought into the different grades classrooms of the Waldorf elementary school. Kindergarten and grade one classrooms, for instance, are known for rose-colored walls and features, grade two for vermilion, grade three has yellows and golds, grades four and five experience the green hues, grades six and seven the indigo, and sometimes grade eight teachers offer up the hints of violet. Rudolf Steiner's pedagogy also indicated how specific colors for each day of the week, associated with planetary influences, have particularly positive effects on a child's soul. They are: Sunday/Sun/White, Monday/Moon/Violet, Tuesday/Mars/Red, Wednesday/Mercury/Yellow or Gold, Thursday/Jupiter/Orange or Vermillion, Friday/Venus/Green, and Saturday/Saturn/Blue Indigo.

When a child leaves one grade for another, the focus on the previous colors and features slips into the unconscious or "goes to sleep" in favor of bringing attention to the new stage of development and its colors and soul features. When a child graduates from high school, the soul has been saturated in an affinity for light in its full human spectrum. The physics of light have become known organically to the child's inward soul, and in outward skill as scientific concept and artistry. Later in high school, some of those physics features of light become more conscious.

Example of the Light of Higher Thinking for the Benefit of Humankind

A heavy environmental darkness facing the whole world in the last decade inspired a profound thinking process of light in a young Netherlands man at the age of his soul's node, eighteen and a half. Boyan Slat was a student in aerospace engineering, and deeply troubled about the increasing levels of plastics being dumped in the world's oceans. In 2013, he left his studies to devote himself to the creation of the Ocean Clean-Up Array,[37] a system used to filter massive amounts of plastic debris out of oceans for recycling. It was launched in 2018 from San Francisco out to the Great Pacific Garbage Patch,[38] a region of ocean plastic between America and Japan.

In what anthroposophy would term a Michaelic feat, referring to the forces instilled by Archangel Michael to help human beings to put iron-will resolve into solutions that bring light to darkness,[39] Boyan stepped up to the fears of environmental degradation with brilliance. He met his challenging feelings and imaginations around a dying earth by turning the pain toward the light of innovative thought.

Boyan clearly tapped his seven life processes to their highest state, that of creating something new and useful to all of humanity. His unhindered positivity and brightness about the deadly subject of the massive increase of plastic affecting all of ocean life directed his radiant focus and engineering interests toward solutions for the well-being of all of humankind. This led to tremendous collaboration with others worldwide to bring his ocean-cleaning vehicle into working reality in September 2018.

A person does not have to consider himself a Christian seeker to behold the light of sun (Son) guided, or Christ-conscious thinking today. Our times allow us freedom and individual dominion to come into the light for ourselves and direct it for good or for selfishness. Yet the nature of this path—one where a great suffering brings to light a higher, inspired insight and action out of the efforts of an individual in lawful, spiritual timing to address a threatening darkness—is strongly reflective of Christ consciousness at work.[40]

String of Pearls

In the ensuing section, and in the following three chapters, I share several biographies of individuals who have traveled the paths of Pearl Children and Adults. Their destinies brought them into the light of Waldorf communities or anthroposophical work in one way or another, at different ages. Since the issues of the Pearls can still be stigmatizing in some places, or during some political eras, I have used pseudonyms in place of real names. I have also changed some details in the stories to protect identity.

Biography: Sarah, age 67: Pioneering, Despair, and the Soul's Cathedral

A young American Pearl Youth, whose mother's desires and needs indirectly resulted in family chaos and violence for a time, found purpose in her elder years by allowing herself to be her own person following a lifetime of not feeling valued by most people.

Sarah struggled her way through confusing parent divorces in a time in America when family breakup was still rare and considered anathema to society's beliefs of goodness and virtue. Years after her family divorce, Sarah found herself as a young adult in despair and suicidal thinking. Today, with the wisdom of many years behind her, Sarah speaks of finding increasing levels of love within herself. A few years ago, at age sixty-seven, she began a new love relationship and started to find her voice through a longtime passion for painting.

When I first met Sarah at a college in the United States, I immediately sensed a connection with her and with a younger Pearl Adult involved in Waldorf life whom we both knew. As happened frequently in life when I unknowingly met people who had grown up in divorced families, I resonated instantly with Sarah.

We were travelers on the same train, as far as the soul is concerned. Her view as a Pearl Adult was perhaps from a booth a few lengths ahead of mine, and maybe on the other side of the train from me, or even from a different cabin. Yet, some of the soul-culture landscapes we'd seen along the way had been jotted and journaled with recognizable hallmarks and nuances. Each of us could, metaphorically, share mental canvases and sketches from the emotional tracks of romantic idealism, stark realism, abstract cubist-emotionalist-reductionism, literalist existentialism, and back to simplified, romantic, masterclass pieces.

An elder now, Sarah can claim a ripe sense of the cycles of our times and the need for Pearls to trust beyond what can be seen in front of us. Sarah has realized the importance of accepting part of what just "is" in life regarding the parent divorces she grew up in. She values the human reality today of ongoing personal development, self-reflection, reversals of opinions and points of view, and general individual and social improvement. Now, she can bring more of herself into her expressive art paintings.

Sarah's existential pain in childhood lingered long into adulthood in her feeling life or *astral body*,[41] a term defined and discussed more in Chapter Seven. It was triggered following a secretive affair her mother started with a neighbor while still married. That affair became public when Sarah was a teenager.

Sarah grew up in an austere Christian farm family in the early 1950s. Emotional or physical closeness weren't features in her family though Sarah remembers the quick, catch-up naps with Dad on the floor of the living room during haying season on the farm.

Just into teen life, Sarah became aware that her mother was having intimate relations with a married man who would come to dinner with the rest of her family. Her mother's absence in the evenings, and the chocolates and jewelry she returned home with, left Sarah convinced that her parents' relationship was in jeopardy. This was affirmed one night at a home dinner party when she witnessed the male neighbor and her mother playing a foot-rubbing game under the table.

Unresolved Shock as Trauma

Sarah felt shocked, numb, and confused. A sense of shame told her that it would be challenging to have the word get out in the close-knit community. Sarah's boyfriend found out about the affair and his family members told him not to date her anymore. Nevertheless, the youth worked out secret ways to stay in relationship with her.

In time, a community member exposed the affair to Sarah's father, yet it continued despite the open knowledge until the neighbor's wife discovered it. Within a year, the stress of the infidelities landed Sarah's mother and her lover in the hospital with separate illnesses. The neighbor returned to his wife, and friends and family members abandoned Sarah's mother.

Exposure to Abuse

Sarah's parents divorced and her mother remarried. In mid-adolescence, Sarah moved with her mother and stepfather to a distant country. Her stepfather began beating her mother regularly. Sarah was shocked and lost her trust of the man. She became intensely ill and was hospitalized, returning to the US and her newly remarried father after many months. She remembers changing from the family's religious, Christian faith to become strongly agnostic.

Fractured Trust Frameworks Can Lead to Suicidal Ideation

A few years later, Sarah and her boyfriend prepared to marry, with a secret engagement, a wedding dress purchased, and bridesmaids committed. The young plainswoman experienced a dark foreboding shortly before the wedding, and she felt that she could not trust a marriage for herself. She and her longtime boyfriend broke up. Sarah tells her story matter-of-factly now, from years of getting an objective handle on some overwhelming feelings.

Sarah soon left her hometown and entered college, where she fell in love with a married student. At first, she was enamored by his attention. Yet, his insistence on seeing her while still in a relationship percolated in Sarah some deeply uncomfortable feelings of confusion and anxiety around relationship betrayal. The young man's attraction led him to divorce his wife and pursue the curious young woman from the farm belt state.

For a while, the interest of higher education bonded the young students. Inspired by her boyfriend's studies, Sarah studied art history. She contemplated forgiveness toward her mother since she now understood how someone could fall in love with a married person.

In time, however, Sarah's relationship with the divorced student dissipated. She entered a lonely and depressed time of soul searching. She hit a serious emotional low and, desperate for some life meaning, decided to give herself six months to find it, or she would not continue to live—she would take her life.

This vow led Sarah to push through crippling despondency. Leary, she considered joining a church but sought some answers at a bookstore instead. There she met a man who encouraged her to read a different kind of spiritual book than she had read before. For the first time in her life, Sarah found herself absorbing everything possible about spiritual values. She remembers uncontrollably crying while reading the words of soul wisdom. Many dream messages started to come to her where she heard an angelic voice talk to her about Jesus, telling her that love was the most important thing in life. Heart-illumined thoughts, unfathomable before that, ignited her imagination.

Opening Spirit Space, Seeking Soul Meaning

Sarah allowed herself some retreat or hut time and then began a period of spiritual seeking. She took up healer training, married a spirit friend, traveled in Asia, and continued to learn about herself and loving friendship. When she returned to the US, she and her husband went their separate ways, becoming amicably single once again.

In her travels, Sarah had met a spiritually oriented man who stirred the thought that Sarah would make a good educator. In a new stage of self-discovery, Sarah took up Waldorf teacher training and became the teacher for a class of young students on the west coast. In time, she entered a long and stable position in school management with a community of warm, skilled, striving, and willful souls.

She found herself knitting together her spiritual awareness and profound esoteric experiences through the cosmology, philosophy, and pedagogy of Rudolf Steiner. The woman from the seemingly simple, country life, found herself resonating with how spiritual development around the world intertwined with the evolution of human consciousness. She also began to understand personal and collective karma.

On one level, Sarah's soul experience as a pioneer in the child-of-divorce consciousness in these new Consciousness Soul times, is reflected in the ideas of Robert Assagioli's "Cosmic Egg"[42] psychotherapeutic theory. Assagioli, an Italian psychologist, was a contemporary researcher in the lifetime of Rudolf Steiner. Assagioli's work was developed more in the 1980s and 1990s by American researchers John Firman and Ann Gila. These researchers expanded the knowledge of the human psyche as being whole, enclosed, and conscious, with parts emerging out of lower, middle, and higher sub-consciousness impulses.

These impulses arise depending on present needs, traumas, and deep, inner-investigative work. Inner distresses, or "bids for attention" as they called it, are often unrecognizable from the outside world. They come from sub-personalities within our normal psyches, and seek for nurturance, healing, or evolution.

Sarah's suicide contract with herself in early adulthood is an example of one level of her consciousness making a bid for attention with another, to find meaning in life from a different perspective. She had absorbed and likely assimilated by then a darkness from her family experiences that had to be rooted out by her own efforts, despite the low energy and depression that she felt from relationship pain.

Something new in her Christ consciousness was piqued by the spiritual book that came her way in her darkest time. This allowed Sarah to begin to bring integration to her psyche and greater wholeness to a part of herself that was insecure and fragile from early experiences. She had become too rooted, unconsciously, in dark, family soul pain.

Without Sarah's cry to another level of her own conscious self, to find some life meaning, which then seemed to come about through an unexpected angelic level of awareness, she may not have survived her emotional turmoil. This, however, was only the start of her soul searching.

In some forms of Eastern spirituality, dark thoughts in the unconscious mind are called *samskaras*.[43] In anthroposophy, they are darkly acquired inner capacities, or the "double,"[44] a composite of our less evolved natures that are not necessarily consciously observed in us. They obstruct a person from the middle road of conscious and courageous heart warmth in the face of adversity. Sarah was caught between what anthroposophy calls Ahrimanic[45] heavy, controlling thinking and Luciferic[46] higher, escapist beliefs.

The controlling thought to kill herself was met in balance with a high striving for spiritual enlightenment. Her overcoming of death thoughts (Ahriman) and the desire to escape somewhat aimlessly to other countries (Lucifer) to feel better about life, brought her, through an angelic force, into a series of tempered Christ-conscious relationships. Striving to meet the other in her heart strengthened her I-being, allowing her to come into emotional balance with herself and find meaningful work in a Waldorf school community.

Sarah took her needs for meditative truth to Buddhist groups for a time while holding complex managerial duties at work at the Waldorf school. She had built a firmer foundation for herself in her new job, feeling that she could expand herself in community and in spiritual understanding. She also felt ready for a relationship again. She married an anthroposophical community member.

Since certain themes and practices in Buddhism hold an important place in anthroposophical understandings, Sarah felt welcomed to find a renewed sense of spiritual trust in Christ consciousness in her work and relationships. This came as a surprise to her after much early trauma and her ensuing renunciation of unevolved Christian beliefs. She was married now to a real friend and settled into substantial and rhythmical community work for over two decades.

Following the death of her husband several years ago, and her retirement from the Waldorf work, Sarah has picked up some connections to her early life through a new love relationship with a retired military man. She feels in a relationship now with a friend that she can "let down" with and relax, even as she soothes some anxieties concerning elder economic uncertainty.

It was trying for her at times later while supporting her dying mother. She navigated burnout in the bittersweet moments together. She still felt the sting of hurt when she wanted something from her mother or from the heart of another person and it wasn't forthcoming. However, she didn't feel so consumed by overwhelming feelings or self-doubt.

Life Spirit Age: Arriving on the Wings of Your Angel

Sarah feels that she learned in hard circumstances that she absorbed some of her mother's emotional wounds. She sees how her mother needed substantial caretaking and struggled to give love unconditionally to people when Sarah was a child.

Sarah notices now how expectation causes the human double to come out and judge others by our unmet needs and desires. Sarah found over the years that much that she berated herself for, as if something was wrong with her, was not her own vice, and she needed to learn acceptance around her struggle to see that. Meanwhile, that self-doubt had given her dark double some dangerous thoughts to feed on.

This unconscious Pearl behavior of absorbing the pain of the parents and believing that the Pearl is tainted or un-whole because of the divorce, is common for many Pearls. Parents and other adults often tell them that they are not to blame for the divorce, but self-blame is rarely the issue. Most Pearls don't really think of themselves as having caused the divorce. Children are innately aware of their own innocence.

To them, it was not what led to the divorce that caused so much stress in their souls; rather, it was what was put in the place of the whole family—often negativity, awkwardness, court battles, insidious soul destruction of the other, and societal stigma. It was also the lowered sense of grace and spiritual worthiness they felt imposed, often by harsh, religious judgment and uncompassionate society or community members.

Boundaries Get Lost in Insecure Attachment

Sarah knows now that an insecure child can't discern about her parents. Children are like sponges and can't always tell what's *mine* and what's *my parents'*. Pearl Children can take a long time or a whole lifetime to become clear about emotional parental boundaries and differences, depending on the intensity of the conflict in the family originally, and the level of abuse and other harms involved in the divorce and family separations. This insight is borne out in family counseling research on children and adult children of divorce today.[47] Pearl Adults can also benefit from understanding developmental stages and phases that happen throughout adult life.[48]

Creating Safety "All in Your Head"

In the developments of new psychotherapeutic interventions in the last few decades, it became questionable whether the use of thinking strategies called cognitive behavioral therapy (CBT),[49] to prepare children to cope with the divisions in the family and the losses of caregiving, was bringing the right care for Pearl Children and Adults.

Children's nervous systems were becoming overly pressured: a) from thinking too much or too complexly about emotional and relational politics and survival strategies in two or more homes; b) from keeping mentally straight about two or more parental behavioral disciplines; c) from thinking about having to see the therapist to think up ways to rethink and cope when one or other parent changes the behavioral thinking in mid-practice; and d) cognitively overcoming worry about school work, classmates, extended family relations, community issues, and any other of the myriad necessities that Pearl Children are often asked to think too much about today as they grow.

Regularly, many Pearl Children are today medicated for nervous-system problems, while left in the same therapeutic driver's seat of overthinking. They are encouraged to take pills for nervous strain and then continually strain their nervous systems with conscious strategies for coping with family divorce that are too early for their developmental age and stage.

What has been missing is the offer of ongoing, unconditional presence from safe adults who gently listen, wait, comfort, and offer deeply accepting warmth and inner nurturing.

These are experiences that unconsciously settle in the soul and help the Pearl Child, youth, or even adult with effective ensoulment and incarnation.

Creating a well of healthy inner memories of warm acceptance, security, and tolerance for Pearls to learn through mistakes and errors without the threat of being cast out of the family the way one or the other parent cast out the other, offers much safer nervous-system stability for a Pearl Child, youth, or young adult.[50] It also offers better soul foundations than regimens of cognitive practices brought too early for a developing child's, or even a young adult's, age and stage of development.

Pearl Children tend to know on some level by adulthood that their inner support resources are thin because they have a "felt-sense"[51] of those resources in others, and they know they can't match up. They can feel magnetized to other people with fuller inner resources, and then feel rejected when the other person doesn't feel met by the Pearl Child in the same way or with the same kind of richness of soul strength. The Pearl's soul strength has often come through many heart and soul interactions with many different parent surrogates and soul brothers and sisters who come and go in their life, rather than from certain emotionally steady or other-honoring family members.

This kind of resourcing awareness is observed now in psychotherapeutic practices such as mindfulness therapies[52] and Hakomi for trauma.[53] Psychotherapeutic trauma work calls this store of good memories a healing resource for the future. Anthroposophically, this kind of noncognitive, resourcing work is best brought through adapted activities meant to sink wholesome experiences inwardly, unconsciously, and appropriately for child development. Practices can be brought more conscious when the child's holistic system is lawfully ready.

For elementary-school-aged children, "curative eurythmy"[54] and "remedial education"[55] practices are some of the anthroposophical modalities that are brought to the soul for unconscious healing, development, and strengthening. (More on this is discussed in Chapter Seven.)

When Pearl Children receive healing and support for a time from cognitive strategies, they can lose the felt sense of comfort and security that therapists hope to instill because the children are required to hold too many intellectualized coping tasks. Much learning for young children is meant to sink in holistically, without thinking, through a layering of warm memories of integrated practical, emotional, and inspirational play and practical experiences with family members, other children, and other safe adults.

Pearl Children must also develop some sense of normal, child-appropriate, age-and-stage skills for functioning well in the world. When CBT therapy is applied without the other inner-layering, Pearls can get ungrounded and overstimulated, losing a sense of an integrated, holistic self.

Adults from safe, whole families, carry unconscious, life-resourcing experiences with them long-term. They need not be overly conscious of them. Responsibilities for caregiving, mutual protection, and mirrored awareness during the child's growth were shared and held between loving and concerned parents, other adult family members, and siblings. This warmth memory sinks in deeply and holds the soul-psyche in emotional safety.

For Pearls, however, the opposite memory of coldness is a layering that can weaken their inner scaffolding. This is most painful for the children themselves. To recover that warmth layering, they need substitute elder relationships if their parents have not found the heart warmth in themselves.

For some Pearl Children, experiencing warmth and love can come from living in nature-oriented, intentional communities with others who have generous hearts and strong relating practices. It is not always easy for a Pearl of any age to feel safety in a community of strangers living together, unless it is a strongly committed group of people working regularly on peace, love, and acceptance practices.

It is important that Pearls still have the chance to develop their own I-natures. Anything can happen in life, and Pearls in living communities have to be able to pick themselves up and walk away from unsafe circumstances and find support, functionality, and grounding again. Some intentional-living community members struggle to allow a person his or her own individuality within the group. Freedom and loyal commitment are challenging polarities to harmonize well yet in living communities. According to Rudolf Steiner, in the future, we'll all be more ready for that.

For now, it can be painfully more difficult for many Pearl Adults, who need to reinforce their ego-I nature for practical-spiritual growth and responsibility, to experience acceptance in some intentional, community-living arrangements. Not having that can lead them to feeling voiceless, powerless, and in dangerous soul decompensation. Decompensation experienced inwardly is not a feeling, but rather a panicky, knowing sense of falling through the cracks of one's own inner and evolutionary soul net.

This is particularly so for aging Pearl Adults, since many are pioneers in society today. Facing the intensity of Western lifestyle expectations of self-sufficiency in old age, when they may have had to use extra inner and outer resources to simply steady themselves enough to be functional in work and relational lives, with little or no family support, can be daunting at best, and overwhelming in the worst case.

Because of the insecurely resourced state they started life out in, no one knows how Pearls' elder years will play out. Since the first wave of aging Pearls in the West has only begun to address aging issues, how they will cope is largely uncharted territory. With better understanding and training in many communities, this could change toward something hopeful for the Pearls who will become elders in the near future and for decades to come. It could help bring about greater facilitation and compassion for Pearls in general.

Committed anthroposophical communities have a chance to help facilitate the elder soul journey of Pearls, if members enlighten their consciousness well about the soul-psyche issues of aging persons with a very new and complex soul structure.

Potential Self-Harm Turns Toward Self-Development

Sarah, the eldest Pearl in this investigation into Pearls and anthroposophy, sees herself today as being in a relationship with a "typical man" who mulls about his feelings and doesn't consider relationship work to be real work. In some ways, Sarah is still holding a lot of the consciousness work on her own, but with help from her communities. Sarah doesn't let too much get her down now.

She recalls one of the most helpful therapy techniques that she has experienced over her lifetime, from Buddhism. It helped her to be stronger about relationships and to not lose a sense of her own nature, even when the others in her life were not emotionally or authentically available. Twice yearly since her twenties, Sarah has participated in three-day emotional-growth dyads working out of Zen Buddhism[56] perspectives. The two people in the dyad ask each other to tell the other who they are, as well as asking, "What stands in the middle, and in the way, of what you are?"

Sarah notices this more intimate relationship work as something that was missing in her many years with the early anthroposophy in America that she experienced. That kind of deeper psychotherapeutic work is part of the next wave of anthroposophy, coming out of new generations of spiritual-scientific researchers and therapists who are intuitively connecting the soul needs of the times with a stronger sense of collaboration and personal connection.

The Buddhist work has led Sarah to explore the anthroposophical wisdom of the spirit self[57]—a life stage that can lead to the realization of *buddhi*[58] or compassionate mind. This is an essential foundation for developing the full I and tapping the greatest gifts and capacities of the Christ consciousness in the distant future.[59]

Sarah recently took up anthroposophical, Christ-conscious spiritual work through rereading the "Gospel of St. John."[60] She feels that she digests ideas better now that she has retired from outer-life work. She enjoys esoteric meditations from the work of anthroposophy, but can't take in much Intellectual Soul work now at her age and stage of the spirit self soul.[61]

Too much intellectual work in the ages from forty-eight and upwards can create a hardening of the soul through an excessive tapping of the etheric life forces for purely earthly life matters. A man, whose body physiology generally holds incarnate forces later into life than a female body does, can safely engage intellectual work further into the spirit self period. It is best if he integrates higher Consciousness Soul work at the same time to keep the I-forces from becoming too ego-centric.[62]

It is not healthy for men or women to be too lodged in intellectual capacities in the later stages of life's denouement. Special spiritual energy is required in the preparation for the dying of the body and the soul's passing of the threshold. Having others hold the space of those lower capacities, which are still necessary in society for some things, is essential for very elder people.

Sarah sees knowledge as crucial work for women today in their earlier adult years, to avoid psychotic breaks over time in their mental health. In these times, without study, she can see that aging women will not understand the advancing developments of the Consciousness Soul era. Without education, they could easily lose touch with the spiritual breakthroughs that will be available for them in the future.

Sarah now reveres the angelic, inspirational image that she received after her exposure to college and higher learning. The image of an angelic being coming to hold her hand, when she was in despair thirty years ago, was telling her that there was more to her life and that she would be cared for if she just took up the challenges.

Luciferic, Ahrimanic, or Wholeness-Centered Christ Consciousness

Sarah felt lost spiritually at the time of her parents' divorce. Until she engaged anthroposophy, she had what she calls a Luciferic escapist approach to her self-development work. She saw herself as gearing spiritually toward getting herself off the planet for good. This was a strong feeling in her thirties and forties. It reveals the anguished feelings that Sarah had about life on earth and the lack of family or dependable people to help her cope with hard feelings and challenging soul realities.

Luciferic impulses, in anthroposophy, refer to those thoughts, feelings, and actions that set a person's will toward escape from the mundane circumstances of earth. It can also entice us to want freedom from people who may not seem to be thriving or very enlivened. Lucifer turns us away from human suffering rather than toward it, trying to notch life up unrealistically to try to erase all human pain.

Luciferic impulses are necessary to a point for a sense of spiritual seeking, and these can assist creative effort. Such impulses turn against human purpose when they become nihilistic against what is earthly, or toward others, out of a sense of pain-induced self-righteousness or arrogance. These impulses can have an ungrounded sense of reality that can easily "go off the rails" and lead to delusions and other psychic disturbances. In yogic terms, this is called "vatta disturbance."[63]

Luciferic tendencies can lead a distraught person, who is not receiving appropriate empathic or compassionate help or care with real life matters, into the psychological state termed "spiritual bypassing."[64]

Ahrimanic impulses, contrarily, have the opposite effect, potentially causing a person to be overly absorbed or even compulsive about earthly, scientific, technological, or materialistic matters. These impulses have a hardening effect on the soul, and can lead to depression, power struggles, and lowered ideals. They can tempt individuals into the general hoarding, claiming, or stockpiling of heaviness in thoughts, feelings, and actions. Greed, control, and hatred are the darkest inward and outward expressions associated with Ahriman.

The middle ground between the Luciferic and the Ahrimanic impulses is the Christ-consciousness impulse. This is seen, in anthroposophical spiritual science,[65] as the most wholesome, loving, peace-fostering, and inspirationally potent place in the soul to live from outwardly and inwardly. It is the steadying ground from where humanistic, original thoughts and creativity based on selflessness can reside.

In true Christ consciousness, individuals developing themselves spiritually do not experience themselves as superior, inferior, or separate, but as vital contributors to the loving and brilliant potentials in human creative change, and in earthly socio-economic development. Deep and sustained healing is available in the Christ consciousness.

Christ Consciousness on New Feet

The kind of Christian belief system fostered in Sarah's religious childhood worked to keep spiritual community members beholden to rigid social codes and a low degree of personal heart and soul responsibility. It echoed olden Christian systems that denied an individual's innate connection to spirit and the right of each soul to take up his or her intuitive path. It also denied the individual's power to repair soulful damage toward others through their own impulses. The individual who had harmed was simply shut out and left to cloister away in penance. Sarah's mother experienced this treatment from the neighbors and Sarah suffered the stigma.

The family divorce, indirectly, set Sarah significantly on her own intuitive path to higher understandings for herself and a life of her own. In the same light of the words of the Christian disciple John, recorded in the Gospel of John, she "took up her bed and walked" (John 5:8 KJV).

Although Christ's teachings spoke of forgiveness and mercy for our "trespasses" and harms toward others, some rigid spiritual communities become intolerant of unique, spiritual aliveness, out of a desire to largely protect passive, material comfort. Yet, like other spiritual masters, Steiner cautioned how too much group activity can put true spirit consciousness to sleep.[66]

Self-dominion and self-responsibility, the two wings of the Christ-conscious spiritual potential today, moved Sarah's Midwest religious understandings forward dramatically in the years following her parents' divorce. It enlivened her experience of spirit in a way that it came closer within her and to the spirit of our times.

Nothing like this ever happens painlessly for anyone. This deeply challenging process today can leave the soul inwardly crying for higher guidance to alleviate unaddressed fears about how to walk one's individual path and take full responsibility for our personal, spiritual evolution now. In Sarah's darkest moment, the light of an angelic presence stirred her from potential self-destruction and toward eventual service in an innovative, longtime institute of learning, benefiting children, families, and adults worldwide in healing and growth.

The painful contract Sarah made to seek meaning in life or die is an echo of the suffering human call that Christ made at his crucifixion: "My God, my God, why hast thou forsaken me?" (Matt 7:46 KJV). Christ died and revealed himself in spirit three days later to assure humanity of what he had promised—that when they sought his help, his forces would remain on and in the earth to be available to the seeker.

The struggles that human beings go through in their path to freedom today lead us on the same journey of the Christ being—except with, generally-speaking, a more extended lifetime than that of Christ's. Christ initiated the individual I in each member of humanity. He was not alone, and yet he did suffer alone in his own way before rising into the full spiritual glory of the godhead. When we feel most alone, we can tap into that light by remembering it in everything here on earth and in others, opening our hearts to warmth of light, and asking for assistance. We begin to take up, without shame, the next stage of the yet unknown journey as the light of renewal reveals it to us, often through others.

When adults who are in emotional pain can find a way to call up Michaelic will, working to trust themselves, heal, or withstand pain, and consider transforming poor thoughts and behaviors toward others, they are beholden in the light. They hold a refined, etheric love at the same time, a subtle sense of warmth light in the heart, and their souls are led along their own path to self-acceptance, personal consciousness advancement, and wider collective connection with others.

The process may seem to be only tiny steps in a struggle with a heavy cross on our shoulders. Yet, the willful action of individually seeking light, in loving tandem with others, sets goodness in motion and contributes to the wholeness of all of humankind.

This kind of Christ-conscious, whole-soul holding is what Sarah experienced while working at an anthroposophical school, helping herself and others around the world to bring their spiritual findings into the light of goodness. The community gave her the place to keep healthy daily rhythms, put attention to what she was absorbing, and allow herself to develop some of her adult age-and-stage capacities in the company of conscious community. She was able to create new ways of fostering innovative education experiences for the future of others.

Out of that anthroposophical institute have come musicians, visual artists, engineers, mathematicians, filmmakers, entrepreneurs, biodynamic farmers, and others, all doing life a little bit differently and following the light to bring similar experiences to others.

In that work, Sarah found herself free to use her intuition professionally, creating and working outside of the box to innovate solutions for the greater functioning of the school and its students. Access to a conscious biodynamic farm offered healthy whole foods through a "community-supported agriculture initiative (CSA)."[67] (Members of a CSA pay in advance for vegetables, fruits, and herbs to support the farmers to live while farming.) Arts activities such as a conscious veil[68] painting process, led painters in her community through unexpected and moving inner-soul revelations in color, movement, and image.

Helping a pioneering school to stay afloat, while working with advanced practices and concepts, took patience. Sarah wrestled inwardly to cope with some archaic influences and the larger economic issues of the day, and it led her to trusting her own problem-solving. Circumstances regularly required her to come up with something new, in homegrown ways.

Sarah found that she had to fight for some of her needs in her position of responsibility to a diverse student population. She waded through the oftentimes painful transitions and transformations that educators endure during generational, economic, and social change. She has learned that the light need not dim, only that it changes colors.

Endnotes

1 L. Waid, and A. Navis, (2016). "Freedom for Thinking: Rabindrath Tagore with Mahatma Gandhi and Kasturba Gandhi at Santinketan," Spotlight (2016), retrieved June 2020, https://spotlightenglish.com/listen/freedom-for-thinking

2 P. H. Wright and K. D. Wright, "Codependency: Addictive love, adjustive relating, or both?" Contemporary Family Therapy 13, no. 5 (1991), https://doi.org/10.1007/BF00890497

3 J.R.R. Tolkein, The Lord of the Rings (Boston, MA: Houghton Mifflin Harcourt, 2005), retrieved June 0, 2020, https://www.goodreads.com/book/show/33.The_Lord_of_the_Rings

4 ASTC Science World Society, "Benham's Disc," (Vancouver, BC: Science World, 2020), retrieved June 0, 2020, https://www.scienceworld.ca/resource/benhams-disk/
R. Steiner, Intuitive Thinking as a Spiritual Path: A Philosophy of Freedom (Classics in Anthroposophy), trans. M. Lipson (Great Barrington, MA: Anthroposophic Press, 1995).

5 R. Steiner, Intuitive Thinking as a Spiritual Path: A Philosophy of Freedom (Classics in Anthroposophy), trans. M. Lipson (Great Barrington, MA: Anthroposophic Press, 1995)..

6 R. Steiner, "Nutrition and Health: Two Lectures to Workmen" (lectures, Dornach, 1924), retrieved June 2, 2020, https://wn.rsarchive.org/Lectures/GA354/English/AP1987/NutHlt_index.html
R. Steiner, Nutrition, Food, Health, and Spiritual Development (East Sussex, UK: Rudolf Steiner Press, 2009).

7 S. Shilpa, and C. G. Venkatesha Murthy, "Understanding personality from Ayurvedic perspective for psychological assessment: A case," Ayu 32,1 (2011): 12-9, doi:10.4103/0974-8520.85716

8 E. Yong, "A Shocking Find in a Neanderthal Cave in France," The Atlantic Monthly (May 25, 2016), Retrieved May 10, 2017 from: https://www.theatlantic.com/science/archive/2016/05/the-astonishing-age-of-a-neanderthal-cave-construction-site/484070

9 C. M. Trine, The New Akashic Records: Knowing, Healing, and Spiritual Practice (Portland, OR: Essential Knowing Press, 2010), retrieved June 20, 2020, https://www.amazon.ca/New-Akashic-Records-Spiritual-Practice/dp/098251980X
R. Steiner, The Fifth Gospel: From The Akashic Record (Forest Row, UK: Rudolf Steiner Press, 1985).

10 B. Singer, A. McCarten, P. Morgan, G. King, et al., "Bohemian Rhapsody," (Beverly Hills, California: Twentieth Century Fox Home Entertainment, 2019, retrieved June 20, 2020, https://www.worldcat.org/title/bohemian-rhapsody/oclc/1085383722

11 C. S. Anderson, "Four Noble Truths: Buddhism, Practices, Applications, and Concepts," Oxford Research Encyclopedias (August 2016), https://dx.doi.org/10.1093/acrefore/9780199340378.013.180

12 D. Kent, "The Effect of Music on the Human Body and Mind" (senior thesis, Liberty University, Lynchburg, VA, Spring 2006), retrieved June 2, 2020, https://digitalcommons.liberty.edu/cgi/viewcontent.cgi?article=1162&context=honors
D. A. Gentile, Media Violence and Children: A Complete Guide for Parents and Professionals (Westport, CT: Praeger, 2003).

13 V. Mather, "What Is Big Air? It's the Olympics' Newest Snowboard Event," The New York Times (February 19, 2018), retrieved June 2, 2020, https://www.nytimes.com/2018/02/19/sports/olympics/big-air-snowboard.html

14 "Christian Rosenkreutz," Wikipedia, retrieved June 2, 2020, https://en.wikipedia.org/wiki/Christian_Rosenkreuz

R. Steiner, The Mission of Christian Rosenkreutz: Its Character and Purpose, trans. D. Osmond (London, UK: Rudolf Steiner Press, 1950), retrieved June 2, 2020, http://wn.rsarchive.org/Lectures/GA130/English/RSP1950/ChRose_index.html

15 M. P. Pearson, Stonehenge – A New Understanding: Solving the Mysteries of the Greatest Stone Age Monument, reprint edition (New York, NY: The Experiment, LLC, 2014).

16 "Xochicalco," Encyclopedia Britannica, retrieved June 2, 2020, https://www.britannica.com/place/Xochicalco

17 R. Steiner, in T. H. Meyer, Ludwig Polzer-Hoditz – A European: A Biography (Forest Row, UK: Temple Lodge, 2014): 203.

18 A. Hart, "Lighting in Orthodox Churches: Liturgical Principles and Practical Ideas," Orthodox Arts Journal (August 27, 2015), retrieved June 2, 2020, https://orthodoxartsjournal.org/lighting-in-orthodox-churches-liturgical-principles-and-practical-ideas/

19 D. Merezhkovsky, Der Antnarsch des Pöbels (Tr. H. Horschelmann) Munich & Leipzig 1907.

20 R. M. Querida, Golden Age of Chartres The Teachings of a Mystery School and the Eternal Feminine, (Ediburgh, UK: Floris Books, 2008), retrieved June 20, 2020, https://www.rudolfsteinerbookcentre.com.au/product/3924/BGolden-Age-of-Chartres-BI-The-Teachings-of-a-Mystery-School-and-the-Eternal-FeminineI-QUERIDO-RENE-M

Harris and Zucker, "Cathedral of Notre Dame de Chartres." (Youtube video), retrieved April 27, 2017, https://www.youtube.com/watch?v=vAtQB9wLkUA

21 H. Raske, The Language of Color: Rudolf Steiner's Painting and Glass Windows in the First Goetheanum (Dornach, Switzerland: Walter Keller Verlag [Publisher], 1987).l

22 C. Grey, "Hadrian the Traveler: Motifs and Expressions of Roman Imperial Power in the Vita Hadriani," História 35, e85, https://dx.doi.org/10.1590/1980-436920160000000085

H. A. Ginsberg, "Hoditz/Hadrian/Pod/6th Layer," Reverse Ritual (April 8, 2016), retrieved June 2, 2020, http://reverseritual.com/hoditzhadrianpod6th-layer/

R. Steiner, "Signs and Symbols of the Christmas Festival: Lecture I, Birth of the Light" (lecture, Berlin, December 19, 1904), retrieved June 2, 2020, https://wn.rsarchive.org/Lectures/SignSymbols/19041219p01.html

23 R. Wilkinson, "Anthroposophy," Rudolf Steiner: An Introduction to his Spiritual Worldview (East Sussex, UK: Temple Lodge Publishing, 1993).

R. Steiner, Materialism and the Task of Anthroposophy, trans M. St. Groar (Spring Valley, NY: Anthroposophic Press, 1987), retrieved June 2, 2020, http://wn.rsarchive.org/Lectures/GA204/English/AP1987/MaTask_index.html

24 R. Steiner, World Economy, (Dornach, Switzerland, 1922), Rudolf Steiner Archive, retrieved May 10, 2017, http://wn.rsarchive.org/Lectures/GA340/English/RSP1972/WldEco_index.html

25 F. Wilhelm and M. Heising, Dancing With Maya: Between Reality and Illusion, Embracing the Power of Uncertainty (Brewster, NY: Zero & One, 2015).

26 R. Steiner, "The Problem of Faust: The Romantic and the Classical Walpurgis Night" (lectures, Dornach, 1916–1919), retrieved June 2, 2020, http://wn.rsarchive.org/Lectures/GA273/English/UNK1930/ProFau_index.html#sthash.uuF9a9Ck.dpuf

27 B. Harris and S. Zucker, "Rodin: The Gates of Hell" (video, 2017), Khan Academy, retrieved June 2, 2020, https://www.khanacademy.org/humanities/becoming-modern/avant-garde-france/avant-garde-sculpture/v/rodin-the-gates-of-hell-1880-1917

28 B. Schwarm and L. Cantoni, "Don Giovanni: Opera by Mozart," Encyclopædia Britannica, retrieved June 2, 2020, https://www.britannica.com/topic/Don-Giovanni-opera-by-Mozart

29 L. J. Fernyhough, "Companioning the Codependent: Exploring the Role of Spiritual Guidance in Client Recovery" (thesis preview, Sofia University, Palo Alto, CA, 2014), retrieved May 10, 2017, http://search.proquest.com/openview/554a9e493884ae495aa1a76635d9564d/1?pq-origsite=gscholar&cbl=18750&diss=y (page no longer available).

30 R. Steiner, The Universal Human Being: The Evolution of Individuality (Hudson, NY: Anthroposophic Press, 1990), retrieved June 2, 2020, http://wn.rsarchive.org/Lectures/UniHuman/UniHum_cover.html

31 R. Steiner, "Cosmogony, Freedom, Altruism" (lectures, Dornach, October 10, 1919), retrieved June 2, 2020, http://wn.rsarchive.org/Lectures/19191010p01.html

32 J. L. Eastlake, tr., Goethe's Theory of Colours (London, UK: John Murray [publisher], 1840) retrieved June 2, 2020, https://archive.org/details/goethestheoryco01goetgoog

33 "Theory of Colors," Wikipedia, retrieved June 2, 2020, https://en.wikipedia.org/wiki/Theory_of_Colors.

34 R. Steiner, The Arts and Their Mission (Spring Valley, NY: Anthroposophic Press, 1986).

35 Steiner, The Arts.

36 Steiner, The Arts.

K. Rudolf, "Art in Therapy: A Synthesis of Anthroposophical Speech and Painting Therapy" (2005). Exploring the World in Colour and Speech, retrieved June 2, 2020, http://www.exploringtheword.com.au/-therapeutic-art/art-in-therapy

M. Altmaier, Der kunsttherapeurtische Porzess: Das Krankheitstypische und die individuelle Intention des Patienten am Beispiel von Rheuma und AIDS – Buch gebraucht kaufen (Stuttgart, Germany: Verlag Urachhaus, 1995).

Steiner, "The Evolution of the Cosmos," Esoteric Science

37 V. Venema, "Dutch Boy Mopping Up a Sea of Plastic," BBC News Magazine (October 17, 2014), retrieved June 2, 2020, http://www.bbc.com/news/magazine-29631332

38 National Geographic Society, "The Great Pacific Garbage Patch," (Washington, DC: National Geographic, 2020), retrieved June 20, 2020, https://www.nationalgeographic.org/encyclopedia/great-pacific-garbage-patch/

39 R. Steiner, The Archangel Michael: His Mission and Ours : Selected Lectures and Writings, (Great Barrington, MA: SteinerBooks, 1994), retrieved June 20, 2020, https://books.google.ca/books/about/The_Archangel_Michael.html?id=fqdDsKX4qdYC&redir_esc=y

40 U. Seiler-Hugova (2011), Colour: Seeing, Experiencing, Understanding (Forest Row, UK: Temple Lodge, 2011).

41 A. Blanning, "The Astral Body: Breathing Archetype and Awareness into the body's Physiology," (AnthromedLibrary, 2020), retrieved June 20, 2020, https://www.anthromed.org/library/2018/8/12/the-astral-body-breathing-archetype-and-awareness-into-the-bodys-physiology

42 J. Firman and A. Gila, Assagioli's Seven Core Concepts for Psychosynthesis Training (Palo Alto, CA: Psychosynthesis, 2007), retrieved June 2, 2020, https://www.synthesiscenter.org/PDF/Seven%20Concepts.pdf
K. A. Lombard, "Visions of God, the Cosmos and Humanity," Love and Will: A Psychosynthesis Approach to Living (September 7, 2015), retrieved June 2, 2020, https://loveandwill.com/tag/cosmic-egg/

43 P. R. Tigunait, "What Are Samskaras and How Do They Affect Us?" Yoga International, retrieved June 2, 2020, https://yogainternational.com/article/view/what-are-samskaras-and-how-do-they-affect-us

44 R. Steiner, Secret Brotherhoods and the Mystery of the Human Double (Forest Row, UK: Rudolf Steiner Press, 2004).

45 R. Steiner, "The Balance in the World and Man, Lucifer and Ahriman: World as Product of the Working of Balance" (lectures, Dornach, 1914), retrieved June 2, 2020, http://wn.rsarchive.org/Lectures/GA158/English/RSPC1948/BalWld_cover.html

46 Steiner, "The Balance."

47 D. Goleman, Emotional Intelligence: 10th Anniversary Edition, Why It Can Matter More than IQ (New York, NY: Bantam Books, 2006)

48 B. Lievegoed, Phases: The Spiritual Rhythms in Adult Life (Forest Row, UK: Sofia Press; Rudolf Steiner Press, 1998).

49 A. Huguet et al., "A Systematic Review of Cognitive Behavioral Therapy and Behavioral Activation Apps for Depression," PLoS ONE 11, no. 5 (2016), https://doi.org/10.1371/journal.pone.0154248

50 G. Moroni, "Explaining Divorce Gaps in Cognitive and Noncognitive Skills of Children," Editorial Express (2016), University of York, retrieved June 2, 2020, https://editorialexpress.com/cgi-bin/conference/download.cgi?db_name=RESConf2017&paper_id=435
M. Finklestein and D. M. Thom, "The Underprepared College Student: How Non-Cognitive Factors Influence Academic Preparedness," Journal of Studies in Education 4, no. 1 (2014), https://doi.org/10.5296/jse.v4i1.4764

51 P. Payne et al., "Somatic Experiencing: Using Interoception and Proprioception as Core Elements of Trauma Therapy," Frontiers in Psychology 6 (2015), http://doi.org/10.3389/fpsyg.2015.00093

52 R. Oritz and E. M. Sibinga, "The Role of Mindfulness in Reducing the Effects of Childhood Stress and Trauma," Children 4, no. 3 (2017): 16, https://doi.org/10.3390/children4030016

53 R. Bageant, "The Hakomi Method: Defining Its Place Within the Humanistic Psychology Tradition," Journal of Humanistic Psychology 52, no. 2 (2012), https://doi.org/10.1177/0022167811423313

54 R. Steiner, Curative Eurythmy (London, UK: Rudolf Steiner Press, 1983), retrieved June 2, 2020, http://wn.rsarchive.org/Lectures/GA315/English/RSP1983/CurEur_index.html Centro Lanzarote. (n.d.). "Curative Eurythmy: The Movement Therapy of the Anthroposophical Medicine," Centro Lanzarote, retrieved May 10, 2017, http://www.centro-lanzarote.de/en/downloads/CurativeEurythmie.pdf

55 A. E. McAllen, The Extra Lesson: Exercises in Movement, Drawing and Painting for Helping Children in Difficulties with Writing, Reading and Arithmetic (London, UK: McAllen, 1974).

56 C. Beck, Everyday Zen: Love and Work, (San Francisco, CA: HarperOne, 2007), retrieved June 20, 2020, https://www.amazon.ca/Everyday-Zen-Charlotte-J-Beck/dp/0061285897

57 R. Steiner, Theosophy : An Introduction to the Spiritual Processes in Human Life and in the Cosmos (Great Barrington: Anthroposophic Press, 1994), retrieved June 20, 2020, https://www.goodreads.com/book/show/864618.Theosophy

58 R. Steiner, Theosophy : An Introduction to the Spiritual Processes in Human Life and in the Cosmos (Great Barrington: Anthroposophic Press, 1994), retrieved June 20, 2020, https://www.goodreads.com/book/show/864618.Theosophy

59 A. J. French, "The Christian Mysteries and Modern Consciousness" (electronic thesis, The University of Arizona, 2017), retrieved June 2, 2020, http://hdl.handle.net/10150/579325

R. Steiner, Christianity as Mystical Fact and The Mysteries of Antiquity (West Nyack, NY: Rudolf Steiner Publications, Inc., 1961).

60 D. Brunsvold, "Rudolf Steiner Lectures: The Gospel of St John, Lecture 1" (YouTube video, Audio Enlightenment, 2013), retrieved May 11, 2017, https://www.youtube.com/watch?v=Dihucr2RCjg (account closed, video removed).

R. Steiner, "The Gospel of St. John" (Lectures, Basle, Switzerland, 1907), retrieved June 2, 2020, http://wn.rsarchive.org/Lectures/GA100/English/LR1942/GoJonB_index.html

61 R. Steiner, Theosophy

62 J. Johnson, "Anthroposophy and Rudolf Steiner: A Brief Guide for the Perplexed," Evolve + Ascend.com (February 27, 2017), retrieved June 2, 2020, http://www.evolveandascend.com/2017/02/27/anthroposophy-and-rudolf-steiner-a-brief-guide-for-the-perplexed/

K. Kaine, "I-Connecting," Soul Questing (2017), retrieved May 11, 2017, https://i-connecting.com/ (article no longer available).

63 M. Sathyan, "Vatta Pitta Kapha and Prakruthi in Ayurveda," E-Zine Articles (October 14, 2008), retrieved June 2, 2020, http://ezinearticles.com/?Vatta-Pitta-Kapha-and-Prakruthi-in-Ayurveda&id=1581711

64 C. S. Cashwell et al., "The Only Way Out is Through: The Peril of Spiritual Bypass," Counseling and Values 51, no. 2 (2007): 139, https://doi.org/10.1002/j.2161-007X.2007.tb00071.x

65 R. Steiner, An Esoteric Cosmology: Evolution, Christ and Modern Spirituality. (Paris, France: Rudolf Steiner Press, 2008)

R. Steiner, The Spiritual Guidance of the Individual and Humanity: Some Results of Spiritual-Scientific Research into Human History and Development (Great Barrington, MA: Anthroposophic Press, 2011), retrieved June 2, 2020, http://wn.rsarchive.org/Books/GA015/English/AP1992/GA015_index.html

66 D. Brull, The Mysteries of Social Encounters: The Anthroposophical Social Impulse (Chatham, NY: AWSNA Publications, 2012), retrieved May 11, 2017 from: http://spiritoftheearthfarm.org/Brull1.pdf (PDF removed).

67 J. Poppen, "What is Biodynamic Agriculture?" Society for Biodynamic Farming and Gardening in Ontario (2016), retrieved June 2, 2020, http://biodynamics.on.ca/about/

"What Does Community Supported Agriculture (CSA) Mean?" Biodynamic Association (2016), retrieved June 2, 2020, https://www.biodynamics.com/content/community-supported-agriculture-introduction-csa

68 L. C. D'Herbois, "Painting with Veils," The Anthroposophical Review 3, no. 2 (1981), retrieved June 2, 2020, http://www.waldorflibrary.org/articles/699-painting-with-veils

CHAPTER SIX

Anthroposophical Human Development

Ways that the soul finds an authentic, incarnate home in the body through the long human development period called childhood. Insights into how family divorce can throw a growing child's soul cycles and healthy inner patterns out of balance, causing soul-psyche (psychological) distortions. How to cultivate healthy understandings and practices for life transitions.

Just as in the body, eye and ear develop as organs of perception, as senses for bodily processes, so does a man develop in himself soul and spiritual organs of perception through which the soul and spiritual worlds are opened to him.[1]
Rudolf Steiner

Rudolf Steiner observed that phases of human development happen in seven-year stages, starting from birth and ending the earthly cycle at death.[2] These stages represent cosmic timings within which certain inner forces unfold and bring about capacities that naturally move a person into learning and whole capacity growth. This process also inwardly layers, within the soul, many rich resources for supporting lifelong "humanness" skills. Broad social experiences support perspective and discernment for older children and youth, preparing them for an adulthood of reasoned thinking, clear intuition, imagination, and inspiring initiatives.

The pure wonderment of early childhood, from birth to age seven, is both soberly and joyously celebrated by parents and caregivers. The responsibilities for protecting early childhood development can seem daunting. Making the time and space to allow small children to play and explore, especially in nature, is paramount to wholesome childhood growth. It is the foundation of anthroposophical thinking and Waldorf pedagogy.

Early childhood is a time of unabashed physicality for small children, with the full-on exploration of sensual forces and with little responsibility except to grow and discover. Since so much biological growth is happening, often unseen, this time is deeply important to the formation of life forces and capacities in the child and well into adulthood. Nothing about it is meant to be "adult."

Figure 6.1: Waldorf early childhood supports and environments

The world of the child, from birth to age seven, requires protective spaces and practices that foster the gentle, rhythmical growth of malleable forces in the child. This means surrounding children with nature, beauty, truth, and goodness, and ensuring much sensual exploration of natural materials in their homes or childcare environments. Much indoor and outdoor child play is necessary. Behavior is gently and patiently led and patterned by benevolent adults who bring child-level imaginations, stories, songs, tasks, and rest times at the right moments in the day and evening. Caregivers see children as they are, in long-term development, thus resisting bringing rigorous disciplines upon young children.

Later in child development, in Waldorf pedagogical life at school and at home, children begin a process toward bringing imagination into harmonious, self-disciplined action, leading to clearer thinking in the adolescent years. Children have wholesome experiences to let their earthly senses be filled with goodness and warmth as they begin to engage and cultivate discipline in elementary, holistic, life-skills practices and academics that prepare them to meet the modern times, without the hardening pressures of many modern, adult activities. Imagination reigns at this stage, with hands-on creativity, integrated arts, mathematics that can stimulate creative works later, and sciences that keep humanness directly in charge of material, mechanical, and technological phenomena.

During the middle-school ages for children, around twelve and thirteen, new physiological maturity buds, and the children cultivate a deeper sense of what it means to wish, wonder, and welcome surprises in life. This is recapitulated in high school, through skillfully taking up humanities studies in art, literature, music, and history, and with revelatory exercises in physics, sciences, geography, and mathematics.

These studies are often introduced through the biographies of great souls who rediscovered the poignancy and radiance of life, using their knowledge for the betterment of themselves and others. (Chapter Seven outlines some of these biographies for the adolescent years.)

Waldorf adolescent studies extend earlier school experiences of painting, craft, building projects, and community life into more conceptual understandings in sciences, architecture, pre-engineering sciences, civics, and the art of social encounter. Teen development comes with fully engaging practices in Bothmer gymnastics, and in outdoor activities that respect the adolescent's changing body, preparing students to move naturally into discoveries in biology, and in higher physics, mathematics, and natural sciences.

Brilliance lives on in daily life riddles, experiments, musical choirs, orchestras, dynamic theater productions, seasonal celebrations, and practical tasks. This keeps classroom life full and supporting the class group to organize meaningful, imaginative learning. Teenagers learn how others have formed systems of economics out of the resources of the earth while learning about mechanics through craftwork with metals, wood, stone, clay, sewing, and technological innovation. They initiate entrepreneurial projects of their own.

Youth are introduced to societal innovators and reformers worldwide through experimenting with their ideas. The human issues that historical figures wrestled with are considered and mentally weighed for their connections to modern life perspectives. Their romantic natures (since adolescents naturally feel a sense for the romantic), their soul searching for the important meanings of human life, and the deeply awe-inspiring, intelligent, outward courage in their achievements, are explored in active ways.

Parents Transform as Their Adolescent Children Change

A child's school years are often a time when parents are reminded of their own inner-child care, or lack of it, and their early-life inspirations. This includes the necessary lifelong capacity to be able to be open-minded, reverent, and curious. It's a large and substantial calling for each parent to keep the awe and wonder of youth sacred, while holding their own vast responsibilities of managing the home, work, bills, and any number of other adult-stage, socio-cultural growth objectives and demands.

This multidimensionality of parent capacity is more real and available than many people believe about themselves. That is partially because material-mechanistic thinking in the industrialization era in the West worked to diminish the value of human capacities. Over time, people began to believe that they were less capable than they really were.

Most parents need a great deal of personal processing, support, and guidance to hold soul-spirit perspectives with their growing children. To keep connected with what their children's child-level world is about, Waldorf schools encourage parents to interact with the schoolchildren's activities, to participate in the running of the schools, and to take up seasonal celebrations, studies, and artistic activities together.

Parents often function with various levels of anxiety with their children. They fear that they can't fully know how to foster their children in a sustainably loving, socially flexible, and productive way wherein their children will competently meet a future with sometimes drastically changing needs. Parents know they can't guarantee lifelong wholeness and positivity because they know they're not sure or capable of it themselves at times.

The Waldorf curriculum can sometimes cause them to bump up against unexamined or undeveloped parts of themselves. Yet, identifying their own adult, soul-development needs, learning forgiveness of self and others, and experiencing community support and development can help them learn resiliency and build a social net with which their children can stay connected through time. It creates a buffer and a firmament for children who are launching into a world of technological possibilities, potential materialistic overwhelm, and various body-mind challenges and soul dangers.

Anthroposophical educators work to bring understanding for parents to develop themselves along with their children's development, while teachers themselves develop individually but also in tandem in many ways with students and families. Necessary, character-transforming growth affects everyone in the years of children's schooling. This is the case in general for everyone, in the Consciousness Soul era that we live in today.

Parents of younger children learn that bringing stabilizing, heartwarming, inspiring, practical disciplines to a child, in right timings, and in balance with creative exploration and skill, is a form of sustainable love for their children. Humanities education and academic skills practices are wed in anthroposophical work, as they are in cosmic-earthly nature. Doing so fosters in the children virtues such as strength, industriousness, patience, resilience, independence, and reverence for other human beings.

Within the school community of unique and striving individuals, Waldorf community members prepare children to step into adult life, at age twenty-one, as themselves and as members of a generational cohort, with awareness of the value of other adults in the world and also other generations of younger children. They have the chance to begin to be more selflessly serving with others in a meaningful life once they explore their feelings for socio-economic-cultural issues of society through to age twenty-eight.

Having met the developmental stages of childhood growth in wholeness, the older adolescent stands in uprightness in a world that opens in lustrous revelations as well as, at times, shocking truths. The pre-adult person takes it all in with equilibrium and determination for the good. All of this is can be true for the young Pearl Adult also.

Development Continues Through Adulthood

When a child has achieved a steady, balanced footing in the world, and has developed imagination, feeling, and thinking for wholesome ego tasks by age twenty-one, new layers of adult inner mysteries begin to develop and unfold. An individual's biography, destiny, and innate creative urges are naturally occurring wonders of the body, mind, and soul. They live steeped within one's daily life of activity, at times asleep, fermenting, distilling, and outwardly unfolding. At important, adult life-cycle moments, like underground springs that finally find an outlet to the air and sunlight, distinct aspects of our inner selves bubble to life.

In childhood and adolescence, each seven-year cycle unveils forces within a foundational fourfold human nature. The fourfoldness of the human being involves the physical sheath, the etheric sheath, the astral sheath, and the ego-I sheath. In adulthood, newly unfolding I-capacities bring budding, seven-year-cycle soul tasks that begin to answer profound questions within us over time.

In our twenties, we feel ourselves fully in the world of others, with all of our senses and higher capacities ripe to connect and know the others in our new world, as well as a natural inclination to feel into the life of others who are not normally in our social field. We are back exploring the world but in a much different state than when we were growing children. We intensely sense into everyone else's feelings. In anthroposophy, this strong feeling time is called the *Sentient Soul* period.

In our thirties, we naturally begin to question the way that we are living, why we perceive life the way we do, and why some people or experiences in our lives seem to affect us profoundly while others seem not to be of remarkable interest. We strive for higher learning and develop our *Intellectual Soul*, hoping that it will help us navigate the complexity of life.

Yet, the Intellectual Soul period can feel full of great struggle or suffering. Often, in our mid-thirties, we may unconsciously begin to ask our souls what the purpose of life is. We enter another profound era of individual awareness called the *Consciousness Soul* period. This is a time when self-reflection, and the inner understanding of why we are what we are as human beings, become important focal points. We can begin to wonder if there is more to life than the practical, day-to-day issues, and what is just directly in front of our sight or stimulating outer senses. This often happens if we lose someone close to us at this stage of life.

At certain adult stages, sometimes through brilliant moments or events while at other times through crises, or quiet, inner experiences, we feel ourselves and this life to be something deeper, vaster, older, or more complicated and mysterious than what we ever considered before. We can also, at times, feel overwhelmed by the sufferings of others, and we might feel an impulse to reject much of the routine society surrounding us.

By now, insights and answers to more existential life questions can't necessarily be answered by our family members or people who have known us long-term. We begin to tap a kind of knowing about which we don't fully understand the source. Intuition can become a well and resource for new actions and ideas.

We may also begin an inner struggle with our own dragons of resistance to change or to certain harder realities about a maturing life. This humbles us, but it can also leave us in moments of thinking that so many things we felt so sure of are irrelevant to what we face now. A great inner wrestling begins to free up thought and heart space for higher soul and spirit cultivation. We learn to reach out to others while reaching inside ourselves as well, to reconstitute. We sometimes have experiences now that we say are turning us "inside out and upside down." We undergo a metamorphosis, and at various life crossroads, work or career issues can conflict with feelings for something more broadly meaningful.

Often in marriages or long-term relationships, this need for new growth is projected as something lacking in the other partner. One partner or the other begins seeking meaning through other people who seem to have a higher or deeper degree of realization in the areas that the married partner has cultivated. In many cases, it plants seeds of frustration, resentment, lack, jealousy, entitlement, or a sense of failure.

This can be even more true in relationships where there is a substantial age difference, representing complex generational differences related to cosmic developments. Therapeutic, anthroposophical biography work can help aid in addressing the feelings arising in this period of adulthood and help the partner to design a soulful approach to inner development that does not have to exclude, demonize, or alienate the other partner.

This may not mean that a marriage will happily or peacefully continue as it has been, or that it will stay together. It may carry on with a different partnership character to it, but it may also dissolve.

Partners who have overly invested their inner resources on the limited human understanding of material wealth-accumulation or fantastic, abstract amusements and entertainments may lack the strong capacities to notice the soul-spirit revelations that arise now. Self-witnessing is needed to help each soul evolve into future fulfillment. That is especially so when circumstances begin to lead adults toward thinking about their own death and the last decades of life.

Yiana Belkalopolos

The Opaline Pearl

The symbolism of an Opaline Pearl, with the mysterious and still-clouded, inner gifts of light in the young Pearl Adult, represents potential and vulnerability. A young, golden, adult heart can seem to be lost beneath the other gems of compassion, justice-seeking, and the striving for a shinier relationship future. Yet, investigating within the fog of sometimes surreal feelings and family circumstances, and outer-world pressures to seek rewards in the materialistic reality, the Pearl can come to accept more of oneself as a beauteous enigma that is as divinely created on the earth as crystals, precious gems, and gold.

Having had the chance to incarnate well in the early development years, or to heal missing pieces early in the child-development stages, this refreshed and wholesome Pearl Adult, despite living out some challenging opposition in the family divorce, can find the grace to come into an appropriate I-being at age twenty-one. This unique and golden I nature is something more complex than Gilgamesh's olden, pearly prize of eternal youthfulness. It becomes a container to bring new soul wisdom, and a spiritual vessel that has the capacity to meet what comes from the future with courage, strength, and emotional resilience.

A new, young Pearl Adult often has an early, mature wisdom from working through some intense human opposites in childhood. Although there can be real grace in this, the young adult can struggle to find meaningful ways to stay aligned with themselves and with the larger adult world. The Pearl compassion and creative maturity that can arise out of excessive challenges in childhood, if not honored or respected by parents or other adults, can get lost in the outer adult world where other adults have less of that compassionate and insightful development. A sense of loneliness, betrayal, and alienation can be reinforced.

For others to recognize what lies precious in the Pearl heart from the early family pressure can take significant time, healing, and quiet presence, since the Pearl many have had to become significantly guarded for survival. Spending the time to get to know the more golden inner qualities of a Pearl Adult is not a waste of time, however. Pearls are often very grateful for adult, humane empathy and will offer goodness in return in ways that they can, or in ways that others offer warm, open-door opportunities.

All souls hold soul-spirit wisdom that is as valuable in life as those things that benefit people out of sheer material worth. Yet, most Pearls are not so grand as to suggest some sort of self-glorifying exceptionalism over others, purely because they have grappled with some challenging dragons. Humility often still holds the reins in a Pearl life, unless that person has been driven so far in trauma to be unable to self-regulate well at all. In this case, the trauma clouds the gifts, making them opaque, or not very clear, to others.

The young Pearl Adult's potent gift is the enfolded chalice of an opening heart and inner hut space that will ripen over the years and through many challenges. Pearls raised in conflict have often been thrown back upon themselves early, sent into the hut, and into the investigation of what has happened to love, and why. This has not always been conscious in them, but at their Consciousness Soul stage, much can reveal itself as reasons for personal, earlier actions. They come to ask the question: "Who am I and why do I experience this kind of suffering?"

Since the Pearl, like others, will encounter many oppositions in life, those who bring kind light to them also bring hope to ripen their heart maturity. That hope is that other people will help that person to feel the human valuing that they didn't feel in a heart-hardened, or coolly disregarding, family experience.

Adulthood today promises the gold of the Consciousness Soul era, that precious substance of self-awareness and soul-spirit understanding, as well as the ability to transform awareness into healing and into a warm and even brilliant goodness in service to others. This is true for anyone who opens to it.

Often, Pearls have had no option but to be opened up. Years of surviving and striving in the middle of parent and family conflicts have brought many Pearls out of a shell of comfort early. Often they've been thrown into the light of Christ consciousness, knowingly or not, and directly or inadvertently into asking strangers for divine guidance.

Some have learned to express the gratitude that they feel about this safely. Others can feel awkward to do so since responses in the past to their childlike grace have been harsh. A hurt, for a Pearl, can go more deeply for a while than one for someone who had firm and loving family support.

As emotionally painful as some of those moments can be, there is a gift in the Christ-like suffering that every human being can experience at times. When we open our hearts and minds in times when we suffer most, engaging our courage despite the angst that can arise in it, and ask the questions that can help us get safer, more grounded, more compassionate and self-responsible, a higher grace can be present. Our needs can begin to be met differently than in the past.

This does not exclude the Pearl's need to put up boundaries when someone they seek help from closes his or her heart or seeks to harm. Pearl Adults strive not to stay shut down when they feel hurt, but rather strive to keep flexible and ask questions, taking up suggestions to see for themselves their effectiveness without forcing themselves to accept anything that may continue to harm their life forces. Finding ways to truly express the pain and suffering that is occurring inside of them is paramount to being understood and receiving appropriate help. This self-dominion is crucial to the well-being of the Pearl soul in these times.

Many blocked hearts and souls are still struggling to open to even the smallest inklings of the golden Consciousness Soul gifts of our modern times. Opaline Pearls can obscure inner light if they get too shut in with their pain and do not seek healing and clarity. At times, the task to pull up the will forces to do so seems impossible. Yet, today, we can take comfort that many Pearls now have surfaced out of some very dark times, and have grown, learned, and succeeded at life challenges to experience truly meaningful joy, love, peace, and a sense of self-creative agency. After decades of experience in a new human culture, Pearls can help each other to overcome obstacles more capably now.

Without asking for help, and humbling to receive love and support, the radiant, etheric, workers in the lower and higher worlds, who are many, can't help to instill angelic support into the Pearls' growing hearts and life experiences. (Volume II speaks more to the practicalities and biology of the expanding human heart.)

Table 6.1: Human development stages table

The following are the generally indicated ages and stages of child and adult development, in accordance with indications set out by Rudolf Steiner. (This is not consciously taught to children. It is work that informs the people involved in the children's growth and healing.) Also shown are the later stages of adult soul and spirit development, indicated with short descriptions.

Birth-7	Physical sheath	The discovery of the body's capacities.
Age 7-14	Etheric sheath	Life forces and imaginations open and develop.
Age 14-21	Astral sheath	Feelings for life, and mental conceptualization capacities, unfold.
Age 21-28	Sentient Soul	Emergence of the full, healthy ego or sense of individual I.
Age 28-35	Intellectual Soul	Individual and collaborative thinking opens, as well as more world comprehension.
Age 35-42	Consciousness Soul	Deeper self-awareness and awareness of one's compassionate inter-connectedness to others and the world.
(Anthroposophy uses Eastern spiritual descriptors for the next three stages.)		
Age 42-49	Spirit Self	Beginning of a dedicated life of higher virtue in everyday actions with others. Sense-free thinking begins. In Eastern spiritual language, this is the beginning of the Manas[3] stage of spiritual development.

Age 49-56	Life Spirit	Capacities for empathy and feeling into the "other" and much that another feels. Comprehension of how one's karma affects all living things. Fuller awareness of old, cycling, and spiritually harmful thinking, as well as the subtler bonds of unfree, materialistic thinking. Complete cultivation of the higher self or inner witness. This indicates the Buddhi[4] stage of spiritual development. Consciousness of the challenges at the threshold of death.
Age: 56-63	Life Spirit, to become Spirit Man	Resonating in openness with general humanity in the far future, this represents the Atman stage of spiritual development, or the full Christ consciousness as undivided oneness with higher source. Fully compassionate service to one another. Complete selflessness. The etheric heart is full, and energetic resonance comes at refined levels of oscillation capacities mostly unperceived or not sustained in our present times.

Anthroposophical Early Childcare and Waldorf Pedagogy

The following discussions of anthroposophical care at different ages and stages of human life are necessarily brief in this foundational book on the diverse soul issues of children of divorce. Throughout the remaining chapters of this volume and the initial chapters of Volume II are references to help caregivers to deepen their insights.

It is important to remember that Dr. Steiner warned people not to be absolutist with his insights, suggesting that they look at some of his lawful indicators for our spiritual times, and then see what the light of individual, soul experience and higher thinking can add from various angles of a person's subjective and objective perspective. Steiner knew that parents needed to do their own research on themselves and their children and, if done with an earnestness beyond a superficial understanding, parents will glean valuable insights about themselves and the souls of the full human beings that are growing into maturity before them.

Most experienced childcare workers and parents would agree that it is challenging for them to be objective about the children in their care while offering appropriate bonding for the child's stages of development. It is essential practice to do so, however, to prepare children for a truly free adult life of soul-spiritual, and practical, responsibility.

In the myriad tasks of supporting child growth, caregivers often can't see the young ones as whole beings who have future tasks that won't be fully apparent to the adults in their lives. The adults must hold family histories, temporary societal constructs, and their own generational issues looser now in Christ-consciousness times. That was not the case in the past when religious law worked to nail down and strictly enforce rules for human beings living into descending incarnations.

Child-raising today must work to provide wholeness in the child's incarnation process so that inner-soul substance is nourished well throughout a lifetime. Yet, in a time when souls are preparing the long process toward ascension, any caregiver thoughts and expectations on the young that get hardened, rigid, or dismissive of individual soul aspects, serve to bind and inhibit, rather than free that child in adulthood.

Caregivers can forget that everything in life is evolving in cyclical progressions and moving patterns, within rhythmical cosmic *breathing*, as with the movements of the earth, the other planets, and the slow spirals of the sun's solar system itself. Those cycles are changing and progressing human consciousness. Change must be embraced with level-headedness but not rigid backward clinging.

Soul Care in Prenatal and Early Post-Birth Months

Although the soul is present at a certain point in an embryo *in utero*, the human stages of development discussed here begin with the human being's earthly birth. (The scope of this book cannot reach with meaningful depth into prenatal awareness. However, Dr. Jaap van der Wal of the Netherlands[5] has extensively researched, with anthroposophical understanding, the life of a child while in embryonic development.)

Caregivers working anthroposophically with birth issues—be they parents, doctors, surgeons, nurses, doulas, massage therapists, nutritionists, or physiotherapists—tend to pay careful soul attention to a child's experience pre-conception, as well as after birth. Children *in utero* can be developmentally affected through various abuses and stresses in the home and family, including mental, emotional, and physical violence. If a pregnant mother uses harmful substances to try to ameliorate stress, this can have lifelong damaging effects on a child's well-being. This is well-known from decades of experience, research, and study in embryology and other pediatric sciences on substance addiction and issues such as fetal alcohol syndrome.[6]

In anthroposophically informed, post-natal infant care, as well as in Waldorf early childhood nurseries and kindergartens, the full extent of the human growth stages for an individual child, from conception, are carefully considered. The child's full development life, including adult development stages, is viewed and held in the light of spiritual lawfulness, in open reverence and awe.

Adults wonder what the children's souls bring with them and what choices they will make as adults working their soul ways into the fold of humanity now and into the future. Children's natural interests, capacities, and higher purposes are respected at each age, although the choices a child makes must be firmly mitigated through parent nurturance and protectiveness until the mid-adolescent stages. That firmness changes as the adolescent gets older.

Anthroposophical developmental awareness acknowledges that if some developmental need in one age and stage of life is missed or distorted, it can cause psychic or even physical disturbance and illness in that seven-year period or in later stages, particularly after age forty.[7] Since healthy foundations are so important for a young child, who learns the habits of home life by mimicking the adults, the parents and caregivers in a child's home require a level of conscientiously high, deeply honest, and consistently warm presence and responsiveness to the child. Strong will forces tempered by loving humility are essential.

In anthroposophical home-care therapy with divorcing families, healthy in-breathing and out-breathing are patterned for parents who have childcare responsibilities. Parents may be guided to notice their breath and are encouraged through practices to overcome chronically held, quickened, or unnaturally controlled breathing. This is an essential first check-in with the seven life processes, to get a snapshot for how the parents' other balancing soul forces might be affected.

Curative arts therapy for parents, such as curative eurythmy, can help parents to safely unwind, boost their health and immunity, and focus beyond mundane work or caregiver tasks. Curative eurythmy practices that assist parents to work opposites can help each to see their children beyond their ex-spouse conflicts. Curative eurythmy is a complex holistic art that tailors practices to individual needs and is best left to one-on-one work with qualified practitioners, though some short, free courses are often offered on-line through experienced eurythmy healers. A gentle curative arts practice that nursing mothers can arrange well on their own at home involves simple watercolor painting, perhaps with some instruction from a therapist by phone or in a few initial creative expressive arts sessions.

Teachers and caregivers working specifically with Pearl Children in the home and in the community, model wholesome and loving goodness while carrying out with the children the daily tasks of cooking, cleaning, singing, and storytelling. Remedial teachers and psychological therapists can observe Pearl Children in regular and extensive outdoor activity and free play, while attending to routine daily tasks and craft-making themselves.

From grade school and onward, a young Pearl Child who has experienced serious soul distortions earlier in life can find healing and redirection through anthroposophical remedial education, active psychotherapy, and work with eurythmists, painting therapists, and craft-makers trained in the developmental needs.

They may need an ongoing, warm and nurturing hut corner to retreat to at times to soothe rattled nervous systems. It is a tricky conversation, but an essential one to have, regarding any Pearl's needs for hugs and safe touch from safe adults, be it at school or in healing environments outside of the home. One possible way to protect child safety in such cases is to have a second adult present as a witness to touch/hug times for children younger than the legal age of consent.

Regularly educating Pearls on safe touch is key for their ability to set adult boundaries. As awkward as this may seem, it is far more awkward and unhealthy for a Pearl to receive very minimal healthy touch throughout their development years. It is well-known in neuropsychology that safe touch is essential to cultivating vagus-nerve strength and resourcing memory.[8]

"To Remedy" is Greater than its Parts

The word "remedy" has its Greek origins in the knowledge of the goddess Iaso, the daughter of the great healer, Asclepius.[9] Iaso was known to have a holistic connection with nature and varied roots, stems, branches, leaves, and blossoms.[10] The healing and sense-restoring aromas, colors, and glistening light auras, for instance, of a spring peach tree, are the result of the whole mysterious series of years of growth before that peach tree fruited and ripened. Healing and growth for children takes in that same wholesome history and knowledge.

The life processes for that peach tree may have begun with organic seeding four or five years prior, or perhaps from a graft of one tree twig or scion onto a host trunk, or from a greenhouse seedling. Rooting, stemming, branching, budding, blossoming, releasing, dying, and overwintering continue year after year for the peach tree. At some point, it is mature and ready to give valued fruit. It is this way in some regards for a human being, although the "fruits" are the capacities of the human I to sustain decades of profound change and actions of goodness in the world. The importance of a peach is not only in the fruit that comes to ripeness in the summer days, but also in the whole life process of the tree.

In various phases of the peach tree's growth and dying-away, beauty and light are created. They are in the glowing juices in a summer-cut peach or in the pink-saffron, lilting autumn leaves. The springtime processes of the whole plant work in tandem with the sun's forces and angles. If a young tree stops giving fruit, the farmer is likely to look to the soil that nurtures the whole tree to see what remedy is needed to bring the fruit back. They know that warmth informs the roots below the ground in winter and spring, as does sufficient clean water and many mineral nutrients. Appropriate sunlight brings messages to the elemental spirits of the plants. This brings a renewal of visible and more tangible expressions of light in the seedlings, stems, leaves, buds, and blossoms.

A young, developing child experiences a resonance in the soul, very astutely, with the elemental impressions of nature, as with the cycles of growth and fruiting of the peach tree.

Remedial Education

For traumatized children, finding appropriate remediation that keeps a child rooted in nutritious warmth, fed by the springs of love and bathed in the sunlight of a well-fostered ego-I, takes a holistic and often societally involved approach to well-being. Too often, young children who have been harmed by one hardening, materialistic practice are given other similar materialistic approaches for healing, and the soul remains cold and unnourished.

Pharmaceuticals, the sensory impressions of a child playing with hard-plastic play toys, or being sat in front of a television for hours, or given an iPad to "speak" regularly to family members, are materialistic approaches to palliating a thin or even somewhat deadened soul. Rather than nourishing the soul, they can assault a child's inner impressions on gross and subtle levels. Genetically modified foods also play havoc with the body-soul complex.

Alternatively, anthroposophical remedial work can be integrated with psychotherapeutic interventions for developing Pearl Children through *seeding* and *rooting* practices such as:

- forms of rebirthing activities,
- grounding exercises of having the child gently and intentionally roll on soft ground or in a sheet or blanket on a carpet,
- helping a child center the life forces with an exercise of rolling a warmed copper ball down the front of the body as the child is sitting stretched out lengthwise on the earthen ground or floor,
- through strength-increasing, full-body crawling on the ground,
- the agility work of lifting a marble from the ground with one's bare toes, or
- through drawing spirals in sand with the big toe of the right foot.

(These practices work with different-aged children.) These exercises can follow a heart-warming fairy tale, fable, myth, or legend, depending on the child's age.

Mindful, present, and conscious activities that strengthen, *branch,* and *leaf* a child's explorations with embodiment, coordination, rhythms, and connection to spatial life forces, come through leg and arm play that crosses the midline, beanbag coordination practices, copper-rod sequences, ball play, and other consciously designed games. Form-drawing activities with crayons contribute something to the child's *budding* sense of contained form, movement, habit, and rhythm in a form-drawing visual expression.

Forms can be moved later into artistic efforts, or into the moving forms in eurythmy activities and even performances with other children. Or they might become the insignia on a finely finished artisan craft, created by hand, such as a wooden stool, canoe paddle, or chest.

Natural, steadying, flexible, and affirming remedial activities, which from a child's-eye view can seem like absorbing play, give a child a chance to find natural breathing again, help the child to have an inward connection, and engage body-soul integration for the opening physical, etheric, and astral sheath stages of life.

Innate Trauma Resourcing Activity: Crawling Infants and Early Toddlers

For a very young child, crawling in "crawl-friendly," warm and welcoming rooms with carpets, small bridges, and low platforms made of natural materials, is an appropriate age-level activity.

An infant or early toddler can crawl in warmer weather seasons in safe and energetically protected places such as quiet, sunlit glens at a farm or on the grass at a park.

In a nursery care setting, a crawling room can be adapted to allow for moments of regression for a child who experienced parental conflict trauma in infancy or *in utero*. A hot water bottle wrapped in a pillow sheet of natural hemp, raw silk, or flannel cotton fabric, with a few dabs of comfrey oil on the sheets, is good to have in the room for cuddling. This comfrey pillow is set on a sheep's fleece in a sturdy, custom-made, infant-bed or low cradle on the crawling floor—ready to crawl into if the child triggers into a crying moment or a fear eruption that causes a lash-out at another toddler.

The child can be encouraged to crawl, "like a kitten," onto the aromatic bed for a few moments of back or neck massage. Gentle, colored fabric can drape over the bed like a tent-awning, creating subtle body protection through a sense of enclosure, and to gentle-down the lighting in the play space. Warm water play, set up in a low wooden tub in the room on a natural-material, absorbent mat, is also helpful. Caregivers can offer a few minutes of hand, arm, forehead, and foot washing with natural sponges and warm, vanilla-essence water. Towels warmed by a hot water bottle can be readied before the child starts play crawling. A warm towel wrap is used to dry feet and hands, or to bundle around an unregulated child, after the healing water play.

Kindergarten

Puppet plays, doll play, and nature-table activity in therapy, for kindergarten-aged children, allow the toddler and young child to project onto play stories what needs to move emotionally inside of them. Kindergarten teachers, parent assistants, and therapists create a warm, inviting, and safe space, and maintain a natural rhythm to their breathing and activities.

This naturally holds the child in a pattern of soulful developmental processes. Children see adults cooking wholesome foods and making natural snacks in the home-like kindergarten environment. Helping with chores, such as folding newly washed and dried laundry, gives a child responsibility and a felt sense of purpose.

At set stages in the day, simple songs, verses, and therapeutic fairy tales are shared for the young souls to absorb healthy sounds and enter into heart-stirring and lively imaginations. Gentle lyre or pentatonic flute music in the fifth key is an important part of the therapeutic landscape of an anthroposophical kindergarten. Rhythmical and stomping eurythmy movements can be brought for several children at once to help the trauma-triggered and dissociated child to feel earthed again.

Early Elementary Grades and Pre-Adolescence

A Pearl Child may be given playful or structured curative eurythmy practices accompanied by verses in heightened speech, for moving primordial vowel and consonant sounds through the body. Later, elementary or high-school-aged children may hear similar but advanced themes in verses spoken in lyrical, epic, or dramatic speech.

Acoustic musical accompaniment for activities throughout the grade-school years instills healing, resourcing memory in the soul. Later, grown children learn to communicate interests, needs, and thoughts with empathic and multidimensional, nuanced complexity, from having heard natural, soul-enhancing music throughout childhood.

At various ages and stages of childhood, general classroom activities brought by adults in conscious rhythms—such as beanbag passing games with verses, walking in poetic meters, or tapping out rhythm-stick games—meet children where they thrive in natural child growth, and in their twelve senses, temperaments, life constitutions, and seven life processes. Therapists can work with traumatized Pearl Children using such practices in group therapy sessions with safe family members.

Adolescence

For the child in adolescence, integrated, body-cognitive work through Bothmer Movement and Spacial Dynamics exercises can be helpful to tune teenagers up in holistic ways to balance changes happening on many levels of teenage-life adjustment. More complex craft and sculpting work in clay, metal, wood, and soapstone, as well as therapeutically tailored literature and music explorations, weave together processes to help a Pearl Youth to stay attuned with the cosmic-formative forces in their soul. (Chapter Seven offers much in-depth discussion on adolescent concerns.)

Right Timing

Parents of Waldorf school children are often surprised at how easily and naturally their children move into new skills and capacities at different ages and grades. This is because Waldorf teachers, healers, and therapists only bring what is appropriate at the right age and time, avoiding straining young children too early or leaving them unmet with the right stimulation when their advancing souls are inwardly hungry for it.

Therapeutic interventions for a Pearl Child with trauma, who needs emotional support and life-skills navigation, can integrate the natural timings and work of childhood development with a counselor's awareness of the unique missing or distorted pieces that the child needs remedied. Therapists need to monitor ongoing considerations for development and what may be happening in the parent divorce conflicts that set development back. Tracking child oscillations in development helps a therapist tweak practices when they notice a child unconsciously blocking progression, or significantly regressing.

Yiana Belkalopolos

Divorce in the Time of Play and Integrity Establishment

Growth and life-skills theories in the Western paradigms of psychology have not tended to look at adult life-rhythm, developmental patterns, and how these are influenced by soul-spirit cycles. Some transpersonal psychology perspectives have begun to consider the whole picture[11] of both child and adult development. In Western functional, behavioral, and developmental psychological theories, such as those of German-born psychologist Erik Erikson,[12] ages and stages of human development are given some attention.

Erikson applied practical-emotional criteria to human development stages. He considered that children work on the development of hope or mistrust up to age one and a half, autonomy or shame by age three, initiative or guilt until age five, industry or inferiority from age five to twelve, and identity versus role confusion from ages twelve to eighteen.

It is questionable if these are true perceptions regarding the souls of children, from an ego-I point of view, since in early childhood, children mostly mimic adults because they have no fully developed ego of their own. Erikson's developmental processes tend to hinge on expecting children to integrate set societal rules and observances, rather than on purely natural child development. Rather than developing curricula and child tasks at home to meet outer systems, anthroposophical approaches meet the soul through inner understandings of human development and individual agency first. Practices in anthroposophical human development help children and youths to be themselves, while understanding the broad needs of society and of individual others. These developed young people arrive to adulthood with the freshness of energetic capacities that can both help to sustain appropriate societal systems as needed and have the natural human capability to create and innovate new developments in societal systems as called for in evolving realities.

In the Erikson model, children are judged early, prior to the development of their full I, on what is autonomy or a lack of it, initiative or its absence, industry or something that doesn't stand up as such in the immediate view of societal industry, or on roles to play out in life when the spirit of the modern times doesn't necessarily confine anyone to distinct, old, societal roles. Erikson suggests that ego-integrity is a development for ages sixty-five and older. However, according to Steiner, if children are raised appropriately in soul-development stages in childhood, they arrive at the ability to uphold ego-integrity at age twenty-one—forty-five years earlier.

Erikson's thinking process seems to leave full adult responsibility to later life maturity, and potentially infantilizes young adults. A belief that the development of the autonomous self only comes later in life reflects the desires of the capitalist class of the industrialization era. Then, it was not propitious for industry owners to have a workforce of people who could think for themselves, since that would not make for adults who would easily subsume their greater capacities to the needs of automation and the running and upkeep of machines and the industrial-capitalist, elite leaders.

On the flip-scale of healthy, modern, child-development practices are the highly popular modern mindfulness[13] and somatic therapies for children that work from intuition-based healing, putting children mostly in adult practices of discovering their own healing for themselves through "listening" to what their body tells them and through forms of meditation. This can bring too much intellectualism and self-consciousness to a child too early. Meditation is not recommended early in the healing of a traumatized child because it can open a child up too much at a time when the child really needs to redefine boundaries and find a sense of unconscious safety again. These practices can work against attempts to integrate incarnation practices and lead to a too finely attuned and strained nervous system in young or middle adulthood.

Some therapies, such as sound-deprivation practices,[14] or nature-bathing, ecopsychology practices[15] are suggested for Pearls, from time to time in their development years, to assist with cutting out sensory over-stimulation and to bring calm to emotional/mental overloading or triggering. Creative-expressive therapy[16] is sometimes child-age-and-stage appropriate. Another popular therapy in the West today, somatic, Mind-Body Resonance[17] can be helpful for young children if the body-consciousness of it is brought through imagination, puppets, verses, and age-appropriate stories about other children. (More on modern Western therapies for used for Pearls is discussed in Volume II)

Punishment and Judgment Hinder Development

The occasional therapist and parent today will resort to old, functionalist, and authoritative strategies to develop a child toward a mechanistic approach to life, with no rights, few independent responsibilities, and little higher mental-emotional-artistic sensitivity or capacity. This is when an insecurely attached Pearl Child with strong feelings is told to simply "man up, be still, and take the punches" to become purely physically responsible to a materialistically oriented, societal role-belief and structure.

This kind of raw, authoritarian mental abuse and imprinting, posing as psychology, came out of attempts to orient people toward working like machines on machines, or toward a future military life of running weapons machinery to kill people. It was a step above a heavy farming mentality, wherein an adult was meant to match, in an animalistic way, the strengths of farm animals and heavy physical work on the wide expanses of land in the constant barrage of the elements. A person was expected to orient their soul-psyche to little more advancement than an ox or bull. Little higher development in the arts or social realm was considered of interest or importance. Spiritual life was either nonexistent or a mostly religious one of blind faith to keep some order and imposed peace in the village.

In such a mindset, what a developing Pearl Child feels about the parents' conflict, or what he is missing in relational and soul-spirit understandings, is considered irrelevant. It is a dangerous psychology that diminishes the soul in order to make a person blindly servile in the face of neglect, like a loyal dog, and unfree to think, feel, and act for oneself.

This punitive, reductionist approach has served to create developmentally blocked and empathically unresponsive persons who easily project violent, put-down tendencies and fantasies onto others.[18] It is a process meant to keep a child unnaturally tied to an old, militaristic, descending-life consciousness. It has nothing to do with assisting a child to develop good skills or higher capacities to raise above a materialistic, animalistic life. With this non-thoughtful psychology, a Pearl's humanity is easily set up for lifelong self-abuses through medications and substances, and vulnerability to the abuses of other people.

It is clearly known that the human nervous system no longer functions on punitive, purely functional development mindsets. Pushing a substance abuse life on a child is a distinct sign of an overly Ahrimanically driven or Luciferically stimulated approach to parenting.

Behaviorally punitive measures, such as spanking or slapping a child, are based on old-world traditions, uninformed by any progressive, healthy study on child psychology. These acts simply send a Pearl into neurological, amygdala-based, danger reactions that set up harm programming in the brain and result in neurological burnout. We see these effects today on thousands of young and elder army veterans in the West, who commit suicide as a result of not being able to integrate the horrors they have experienced with a firm, inner, and healthy ego-I nature. They experience full-on ego disintegration that has no safe foundations to rebuild on when they are thrown into post-traumatic stress disorder.

This punitive, reductionist approach to child-raising also undermines the integration of newly acquired habits and skills into the child's innate and automatic consciousness. It makes the child or youth fearfully self-conscious and servile to a domineering parent. The child cannot become wholly scaffolded as an individual self, with unconscious, good habits that can sustain the grown person without substance abuses and without regularly straining the nervous system.

This kind of punishment can distort a Pearl Child's ability to trust, right down into physiological blocks. With a parent who may have already weakened the child's trust bond through the divorce actions, or through ongoing tension and conflict with the other parent, this can become a soulfully fitful experience for the child, and even terrifying. The terror can get "buried" in the psyche until years later when some crisis unleashes a Pandora's box of dis-regulated adult emotion, including hateful violence that might have been the ideal of the military-minded parent but which is not appropriate for the times or for a civilian life.

When children can't trust the main caregivers in their early life to hold their hearts in as great a value and concern as any other consideration about human life, children will not form trust with even respect-worthy people in society. In the worst reaction from the distortions of human ego and power in children's early lives, the children can grow up to be adults who come to believe that they have the right to life and death purely on their own terms, with little regard for anyone else.

This is so because the adults around these children have not proven to be respecting and thus worthy of the children's truly human needs and efforts. The whole experience of these children's development years was of being treated in a way that was not human for our times.

In essence, their souls must rebel or be destroyed in the absence of any true heart, soul, or human spirit inspiration.

Adult and Child-Development Boundaries Get Crossed in Divorces

Another development challenge for Pearl Children is when parents, and people in elder generations, impose a higher level of spiritual development onto younger people than is appropriate to their age and stage. When boundaries between adult and child become too permeable or completely nonexistent, a child can't clearly achieve what is needed for their soul development because an adult is imposing adult-level practices or functions onto child capacities.

These children lose themselves and cannot build functional egos to meet life with self-sustainability and responsibility in the world. When the parent does not behave as the compassionate and appropriately boundaried adult, overwhelming the child by disregarding the child's own capacities, limitations, and protective boundaries, psychic distortions and other levels of soul entanglement and damage set in. Often, Pearl Adults spend a great deal of unconscious time in confusion about their own sense of purpose, capability, self-worth, and needs.

Midlife

Older Pearl Adults can naturally come to higher stages of adult wisdom development, particularly after age forty-two, like anyone else. Many were exposed early to experiences that later gave them a sense of expanded humanitarian consciousness. They've seen beyond the veils of outer or exoteric society and been exposed to the deeper suffering truths of many, if not most, people in the world on one scale or another. They may begin to have revelatory moments where their life struggles seem to have some purpose that is exactly the same as the greater purpose of all of humanity.

They see how a human life is fuller than simply the job-life, functionality-perfection ethic promoted to them earlier in life, one that was too often framed within a hyper-materialistic, industrial-complex, employer narrative that wasn't soulfully whole then and not particularly realistic now. They may see that too much family and relationship life, and healthy child development, was sacrificed on the altar of mindsets of mass production, destruction and waste, rather than human meaning, environmental holism, and the responsible sharing of earthern resources, manufactured or grown goods, and human honoring services that serve both individual and universal goodness.

Pearls can grow like anyone else in consciousness and understand the sufferings and redemption spoken of and written in the many great spiritual texts – whether they've actually read them or not. Particularly, they can begin to comprehend the Western, soul-spirit path that the Christ had to take to reveal the mystery of the Holy Spirit. That is the spirit capacity that permeates all spiritually striving people in the Western occult world, taking them through suffering and returning them anew to the consciousness of the life-radiant and heart-warm light inwardly and outwardly, regardless of religious, racial, cultural, or gender affiliation.

A more selfless perspective on Pearl suffering unfolds from a knowing inside them that seems vaster than simply thoughts, feelings, sense-world impressions, or opinion-based, societal beliefs. Mysterious capacities and necessary, individual rites and practices can reveal themselves to the suffering soul. Elder Pearls may still need help sometimes, due to past, unaddressed stigmans and missing pieces, to bring themselves safely and more whole into a renewed soul-spirit light with others, for our times.

By the ages of forty-nine and older, a disciplined practice of the anthroposophical Eight-Fold Path[19] of meditative focus can become a helpful support to those higher Pearl intuitions, imaginations, and inspirations. The six exercises[20] for patience, character, and insight into higher spiritual states of spiritual m*anas*, b*uddhi*, and a*tman*,[21] can begin to show a Pearl individual the connections to higher-world knowledge in natural and psychically safe ways. These understandings are related to higher Hindu, Buddhist, and other spiritual path understandings.

Maturing Pearls are often wholly capable of personal, spiritual understanding through their own efforts, with soul-groundedness, a purified emotional life, an ability to stand alone if necessary, and the ability to experience greater tolerance with others with a sense of compassionate connection with the very human condition of all people of the world.

With supportive community to both call on and support, this maturing Pearl can recover some lawful life forces and experience the humble, inner stability of ego-I strength that need not tip over into unbalanced egoism. They can be seen for more of their higher selves, soaking up some of the missing earlier developmental pieces and coming anew into later spiritual processes. They can prepare better for the life denouement stages toward death than perhaps their early life prepared them for younger adult life, and become part of the wholesome stream of others assisting youngers toward life, and elders toward the death passage, with love, patience and empathy. Pearls can experience more of their true soul incarnation purpose while moving closer toward their end-of-life excarnation process. This "recovery" can bring the most precious embrace of spirit for Pearls, having experienced a healing that can be truly miraculous to the soul and healing aspects that they may have never been safely able to open to prior, including positive states of love, truth, and compassion.

The unique developmental considerations for a grounded, loving, and upright *incarnating* human being, from infancy through middle childhood, and into the full sun-life of the early and middle adult years, are much different than the needs of a person focused on *excarnation* later in elder, adult life. The levels of this vast human spectrum become very apparent after the late forties. Highly traumatized, older Pearls, who have not had the appropriate healings and support, often relate more to the excarnating or dying stages of life. In these Christ-consciousness times, their healing needs can be helped and tailored by therapists and community members by bringing about experiences wherein they can retrieve some aspects of missed life development and awareness while being given allyship and support in later life spiritual development.

In the West, the holistic, well-developed, incarnating and excarnating human being, noticeable often in their wise, gracious, and reasonably self-sufficient, elder stature, is someone who has used the knowledge and karmic experiences of earlier life development to enliven further goodness on the earth together with others. From midlife into the elder years, that person turns to higher understandings of a universal and selfless spiritual nature.

That person in older age addresses the "downsizing" period of life denouement and retirement. A person begins to focus on excarnation into the heavenly worlds where an ego will have no bearing except for what the human being has instilled in the soul through higher I discernment, personal responsibility toward others, and actions of goodwill on the earth.

Elder Development and Eastern Excarnating Practices

Some Eastern spiritual practices promote the excarnating life perspective, which is most appropriate for elders who have reached the Life Spirit development stage, throughout a lifetime. It is seen in the yogi who feels longing and desire for life beyond the earth, based on an ascetic consciousness and early religious understandings of clairvoyant memory. Yoga reflects a time when human beings deeply experienced themselves as being at one with gods that were external to them.

True Eastern yogis believe that excarnation is the prime focus of life. They live for an individual but renunciate life, or they lead a group of student souls, wishing for perfected ascendance in practices that can help them reach the *atman* state in time and not incarnate any more. They tend to live quite austerely.

This is not the same for most Western yogis, who have a great deal of wealth supporting their lives and who do yoga more for health and well-being. Western yogis benefiting from a Western-world materialistic occult life have a different process that can get tricky to navigate today with appropriate soul clarity and responsibility. In the future, all true spirit practitioners, of all denominations, will become more resonant with the highest state of *atman*, and differences between paths, and even soul regions in the world, will begin to disappear.

In Eastern yoga, nondistinct elders have cultivated a sense of unity through a patient, egoless life led by following and serving leaders with higher developed egos, or through simplistic and mutual, indistinct soul disciplines in spiritual, living communities such as ashrams. Most excarnation-focused people are not able to speak as fully formed I-beings. Since they have a longing desire to leave the earth as completely as possible and not to reincarnate, their effects on younger souls arriving onto the earth, to carry out incarnating soul functions and development, must be discerned carefully. Some true, higher gurus in the East can do this for others in the lineage of their soul path.

People leading poor or immature Eastern practices in the Western soul regions of Europe and North America can cultivate dangerous dependence in others, while promoting themselves as having the ultimate guiding eye of the false master. Sadly, people have been quite harmed spiritually by some cult spiritual types who set up elaborate systems of spiritual practices and gatherings that turn out to be abusive and unfree. This happens also in some Christian-based faith groups. Pearl elders must be supported and also very discerning when deciding how to manage their elder spiritual life.

Although, ultimately, we all excarnate into the heavenly worlds for a time, and all souls will eventually leave the earth, some Eastern practices of old entice the devotee not to think for themselves in life and not to seek any individual life expression. Some Christian-promoted systems walk the slippery-slope line with this also. Spiritual organizations that offer practical supports to their members but without the freedom to come and go in the regular world as they choose, or groups that espouse absolutist theory that leaves no room for an evolution of conscious, individual thought, are the most dangerous in the West in these times.

Pure, mature, selfless, and universally minded spiritual practitioners, who can help run practical communities for and with others without infringing on members' free choice, are rarely found today, even in the east. That is because the I-nature in individuals is still developing, even in otherwise very astute, spiritually devoted people. Although many Westerners go to the East in their late life to live in intentional spiritual ashrams and the like, most are run today by independent thinkers who choose to function interdependently, with several leaders of conscience practicing spiritual and karmic discernment together and fostering more capacity and development in others. Many help people who are poor, sick, and dying.

Since the excarnation-oriented person living in the West, and away from Eastern altruistic life, may lack a voice in life, such a person can also lack sufficient means for taking care of their practical survival needs in the Western or Eastern worlds. This is especially so if they chose a turn in their path that doesn't fit the Eastern-minded community because it is not a truly universally oriented community. This suggests reasons why anthroposophically-based, cosmopolitan, and Michaelic communities for intergenerational living, working in Threefold ways, is important for our times, throughout the world.

If leaders in undeveloped organizations strive for higher states of spiritual development, their words may repeat what the master or guru has spoken in the past, rather than reflecting the present moments and needs. They do not necessarily reflect the individual, moral, and spiritual learnings that have come through their own unique and far-reaching activity in the world, or from taking personal responsibility for harms done to others. They may not reflect universal perspectives in their thinking, and they can relegate real soul development to a secondary place to spiritual development.

That does not mean that their efforts are never good or not bringing them along to greater development, in time. It does show, however, the challenges and dangers for elder Pearls who join Eastern excarnation communities due the lack of more developed Christ-consciousness communities in the West so far.

Elder Western-World Practices of Incarnation

Almost in polarity to Eastern soul life, the requirements of incarnate soul practices in peoples of the West have the purpose of developing full, individually responsible capacities. With that full I development, a person can more freely enter whatever regions of universal and relational experience and understanding the soul deems for itself to be necessary for the fulfillment of their calling or destiny on the earth. An elder Pearl may see later life as a time for working out the karma of past lives, as well as working to prevent the accumulation of unhelpful karma for a future one.

The challenges and dangers in Western soul life occur when the individual falls into the egoistic distortions of applying spiritual truths to earthly sensual desires and heavy materialistic-mechanical attachments. However, karmic restitution is always available if the individual applies their will strongly enough to work for redemption. This depends on the strength of the real ego-I development in that individual. It can be harder to do as one gets older, due to waning energies.

Elder age, in this case, can involve spiritual learning while making up for harms done in one's lifetime when one had less time to pay attention to one's karma because of work life, child-raising, or other family and societal duties. The more realized the soul, the more a person will have been making amends and adjusting along the way in life. The elder works toward softening the heart, and developing creativity and a greater sense for compassionate action, while the mind works toward naturally alleviating pain as much as possible as the body crystalizes more due to aging and dying issues.

If a Pearl elder has had the opportunity to find an anthroposophical living community that understands Pearl issues and is supportive, this elder can free up some time and energy to review life in a backward order, to clean up some awareness of what their individual life has meant to others, as if looking back toward others from the spiritual world with a freed heart and soul and without too many strains on the body. Anthroposophical doctors living in intentional, anthroposophical living communities can help elders with the physical body adjustments of aging and dying.

The Pearl can contemplate the ancestors who have earlier passed the threshold of death with a greater interest regarding what one's own life has done to help further the understandings, skills, and capacities of other family members and loved ones here and across the threshold. The Pearl can even begin to imagine what tasks have been hard or impossible to take up this lifetime and to consider what the Pearl might need to take up in the next life.

The fullness of the adult development ages and stages, including elder incarnation and excarnation developments and needs, are not directly taught to developing children in Waldorf schools or anthroposophical communities, as it is not appropriate for the early, incarnating child or youth. Nor is it necessarily appropriate for young adults and new parents, who are not yet into the Consciousness Soul stage of life where the considerations of the later stages or the denouement years of life are not in right timing for them personally.

If tragedy, crisis, trauma, or grief-filled loss stirs their souls earlier to higher understandings, healthy processing will usually bring those interests to a settled and less conscious place for a while. In that way, appropriate soul-development stages can work in more lawful rhythm and timing.

Unfolding Human Development

The coming chapters distinctly discuss different child and adult development stages, starting with questions for counselors and caregivers to ask about the Pearls in their care regarding the seven life processes. Specific input is offered regarding Pearls, followed by biographies of Pearls at different ages and stages who have experienced Waldorf or anthroposophical life.

Birth – 7: Habits, Routines, Traditions, and Physical-Sensual Explorations

A time of vastly envigorated formative forces working in the child, often imperceptible, needing caregivers who offer protective holding, gentleness, sensitivity, beauty, color, naturalness, well-patterned habits and rhythms, and the patience to support a child's undisciplined exploration.

Seven Life and Learning Processes Check-in:

How does observation evolve in the infant and toddler? How is the small child breathing within the environments and with the primary caregivers and immediate family members? Does the child tend to be in a natural, relaxed breathing, allowed to flow with a naturally observing and interacting pace? Or is the child consistently in stress, with breath either too short, held in, or too exhaustively outflowing?

Parents hold the early life of the child by establishing safe, predictable, and trustworthy habits for life. This includes regular meals at times of the day that work in harmony with natural circadian laws of human biological functioning. For instance, the body is known to digest, assimilate, and distribute food nourishment better after seven o'clock in the morning, in mid-afternoon, and prior to ten o'clock in the evening. Eating at other times of the day can cause strain on the body's organs and chemical/hormonal rhythms.

At other times, the body is resting, repairing, or cleansing its organs for the next round of digestion, assimilation, and distribution. This works differently in an infant than a toddler or older child, yet the processes themselves are working into natural daylight and night-time rhythms.

People the world over tend to eat in some level of rhythm with the daylight and nighttime. They have meals in the morning, often at noon, and later, a few hours before going to sleep for the night. When young children go to bed early and at regular bedtimes, allowing digestion and physical body repair to happen naturally, as well as allowing the ego and astral body to let go into higher realms during sleep, children experience greater whole energy, better moods, and lifelong physical, etheric, astral, and I-being health support. These habits are established early for the child through the parents' own patterns of good habits and healthy self-care disciplines. Habit formation is key for young children and a significant task of the first seven years of life.

Habit Life Pulled from Under, and the De-Scaffolding of the Will

It is common for Pearl Children to have confusion around the basic kinds of habits and routines that serve to stabilize their lives and the lives of other children and families.[22] If, for instance, in the case of a single-parent custody agreement where one parent has visitation rights, the live-in parent may set up habits and routines while the other parent lets those habits, routines, or rules go undisciplined.

Even if this easing up of home rules is perceived by a weekend parent, or the infrequently visiting parent, to be a kind response because that parent is trying to make up for some of the hardship of the divorce on the child, it is not good for the child. Internally the child begins to distrust or disregard habits or routines in general that normally offer growing children a rooted, structured sense of safety and well-being.

Re-instilled, well-kept habits can be destroyed later if another significant trauma retriggers old divorce distrust in the child. The opposite experience can also happen, wherein the child becomes compulsive or obsessive about keeping routines and habits in an attempt to "hold on" in the face of loss. The child can lose self-regulation then if someone attempts to ameliorate the child's obsessiveness.

Bringing authentic discipline to young children in an antagonistic divorce can be discouraging for each parent. Without diligence, it can establish a strategic game-field for parents' blaming stances toward each other when child behavior problems arise. It can also set up harsh criticism or violence against the children when they exhibit characteristics of the opposing parent.

This can be the beginning of a very destructive soul experience for the children in the middle, seeding the roots of confusion, as well as literally an inwardly felt experience of assault on the child's sense of safety, internal rhythm, and justice.

Early habit life routines for young children are known to become internalized for years later. Many child-development researchers, including anthroposophical practitioners and researchers, consider the habits of early childhood to be formative for the rest of that person's life.[23] A continually deconstructed and reformed, or a casually implemented and loosely upheld habit life for a young child of divorce, due to parental disagreements, can cause a child to have a consistently triggered, insecurely established sense of attachment to both parents, or to anyone. Sadly, for some Pearls, that can carry over later to social life, work life, and earth life, in general.

In anthroposophical understandings, the habits of childhood help the evolving human being to incarnate well on the earth and manifest a proper footing to realize one's destined path. With insecure habits, incarnation is uncertain, and the destiny of the soul's path can become completely obscured and missed. It is a damaging issue for all of society when souls cannot fulfill their spiritual contract in life.

In her book, *Putting Children First*,[24] Joanne Pedro-Carroll notes that this insecurity in a child's psyche can lead to an outer sense of lack of control, which then manifests as poor socialization in school or social interactions. The child experiences shame, humiliation, and isolation. For some children, if unchecked in adolescence, this can lead to deeply troubled actions and rebellions, with a disregard for authority overall, as well as a complete disinterest in or even awareness of healthy self-care.

Directed activities cultivated early in a child's life offer confidence. Through that stability, a child can build personal character and test themself safely in relationship with people in that child's generational group and in the bigger world. Self-protective and life-affirming inner modalities are developed through habits that can be modified through experience when the child has developed fuller capacities in early adulthood.

As children get older, some routines and habits can change in a healthy way. A child can have a later bedtime at fourteen years old than at seven. The youth may not do as many chores at home at seventeen years old because the youth works a part-time job two evenings a week and has music practice on a third evening. That Pearl Youth also has a need to spend time with friends some afternoons or stay late at school to work on projects.

When one parent negates the reasoning for why the other parent has allowed some habit changes in the child's life, without finding a compromise with that parent, then it is often the child in between who has to do the more complicated negotiating. Ex-spouses can work to blatantly destroy a child's sense of "common" sense about the child's needs and habits, since neither parent is working in "common" with the other to sense out the truest and most whole needs of the child.

This can cause the child to become a sophisticated juggler of circumstance before the child's nervous system can develop executive functioning authentic to such sophisticated and politically complicated reasoning. The child can hit a wall inside instead of coping, and then rebels and does whatever the youth feels will shake one or both parents up, even if it means unconsciously hurting or resorting to self-harming. If the political battlefield nature of the parent's responses continues, the child could end up in chronic, distrust-based, behavioral difficulties.

A consistently destabilized habit life in the child-development years can destroy any personal sense of self-dominion and leave the child, youth, or early adult chasing outer idols, ganging up with others, or "crashing" into psychological or physical disease. Triggered, disruptive memories from consistent destabilization can so badly veil the Pearl's capacities that the youth is often regressed in a younger child development state, often noticeable in a little girl or little boy voice. Pearls of various ages can flutter in the winds of others' desires, actions, and intentions,[25] if no authentic and trustworthy habit base is set in unconscious memory.

Some of these children, in adulthood, know that they want to feel inwardly connected in rhythm with themselves, others, and the natural rhythms of nature. Soul memory from past lives can help hold important soul-knowing in their inner consciousness. Pearls, like anyone else, need to feel like, and actually be, accepted as integral members of the collaborative effort of life with others. Yet, they don't feel obliged to give themselves over to anyone in soul-destructive ways. They've simply been through too much soul destruction already in childhood. Some others, however, never gain a grip on healthy awareness for themselves. Most fall somewhere in the middle. Habit support develops trust and habit destruction leaves little upon which to found one's trust.

Since many parents of divorce have tried to tip or weigh their child's favor toward themselves by tearing away at the beliefs of the other parent, or by letting the child choose whatever he or she wanted to do too often. They find it hard later to take responsibility when they hear from the child that the child felt abandoned.

The young person was left to make decisions without fully developed capacities. Too young to meet issues with full forces, to foresee problems, or to discern consequences appropriately, the Pearl as an adult can struggle to know what moral, and ethically well-negotiated behavior between people is. What I call "regulation-abandoned" children may or may not be able to glean a real sense of what "healthy" or "regulated" actually feels like.

This is especially so if they are left only to their own instincts in uninspiring social landscapes, poorly planned and architected city streets, toxic buildings, eating genetically modified or denatured food, indiscriminately listening to music or noise, regularly exposed to overly bright lights, or addicted to television, tablets, mobile phones, and computer games.

Without harmonious habits, environments, and sleep, a child cannot grow into an adult with a sustainable and fully functional life rhythm. This can double the inner sense of lack and spin the psyche into a decompensated nightmare.[26] Life literally feels like hell. Too often, this is when medications are prescribed, or the Pearl Adult is essentially forced into eating disorders or substance use or abuse to numb and bring stillness to the chaos and pain.

Ages 7 – 14: Etheric Life Forces: Imagination

Forces that worked extensively to form the physical body of the child in earlier years are now, from years seven to fourteen, more freed to allow the child to begin to explore, imaginatively, the social and practical world of a child-oriented school (or home-schooling) community. They begin to practice how human life in the world is functioning in relationship to natural resources and other children, and what they can create with them be it through growing a garden, crafting, making plays out of stories, drawing figures and painting or sculpting, and dancing patterns together. Basic, lawful disciplines associated with mathematics, reading, and sciences structure a child's life more, but through the still tender, formative imaginations of nature's elements and rhythms, and through more sophisticated social experiences, for instance, in games and musical instrument work with others.

Seven Life and Learning Processes Check-in:

How is this child relating to the new surroundings of grade school and other children who are also meeting discipline in a new way? Does the child behave as if feeling safe and trusting with others? If not, what are the extra little moments, check-ins, or haven times that the child may need to process grief, frustration, fear, or even tiredness creatively?

Is the child too tired at times when other children are energetically warming up to activities of the day? How can the child be included in the activity while being respected for the need for less stringency and more restfulness or relaxation in the learning time? How does the Pearl warm up to new activities, transitions in the day, and conflicts between other children? Does the child need a warm, transition food or drink upon arriving at school, or after leaving the classroom?

Can the Pearl express normal fears and worries through questions about what is happening, or does the child become aggressive, compulsive, or shut down when experiencing other children's social conflicts? How can this Pearl be helped to calm nerves in ways that seem like play, and even like enjoyable learning?

What calming sounds does this Pearl need to hear or create and take into memory? What scents, textures, or elements does the child need to spend some immediate or transitional time with?

Is the Pearl getting imaginative time in places that allow safety? How is the light in the room affecting the child and does the Pearl need some rebalancing colors to focus on for a portion of the day?

General Transitions and Developmental Stage Transitions

A practice that I call *transition-therapy*, evolving from Western psychology studies, anthroposophical remedial-curative indications, and my experience as a Pearl myself, can have supportive and healing effects for children of divorce.

In Chapter Two, we saw how transitional needs can focus on the seven life processes, right down to how the child is helped to "warm" the inner senses while leaving home for school from one parent's residence and then making their way after school to the other parent's home. Seen in contrast through the following lemniscate images, the crossover period for a child leaving one parent's home/family to school, and on to the other parent's home/family after school, is relatively stabilizing when parents who are former spouses are mindfully working together in the co-parenting arrangement.

Figure 6.2: General Life Transitions Lemniscate

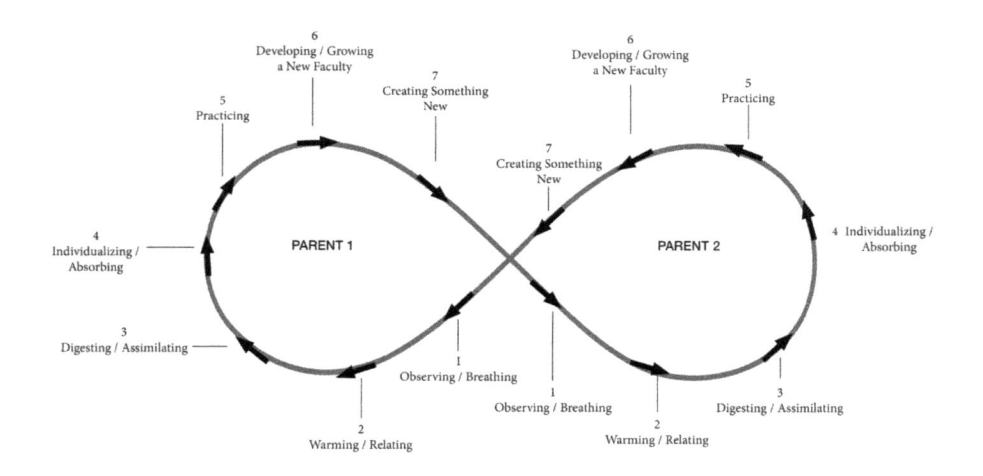

The Pearl and the Hut

Despite some stress level, the child's process, represented in the General Life Transitions Lemniscate, is flowing and mostly uninterrupted. It can be gauged as similar to when a child felt some normal nervousness on the way from school to stay at a grandparents' house overnight. The smells and décor of the home and the routines of the elders may seem familiar but somewhat different to the child's, or the Pearl may find the grandparent's barking dog annoying compared to his quiet family cat. With the cooperative and sensitive adult family members attending to the child's needs and fears, these stressors are low-grade and don't inhibit the sense of being attended to and safe. The atmosphere and the soul sense between the adults do not hold significant destructive tone or any gesture of non-acceptance. The child feels secure and loved.

These small contractive adjustments are dissimilar to those we saw in Chapter Three, in the experience of Pearls whose parents resonate conflict.

In the cooperative model of parents raising children in a respectful, co-parenting situation, the child in general life transitions, even if they are somewhat stressful and bring some emotionally triggering periods of adjustment and anxious feelings, is supported and attended to by each parent effectively. These periods are addressed by parents using the seven life processes to check in about what might be challenging the child's ability to adjust. In this case, the child, with no sense of threat because the child has experienced respect and stability from the parents and has not had adult-level conflicts or tensions brought upon the child, can smoothly move into the sense of safe and expansive space of child-level interests in either home. The child may have had to overcome minor adjustments or moments of awkwardness but innately trusts the support of each parent to help them manage the transition.

Figure 6.3: Child High/Low Cross

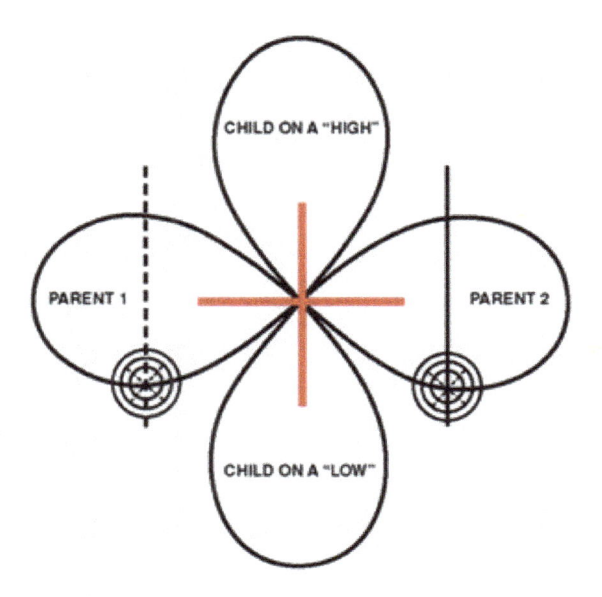

When a co-parented child's transitions between parent homes are met with hard, conflictual or judgmental stances in the parents (represented on the transition lemniscate by the circles with xs inside), the child suffers from adult-level issues and soul abuses. When both parents offer such conflictual responses, even if they think they are covering it up somewhat, the tenderly growing child can experience trauma triggering. This destabilizes the insecurely attached child even more, and can begin an inner soul pattern of unconscious stress that sets the child's neurological window of tolerance into sweepingly toxic highs and lows.

This may not be initially perceived by the parents because the child works unconsciously to protect against parent harms, hiding what is actually happening inwardly. The child cannot yet have consciousness of what is happening inside, but seeks safety first. The child experiences inward extreme needs for excitement or escape, and/or low dives of depressive mood and a loss of will to cooperate or desire naturally joyful experiences. Some children end up in a constant state of protectiveness that exhausts them later in life.

When a child, who is transitioning between parent homes in a divorced parent situation, is met at one home or both homes with blatant or insidious expressions of criticism, judgment, or outright conflict against the other parent, the child can not transition appropriately psychologically. The child's soul-psyche registers threat. The child may directly experience criticism from one parent about how they are acting, having been under the influence of the other parent, or they may experience the hardened boundary being projected toward them in a superficially covered way.

Children register far more inwardly than is often in a parent's awareness. The child innately experiences the injustice toward them but has no safety or capacity to do anything about it. The natural soul tendency will be to escape the injustice, by acting out, or by hiding away or stuffing down feelings that then energetically cause a depression of the child's spirits or will forces. The child jumps high or low inwardly or outwardly.

This is so even if the parent moves out of the conflictual stance and applies the seven life processes afterward, particularly if one or both parents bring this resistant stance to the returning child regularly.

Child-of-Divorce Balance or Distortion Chart Series (CoDBoD Charts)

The Child-of-Divorce Balance or Distortion Charts (CoDBoD Charts) below show the differences between child stability when parents cooperate well in the home, and when parents work through conflicted divorces.

The colorful backgrounds of the charts show colors associated in anthroposophical child-development theory with ages and stages of development. Chart 6.2 simply familiarizes the reader with those stages, the grades associated with each color and stage, and the soul sheaths that are opening at the different stages: physical, etheric, astral, and ego-I.

The seven stages outlined in the CoDBoD Chart here represent the developmental milestones for the child soul through the school years. Each is outlined according to a child's school grades, going from ages 3 – 7 for kindergarten and ending in a generalized category for the adolescence years, corresponding with the full development of the ego-I. At the bottom of the chart are references to the twelve senses that are being fully developed in the stages of life in accordance with children's ages.

Colors here are esoteric, highlighting the underlying soul nature of color influences on the grade-school years and the children's ages. Red is grounding and stabilizing, orange-vermillion stimulates joy and a sense of creative care-giving toward the other, yellow is energizing and inspires the imaginative adventurer toward creative initiative, green embues the heart with both strength and tenderness, blue supports a cooler sense of conceptual thinking, and purple-violet is altruistic and compassionate for the sake of all.

Chart 6.4i: The Child of Divorce Balance or Distortion Charts (CoDBoD Charts), Backdrop -- Developmental transition stages according to anthroposophical philosophy and pedagogy.

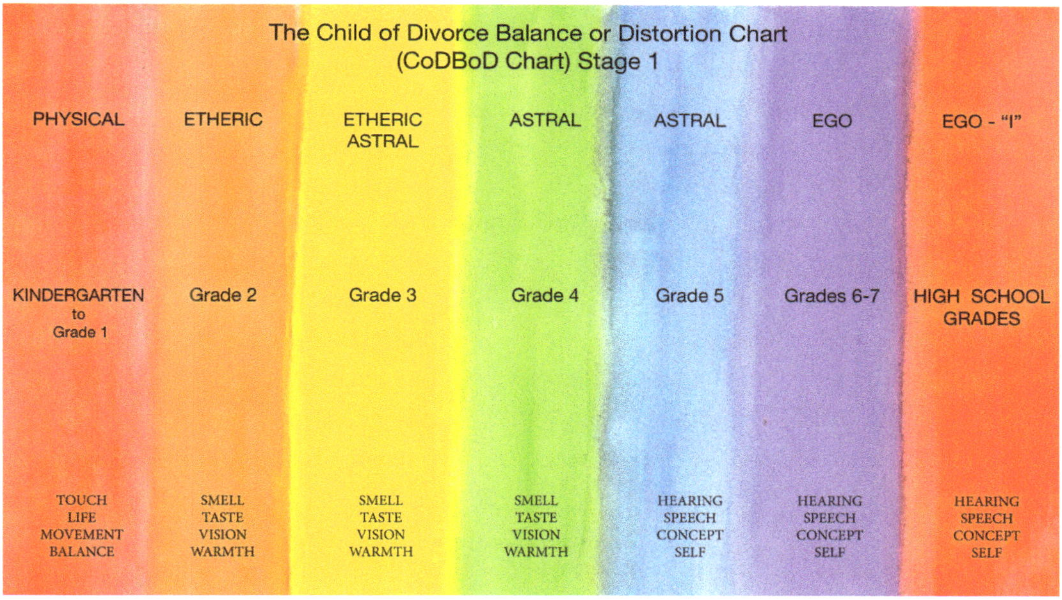

			The Child of Divorce Balance or Distortion Chart (CoDBoD Chart) Stage 1			
PHYSICAL	ETHERIC	ETHERIC ASTRAL	ASTRAL	ASTRAL	EGO	EGO - "I"
KINDERGARTEN to Grade 1	Grade 2	Grade 3	Grade 4	Grade 5	Grades 6-7	HIGH SCHOOL GRADES
TOUCH LIFE MOVEMENT BALANCE	SMELL TASTE VISION WARMTH	SMELL TASTE VISION WARMTH	SMELL TASTE VISION WARMTH	HEARING SPEECH CONCEPT SELF	HEARING SPEECH CONCEPT SELF	HEARING SPEECH CONCEPT SELF

The Child-of-Divorce Balance or Distortion Charts (CoDBoD Charts) Backdrop shows the anthroposophical ages and stages of school-age children prior to high school. Each imperfectly defined age and stage is given an esoteric color to represent it, just as each Waldorf classroom is painted in a corresponding esoteric color. Each color suggests the recapitulation of the human consciousness stage associated with that age and stage of the child.

For instance, the kindergarten and grade one children are still in the fairytale consciousness and a gentle, soft consciousness with little ego. This is similar to the Indian cultural epoch, when little color was perceived by human beings except a kind of hazy rose color. Grade two corresponds with the Persian epoch when another color, vermillion was perceptible as was a sense of a more joyful and careful exploration of the world around oneself.

Grade three reflects the mustard-yellow sense of the Egyptian epoch when human beings dug deeper into working the sun-drenched earth, green is grade four and the more impassioned-heart Greco-Roman period when humanity found itself balanced in a new ego, while blue is grade five and the Anglo-Germanic individuation color.

Violet is for a future, very spiritualized, Russian epoch and can correspond to grades six and seven, as children prepare for a high school future when altruism in cultivated more toward the end of the adolescent journey. High school stages are represented with the red again, as a recapitulation of a new grounding period into the adolescent years begins.

Chart 6.4ii: The Child of Divorce Balance or Distortion Charts (CoDBoD Charts), Overlay 1 -- A whole-family, child-development scenario, or a healthy seven life processes, co-parenting situation for a Pearl Child.

In this next representation of the CoDBoD Charts, Overlay 1, the purple line represents the child. Married parents, unmarried parents in stable relationships, or parents in respectful, mindful co-parenting, are shown as green and orange lines. Although the parents move toward and away from each other in natural, relationship individuation and breathing, they come together regularly and consistently on the important matters. The child's life is stabilized by the parents' processes of coming together and affirming routines, habits, cooperative decision-making, and loving attention to the children and to each other.

The purple child line shows the steadying and calming effects that attentive parents bring into the child's unconscious to support the child's whole growth and development. In a divorced, co-parenting situation, this steadiness is still generally possible, with each parent cooperating and keeping sensitive to the child's seven life processes. (Lines and transition points are deliberately imperfect to reflect the organically human nature of transitions and developments.)

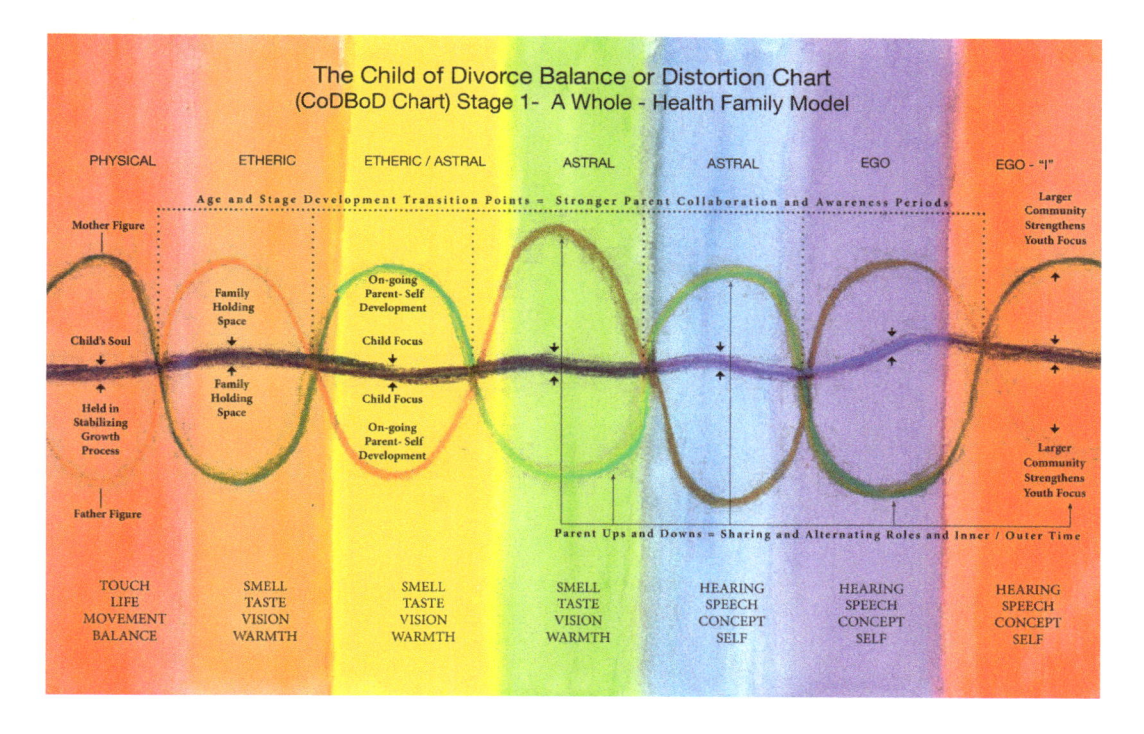

[Chart: The Child of Divorce Balance or Distortion Chart (CoDBoD Chart) Stage 1 – A Whole-Health Family Model]

The Child of Divorce Balance or Distortion Charts (CoDBoD Charts), Overlay 1, shows a stabilizing process for children who's parents work respectfully and compassionately to mitigate child stressors through the child development years. Parents work to keep developmental transitions and life challenges at a child-appropriate level as they develop their own increasing sense of individuation and autonomy, increasing the inter-dependent nature of family. The child can trust a protected growth period, especially through the years up until later adolescence.

Chart 6.4iii: The Child of Divorce Balance or Distortion Charts (CoDBoD Charts), Overlay 2 -- A child's development caught in the unsteadying influences of parent conflicts during and after divorce.

The Child of Divorce Balance or Distortion Charts (CoDBoD Charts), Overlay 2, shows disturbing distortions that begin to happen when parents who divorce can't cooperate or tame antipathies toward each other for the sake of their own development and the child's.

The child, represented by the purple line, experiences unsteadying divorce conflict between parents. One parent (green line), experiences strong emotional upheaval, seeking support while forcefully protecting the child and fighting to have the child follow certain life beliefs and strategies. That parent's emotional presence to the child convinces the child that they are more understood with that parent, and the Pearl chooses to be with that parent for now.

The other parent (orange line), steps back to assess personally and to try not to distress the child further. That parent acts as a net below the child to catch the Pearl if they are falling into depressive or reactive behaviors in the presence of the other parent.

If the first parent's reactions become a set pattern of astral one-upmanship or escapism toward the other parent, the vulnerable child who is trying to stay close for emotional sustenance, can begin to feel emotional overload, abandonment, or even depression. The child may voice a desire to connect more with the other, seemingly steadier, or more available parent. That parent may seem more stable due to being without much of the parenting responsibility so far. The child's connection moves down to the orange line.

The second parent, perhaps in connection with a social system, attempts to raise the child up from depression, making life at home light and happy, with many fun things to do. That parent may appear to the child to be cooperative with the other parent during court hearings, although behind the scenes, that parent fights for exclusive or increased access to the child. If the second parent wins access, there could be more parent infighting on a subtle level. If that parent loses, the child is further destabilized by not being able to be with the other parent who on the surface, or from memory or in the child's imagination, may seem more enjoyable to be with.

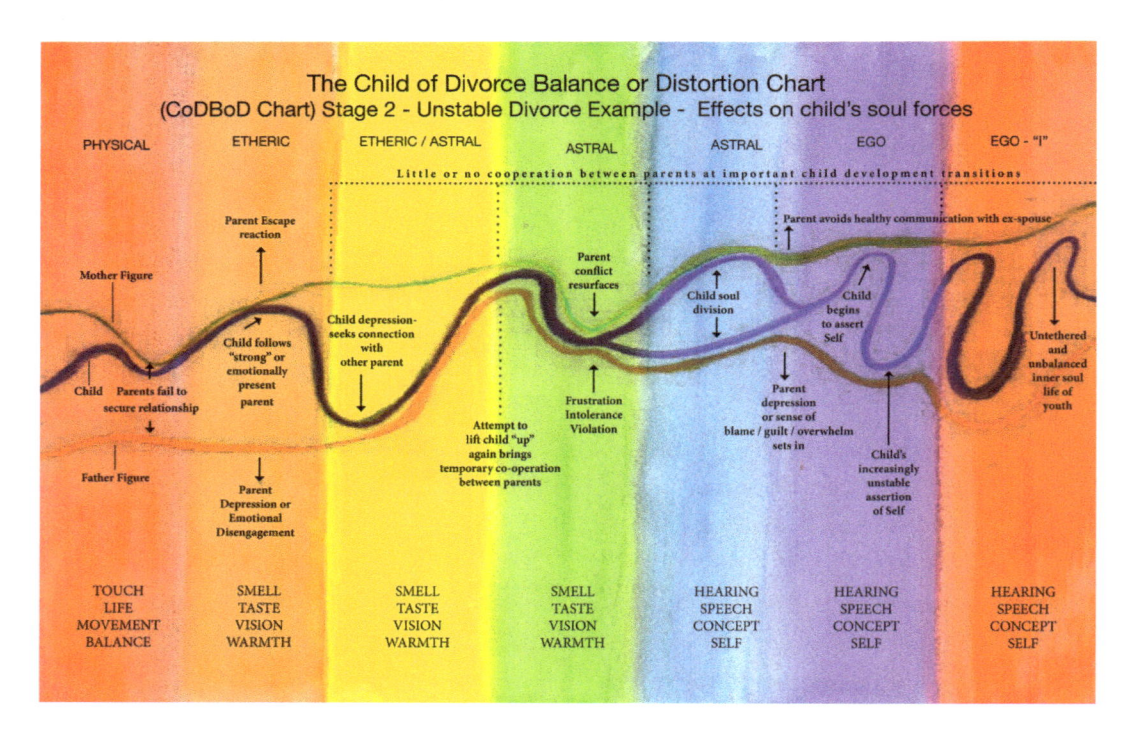

The Child of Divorce Balance or Distortion Charts (CoDBoD Charts), Overlay 2, shows the destabilized child in a divorced parent situation where parents are not cooperating or managing co-parenting well. The child becomes a wavering, destabilized soul force following the mood swings of the adult parents. The child/youth is unable to incarnate appropriately within a growthful, child-level family environment. Without appropriate stabilizing forces that allow the child/youth to be back in appropriate child-level development, the child/youth will mimic adult-level soul-psyche processes until he or she burns out on some mental, emotional, or physical level.

To avoid this and numb or escape the pain, or to try to find a childhood again, the child/youth may run away from home, get involved with manipulative people who seem to have his or her best interests at heart while introducing the child/youth to drugs or other additive or dangerous practices, or may fail to function well at school or in other social environments. All of the dangers of being an alienated, "lost" soul can set in if societal supports don't catch the child/youth in the struggle to reclaim missing childhood stability and relational pieces.

Often, at some point after legal battles, a parental conflict flare-up arises based on past, unresolved issues. Neither parent takes up the conflict from a new place of tolerance, understanding, and humane acceptance toward the other. The child feels soulfully split now. The child may also be in other natural, childhood development challenges at the same time. The Pearl experiences overwhelm in many, fourfold ways.

What is naturally an awkward time for any child in development transitions can become a point of neglect for this child. The parents are too busy hashing out their ingrained adult-conflict issues. The child is not strongly soul-developed to individuate fully from either parent yet. The Pearl is struggling out of some early, conscious awareness that they are not getting the appropriate support from either parent. The Pearl experiences a split in parent loyalties and attention. The child is drawn out and away from personal development and can literally experience moments of psychic splitting, even to the level of schizoid psychosis.

Finally, at later stages of development, if the parents can't bring some cooperative harmony between them, the child's inner resourcing is lost, and the Pearl is not incarnate enough with a wholesome inner constitution, to meet new child development stages in steadying and strengthening ways. The Pearl's behavior can become highly troubled and even erratic.

If the Pearl's parents armor their positions and different expectations of the child, and if the child has no other strongly objective adult who can hold important wisdom and support, the Pearl becomes frozen, or on the other polarity, highly reactive.

The Pearl may not at first seem so disturbed, since school frameworks and other social systems may be holding the child together. The Pearl is, however, consciously or unconsciously deeply aware of the loss, neglect, and abandonment of peace and love in the family. Authentic fortitude is replaced with distrust and displayed in the child in a wavering, high-and-low existence. The older child's ability to self-regulate emotion, and to use executive planning and self-concept to mature into a full ego-I being, experiencing natural confidence in the child's own life decisions, can be seriously undermined. The Pearl's mental, emotional, or even physical judgment can get very risky.

Adolescent Transition Risk

One of the hardest developmental stage transitions for the Pearl Child can be from the pre-adolescent developmental stage, ages 12 – 14, into full adolescence from ages 14 – 21. Soul movements then, between antagonistic parents, can be like tightrope walking or stepping on emotional landmines.

Figure 6.5i and 6.5ii: Review of the child at risk crosses

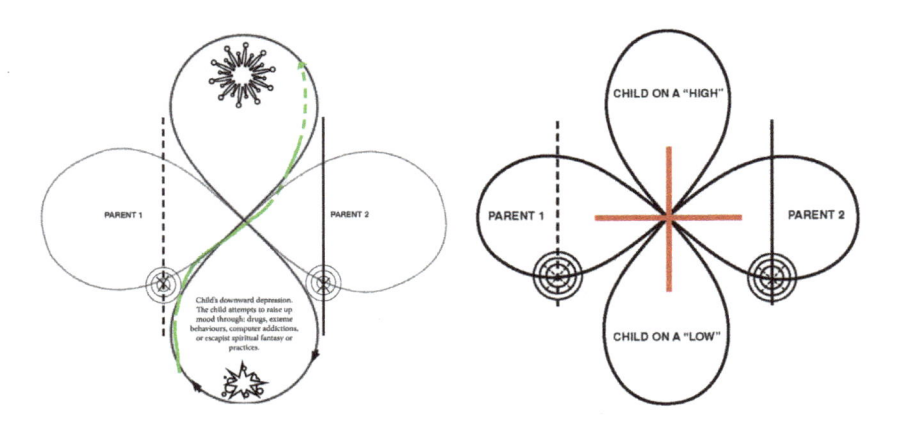

Referring to Figures 3.17 and 3.18 from Chapter Three, at the cross-stage where a natural contraction regularly happens in Pearl life, a Pearl Youth who is psyching themself up to move from one more comfortable parent environment/experience to a less known or less warm experience with the other, might endure a harsh and harmful contraction in the youth's already unsteady soul.

The youth may face any number of hindrances to normal processes, including an emotional blockage that shuts down creative thinking, sparks roller-coaster emotional volatility, or even lead to a serious physical or psychic crisis.

A Pearl Youth may be in a situation of crossing over to the other parent's home while needing to know how to trace the seven life processes alone inwardly. Until now, the parent may have been loosely holding that process. At the father's house, for instance, if routines and understandings are disordered and less harmonious to the youth's needs than at the mother's home, the Pearl's own natural, pre-adolescent state of disorder at times can seriously throw off the parent home transitions and seven life processes attunement. (This could happen the other way, moving from more harmony with the father to more awkwardness and a less orderly or trustworthy experience the mother's place.)

It is important to be reminded how important a sense of sanctuary or a hut space is, even for adolescents, in each home. In adolescence, this is especially so when life outside of home can feel the opposite of sanctuary on a regular basis.

With poorly attending parents, the frustrated Pearl Youth, who never feels fully safe with the parents' tensions, may try to fight, or vehemently negotiate with one parent or the other to override a firm boundary set by one or another parent, so that the tired youth does not have to re-attune natural processes all over. This is something that an adolescent can inwardly register as deeply unfair and energy-consuming. There is a natural tiredness in adolescence due to the major growth and transformation process happening physically, mentally, and emotionally.

Sadly, this fighting to keep a sense of self-order in the homes of one's divided parents is common for Pearl teens. Outside of the home, Pearls are very often highly sensitive about what is different in them compared to what they notice as more relaxed, whole-family youths in their peer group, although they may not be able to express their discomfort in words.

Lofty Neglect

Another difficult lemniscate scenario that seems prevalent for Pearls, in developmental stage transitions, is when everyone involved tries to not notice or address complex feelings in the teens in the crossing over between parent home periods. Parents might think that they are being super-kind with the normally disorganized and awkward pre-adolescents or teens. Yet, the youths can feel that the adults are being superficial about their needs. Or, they are so numb, they are on limited function mode in one or more important areas of development.

Adults often find talking with pre-adolescents hard anyway, and with Pearl teens, it can be extra awkward due to the often-troubled feelings those teens deal with regarding their family. A dissociative and disincarnate confusion, uncertainty, or even light-headedness can arise in the youth that the young person neither understands nor can cope with when adults try to stay cool to match their energy. They actually need an adult who can really warm up to what they are experiencing.

In this scenario, while everyone gives everyone else space to not feel conflictual and to try to honor the adjustment issues, the risk is that the youth can inwardly feel like a floating balloon, suspending some natural life processes in an airy way. No one is willing to fully adjust to the youth enough to bring the balloon back and anchor the strings well in a warm, balanced, and soul-nurturing way. Everyone's behaving as if they are on eggshells for the Pearl's sake, but it's not really what the youth needs or wants.

A counselor or counseling group can help the pre-teen to "portage" through the new age-and-stage transition. This is done through biographies, arts, and some practical craft related to the child's changing likes and dislikes. Much work can be needed in supporting the child to cope with organizational tasks without feeling low about themself when adolescent biological issues cause the best efforts at organization to get scattered. Coaching with humor, consistency, and helping the child with resilient self-forgiveness is important. Preparing the Pearl's parents for the specifically awkward adolescence of Pearls is also important.

A female child growing into pre-adolescence who has little connection to the mother in the divorce arrangement, and who easily transfers the need for feminine role modeling onto a female class teacher, could have real transition troubles when the pre-adolescent or middle-school youth moves to the more independent high school. If the parents can foresee this early enough, then the youth might need to see a counselor for a time before, during, and after the transition. The girl may need to be visiting with the high school teachers ahead of time, one-to-one, to feel welcomed and understood better through biography work. The youth may require help to form a relationship with a high school counselor, as well.

This Pearl Youth may benefit, six months before joining high school, from joining an outside group or team for young women, where the adults in charge are screened for their child-development understandings. A parent can enlist a counselor to help the child to identify the right kind of group or persons to get support from before the high school transition, based on Pearl Youth understandings. The youth can also be supported to ask the previous, middle-school teacher to offer some visitation time with the Pearl through the high school transition.

Creating a space in at least one home that represents a stepped-up studio-hut or haven of creative expression and comfort for the youth is helpful. Assisting the child to order and archive crafts, paintings, and projects created in the middle school or senior elementary school, during hut time, can provide time to talk about transitioning needs that the Pearl might be thinking or worrying about.

The thirteen-year-old boy who has an estranged relationship with his father, or who may be struggling with his gender orientation, may need a hut space that gives the opportunity to learn about meditation, creative expression, sexual diversity, or personal self-care. The youth might need a kind of hobby-shop space. The hut space of childhood needs to change for a teen. It needs to grow up, with some extra-level supports such as a good music system with favorite music, a video-system that is not necessarily fed to the internet, food, and anthroposophically designed, child-play therapy[27] features that reflect older youth interests.

These can include art materials, items to construct other items, such as jewelry tools, sculpting tools, driftwood, an adult easel with paints, stones, beads, crystals, copper-work tools and sheets of copper, old model-making materials, old electronics components to putz around with, colorful modeling wax, small metal pipes and metal clippers, fabrics and a sewing machine, soapstone for carving, clays and possibly a potter's wheel, writing journals, personally directed and recorded stories or songs from friends and family members, instruments, and a good sofa to chill on when tired.

Access to a full, backyard workshop for metal or woodwork is also a good hut space for any adolescent. Depending on one's resources, it could be a full sewing studio with space for friends to visit, a personal theater, or a greenhouse. Personal space in adolescence almost always involves having the opportunity to invite at least one friend into one's sanctuary space to have relaxation time with and to confide in. Unbiased, adult check-ins about this relationship can be meaningful as long as they are not intrusive or disrespectful.

Boundaries around hut use need to be negotiated respectfully between parent and adolescent. Parents of Pearl Youths can each strive to acknowledge the youth reverently but also in a connecting and well-incarnate way by planning invited meet-ups to visit the youth in the studio-hut, spending some time simply observing, listening, or affirming for the youth what they are doing, thinking, or feeling, without judgment. Introducing inspiring and responsible community members to meet up with the youth, to say hello, can mean a lot and can light some ideas and connections that foster growth.

Youths feel safer to reveal more of who they are and what they can offer to life when a parent can simply offer quiet, unconditional empathy and presence at important times. In divorce, when the parents can manage forgiveness and respect for the other's failings and struggles, the youth will in time not feel the need for so much studio-hut space for personal, healthy soul growth. The Pearl will have restored some confidence in love, in relationships, and with a foundation of personal creative capacities, work, and independent life skills.

This picture may seem frustratingly utopian or very energetically awkward and unmanageable to some divorced parents. This is partly because it places the higher conflict-resolution work on the adults, where it belongs, while leaving the youth in their own, age-appropriate processes and burdens. Yet the short-term years of discomfort for the parents can make the big difference to the child between a lifetime of distress, psychological imbalances, outer-life failures, and soul regressions, or a life of a developing, capable, and responsive adult.

The latter is one who can forgive with compassion and step up to life's hard issues with a determined will, personal creativity, and confidence. That Pearl can engage with others in social life and in the struggle of living a life that is more than just a base-line war and a jealous, survival battle.

The Parent's Reckoning

In time, many divorced parents come to some sense of what their own necessary hut time, or lack of reflective space and self-development time was all about, once they were away from their former spouse's concerns. Often, that is when they learn for themselves that the other partner was not fully responsible or to blame for the divorce or their discomforts. They also learned that their Pearl Child could not possibly meet what other children in whole families were doing without the loving and accepting supports of whole families. Once parents clean up their own issues, they can see their children's issues and needs much more clearly.

To manage an adult-life connection with their grown-up Pearl Adult in the future, parents may need ongoing hut time themselves, or opportunities to do their own work with counselors or mentors. They are going to need to rebuild a different relationship firmament with their Pearl Adult children. Adolescence was the kicking off point for a new consciousness regarding this human being before them. If they failed then, they're going to have to do significant repair work not to lose the Pearl Child completely.

If the youth's childhood had few stable habits, the rest of the life cannot be expected to match traditional soul-development expectations, unless the parent can provide healing reparation about the past and instill something better in the relationship now—while not infantilizing a grown adult Pearl. There is nothing simple about such a process, but with a strong heart will and a mature adult consciousness, it can be done.

Some questions for adults to ask if the divorce leaves the Pearl Youth exposed continually to a subtle war of wills between the parents:

- What whole elements in this youth have been inwardly disrupted and what must be rebuilt for sustainable health, including the youth's heart capacities, beyond just being strong and stoic?

- Is something in this divorce evolutionary and timely in the bigger picture of history, or is it all purely destructive or unfortunate? How can the Pearl Youth turn the adversities into strengths that can be realistically sustaining?

Clearly, many Pearls need some softer and kinder cushioning in their development because of the harsh extremes they have faced in their own family life. This is not saying, or stigmatizing, that the Pearls are looking for a cushy life. More is to be said later about this balancing, and the dichotomy between gentling and hardening in our times. For now, we know for certain that traumas need healing, and the following biographies, based on each developmental stage, can help adults involved in or on the sidelines of family divorce offer better support to Pearls and avoid unintentionally poking sharp objects into the Pearl's healing wounds.

Biography: Priya, Age 11: Second-Generation Pearl Child

Priya, at eleven years old, had been experiencing her parents' marital breakdown for four years. Two years ago, her father moved away from the family home. Her parents told her and her siblings that this arrangement was created so that her parents wouldn't fight any more. The news was brought to them with an age-appropriate story that her parents shared. Priya and her siblings had been witnessing physical and verbal fights, and insidious, soul-destructive comments between her parents over many years.

Each parent had worked individually and together in group therapies to overcome distrust and hostilities. They attributed some of that to what they themselves had witnessed growing up in the poor parental models of their own divorced parents. They each experienced neglectful as well as violent care during and after their parents' divorces.

As a child with a balanced temperamental nature, strong etheric forces, and a stable constitution from wise anthroposophical community holding, Priya has managed to adjust emotionally well to the family life changes compared to one of her older siblings. Her father's move away was initially painful and unsettling for her. Her reaction to the news of her father's move was of deep fear that she was losing her father forever.

This is a fairly normal response in a Pearl Child's thinking, but it is a cognitive distortion in psychological theory called catastrophizing.[28] The seed of chaotic abandonment issues could have been cast for Priya, considering some of the distortions that her own parents have had to work through out of their own parents' divorces. Her older sister has relied on going to live with a distant, extended family member to provide the hut space for her to heal and safely be herself. She had witnessed too much parent violence to feel safe in her adolescent transition.

Had the entire family not been so integrated into Waldorf and anthroposophical community working in simple and sophisticated ways, and with substantial family wealth to provide ongoing foundational support for the whole family, Priya's trauma could have settled inwardly in less whole ways. Second-generation Pearl Children can become even more traumatized when their Pearl Parents don't know how to hold relationship space and then trigger in their own pain from their own Pearl Child challenges and memories from the past. Priya's own Pearl

Parents couldn't help themselves as easily, but they knew to get help for their children as soon as possible when their own marriage started to deteriorate.

Anthroposophically, Priya's Pearl circumstances are more ideal, in that the child, after the change of teeth at age seven, began to be soulfully considered in a different way by her inherited parents. After the loss of the baby teeth and the emergence of the adult teeth, a child in the anthroposophical light becomes more of a member of a holding and fostering community than the possession of one's immediate family members.

Being loved, aided, and guided by anthroposophical teachers, artists, mentors, friends, craftspeople, farmers, entrepreneurs, Camphill community members, and extended family members, meant that Priya's parents' problems could not have as much effect as they might have if the family were isolated or in a not so conscious community. A new level of living is being fostered in intentional and conscious community in this family's case, one that is emerging more in our times and one that anthroposophy foresees mostly in the distant future.[29]

Endnotes

1 R. Steiner, "Chapter III: The Three Worlds, the Soul World," Theosophy: An Introduction to the Supersensible Knowledge of the World and the Destination of Man (Forest Row, UK: Anthroposophic Press 1972), retrieved June 3, 2020, http://wn.rsarchive.org/Books/GA009/English/AP1971/GA009_c03_1.html

2 G. O'Neil, The Human Life (Spring Valley, NY: Mercury Press, 1990).
R. Monte, "The 7-Year Cycles of Life" (2017), retrieved June 3, 2020, http://www.tommonte.com/the-7-year-cycles-of-life/

3 Theosophical Society of India, "Atman, Buddhi, Manas," (Chennai, India: Theosophy World, 2020), retrieved June 18, 2020, https://www.theosophy.world/encyclopedia/atma-buddhi-manas

4 Theosophical Society of India, "Atman, Buddhi, Manas,"

5 T. Meyers, "A Day with Jaap van der Wal," Anatomy Trains (2015), retrieved June 3, 2020, https://www.anatomytrains.com/blog/2015/09/30/a-day-with-jaap-van-der-wal/

6 K. Nash et al., "Identifying the Behavioural Phenotype in Fetal Alcohol Spectrum Disorder: Sensitivity, Specificity, and Screening Potential," Archives of Women's Mental Health 9, 4 (2006): 181–184, https://doi.org/10.1007/s00737-006-0130-3

7 R. Steiner, A Modern Art of Education (Great Barrington, NY: The Anthroposophic Press., 2004): 117.

8 M. Changaris, Touch: The Neurobiology of Health, Healing, and Human Connection (Mendocino, CA: LifeRhythm Books, 2015).

9 M. Cartwright, "Asclepius: Definition," Ancient History Encyclopedia (June 0, 2013), retrieved June 3, 2020, http://www.ancient.eu/Asclepius/

10 Atsma, "Kheiron," Theoi Project, https://www.theoi.com/Ouranios/AsklepiasIaso.html

11 G. Hartelius, "Transpersonal is a whole person psychology (Editor's Introduction)," International Journal of Transpersonal Studies 35, no. (2016). http://dx.doi.org/10.24972/ijts.2016.35.2.iii

12 David L., "Erikson's Stages of Development," Learning Theories (July 3, 2014), retrieved June 3, 2020, https://www.learning-theories.com/eriksons-stages-of-development.html.

13 C. Mace, "Mindfulness in psychotherapy: An introduction," Advances in Psychiatric Treatment, 13, (2007), 147-154. doi: 10.1192/apt.bp.106.002923. Retrieved May 30, 2017, http://apt.rcpsych.org/content/13/2/147

14 A. Kjellgren and J. Westman, "Beneficial effects of treatment with sensory isolation in flotation-tank as a preventive health-care intervention - a randomized controlled pilot trial," BMC Complement Alternative Medicine, 14:417, (2014), doi: 10.1186/1472-6882-14-417. PMID: 5344737; PMCID: PMC4219027.

15 Z. R. Luo, "Post-Traumatic Psychological Resilience in an Eco-Psychology Perspective," Advanced Materials Research, vol. 664, Trans Tech Publications, Ltd., (2013), 331–336, doi:10.4028/www.scientific.net/amr.664.331.

16 S. Tortora, "The Need to be Seen: From Winnicott to the Mirror Neuron System, Dance/Movement Therapy Comes of Age," American Dance Therapy Association: Marian Chace Lecture 33, no. 4 (May 2011), http://dx.doi.org/10.1007/s10465-011-9107-5

    N. D. Cook and T. Hayashi, "The psychoacoustics of harmony perception," American Scientist 96, no. 4 (2008): 311, https://www.jstor.org/stable/27859178

17 S. McConnell, "The Evolution of Somatic IFS," Internal Family Systems (May 6, 2011), retrieved June 3, 2020, http://www.selfleadership.org/blog/evolution-somatic-ifs/

18 E. T. Gershoff, "Corporal Punishment by Parents and Associated Child Behaviors and Experiences: A Meta-Analytic and Theoretical Review," Psychological Bulletin 128, no. 4 (2002): 539–579, https://doi.org/10.1037/0033-2909.128.4.539

19 "The Eight-fold Path and the Six Basic Exercises," Center for Social Sustainability (2010), retrieved May 13, 2017, http://www.humanviewpoint.com/images/Eight_plus_six_exercises.pdf (site unavailable).

20 "The Eight-fold Path," Center for Social Sustainability.

21 "Atma-Buddhi-Manas," Theosophical Encyclopedia, retrieved June 3, 2020, https://www.theosophy.world/encyclopedia/atma-buddhi-manas

22 J. Fuller, "Helping Children Sleep When Parents Split Up," Slumber Baby, retrieved June 3, 2020, http://www.slumber-baby.com/helping-children-sleep-parents-divorce/
    N. Zill et al., "Long-Term Effects of Parental Divorce on Parent-Child Relationships, Adjustment, and Achievement in Young Adulthood," Journal of Family Psychology 7, no. 1 (1993): 91–103. https://doi.org/10.1037/0893-3200.7.1.91

23 C. Kleinsorge and L. M. Covitz, "Impact of Divorce on Children: Developmental Considerations," Pediatrics in Review 33, no. 4 (2012), https://doi.org/10.1542/pir.33-4-147

24 J. Pedro-Carroll, Putting Children First: Strategies for Helping Children Thrive Through Divorce (New York, NY: Avery, 2010).
    J. Whitten, "Putting Children First: Strategies for Helping Children Thrive through Divorce. (Review)," PsychCentral, retrieved June 3, 2020, https://psychcentralreviews.com/2016/putting-children-first-proven-parenting-strategies-for-helping-children-thrive-through-divorce/

25 A. C. Jones, (2016). "Stop the Spiritual Bypass—Stay Human," Elephant Journal, retrieved June 3, 2020, https://www.elephantjournal.com/2016/11/cat-stop-the-spiritual-bypass-which-robs-us-of-our-humanness/

26 "Decompensation," Wikipedia, retrieved June 3, 2020, https://en.wikipedia.org/wiki/Decompensation

27 N. Rye, "Child-centered play therapy," International Center for Rehabilitation (2010), retrieved May 2017, http://cirrie.buffalo.edu/encyclopedia/en/article/275/ (page no longer available).
    R. VanFleet et al., Child-Centered Play Therapy (New York, NY: The Guilford Press, 2010).

28 A. Bonfil, "Cognitive Distortions Definition of Catastrophizing," Cognitive Behavioral Therapy: Los Angeles (2015), retrieved June 3, 2020, http://cogbtherapy.com/cbt-blog/cognitive-distortions-definition-of-catastrophizing

29 R. Steiner, "Preparing for the Sixth Epoch," (Dusseldorf, Germany, 1915), Rudolf Steiner Archive, retrieved June 0, 2020, https://wn.rsarchive.org/GA/GA0159/19150615p01.html
    J. Porter, "By Intentional Communities, for Intentional Communities," Foundation for Intentional Community (May 12, 2017), retrieved June 3, 2020, https://www.ic.org/by-intentional-communities-for-intentional-communities/

CHAPTER SEVEN

Adolescence and Bridging the Abyss: Ages 14–21

Initiations into soul sophistication begin in adolescence, as do some of the greatest danger times for youths growing up in divorced families. Biographies and modern alchemical wisdom paint a fuller picture of how Pearl Children and Adults approach life from the place of an inner wound. Mythology, the arts, and practical stories, lit by imagination, intuition, and the inspiration for overcoming personal suffering, become vital healing forces for child-of-divorce trauma wounds. Inspiring, and deeply human, adult role models become torchbearers for youths to emerge into adulthood with robust egos capable of sustained efforts of self-care, adaptability, practical capacity, and selflessness.

> *Receive the children in reverence; educate them in love; let them go forth in freedom.*[1]
> *- Rudolf Steiner*

Modern Western adolescence could be hash-tagged: "#TnT – Transfiguration and Torpor." A new aspect of a youth's whole being is emerging through remarkable change and growth forces in the body and soul. This inward and transfiguring activity sparks powerful impulses of creation and sexual procreation that grip some unsuspecting teens in levels of risky excitement and emotional fireworks; thus, #TnT!

Others may feel the changes as waves of creative urges, sleepy romanticism, or moody, self-image experimentation with dreaded disappointments bringing torpor. The array of potential soul expressions in adolescence can bring the refreshing and hopeful renewal process that is natural and wholly available at this stage of life. Yet, at the other end of the spectrum, it can become a burdened, confusing, unfree exercise in frustration and maladaptation.

Adolescent life for Pearls can quickly become politicized by parents and others. The way that each parent consciously holds his or her hopes for the youth, or otherwise controls a youth with a parent agenda or vision that is authoritarian rather than well-authored, compulsive rather than compassionate, or rigid rather than renewable, can be demeaning and restrictive to teen development.

Teen Development Restriction versus Teen Development Growth

Authoritarian parenting	Well-authored parenting
Compulsive parenting	Compassionate parenting
Rigid, traditional conception	Renewable, progressive perception

Well-authored parenting means the parent has well-developed executive capacities and can plan, self-regulate, and consider options with patience. The parent can help the youth to sketch out ideas and conceive sets of priorities before launching full-out on initiatives. A parent can rehearse a "scientific process"[2] with the youth, fully regarding the youth's interests and impulses. The wise parent instills trust by being willing to see the youth more separately from who the parent has known the child to be before, guiding the teen's interests without leading them.

In a scientific process, the parent elicits or simply hears out the youth's hypothesis for an idea or plan to do something. The parent encourages the youth to investigate a deeper feeling for a question the youth holds about an idea and how it relates to the youth's life as well as the well-being of others. The parent asks the youth to consider materials, costs, and the method of executing the plan, encouraging the youth to experiment with the idea gradually in the first attempt.

The parent listens with deep interest to the youth's observations of how the activity unfolded and gives feedback on what the parent heard the youth say. The parent checks in with the child's feelings and needs, then patterns how a person "authors" one's experience well by contemplating on the youth's thoughts about the original plan, and on the further reflections that result from experimentation, before commenting.

The parent patterns synthesizing the results and process with new questions, presenting other sides of interest regarding the methodology, materials, or hypothesis, and expressing wonder at how the youth has thought of other practical or creative, potential perspectives. The parent may suggest that the young person document the activity in some way. The parent strives to share the insights of inspiring people who have tried something similar or related before.

The parent encourages the teen to follow through on the plan again and see what other insights, feelings, or needs arise—offering to be there to consult, as well as to help the teen to network with other consultants when needed. The parent asks the teen after several tries how ready the youth feels, on a scale of one to ten, to take the activity up freely themself. The parent stays connected until the adolescent feels ready to take the process up independently, with the reassurance that if the youth still wants to consult later about the activity, the parent will consider it meaningful to be there and helping in whatever way the parent can.

This process can happen when a youth is trying out a new summer job, dating someone for the first time, designing a basketball team logo, or preparing some complex, innovative performance art/light-tech/overnight camp-out experience with friends in the spring, out on friend's uncle's woodlot or on a farm-community acreage.

The possibilities for what different teens will come up with as interests and initiatives are endless, and parents need to keep creative and honorable minds to encourage the soul of this young person to find its own process. Supported with a sense of manageable freedom for the task, the teen will find the inner and outer resources, relationships, and ways toward the realization of a project, work experience, creative dream, or other life-destiny fulfillment. Adults need to guide a youth to be grounded and responsible with the economics of an adventure, including with good bookkeeping practices, since practical, financial awareness is essential to teen development. Bringing detailed awareness of the rights of other people involved in one's dreams and projects is also important at this stage.

When parents stay open to a well-considered teen activity or adventure, and pattern collaboration with other parents and other adults who are involved in assisting the youths to fulfill goals, they inspire trust in youth who are then inspired to be trustworthy themselves. Offering trust, helping to scaffold the adolescent's thought processes, and offering chances to role-play and test out scenarios ahead of time, are crucial to helping to build the higher, executive-mind neurology in the youth. Helping a youth review feelings, needs, options, and possible outcomes is a loving way for a parent to be present to the teen's self-dominion in decision-making while not imposing personal opinions, judgments, or purely personal agendas.

Depending on the teen's maturity and age, general life contracts may necessarily be worked out around such things as regular parent-youth communications, curfews, love-first/no-fault emergency procedures if the adolescent finds him or herself in trouble with a gang, drugs, alcohol, or sexual abuse, and arrangements around youth project finances.

Compassionate parenting is a reversal of the belief that every mistake that a child makes is somehow a fault. It reroutes a parent's perspective from the materialistic view of the child as an unfree agent of the family, and a programmable, perfection-machine geared to learning the skills to match himself up to a highly evaluated, mental-physical process worth a certain salary or expected social value in the eyes of family members.

Instead, compassionate parenting means viewing the adolescent as a free, soul-spirit being that can meet and be part of designing, in an entrepreneurial way, the evolving life that the youth is living in the world. All souls, along with the other members of their cosmic generation, bring new and evolutionary information to the collective society, as well as karmic tasks, to work into the world. This is for a relatively short time on earth, and a person can become easily distracted and suppressed from bringing their appropriate talents and insights forward, which becomes a loss to society as a whole. Learning what to do to avoid such diversions is part of the character-building of the youth in his lifetime.

Souls are finding their ways to sustain a lengthy living process here on earth, but also, for much longer in the spiritual world again. The early development tasks for parents are to root the youth well enough that the full adult soul can get to work on karmic deeds. They are prepared to notice, clean up, enliven, and transform old, human devolution debris that might be clinging from a past lifetime, preventing a modern person from loving fully, taking responsibility among others, and returning well to the heavens again at the end of this lifetime's journey.

The incarnating child soul strives to feel a soulful connection with others. The maturing soul also works to get a personal and collective sense of what harmful, old impressions are invested in the soul that need to be lit up and brought to healthy, contemporary goodness. This process happens in adulthood if childhood development goes well. If that child has been hindered by trauma, the soul tasks can be unsteady, intermittent, or filled with regular distress.

A well-cultivated adult (who can be from any socio-economic-cultural background), will also have the chance to see, in time, with a cleansed soul, some gleanings of the future and what the soul ought to prepare itself for and carry in consciousness over the threshold of death for another time. Only an individual soul can know that calling fully for oneself over time. Regularly in the West, souls in these times are clouded in earthly materialist perceptions, bringing suffering and even vengeful inclinations toward others. People may make many attempts to "clear the slate" to see a more whole and higher "truth" for themselves again.

Since the true seeing and tasks of an incarnating soul can be intense, challenging, and distinct for every human being, it is loving to bring real care and concern for a youth's struggles, rather than an attitude of pressure about perfectionism, absolute right and wrong, or mechanistic programming. Offering insights and practices to help any person to keep aligned with the spirit and soul during a lifetime of working into the world in various ways represents the Consciousness Soul and Christ-conscious, higher brotherhood-sisterhood working of our times.

Renewable, progressive perception can be one of the hardest tasks for the parent of an adolescent. A responsible parent spends much of the child's upbringing creating reasonable stability around the basics of life, and in a mindset to foster practical, physical, and mental wholeness in that child's adulthood. In adolescence, the child's inner biology, as well as soul-destiny purpose, is creatively charging up, while growing, refining, and paring away some excess neurological "nesting." This new being is going to become an interesting juggler of old and new human themes.

Much of the newness of this child's generational offering to society, and this individual's path of destiny, as contracted in the spiritual world during the soul's last sojourn there, is esoteric (hidden). It will be revealed in adulthood over time. Parenting with the courage and presence of mind to hold the child's future as an open question is the way to renewable, progressive, soul attunement.

If the childhood upbringing has been whole and truly facilitating, the youth will know and show some substantial inklings about the youth's own life destiny by the time the youth is between the ages of eighteen and twenty-one. Until then, the youth's sense of purpose can still be vague or dull. A parent needs to begin to have a more open mind about this child in adolescence, reorienting thoughts and unconscious expectations, and earnestly opening to understanding and fostering what the youth is discovering and balancing while the parent continues to do the same.

Fostering Teenager Executive Mind

Adolescent politics become fairer, and in better relationship when parents are conscious about their work with this emerging adult. Through mutually creative and open negotiations of actions with the emerging adult, including responsibility-planning, the youth can be greater supported in cultivating right-relationships with others in life. This includes learning to hold oneself appropriately with both authoritative community members and with those who are only just developing a sense of personal, self-dominion. They learn responsible, collective, collaborative interaction with others at work and in the social realm.

This can also help youth to learn to begin to build relationships with people such as police, youth support volunteers, fire department workers, paramedics and other first responders, professional and emerging artists, and any array of entrepreneurial and business involved adults in the community or wider society. Some of the best scenarios for this are when a youth can arrange to spend some mentoring time with such community members, or when community leaders can participate in a youth project.

The adolescent has the chance to be inspired and feel inclusive within the wider, adult, societal structures surrounding youth life. The adolescent can still feel safe to test personal limits and interests, expanding capacities to widen those limits. The cooperating adults agree to help bring some adolescent experiments into society, and to assist youths to observe their own initiatives, their results, and to encourage some self-reflection.

By later adolescence, projects that a youth brings forward to society mustn't be simply childlike and self-focused on the teen's own or generational interests. These tasks need to come out of the adolescent's deeper feelings about the other people of the world. It is about collective world and societal needs, and the changes that each youth has spent some energy reflecting and imagining into, even if he that requires wrestling with new and more complex feelings. (Appropriately, a form of ancient Greek wrestling is taught in some Waldorf high school gym classes—as a metaphor for life.)

Engaging some King Arthur and his round table[3] types of knightly discussions and activities around ethics, honor, and initiative, or participating in an indigenous, male-and-female governance council[4] to examine societal fairness and justice, young people learn to bring an inspiring, creative idea into practical working in the world with awareness of the needs and insights of others who are different from themselves.

Through collaboration, and adult modeling of objective thinking and perspective seeking, youth put more conscious will into action. Relevant social follow-through, with a mutual council of adults and youths, can take young, emerging adults through one of the most important tasks of teen life—the ability to plan and act collaboratively and executively, taking responsibility for outcomes without punitive repercussions in the face of mistakes.

Youth need acknowledgment that they have been heard and that their parents and other adults have considered their views with more interest than a quick and passing thought. Integral communication from self-reflecting adults around them, on a consistent basis, can prepare the teen for critical, lawful, and resonant thinking and behavior in society that stays associated with real freedom for all, including the freedom needs of the sick, disabled, and the elderly.

This can also mean important sharing, and emotional-behavioral contracts, around, for example, learning safe car-driving practices, or committing to understanding and communicating appropriate consent, intent, and feelings when romantic or sexual interests with another person are piqued.

For teens who make harmful mistakes (ones that don't have serious societal consequences that can bring incarceration), a restorative justice approach involving cooperating adults gives adolescents the opportunity to do monitored community service if teen neglect, over-exuberance, or rebelliousness causes unexpected harm to others. Stealing or doing damage to public or private property, in the middle of testing one's egoic desires out in adult life, still require lawful consequences.

For instance, a weekly, teen music-dance-spoken-word party, in the backwoods or yard of a family property on Friday nights, begins to annoy one neighbor because of regular noise and careless driving on the highway on the way into the property. The neighbor decides one Friday night to confront the teens on their behavior, for safety reasons. A group of teens react to the middle-aged neighbor's stern tone of voice later by openly urinating on her back porch, dumping empty beer cans at the end of her driveway late at night, and burning her wooden birdhouse for the drunken fun of it. The next Monday, the neighbor calls the high school to report the incident since she knows that some of the adolescents come from that school.

A responsive meeting is called once some students are identified, and community members discuss what can accommodate reparations to the annoyed neighbor. Their goal is to offer the teens a valuable opportunity for reflection, problem-solving, and wisdom-testing regarding gauging their levels of generational freedom, while learning to value the needs of neighbors and older persons.

The teens contract to meet with the neighbor, parents, and a counselor to hear out feelings and concerns. The teens still want to party, and the woman wants a quiet night with no garbage on her property the next day. The teens learn that the woman used to work as a cleaner at concert stadiums for years to take care of her son after she and her husband broke up because of alcohol abuse that neither is involved with anymore. She had met a lot of interesting and creative musicians at the concerts, but she was always hearing loud music late at night and later, had trouble hearing due to ringing in her ears. For most of the last ten years, she's only managed about five hours of sleep at night.

She used to collect huge bags of empty beer cans, alcohol bottles, and other garbage in the bleachers, and the smell of alcohol now makes her stomach sick. Even more so since her son died early in his forties from liver cancer from an alcohol problem when he himself started a music band that was always on the road.

It becomes clear that the woman clearly cannot maintain her health with teens playing loud music in the yard behind hers. She appreciates that young people love music and need the chance to have a good and creative time with it safely and independently. She suggests that the youths find another venue for their fun, but they are reluctant because they don't know anywhere free or interesting to do so in the neighborhood. The woman offers to call an old friend in the music business who may know of a spot where the youths can enjoy their Friday nights.

Sure enough, a sound man knows of another teen at another school in the neighborhood whose parents built him a studio with full sound equipment, but he doesn't have a band. He is known through a parents' group to be an exceptional guitarist but never seems to get his music out to others since he's a bit shy and even overwhelmed sometimes about doing the tasks of a band. When he was fourteen, his father fell off a ladder, breaking his back, and leaving the teen to do a lot of family organizing tasks. The sound man asks if he can introduce the teens to this other youth and have a night of discussion about music production, past and present.

Soon enough, the adolescents are sharing talents, becoming good friends, and getting some people, including adults, out to their venue to hear their songs and see who they are.

A band emerges with a poster and logo that the band members put inspiring, creative will into. It depicts crushed beer cans nailed to a shepherd's staff stuck in the ground. Old, green-moss-covered, wooden bleachers sit in the shadow of a blue-lit, small-town ballpark. Sitting on one side of the bleachers with a soft beam of saffron-gold light back-lighting is a young woman with yarrow hair holding a microphone to the partial silhouette of a young man who faces her. He is sitting on the bleacher step below with his head inclined down, exposing his bare back and neck.

They are painted to look as if his rib bones are a stairwell heading toward the light that the young woman sits in. The image's focus is on youthful light and compassion, with the "crippled" young man beckoning the young, angelic-looking woman. The band's name has become "Bones Speaking." The dark-light imagery, raising its message into something heartfelt in a mysterious and romantic kind of way, has freedom as well as appropriate, age-and-stage elements of adolescent art. A profound creative endeavor has emerged for the youth through adult cooperation and mutual understanding.

The Wild-Horse, Dark Double

There is little rest from wrestling with the dark double nature in parents while raising adolescents. The struggle to rein in one's own latent adolescent behavior, while raising youths, is an important parent task. Unmet adolescent needs in the parent need to be met away from the youth, and possibly with counselor help to get updates on neurological and Consciousness Soul self-care. This can bring profound grace in time if parents stay honest and growing within themselves. Otherwise, generational boundaries and tasks get confused and distorted.

The parent dark double often shows up as adults who act more like their rebellious or risky teens than their own children. Parents can easily muddle their consciousness with their adolescents, allowing their children's adolescent years to become a ground of leniency so that parents can cut themselves some slack, regress, and relive their own awkwardly attached or dysfunctional aspects of youth. Their own children end up uninspired at a very important time for them to have ideal adult mentors.

When parents don't address their own soul-psyche development issues separately with healers who can distinguish appropriate age-level developments, they risk imposing their old issues and suffocating the youth's natural energies for what they must meet in life now. For a while, parents may think that disregarding discipline for their adolescents, and laughing off troublemaking or escapism, may provide joyful entertainment for everyone. The enjoyment usually runs thin when a wake-up conflict, criminal event, serious accident, or lost job or career opportunity for the youth or the parent grounds people painfully or even devastatingly, returning each person to their appropriate responsibilities and age-and-stage work.

Transfiguration And The Inner Temple

The transfiguring of the child body into a full adult body, which will carry substantial humane life for decades to come, as well as providing a home for an ongoing, inspired soul, represents the completion of the inner temple framework in the adolescent individual. That temple—a development forward from the hut—becomes the inner place to hold ongoing nurturance and upkeep for the healthy, individual I-being.

Coming now on the mature side of adolescence, a budding, I-informed adult can feel that one has come through a mysterious life initiation toward a wholesome life with many dimensions and capacities primed. This can give the young adult Pearl self-dominion and lifelong options for how that adult feels called to enliven life and manage the practical details of daily life soulfully with others.

On the flip side of that kind of older-adolescent-to-adult-transition potential, many Pearl Youths in the past have come through their teens with only the barest of I-capacities intact, having been overpowered by others' egoic tendencies. As adults, they may severely suppress their own nature to please others, or they may become easily reactive. They may come into adulthood bound in the power games of adults, higher strategizing with the tools of negative, manipulative limitation, and a with a focus on self-protection, intrigues, and imposed, entitled attachments with people rather than respectfully negotiated ones. They may enter adulthood blocked about the essence of true love and oblivious to true collaborative, human well-being.

Youthful Alchemy

Concurrent in older adolescents who are abounding in new physical potentials is the staggering capacity for mental sophistication, which may or may not be apparent to other adults, depending on the youth's development and or/opportunities so far. For a while, those potentials seem hardly able to keep their soul aspects and talents together, coordinated and flourishing, when at a younger age, these youths as younger children seemed to have life far more integrated.

Back then, mom and dad, or caregivers, teachers, or other society members, were holding more of the responsibilities around the youth's life. Now, youths maneuver among academic studies, trades training, peer networks, intimate friendships, special interest projects, class trip planning, team organizing, part-time job juggling, entrepreneurial and artistic interests, and full-on, life-management work—all more fully on their own.

Working every angle of themselves in these older adolescent times brings a profound transformation in the youths. Simplifying may seem like an easy option at this age, yet these complex activities help to shape many important future capacities, including the executive functions of the brain that strengthen lifelong, personal guidance. When parents and other caregiving adults learn to bear the transforming fire of these adolescent times, staying with the hard work of change, all tend to benefit better later. What seemed like lead and teenaged torpor at age fourteen is alchemized to gold by age twenty-one when an adolescent is fostered well.

Prefrontal Cortex Brain Development

In the teen years, profoundly life-giving hormones and organic chemical reactions work the whole adolescent and young adult into a brilliant new force. The residuals of this growth are the dying-away of old brain cells and neural connections that won't be needed in the next stages of the life journey.

Whatever gets the most attention or resistance from adults during these times may inform brain development, but it may also diminish the youth's growing neurology and vagus-nerve functions that inform many body functions as well as soul-spirit scaffolds. More study today is showing the effects of trauma on adolescent brain development in the very important, prefrontal, executive functioning area of the brain.[5]

A young, trauma-bound Pearl Adult can ride the early adult years as a person both driven and unfree, who is in a constant state of angst and hoping to be loved, soothed, and admired by others. Or, the adolescent may skip valuing any sense of love and go right for the metaphoric jugular in getting needs met with others in whatever way the young adult can get away with. The young adult Pearl may have no clue that poor actions tend to come back upon a person at some stage in later life.

Anthroposophical therapeutic tending and guidance for Pearls in adolescence seeks to help youth enter young adulthood with capacities to engage life both well and freely, with the knowledge that what they apply themselves to can work for their betterment or their decline. Counselors work to help Pearls in young adulthood to hold their neurology whole and calm when they meet the challenges and the many people in life who might not extend the love and acceptance that they need.

With this kind of *free-holding*, young adult life takes on an artistic, self-entrepreneur approach. The adult can see and chose the practical canvases, the colors of life, imaginations, and feeling expressions that reveal life's soul significance (or insignificance at times), and the experiments and processes needed to bring the greatest effect to one's own needs and to those of others at the same time.

The *metaphoric* artist (since a person can be an artist while working in seemingly non-artistic professions and activities) means being someone who is practicing being in full charge of oneself and responsible for one's creative landscape, but with an equalizing, humble awareness that one never lives in a vacuum, and that an artist is as vulnerable to needing relationship and requiring understanding for others as anyone.

Life will have many turns, and the young Pearl Adult, out in the world, could experience emotionally charged times. The life metaphor of roller-coaster hills, deeply peaceful ponds, innocent and enlightening sunlit forests, or clouded, enraged ocean horizons is a world reality for all beings. And so, an enlivened Pearl life, as with a life for many other people with traumas or other significant soul-development challenges, is a vigilant process of keeping hold of one's reins while at times feeling like one is riding an impetuous steed that one can't quite control as well as one would like.

Yet, with awareness, helpers, and soul-psyche tools, it does not need to be a dull or deadened life journey. All experiences, in time, will bring the needed self-awareness that a Pearl can use to enrich more self-dominion, good relationships, and healthy neurological and spiritual growth in adulthood.

Yiana Belkalopolos

Torpor

The young adult, having come through adolescence, is equipped, at one end of a spectral polarity, to lead an innovative life of sustainable and mutually invigorating relationships. The opposite pole is daunting to the soul, with a young adult recovering, sometimes constantly, from low mutual human respect in exchanges with others, and being survival-focused on material accumulation and inadequate feelings that can lead to the opposite—hubraic self-glory. No one suffers more for the strains than the young Pearl Adult. The soul emptiness can start to manifest a kind of dark, phantom-being if others are not there to give loving support and encouragement.

Most adolescent youth strut and meander in the inner-soul dance of *sympathy* and *antipathy*—what they are attracted to and like, and what they are repulsed by and dislike. By age twenty-four, if held well, young persons have had good mentors and inspirational examples of soulful adults to help them understand how to be with these inner tensions of likes and dislikes without attempting to attach too heavily in one direction or avert too fully in the other. Pearl Adults are still vulnerable in this respect, when they can't manifest the right support or self-holding to keep even and balanced.

Some signs of the torpor of adolescence that can extend poorly into adulthood are when your daughter, who at a younger age was endlessly energetic, regularly crashes in bed for half the weekend, and at the worst times, such as when you had agreed to go out together to choose wedding gifts for her older sister's wedding. Her sister is disappointed and venting to you about her lazy sister because she knows it's not right to get on her little sister's case. She would like you to do it.

The adolescent overate sugar-coated licorice strings at a friend's house Friday night (and was likely smoking pot but you're not certain) and can't get up the energy for two days to fulfill a family agreement. Her liver is gummed up and camped out in cleanse mode. She wants to watch woeful videos in bed. What's worse to her, though she doesn't want to talk about it, is that her skin is breaking out in acne, like it always does when she eats sugar. She's miserable.

Since she hasn't been getting the right attending in her Pearl circumstance anyway, she's not interested in what you think is good for her. She feels you're nagging, and she could be right. She can't see the hormone-candy-toxin connection that's making her feel that she's steeping in a witch's stew. Instead, she's preferring to get at her pain with you by projecting that you're the witch for saying anything about her predicament and what she sees as a superficial issue—her physical health. Her sad and depressed alienation is more important to her right now. On one level, she's right.

She knows it's something deeper, but she doesn't know how to express it or cope. Her teenager mind is in conceptual thinking now, and unconsciously she's just getting used to it. If it hasn't previously been safe to talk about her needs, when she was two or three years younger, now that she's fourteen, the exit from the torpor won't happen easily. She won't necessarily respond the way your married friends' teenagers do. Many teens are uncertain who they are because they are inwardly changing in many profound ways at once.

Trying to move into conceptual mind without the base of a wholesome sense-life, honored feelings, supportive and dependable caregivers, and imagination-rich inner resources cultivated early in life, is likely going to send a Western Pearl female, with child-bearing capacities and an estrogen-dominant physiology, all over the emotional map.

She could resort to strategizing and manipulating to get her truest needs recognized, rather than having the ability to network for her care in a whole and proactive way. It's likely that she is not aware of being manipulative, and feels a level of suffering, with the sick feeling of not really knowing how to trust others or herself to manage her emerging adult life. She may try to find someone who will manage everything for her—leading to dependency and potential domestic abuse issues in relationships.

Another expression of the inner chaos can be the advent of eating disorders in a female youth (which can also happen for male youths). Eating disorders can be an unconscious attempt to revert to child body and resist inner body maturation because the neglected youth doesn't feel ready or capable of it.

A different example of the torpidity setting in at the middle stages of this teen transfiguration is when the adolescent returns the most bewildered response and moodiness to a parent's request to close up the iPhone (after the teen's been on it for an hour-and-a-half) and help prepare the meal to which she has invited her five adolescent cousins.

The teen's eyes gloss and gleam, and she wonders what old reality her parent is contorting in. Why would her mother think it is more important to chop vegetables than tweet with the same cousins who are coming to dinner to get ideas for the school-video fashion outfits they're making next week? They can make food later!

The parent is wondering if the child is on drugs since it's an hour before dinner time, six hungry adolescents will soon descend on the kitchen needing to eat a substantial meal, and the chore request of the adolescent daughter was gently and reasonably made. The youth was the one who asked for the family gathering. Why will she not move off the sofa now in time to get food ready? Winging it in the final hour in a small kitchen with everyone there isn't going to cut it for mother.

The teen, rather than cooperating, slowly gets up from the coach to forage some cheese in the fridge rather than taking out the foods that need to be prepared. She hangs out by the windowsill, popping bocconcini cheese balls and watching the birds at the feeder, nonchalantly mentioning the crow that someone knocked dead with a slingshot down the road three days ago.

You, the responsible parent who's hyper-pressured now, would do well to take another breath and renew your tactic, since this laziness, macabre-mind, and fogginess in this sixteen-year-old is a real, potential sign of biological, hormonal loading, limb growth, or brain neurology warehousing. The youth is not really asking to be pandered to and is not lazy or being a princess or gothic about things. The adolescent may have truly forgotten the agreed task on the way from the sofa to the fridge. It could easily be that, on this particular afternoon, her many developing inner forces have chosen to do some sophisticated tasks at the same time that the family members are expected for the earlier-planned dinner get-together.

Another torpor scenario for a set of former-spouse parents to cope with might constellate around addressing their adolescent son's unpaid car insurance bills. Each parent is left aghast that their recently fitness-emasculated, moody seventeen-year-old has forgotten financial common sense. He's been funneling most of his part-time job earnings into body-building supplements and caffeine drinks they didn't know about. As a result, the car insurance hasn't been paid, and the insurer is threatening to cut off coverage. That would end the part-time job, since the teen needs the car to get to work that is a distance away.

While the parents fear that the youth has lapsed into hormonal fever, the expansive-minded adolescent (raised for several years with his parents in exotic locations in Bolivia and Argentina) is thinking about his skiing trip at Christmas at Mount Washington, Oregon, and how he's going to sell his car anyway to pay for that adventure. He seems to have forgone the notion that the insurance company doesn't care what his plans are three months from now. The insurance company's prepared to shut him down, and how will he get to work now to pay for a vehicle, trip, or any other of his self-directed interests and activities?

When confronted with the problem, the teen seems lackadaisical about it and unconcerned about the urgency of paying off his two lapsed bills. His mind may, in fact, understand the importance of the issue, but in the moment that his parents address it, his body is pulsing in powerful, dopamine serenity after a barbell workout. He can barely move his legs right now, despite the strengthening cross-fit practice he just did, because inwardly, his body chose this moment to spark another growth surge in his leg muscles.

He thinks he can put his next paycheck into the bank to cover the payments, but he can't seem to get himself to say that to his parents because his head is pounding with elevated sexual surges. He doesn't entirely understand what to do or say. He seems in a strange and impudent daze, from his parents' perspective. They're anxious about how to get their point across.

The teen silently wonders if he was really meant to be born to such niggling, civic-minded parents who don't know how to have fun. Again, before one or other parent loses their cool with the adolescent, each may decide to have a chat after the youth has had a shower and cleaned up, and while eating a grounding dinner.

Divorced parents need not to be over-stressing adolescent discipline points, having too much of a talk-over, when the other parent has already had the talk. The teen heard it once and may resist hearing it again from the other parent too soon after. It's tricky in a split family. The Pearl Youth may easily rebel rather than cooperate if divorced parents don't cooperate and coordinate on important discussions.

Confusion and fear can set into the parent who can't discern if this is just adolescent torpor in the natural metamorphosis, or if this is a sign that the youth will become a steroid junkie or a credit liability. Similar confusion and dread can set in for the teen that the parents will never understand his life goals.

According to his feelings one day, he tells a parent that he wants to be a travel agent and maybe a pilot one day if he can make enough money to pay for flying lessons. The other parent hears he's preparing for a nature-sport business promoting internationally informed fitness programs. When his parents fight over what he's doing with his life, he wonders what the point is in talking to his parents about anything. Then the depressed torpor sets in.

Overreaction is a common issue for Pearl Adults and parents on both sides of the parent-teen dichotomy at this stage of life. Patience and deeply listening to this emerging adult's struggle are essential at this point in life, without making it a parents' struggle against each other.

Adolescent Design, and Rearranging Parenting Templates

Anthroposophically guided adolescents are seen and understood to be in transition and unique self-design. Adolescents, in general, need more time away now from their parents, but in inspiring activities. They are introduced to greater dimensions of the seen world, as well as some of its unseen complexities. They need refreshing experiences in history, geography, mathematics, physics, humanities, biology, arts, and sciences. They also need to get out into nature's elements to renew and test themselves, be it on winter camping trips, or with a gap year of living on a biodynamic farm in another country. The potential for this depends in part on the socio-economic situation of individual families or a school's philanthropic funds, geographic locations, cross-cultural arrangements, and school agreements.

The universal perspective of Waldorf education and anthroposophically conscious therapists, trainers, and caregivers, teaches the adolescents the need to visit new places with new people, even if it's in their own town or city. High school classes often go on mutually planned trips to other places or countries to do philanthropic work, such as building playgrounds for children in Africa and Chile. They may also do study exchanges. Learning more than one language in the early, grade-school years makes this more possible.

Many German adolescents in Waldorf schools in grades eleven and twelve travel to other countries to Waldorf high schools for a year of education-and-life exchange. Schools in other countries have begun to take this practice up as well. Students live with other Waldorf student families while keeping up on the Waldorf high school curriculum. The course of study is similar in most Waldorf schools because the curricula are based on universally human themes geared to youth-level development.

Yet, a family exchange for a Pearl Youth can be a painful reminder that the Pearl can't meet any standard, whole-family requirement to host youths from other countries. Having an exchange student stay with a youth in a single-parent family, with a conflicted family scenario, is less likely to be a consideration. This may require different thinking in the future, and efforts to find ways to make exchanges work out for Pearls too, with special arrangements and considerations.

In Waldorf schools, inspiring teachers also regularly travel from school to school or among world communities, sharing practical and creative skills, as well as biographies of great people that the students might never hear of otherwise.

Emotional Regression

Since traumatized Pearl Youth often find themselves wavering emotionally over what it means to be fully responsible for themselves, they can have regular occasions of regressive desires for their younger life. These moments can come out as immature behavior just when the adults around were hoping for the opposite. Parents who are attuned to the struggles of Pearl adolescents can allow for some immature dips backward while supporting the return to appropriate age-and-stage wholeness. They can connect with the feelings and fears of the youth, as well as missing development pieces that are holding the youth back. They can work on new relationship skills and practices to help bridge from one stage to another.

When primal or other historical re-enactments that adults outwardly celebrate in the culture get expressed in adolescents, such as in *Game of Thrones* cultural imagery, or in Nordic Odin mythological obsession inspired by the *Vikings*[6] TV series, parents can ask themselves what the youth is trying to *earth, stabilize, cling to,* or *idolize* inside by mimicking adult cultural icons. A teen may be want to assuage, or reinvent, something triggered inside of himself that represents undeveloped, or missed soul-scaffolding from the past. Parent neglect of teens, through putting too much emphasis on movie or computer game characters and scenarios and not enough time into real-life activities, can trigger regressive behavior in the adolescent.

Fights And Power Struggles

Sudden, fiery, and even brilliantly passionate emotion, as well as mental lobbies from some Pearl Youths toward parents about why they absolutely must do or have something different this week than two weeks ago—and not the same thing that their best friend has but not too different either—can leave the adults around them stymied and even in a quiet fury themselves.

Without presence of mind, parents forget that they can't ultimately win practical, emotional, or even mental arguments with this child anymore, and they shouldn't. Too many things are happening with a brand new engine, so to speak, in a teenager. They need to be fresh.

Many things may be happening here, but here are two possibilities. Firstly, the consumerist approach to life can set in with a youth who sees one divorced parent or the other often trading subsequent life partners. If the adult appears to be going consumerist in relationships, the youth may do the same with the parent, as an irreverent and unconscious backlash. This shows up in the youth's inability to substantiate relationships, and thus, the frequent grasping for new material items, experiences, adventures, or ways to get people to like the Pearl.

Secondly, the adolescent is feeling inadequate in comparison with peers, as is normal to a point through adolescence. It can, however, get to a level with a Pearl Youth of heavy self-criticism and criticism of parents or others, with the youth not consciously knowing how sabotaging that can be to the youth's ability to fulfill personal needs. It can be an expression or "externalization" of how the youth is "internalizing"[7] the harsh criticism that the parents engaged in between each other.

Youths must have some experiences of win-win now with others, to trust that they can experience the empowerment of creative, and increasingly conscious, ideas later in the greater world. Souls know that they will be called to the concerns of the wider, societal collective in some way, and adolescents look to taste something of the full potentials of their future selves, even if some aspects of their souls don't ripen for decades. Youths will meet many people in the future who will see things differently from their parents. Parents need to try not to influence their adolescent children based purely on personal or colloquial views. What parents can do for themselves is arrange their own opportunities to grow in humanness, adapting personal boundaries and continuing to offer support and networking help to the youths. Youth need to be inspired by parents and other adults who are fulfilling a meaningful soul destiny that also includes the challenging personal growth work and ongoing connection activity with others.

Inclusive Leadership Starts at Home

Adults must allow themselves to be led into the teen's inner vision often, rather than being the unchallenged leader of their children. Without deep trust in themselves through a good investment in their own generational, soulful, and spiritually lawful child development, parents can lose touch with what the teen's soul calling in life is really about at different development stages.

Parents often forfeit the mature heart substance that would carry their connection with their adult children in adulthood, and free of unnecessary familial attachments and material bonds. If parents can't adapt, the young adults will try to break free in some way out of levels of suffocated, "I" anger.

This is not the same thing as saying that young adults no longer need to consider their parents' feelings, sufferings, or needs for connection in the future, or that they should act in complete aversion to celebrations of family historical times ever again. They don't have to denounce family holiday celebrations every year, although they must have the free choice now to participate or not and to negotiate get-togethers to reflect their interests as much as their parent's likes and dislikes. Expecting that sympathies and antipathies can and often will arise, and handling them with well-negotiated, soul-perspective can help the adults manage in new ways together.

Adolescents are a new cosmic generation in the fold of life, different from their parents' generation, and they will bring some approaches to life that are unique. The full results won't present themselves in some of these emerging adults until they are in their individual Consciousness Soul stages between the ages of thirty-five to forty-two. Toward late adolescence, parents aren't excluded from the youth's life now, but they are not going to remain the main attachment focus either.

Yiana Belkalopolos

Threefold Human Being

Slowly becoming authentically adult is revealed in adolescence to be no easy feat or runaway ball game, yet there is something purposefully exciting about later adolescence. When guided with an anthroposophical awareness of an extra layer of threefoldness[8] within the fourfold human being—the awareness that a person continually bears the soul functions of thinking, feeling, and willing within the physical, etheric, astral, and I-nature—many golden gifts for a lifetime can mature.

When young Pearl Adults become parents themselves, or when they reach the ages of thirty-five to forty-two, they will review their earlier childhood and want to reminisce mentally (thinking), emotionally (feeling), and even physically (willing) through visits to old family haunts or in recreated, or renovated, family experiences. This is a form of group soul-life reflection (*Ruckschau*)[9] that is only healthy if it does not entangle old, family age-and-stage relationships. Until then, parents who have helped the children to ensoul their early stages naturally and substantially, and who have made reparations for harms done, can let go of the past and learn from their adult children now in more of an unconditionally loving, in-the-moment, friendship stance.

The healthy and wholesome new adults will not be a replica of the adults around them, but not alien either to the practicalities of the societal life that is already established. The don't have to live in shame about what the society is they are entering, imperfections and all, nor afraid to be greeting society anew and differently. Knowing that they will be tested, and familiar with wrestling with feelings and constructing responses with wholeness (instead of simply impulsing raw ambitions or opinions), this adult can stand independently and make the decisions that young adults can handle. The Pearl Adult feels confident to ask for collaboration and assistance if some of those decisions bring challenging consequences or feedback. They don't harshly berate or harm themselves over life's errors.

Many Pearl Parents intuitively know that their children are going to go through some hard, early-adulthood emotional turmoil in the Sentient Soul period. Too many push the youths to try to bypass that period by insisting that they pursue higher intellectual education directly out of high school. Other parents do this too. Many anthroposophical youths today are saying no to this. They are keeping their early adulthood away from school to allow their feeling life to breathe appropriately into adult life before making higher intellectual plans that actually suit a later adult development period, around ages twenty-eight to thirty-five. Pressuring for high academics immediately upon entering the Sentient Soul years can thwart the soul and often represents the parent's discomfort with their own feeling life. It can send young adults into eating disorders, addictions, suicidal ideations, or deeply buried resentments that surface with great adversarial power later.

Two anthroposophical young adult initiatives—the YIP program in Sweden[10] and Free Columbia in Harlemville, New York[11]—have addressed the early adult Sentient Soul period insightfully. Through travel and learning initiatives steeped in self-designed, creative activity and close, respectful, social-relationship cultivation, these young adults have had an experience of the freedom to discover the Sentient Soul that many others could benefit from today. One young adult group hiked, camped, created, and studied together through the woods of Sweden and all the way to Greece in a trip that took several months.

Tightrope Walker

Adolescents soon become aware of the dangers and darker temptations of becoming adult. These can be experiences such as the sexual abuses and work-life cultural discriminations that young women and men frequently experience in societies around the world. It can arise in the confusing reality for a young person to be faced with a longtime friend who has fallen into a serious fentanyl addiction following a sports accident that left them in intense pain.

A young gay teen may or may not find a peer group to support feelings and needs, and he soon learns of an LGBTQ+ community member who took their own life because of the same kind of alienation. Many teens today are aware of violence in their own towns and wars in the world, through exposure to media and the internet.

Keeping the lighter side of life inspiring for youth when they meet the dark side is practical, and it is also the higher heart work of Waldorf high school teachers, specialists, healers, anthroposophical therapists, and counselors today. Dark ways are transformed by awareness, revealed as degrees of hues and tones that are naturally cast around the light of being human. Waldorf high school art classes feature work on light-shadow contrasts. Drama work is also excellent for revealing the transformation from darkness into light in human characters. It can also show how characters who are superficially light are brought down to earth through the understandings of the shadowy sufferings of people in life and the challenges that create mature human character. Heavy, fallen characters are also given the chance to redeem themselves and show themselves in the light again.

Adolescents notice the shadows of adult selfishness quickly. Adults often send this awareness underground in themselves when they have no skills to deal with their own dark shadows. Usually, these surface in adult awareness later, one way or another. The dark double in us festers if unaddressed, and others often notice it easier than we do ourselves. They are mirrored in our subtle actions toward others. Unaddressed dark issues can become lodged and sabotage the person's long-term health and growth.

These stuck places are heightened and extra-confusing for some Pearl teens, who saw their parents inappropriately work with their dark doubles, and who begin to care significantly about their relationships with their peer group. They need to learn self-compassion and to repay their outward efforts by firstly applying self-care, self-reflection, and self-understanding when their actions bring them self-destructiveness and poor judgment. Adult mirroring and guiding, as well as respectfulness and compassion toward the youth as the Pearl heals and attempts a relationship repair with someone, raises being human to a wisdom-informed, artful expression of inspirited adult life. It is a tragedy when youth feel no inspiration from adults.

It helps a youth to know how to bring warm and loving iridescent moments and ways into their actions with others that are wholly good and worthwhile in the world today. When adults truly care to mirror, and not blame or condemn youth, and can have the patience to stand by them as they follow through on new challenges, all of society benefits from the soulfully initiated new adult who emerges later.

Sleep

Another consideration for adolescents regards how their early, well-cultivated sleep habits and daily routines can vaporize seemingly beyond the sun's range for these newly nocturnal creatures. The cool, female Pearl, moon mama of teenage society, up in her lonely castle tower late at night, or the male Pearl peacock in his monastic, music app download chamber until the wee hours of the morning contemplate the painful abyss that they must overcome through life. They need to know that the task of overcoming feelings of the abyss won't feel so moody and brutal if they let their physical bodies rest and their higher subtle bodies go off to commune with spirit in the starlit, sleep-time.

They need nighttime rest to restore bodily functions and to prepare unconsciously in the heart for molding a new space that must be opened to manage their childhood feelings around love so they can begin to have more mature experiences of love. Their parents' love (*storge*) was only one kind of love. They will explore sexual love (*eros*), friend love and love for creating their own family (*philia*), as well as mature, non-dependent, universal love (*agape*).[12] This can make for long, distilled evenings of remembering the experiences and feelings of the day and trusting enough to let the mind quiet down into nothingness, and the body relax overnight.

Pearl Youth

The teenage years for a Pearl Youth can offer a temperate, whole, organic and self-constructive period. Yet, in the age of the internet and an increasing, all-pervading, mass cyberculture, they can also be a time of intense distortions around new inner sensations and interests. Raw, emoticon-stiff, emotionally removed experiences of having their awkward feelings whizzing through social-media spheres in the middle of school-time lunch periods, quickly become fodder for ridicule or bullying. Inner loneliness can be a significant concern for Pearl Youth when they have frustrated social skills to build on with other teens, or when social fears alienate them from reporting damaging internet interactions with other youths.

These young people, in the refining and revelatory older adolescent years, can have a smoother ride when parents, in league with community, manage to connect more frequently with these youths, using cyber-awareness themselves, and with warm objectivity about compassionate, worldly concerns. Adults addressing the outer life of Pearls in objective and collective student venues, with warm-hearted world sensitivity, can integrate a tone of soulful, unconditionally positive acceptance of youth, but with an ethical filter. This can make a huge difference to the Pearl Youth's sense of self-validation and loving inclusion.

Competing with an adult for "super-coolness" is not what the Pearl needs with a school counselor or any other adult in these modern times. Youths need to engage continually with adults about the questions of:
- Why and how do these computer games, apps, tech devices matter to you?
- What are the harmful consequences of their usage?
- How do you expect to cope with the dark side of this item or these consequences?

Adults need to listen to see if their answers, or the answers of the adolescents, reflect humanness, potential heartfelt selflessness, or an escape and feeble attempts to deflect responsibility for tech usage toward other people and adults.

Parents of Pearl Youth can hold loving awe and open wonder in their lines of questioning with their adolescents. When their teen's actions and behaviors seem to threaten their adult thinking, they can remember the polar ping-pong the child is in. They work to help normalize passing adolescent phases, reminding youths of the unique light-connection to their individual I-being.

Parents need to show their cool adolescents warm love without old sentimentality. Pearl Adults will revisit that warmth as inner resourcing in times when the coldness and harshness of society threaten to overcome them. They need these experiences of mature love. Rather than having divorced parents creep into behaviors of blaming the other parent for the strange actions and utterances of their adolescent on the internet, they wait, care, listen, seek understanding, and make reparations when necessary.

Also, the *coolness* that teens expect of each other can be too harsh for a Pearl Youth, who may not be emotionally mature enough to meet his peers in the increasing objectivity expected in early adulthood as a result of conceptual thinking. Each parent needs to warm sufficient love feelings around the adolescent, likely more so than for some other teens, while holding that love like a radiant lamp, and not like an all-consuming fire. Warmed in the blood, the youths can metabolize within their own lives what moves their will to contribute to goodness in the world while not becoming intolerant of either parent.[i]

The following are descriptions, visualizations, and biographies for the adolescent years, in the light of Rudolf Steiner's fourfold human being, and the physical, etheric, astral and ego-I necessities of uprightness.

---

[i] That is a highly mature spiritual task for a Pearl with one or both parents who may have been incarcerated for serious crimes. It is not one to take on alone, but rather with mature social workers and highly reputable, human, soul-spirit guides.

Ages 14 – 21: Astral Period: Feelings, Desires, and Mental Concepts

Figure 7.1: Alchemy and a maturing soul chemistry within

Seven Life and Learning Processes Check-in:

Is this youth seeming overwhelmed in the physical, etheric, or astral systems, by the changes in new adolescent life? Does the Pearl digest life experiences with daily conversations with family members, friends, teachers, coaches, or counselors at the school? Is the youth getting individualized opportunities to assimilate what she is learning while integrating intuitions and needs?

Are options and concepts being brought to the Pearl that only express the nature and abilities of whole families? Is the youth being ghettoized or being included in discussions with others about how they see things differently, coming from whole families?

Do other youths seem unable to digest or relate to where the Pearl is coming from?

Do groups of friends include the Pearl's feelings and needs? Do other youths mock or criticize the Pearl, avoiding appreciating aspects of this youth's character that may seem more open, warm, and soothing? Is the Pearl shy, tentative, or removed when the more natural teen experience is for peers to act "in" and coolly collected with each other?

Does the adolescent see themself as a significant contributor to the school, soccer team, dance class, or various planning get-togethers for youth social activities or friend's birthday celebrations?

Can the adolescent recognize times to ask for help to withstand and deflect taunts and jibes, or testing by peers? Is the Pearl having ongoing conversations with mature people about how the youth sees these social activities happening in the outer life and among others in friendship circles?

Is the Pearl able to identify sexual feelings and discuss and find mirroring about healthy and personal values and boundaries around sexual relationships and consent?

Are older teens an enigma to this Pearl, leaving the youth feeling separate or divided inside about their place in different kinds of relationships? Is anyone else aware of the Pearl's potential feelings of unrealized family capacities and missing experiences? Does the Pearl act confused about parenthood in general as the youth develops the ability to have children?

Does the adolescent have a strong inward sense of a path as a caregiver or as a society worker and contributor? Is the Pearl aware of support systems in place for adolescents and teens, such as school counselors, after-school groups or team leaders, other parents, extended family members, and youth-oriented organizations?

Does the teen feel capable of the negotiating and collaborating skills needed to live a natural life of contributing, giving, receiving, offering help, asking for help, and being able to radiate inspiration and seek inspiration from others when their own light is low?

Do you as the parent, guardian, or caregiver notice your own gender awkwardness arising? Are some confusing gender questions arising in you that the Pearl Youths might be wanting connection about, but that you are not skilled or knowledgeable about yourself?

Biography: Mathias, Age 18: Parental Alienation

Mathias lives in Germany, where he was born and where his parents met and did not marry. They dissolved their relationship when Mathias was two years old. His mother raised him with citizenship in Germany and another Western country.

Mathias had summer vacation visits in other European countries with his foreign-born father and his father's new family, over many years. His father is an innovative craftsman. His mother, striving in the fine arts world, raised Mathias with the help of a Waldorf early childhood and grade-school education.

Both of Mathias' parents lived in tight economic circumstances, with his father, a contractor with employees, doing better financially than his mother. His parents carried on financial and emotional jealousy and animosity throughout Mathias' growing years that seeped into Mathias' awareness despite outward appearances of considerate co-parenting. Mathias' mother, a sensitive woman with a strong, matriarchal mother, often emotionally manipulated her son about her loneliness and her need to keep Mathias in her life for her own self-care. She would talk his father down.

Although Mathias thrived in lower school, he struggled socially in high school and became addicted to computer gaming as soon as he was old enough to use computers. (Computer work is restricted in some Waldorf schools until the adolescent years.) At the same time, Mathias became obsessed with marijuana.

During the economic downfall in the West in 2008, Mathias's mother sent fifteen-year-old Mathias to live on a long-established and reputable community farm in the country of her second citizenship. There, a strong father figure held sway on the farm and Mathias thrived through his connection with the farmer's son and the son's friends, who also regularly smoked marijuana. Mathias, a meticulous young man with a melancholic nature and enthusiasm for learning carpentry and architecture, loved working on the farm and with the farm animals.

Mathias was also exposed to a sophisticated musical and theatrical culture while living in the country. With some other young farmworkers, he discovered the liveliness of the farmer's bakery business while preparing and selling whole-made foods from the land. Later, he returned to Germany where austere economic measures were in place and his parents' economic circumstances were challenged.

In his seventeenth year, on a trip back to live in another part of his mother's second citizenship country, Mathias was now addicted to cigarettes, frequently smoking marijuana, and determined to start driving. He was not going to school then. He lived among Waldorf community members and worked with a carpenter to get money to pay for a starter car and gas.

In the process, Matthias opened to some counseling with me to normalize Pearl Youth issues, feelings, needs, and missing pieces. I spoke earnestly with his parents in Germany to help them to overcome their animosity and bitter estrangement. Out of that, Mathias returned to Europe to live with his father's family. He apprenticed with his father in carpentry and architecture while having an experience of a more whole family for the first time in his life. Mathias took up reading the mythological Waldorf high school story of *Parsifal*.[13] Marijuana use became less of a crutch.

The Parsifal story is about a young knight whose undeveloped ego forces and exuberant willfulness lead him to miss asking the right question of a masterful but ailing king. His error leads him into perilous yet profound adventures and relationships that teach him life lessons. In time, life brings him back to where he started, more certain to and ready to seek empathic understanding of other's sufferings, but with some of his own, deeply experienced life wisdom. With the humility and grace now to seek a purposeful life with compassionate awareness of others, Parsifal wins the hand of a beloved princess and the right to rule the kingdom.

Adolescent Visualization: Ship in a Storm

In anthroposophical child development, adolescence moves a child from the second seven-year stage of growth, called the etheric stage from ages seven to fourteen, into what is known as the astral stage from ages fourteen to twenty-one. A youth's feeling forces can be deeply inspired toward a still naïve but idyllic goodness, or dulled toward the other pole of potential suppression, anger, rebellion, and possibly disillusioned depression.

In the earlier full blossom of the etheric years, the child filled up with life forces and was strong in imagination. The child had healthy habits established in basic self-care, hygiene, self-discipline, and social cooperation. In the Waldorf lower school grades, the child lived into the fully integrated, whole-body, heart-and-mind capacities available biologically prior to sexual maturation. The child lived imaginatively, with plenty of artistic opportunities, dynamic physical play, and movement activities in eurythmy, Bothmer gymnastics, and sometimes, spatial dynamics.

The child's mornings were filled with reverent music, verses, stories, and structure-building skills. The Pearl Child ripened some imaginative, practical capacities in gathering, sorting, forming, researching, identifying, articulating, memory-strengthening, and relating with much of the natural world and its material organizations and laws. Ideally, the Pearl's life had been sculpted by parents' warmth, nurturing, and hands-on engagement at home. The natural sense of the rhythms of nature and the cosmos were established and attuned by yearly festivals. The Pearl also learned to be in regular engagement with many of the same peers in class for years. (Waldorf students in grade school mostly stay with the same teacher through grades one to seven.)

Depending on many factors, such as the child's cultural, religious, or economic background, as well as the breadth of the family and community relationships and even the geography of the region, the child has been introduced to a certain level of outer-world experiences. By adolescence, the Pearl has likely had many kinds of experiences in more superficial human interactions outside of home. The child may have inwardly invested some sense of a free, moral, and ethical patterning as a result of the influences of certain important and responsible adults in the child's life.

With the emergent development of the astral realm of deep feelings and desires that opens in pubescence, the youth begins a seven-year chrysalis phase of highly sensitive transformation. Mixed with a bodily experience of unsettling neurological, hormonal, and chemical changes, the youth trustingly orienteers through a forest of uncertain impressions, joyous stirrings, awkward sensations, thick entanglements, inspired insights, and unfamiliar yearnings. For many Western-world adolescents, and increasingly more in other world regions, these seven years of development also represent a period when the adolescent becomes the driver of a powerful and dangerous motor vehicle.

Higher-thinking capacities begin to move the youth into levels of capacity that only human beings can claim. This young person's world of nature, animals and the lower senses can become challenged now, as the youth seems to reject or distance oneself from parts of this earlier world of earthly life connection, embracing it from a cooler and more thoughtful and conceptual perspective.

The adolescent may seem to be dropping interest in earlier experiences altogether, taking life all in now from a less engaged, conceptual, and objective distance. Suddenly, some things of childhood can seem to the youth somewhat insubstantial, or perhaps the opposite—too weighty. In little steps over several years, life begins to feel refreshingly new and exciting, while some past experiences, which were fine or profoundly enjoyable at a younger age, are now unacceptable, frustratingly "dense", "boring", tiring, or not worth the same effort now. Male and female-bodied youths portage these new waters both in similar and in different ways.

Some youths today actually experience a sense of gender melding, not identifying strongly as male or female, but more gender neutral or undefined. Since humanity is in an ascendance pattern now and beginning the stages of a return to androgyny in the future, this will make sense to some and be confusing to others.

The newly emerging youth begins to take what has been imagined and practical when younger and moves this into more functional, conceptual symbolism. This, as with the study of algebra, represents earlier imaginations and hands-on activities in life being transformed mentally into symbolic, complex, and managerial knowledge. Later, this conceptual thinking becomes the ability to understand and discern, for instance, that an (0) on an accountant's sheet may mean "no taxes on that income," or "balanced financial credits and debits," or "a space to be filled with future data." It does not just mean zero or nothing. It has meaning, depending on what meaning someone has given it, although the symbol itself, in basic, early-childhood thinking, meant a ring, a hole, or no thing is here.

This new, efficient, and diversified ability of the child, to conceptualize a symbol for something that the youth now wants or needs to represent, based on something not actually in the room or in the youth's hand or vision, is the new land of higher *conceptualization*. Without careful inspiration and guidance in this time, a youth can begin to lead a life of abstraction, rather than one still in balance with very human and nature-based interactions and responsibilities, and with creative, loving relationships.

These new capacities for understanding life open in ways that the child could never have experienced fully alone before. This new stage brings, for instance, the ability to foresee, plan, or manage the amount of time or energy that a project or goal might take without enacting the actual steps to first do it.

At the same time, as the adolescent's mind is changing its ability to see the world in more complex, representational forms, the young teen's body begins to pulse with the newness of procreative powers. It becomes filled with urges seemingly beyond the capacities of the mind. These new insights begin to expose the adolescent to the wholeness and existential meaningfulness of life, birth, human death, and the cycles of regeneration.

For many youths, adolescence in the West is a time that also brings a desire for experimentation with levels of higher consciousness and spiritual highs that teens often strive to reach through marijuana, alcohol or other substances. This adolescent time of testing the reaches of one's higher abilities and understandings, bears the markers for poor risk-taking, addictions, and emotional wounding. This often happens through painful peer relationships, and group strife, if strong adults are not present in the right way to help buffer as well as co-engineer this age and stage of youth.

Visualization: Out of Imagery into Feeling – Clipped by Concept

To have a sense of the transition to older adolescence for a Pearl Youth, a visualization activity can bring some awareness. Imagine yourself, in this moment, sensing and feeling as a youth entering adolescence, moving from imaginative thinking into higher conceptual thinking. Bringing an artist's eye to your imagination, you are aware of a seascape ahead of you with golden sunlight raying through a darkening, cloudy sky. A magnificent ship is docked nearby. In the distance are green, mossy coves with mounting waves thrusting down upon driftwood-strewn beaches.

There is a sense of natural, beautiful, and colliding forces in the ocean waters of the feeling life, and in the cloudy skies of thinking. This new, conceptual I-being is going to navigate in time with clarity through the distracting and practical-sensual challenges of life's material concerns. The challenges of the tasks at hand are like mounting storm waves laying the fearful heart bare and exposed to majestic peaks but also deep, primordial fjords.

Something about the view ahead seems olden and ominous, and not for his soul now. The youth wonders how to grasp some truth in all of this for the times, and to forge a character worthy of containing what arises in dreams. The youth pierces rising fears and anxieties with clear plans that seem like lightning crackling through thunderous clouds. The youth strives to be natural while not succumbing to fear, choosing a sometimes clear, sometimes wavering course of action significantly different from the brutal captains of history. The youth aims for survival and grace, as well as a healthy love for the other crew members' safety and well-being. This may cause the youth to have to go off charter at times and recalculate the navigation plans, but the adolescent has been guided to take certain diversions in stride, undaunted by messy old imaginations and legends of calamity.

Imagine this seascape representing the inner and outer feeling experiences in the elder, adolescent Pearl upon entering this new world of teenage astral testing on the high seas of socio-relational confusion. Awkward, emerging, and reconstituting mental capacities for organizing complex experience into efficient, rhythmic, and responsive action are more loosely tethered to this child of divorce than what a more whole-family youth might have as early-life, foundational strength. Insecure nervousness from the past can leave the youth less certain of triumph in these exciting but also daunting life adventures. The youth may unconsciously try to shy from all that natural, human soul-potential says that the Pearl can step up to in the best and worst moments. A shadowy sense of failure, harkening from childhood years, may hound and haunt this Pearl's natural ambitions to meet the world with a capable and whole-minded spirit.

This worried youth, sailing headlong into the unbounded and frigid waters of *cool* (conceptual) adolescent experience, may feel a lot of maturation as a rude awakening at worst, and as a real headache at other times. Unlike the youth with the well-attended and scaffolded courage and grace cultivated from close and accepting parents, supportive extended family, family friends and connected community members, this young person may be hauling sail on a raw nerve. The Pearl's refined and guided mental-framework-hull (a metaphor for the frontal brain cortex), for debating different future scenarios in exciting and foreboding seas, is not nearly as bolstered as some peers from whole families, despite having strong potentials and capacities otherwise.

The Pearl will require firm moral focus and presence, assisted and inspired by wise strangers and gifted navigators along the way, in order to hoist in the ropes of self-sabotage when they loosen from the less firm ego-I deck. Some self-glorifying that arises, by necessity, out of the Pearl's need to acknowledge outwardly and advertise personal over-comings and successes that go unnoticed by the family of origin members, must still be monitored and reined in for the very dark shadow that such behavior could develop into. Some hubraic reactions are rational and inevitable for a neglected soul and can represent an attempt to rally depleted energy.

Untethered, the youth can be led beyond the good fold of benevolent collaboration with others. That could feel deeply inwardly disappointing to the Pearl, whose attempts to feel a sense of belonging with others may have already brought significant grief. In this sailing metaphor, the other crew members may lose faith in the companion that they need to trust to help them get through the challenging seas ahead. They relegate the youth to the simplest, servile tasks and the youth's self-dominion gets abandoned.

The youth's decompensated energies need attending in different ways than other youths in whole families. The challenging self-balance tasks the youth is unconsciously struggling with represent hard work that needs to be acknowledged. In addition to the strife-filled inner work going on, the teen may spend much time alone away from school and youth societal events, exhausted and unsupported. Attempts to compensate for neglect can come out annoyingly to others, but they need to be gently checked and lovingly buffered by good and kind helpers if the youth is to come to real strength in the good work of cooperation and shared leadership—both significant tasks for all souls in our times.

With an unshakable trust in the cooperation of the venturing companions, in any weather and in the presence of whatever is brought in uncontrollable circumstances (a trust that is less easy to cultivate for a Pearl), this youth has the potential to meet great callings in life like everyone else. However, this rosy picture is not how many Pearl Youths today enter this stage of life.

Adolescence is its own world of human expansion and adventure, and yet it is what many parents of Pearl Youth see strictly as training grounds and battle-readiness prep for future jobs—the more tech-advanced, the better. Teen life, in many distracted parents' minds, is an unfortunate detour from the work of gearing up for the pursuit of full-time engagement in filling bank accounts, learning the complex game of paying rent or owning mortgages, being a sports hero or heroine, or following mom and dad's footsteps into a social game full of strategic contracts and power-over conflicts.

Yet, that youthful Pearl's future could hold a new and more supportive vision along the lines of Rudolf Steiner's anthroposophical view of the developing and emerging human being who must come through suffering, and who is not lesser for it. In this way of thinking, anthroposophically minded people can renegotiate the way people care to live in association with others. That can include new approaches to an energy-sharing life (as in solar farm communities, for instance), conscious finance and resource sharing (CSA food cooperatives, conscious small entrepreneurial efforts supported by loan systems such as those cultivated in Rudolf Steiner Finance [RSF][14], and intentional living-space sharing such as in eco-villages).

With the higher, conceptual mind in place in a Pearl, and practical, life-skills capacities developed and supported, including self-care skills, the challenging material-financial issues can be much less of a focus for the young Pearl Adult's energies. In a conscious, supportive community, the social organism can make room for more morally and soulfully helpful inspirations between living companions. Youth could be planning a future with people who behave more in honest brotherhood and sisterhood than what many divisive parents of Pearls were able to arrange with angry and bitter hearts.

By mid-adolescence, a Pearl Youth is often already entangled with the heavier sides of socio-political heart pain, with a soul weakened and endangered, right at a portal time in society with people engaging some of the most massive technological, cyber-dominated mechanisms ever imagined by mankind. A Pearl Youth's ability to see humanness within the exciting but also potentially ruthless and freedom suppressing machinations of our times is daunting. Rather than living into natural human rhythms and relationships, some may become emotionally disconnected and too invested in computer games, internet news, social-media bullying, and increasingly alienating experiences of peer disconnection. They might even find themselves in an escapist, anti-hero cultural life, or stuck in underworld, gang initiations.

Keeping in mind and applying all that has been mentioned in earlier chapters about the twelve senses, temperaments, life constitutions, polarities, artistic engagement, and the seven life processes, five important signatures of anthroposophical healing can particularly benefit the adolescent child of divorce.

These are: a) *creative engagement with nature,* b) *movement and role-playing,* c) *emotional intelligence and education in peer interaction* that identifies negative, tribalistic tendencies as opposed to healthy, peer group actions, d) *exposure to "grace" in adults* through meeting inspiring adults working in the arts, non-profit organizations, philanthropic centers, and progressive, social development groups and businesses, and e) *meditative exercises and mindfulness lessons* for creating hut space when necessary to guide the teen toward self-awareness and emotional resourcing when the technological world threatens to become overwhelming.

Creative Engagement With Nature

Therapeutic work for Pearls can entail nature-oriented, out-of-school, adult-mentored, and self-designed group encounters. Adolescent learning opportunities that take the youth away from the desk and into the real laboratory of life can have a meaningful impact in an increasingly computer-dominated world. It is helpful to always keep in mind that a sensitized and respectful presence and tone in the facilitators is paramount to the trusting relationships so necessary for Pearl Youths.

An exciting adventure in nature such as a class camping trip with canoe portaging, can teach a youth a great deal about geography, biology, social studies and the physics of light, warmth, and energetic force. Outdoor activities with other youths, which don't give time for inner emotional check-ins, can turn back on a Pearl Youth if the youth becomes unconsciously destabilized at the evening campfires by experiences or emotions that other teens might not take so sensitively because they feel more secure inner resourcing. The bantering and discussions can expose the youth to a missing piece in the Pearl's own family relations and relationship development that can sit open, raw, and bewildering.

A Pearl Youth is often having to do inward personal checking, either consciously or unconsciously, to hold themself in an emotionally grounded way in situations with other youths. The Pearl can feel left out and unable to relate to the nuances of the conversations, jokes, or certain playful interactions. Often, much more work is going on inside of a Pearl than what other people are aware of. It is not fair to say that the youth is just taking everything too personally. Rather, the Pearl is a rightful person taking in what can be digested and processed about the social life with a home-safety net that may be full of holes.

More realistically, the Pearl is unconsciously working for balanced thought while wondering what it is that others are doing socially, and seemingly more successfully or harmoniously, than what the Pearl Youth knows to do. How others behave can feel alien and awkward, even if their approach to life appears to the Pearl to be more connected and stabilizing. The unconscious confidence of the peers can be confusing since the Pearl Youth's inner sense of self may be regularly wavering or oscillating, feeling edgy and anxiety-causing. A level of unhealthy, critical, self-consciousness can set in.

Teachers, school guides, group leaders and other adults in the lives of adolescents, who are not Pearls themselves or have not experienced such family alienation, are rarely challenged to be as self-responsibly aware in every aspect of their lives as these children are. They often don't relate, and they may think the youth is too mature for the Pearl's age. An adult many use a put-down comment or try to force a sense of fortitude and structure on the youth that is closer to their expectation of how the youth should perceive the world and behave in it.

The youth can feel that an injustice is being perpetrated since the Pearl is doing everything rationally appropriate to the personal life circumstance to function, bring some self-care, and stand alone in a disorienting family culture. The Pearl has a different framework for objectivity setting up inside as a result of working to overcome the overly patterned and ingrained intolerance learned at home. Community support is needed, but not if the youth feels bullied to be what others expect without others understanding the Pearl's very real challenges, vulnerabilities, and strengths.

Movement And Role-Play

Movement and enactment activities such as physical education, dance, and drama have been typical curriculum subjects in high schools in different modern eras to support adolescent growth. The frequency and levels of instruction and involvement have tended to fluctuate in educational eras since the turn of the twentieth century. Much athletic activity in high schools over the years has become synonymous with strength, fitness, health, teamwork, accuracy, resilience, and cooperation.

However, since the late 1980s in North America, public schools pressed for academic rigor among students at the expense of hands-on learning, humanistic arts programs, cooperative games learning, or laborer-apprentice, skilled-craft classes such as machine shop and home economics classes. Many balancing activities have become largely relegated to after-school activities paid for by parents in clubs and organizations such as hockey teams or ceramics art classes. There, the values of social grace, mutual human respect beyond pure competitive edge, and universal access may or may not be well-cultivated.

Too often speed, competitiveness, efficiency, and tough, dominant endurance are the heralded norms of after-school sports and extra-curricular activities—with little in the way of emotional-mental awareness instruction, sexual assault prevention training, and the cultivation of cooperative systems-building techniques that integrate diverse points of view. Rarely are youths encouraged to develop any of their own new kinds of fitness activities or sports games, at an age when the encouragement of such developments would be greatly inspiring to youths. Grace and authentic, youth-level, heartfelt connecting gets pushed out of the youth's life in favor of an adult, professional-minded, and even falsely tribalistic tradition that is imposed on youths with hyped expectations. For any youth, including Pearls, proving oneself in an adult-rigidified, competitive hierarchy can quickly devolve into ruthless dehumanization.

Speed, toughness, and robotic efficiency become the popular currency, and an increasingly thin soul life becomes the price paid to prepare to live the imposed "dream" of tough dominance supposedly leading to future power, wealth and control over one's circumstances and others. Real joy can become a rebellious aside to the main game of beating everyone else, even when others feign friendship on the outside, or outright resort to bullying. Painfully, too many Pearls know how few true friends are cultivated at school or in sports teams—meaning real relationships of companions who are there to help them from time to time when family troubles knock them down.

The Pearl Youth in high school can feel at times like a humanized transit pass, displaying the "in" ticket for the right to wander among *cool* persons, places, and things, yet wondering what the real destination is, since little touches the heart or warms authentic, soul-spirit connecting with others.

To the depressed Pearl Youth, everything can feel too much like distraction and superficial entertainment. The youth feels social pressure, but inner missing pieces from home life can thwart the Pearl's ability to understand and cope with more social complexity. The politics of school can get the youth down and leave the Pearl feeling confined. The youth can feel inadequate to enter and influence the social sphere. If the youth just ignores the relational realm and focuses simply on skills-building, the Pearl can be unconsciously contributing to an even weaker soul life later in the adult years. This can be exceedingly painful and bring setbacks for the Pearl when the Intellectual Soul stage opens up and inner relationship resourcing is again thin and unsupportive.

Pearl culture has some uncomfortable and challenging changes to bring to the adult world if Pearls continue to have their basic relational needs left in neglect. Recently, the World Health Organization (WHO) determined that the badmouthing that Pearls often experience from one parent putting down the other during and after divorce represents a significant, ongoing health threat, including mental health, to children of all ages well into their adulthood.[15] This highlights a societal issue and potential mass social problem since millions of children, youths and young adults are affected in the West today.

These issues can make the adults around Pearl adolescents very uncomfortable. It is not the fault of the youth, but when society's leadership representatives also neglect the real inner issues of the youths in their communities, relegating them back to the dysfunctional family unit, the child's own dysfunction in adulthood will start to cost society heavily through illness, crime, homelessness, and public disruption. Social media has become a venue for this very kind of societal disharmony, with heavy fighting and hate dissemination among different groups, including blameful male-female relationship conflicts. Not all of this is driven by Pearl issues, but some of it is highly consistent with the issues of divided families.

High school counselors and extra-curricular leaders can work to attune to Pearl issues in realistic and capable ways, compassionately supporting Pearl Youth, and patterning emotionally intelligent social skills for the youths. In youth sports, leaders need to take the moral responsibility to teach grace in sport, for instance, the way that Waldorf schools do.

Waldorf students learn about the Olympic athletes of old, whose heroic status was not simply based on physical splendor and hyper-efficiency in sport, but on a higher-order grace and social responsibility to the *polis* or the society and all of its people. A skilled athlete was not declared the winner if that young person could not measure up equally in human inspirational good standing with others in the consciousness of the times. That included a reverence for the gods or higher cosmic forces. That higher nature showed in the movements of the athletes and in their I-thou interest in the betterment of all citizens and society as a whole.

People leading adolescent youth today are on the front lines of Pearl Youth life, and are more than ever required to be significant role models. Yet, youths need role models who truly get who they are and what they struggle with. Teachers, policy makers, judges, lawyers, and health professionals who have a deeper consciousness of the suffering of these youth can work to stop the stigmatization and blaming that they often experience and start supporting specialized practices that can truly help Pearls to evolve.

A Spacial Dynamics group verse based on an ancient Greek saying still holds much soul meaning for a group of athletic teens, including Pearl Youths. Aristotle's tome, "The hardest victory is the victory over the self!" bears a much greater fullness of meaning than a tribalistic, football cheer-leading chant ("Rah, rah, rah, bush kum bah, go Royals go!") For Pearls, it is often a victory to find and honor a true self firstly, out of the rubble of family conflict, before being able to be the victor, or master, over one's own behavior and life.

One of the features of adolescence is to realize the ninth sense of the all-important sense of connection to the other, learning how to appreciate the grace, strength, and sufferings of other human beings. Role-play enactments, where ancient figures meet up with modern characters in sport and other disciplines, can bring much-needed wisdom and humor in adolescent learning, showing how we see the other today and how honorable humans might have been expected to treat each other in the past.

This might be set up as a video interview in homeroom class, between an historic hero and a modern sports star. It could be an introduction to a staged school debate, in a woodworkshop setting with the historic figure and the modern one working together on a craft project. A grade eleven civics class could have students working in historic-hero and modern-hero roles to design a petition to divorce-court judges about the treatment of children in divorce.

This teen engagement is done while creating interest around how to interact with others in empathic ways with authentic, practical deeds, while in the middle of today's modern pressures. Students question why human interaction is different today than in the past and if it seems that humanity has increased in honor and grace or decreased. Students seek ways to uphold honor and grace now.

More enactments can be played out regarding class systems and culturally different social behaviors using nonviolent communication practices,[16] or Augusto Boal's Theatre of the Oppressed,[17] by teaching political diplomacy, and by offering students practice in trauma responsiveness between individuals.

Emotional Intelligence and Education in Peer Interaction

Coincident with the decline in humanities education and physical-health focus in many public high schools, has been an increase in computer-based violence among North American teens. The systemic cyberbullying among adolescent groups, as social-media outlets such as Facebook and Twitter became popular between 2010 and 2017, was in part a mirror of adult bullying in society. Youth, who regularly experienced one or the other parent bully the other at home or after divorce, are highly susceptible to computer violence. This online activity has become darkly entangled with acts of suicide by youth who have become grossly intimidated or sexually abused by unbridled peer taunting and adult decadence.

Emotional insensitivity comes from not learning early enough that all people experience feelings and needs, and that checking out difficult feelings, to discern issues and make repairs for misunderstandings, is an essential part of an adolescent's life-skill set today. This has led to ongoing harms and thus debates about the leadership ethics in sports and fitness organizations promoted in and out of school for teenagers, including physical and sexual assaults in hockey leagues and gymnastics communities.

Concerns have ranged from the pack, gang, and false-tribalism mentality of team pressures,[18] to convincing youths to see people as products and competitive machines, or to the influences of computer gamers and sci-fi robotics hero-worshippers who inculcate a hardened, counter imagination to industrialization and the cyber-technology surge, rather than a humanistic and more soul-spiritually related one.

Yet, this is not always the case, and good team interactions, such as in the heartwarming story of the efforts of students at Michigan's Olivet Middle School[19] recently, are very worth highlighting. The students in that school planned together to put their full efforts toward getting a football goal for a classmate with learning disabilities, simply to help a vulnerable and less empowered athlete in their midst to have a felt sense of the joy of success in sport that other teammates often take for granted. This is the same kind of cooperative, peer learning in Waldorf high schools fostered along with other, regular high-quality learning.

Exposure to Grace in Adults

Sacred rituals of the past are transformed in adolescence today into rhythmical, conscious actions of inspiration and higher striving between individuals. They have evolved into human activities involving regular practices that progress creatively and support human connectivity.

Distortions around humane activities versus inhumane values in society today abound. They come out of competitive pressures in hyper-materialistic societies with leaders who lie, connive, and behave in outright criminal ways to hold power in society. These influences can push adolescents into hardened, addictive[20] or reductionist behaviors, unconsciously trying to hold onto some sane moral ground while having little healthy modelling to know anything truly wholesome.

Well-integrated physical mastery games such as Spacial Dynamics and Bothmer gymnastics (discussed in more detail later in this chapter), which are taught in Waldorf high schools, can help to remedy some of influences of corrupt adults who claim endless attention on social media and other outward venues.

Adolescents need such modernized, physical activities that work with the grace of the human body and bring youths into gymnastic-type activities that keep etheric forces full and alive within the movements themselves. These movements should be brought in meaningful and fun ways with other youths and adults. Gym activities need to foster humor as well as skill and health.

Having ongoing experiences of live-giving forces moving in the body and between people, when the norm today is too much about putting youths in chairs in front of computer screens, or leaving them to socialize in virtual environments on social media, is essential for giving youth a lifelong sense of how grace moves with them and between them and others in human environments. This will be even more important as human beings begin to interact with increasingly sophisticated, human-like robots.

Waldorf teachers can do well to invite adult public figures of renown into the classroom as guests for short periods of time to participate in Spacial Dynamics activities with the youths. The students and the honored guests can make time within the enjoyable activities to have conversations about what grace means to that guest and how and when they have experienced it in their own lives within society, and with whom.

Intact Family

In an intact family, without generalizing too much, youth develop through situations wherein an adolescent experiences appropriate challenges while having their nervous system *held* well. That means that a growing youth experiences appropriate parent and family support that keeps them balanced and their neurology calmed in the face of sufferings and small or big traumas. This is often a familiar extension from trauma-balancing support and care that was given to the youth in earlier childhood.

Such foundations of peaceful, caring, capable, and resilient attention to a child's needs allow children to develop into maturity with a sense that the world is good and that a person can successfully manage a life of goodness in it, despite obstacles and even traumatic circumstances around them or which affect their direct lives. It is not a delusional state for a youth to achieve adulthood with this awareness. It is, rather, a sign of a well-balanced and supported human character capable of knowing that this person can equalize negative challenges with positive insights, appreciation, and resilient, cooperative efforts with others through outreach and the uninhibited sharing of needs and challenges.

This well-developed adult is excited to learn new things, is creative in daily life, and can arise buoyant in the face of hardship. The young adult is neither caught in too much *gravity*, nor too much *levity*. This person is not tempted to believe that life is too bad nor too good.

This is an ideal, however, and largely inconsistent for many adolescents in the West. For the millions of Pearl Children today, surrogate experiences of intact families coming from foster families, from Pearl's experiences of living with friends in intact families for a time, and the opportunities for Pearls to live in intentional, living communities can be some of the ways that they can have a felt sense of the resourcing, intact family.

How do Waldorf and anthroposophy offer any chance of this kind of a debut into adulthood for children from unstable early family experiences if it doesn't seem realistically achievable today for most people, anywhere? The question urges us to look differently at the shadows hovering over modern life for the new social ways that want to emerge. It is imperative to know how the dark double of a young adult presents itself today and how to appreciate the young person's struggle with it.

Parsifal revisited

Parsifal[1] is a tale studied in Waldorf high schools specifically because it meets, in a mythical-historic epic, the emotion and desire levels of teenage astrality. Parsifal's journeying also reflects the soulful, neurological, and developmental awakenings happening in the late adolescent. The story follows the life of an older youth whose early life was founded in seclusion with his mother in a forest of sensual delights. The boy's father, a knight, had been killed at battle. His mother hoped for her son to avoid a similar fate, so she hid him.

Like the elder adolescent of modern Western times, Parsifal, as a young adult, ventured into the world of worldly knights and took up the challenge of an individual life, albeit at first one of limited responsibility and wisdom. Unsophisticated, he was destined to pursue the desires, joys, and dangers of adult life with strong inner resources from a natural and well-tended childhood, but with societal blinders on.

In his early adult venturing, he misses important messages shared by the women that he meets, gets into battles with others more sophisticated than himself in life and love, and is emotionally blind and acts foolishly in his first opportunity to meet some of the greatest knights of the land. He was oblivious to the detailed social trials in the world and numb to the paths and trials of both the profound and dangerous other adults around him. It was, in fact, essential for this to be so, since the profound forces of consciousness, if welcomed too much and too early, would overwhelm him. Parsifal had to take a grounding path toward personal and collective awareness.

The one requirement that would have made Parsifal avoid significant struggles and harms in early adulthood, but that would also keep him from knowing his own, individual ways and capacities, involved the need for a more highly developed mind than the prior Intellectual Soul epoch could offer. To value a worldview capable of complex executive thought and a personal sense of human compassion—was not yet conscious in him in his earlier childhood cultivation. His prideful will, his simplistic heart, and his limited thinking would all need to be "broken" and reclaimed before gaining enough consciousness to develop mature enough insight to allow him to hold leadership so that others could be inspired and develop appropriately.

Parsifal's story comes at the very beginning of the Consciousness Soul epoch, in the late Middle Ages, when humanity was steeped in the intellect but only budding in other levels of human consciousness. The story of this young adventurer is still valid today because humanity is not yet very sophisticated with Consciousness Soul gifts.

As a symbol of the modern times, Parsifal had to learn the new life lessons directly for himself. The new mysteries required that he learn the hard way to see himself, to understand the needs of the land and others, and to finally value the reasons for compassionately asking the right questions of the most noble and honorable people of the land. In Parsifal's case, this meant asking the ailing grail king, the leader of the noblest order of knights, the Templars, what ailed him.

As a blooming, emergent adult destined for greatness, Parsifal can be seen in his awkward emergence as a younger version of King Gilgamesh of ancient Persian times. That leader was seeking the shining oyster and pearl of boundless ambitions and immortality. He was too unconscious, as a result of his times, to foresee the snakes, and also the righteous challengers, to his blind ambitions. Gilgamesh managed some passions but mismanaged significant others and nearly reneged on his whole higher purpose by falling asleep and allowing a snake to steal his one important treasure, the meaning of life.

Parsifal is an updated version of the Gilgamesh story, now with a European protagonist—a young man protected in childhood from the intrigues and trappings left over from the

Intellectual Soul refinement brought from Greece and Rome into Europe. He is destined to come through the trials of ignorant, early knighthood to earn the key of the future Consciousness Soul evolution. That is, he will become a benevolent leader because he has authentic compassion developed through his own sufferings that have brought conscious wisdom. This wisdom has arisen out of his own, self-directed actions, and not through how others have told him he must be.

The Parsifal story shows the archetypal adolescent's lack of full executive ability in his conceptual development, and thus a lack of mature distance from his overriding lusts for life. Naturally, he is not mentally prepared to foresee the many realities that could provide buffers and obstacles to the already challenging processes of life. It takes a self-created education in life for Parsifal to experience emotional pain for himself, to self-reflect, and thus to be able to soulfully understand the needs of others beyond his purely egoic plans. The medieval story of Parsifal fulfills the Waldorf high school curriculum's recapitulation of human consciousness, which is woven into the grade eleven year.

In a modern Parsifal experience, the biography of Pearl Youth Rubin can bring some insight into how conscious community can help a Pearl Youth through a challenging trauma today, getting quickly onto making amends and picking up the lessons sooner to put greater goodness into practice for the sake of society.

Biography, Rubin, Age 18: Moon Node Wakes Up

Three years ago, Rubin, a Canadian teen, rolled his car in the early morning, driving up a mountain in heavy rain. His car was totaled. He walked away from the car wreck after paramedics and police officers attended to him at the roadside. Rubin, a Pearl Youth, was unscathed, but still obviously shocked and shaken the next day. It was at a time coming up to his moon node[22] age and stage of eighteen years, seven months, and nine days (rounded, due to planetary orbs or halos to around 18 ½ years old).

The moon node or lunar node times in life are when the sun's path and the moon's path cross. This happens twice yearly until, at age 18 ½, they cross once again in the zodiac signs where they originally crossed when the person was born.

The node time highlights a moment of destiny when we look at what is and what isn't serving our individual higher purpose, and to look to our opposite way of doing things to see if there is an answer coming toward us from that opposition. Our modern destiny, and our feelings for our old ways of life, seem to clash, and our highest goal in time is to find the understanding consciousness in the center of the opposites.

Rubin had been out with a friend, close to two hours away from home, and needed to drive back on a highway requiring driving a mountain pass that is well-known in the region for frequent, deadly accidents. He said he had been having "a shitty time" in life for quite a while. He had also been smoking a significant amount of marijuana in that period.

He had stayed up to the early hours of the morning with his friend. Rubin stressed that he was not under the influence of any substances that morning, although he was known to enjoy marijuana and refrained from sharing whether he and his friend had imbibed through the night. He said he was exceedingly tired when he got in the car to drive home on dark roads.

Rubin had noticed himself nodding off at one point on the drive and thought to pull over. He reached for his water bottle for a drink and his driving arm turned in the direction of the water bottle as well. The car started rolling and Rubin blacked out just after noticing himself bearing his head down for protection.

The car rolled at least twice, witnesses said, and tore down three big trees at the side of the road until it came to a stop. Rubin remembered glass shattering, and afterward, the fire trucks and ambulance coming. Rubin had his driver's license suspended and was told he would have to replace the trees.

His grandmother, a longtime anthroposophist, took me to see him the next day for trauma healing. As we worked through a cocooning, warmth process involving blankets, a sheepskin, warm tea, and some cranial holding, Rubin cried and shook out the initial fear and feelings of shame, bringing him some shock relief.

In a trauma event review with myself and his family, he eventually knit together some other traumatic thoughts that he had been having related to his birth father's friend and his best friend's friend, each of whom had died in car accidents.

The heaving grief moments that Rubin experienced in our healing were deeply telling of the unprocessed grief that seemed to be locked in his memory. Rubin shook out some of that somatic impact on his body also. With family around, he was able to retell the event in a non-judgmental atmosphere, and to start to see it in perspective. He could let down gently from his hypertensive, nervous system spiking and come to a healthy, emotional "window of tolerance"[23] in his emotions.

At this stage, he could feel his blood coursing again, his feet on the ground, and the soreness in his knee. He was no longer jumping out of himself in dissociated thoughts. His stepfather learned some compassionate patterning as Rubin and I worked together. I noticed an awkwardness seem to leave the stepfather as he paid deep attention to the healing with his new wife's teenaged child.

It became clear very quickly to me that this was a critical experience for Rubin, to be seen in this holistic sense of crisis by his stepfather and for them to both be shown unconditional acceptance. The stepfather agreed that day to an emotional support commitment with his stepson. Rubin was also able to see his stepfather as a helpful resource person for rebuilding, out of his own feelings and needs, a sense of safe emotional support around his adolescent issues.

In anthroposophical understandings, there is a time in adolescence when we tend to experience a higher, soul-purpose event. It can be very subtle yet inwardly significant to our whole life journey. Today, people often miss the meaning of their first lunar node experience because they are not guided inward in any way to notice it.

The Parsifal youth today is entering adulthood often in a fine, very pure, and innocent way. In a Pearl-oriented Parsifal such as Rubin, he has soul strength for his survival tasks but low trust in the adults around him. I noticed this when I began Rubin's healing.

The trauma could have led him into self-deprecating thoughts and potentially even depression, if he had not had help to bring his nervous system back down from spiking, and an advocate to keep the adults from burdening him with guilt, shame, anxiety, and a sense of foolishness. Rubin's body and stomach went into spontaneous trauma-shaking when we worked through the initial retelling of the accident.

Without a counselor's age-and-stage awareness, and Rubin's anthroposophical grandmother's interest, awe, and wonder for his lunar node moment, he may not have lifted his fear and despondency up very quickly, into the light of potentiality and capability. He could see that the accident could have a positive turn to it because, in his "shitty," lonely time, he was able to open more to his stepfather and find some much-needed, heartfelt connecting.

If Rubin could have trusted his mother's new relationship as something that would be emotionally supportive of him and not just his mother, he might have been able to slow down in the period before the accident and ask of himself: "What ails me?" If his mother had been aware of seven life processes check-ins with her son when the new stepfather moved in, Rubin's emotional insecurity could have been addressed better by the adults.

He might have worked with a counselor to rehearse ways to share his needs with his mother and new stepfather. He may have addressed any number of feelings and issues around his parents' breakup. Yet, this is not the mystery process of our times, to become conscious only from what others tell us. Life must be lived freely, exploring into our own lives and facing the consequences. Rubin's processing happened after the accident, an event possibly brought about by parental alienation. For some levels of safety, Pearls may need help removing some of the more endangering mental-emotional obstacles that are a result of getting caught in the parent-conflict issues.

When his soul node comes around again, close to age thirty-seven, Rubin may be more prepared to avoid crisis by identifying his feelings, attributing them correctly to things that happened in his life, and finding ways to use his feelings in a conscious manner. He may need to learn, in the meantime, to take extra care of himself when inner matters cause him distress. He may learn to stop and check in with himself and with self-reflecting others if he is inclined to take a risk or adventure with a friend when he's not feeling at his best. The key will be not to let the fear from the past stifle his actions into the world from which new insights, directly related to his individual path and choices, can be revealed and from which wisdom can bring innovative thinking for himself and to aid others.

Pulled into Free-fall and Getting Back Up on Wisdom Feet

The Demeter/Persephone myth may be an important recapitulation story in our backward tending, Ahrimanic times. The ancient Greek, archetypal, mystery-school tale of the young goddess, Persephone, and her earth-goddess mother Demeter, dramatically describes their experience with Hades, the god of the dark underworld. Zeus, the ruling heavenly authority in the ancient Greek pantheon, arranged for Hades to have his desires filled for a companion in hell, by helping bring about Persephone's abduction to the underworld.

Persephone, stolen into Hades' world of darkness for months, was rescued back to paradise on the petition of her mother, the goddess of all that lives and grows, but with the caveat that the young maiden would have to return to the darkness of winter every year because she ate forbidden pomegranate seeds while in hell. The contract with the human and the spiritual worlds becomes one of balancing between opposite forces.

The Persephone story represents the explanation of the seasons, when six months of light and life-bringing warmth are overcome by six months of cold and barren darkness. However, it can also reflect the deep feelings and sense of a fall that Pearls can experience in a parent divorce, as well as the task to hold oneself steady in the heart while in the middle of conflicted, opposing views—long term. It can be seen as the Pearl challenge of going back and forth between parent homes, as well as a metaphor for finding the loving, still place between one's individual light and one's dark double.

The practices that took place in the Eleusis feminine mystery school where the Persephone initiations were practiced yearly, were deeply sacred for close to two millennia until their demise through corruption following the birth and life of Christ. The spiritual task back then was to go inward in the autumn, as the sun receded below the equator, and learn practices to honor the goddess of life and earthly creation, as well as the father god of the cosmos, in order to heal and survive until the spring and the return of balanced light.

Priests and priestesses of the Eleusis mystery school were still somewhat clairvoyant and capable of perceiving the cosmic influences on human beings in clairsentient ways. They were skilled with natural herbal remedies and sacred movement. A dramatic play was performed of the Persephone/Demeter story in the sanctified outer temple rooms where many society leaders and everyday people would gather once a year. Other rituals took place along the Sacred Way walking path to Eleusis from Athens. An inner temple held a most secretive image of a mother and divine infant.

Today, a Persephone-natured Pearl must guard against falling asleep in old consciousness and succumbing to dark thoughts of disconnection from the alive and cosmically connected world truth of light and life-giving, heartfelt, etheric forces. The Persephone Youth of today is one who has been exposed early to the dark double side of life through divorced-parent conflicts, especially if they are regularly exposed to parent negativity and drawn into inappropriate, hardened beliefs and thinking. That youth learns the lessons of self-guardianship, employing flexible but self-honoring, protective boundaries and contracting with the higher force in others to balance and manage their relational life issues.

The Pearl comes to know that divine, balancing forces will keep bringing the light and strength to carry on to a new season of love and higher goodness. This person takes self-dominion over affairs, as well as responsibility for harms done out of longings. In time, this

The Pearl and the Hut

person is freed to be able to keep vigilant attendance on their own spiritual development and thus able to help others who may also have become caught in negative conditioning, falling asleep in fear, insecurity, or trauma. This Pearl becomes a compassionate soul-spirit ally when the hardening forces of the world threaten to overwhelm the souls of others. The Persephone matures to the Demeter potential, having benevolent power to help hold back dark, Hades shadows that can threaten to suffocate a broken family.

The following is the Demeter/Persephone myth in full.

Figure 7.2: Demeter and Persephone

Demeter and Persephone

An innocent young daughter, of the great and holy gods, played one day in a meadow flourishing with wildflowers, near her mother, the goddess Demeter. The late-day sunlight had cast the emerald leaves on the surrounding trees into a warm, golden glow. The child, Persephone, being full of wonder and curiosity, wandered playfully across the high landscape, following an evening lark. Mother and daughter reveled in the freshness of the mountain air, noticing the salty scent of the ocean wafting from far below.

Suddenly, before Demeter's eyes, the land began to shake, and a mighty lightning bolt cracked the earth's surface. Out of the burnt crevice rode the horrifying god of the underworld, Hades. Hades arose with bloodshot red eyes, a sleek, stringent physique, and an unrelenting grip on the reins of a black chariot drawn by three steaming black horses.

Demeter stood helpless as Hades, with a quick and sneaky flip of his cloak, enveloped Persephone and pulled her onto his chariot. With a blood-curdling laugh, he charged his horses down again into the abyss from whence he had come, carrying the young girl with him.

The earth closed behind him and Persephone was enfolded into the world of anguish, terror, and wretched loneliness.

Demeter became overwhelmed by grief. For days, she wandered forlorn and lost, barely able to imagine the life of her daughter, imprisoned as she was in the clutches of Hades' manipulative attention and self-absorbed talk of false love. Every imagination of the horror stuck a dagger in Demeter's heart, and she wondered if she could keep her will strong ever more.

Helios, the god of the sun, cast his eyes to the earth mother with deep compassion, and decided to reveal how Demeter and Persephone had been lured into a trap by the workings and strategies of Zeus, the high god of Olympus and Demeter's brother. Demeter learned that Zeus and Hades had made a pact to relieve the god of darkness from his loneliness and despair. He had asked Zeus for a young companion and the ruler of the pantheon of gods had granted the favor through Persephone.

The mother goddess of the crops, herbs, flowers, and orchards fumed with anger. She called on Zeus, the keeper of lightning, in the mountainous heavens. She demanded an explanation for the capture of her daughter. She refused to accept her beautiful daughter's kidnapping as a sacrifice to the god of darkness. When Zeus ignored her petitions to have Persephone released at once, Demeter caused the living forces of the earth to begin to die.

Leaves turned to red, orange, yellow, and to a deadened brown. They fell from the trees. Grasses and grains dried up. Winds and rain blew them flat against the wet ground. Flowers wilted and toppled, and fruits fell moldy in the orchards. Birds gathered in the skies to follow each other far into the south. Soon all was barren and cold, but still, Zeus and Hades failed to comply.

Demeter, heartbroken, began to wander, seeking someone worthy to help her find her daughter. She called on the wise Hermes, the messenger god of higher thinking, to go to the underworld and warn Hades: "If Persephone is not returned in good timing, all of life on earth will be cast in death forever, just as the underworld would like it." Still, Demeter heard no answer.

In the underworld, Persephone was stricken into complacency with the dark god. Hades led her about his world, and the young girl experienced the pain and suffering of the people caught in the grip of earthly shadows, deceptions, ignorance, and selfish desires. Persephone's thoughts reeled, but her good heart kept her awake through Hades' endless, charming maneuvers of sensual love. The more he displayed his hoard of coveted delights, the more Persephone longed for her freedom and the light of day again.

Distraught, Demeter made her way to the well at Eleusis. There, four daughters of King Celeus and Queen Metaneira of Eleusis, met her in a profound state of godly glory and despair. Demeter, unsure who to trust, pretended to be a homeless fugitive, Doso, from a kidnapping in Crete.

The women, amazed at the fugitive's profound natural life forces and radiance in the middle of great grief, took her home to care for their sickly brother, Demophoon. Demeter healed the young boy with ambrosia and sought to make the boy a god, hiding him in a sacred fire at night. Metaneira, too common to see the truth of divine grace in her midst, spied out Demeter keeping the boy in the fire, and cast the goddess from her home.

In the underworld, Persephone, lonely, and losing her will forces for life, chose to eat a few seeds of a pomegranate offered to her by the overbearing Hades. Hades was eternally pleased. To eat of the pomegranate made Persephone forever a mistress to the underworld god.

Meanwhile, earth had laid under wintry, dead cold for months. Zeus began to worry that his sister would truly withhold all life as she had promised, if he did not convince Hades to return Persephone to her mother. He called on Hades and Hermes, and he listened to the messenger god's plan to release the young girl.

Although Hermes had hoped to secure the girl's release for good, he could not override the sacred law of Hades' underworld. Persephone had indulged in the six pomegranate seeds, so she could return to the light of the natural world of the greater gods, but she would have to visit again with Hades every year for six months. During that time, all of life on earth would go into darkness, cold, and gestation. Life would return with Persephone every spring.

The deal was made, and Persephone, wiser and poised in a new way for her responsibilities to the earth and the gods, was whisked out of the underworld by Hades. The dark god left the young goddess in the meadow of her innocence and rushed back to his wintry den. He gratefully anticipated the coming autumn, six months hence, when Persephone would return.

Wisdom in Disaster

The story of young Persephone is significant in the world today of hellish environmental crises, massive politician corruption, and corporate irresponsibility. The modern Hades shows up in many corners of our awareness, including in certain, transhumanist cyber-tech gurus who propose to completely disassemble human souls by using false physics and rationalizations to make the soul seem unexciting and irrelevant. They envision reassembling human beings with computer parts without their real understanding, consciousness, or moral input, despite the harm it could do to truly human and humane life on earth.

Persephone, through the powerful holding and help of her earth mother Demeter, rose with new awareness of the dark side of earthly life and death, and with a sense of capability, resilience, and acceptance of the dichotomies of being godly on earth. This is a significant step, for instance, from Hindu times when, in the Bhagavad Gita, the reluctant Pandava, Prince Arjuna, is told by Lord Krishna not to seek to see all that god can see because he would be overwhelmed by the hellishness. Arjuna had been told that he would not be able to cope with seeing the array of horrors of the world.

Today, many Pearls are already initiated into the negative, dark double awareness through early parent conflicts. With the internet, Pearls can also be exposed to endless horrors and negativity in the real world beyond their capacity to cope and without the necessary protected havens of home and loving family support. Early adulthood holds a frightening imbalance for many of too much darkness and not enough light. Being emotionally capable of seeing both the light and the shadows of life today requires extensive human wisdom (the *sophy* or Sophia part of anthroposophy).

The wisdom story of Persephone can prepare young Pearls to know that they can overcome dark aspects in themselves that seem to weigh heavily and which have come of out of old, less conscious experiences. Pearls need to remember that they have the power to see the brightness of a human spiritual life again. In order to serve humanity well, they need affirmations from life itself that they will one day safely pass the threshold between life and life after death with the peace of consciousness, holding just the right wisdom and integrity for their present times. They will accept that temporary wisdom will change in future lifetimes, but that light will overcome darkness again and again, since spiritually and cosmically, we are born from light and return to it. This is the eternal story in the ultimate word of the gods/goddesses through time and through consciousness changes.

The Persephone myth, in its purity, was a seed story for the future, and significant for our times when the worst images and experiences on earth can be known to all today through the internet. Demeter, the mother, would not lose hope and did not allow great anger over injustices to fully override her godliness and her task to lift others (i.e., Demophoon) up into the light.

Persephone unconsciously knew that her immortal foundations were unquestioned, and she endured, trusted, and strengthened her sense of goodness in Hades, knowing that her discontent, in the cold and heartless winter of her captivity, would pass in time. The goodness that she held onto and percolated in the darkness would emerge victorious in the spring, and ultimately, in the soul-spiritual value of her life.

Persephone's effort to survive the living hell unconsciously by eating some of the seeds of the pomegranate etherically kept her sense of self intact, leaving her in a spiritual contract with the earth and in the depths of her heart represented by her mother, Demeter. The transformation of that heart force today comes from coming through the dark times with individual consciousness buffered by the heartfelt help of the soul sisterhood-brotherhood of our times.

That is the seeding of the all-compassionate and selfless love that Steiner foresaw in the future feminine integration of the New Isis.[24] Some "seeding" souls already have inklings of this more thorough, selfless, feminine integration with the light that will be much more consistently gathered and realized in the future.

It is part of spiritual law that the Persephone story traversed the Egypto-Chaldean epoch into the Greco-Roman epoch when great spiritual events were preparing for the Christ event. The story led to the formation of the Eleusis feminine mystery school, around 1450 BC. The Eleusis school, and the later Ephesus mystery school, prepared priestly initiates for the event of Christ's incarnation and then death at Golgotha, and the resurrection in the etheric, known as the Holy Spirit.

In time, as the Christ consciousness began to percolate among people, the Eleusis school became decadent and spiritually insignificant, as the practices had integrated as needed in human souls, and new mysteries were about to be directly laid upon the soul through the Holy

Spirit of Christ. Yet in the seeds of the Persephone story are, according to Steiner, important elements of the new feminine, Sophia forces coming to the earth very soon, and the more developed feminine New Isis force that will come farther into the future.[25]

The Persephone story, as recapitulated today, is part of the Christ story. It is symbolically about the descent and then rise of consciousness of a healthy and capable I-being out of the awareness of the realm of human suffering, and the subsequent personal acceptance of the need to balance awareness individually. A balanced individual can have the inner resources to help raise others from their soul misery. This well-prepared person can inspire people out of despair in a soul-stirring, somewhat Manichean, compassionate way.[26] They will reverently facilitate others to trust themselves again, and to trust life's eternal love and grace, while accepting and strengthening their soul-sight beyond the earth's temporary love.

Persephone and the Pearls

Today, a Pearl Youth, with a weak foundation, may struggle as hard as Demeter with a dark night of the soul experience. The Pearl might not be able to hold back astrality and may feel a fury that love, and stability, have been demeaned and lowered into a such a dark place in the family. The Pearl may want to curse all of life, not understanding that such actions may harm one's sense of higher love. These are like stages of denial in grief and mourning. Since some changes that are coming up in humanity are exceptionally hard to imagine without strong heart holders and spiritual seers, the new "I" in the Pearl may intensely fight for appropriate guidance, stable home structures, and healthy, loving attachment. Rudolf Steiner acknowledged some forms of anger for their spiritual righteousness potential, though he did not support violence.

In the years since Christ's crucifixion at Golgotha, many leaders of religious orders that did not overcome old thinking and traditions sought control. Many denied the signs of spiritual awareness in others and have even condemned spirit seers or clairvoyants, chaining them with labels that stick even today, such as witches, heretics, and lunatics. If one is not raised with appropriate spiritual imaginations and rational spiritual-scientific investigative ability, then one can become laden with the poor and oppressive imaginations of others. An individual can usually directly spot poor imaginations through old labels that a people carries on for centuries against others without bringing any new insights of love toward them.

The task today is for all people to come to trust, as a prime knowing inside of themselves, that they have the profound, godlike capacity within their own hands, hearts, and heads to meet what comes to challenge them on the earth. This inner reflection of Christ is godlike, and never consistent with egoic selfishness. The inner task now and in the future is to stay human and loving in the working with others so as to realize one's way back to the heavenly consciousness with good heart memory of selfless service to other human beings. In time, individuals will trust the foundation of spiritual strength that a being like Persephone could inwardly hold, despite the sour seeds of destiny. They can remember the spirit-life-giving qualities of those red, blood-like seeds, and be reminded of a profound truth revealed at the death of Christ. More on this is discussed in Volume II.

In Persephone's time, 3,500 years ago, knowledge of divinity was cultivated in a group consciousness among priests, priestesses, and worshippers in mystery-school temples. These reverent practices prepared the soul for what the Christ consciousness would bring onto the earth—the awareness that every individual would come to "Know thyself" inwardly. All human beings can now come to remember the profound divinity of one's soul, and the responsibility to all that comes with acknowledging that in others.

When we have sufficient consciousness of all that we are as human beings, including the challenges of taming our own dark doubles, and the gifts and strengths bestowed upon us through to even the finest levels of reclaimed clairvoyance (something that Steiner said we would be re-cultivating more in the future) we will have access to perceive the light of the heavenly and angelic forces again, here on the earth, through subtle forces.[27]

Modern Persephone Perils

Any Pearl Youth or Adult who is unsupported to the point that the young adult falls into abuse by others, experiences life as a living hell. Young women and men who get abducted into human trafficking rings and are not helped out by society's safety net workers or others, can see that many people around them have not reached selfless divinity enough to know how truly to help their younger brothers and sisters on the journey. These young people are regularly in danger, but no one has figured out how to find them and rescue them. A Pearl is responsible for oneself in early adulthood, but never fully so, or fully expected, alone, to take on the task of self-protection and freeing oneself from the worst transgressions by others. Society makes contracts together to help everyone face horrendous crimes and damaging misdemeanors.

Loneliness and alienation are problematic stages in individuation work. Relationship is imperative, and elder, more developed spiritual community members have a responsibility to help guide younger ones, as well as to listen to what youngers can bring to the world in soulful action. Young Pearls are bringing an ego-I into place just like their elders. Elders haven't survived to be elders without some level of intact ego that was fostered along by others who took responsibility for such stewardship.

"Elders" does not mean people in their oldest ages and stages of denouement in life, though they can at times offer helpful wisdom. Anyone a generation older than another helps build life scaffoldings and also clears a path to heal youngers toward the stages of ego wholeness. A developing younger person cannot be of service to the needs of others or society's future if the people who came before them did not leave good paths with a thought to others to come.

That unsupported young adult may easily dissolve their own healthy habit life and self-care structures, diminishing the founding I-forces, and risking becoming abusive, neglectful, and unfree with others. When helping another, however, elders must maintain firm boundaries at times so as not to become too depleted to be able to help long-term, losing their own soul-seeing and possibly becoming entangled. Therefore, a whole, intergenerational community can offer the most support to people in need.

Except in great old age or when one is gravely ill or very directly dying, this handing over I-responsibility is a constant and unhealthy, egoic temptation. It can allow others' dark double forces to unconsciously control and manipulate a person's energy and hindering their ability to find the light through their own inner will and spirit connection. This significantly matters as one prepares for the passing at the threshold of death. For younger people, daily life can feel like bridging the death threshold as it did for Persephone.

Oscillating Between Worlds – Visualization

The following complex visualization asks the reader to step right into the shoes of Pearl Youths in our times. Please be conscious of the potential need to create a calm space for yourself and to make time for noticing your reactions. Mindfully, take hut time to integrate the feelings and sensations that arise in yourself, with compassion. You may support yourself by having an open conversation about it with someone you feel some trust with, or by finding an activity to shake heaviness up like dancing or shooting some basketball hoops. Use some creative-expressive therapy if you feel stuck on one difficult thought, to re-balance darkness and light.

Let's return to the metaphoric visualization of the seafaring youth who is about to step out into the world of adulthood.

First visualization: An older adolescent youth from a *whole family.*
Second visualization: A teen whose parents are *leading up to a divorce.*
Third Visualization: An older youth in the middle of a conflicted family divorce.
Final Visualization: A Pearl Youth whose grandparents and parents emigrated from India to a new Western country.

1. An older adolescent youth from a whole family.

An elder youth arrives one day to a ship's cabin porthole, gazing out on the sea and onto the sunlit horizon. The youth feels great excitement, quickly followed by a *normal* adolescent uncertainty that doesn't dampen enthusiasm. The youth scans the high cliffs of the fjord, and notices that the hue of late autumn light on the water is stirringly beautiful but also somewhat unwelcoming. It suggests the coming stormy season of wintry cold and hollow winds.

The eerie moment is notched up by a moment of anxiety in the young adventurer, who observes heavy, accumulating clouds in a far part of the skies. Metaphorically, although the youth is pulsing with many different and contrasting feelings, a stable inner *rudder* supports this elder adolescent for the long-run journey. The youth has faith in having:

- some strong and clear capacities to *pay attention* to the often unpredictable seas ahead,

- the ability to *envision* both opportunities as well as obstacles in the inlets and straits that show themselves along the way,
- wisdom to *breathe well* through troubled, fog-filled moments and not let fear rule the mind or stifle the heart,
- confidence to *attempt more than a single option* for action when the winds change, and
- *grace* enough to earnestly connect with others on the deck to receive the help needed when problems arise that the elder youth has no reference or experience for.

The youth *respects* the truthful justice that one is sailing with other human beings for whom this life adventure is just as important for their souls. This person is *willing to step aside or back* at times and let others lead. The mature adolescent *values others' input.* This youth can embrace the upcoming and unpredictable forays of the day, weeks, months, and seasons with an underlying sense of *joie de vivre, trusting* that there are many others who have good intentions and the will for the best outcomes for others.

2. A teen whose parents are leading up to a divorce.

Imagine, secondly, an adolescent whose parents, having been highly conflictual for some time, are finally orchestrating a breakup. The increasingly heated interactions of the youth's parents, and the intense thinking the teen may be doing to try to resolve the family worries, can cause the nervous system to be over-activated. The youth arrives at the metaphoric "ship deck" of life, ready to blow a gasket, but holding on, barely. The youth feels raw from lack of sleep and may be experiencing some stress illnesses such as indigestion, headaches, or tightening body pain.

The Pearl may feel a *nerve death*[28] that Rudolf Steiner noted can happen from over-intellectualizing or overthinking. In a heated moment, the youth swaggers about helplessly, trying to cast blame away from personal pain. The Pearl can act intolerant of people with whom the youth normally has good relations.

In the heart, the youth feels like ranting a heavy-metal music thunderstorm, cranking a hell-bent screech into the seafarer's night, strings busting, with no thought of backup singers to hold any kind of a melody. The youth may feel that there is no way to win and everything to lose. The youth is suddenly willing to put risk front and center, and unconsciously use or abuse the crewmates or anyone else at will to get the job done. The youth can't seem to own that this outraged behavior is actually coming from a mix of fear, sadness, and grief at the parent's marriage failure and breakup.

With everything so new in the family crisis, the youth may have no idea which people to count on to buoy depressive feelings about the family, since the youth isn't very sure of wanting to let anyone know what's happening. The youth's sense of stigmatization can blind them to seeing at least some crewmates as the humane resources or helpers they could be. The youth's sensitive inner being is already roaring with *normal* adolescent juices, while cortisol chemicals flood the danger-alert systems in the lower, animal-brain part of the neurology.

The youth may be cycling with unstoppable thoughts about what the future will bring for home and family in the future.

3. *An older youth in the middle of a conflicted family divorce*

An elder Pearl Youth whose parents are in divorce proceedings or difficult divorce mediation may live out this nautical metaphor for life more as an uncomfortable task to get through than an adventure to cherish. Life is constantly requiring the youth's *strained focus* since the Pearl can only guess what will come clear through the parent breakup. This sailor may start seeing life through an ocean-sprayed porthole full of water beads (water being a metaphor for emotion).

This Pearl is stepping up to sail their new body/heart/mind complex in an imperfectly known world with a consciousness clouded by an overwhelming array of feelings around having parents at court against each other. Some of these feelings can take on macabre forms due to the unmanageable nature of having parents who are often each expecting the system to side with them, while also working hard to prove why the legal system shouldn't side with the other.

Very often, family court can only make a decision for an arrangement of alimony and/or child-sharing with which each parent is not entirely happy. Mediation may get more nuanced details hammered out between parents, but latent grievances can still fester afterward and even for decades in a divorce settlement that one or both parents think is still unfair. The adolescent in this stage of parent divorce is only beginning to conceive, mostly unconsciously, what this is going to mean for the teen's emotional life in the future.

The Pearl may perceive the oceanic life ahead with rapidly *thinning inner resources* and a new, *unrelenting edginess* that the youth may only learn later is a sign of anxiety. The imagination of the windows of opportunity in life dripping with distorted feelings around family can elicit moments of *overwhelm and helplessness*.

In the sailing metaphor, the youth hesitates before setting sail, stuffing down a heaving stomach upset. Suddenly unsure of themselves and also of fellow crew members due to a subtle level of paranoia that can set in with a new sense of family conflict insecurity, the Pearl Youth *lodges powerful fears and anxieties into the subconscious*, unknowingly leaving them to eat away at the etheric life forces.

The youth, trying to captain their own boat, becomes faint at times with no understanding as to why. The Pearl wonders where courage has gone. The youth is stepping out on a much bigger voyage now than what earlier life had offered preparation for. *Self-doubt* looms, frustrating clear thinking, just when the youth longs most for a positive and manageable vision.

The youth in this scenario churns some thoughts over and over, worried about failing and not having parents who may no longer be heartfelt enough to buffer the youth's life setbacks.

If the youth's boat lurches in swirling waters at a channel opening, the Pearl may emotionally regress and want to huddle in the hull, leaving others to the responsibility of steering through life's storms. The youth can feel a sudden shame for not having the will to help others in the way that the youth's innate goodness and godliness would like to be able. The youth's capacity for *personal dominion is wrung-out,* and the Pearl may become dependency-minded without wanting to be so. The freedom to embrace life becomes limited in an unhealthy way, and the youth *may self-sabotage* by severely scaling back goals and ambitions.

If the frayed youth is expected and pressured to step up to normal tasks as usual, without appropriate counseling or other emotional support around the family divorce-court issues, the Pearl may still take the helm responsibly, and even hold well in challenging or dangerous moments, until reaching safer waters. However, when the adrenaline rush is gone, the Pearl can crumble, having over-extended one's energies, feeling let down by life's watery adventures. The young person can become unwilling to step into the vessel (life adventures) with the others again. *Absolute and intolerant emotional reactions* can take the place of hopefulness and supported emotional coping, undermining the natural, unconscious deep faith and inner gratitude that healthy teens mostly feel when overcoming new life hurdles.

4. A Pearl Youth whose grandparents and parents immigrated from India.

In one more adjustment to this seascape imagination for Pearl Youth, let's look at a youth from an immigrant, extended family, in a big city in North America. The youth's family is originally from India. This Pearl Youth of the next generation from the immigrant generation, experiences a breakup in the parents' marriage. Such an experience may have rarely been imagined in the original home country of this Pearl Youth.

The next-generation child hears the condemnation from the grandparents, who live with one of the youth's parents, of what a disgrace the Pearl's parents have brought on the family by divorcing. The divorced parents, however, appear to be civil with each other.

With a family past where couples were expected to work out their problems through tradition, worship, and putting up with hardships together, this youth feels caught not so much in the immediate family dynamic, but in the intergenerational one. The youth, who is two generations and thousands of miles removed from the ancestral, cultural traditions, finds themself entering new teenage territory with an outward easy-going nature but a stern, confused, and inhibited sense of guilt regarding the family-lineage connection.

This results from colliding cultural messages, seasoned with judgment from the immigrant elders about the decision of the parents to divorce. The Pearl is not sure how to be with extended family members, some who agree with the parents and others who side with the elders. Cultural gatherings from the India side become stressful, and the young adult wants to feel peaceful and loving with everyone.

The youth's spiritual culture says not to put energy into heaviness and unpeaceful feelings. In contrast to the smooth-sailing-older-adolescent-adventurer visualization in the first scenario above, this teen arrives at the dock for the journey feeling jumpy. The youth lightly plays around with fellow sailors upon arriving, with smiling positivity and an honest, warm charm. The Pearl is not, however, well-focused on duties or ready to take them up. To relax from family stress, the Pearl did prayers or meditation more than usual that morning and is finding it hard to get serious again about practical matters.

The youth feels sure that all will work out okay, but others around don't feel as confident about the sailing as the Pearl would like them to be. They recognize a bit of spinning, light-headedness in the Pearl but don't know what to do to help the Pearl become grounded again. This youth's meditative/spiritual practices are helping keep the youth's neurology clear of negative impressions about the family tensions, but they also seem to be uprooting and scattering the Pearl. This, despite the youth's reassurances of only being a bit playful before settling into a responsible voyage.

The Pearl senses the boatmates' distrust and feels pain. The youth would never intentionally mess up in a way that would harm friends and workmates. The Pearl feels more substantial and capable than others may perceive, even though the youth shows determination in a less "hard-ass" way due to cultural differences. Not feeling understood, the Pearl can feel rejected, but cultural conditioning may cause the youth to be even more light about it all, or simply release responsibility to the higher authority and become a passive observer and servant on the journey. The Pearl's room for incarnate growth together with the others narrows and the youth risks the cynical or detached ridicule of the Western crewmates.

Returning home, the youth feels sluggish and unaccomplished in the goal to achieve a good standing with their peers. The youth's despondency gives the grandparents reason to mock the divorced parents for failing to support the youth to be more successful in the new country. The wheels of new negative thoughts set the young person to reviewing childhood and then leaping to imaginations of being on the ship's bridge sailing to India and marrying an attractive, modern person there who might be more accepting and understanding.

The youth doesn't notice being a bit numb and exhausted in the stir of all of the conflicted feelings. The youth suddenly imagines shipmates yelling profanities because the Pearl thought to ignore them and wanted to sail far away from their goals and dreams to pursue one's own. Thoughts of the Hindu goddess of destruction, Kali, come to mind, then huge frustration hits for having thoughts of "stupid, old-world India stuff" from the elders.

The youth self-affirms about being a capable, modern, intelligent, and valuable, Western-world crew member here, and gets on social media to apologize to crewmates for absentmindedness. Forgiven by people who really like the youth's amiability and positive energy, as well as the youth's willingness to own up to mistakes, the youth feels positive and accepted again. The Pearl feels valued for the good track record of service demonstrated to the shipmates so far and looks forward to working together again soon.

That night, at dinner with the parent and grandparents, the elders nag about why the youth doesn't show more interest in going back to the old country to work or find a life partner. They needle the Pearl and the parent, saying that the youth might have a more successful marriage union with someone of the same culture. Soon, the youth gets thoughts that say it's impossible to win at life, and the Pearl's will forces drip away in a metaphoric cold puddle of water on the floor, for days afterward.

Documentary

In a contemporary British Broadcasting Corporation (BBC) documentary on divorce called *Mum and Dad Are Splitting Up*,[29] several adolescents speak to the classic pain and sense of abandonment that thousands, if not millions, of children of divorce experienced in the moment of their parents' revelation that they were going to get divorced. As Yasmin Alibhai tells it in an article in the *Daily Mail*, "The children in this documentary seemed like castaways, hungry and thirsty, dying to speak to someone about what happened to them and to ask their parents questions still left unanswered."[30] The documentary producer, Olly Lambert, evokes the image of a long shadow cast over his life when describing his own parent's divorce close to thirty years prior. The retelling of one young teen girl's life is depicted as a family swimming "in a swamp of secrets and lies."

Music and Arts: Budding Adolescent Culture

Imagine the moment when fighting parents decide that they have no option but to stop the marital conflict for the sake of the child. They close their discordant life with a complete stop, at least initially in their minds. They tell their children about the divorce with a sense of finality—because they are angry, "fed up," and done with it all. That break resounds in the child's soul like the moment the lyre player, harpist, or guitarist slams a full hand stop on the strings. The sensation can feel worse than a physical blow to the body because the fuller impact lingers interminably if there is never any healthy resolution. A dead, flat finish.

The lead musicians have bowed out and are heading in opposite directions, to melodies of their individual making. The youth stands alone with dissonant, raucous, or even grotesque music of old still inwardly playing and unnoticed on the outside. Adults can handle the hard-rock chord finale, even if it's angry, if they have a healthy ego-I to guide their self-healing after. Children in development cannot. For them, imagination and memory can go into overdrive.

At the height of new family divorces in the 1970s and 80s in the West, popular music heavily moved toward chromatic or tension-riddled themes and lyrics, often having no sense of resolution. Heavy metal music is an example of such music that rose as a dark counter to hippie music in the 1960s. It shadowed earlier classical music themes such as in Bartok's *Third String Quartet*,[31] popular in 1920s Europe. Music with much challenging oppositional resonance revealed Bartok's estrangement from harmony while he attempted to resolve musical tensions reflecting the deadly, oppositional economic and political issues of the First World War.

Recently, psychoacoustics theory[32] has suggested that sound, stable, resolved chords in music bring a biological harmony to the listener. This can bring some insight to working with adolescents who are in the middle of family divorce, or who are trying to express something about it through their music. Melissa, in the next volume, found classical music exploration helpful during her adolescent years in a divorced family. Playing the cello and traveling to other towns to play in concerts brought her some needed relief from tensions at home.

My own classical dance and joyful musical theater experiences as a teenager, away from both of my parents' homes, brought me grace and life-saving memories later in life. Balancing the adolescent soul with music is an important part of the Waldorf high school curriculum. Music explorations with a teen in counseling can bring some earnest meaning to the heart. In the classical music genre, an off-tonic piece like Beethoven's *Piano Concerto No. 4 in G Major Op. 58*[33] can bring a welcome resolution out of discord.

The range of music that can tap into a youth's soul and move him or her to a sense of connectedness is vast. Yet, some music choices offer more harm than good, especially music that plays too much on dark moods. Encouraging Pearl Youths to have conversations about the music they listen to and what moves them and why, without expecting answers, is a healthy way to keep curiosity alive in the youth. Leaving the questions and answers open-ended avoids oppressive judgment while helping accustom a youth to being consulted about choices.

Letting a Pearl Youth know that you value what he or she is thinking, or what he or she is trying to work out inwardly, is important to cultivate positive self-esteem for Pearls, based on something relevant for the adolescent even if it is not well-defined or confirmed. Music, though, like anything, can take a youth too far out of oneself. Consulting youth about their music interests, past and present, can bring them more present to their own capacity for self-investigation about personal expression, artistry, emotional resilience, and the ability to research what their individual, soul culture is about.

A counselor can also ask a Pearl Youth to imagine a piece of music created just for them, and what it would be like, in detail.

Eurythmy

For some adolescents, eurythmy lemniscate movement activities enhanced by music, and with verses that transition imagination toward inspirations, can bring the emotional life into greater balance. Moving back and forth between clear, opposite gestures, in the form that resembles an infinity symbol (shown below), can help Pearl Youth gain some sense of personal, emotional boundaries and inner holding, after a parental divorce. The youth can find oneself in the transitions and intervals in between the opposite gestures.

Figure 7.3: Eurythmy lemniscate

In another feature of eurythmy work, a teen can find ways to step around or back from parent-conflict moments, returning to them in cycles and with enhanced energetic forces through reinforcing gestures. This can resemble some Eastern Aikido[34] practices that teach a person the ability to conserve energy, step out of energetic harm, and keep a breathing flow in the middle of confrontation or tension.

A youth can safely work through some releasing and balancing gestures and movements that harmonize brain responses while also allowing certain choreography to move the Pearl through complexity, gracefully. Eurythmy works with breath alignment and movement to bring natural breathing practices into harmony with the soul. It can be gently healing and stabilizing to a distraught neurology.

One aim in eurythmy for Pearl Youth can be to help the youth to work through the oppositional lemniscate with reminders of the beauty and soulfulness of cosmically lawful, symbolic patterns. Initially, it is up to the healer to observe the gait, stances, defenses, refusals, and any other reactions the adolescent may have to moving between polarized opposites. Then, working lawfully attuned movement over time can resource the soul with new, helpful felt-sense patterns, even if they go less conscious for periods later. For an older youth, the lemniscate can be moved into a more complex, rose curve geometric pattern.[35] (The rose is a symbol of the Christ-conscious, etheric heart.)

The therapist can help the youth to choose music for movement practices, and also accept and relate to choices of music that the therapist makes. The understanding should not be made intellectual, but rather imaginative and left with open riddles to contemplate. The music and story of Wagner's Parsifal opera[36] are filled with opportunities for bringing open questions that leave inspired wonder.

Figure 7.4: Eurythmy working the lemniscate at points of polarized blockages

Through eurythmy practices, the teen practices relating to a sense of the other, in a way that leaves the youth free, with skills to revive their own I-forces if an encounter with a conflicted parent threatens to be draining to the etheric forces. The movement, music, and verse work can provide the youth's I-nature with energetic perspective—highlighting similarities and differences between the youth's and the parents' I-natures.

Choreographed sequences can help the youth feel the sense of moving backward from a conflict point, coming around to see the other person's point of view for a moment, and then backing out and around again, to make the passage past the conflict point with fresher perspective on what they youth's own needs are about. Without overly cognitive or intellectualized impressions coming into the youth from adults, the Pearl learns how to hold themselves while others freely weave their own karmic tasks in the world surrounding the youth.

Figure 7.5: Eurythmy and conscious color applications

In performance eurythmy, beautiful gestures of geometric patterns and color, forming connectedness, and woven in simplified expressions of planetary movements, sacred form drawings, Celtic knots, and many other valuable creative expressions, help the youth to internalize a felt sense of human etheric life dynamics and willful lawfulness. This can bring some balance in the exposure to parental conflict energy through something called the *counter-image* or *after-image*.[37] A youth takes a hardened, parent conflict gesture and translates it into its opposite, counter-image movement. The youth also enlivens the heart by moving with the imagination of a sacred lemniscate passage between the ventricles of their own heart.

Figure 7.6: Lemniscate in the human heart[38]

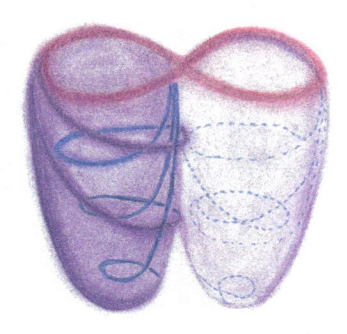

A counselor can encourage one or other parent to do eurythmy activities, helping them move uncomfortable feelings about holding the space between polarities, and finding ways to soothe tensions individually. Working with one parent, with the thought to entirely dismiss the other parent, can reinforce a consciousness of alienation that a Pearl Youth can easily pick up on. The counselor helps a parent to find space in their own polarization consciousness and then ease conflicted beliefs about the opposite pole, through enlivening movement first.

Figure 7.7: Eurythmy working polarities with openness

Working with a eurythmist or anthroposophical arts facilitator, a counselor can help parents to develop rhythm and balanced, expressive practices about their discomfort, and bring perspective regarding appropriate responses for the age and stage of their youth's adolescence. The eurythmist can also bring movements that help the parent get a felt sense again of the developmental differences between the last years of adolescence and early adulthood.

Movement and Verse Work for All, Including Therapists

Lemniscate work can help the teen to visit various temperamental moods and oppositional archetypes through accompanying eurythmy verses or with music chosen together with the counselor or curative eurythmy therapist. Opportunities to experience invigorated stillness are important in anthroposophical counseling, eurythmy, and spiritual work. A Pearl Youth learns to pause and breathe before reacting to a parent slight or to conflict statements that a parent might share about the other parent.

This could be achieved in one instance with an *etheric* and *poignant* pause, at the *still-point* crossing between the loops of the lemniscate. This still-point has the aliveness of the meditator, who gathers presence and life-force connection, before moving into action.

Here is a foundational verse given by Rudolf Steiner, to be spoken while standing in a five-pointed star, for grounding and centering, before entering into the eurythmy lemniscate. It could also be used at the center crossover in a moment of more still, mindful pausing.

I think Speech
I Speak
I have Spoken
I seek myself in the Spirit
I feel my Self in my self
I am on the path to the spirit,
to my Self.

- Rudolf Steiner

Since harmony is a challenge for children living in the middle of parental conflict, I suggest strong in-and-out movement work with the "Buh" eurythmy gesture for regrouping and a sense of personal holding, and the "Ah" gesture for release to the divine.

Figure 7.8: Gabrielle Armenier in Ah and Buh gestures

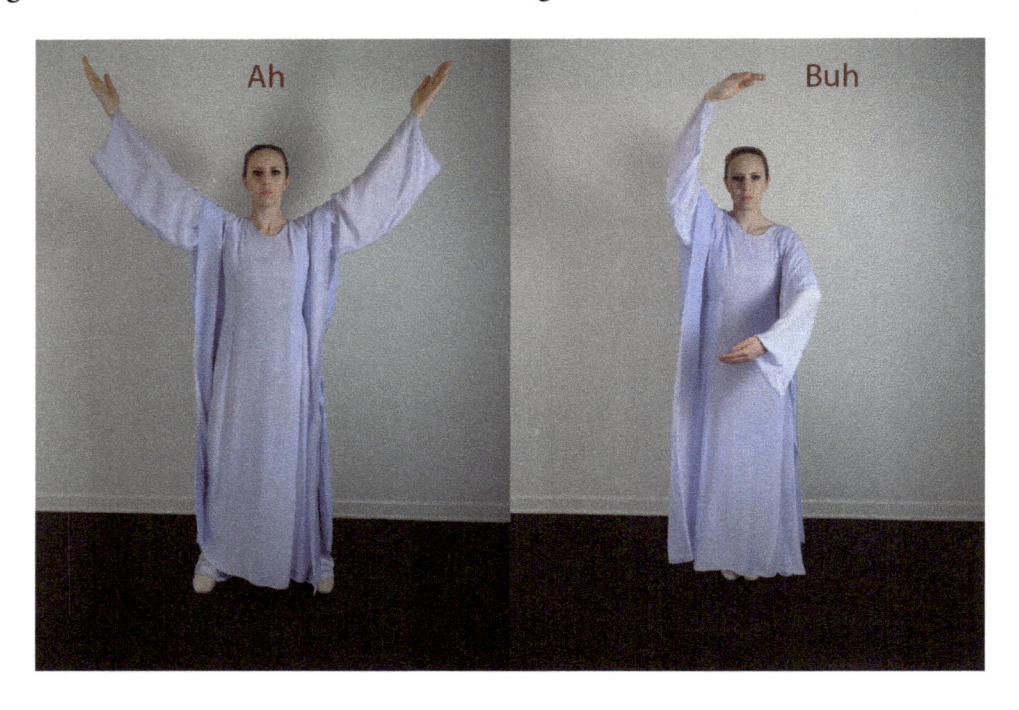

Curative eurythmy exercises with copper rods, to feel the difference between stiff, flexible, and permeable personal boundaries, can also reveal a youth's needs, potentials, and limits

Verses for Strengthening Soul Forces

Rudolf Steiner gave many verses for many different needs and occasions. Here are some given for older youth and adults, to strengthen their own forces while working with challenged children or others.

Spirit Triumphant
Spirit Triumphant
Flame through the weakness
Of irresolute souls.
Burn out self-seeking.
Enkindle compassion.
So that selflessness,
the life-stream of humanity,
may flow as a well-spring,
of spiritual rebirth.
- Rudolf Steiner

In World Tribulation, Times of Trial

In world tribulation,
and times of trial,
if we can nurture in the
soul's deep, inmost core
the strength to sense
the power of spirit beings,
such heart-striving will keep
life's reins within our grasp
- Rudolf Steiner

Michaelic Verse

We must eradicate from the soul
all fear and terror of what comes toward us
out of the future.
We must acquire serenity in all feelings and
sensations about the future.

> We must look forward with absolute equanimity
> to all that may come,
> and we must think only that whatever comes
> is given to us by a world direction full of wisdom.
> This is what we must learn in our times.
> To live out of pure trust
> in the ever-present help of the spiritual world.
> Surely nothing else will do,
> if our courage is not to fail us.
> Let us properly discipline our will,
> and let us seek the inner awakening
> every morning and every evening.
> - Rudolf Steiner

Figure 7.9: The creative lemniscate that maintains form

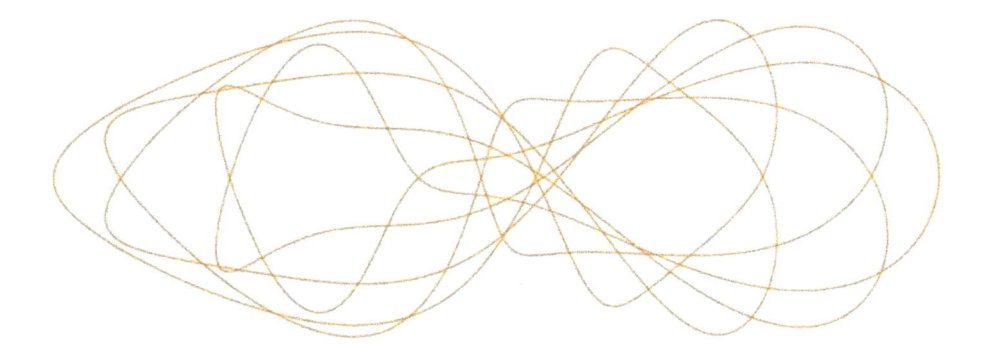

When Parent conflict and restriction are not too great on the adolescent, he or she may turn to any number of creative-exploration movements at home. Youth creativity can wreak havoc on parents who have not strengthened in their own forces, including in wise and compassionate ways. Parents who are working the soul work themselves, who feel whole and centered in their own ego-I forces with a higher consciousness awareness, can enjoy the creativity of the youth in their attempts to stay connected to each parent while keeping personal, etheric forces alive. Otherwise, a youth will need hut space somewhere at home to practice eurythmy movements and verses on their own.

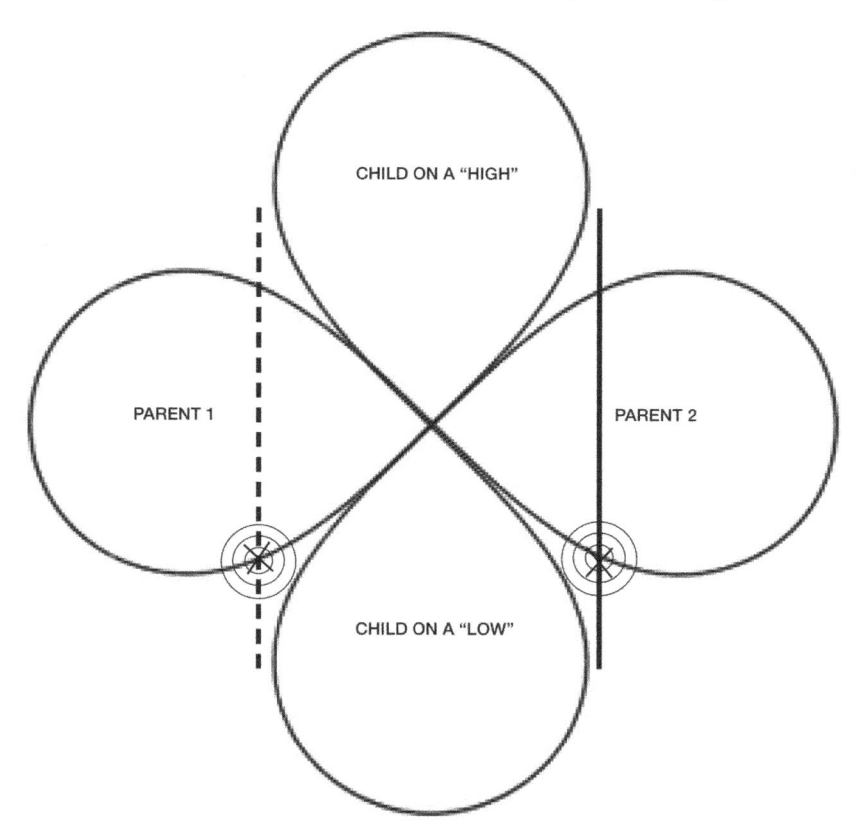

Figure 7.10: Lemniscate, with Pearl between conflicted parents, is a geometric rose curve

[Diagram: Four-lobed rose curve with lobes labeled CHILD ON A "HIGH" (top), CHILD ON A "LOW" (bottom), PARENT 1 (left), PARENT 2 (right). Xs in triple circles appear at the lower intersections between the parent and child lobes. Vertical dashed line on the left and vertical solid line on the right.]

When a Pearl is caught between conflicted parents where conflict impacts them from both sides, the Pearl escapes into a pattern that is geometrically the beginning of the rose curve. In time, this pattern can elaborate into a full rose, through a Pearl's willingness to keep moving through the pain through inner investigations into spiritual life to help cope with suffering. This is a significant spiritual initiation of a high order. It is when true, selfless love can blossom despite the sometimes overwhelming challenges.

Without strong, whole parents who are working to keep their adult development issues clear with their children and youth, the developing youth who is determined to realize a better life has little lawful option but to go into the adult-level lemniscate cross earlier than is appropriate for self-development. This creates, geometrically, a 2/1 parameter Rhodonea, or rose curve.[39] (Xs in triple circles represent the points where a child or youth experiences a parent being conflictual about the parent at the other home.)

The above diagram shows, in a psychological metaphor, how mathematical lawfulness determines that the Pearl's parent conflict often guides a youth's soul movements into an opposite polarization from the parents. Although the rose curve can bring protective benefit and foster healthy individuation for the youth or young adult, it can bring harm if it happens too early in development and for the wrong reasons.

At a higher spiritual level, inner rose curve activity can bring an authentic association with the Rosicrucian Rose Cross that relates to higher, Christ-consciousness practices. However, this represents very disciplined, complex, inner spiritual work. As shown in earlier chapters, being thrown into sophisticated spiritual levels of behavior too early, out of seeking a way to counter the youth's despair to be free of his or her parent's hardened stances, can risk bringing harm in the youth's nervous system.

Jaimen McMillan's Spacial Dynamics™

"Spacial Dynamics" was developed by American movement specialist, Jaimen McMillan. A world-class fencer, he created the discipline of Spacial Dynamics out of an intensive study of the principles of self-mastery.

Figures 7.11 & 7.12: Jaimen McMillan in space/time motion

Since its founding in 1985, Spacial Dynamics has made major contributions to the fields of physical education, movement therapy, group building, leadership, and world peace.

The discipline is based on nature's growth-forms such as spirals, vortices, lemniscates, and inverted spheres to enhance a person's ability to move. The work addresses all levels of a child's and youth's developing needs. It meets the body with grace and stimulates the soul and spirit with a span of spaciousness, allowing the youth a sense of free self-connecting and communicating, as well as a way of safely relating with others and a vaster meaning in life.

An expert in the plane-based Bothmer Gymnastics system,[40] McMillan championed these separate and mutually supportive movement disciplines to meet the needs of the growing child. Bothmer Gymnastics[41] and Spacial Dynamics are two parallel pillars of movement education taught in Waldorf schools throughout the world today. Exercises support a healthy progression through life and are helpful when developmental steps are missed, or when a child is emotionally or somatically stifled.

Figure 7.13: The hand as growing tree: Jaimen McMillan with kindergarten children

In practice, the goal of Spacial Dynamics work is to help each child to take her or his own next step. It has proven effective both in movement education and in movement therapy, weaving together not-yet-integrated reflexes into fluid movement patterns. It is an aid to movement for children working through trauma.

Figure 7.14: Learning tender touch in verse and imagination

In the movements, the goals of ancient Olympians shine through. They celebrate grace, human dynamics, and the dignity of the human gestalt in harmonious and archetypal activities that harken to the ancient Greek Parthenon. (With Thom Schaefer, McMillan developed the fifth-grade Greek Game/Pentathlon model used internationally in Waldorf Schools.)

Figure 7.15: Greek Olympics, 2006

Children's bodies, hearts, and minds are harmoniously attuned through tossing a javelin or discus, manipulating wooden rods, or masterfully using the body in space itself through enjoyable, special games and activities that highlight a developing, mature deportment

Children experience most Spacial Dynamics activities together with others, spanning from early childhood through adolescence. In increasingly intricate forms, the wonders and possibilities of the human form are celebrated.

Figure 7.16: Establishing personal space

A Pearl Youth, coming into his or her I-nature, can practice myriad Spacial Dynamics activities to affirm his or her own personal space, and to move on to mastering interpersonal space. From there, the youth can become a contributor to ever-widening, rippling social spaces.

With this comes the cultivation of an inner space where youth learn to create the peace of an inner temple or cathedral, built of soulfully crafted and enlivening physical activities. They enliven spaces that build individual form, functional strength, social grace, and cooperation with others. Through the *Hands in Peace*[42] movement, Spacial Dynamics leaders have brought movement-based peace initiatives to all world continents, for children who have experienced conflict and trauma.

Modern adolescents still emerge from childhood like the Parsifal lad—raised in the proverbial forest and now testing their human and humane skills to enter knighthood and the complexities of civilization.

Figure 7.17: Learning to choose where and how to meet a challenge

Or, they come as the ancient Persephone priestesses, called to witness the pain and grief of the darker underworld of life. The adolescent strengthens core resolves through a new active life of weaving between the darkness and the light.

Figure 7.18: Courage: Walking a gauntlet of thrown staves

In maturity, youth come to nurture their own emerging adult beings well, helping others to do the same, while fully participating in lifting all in the community and in society, as well.

Figure 7.19: Hovering trust, grounded in group support and safety

In the past, youth were initiated in certain movement arts: Parsifal with the sword, and Persephone through a form of ecstatic dance. Today, Spacial Dynamics brings a modern form of differentiated movement training for the modern adolescent. It helps youth initiate their own movement with growing focus, direction, and clarity within the intrigues and confusions of our times.

Figure 7.20: Individuated movement

Yiana Belkalopolos

Drugs And Alcohol: Object Relations Or Spiritual "Highs" Seeking God

The temptations to have excessive endorphin brain chemical escapes, to make the pain of a divided home and family life feel better, can bring a Pearl Youth into contact with substances that are powerful and deadly if abused. Common street drugs, mixed today with deadly levels of fentanyl,[43] for instance, are easily available and daily killing young people through sometimes minor doses.

The beta-endorphins released by this drug, which was originally used to treat post-surgery patients, can relieve pain. Yet, as with all opioid drugs, they give a false sense of security and, today, are often so potent that death is imminent without a very quick administration of Naloxone[44] antidote. For people who grew up with insecure family attachments and connections, taking opioid drugs is a turn toward help that can easily have a lethal outcome. In a way, for some Pearls, it has become a game of Russian roulette—a kind of carefree gamble between a short-term experience of calm and bliss, and death.

Drug use can reflect a youth's desire to return to natural endorphin[45] brain health that would be present if they had received appropriate maternal bonding and ongoing paternal calming in frightful times throughout the childhood years. The same warm mirror neuron, good feeling that a baby has in the arms of a loving mother is associated with endorphins flowing in the brain.

Sadly, not all children have this warmth and calm closeness from the start of infant life, making some children even more at risk for substance abuse later. The soul knows what it needs, but the earth life may or may not provide it. Going to substances can be a trap, but initially, for young brains on fire, it can seem like a necessary or easy option.

Endorphins are released in the brain through one-to-one eye contact between a baby and a mother, gentle father, or caregiver, through physical adventures and exercises where people share closeness and touch, in positive or joyous moments in general, and through exercise and loving, intimate, sexual stimulation. Endorphins are chemicals released from the regions of the pituitary, hypothalamus, and pineal glands in the brain.

When an adolescent can't endure or calm a churning gut or strained thinking, that youth can easily be swayed to turn to substances, legal and illegal, to calm the chaos and pain. Distressed adolescents are often prey to dealers looking to get these youths hooked on the pain-killing effects of drugs. Alcohol, although legally endorsed for use by many people in the West socially and for relaxation, can have a debilitating effect on the soul, robbing it of its individual nature. The real ego kept dependent on externally derived elements of water and fire with alcohol becomes dulled through inappropriate neuron firing and weakened thinking. This becomes distorting and corrosive to various life elements in the internal organs.

According to anthroposophy, alcohol creates a false ego,[46] a "being" capable of states that an undeveloped ego-being is too afraid or awkward to meet on their own, sober terms. It takes hard will-force work to create strong and sustainable capacities from within oneself. It requires great self-discipline to practice mindful ways toward relaxation that can sustain the inner organs much longer than substances, and more freshly throughout life.

Although drinkers often feel that they open themselves more after a few drinks, alcohol frequently moves people to open to lower urges and actions that only receive their higher reckoning later. Until then, the alcohol has taken over so much of the real nature of the person that he or she can no longer discern personally or socially responsible actions free of dependency and addiction.

Alcohol can also distort the hormonal nature of the human being, and that can suffocate the lively impulses of the body's creative juices. Instead of rising to the feeling and willing life forces coursing through the healthy veins of one's body to sing, dance, create, construct, play, and engage in any number of healthy ways socially, alcohol can often drown or dampen these into unnatural and socially restrictive behavior. The drinker loses the ability to create oneself anew out of their own interests beyond lower urges and fantasy.

If on the flip side, a drinker uses alcohol to calm in order do creative activity, the false ego can fall into a kind of hubris regarding a true capacity to cope with a creative nature, and the alcohol becomes a dependent relationship, dominating the source of creative activity. The person requires increasing levels of alcohol to create, rather than having wholesome practices for building substance within oneself to withstand creative life and social pressures, as well as the enjoyable engagements that can come out of it. Alcohol can disguise the inspiring messages and signs that a creative being naturally gets out of the socio-spiritual world, insights that can help a person to adjust life to new stages of self-management and more effective socio-economic abilities.

Tragically, we have seen this destructive effect on many popular artists who have lost their creative lives to alcohol at young ages. The popular English singing star, Amy Winehouse,[47] comes to mind. A remarkable musical talent, she died at age twenty-seven of alcohol poisoning after years of alcohol abuse. A whole roster of great musical talents succumbed to deaths attributed to alcohol, or alcohol-drug combinations.

For youth who are trying on a newly formed and vulnerable ego-I for the first time, popular artists and adults who use alcohol to create their images can be false role models for the budding, creative, and capable young adults. These young people cannot necessarily fully see, or feel for themselves, into the whole story of life's ages and stages, and thus cannot see the long-term effects of substance use on the soul forces.

Today, parents can get confused about their youth's mental and emotional maturity because young people see so much of the adult world on television, social media, and in movies. Too often, we take real moments of soul distress with a joking aside: "Oh, he's just being rad or hard-ass crazy." Meanwhile, the youth has been following the actions of adults whose lives are secretly overrun with substances. The adults in their lives have had no true higher ego to inspire the youth appropriately toward soul-spirit strength.

Suicide

The complexity of suicide ideations, attempts and completions is greater than the scope of what this book can address, but its mention in the discussion of high-risk activity for alienated Pearl Youth is important to consider. Suicidal thoughts can represent a break with trust about the value of one's life experience and/or one's capacity to meet the real challenges of life. These can be an attempt to return to something considered more bearable than earthly life itself. It is a sad, false reasoning because earthly life is the only place to cultivate soul-spirit resiliency capacities. Thus, too often, suicide in youth becomes a karmic statement of the lack of support, protection, or wisdom needed to guide youth-resiliency appropriately.

Most counselors and researchers who have extensively worked with suicidal people, and have worked with the research on the issue, suggest that the exact nature of the external and internal events that bring about suicide completions are unknowable.

Family members of suicide "completers" often sense that feelings of overwhelm, numbness, shame, disgust, alienation, confusion, disillusionment and fear were some of the factors that the family member inwardly struggled with before taking his or her life. Adolescent biology alone can stimulate feelings to an intense new level from those experienced in childhood. Youths often need help to normalize some powerful feelings newly experienced as teens.

Since it is known that suicide risk for adolescents and young adults is high, particularly in the modern Western world, holding the awareness of these kinds of struggles with new or complex feelings is key to any anthroposophical healing initiative with Pearl Youths.

In adolescence, a more complex biological system means more is going on in the body just at a time when working toward individual clarity means moving away from the mother and father attachment figures. Under the kind of school and career pressures happening in the West today, with extreme competition sometimes for few jobs, a teen can feel little sense of open or free inner space while acting within the outer-world demands.

If the nervous system is pushed to overrun higher than its natural stages and capacities, it will in time shut down, burn out, or rebel. From an emotional and neurological perspective, the teen is at risk of *hyperarousal* followed by a deep fall into tiredness or depression called *hypoarousal*.[48] The teen may become manic inwardly or outwardly and then fall into numbness after. Anyone who is not tuned to suicide risk can ignore or misinterpret the signs of momentary psychosis setting in.

Normally in adolescence, there is some level of emotional surge-and-dip behavior for the youth as a new adult body slowly forms into a new homeostatic state of balance. The more that unnatural developmental pressures meet the Pearl adolescent from outside—such as the divorcing parent's court battles, repressed interfamily communications, parental mood or personality changes, and the tender as well as threatening dynamics of parental dating—the more the unfolding natural capacities and timings of the adolescent can become overwhelmed or blocked.

This can lead to unbearable inner tensions or the experience of the teen's etheric forces and will forces dropping out or seriously depleting. The youth's emotional energy is drained toward adult and societal issues having little to do with the youth's and taking away from a youth's vital developmental needs. Pushed too close to the edge out of soul-thinness resulting from not being seen or heard appropriately and thus not getting useful reflection back, the youth could try to drop right out of life.

Biography Revisited: Sarah, 70: Overcoming Suicidal Thoughts

Sarah, whose biography was shared in Chapter Four, found herself feeling suicidal when she was twenty years old, just a few years after her parents' divorce. The divorce had brought a great deal of stigma in her time and resulted in a transnational home upheaval in her adolescent years, as well as her exposure to a violent stepfather. This was likely very shocking to Sarah's emotional and nerve-sense life, and a stun to her sense of normal habit life and routines at a very delicate youth development phase. As Sarah strove to meet the maturity of her early adulthood, she was dangerously depressed, feeling completely alone, and angry at God and religion.

> I started asking myself, "What is the meaning of my life? Is my life worth living? Am I just a piece of sand on the beach of life? Why don't I have any friends? Why, why, why? Everyone had two eyes, two ears, blood, peed and pooped, I rationalized, but why could someone be the President of the United States, and why was someone like me even alive?" I got nowhere with these questions except in deeper aloneness.
> - Sarah

Some Pearls can have extreme pain like this, followed by a "saving-grace" kind of transpersonal experience, spontaneously moving them out of despondency and depression. In Sarah's case, she had a dream that felt as if someone had grasped her soul out of the dream world and was holding her hand and telling her not to worry, that she would be helped. To her, it was an experience of the angelic world (perhaps even a message from an ancestor), that shook her out of a dangerous mood state. Yet, the climb back up out of mood disorder can be a long process, with many pitfalls, triggering early emotional pain and temporarily exhausting one's will forces.

Sarah's dream message might be seen transpersonally and anthroposophically as a sign from the higher soul, or as an enlightening moment supported by beings across the threshold of life and death. Rudolf Steiner spoke of the spiritual phenomenon wherein one takes a thought, prayer, or wish into sleep at night and can receive a kind of message from the spiritual world upon waking.[49] Many deeply suffering people make a savior wish, prayer, or call-out, hoping for help to manage their overwhelming heartache and heavy emotional states, and great numbers of people undeniably claim to have been answered in some way, either directly upon waking or sometime shortly after.

Others can have a kind of suicidal pain that so alienates them from any sense of higher self-worth within themselves and with others that they move into a surreal, abstract, delusional, or even schismatic state of mind. This is when they cannot interpret, rationalize, or self-affirm through their dreams or higher visions. This can create an extreme care situation, and the youth might need to be hospitalized for a time to assure that the Pearl gets the attention and exposure to the life rhythms and moral support needed. Other people, like Sarah, catch a sign of grace that moves them into clarity and action to find a way to cope and heal.

With what is known today about Takotsubo Cardiomyopathy (TC) in the heart walls (where one ventricle or one side of the heart's ventricles can fall weak in the middle of emotional heartache while the other side struggles to maintain normal functioning), this can result in overwhelming impulses in the body-mind complex. Adding this to the circumstances of an adolescent who is also experiencing the deadening of some brain cells while others are trying to find the healthy messages to form a well-coping, planning, and executive structure, one can see the potential suicide dangers for disaffected youths.

Depending on the teen's or the young adult's level of self-acceptance and esteem, that youth can interpret deeply buried or raw heartache as a kind of self-execution—self-hating about an inability to feel okay with life's struggles and wondering why other people can't notice their silent despair. Fear around why the heart hurts so much can restart cortisol chemicals flooding in the teen's nervous system, just when the youth least knows how to reach out for help.

In history, humanity experienced a great flood, in a real experience in antiquity, and through the stories and recollections of others. Today, we experience frequent internal emotional micro-floods from our physiological responses to ongoing world traumas. Still, as before, we can be led in such moments to a vision or message of higher spiritual purpose and meaning. Some teens, however, may not have enough soul-spirit foundation to trust when a sign or inspiration of hope comes in a moment of despair, or they may not know how to interpret it.

Running Away from Hardship, Abuse, or Neglect

Highly stressed teens can try to leave home too early out of feelings of desperation. They can get into sexual relationships out of the desire to find someone to take them away and take care of them, giving them a parental-endorphin experience with a partner that they missed in their childhood.

Some adolescents may have a child at a very young age, wanting to experience a return for a time to the happy, natural, and warming experiences of childhood and early nurturing. Childhood oxytocin hormones, coming in mother's milk and also from the experience of being lovingly held or hugged, can create a warm bliss feeling for a while between mother and baby, and later between a person and their various friends, family members, and intimate partners. The raw need for this in a Pearl who experienced too much hardened conflict at home, and the lack of prefrontal brain development, can prevent a young person from being discerning about intimate partners and sex, and of long-term child-raising issues and needs. The bliss "hit" is only temporary, but the pressures of child-raising are long term and the Pearl may not be ready or capable of such important considerations.

This seeking for the primal, infant, or pre-birth experience is a known trauma processing response.[50] In high traumatic stress, if a person recedes unsupported into an infantile or child state, or while feeling in an unsafe environment, then greater states of stress, panic, or alienation can result, and emotions can become dysregulated and out of control.

This is one way that a downward spiral of moods and the inability to cope can set in. Sadly, this often leads to illusions about the return to innocence, which are lived out for a while until more stresses burst the bubble of ideation in a person who has not been supported to find life-coping skills and circumstances for resilience.

Often, this is how the intergenerational transmission of divorce can happen in families. Adult children of divorce repeat the pattern of divorce of their parents when their attempts to have children and create meaningful relationships fail to soothe their initial trauma or stress.

Co-Ego-Based, I-Therapy

Anthroposophical therapists working with pre-teens (pubescents) and adolescents on divorce issues could work with the divorced parents concurrently, through a transpersonal approach adaptable for both. A sensitive approach for divorced families could have children or teens working individually or in sibling therapy, and the parents working individually with therapists.

Here, it is helpful to borrow from a transpersonal model originally developed for divorcing parents based on Elizabeth Smith's work with a trans-egoic model[51] for processing death or grief. It can be adapted and applied through what might be seen anthroposophically as a co-ego approach.

It is likely that parents caught in divorce battles are themselves missing some developmental ego-I pieces. Had full development been in place, parents may have handled the stresses in the relationship better. In their incomplete upbringings, they may have had little positive, inspiring, or calming attachment health. Smith and Gray view trans-egoic transpersonal therapy with divorcing adults and their adolescent children as having four stages of awareness and work, each with two phases. These adult themes are:

- *Normalization of Death:* confronting relationship mortality and resolving grief and unfinished business in the divorce relationship,
- *Faith in the Existential Life*: finding a greater meaning in life and coming to terms with "Who am I?",
- *Ego Disattachment:* release of the old me and reframing and disidentifying with a previous sense of self, and

- *Self-Transcendence:* acknowledging the new self, overcoming idealization of the early family relationship, and discovering one's new mission with acceptance and joy in the new identity.[52]

One danger with the trans-egoic approach, if it is not facilitated with awareness of developmental needs in youth, is how it can encourage a spiritual or fantastical-bypassing in the adolescent if adult-oriented practices and understandings around relationship closure are encouraged for the youth. Another is the possibility for a parent's new "identity" to move unrealistically beyond wholesome, child-development needs, leaving the child in classic divorced-child neglect.

That neglect refers to the absence of caregiving that truthfully meets the child where the development process is healthiest for that youth. A happier, healthier parent means little if that happiness is based on things that can't authentically support the youth's health and well-being. Divorced parents often involve themselves in many new personal-needs activities to get their lives coordinated again in a new single life. This can lead to setting aside normal soul processes for a youth's life stage, hoping that a basic-needs approach to the adolescent at home will be enough, such as food, clothing, shelter, and some extra fun time when possible. Adult adjustment and youth adjustment to traumas and emotional upheaval have different features.

When the parent's relationship and life adjustment needs take precedence over the youth's, the youth's growth is made more austere or ascetic. This can have long-term repercussions.

Stuffing Feelings and Needs

Many Pearl Youth take emotional issues inward, repressing their feelings or voice out of a natural lack of ability to identify what is feeling hurtful. What needs to be held in fullness by the adult in the middle of a parent breakup is too often soul-thin and even repressive. What is going on in the adolescent's whole transformation into adulthood is profound and too great to add adult responsibilities onto youth as well. The youth can easily become overwhelmed.

Newly single parents often try to make a youth understand that mom or dad are not able to do so much for them now because each parent is busy working more to take care of two households and increased expenses on things that were previously shared. If the youth rebels, often a subtle implication is put out that it is the other parent that is not doing enough, or that the youth is expecting too much now.

It may be true that one or both parents miss holding appropriate developmental foundations and structures for the youth. Each parent may be cutting corners on time spent attending to the youth due to outer pressures faced by single parents, or as a result of spending time courting another partner. Adult needs now override the youth's real development support and, often, real emotional struggles.

Sometimes a parent resorts to a punitive approach to the youth if that youth naturally acts out to get parent attention. The youth experiences a deep inner sense that something important in the soul is being missed. The youth's soul will intensely feel the unfairness of this if what is neglected is significant soul-development work or support. The youth unconsciously knows that some inner scaffolding for lifelong capacities is in jeopardy.

Divorced parents who don't form new relationships that offer real child-development support usually depend on the child's school environment to serve the child's holistic needs. A Waldorf school is more equipped to do that, but it can't do it all. In my own experience as an elementary Waldorf teacher, Pearl Children in my class often returned to school the next day, or after the weekend, with weaker or more quickly dissipated energetic forces than the children from whole families. They had often not had appropriate development practices, rhythms, or routines upheld at home. Often the parents arrived frazzled and in various states of disorganization themselves.

The same scenario can play out for high school adolescents, with parents naturally less present in the school environment, and sometimes neither parent showing up for important sports events or cultural celebrations. Sometimes a teen is given money as compensation for the absence of the parent or other adult family member attending.

A skilled anthroposophical counselor working with divorced families holds three levels of consciousness. One is to bring child-development needs-awareness in therapy with the youth. A second involves bringing interventions at various levels of need for parents who may have missing pieces from different ages and stages. An important third level of working with the parents is to ensure that the parent knows what it is that the youth is working within their own soul's age-and-stage level. This helps to keep development lines, and healthy, adult-youth needs and boundaries clear.

Young adults, or even older ones, who have had to hold their own development stages too much on their own, can regularly show up weakened and energy dissipated in society. Without appropriate support, and the intra-sharing of souls who have deeply compassionate hearts around other's suffering, Pearl Adults, who carry a new story for our times, are frequently dismissed by other adults as being not fully legitimate people showing up and contributing to society. Others don't feel a full felt sense about them. They think that there is something intuitively wrong with the other person, and thus that person ought to be avoided. Imagine the added pain for the Pearl who already knows that he or she feels different and suffers accordingly.

Perhaps that is why many Pearls look to doctors, nurses, mature spiritual leaders, or psychotherapists for the human compassion that they didn't experience at home. More developed and selfless people don't expect to feel a harmonious, physiological, felt sense with other people in order to accept and help them. They don't tribalize about who they help or work with.

For instance, a majority of nurses help whoever comes to the hospital room and hold a humanly compassionate vision of the people in their midst—whatever physiological or energetic state their patients are in. They naturally maintain a high soul-spiritual calling. They don't have to feel fully resonant with a patient in order to be willing to help that patient. They don't have to feel that a patient is just like them in order to help them to heal. That level of selflessness is necessary to help some Pearls with emotional management, practical living circumstances, and various other efforts in life.

Age-Appropriateness and an Anthroposophical, Co-Ego Model

Anthroposophy naturally addresses trans-egoic practices by recognizing that divorce too often triggers a life initiation in both parents and children, whether the lessons of the initiation are accepted and integrated or not. Touching fundamental or core human soul-psyche concerns, which often arise as the impetus for change in a relationship, often stimulates developments associated with complex soul and spirit issues.

Many divorcing people misidentify something needing to develop within themselves and blame the spouse from holding them back from what they want. A whole process of blame and game begins in an attempt to override difficult feelings and personal realities, and to try to get more of what one desires rather than what one truly needs.

Often, a lack of empathy and selfless help cultivated between spouses, for the struggle of being a human being and feeling personally inadequate to the task at times, is more of the honest theme of what's going on when a relationship breaks up. Today, much honest soul nature in people in the West is buried under layers of fantasy-minded ambition and pressures to uphold a societally and culturally constructed personality based on economic agendas.

Yet, years of hindsight from divorced adults have now shown that it was often the painful challenges that their children went through after family divorce that woke parents to learn life lessons that went beyond material needs and desires. They learned to transcend some of their lower ego directives, so their children could experience a safer sense of love, commitment to meaningful ideals, and some inner peace.

They often eased up on the former spouse in time and recognized that each partner had issues to deal with and overcome that had nothing to do with one trying to harm or suppress the other. However, there are still parents who divorce who never entirely give up blaming the other person and never own any poor relational or personal development issue of their own, or a lack of real interest in making positive change for their own human betterment or for the sake of the children.

When parents demean the other parent to the youth, they often say they expected more from the other spouse than the spouse was capable of or willing to develop. The parent usually tells the child what the "right" behavior should have been. However, that outcome was not successfully executed by the parents together. It is an idea that has not had any appropriate successful process toward manifestation, but the child is expected to side and agree with the blaming parent anyway or risk being blamed or rejected in some way also. If both parents engage in such blaming or behavior, the Pearl Youth is put in a very hard place of both human and soul-spiritual confusion.

Yet the ideal and right way of relationship is only in each parent's imagination, unless it later becomes manifested in a new relationship. Too often, what divorced parents come to realize with maturity or hindsight is that they never fully realized the relationship of their imagination, and that real relationship either eluded them entirely in life, or they settled for something more honest and/or humanly accepting in time because they became more mature about themselves and life.

The transcendent or ideal relationship that divorced parents expect their teens to believe in is often based on clouded beliefs and understandings about human nature today. This distorts a young person's ability to accept one's own flaws and see life as a process toward growing into being a more mature and realized higher being—with another person going through similar development alongside them. The teen can take this as meaning that they have to be perfect and ideal right away in relationship or they are failures worthy and deserving of rejection by others.

Youths who are just developing healthy egos can't possibly measure up to the relationship perfection imaginations of their parents, since they are entirely different souls in a different generation with different tasks that will work out differently in their adult-life culture and relationship expectations. Only truly moral/ethical ideals can support a child and youth in life, and the parent who claims the higher moral ground through blame and judgment of the other, has to live up to a higher ideal in a real and manifest way in relationship or betray the trust of the child. Since perfection is a spiritual ideal and only archetypal, not human, the child or youth is set up to become disillusioned and disappointed.

Pearl Children are often left with sheer gaps in relationship skills and can come to live out of high relationship ideals that have no substance to back them up. They need people who can pattern the harder work involved for respectful relating, for feelings and needs negotiations, and for boundary contracting with the partner who is not the same as themself. Pearls need to learn how couples do this without losing the warmth and empathy that keeps hearts connected on higher levels than the purely material and physical ones. Many Pearls didn't see this at home with their parents or families.

Too often, it is the young Pearl Adults who notice the lack when they reach their real ego-I stages in their early twenties. In their Sentient Soul twenties, too many Pearls struggle to stand and hold themselves in the world with missing relational developmental pieces. They distrust in what their parents set them up for in relationship, but also have no real idea of how relationships work.

The problem is that those developmental skills and experience pieces needed to settle into the soul in right timing earlier in life, and unconsciously, before the children became adults. Making a twenty-year-old too conscious of themself is also putting them out of developmental lawfulness. The Consciousness Soul period of adult development does not appropriately open until around age thirty-five, once life experiences have scaffolded some inner-soul substance that can hold the young adult enough to expand consciousness appropriately without straining the nerves and pushing the higher nervous system into function before the youth is ready emotionally, mentally, and experientially for that.

In the West, where the "melting-pot" belief system of "anything goes" child-raising has left children exposed too much and far too many adult-life problems far too early, the rates of mental health problems, nervous-system disorders, and pharmaceutical interventions are astounding.

Until age twenty-one, children haven't formed a full ego yet to help them stand up well and selflessly with very individual others—and not lose the core needs of self-care and respectfully negotiated boundaries that a true ego-I holds. They also can't be self-generating and in their appropriately sustainable, creative selves. If children are pushed too much to accept adult-level transcendence, they can become, in adulthood, like empty vessels bobbing in someone else's ocean. They are often awash in emotion, partly because they can't find their own footing, don't know themselves well, and have no capacity to take responsible actions for themselves in the practical world. Washed out too often, they can come to believe that they are both helpless and hopeless.

If the child's higher spiritual forces have been stirred awake out of trauma, fear, and grief, and are not allowed to go back to sleep properly until the right later ages and stages, Pearl Youth can naturally and unconsciously fixate on higher knowing in a locked-in, escapist response to pure emotional pain. In this scenario, spiritual bypassing becomes an obsessive-compulsive go-to. The youth's ability to incarnate well and consistently and maturely function in the world in relationship with others, and particularly others who are not direct reflections of themselves, is missed.

To use a craftsperson metaphor, these Pearl Children end up overworking their forges (neurology). After being worked for a while, the neural "workers" start to get tired, and metal tailings begin to lay a lasting cover of dust (cortisol spills in the brain) in the workspaces. Blunted tools are left lesioned in vices (cerebral gaps form in the brain neurology from burned-out chemical firing systems), and empty boxes (memory cells) are stacked on shelves without enough resourcing, practical and reusable product in them.

The shop becomes dull with residue, stagnant, and everything sits, waiting and dated (toxic memory). The worker has to go on strike (hospitalized or put on dulling medications, possibly). The company managers are soon on the warpath (parents and society frustrated about what is wrong with the young person and confounded as to why this youth won't get a proper life into gear). It is far less that the youth doesn't want to step up to life, but rather that this Pearl can't. The nervous system is on shop shutdown from regular, toxic overload.

Heroic Ex-partners Step Up and Do the Work

Concurrent, co-ego therapy, where the child is in therapy and a parent or both parents are in their own therapy and psychoeducation work, helps to address similarly undeveloped stages and processes in both the parent and the child. This therapy works in appropriate, age-and-stage-honoring ways. This way, the adults manage to stay adult while the adolescent stays in a youth-level developmental cycle. Parents learn how to compensate for the things that the child is missing, keeping their own missing-pieces work under their own authority and helping the adolescent do the youth work. Adult-level work is not projected onto the child, eating up a youth's developmental energy.

Assisting parents to see the broader soul capacities being called up in themselves and in the life of their children, in the middle of sometimes chaotic feelings and confusing changes, can help them to enliven a sense of interconnected wonder. That is deeply necessary today in the face of increasingly materialistic influences and distractions to the soul work. A more updated and ideal consciousness from parents, coming out of their own therapy and psychoeducational work, ameliorates some raw lower impulses triggered by the divorce, and can help everyone to open more heart space.

The Pearl is unconsciously helped while the parents knit higher prefrontal-cortex thinking abilities with cognitive behavioral[53] psychotherapeutic techniques, for instance, to reach greater self-understanding and mutual compassion in the situation. When parents process some of their own higher-mind, prefrontal cortex consciousness to regulate desire issues, they can come into more heart and soul balance and help their adolescents.

Too often in divorce, parents dive into lower mind, sensual-emotional body issues, or material concerns—just as the teen is needing higher-mind consciousness in the parents. Parents who upgrade their soul capacities while the adolescent upgrades in the right way, allow more growth for everyone in the future. Consciously keeping up on self-development and pscyhosocial understanding of other generations can bring hope for each family member to live into a different kind of family peace, respect, and balance.

Saverio and his former wife, in Volume II, are managing this new level of cognitive, co-parenting and it is truly a loving, courageous, soulful, and creative experience to behold. Both parents have learned that the freedom to choose for oneself in life does not mean freedom just to walk away, hate, use, or abuse the other, or negotiate uncomfortable relationships through dismissive, annihilating, or inferiority–superiority power struggles. Everyone in the split-up counts, everyone is heard and valued, and every individual's needs are supported to as reasonable a degree as possible.

Practices and Biographies for Inspiring Teens

Normalizing the feelings associated with the dissolution of family when a divorce happens, including the very difficult feelings around the dissolution of the relationship a youth had previously to each parent, is a delicate process and should be done with great care and countered with inspiring biographies. Stories of poignant young souls who learned to function well in life following battles, loss, extraordinary and quick change, and also grief, offer a teen an opportunity to speak to the grief of lost innocence, and the painful work of overcoming a shaken will and bringing it back to strength.

The autobiography, *I Am Malala: How One Girl Stood Up for Education and Changed the World*,[54] is the story of a Pakistan teen girl, shot by Al Qaeda terrorists, who has recovered to become a world peace activist and a member of the United Nations. Although others around her world were killed by Taliban terrorists, Malala's courage in the face of life-threatening challenges saved her and moved her life forward in expansively positive and growthful ways. This is a profound one to bring to a world-wizened youth. It is a story that acknowledges that danger and death are real, but which also points to the enlightening strength and expansive life and love that can arise out of trauma.

Another good biography of humanness along the way to creative success is Gordon Parks' *Voices in the Mirror: An Autobiography*.[55] Parks was born into black poverty in the United States, where death and darkness in the world of Afro-Americans abounds. Yet, through his artistic nature, Parks became a writer, musician, filmmaker, and acclaimed photographer.

Faith in the existential life is present in William Grill's prize-winning book *Shackleton's Journey*,[56] and in Michaela DePrince's, *Hope in a Ballet Shoe*.[57] *Shackleton's Journey* is created from paintings and pictures, and tells the story of the explorer Ernest Shackleton's journey crossing Antarctica from one sea to another sea, via the South Pole. The ship in which he is sailing, the *Endurance*, gets stuck in the ice and the crew is left to a treacherous journey over land and then by lifeboats to reach South Georgia. The author, having dyslexia, created a story to unburden the conceptual mind through a picture-book telling of an adult epic. It is appropriate for a teen who may be in some emotional strain and cognitive thinking overload, but needing inspiration about a tough journey to talk about at the same time.

Hope in a Ballet Shoe is a book that traces a child's experience of suffering from what could have been a soul-destroying childhood of abandonment and abject poverty, to a life that allowed the child to live fully into her own skills and talents. International ballet star, Michaela DePrince, was orphaned as child growing up in Sierra Leone, when her father was shot by rebels and her mother died of starvation.

Michaela was adopted from an orphanage in Africa into an American home and has become a foremost dance inspiration in the ballet world today. This book can be helpful for children of divorce who feel adopted into a blended family, where finding their own sense of self after heartbreak, loneliness, or emotional struggles can be a mixed blessing leading to strength in one's adult life later.

Ego-detachment is a step to a free selflessness and is different for a parent and a youth. It happens when we cultivate the sense of other enough to see our actions as part of something bigger than ourselves. Ego-detachment can be understood in the modern novel called, *The Boys Who Challenged Hitler: Knud Pedersen and the Churchill Club*,[58] by Phillip Hoose. This is a thoughtful story of how some English youth worked together to stand up to the soul-damaging reality of genocidal war being promoted by Adolf Hitler at the time of the Second World War in Europe.

The novel does not seek to hide the darkness of the outside world from adolescents. It shows, however, how the youth themselves had the will and the higher, trans-egoic inspiration within themselves to plan well and work together to bring positive change into the world in exceedingly dangerous times. This novel offers much content for counselors, teachers, parents, or other close adults to explore with the youth. It addresses feelings of grief, overwhelm, and fear, as well as reticence, faith in one's higher feelings and thoughts, and the love of brotherhood cultivated between English boys to rely on each other and be there in strength when others were falling.

Finally, unhealthy *self-transcendence* is represented in the novel *Hole in my Life*[59] by Jack Gantos. Gantos was a young adult who wanted to go to college and become a writer, but he didn't have the money. To fast-track his education, he became a sailor and hashish dealer in New York until he was caught dealing and was sent to jail for six years.

Gantos, a prolific and realized writer today, tells his story of struggle and confinement in prison during his early adulthood. Through some gritty, dissociating moments, Gantos shows how he overcame his own restless and crazed ambitions to apply himself to the one thing he really wanted to do—to become a successful storyteller through novel writing. By dedicating himself more to the goodness in his own self and abilities, transformed his worst enemy, the undisciplined part of himself. He had to find the way to his own self-discipline, one that resonated with his individual soul journey.

North, South, East – Meet West

A counselor, cultivating therapeutic alliance with a youth whose trauma has put them into a regressed state, must still address the complex world the youth will step into in adulthood. An initial approach can be to use a technique derived from studies of nonlinear, nondirective cultures first to support the childlike quality of the regression. Creative play therapy helps a youth or young adult to re-instill wonder in life and in worldly themes. (Some South American, Asian, and Mediterranean cultures are nonlinear and nondirective.)

In this regard, a counselor can prepare some activities of child-centered play therapy for the youth, such a sand-tray therapy.[60] Carefully chosen toy items from around the world, placed in a sand tray for the youth to mess around with and create story scenarios, can be unassuming for a regressed youth in the first few sessions with a therapist.

The youth is simply invited to move items about the tray in whatever way appeals to him or her. The most important part of such therapy is that a caregiver simply witnesses for the youth what is happening in the youth in connection with the sand-tray figures and implements. The therapist or caregiver offers non-judgmental, unconditional, and positive commentary and reflection.

Creative play therapy techniques brought out of a cultural approach that is more linear and directive can be helpful, once trust has been built in the relationship. It firms up some inner discipline and clarifies needs in the adolescent soul. (Chinese, German, and Anglo-Saxon cultures are more linear, directive cultures.) This helps to strengthen the balance of practices in the universally human, adult world into which a youth must grow. Non-direct play therapy allows a Pearl to move out of regression at the Pearl's own pace. The therapist continually observes and checks in regarding the youth's seven life processes.

The following is a threefold, directive process:
- Inviting the youth to look over a music collection, reflecting constructively and artistically on some universally human themes.
- Asking the youth to create a response to that music, with help at each stage of working out that creative response.
- Welcoming the youth to reflect on the process with the therapist and creating an art or music piece based on the reflection.

The Pearl Youth may choose to respond through music on an instrument that the youth plays, or on one that is in the therapy room or at home. A different response could be through craft, a construction project, sculpture, cooking food—anything that lends itself to creative expression. If the youth doesn't initially respond to self-initiated creative expression, the Pearl can work from gathered images to create a music video cover based on a band or performer that the youth likes, or one for a spoken word performance that matters to the youth.[ii]

A keen musician might be encouraged to create a music video with a friend or family member that feels meaningful and expresses interests and frustrations. Or, the youth might create a whole new musical instrument, or even a new musical genre to perform at an open-mic gathering or a newly organized youth-music venue. The only criteria are that the project be exploratory and skillful. An element of extended practice is involved. The youth can practice in sessions with the therapist, as well as more individually if the Pearl is seventeen or older.

Whatever the selected project is, after its completion, the youth works to review it with the therapist after some breathing time. Three to four weeks is a good spell to let the project rest before revisiting it. The intentions in the project are threefold:
- to increase awareness of how a youth can address opposite impressions creatively,
- to reflect on how being skilled at the project feels different from being exploratory, and
- to gauge the youth's reaction to other people seeing or hearing what creative response the youth has been working on.

People who experience the response don't need to know what the stimulus was at first. Later, the therapist and youth can discuss reactions and responses given by others.

Working with structured creativity and unstructured creative work helps an adolescent get comfortable with the same experiences in family and societal life. Working with skilled artistic effort helps the youth be able to focus on practical activity and consider creative responses, sometimes spontaneously, in the middle of experiences that may seem chaotic. The youth is

---

[ii] Two or three options of how to go about the process are recommended. Let the adolescent come up with options using a scientific process approach with a hypothesis of what it might look like when finished, gathering materials, deciding on a method, experimenting, observing results, reorienting their thinking to what was discovered, synthesizing feelings about how things turned out, and forming a new idea out of the original hypothesis.

supported to not lose touch with themself in such circumstances and to have ways to cope and carry on productively and bring inspiration for oneself and others.

Projects can be big or small, depending on a youth's network and resources. The youth can work on how to be interdependent about social and societal networks and resources to get a project done. In this way, a youth's soul capacities are broadened, and a network of support can be expanded. The therapist regularly supports this learning with empathic feedback.

What used to be a time of connecting a youth only to a local community or nation, must now be one of helping a youth relate to a community of world citizens, since most countries and communities today encompass people of several nationalities. Looking into biographies of different world artists can help the process along. The youth can also work through what someone from another culture might take away from experiencing the youth's creative response. Fears and concerns can be worked through with the therapist.

The therapist holds the intent to strengthen the youth's capacities to keep in relationship with others, and other points of view, while affirming the youth's own skills, capacities, needs and sense impressions at the same time. Together, the youth and therapist work to build multi-capacity skills and relating techniques at an adolescent developmental level.

The youth gets to work the soul substance of creating something meaningful while relating with an empathetic and consistently available adult. They work through anxieties or insecurities about how to meet others while being functional and productive in life also. A counselor helps build the inner, safe hut that this Pearl will need to carry around inside the soul throughout a full-on life. The youth is also attended to in negotiating needs and in recognizing and attending to the creative and expressive needs of others, learning to protect varying levels of energy gracefully with firm, flexible, or permeable boundaries.

The Silenced Youth

If no-talk therapy[61] is initially necessary with an adolescent, the counselor can have some paintings or posters of in-progress artwork in the therapy room, done by other teens. The therapist might play interpersonal music produced by other young people as therapeutic support from peers. Or a therapist can hold an empty-chair[62] dialogue with a notable cultural figure who clearly understands broken hearts, empathy, and emotional responsibility to others, such as a singer-songwriter Adele in the song "Hello."[63]

In empty-chair work, a therapist or a client sets a chair in the room and imagines someone sitting in that chair with whom they would like to share some difficult feelings. Clients rehearse how they might talk to someone they are struggling with emotionally. Or, they simply work to identify feelings and problems that they are having in life and how to talk about them with another person. The therapist encourages the client to find their voice with the imagined person in the empty chair. A Pearl can use the empty-chair technique to practice a dialogue that the youth might want to have with a parent, a teacher, a friend, or someone from whom they would like to seek help.

With a no-talk adolescent, the therapist can have a conversation with a respected empty-chair figure about how that person worked with difficult feelings and transformed them into a creative project with a friend who understood them. The therapist provides the voices for the empty chair 'person' and anyone else in the empty chair dialogue, guessing at some thoughts and feelings as well as helpful actions. The therapist guesses and then reflects that the guess might be wrong or only partly true, giving the impression that he or she is not trying to put definitive words or feelings in the empty chair "guest's" mouth. This can be a warming up process to help a no-talk teen know that the therapist is there to work to understand the youth and to help make something hopeful and good from the pain that has locked up the adolescent's voice.

In a community of people who play instruments together, a therapist could have local recordings of youth music to play in the therapy room. Better still is if the therapist can play some music that the therapist created and talk about the feelings, challenges and processes of bringing thoughts and feelings into vocalization, perhaps with some insights learned from other community youth. The therapist can then begin to open a door for the youth to express the struggles that the Pearl is having finding their voice.

The no-talk youth is stuck, so having one or two interest items that move in the room can provide interesting points for the therapist to refer to and reflect quietly about in the youth's presence, while also talking generally about the life of Pearls. A motion lamp, a creative, hanging chalice in which the therapist can light a flame, a pet, some avant-garde fountain, something on an up-and-down moving pulley, some kind of a balance beam on a fulcrum, or sprouting seeds in unusual planters, can unconsciously suggest the important liveliness of activity and expression.

Taking a sensitive, introvert's approach works well with no-talk teens, initially. A therapist can quietly share about unfinished creative works in progress in the room as a way to connect with the adolescent's age-and-stage timing and the sense of acceptance that meaningful things in life don't always come across as complete or fully understood yet, or not expressed enough emotionally, but that the state of "emerging" is valued and appreciated.

Something has sent this youth inward, and there is a world inside that the Pearl is protecting. It's an inner landscape as well as a hut that the youth has created, usually unconsciously, for protection. This youth, in silence, is often energetically gauging the therapist, sensing if the inner landscape of the therapist is earnest and safe ground.

A therapist with a no-talk client, working as explorer on *fresh and protected land,* needs to:
- Show trustworthiness and be prepared to be called up in time on why he or she should be trusted,
- Share honestly about why the therapist is a therapist, and what brings the therapist here with this person,
- Make expectations and non-expectations clear,

- Explore some purely human awareness of what many of the young people that the therapist has worked with seem to experience in life (keeping specific names and identities confidential),
- Check therapist power postures, gestures, voice tones, and assumptions,
- Prepare to be moved, developed, and at times, unnerved by being out of a comfort zone,
- Commit to walk what the therapist talks or explain individual divergence or adaptation reasons, and
- Do personal self-care work while also sharing insights on self-care with the Pearl.

To initiate some more unconscious discovery with a vocally blocked teen, a therapist or caregiver can touch on some dream work,[64] drawing attention to an artistic sculpture or an indigenous painting, or maybe some drumming music that have all been created out of a dream the artist had. A photo of clouds can also be explored. In my case, a dreamcatcher[65] in the room, in the tradition of the culture of the First Nations Qu'Wutsun community where I practice,[66] has provided a focus for discussing the values and details of dreams.

All abstractions shared or discussed about dreams need to be explored to find emotional information and a connection to practical, daily living and relationships. A therapist can also discuss with the youth any faith-based, religious, or spiritual connection that the client raises about dreams, with an open-ended approach of inquiry and interest, or of sharing insights from others, but without imposing beliefs.

Figure 7.21: First Nations dreamcatcher

A therapist might wonder out loud, in the presence of the silent youth, what the dreamcatcher might be about, and how other people elsewhere symbolize capturing dreams. The therapist can mention the importance of protecting healthy sleep in order to cultivate a better dream life. This can lead to some commentary on what the therapist knows about sleep problems with Pearl Youth.

Therapists offer ideas about practices that Pearls have used to get prepared for sleep, to cope with sleeplessness, and to notice and log dreams or thoughts in the morning that come in the night. They encourage youths to come up with a poem, or some creative logo, or a clothing meme related to the dream.

A Waldorf school counselor can share a myth and ask if the Pearl thinks a myth came out of someone else's dreams. The therapist asks the youth to think about it but ensures that the youth doesn't need to respond now or without sitting with the question for some time. The therapist might share a response that another, unnamed youth once shared on the same topic, including what that response meant to helping that youth work through a problem. The therapist can also share some positive development experiences with other youth who overcame not feeling able or willing to talk.

In other sessions, the therapist can show the chalkboard artwork of David Newblatt[67] in his illustrations of the magical Parsifal tale. Together with the youth, the therapist can explore what kinds of dreams must have come, and how, for the artist to create such images. Together, they can wonder what kinds of images show up in the culture today that might have come from someone's dreams. This can introduce the notion of dreams telling us an important story about ourselves personally or culturally. The therapist can read sections of the Parsifal tale to the youth, or record chapters for the youth to listen to at home.

To address a perceived need for groundedness in the youth, the counselor might encourage the teen to sculpt, with clay or soapstone, certain images that might have come from dreams in, for instance, the Greek Odysseus legendary myths, or from Nordic, Assyrian, or Celtic tales. The therapist might encourage the youth to take walks in nature, with a friend or the family dog, to get inspiration for the sculpture, getting a sense of the life of ancient peoples who spent a great deal of time close to nature. If the youth expresses interest in outdoors experiences, the therapist can discuss safe groups to join or safe ways to be in nature alone.

If the youth begins to open up in the dream process, showing practical approaches to sculpture, such as sculpting dream-evoked earthen pots, sculpted solar-lamp holders for the walkway to a house or for a youth center's front lobby, or willow-branch-sculpted furniture, can inspire youth will forces and an entrepreneurial capacity. The youth and the therapist can plan a project. The therapist shows some examples of inspiring sculptures and discusses the biographies of the creators with a focus on emotional life issues the sculptor was known to overcome or engage creatively.

If aspects of a project are beyond the skills of the therapist and the client together, the therapist patterns networking, collaboration, and resource-raising with other community members. The adolescent gets reflection and insights into how to promote projects of interest in ways that protect the youth's creative inwardness. The youth is learning how to protect creative boundaries but give out to others some inspiration for the project at the same time. The Pearl can work on how to keep up the inspiration to follow a project of interest through to completion, even if the youth's boundaries get challenged, or if setbacks make the youth want to retreat and go silent again.

With the therapist, a silenced Pearl Youth can work through rough feelings and rehearse how to authentically tap thinking, feeling, and willing by working with simple wood-whittling that moves into more complex projects, through wax sculpture, knitting, culinary arts, fashion designing, or any number of other craft-based ways to express themes. Themes might address a) divisiveness, b) rebuilding from destruction, c) bridging, or d) cultural fusion.

The youth might design testimonies and affirmations to put onto car stickers or posters geared for other struggling youth. These can serendipitously be posted in special teen places where youth like to go to be away from adults for a while. This could easily lead to discussions of social beliefs, personal identifications that might be inhibiting the youth's voice, and family myths. It can also address the value and purpose of public art.

Processing in such ways help a youth discern how to express while not annihilating the expressions of others. Working with messages on the same theme from three to six points of view helps to ground and balance communication practices. It also aligns with important sacred geometry for our times, which is discussed more in Volume II.

Adolescents will need strengthening in their esteem to cope with a society changing its values about the treatment of women's sexuality and mothering. By example, a Pearl Youth might work with a mixed-media totem sculpture depicting a young woman walking through wombs depicted as holes in both her mother and her father. The question in the artistic piece could be: "What is a baby when family love is missing? Without love, what is a mother or a father?"

Reaching In and Out – Crafting an Inner Safety Net with a Mentor

Doing practical activities like cob-oven building, sculpting, knitting, sewing, jewelry-making, or felting "object-relations"[68] items, while in an inclusive group with emotionally aware adults and other youths, can assist a Pearl Youth to experience soulful people and network supporters while engaging the will in mutually valuable projects.

Pearl Youth need to work with real earthen substances and skills in life, rather than just playing or socializing on computers. They require time with adults who know how to hold and share soul substance fluidly and respectfully out of having developed strong relationship skills. Pearls need ongoing inspiration while hearing about human relationships, and while practicing skills to manage good relating well. They often need help finding the middle way between feeling rigid antipathy toward others or sometimes painful sympathy. They learn how boundaried but active empathy is a heartfelt and upright place from which to work. They learn to move into good actions out of valued and transformed feelings and needs. They also practice positive ways to ask others for help.

This tempers Pearl Youth from engaging unhealthy states of fantasy and dissociation. Practical but imaginative work keeps them out of spiritual bypassing while they learn about self-care, communion with others in the middle of tense frustration, and how to safely move from worried thoughts of injustice to skills of effectiveness that create more just and fair circumstances for them without denying justice for others.

Transferring, for a time, some relationship felt-sense needs to an empathic adult is a known need for some more unstable Pearl Youths and for many Pearl Adults who had little help with their divorced-parent issues earlier in life. Practicing skills and creative tools with those surrogate parents, who can tend to the Pearl's mental and emotional needs in the most unconditional ways as possible, heightens a very stricken Pearl's inner resources. They can more effectively move through the emotional and psychological blocks that arise from lacking a cooperative family. This temporary transference strengthens a Pearl's ability to trust elders in good ways to meet many kinds of personal needs, and to learn to share life with the needs and ambitions of others. Transference management takes a skilled therapist or social worker.

A trained therapist can aid the youth to take in what is needed from the adult and leave the rest, respecting the therapist's needs at the same time. Therapists help some Pearls have a mature experience of parenting that they sorely lacked. It requires a strong, I-experienced person at times, who has a network of other supporters who share resources, connections, and experienced understandings of the issues. Every once in a while, a well-attuned foster couple, or a counseling couple, comes along who offer that direct relationship patterning that the Pearls often deeply long for in a surrogate experience.

Sometimes, a temporary retreat or series of retreats with a skillful couple, or couples, rather than a formal adoption, is like gold to the Pearl adolescent and young adult. The youth can experience real male-female relationships working daily in a home or home-like setting. In such circumstances, a youth can learn or re-learn some mundane but very helpful home-life skills that may have been missed, from housecleaning to food preparation, to fixing a leaky tap to building a garden fence.

Learning and developing through skilled craftwork shows the youth the need for patient considerations of what the youth intends and how to work toward an intended outcome. They also learn how to manage feelings and negative thoughts when something one intended doesn't work out as effectively as one had hoped. The youth learns to value and appreciate the people supporting the youth's efforts while adjusting expectations and hopes and making the most of the effort without closing off from the possibilities that something even more effective or emotionally rewarding can and likely will develop in time with more life experience and more fully developed relationships.

Managing disappointment without pillorying other people in one's life when things go wrong is an essential life skill. It helps them with life visioning, collecting impressions of meaning, acquiring needed materials and resources, accepting the need to ask for informed input from others, cherishing the value of reflection on misjudgments and honoring personal growth through making amends or corrections, and sharing heartfelt kindness toward others who also go through disappointments, setbacks, or frustrated goals.

Pearl Youth learn to practice inner mantrams and engage encouraging self-talk that they may need to propel them through blocks, setbacks, and reconsiderations. They come to celebrate important steps along the way to completing tasks fully. These experiences log in the soul a sense of a heart firmament without getting hardened. Such practices strengthen an inner temple of courage, self-trust, competence with others, and skill in managing mutual boundaries. They also contribute to a hopeful fortitude and faith in one's own worth.

The Life-Hardened Youth

In the presence of a tight, heart-closed youth—who may have shut off socially after experiencing too much aggression in life, or who has erected furious protective barriers against relationship dysfunctions—a counselor needs to know how to bring both gestures of ethical firmness and compassionate softness. These Pearls usually need help with practical basics, such as a home, safety, sufficient nutritious food, transportation, and even clean clothing and hygiene products. They may have poor day/night rhythms, and they can be very ritualistic about some practices or beliefs. They often expose themselves more regularly and more harshly to the natural earth elements, such as putting themselves out into a strong windstorm to feel alive, or trudging through a serious snowstorm to see a friend when most people would stay in. They may take greater risks than the average person their age.

A therapist meets this youth in an earnest way that responds to hardship with compassion and respect. The youth has garnered protectiveness for real purpose in response to early experiences. The hardenedness needs to be accepted before it can be transformed. This youth is working through the warrior and guardian human archetypes. Archangel Michael activities can help with this. Visioning slaying a dragon that is dislodged from inside of oneself, while simultaneously envisioning oneself as whole and filled with honorable light, in the presence of an angelic being who had to do a similar act, is reassuring to a hardened youth.

In early therapy with these youth, the therapist inwardly holds the following vision for the youth.

Verse for Michaelmas

There is a knighthood of the twentieth century,
Whose members do not ride through the darkness of physical forests of old,
But through the forests of awakened minds.
They are armed with spiritual armor.
And an inner sun makes them radiant.
Out of them shines healing.

Healing that flows from the knowledge of the image of man as a spiritual being.
They must create inner order, inner justice, peace and conviction,
In the darkness of our time.

- Karl Konig

An older youth can memorize the verse over a period of discussions with the therapist or caregiver on the images and actions inherent in the verse. It is helpful to have a warm but also radiant and firm image of Saint Michael in the therapy room.

Figure 7.22: Archangel Michael

The youth can be encouraged to share what thoughts, feelings, and impulses to action arise from seeing the Saint Michael image. The concept of an overarching higher guardian can be discussed, with sensitivity to who the youth sees as personal guardians. If a perceived guardian seems very dark and hardened, the therapist asks curious questions about this. A theater role-play can be set up with the youth and an actor playing St. Michael as the youth's guardian. The therapist acts as the observer and unbiased commentator, in the way that child play therapy works. The youth and the actor can work to role-play scenarios wherein the youth finds ways to use the strength of Michael in gentling ways and softening moments. Working with how to make safe relationship connections will be key.

The therapist can share knighthood themes, verses, and stories, such as from the Arthurian legends. The Pearl is encouraged to share what the youth has experienced as knighthood behaviors from others, or if the youth has experienced these in themself. Stories of Arthurian characters can be compared to people in the youth's life, seeking to find the humanness and wholeness in those people. The therapist might also examine the gentler, nurturing feminine beings who supported the knights, the king, and the feminine aspect of Saint Michael. The goal is to find ways that the hardened youth can create inner relaxation, and a mentality of self-nurturance and healing without losing the strength of the inner protector.

The therapist and youth can explore the notion of valor. The youth and the therapist reflect on the Waldorf Knighthood Code of Honor. This youth has likely already had to be a lone knight for much of life, protecting themself and possibly others in the family, as well as come-and-go friends or acquaintances who were also having harsh experiences. The youth needs to know about the knight of light, and about the color of the roundtable characters as well.

This youth has usually been forced to be an adult before the youth could be a child, and perhaps given too much imagery of black, gray steel, or other dark, shadowy impressions. This Pearl will not let go enough to balance toughness until life helps the youth have real imaginations of something to which a softer-hearted but safe soul can relate.

Waldorf Knighthood Ceremony Code of Honor: Age 12–13

In the presence of the assembled community of Lords and Knights, I swear:

To serve God and to follow the path of Christian goodness.
To be true and faithful to myself and the humanity in others.
To show courage, courtesy, and generosity.
To show respect and honor my enemies as developing individuals.
To protect the defenseless and to assist women and children.
To honor the women as much as the men of the court.
To regard my honor higher than my life.

To be true to this oath whether I am alone or with others.

The therapist who holds the inner gestures consistently and rhythmically of the full elements of earth, water, air, fire, and ether—while bringing practices for empathic warmth, boundaried strength, and inspirational light for learning new things and opening to heartfelt compassion—can meet the hardened, too-earthed, youth "where the youth is at" without sinking into unhealthy, hardened, and even animalistic nature.

Creating just the right, inner-effervescent readiness, without attention-seeking, while attending strongly to the youth's trauma-vigilant behaviors, and patiently letting the adolescent set the pace to open up (and being prepared to meet his or her anger and rage at times), a counselor can energetically and inwardly reach this hardened youth long before outer changes become apparent.

A therapist who can tend to this youth while holding the positive awareness of what is possible in the youth's healing, allows safe space to open up between them slowly. The youth will find ways to offer up heavy life issues to observe with the therapist, even if they come out for a time as words or feeling expressions that seem like sword flashes coming at the therapist.

A therapist needs training to know how to hold this energy while also detecting if the youth is too close to a violent outburst. The therapist always looks for and speaks to positive qualities and hard-earned skills that the youth exhibits, while reflecting, with supportive skills-building, what the child is lacking and covering up with anger and fierceness.

Accompanying a hardened youth to experience, with others, various creative and practical activities of fire and earth is a potential therapist intervention, and crucial for some hardened children. They need to learn to put anger and rage into practical artistry, coming to know how to give the anger and rage they absorbed from witnessing parent violence or conflict back to the darker earthen forces that evoked it, without projecting it onto other human beings. Biodynamic farming can be effective for that.

A fiery activity—such as forging with heated copper as Waldorf teens do in grade ten chemistry class, building an outdoor forge or rammed-earth oven together with others on a biodynamic farm property, or glassblowing in an artisan-glass shop with insights from a Waldorf grade-twelve, light-and-color block lesson—needs to be rehearsed ahead of time with the youth for safety and to knit some prefrontal-cortex, executive-mind, neural-canals for self-restraint.

The therapist and youth can design escape plans if the youth starts to feel triggered in an activity and needs to step away from a class or group. The youth gets backup for escape, such as a planned ride home, for a time. Healthy escapes need to be designed, such as planning an activity of watery, airy coolness that the youth can turn to if working with the fire-earth activities becomes too overwhelming. In a rural area, planning a forest zipline splurge, a kayak day at the lake in the spring or summer, or a snowshoe frisbee session in the wintery park, with nourishing snacks brought along, can keep a youth's mind in balance.

The youth is supported to ask friends or community adults to help meet needs. The Pearl thinks of ways that won't be exhausting to give back in appreciation for the help. The therapist and youth work to network needs among community members to see who can offer up a releasing experience for the youth when needed, something like a Big Brother or Big Sister[69] activity. Meet-up networking among adults who know each other well can help with this, and the youth is encouraged to work on that with them. Anthroposophical communities can offer suggestions, planning ideas, encouragement around implementation, and respectful people to help with reviewing afterward.

In the city, an Aikido-flow healing session can be planned at a dojo. A rafted-ice-sculpture afternoon using ice cubes, wooden floats, and kettles of boiling water can be arranged on a local creek.[iii]

A Saturday afternoon can become a day of flag sculpture projects using banners stamped, at a silk-screen artist's studio, with mindful expressions related to air, breath, and wind, and tied to trees in a park. This can be planned with city councilors as a youth advocacy event, or the banners can be offered to a conservation park. The therapist helps the youth to get support from public officials and other artists for such projects.

The youth, feeling welcome to access activities that give creative voice to the fullness of Pearl needs, while addressing developing needed skills that are harder for the youth to develop, can begin to enlighten their inner hardness and protective issues, while freeing heart and soul forces to express gratitude and the will to cooperate with others. The youth develops new constructive processes at the same time, rather than destructive ones.

Eruptions at School

Imagine a Pearl Youth who has arrived at school after lunch following an iPhone call to the absent parent of the week, where the conversation triggered feelings of old parental divisiveness. That youth, arriving to a physics class investigating the nature of fire and light, could easily project a fight reaction from the parent disruption into an excitable experience of working with the fire element in class.

The youth might unthinkingly launch into some riling behavior with the youth at his study station due to a regressive feeling memory. Without some understanding and gentle framing check-ins with the youth, the teacher or other assisting adults could unexpectedly fuel a buried emotional trigger in the youth, to which the youth reacts by setting aflame more than what is in the science experiment methodology.

For the teacher to regain control of the classroom mandate, the youth may have to be called in by a school counselor to cool down. Having an activity in the therapy room that directly balances elements can be helpful. Water and air balance fire and earth. A Bunsen-burner experiment is fire and air. The counselor can quickly balance that in the counselor room with

---

iii   The youth compiles ice cubes and compostable materials on a small raft the youth and adults have hammered together to float. The youth pours hot water in places on each ice cube pile, letting imagination open to what the youth sees. The youth photographs the sculpture, then floats it down the river or creek for others to experience.

something that employs water and earth. This could be something as simple as offering an enjoyable drink and a half a sandwich.

The counselor might need to invite the youth out to the quiet side of the parking lot to have a 20-minute, valiant water-gun assault on the counselor's vehicle—cleaning it off in the process. The counselor gets the car cleaned, and the youth gets to vent safely with an adult closely tending. The counselor highlights moments of knightly valor in the youth's agreement to cooperate, leave the classroom, and engage in a more appropriate rant with an empathic and responsible adult to diffuse the hard feelings.

Back in the therapy room or hut space, they reflect on how actions in the Bunsen-burner class might have been different through remembering the code of honor when a parent conversation triggers hard feelings. An older teen can begin to rehearse the Knighthood of the 1st Century Michaelmas verse with the therapist.

Hormone Strengths – Hiram, Warriors, And Ennobling Activity

A helpful, earthing activity for a youth is to visit a story from history. The therapist prepares the youth for the sometimes-awkward discomfort of slowing down anger or fear in order to think. He says that they are going to mine something important from history, but that when they go back in time, everything gets slower because many things in the past were slower. They work on a breathing exercise to prepare for the story and to get the youth's breath into balance.

An anthroposophical, psychotherapeutic framing for mid-adolescents is to encourage the adolescent to solve riddles, for instance: "Who was the mightiest metal forger in history? Who changed fiery metal into light?" This can bring up a backward review moving from twentieth-century inventors, to Middle Ages swordsmiths, and eventually to famous metalsmiths such as Hiram in King Solomon's time.

Linda Jeffrey has written a touching account of grief related to how King Hiram, the great iron forger and builder of the Temple of Solomon, starting in 980 BC, lost his father in a metallurgy accident when Hiram was eleven years old.[70] It is a helpful story to work with estranged Pearls who may be holding grief about not feeling parented appropriately, or at all, by a biological father.

The story of Hiram can lead to a transpersonal discussion of how, in modern times, the Archangel Michael urges people to turn their grief into strength, and manage their own inner dark feelings, but not by harming themselves physically or personally. Michael petitions human beings to use higher thinking and heartfelt words and actions to overcome feelings inwardly that evoke imaginations of war or bitter conflict.

This can be worked playfully for a younger teen to lighten up a very hard week, month, or year of tensions between parent homes. A therapist can work with the adolescent through eurythmy, copper-rod activities, stick-play, or choreographed sword-fighting activities. Dragon images can be created, with labels pinned to them with feeling-related words often associated with harmful feeling reactions, such as jealousy, resentment, disregard, supremacy, insidiousness, and loathing.

The youth and counselor work to identify as clearly as possible what kind of sensations a person can have inside in relation to such feelings. They try to discern when these feelings arise. The youth takes up a physical wooden sword that has significant weight, to create actions in the air for each word, parsing each word, slowly, with imaginations of what one can do in real, inner action and outer service for others. This offers a physically-felt rehearsal of forging a hard feeling into something of positive accomplishment. The youth feels the weight of the sword like the weight of responsibility, then uses sword actions in every non-weapon-like way possible—such as a laser to cut metal, a scythe to cut wheat, a plank to artistically nail into a building construction, a high-jump pole, a skateboard, or a canoe paddle. The youth looks for alternative actions that go with each feeling that they have explored.

This can be highly transformational for a Pearl Youth if the youth sees an adult stick close and accepting through this experimental, physically releasing, alchemical thinking process.

Later, as the youth builds more therapeutic trust, the counselor can address romantic feelings associated with adolescence. Reciting passages from Shakespeare's Twelfth Night[71] can add some objective distance to romance, as well as levity and flair, through this emotional, swordplay story of grief, confusion, and the disguised lovelorn issues of Olivia, Orsino, and Viola.

At the adolescent level of about age fourteen and fifteen, drama work and explorations can allow blocked feelings to arise and help the brain to restructure thinking, feeling, and willing impulses. All aspects of being fully human can be played out on the stage, in a drama room, or in role-play therapy.

Doing set and stage construction work, as well as sound and light effects, brings thoughts and feelings into a physical construct. A set design is its own sculpture, or even several sculptures for different scenes. Working all of the elements of theater and drama give a youth the chance to play it all out as an adult before becoming fully adult.

Full-production drama work, even on a small scale, offers opportunities to bring all elements into character development for adolescents. Plays are worked in every grade of Waldorf schools. Rudolf Steiner wrote four profound mystery plays for adults, full of the dramatic struggles of the soul depicted through compelling characters: The Portal of Initiation (1910), The Soul's Probation (1911), The Guardian of the Threshold (1912), and The Soul's Awakening (1913).[72] The plays are staged regularly throughout North America and Europe, especially at the Goetheanum, home of anthroposophy in Switzerland. Anthroposophical therapists are urged, for their own strengthening consciousness, to familiarize themselves with at least one of these plays.

Alchemy

When the rite of adolescent passage is full and wholesome, the child emerges as an individual woven into rich soul history, steeped in present capacities, and undaunted to step up to future experiences. Alchemically, the youth is capable of warm relationships replete with a) the right soul *salt*, or firming forces, b) appropriate *mercurial wisdom* or heightened thinking, and c) with the refined touches of *soul sulfur* to generate a warm, pungently heartfelt inner sense of both self and selflessness.[73] The youth can have some acceptance and ease with themself.

Adolescence, by its nature, is wrought with both golden glory and dark dangers. Anthroposophical psychotherapy, medicine, adjunct therapies, and pedagogy address the gravity and levity[74] of this childhood period by weaving many levels of consciousness into teacher preparation work, therapeutic specialist interactive collaborations, cross-cultural sharing, and hands-on, fully engaged work with growing young persons.

Conclusions

Marriage and relationship breakups are never easy on the psyches and souls of the people involved if they are honest with themselves. The divisiveness can bring about wrenching inner struggles toward wholeness and a faith in life or others again. When those breakups are significantly conflicted, even if the children in the middle do not directly see or experience outward conflict and violence, the disconnect is still very potentially damaging, and affecting those children in their inner sense of development toward being loving beings.

When the divorce doesn't resolve the parent tensions, as it rarely does, then the children are regularly exposed to challenges that are adult-level, and that has proven very problematic for young beings who are essentially still meant to be in the protective "nest," away from the harsher and hardening adult-world realities. Decades of complex research on homelessness, addictions, suicide, and various other mental health-related concerns have borne this out.

According to Rudolf Steiner's deep, complex, and comprehensive research on child and adult development, that which affects the hearts of human beings is essential to whether their lives thrive or dive. The emotional roller-coaster rides, or outright chaotic inner lives of many children of divorce, reflect each soul-psyche's great challenge to free itself from dark negativity and find the positive light of human truth and connection again.

Often, many of the harmful effects of the negativity are not outwardly noticeable, as younger children seek to appease their conflicted parents. However, what happens in childhood can have serious repercussions for Pearls later in adolescence and far into the adult development stages.

Volume I

Much of what has been shared in this first volume of *The Pearl and the Hut* stands alone. If childhood development is approached in the ways indicated with foresight by Dr. Steiner a century ago, and elaborated now by thousands of anthroposophical workers and Waldorf teachers, doctors, therapists, and pedagogical researchers, much in the heart and soul will be supported to act as wholesome foundations for Pearls worldwide. The indications and practices in this book can offer a resourceful holding for Pearls to manage well through both the joys and challenges of a full adult life.

The children of division can find the anthroposophical connections that they need and, in the fullness of their adult lives, begin to become the radiant and opalescent Pearls of wisdom that is their natural, human birthrite.

Pearls learn to understand their childhood missing pieces better and can begin to find ways to make up for them. As wholeness increases, they learn to hold appropriate boundaries with others when necessary, but also to have the resilience to make those boundaries flexible and open to others' perspectives, seeking not to dominate or conquer those who oppose their thoughts or ideas, while not giving away their own sense of self to anyone else's consciously or unconsciously domineering theory or belief and still cooperating for the best outcomes for all.

By taking in the ideas and heartfelt understandings in this first volume, Pearls can know that they are truly not alone in the earthly realm and in the soul-spiritual realms, and that they belong on this earth for a purpose that is as valuable as that of all other human beings.

Volume II

Rudolf Steiner's complex yet highly relevant insights for our times were presented over several years in six thousand lectures, thirty books, and countless private conversations that were later recounted to others over many years. Much that is in these lectures, which shared how to support children in their physical, mental, emotional, and soul-spiritual growth and education, became elaborated by Steiner in his insights on the ages and stages of adult developmental life that follow childhood.

These insights start with the sentient or strong feeling-life period of young adulthood from ages twenty-one to twenty-eight and go on into the ages after sixty and well into the following physical denouement period when the spiritual life becomes the most dominant as people prepare for death and the soul prepares for a rebirth into to the heavenly world beyond the earth-cosmos threshold.

Volume II elaborates on these stages and, once again, offers the biographical stories of other Pearls who have been through these various adult stages of development with some anthroposophical connections and awareness. It also holds information on Western psychological theories that support Pearl wholeness, an elaboration on Platonic solids metaphors for psychological stability, a very new, modern, and relevant perspective on the Cain and Abel story, and profound insights from Rudolf Steiner on the growing etheric heart.

With the increasingly mature soul-spiritual knowledge presented in the companion text to Volume I, which still works into practical life, Pearls can, in freedom, choose to become guides and helpers for others to know how to bridge divides and bring love consistently into the world for themselves, and together with others. They can do this in true humanness, not expecting perfection from themselves or others, but rather knowing that we as human beings are in a state of "becoming" our greatest selves.

In my own life, and in the lives of some other Pearls discussed in the two volumes of *The Pearl and the Hut*, these higher insights became crucial for a sense of well-being after the important age of thirty-three. Volume II of *The Pearl and the Hut* looks at many profound aspects of the development of the adult feeling life, intellectual life, Consciousness Soul life, and then the inner world of greater soul maturity and the attainment of higher soul-spiritual wisdom, strength, and peace.

Though this content was originally contained in one very large volume, wise helpers suggested that it be portioned into two books for more ease of understanding, for individual's pocketbooks, and to contain any overload of information all at once. Having the content in two volumes also allows a sense of the important differences between child soul development and that of adult-level development.

Although a Pearl reader will have a great deal of substance to work with from Volume I, which can offer sustenance for years into adulthood, I offer the awareness here of another book that shares more ongoing assistance for times of adulthood strife and confusion that inevitably challenge us all in adulthood to grow. It is offered in freedom. No one should feel pressure or lack if they have no access to the next volume, since much is available from many different sources outlined in Volume II to help a Pearl to know the higher developmental insights and work.

Those who choose to read both volumes will come to learn how to reach out in effective brotherhood-sisterhood to each other when the effects of outer-world machinations threaten to unbalance human souls in general. They can effectively engage their hearts in wholeness to dance and navigate through tensions and to also hold strong and loving protective space for children and younger people when necessary.

It is my intention that Pearl readers of either volume will know without a doubt that they are genuinely loved and entirely capable of whole-hearted love toward others.

Endnotes

1 R. Trostli, Rhythms of Learning (Great Barrington, MA: Steiner Books, 1998).

2 L. W. Lake and S. L. Bryant, "The Scientific Method and Earth Sciences," Journal of Energy Resources Technology 128, no. 4 (2006): 45–246, https://doi.org/10.1115/1.2358150

3 J. Steinbeck, The Acts of King Arthur and His Noble Knights (New York, NY: Penguin Classics, 2008).

4 B. A. Mann, Iroquoian Women: The Gantowisas (Bern, Switzerland: Peter Lang, 2006).

5 M. D. De Bellis et al., "The Biological Effects of Childhood Trauma," Child and Adolescent Psychiatric Clinics of North America 3, no, (April 2014): 185–222, http://doi.org/10.1016/j.chc.2014.01.002

6 Vikings, written by M. Hirst (Wicklow, Ireland: Ashford Studios, 2013 – 2020).

7 J. A. Graber, and L. M. Sontag, "Internalizing problems during adolescence,"(Hoboken, NJ: John Wiley & Sons Inc, Handbook of adolescent psychology: Individual bases of adolescent development, 2007), 642–682, https://doi.org/10.1002/9780470479193.adlpsy001020
V. E. Cosgrove et al., "Structure and Etiology of Co-occurring Internalizing and Externalizing Disorders in Adolescents," Journal of Abnormal Child Psychology 39, no. 1 (2011): 109–123, https://doi.org/10.1007/s10802-010-9444-8

8 R. Steiner, The Foundations of Human Experience (Hudson, NY: Anthroposophic Press, 1996). Hudson. NY.

9 Steiner, Foundations.

10 "YIP: Jarna," International Youth Initiative Program (2017), retrieved May 16, 2017, http://www.anthroposophy.org/articles/article-detail/how-then-shall-we-live-1306/ (article has been removed).

11 "Practical Investigations of Art in Relation to the Spiritual Aspects of the Human Being and the World," Free Columbia (2008), retrieved June 3, 2020, https://hawthornevalley.org/project/free-columbia/

12 M. Sol, "Eight Different Types of Love According to the Ancient Greeks," LonerWolf (2017), retrieved May 16, 2017, https://lonerwolf.com/different-types-of-love/

13 C. Kovaks, Parsifal and the Search for the Grail, (Edinburgh, Scotland: Floris Books, 2002), retrieved June 18, 2020, https://www.amazon.ca/Parsifal-Search-Grail-Charles-Kovacs/dp/0863153798
R. O. Moore and A. Ordway, "The Mirror Without a Face: The Assessment of Parental Alienation Among Children of High-Conflict Divorces," Vistas Online: ACA Knowledge Center (2013), retrieved June 3, 2020, https://www.counseling.org/docs/default-source/vistas/the-mirror-without-a-face.pdf?sfvrsn=6

14 S. Finser, Money Can Heal: Evolving Our Consciousness: The Story of RSF and its Innovations in Social Finance (Great Barrington, MA: Steiner Books, 2006).

15 W. von Boch-Galhau, "Parental Alienation (Syndrome): A Serious Form of Psychological Child Abuse," Neuropsychiatry 32, no. 3 (September 2018): 133–148, https://doi.org/10.1007/s40211-018-0267-0

16 M. B. Rosenberg, Nonviolent Communication: A Language of Life. (Encinita, CA: Puddledancer Press, CA, 2003).

17 A. Boal, Theatre of the Oppressed, (New York, NY: Theatre Communications Group, Inc., 1993)

18 R. Brokamp, "Professional Sports: A Waste of Time, Money, and Energy?" Get Rich Slowly (2019), retrieved June 3, 2020, http://www.getrichslowly.org/blog/2012/05/02/professional-sports-a-waste-of-time-money-and-energy/

19 Olivet Middle School (Facebook video, 2016), https://www.facebook.com/aimediaAUS/videos/10153681021824220/?pnref=story (post no longer available).

20 A. L. de Grace et al., "Exploring the Role of Sport in the Development of Substance Addiction," Psychology of Sport and Exercise 8 (January 2017): 46–57, https://doi.org/10.1016/j.psychsport.2016.10.001

21 V. W. Setzer, "A Parsifal Block Lesson at Escola Waldorf Rudolf Steiner de São Paulo," Instituto de Matemática e Estatística da Universidade de São Paulo (1994), retrieved June 3, 2020, https://www.ime.usp.br/~vwsetzer/parsifal.html

22 Donato, S., The Effect of Lunar Nodes on Human Biography: Waldorf Journal Project (2015)., retrieved May 16, 2017, http://www.waldorflibrary.org/journals/24-waldorf-journal-project/933-waldorf-journal-project-2-the-effect-of-lunar-nodes-on-human-biography

23 F. M. Corrigan et al., "Autonomic Dysregulation and the Window of Tolerance model of the effects of complex emotional trauma," Journal of Psychopharmacology, 5, 1, (2010), 17-25. Doi:10.1177/0269881109354930, retrieved May 16, 2017 from: http://journals.sagepub.com/doi/abs/10.1177/0269881109354930

24 R. Steiner, "The Search for the New Isis, Divine Sophia" (lectures, Dornach, 1920), retrieved June 3, 2020, https://wn.rsarchive.org/Lectures/GA202/English/MP1983/NewIsi_index.html

25 R. Steiner, Goddess: From Natura to the Divine Sophia, Pocket Library of Spiritual Wisdom (Forest Row, UK: Sophia Books, 2002).

26 R. Steiner, "The Manicheans" (lecture, Berlin, November 11, 1904), retrieved June 3, 2020, https://wn.rsarchive.org/Lectures/19041111p01.html

27 R. Steiner, "Background to the Gospel of St. Mark: Lecture Twelve, Mystery Teachings in St. Mark's Gospel (lecture, Hanover, December 18, 1910), retrieved June 3, 2020, http://wn.rsarchive.org/Lectures/GA124/English/RSP1985/BakMrk_cover.html

28 "Kaspar Hauser," Initiative for Anthroposophy (January 2014), retrieved June 3, 2020, http://initiativeforanthroposophy.org/wiki/kaspar-hauser/

P. Tradowsky, Kaspar Hauser: The Struggle for the Spirit (Forest Row, UK: Temple Lodge Press, 2012).

29 O. Lambert, "Mum and Dad are Splitting Up," Voices in the Middle (2017), retrieved May 17, 2017, https://voicesinthemiddle.org.uk/story/mum-dad-splitting-up/ (article no longer available).

30 Y. Alibhai-Brown, "What divorce really does to children," Daily Mail (September 4, 2013), retrieved June 3, 2020, http://www.dailymail.co.uk/femail/article-2411830/What-divorce-really-does-children--shattering-words-If-youre-divorced-thinking-testimony-shake-core.html

31 R. E. Rodda, "String Quartet No. 3, Sz 85," The Kennedy Center (2018), retrieved September 4, 2018 from: http://www.kennedy-center.org/artist/composition/3856 (page no longer available).

32 Cook and Hayashi, "The psychoacoustics of harmony perception," American Scientist.

33 M. Uchida, "Beethoven - Piano Concerto No. 4 in G Major Op. 58" (YouTube video, 2013), retrieved May 16, 2017, https://www.youtube.com/watch?v=9a7XiHRjTGI (video unavailable).

34 P. W. Boylan, "Aikido as Spiritual Practice in the United States" (thesis, Western Michigan University, 1999.), retrieved September 4, 2018, http://www.aikiweb.com/spiritual/boylan2.html

35 A. M. A. Oam, "Four-Leaved Rose," Maplesoft (2016), retrieved June 3, 2020, https://www.maplesoft.com/applications/view.aspx?sid=87677&view=html

36 R. Wagner, "Richard Wagner: Parsifal (Bayreuth Festival 2012)" (YouTube video, 2012), retrieved June 3, 2020, https://www.youtube.com/watch?v=bTaQu7ivsRM

B. Shwarm, "Parsifal: Opera by Wagner," Encyclopædia Britannica (2014), retrieved September 4, 2018, https://www.britannica.com/topic/Parsifal

37 B. Urieli, H. Muller-Wiedemann, Learning to Experience the Etheric World: Empathy, the After-Image and a New Social Ethic, (Forest Row, UK: Temple Lodge Publishing, 2000).

38 J. W. Rohen, Functional Morphology: The Dynamic Wholeness of the Human Being (Hillsdale, NY: Adonis Press, 2007).

39 Oam, "Four-Leaved Rose," Maplesoft.

V. B. Garrett, "Space Is Human," Movement Academy Project (2011), retrieved June 3, 2020, http://movementacademyproject.com/2011/12/28/space-is-human/

40 V. B. Garrett, "Space Is Human," Movement Academy Project (2011), retrieved June 3, 2020, http://movementacademyproject.com/2011/12/28/space-is-human/

41 V. B. Garrett, "Space Is Human,"

42 V. B. Garrett, "Space Is Human,"

43 M. M. Young et al., "The Rise of Overdose Deaths Involving Fentanyl and the Value of Early Warning," The Canadian Journal of Addiction 6, no. 3 (December 2015): 13–17, retrieved June 3, 2020, https://www.csam-smca.org/wp-content/uploads/2016/01/CSAM-December2015.pdf

44 T. Calas, et al., "Naloxone: An Opportunity for Another Chance," The Journal for Nurse Practitioners 12, no. 3 (2016): 154–160, https://doi.org/10.1016/j.nurpra.2015.10.025

45 A. S. Sprouse-Blum et al., "Understanding Endorphins and their Importance in Pain Management," Hawaii Medical Journal, 69, no. 3 (2010)

46 R. Steiner, "Steiner on Alcohol. Spiritual Science is Practical," (2007), retrieved May 16, 2017 from: http://888spiritualscience.blogspot.ca/2007/10/rudolf-steiner-on-alcohol.html

R. Steiner, "Problems of Nutrition (lecture, Munich, January 8, 1909), retrieved June 3, 2020, https://wn.rsarchive.org/Medicine/Nutrit_index.html

47 "The Tragedy of Amy Winehouse," Amethyst Recovery Center (2015), retrieved June 3, 2020, https://www.amethystrecovery.org/the-tragedy-of-amy-winehouse/

J. Courtney, "Back to Black: An Exploration of Amy Winehouse's Music and Addiction," JMU Scholarly Commons: Senior Honors Projects, Spring 2015, Paper 47, retrieved June 3, 2020, http://commons.lib.jmu.edu/cgi/viewcontent.cgi?article=1084&context=honors201019

48 D. J. Siegel, The Mindful Therapist: A Clinician's Guide to Mindsight and Neural Integration (New York, NY: W.W. Norton & Company, Inc., 2010).

P. Odgen, et a Trauma and the Body: A Sensorimotor Approach to Psychotherapy (New York, NY: W.W. Norton & Company, Inc., 2006)

Kerr, Living Within Your Window of Tolerance.

M. Elaine, "Analysis of the Real-World Application of Sensorimotor Psychotherapy for the Treatment of Complex Trauma," St. Catherine's University: Master of Social Work Clinical Research Papers, Paper 172 (May 2013), retrieved June 3, 2020, http://sophia.stkate.edu/msw_papers/172

49 R. Steiner, The Experiences of Sleep and their Spiritual Background," (Stuttgart, Germany, 1922), Rudolf Steiner Archive, retrieved June 16, 2020, https://wn.rsarchive.org/GA/GA0218/19221009v01.html

50 H. N. Lokko and T. A. Stern, "Regression: Diagnosis, Evaluation, and Management," The Primary Care Companion for CNS Disorders 17, no. 3 (2015). https://doi.org/10.4088/PCC.14f01761

51 E. D. Smith and C. Gray, "Integrating and transcending divorce: A transpersonal model," Social Thought, (1995) 18, 1, 57-74, DOI: 10.1080/15426432.1995.9960215

52 Smith and Gray, "Integrating and transcending divorce," Social Thought.

M. C. Kasprow and B. W. Scotton, "A Review of Transpersonal Theory and Its Application to the Practice of Psychotherapy," The Journal of Psychotherapy Practice and Research 8, no. 1 (1999): 12–23, retrieved June 3, 2020, https://www.ncbi.nlm.nih.gov/pmc/articles/PMC3330526/

R. Bento, "Aspects of Rudolf Steiner's Psychosophy," Rudolf Steiner College (2014), retrieved May 16, 2017 from:

http://www.rudolfsteinercollege.edu/news/aspects-rudolf-steiner%E2%80%99s-psychosophy.

J. Messerly, "Summary of Maslow on Self-Transcendence," Reason and Meaning (January 18, 2017), retrieved June 3, 2020, http://reasonandmeaning.com/2017/01/18/summary-of-maslow-on-self-transcendence/

53 D. David, et al., "Why Cognitive Behavioral Therapy Is the Current Gold Standard of Psychotherapy," Frontiers in psychiatry, 9, 4, (2019) 29, doi:10.3389/fpsyt.2018.00004

54 M. Yousafzai, I Am Malala: The Girl Who Stood Up for Education and Was Shot by the Taliban (London, UK: Orion Publishing Group, Ltd., 2013).

55 G. Parks, Voices in the Mirror: An Autobiography (New York, NY: Three Rivers Press, 2005).

56 W. Grill, Shackleton's Journey (London, UK: Flying High Books, 2014).

57 M. DePrince and E. DePrince, Hope in a Ballet Shoe: Orphaned by War, Saved by Ballet. An Extraordinary True Story (London, UK: Faber & Faber, 2014).

58 P. Hoose, The Boys Who Challenged Hitler: Knud Pedersen and the Churchill Club (New York, NY: Farrar, Straus and Giroux, 2014).

59 J. Gantos, Hole in My Life (New York, NY: Square Fish, 2012).

60 S. A. Armstrong et al., "Humanistic Sandtray Therapy with Pre-adolescents," Journal of Child and Adolescent Counseling 1, no. 1(1): 17–26, https://doi.org/10.1080/23727810.2015.1023167

61 M. B. Straus, No-Talk Therapy for Children and Adolescents (New York, NY: W. W. Norton & Company, 1999).

62 W. Drake, "What Is The Empty Chair Technique And Why Do Therapists Use It?", (Mountain View, CA: Better Help, 2020), retrieved June 20, 2020, https://www.betterhelp.com/advice/therapy/what-is-the-empty-chair-technique-and-why-do-therapists-use-it/

63 J. M. Cunningham, "Adele: British Singer-Songwriter," Encyclopædia Britannica, last updated May 4, 2020, retrieved June 3, 2020, https://www.britannica.com/biography/Adele

64 E. M. Eudell-Simmons and M. J. Hilsenroth, "The Use of Dreams in Psychotherapy: An Integrative Model, Journal of Psychotherapy Integration 17, no. 4 (2007): 330-56, https://doi.org/10.1037/1053-0479.17.4.330

L. Ruwoldt, "Dreams and Nightmares in First Nations Fiction" (doctoral dissertation, Universität

Greifswald, 2017), retrieved September 25, 2018 from: https://epub.ub.uni-greifswald.de/frontdoor/deliver/index/docId/2111/file/Dreams+and+Nightmares+in+First+Nations+Fiction_Ruwoldt.pdf

65 D. G. Barrett, "Dream Weaver/Dream Catcher: The Older Child and Analyst at Work," A Topical Journal for Mental Health Professionals 36, no. 3 (2016): 242–254 https://doi.org/10.1080/07351690.2016.1145976

66 "Quamichan," Wikipedia, retrieved June 3, 2020, https://en.wikipedia.org/wiki/Quamichan

67 D. Newblatt, "A Foot of the World Conference: What ails thee brother: Parzival as the herald of the consciousness soul of our time," (Plumstead, Capetown, 2018), retrieved June 20, 2020, http://www.aswc.org.za/images/What%20ails%20thee%20Brother%20-%20Parzival%20as%20the%20Herald%20of%20the%20Consciousness%20Soul%20in%20Our%20Time%20print.pdf

68 K. R. Silk, "Object Relations and the Nature of Therapeutic Interventions," Journal of Psychotherapy Integration 15, no. 1 (2005): 94–100, https://doi.org/10.1037/1053-0479.15.1.94

"Object Relations," GoodTherapy (2018), retrieved June 3, 2020, https://www.goodtherapy.org/learn-about-therapy/types/object-relations

69 "Program Partners," Big Brothers and Big Sisters of America (2018), retrieved June 3, 2020, http://www.bbbs.org/program-partners/

70 L. Jeffrey, "Death Built a Temple," The Grief Experience: Blog (January 27, 2012), retrieved June 3, 2020, https://thegriefexperience.wordpress.com/2012/01/27/death-built-a-temple/

71 J. M. Pressley, "Twelfth Night; or, What You Will," Shakespeare Resource Center, retrieved June 3, 2020, http://www.bardweb.net/plays/twelfthnight.html

W. Shakespeare, Twelfth Night; or, What You Will , (London, UK: Penguin Classics, 2015).

72 R. Steiner, Four Mystery Plays (London, UK: Anthroposophical Publishing Co., 1925).

73 R. Steiner, "Salt, Mercury, Sulphur" (lecture, Dornach, January 13, 1923), retrieved June 3, 2020, https://wn.rsarchive.org/Lectures/19230113p01.html

74 P. Matthews, "Space Is Human," Movement Academy Project, (2011), retrieved May 16, 2017, http://movementacademyproject.com/2011/12/28/space-is-human

Yiana Belkalopolos   B.A.A., B.Ed., MATCP

Yiana is a registered, private practice clinical counselor in British Columbia, Canada. She took her master's degree in Transpersonal Clinical Psychology in Palo Alto, California in 2015. She has worked as a certified public-school teacher in Toronto and in the B.C. Gulf Islands, and as a Waldorf school teacher in the Canadian Rockies.

As a dancer, singer, theatre artist, and playwright, Yiana led and co-led community arts and healing arts initiatives in Canada, Mexico, and India. She is on the Dean's Honor List at the University of Toronto and won the CBC Regional Director's Award for Best Radio Documentary on palliative care in 1988.

Her on-going volunteer support for children and their families has included seventy-six children in an orphan home in India, war refugees, people coming through the foster-care system, and Coast Salish First Nations families. She has spent twenty years as a student of the silent Ashtanga Yoga spiritual teacher, Baba Hari Dass, and has been a student of Rudolf Steiner's Anthroposophy since 2003. She is a member of the BC College of Teachers, the British Columbia Association of Clinical Counsellors, and the Anthroposophical Society of Canada.

CPSIA information can be obtained
at www.ICGtesting.com
Printed in the USA
BVHW020353230122
626043BV00001B/1